Bamboula!

BAMBOULA!

The Life and Times of
Louis Moreau Gottschalk

S. FREDERICK STARR

New York   Oxford
OXFORD UNIVERSITY PRESS
1995

Oxford University Press

Oxford   New York   Toronto
Delhi   Bombay   Calcutta   Madras   Karachi
Kuala Lumpur   Singapore   Hong Kong   Tokyo
Nairobi   Dar es Salaam   Cape Town
Melbourne   Auckland

and associated companies in
Berlin   Ibadan

Published by Oxford University Press, Inc.,
200 Madison Avenue, New York, New York 10016

Oxford is a registered trademark of Oxford University Press

Library of Congress Cataloging-in-Publication Data
Starr, S. Frederick.
Bamboula! : the life and times of Louis Moreau Gottschalk /
S. Frederick Starr.
p.   cm.
Includes bibliographical references and index.
ISBN 0-19-507237-5
1. Gottschalk, Louis Moreau, 1829–1869.
2. Composers—United States—Biography.
3. Pianists—United States—Biography.
I. Title.
ML410.G68S7   1994   780'.92—dc20   [B]   93-11539

9 8 7 6 5 4 3 2 1

Printed in the United States of America
on acid-free paper

Preface

This is a book about the American composer and virtuoso Louis Moreau Gottschalk (1829–69). In the history of American music and culture Gottschalk's position today is that of a footnote, albeit a big one. He is known by only a small number of his three hundred compositions and his brief but dramatic life is summed up in little more than a few pat formulas.

Gottschalk, we are told, was a virtuoso who wrote a few promising pieces that somehow anticipated ragtime and who otherwise led a rather messy private life. The American public adored his music, yet he failed to develop his talent and, after a promising beginning, contented himself with churning out sentimental potboilers. He was an American original, to be sure, but certainly not so major a figure as to be placed in a musical pantheon along with MacDowell, Ives, Gershwin, Carter, Ellington, and Cage.

This book offers a broader picture of Gottschalk. It accepts him as an innovative and meritorious composer of works in various genres who strikingly anticipated American tastes well into the twentieth century. It recognizes that he was both an arch-romantic and a rationalist, a sentimentalist and a pragmatist, at once America's first regionalist composer, its first multiculturalist, and its first true nationalist. Above all, it sees Gottschalk as a Jacksonian democrat who believed in art by the people and for the people yet who, at the same time, was the bearer of a new cosmopolitanism.

During Gottschalk's lifetime Americans for the first time erected Culture as an absolute, the possession of an initiated and favored few.* Gottschalk resisted this tendency. Even though he had no illusions regarding the public's tastes, Gottschalk welcomed and fostered the penetration of popular music into loftier realms, just as he toiled endlessly to bring his brand of "classical" music to the mass public. His lifelong battles

---

*Raymond Williams, *Culture and Society: 1780–1950*, New York, 1958, p. xvi.

against the new elitism ended in failure, yet they impart to his story a peculiarly modern cast.

It is not the purpose of this book to reinterpret the sweep of American culture in light of Gottschalk's contributions. Its more limited mission is simply to present what is known of the life and music of this New Orleans–born artist, and thereby to rescue him from the clichéd formulas that have obscured him from view and distorted our appreciation of his music.

Acknowledgments

One fine autumn day in 1991 I found myself in the largest psychiatric hospital in France, the Centre Psychiatrique, in the ancient Picardy town of Clermont-sur-l'Oise. Opposite me, attired in white, sat the hospital's archivist, who regarded me with undisguised suspicion. "You are interested in an American who was here?" he asked. "Yes," I replied, "a very important musician named Gottschalk." "But don't you have psychiatric hospitals in the States?" he inquired. "Of course, but this was in 1848," I replied. "Besides, he wasn't a patient. Just visiting," I explained. "And why would anyone want to 'just visit' here?" he bore in, now clearly skeptical. "Well," I explained, "the person I'm interested in was a personal guest of your director." "Of course," sighed the archivist; "we hear that all the time." "Yes," I retorted, "but in this case Gottschalk was truly a guest, and he wrote some wonderful music while here." "Sure, sure," I was told. "Just like Beethoven over in ward three or Berlioz down in the brick building."

In the end, the archivist explained to me that he would need permission from *monsieur le ministre* to release a patient's records. Then, in an ominous effort at sympathy, he invited me for tea and "a nice chat." Only with the intervention of Claude Teillet of the Société Archéologique et Historique of Clermont-en-Beauvaisis was this little mess untangled.

To write a biography of Gottschalk is like climbing Mount Everest: one can do it, but only with a lot of help and support. While many offered generous assistance, I am particularly indebted to those brave souls who had set out on this path before me. The late Robert Offergeld, a splendid raconteur, whetted my appetite, and through Dr. Marc L. Spero, Offergeld's executor, I eventually had access to his notes. Dr. Francisco Curt Lange of Caracas, Venezuela, provided steady encouragement, as well as voluminous materials gleaned from a half century of research throughout South America. Dr. John G. Doyle of Mansfield College shared his unparalleled knowledge of Gottschalk bibliography. Suzanna Lix, a grand-niece of Gottschalk's early biographer, Vernon Loggins, prowled through her attic in Gatlinburg, Tennessee, to recover notes and papers helpful to the project. Over many years, Richard Jackson of the New York Public Library gained a formidable but not uncritical knowledge of the New Orleans–born composer, all of which he shared willingly with me. Marcello Piras of Rome made available the interesting results of his investigations there. In recent years, no one has more diligently researched Gottschalk than Dr. Clyde Brockett of Christopher Newport College. He not only shared the fruits of his labors with me but provided valuable suggestions at all stages. Leann F. Logsdon of Atlanta, Georgia, made available to me her excellent but unpublished study on Gottschalk and Meyerbeer.

Among the most ardent Gottschalk researchers has been his collateral descendant Lawrence B. Glover of East Brunswick, New Jersey. An environmental scientist by profession, Glover became a historian and genealogist of necessity when he inherited a mass of Gottschalk papers. He placed both his expertise and his papers at my disposal.

Vast troves of Gottschalk material probably survive unrecognized in secret places. That which is known is accessible thanks to the labors of archivists and bibliographers in many countries. In France, for example, there is the staff of the music division in the Bibliotheque National, while in Switzerland there is Mr. Olivier Conne of the Archives Cantonales Vaudoises in Chavannes-près-Renens. My old friend Dr. Alexander Fursenko and musicologist Victor Lebedev in St. Petersburg located important materials in Russian archives, while Professor Anne Swartz of Baruch College, City University of New York, exhumed rarities in Warsaw. Gloria Goldblatt, author of a fascinating but unpublished biography of Ada Clare, turned up important papers touching indirectly on Gottschalk and has kindly shared these with me. My gratitude to each is enormous.

Naturally, the bulk of Gottschalk documentation is in the New World. Particularly valuable to the biography was my research trip to Cuba where, thanks to the generosity of Maria Teresa Linares Savio, Director of the Museo Nacional de la Música in Havana, and also to Tomas A. Pinella y Serrano of the Ministry of Foreign Affairs, I had rare access to archives. Three fine Cuban scholars shared their unpublished research with me, to my benefit. Hearty thanks, therefore, to musicologist Rita Maria Castro y Maya, an authority on Gottschalk's operas; to Cecilio Tieles, who rediscovered the composer Nicolás Ruiz Espadero; and also to Zoila Lapique Becali of the Biblioteca Nacional José Marte.

In Puerto Rico I received priceless guidance from Gladys E. Törmes at the Archivo Municipal in Ponce; Brunilda Ramirez of the Museo de la Música, also in Ponce; Gloria Vega, Director of the Biblioteca General de Puerto Rico in San Juan; and Raphael Santiago at the Archivo General.

Similar help was provided by the staff of the Archive Departementale at Basse-Terre, Guadeloupe; the Bibliotheque National in Port-au-Prince, Haiti; and the Biblioteca de la Escola Nacional de Música in Rio de Janeiro, Brazil. There is no more knowledgeable authority on Gottschalk in Puerto Rico and on Puerto Rican music generally than Professor Donald Thompson of the University of Puerto Rico, and none could have been more generous with his help. For insights on all aspects of Caribbean and Creole culture, I am especially grateful to Professor Réginald Hamel of the Université de Montréal.

It would be impossible to thank individually every staff member of every historical archive and town library in the United States who helped me. Among those to whom I am particularly indebted, however, are Joyce Anne Tracy of the American Antiquarian Society, Worcester; Elizabeth van den Berg and Judith D. Harvey of the Free Library of Philadelphia; Vaughn L. Glasgow of the Louisiana State Museum; Sally Reeves of the New Orleans Notarial Archives; Francis O'Neill of the Maryland Historical Society; Katheryn Metz of the Museum of the City of New York; George Boziwick of the Music Archive at the Lincoln Center Branch of the New York Public Library; as well as staff members too numerous to mention at The Historic New Orleans Collection, the New-York Historical Society, the New Orleans Public Library, the Western Reserve Historical Society in Cleveland, the Cincinnati Historical Society, the Bancroft Library in Berkeley, the South Carolina Historical Society, and the Boston Public Library, to single out but a few. And what about Dr. Don J. Young of Sandusky, Ohio, who dug out treasures at the Follett House Museum on Gottschalk's several visits to that city? Or Professor James Kimball of Geneseo, New York, who did heroic bibliographic work on Gottschalk in upper New York State? Or Harold Linebach of St. Louis, who shared his priceless archives with me? To all of them I offer sincere thanks.

A number of special friends and colleagues have provided timely advice and encouragement on the biography, among them Professor John J. Joyce Jr. of Tulane University; Professor Lawrence Gushee of the University of Illinois; Professors Geoffrey T. Blodgett and Steven S. Volk of Oberlin College; and Gunther Schuller, composer, musicologist, and editor, of Newton Centre, Massachusetts. Their great gifts as teachers should not be judged by the meager efforts of this one student. Above all, I want to acknowledge with deepest respect and affection the immense help provided by pianist and historian Vera Brodsky Lawrence of New York.

That it was possible to conduct much of the research for this book from a Midwestern American town of seven thousand inhabitants attests to the competence of Daniel Zager, librarian at the Oberlin Conservatory of Music, as well as his assistant, Carolyn Rabson, and of Valerie

McGowan-Doyle, head of inter-library loans for the Mudd Library at Oberlin College. A team of student research assistants at Oberlin College deciphered the unintelligible scratchings of nineteenth-century writers and translated the sometimes florid prose of the era into English, in the process gaining impressive expertise. Among these were Robert Theodore Seaman, Marcos P. Natali, Paul R. Dreifus, and Alejandra del Castillo. Thanks also to Roberto Lazo of Oberlin; Aryel Sanat of Washington; Ian Linbach of the College of Wooster; and Melissa Hensley of Washington University, St. Louis, for their help in this area. Adriana Acurio of Lima, Peru, made important Gottschalk discoveries in her home town.

It was necessary to call on the special talents of many in the course of preparing this book. Without Judith Bethea of New Orleans, for example, it would have been impossible to mine that city's labyrinthine Notarial Archives with any degree of success. Richard A. Sherlock, Oberlin's photographer, prepared the illustrations and proved a master at recovering images from pale negatives.

I offer thanks, in lieu of a more public confession of guilt for the agony I caused her, to Connie Cooksey Gardner of Stowe, Vermont, who saw the manuscript through more drafts than were done for Tolstoy's *War and Peace*. In the process, she gave up many hours of practice on the flute—too high a price by far!

Above all, I owe a special debt to the tireless Elizabeth Esterquest Young of Oberlin, who tracked down hundreds of rare publications and living persons essential to piecing together the Gottschalk story, and who took a lively personal interest in every aspect of the project. In the process, this mathematician by training became a fine historian. Gottschalk studies will long be in her debt.

Oberlin, Ohio   S. Frederick Starr
May 1994

Contents

Bamboula!

Chapter One

✖ A Death in Rio

IT was Sunday, December 19, 1869, in Rio de Janeiro, and the body of Louis Moreau Gottschalk lay in state in the unornamented rooms of the Philharmonic Society at 41 Rua da Constituição. The forty-year-old American composer and pianist had died in agony at 4 a.m. on the previous day, after gallantly kissing the hand of the distinguished mulatto physician who had attended him.[1] A hastily assembled team of the best specialists in Brazil had embalmed the body the same night, and the country's leading sculptor, Professor Bernadelli of the Academy of Fine Arts, had taken a plaster cast of the musician's face in order later to do a commemorative bust.[2]

All day on Sunday the Philharmonic's building was jammed with mourners filing past the open casket. Many were in tears over the loss of a man who had only been in their country seven months. Near the bier stood the Chickering grand piano, draped in crepe, on which the virtuoso had given his last performance three weeks earlier. He had faltered while playing his sorrowful *Morte!!* (*She Is Dead*), and as he began his next piece, the immensely popular *Tremolo*, he collapsed over the keyboard.[3] In tribute, the Philharmonic Society's orchestra now performed *Morte!!* before the open coffin. Then the several hundred members proceeded downstairs and out on the street to form the cortege.

That morning the Portuguese, Spanish, French, and English press of Rio had all issued black-bordered front page announcements of the North American's death. Whatever businesses would normally have been open on Sunday now closed out of respect. From mid-afternoon carriages and mourners on foot had been moving toward the city's center, creating a traffic jam on all the streets near the Philharmonic. Only with some difficulty did the cortege manage to form, with Emperor Dom Pedro II's own First Battalion Band at its head.[4] Behind the band walked members of the Philharmonic Society, in full dress and with mourning sashes across their chests. They carried torches, and the smoke lent an eerie cast to the procession as twilight approached. Then came the coffin, carried by eight pallbearers from the Society, several of them pianists and all friends of the deceased. Behind followed still more torchbearers.

The cortege moved slowly through the narrow streets for a mile, finally reaching the large, open Largo da Lapa, adjoining the public gardens. There the coffin was transferred to a horse-drawn hearse, and a procession of hundreds of carriages formed to accompany it southward along the harbor's edge for six miles. It then turned inland toward the Copacabana hills and the São João Baptista Cemetery. Throngs lined the sidewalks, and windows along the entire route were filled with mourners straining to catch a glimpse of the casket.

At the cemetery assembled the largest crowd of all. Representatives of benevolent societies to which the North American had contributed money stood in the front ranks of mourners. All eagerly followed the florid eulogies delivered by the learned Dr. Achille Verejão and Professor Antonio Cardoso de Manezes. Both offered testimonials not only to Gottschalk's artistry but also to his generosity toward educational and cultural institutions in the Brazilian capital. In addition, Dr. Verejão praised the composer for having championed a new Pan-American ideal. "He was an American," the doctor declaimed, and from the White Mountains of New Hampshire to the Amazon had celebrated "the grandeur of the Americas."[5]

When the eulogies were done, the coffin was opened briefly, and the crowd surged forward to look one last time at the mustachioed composer with all the medals and ribbons on his chest. The medals were removed, and the coffin was then closed and transported to a private vault made available by a leading family of Rio. A week later a requiem mass was sung at the church of São Francisco de Paula, and a month after that a second mass was celebrated at the Philharmonic Society's behest.[6]

Twelve years before these events, while Moreau Gottschalk was touring in Cuba, a newspaper in one of the island's small towns had reported that he had died of an aneurysm. Gottschalk, thoroughly amused, wrote the editor a jocular letter assuring him that he was still among the living. The skeptical editor remained unconvinced, and soon his paper issued a colored engraving showing the virtuoso's veiled bust and a broken lyre, with the inscription "To Gottschalk, Respects from His Inconsolable Admirers."[7] Reports of Gottschalk's demise appeared soon thereafter in both North America and Europe. For weeks he busily penned letters to friends and editors in an effort to prove he was still living.

Now, with Gottschalk certifiably dead, the press of Rio de Janeiro issued a fresh set of commemorative engravings in tune with the public's sorrow. One allegorical masterpiece showed the composer lying in state while an angel representing the Philharmonic Society sobs at his feet and three female figures, representing North American, South America, and Europe, stand by mournfully.[8] This maudlin scene faithfully reflected sentiment in the Brazilian capital. Never before had a musician received such parting honors in the New World. "One cannot imagine the sensation that [Gottschalk's] death has caused among the people of Rio," wrote one of the pallbearers. "I have never seen a procession as solemn as Gottschalk's nor such a general sensation caused by any death in this capital of four hundred thousand inhabitants."[9]

Few of those who mourned Gottschalk's death knew or cared that he had played for Chopin, had been lauded by Berlioz, could claim as patron the Queen of Spain, had performed for Abraham Lincoln, and had been received by the presidents of five South American countries. They all loved his music, however. They knew of his "monster concerts" in Rio and revered him as a person, and some had even tasted the "Gottschalk Chocolates" on sale at confectioners throughout the capital. Befriended by the Emperor of Brazil, this New Orleans native had somehow touched the public's hearts wherever he went and had been received as a new kind of ambassador. Throughout South America, and, earlier, in the United States, the Caribbean, and in Europe, he had become a culture hero, a "universal celebrity," in the words of one Rio journal.[10] Gottschalk was the first Pan-American figure in the arts.[11]

Over the next few weeks the Rio press poured forth articles on the deceased musician. Many eulogists resorted to poetry, with one newspaper printing an eleven-stanza poem *To Gottschalk* on its front page.[12] The public's desire for stories about Gottschalk's life and death was insatiable, and no detail too trivial, as was proven by a detailed article devoted solely to the embalming of the composer's corpse.[13] The popular paper *A Vida Fluminense* issued an engraving of Gottschalk's funeral and also a profile view of the supine dead composer, both suitable for framing. The usually irreverent and saucy *Ba-ta-clan*, which had often caricatured Gottschalk during his lifetime, now offered a black-bordered lithograph of the departed during his last days. Gone from his face was that handsome and quizzical look that had captivated thousands. Now his blank staring eyes were set in a puffy face distorted from exhaustion.[14]

Meanwhile, various innuendoes about the composer, most of them patently false, began to circulate. It was said, for example, that only two of the city's three thousand residents from the United States attended the funeral. The clear implication was that Gottschalk was *persona non grata* in his own country or that North Americans were too boorish to appreciate their great artist.[15] In fact, the paucity of North Americans at his funeral is not surprising since many of those present in the Brazilian capital were ex-Confederates, while Gottschalk had supported the Union cause during the Civil War.

A second and more damaging rumor sought to explain the failure of the Brazilian emperor to pay his last respects to a musician whom he had personally befriended.[16] Here the implication was that the composer's purported tie with a singer from the infamous Alcazar Theater had been such that no upstanding and Catholic emperor could pay homage to him in death. Yet Dom Pedro II had been the guest of honor at one of Gottschalk's last concerts and had sent prominent members of his retinue to the composer's bedside after he collapsed. The emperor was absent at the funeral, first, because the entire court had removed to the more temperate summer capital of Petropolis as was the custom during the torrid months and, second, because his wife was still recovering from a serious illness.[17]

Far more intriguing were the various whispered insinuations regarding the causes of Gottschalk's death. The actual death certificate, recorded at the Santa Casa da Misericordia, states laconically that he died of "an incurable galloping pleuropneumonia."[18] A German-born friend, Henri Préalle, quickly transformed pleuropneumonia into a stomach abscess, while a fellow pianist from Brazil lost no time in blaming "a tumor! A stupid tumor! Nothing more, nothing less."[19] Gottschalk's trusted valet, Firmin Moras, accepted the abscess theory but then gravely informed the press that the abscess had been caused by a blow from a sandbag hurled by a São Paulo student who was angry at having had to give up his fraternity house to the touring virtuoso for a performance.[20] Inevitably, a variant of this soon had the sandbag hurled by a jealous husband.

The most titillating explanation of Gottschalk's demise was that he died a "victim of the enticements" of a French actress named Clélie. According to this tale, Gottschalk had met this seductress at a post-concert soirée in the Uruguayan capital of Montevideo during the previous winter, they had become romantically involved, and Clélie had then followed him to Rio. A close friend and subsequent biographer of Gottschalk later wrote in detail of the mysterious Clélie and her fatal influence on the composer.[21] In a striking passage we find Clélie in Rio on the day of Gottschalk's funeral, summoning the biographer himself to accompany her on the then precipitous path to the peak of the Corcobado, high above the city. From this misty summit she is supposed to have watched

Gottschalk's funeral cortege move slowly toward the São João Baptista Cemetery.

A splendidly operatic finale, to be sure, but it begs the question of just what the actress did to cause Gottschalk's death. This, in turn, raises the more basic question of Clélie's very existence. Some have suggested that Clélie may have been nothing more than a figment of the Spanish-born biographer's fertile imagination. This, it turns out, was an overstatement. But if the mysterious Clélie existed, her relationship with Gottschalk is unclear, and her presence in Rio still unconfirmed.[22]

All these tales reflect one solid truth: that Moreau Gottschalk generated a cornucopia of adulation, denigration, and outright myths, both during his lifetime and afterwards.

By December 24, 1869, news of Gottschalk's death reached São Paolo, Brazil, where the jubilant academic community had only recently received the composer. Now, a local composer dedicated a *Marcha funèbre* to his memory, and a São Paulo poet described this New World composer's meeting in Heaven with the European greats.[23]

At nearly the same time, word of Gottschalk's death reached Buenos Aires, Montevideo, Santiago, Lima, and other South American cities where he had been idolized. Adulatory biographies were rushed into print to meet the public's demand.[24] The news traveled swiftly also to Cuba, where Gottschalk and his music claimed a passionate following. The Havana composer Nicolás Ruiz Espadero wasted no time in penning a lengthy tribute to his revered colleague, whom he portrayed as a distinctive voice among romantic musicians. Espadero published his eulogy in the distinguished Paris journal *L'Art musical.*[25]

Even before this, Gottschalk's younger sister Clara had been busy disseminating the sad news among editors in the French capital, where Gottschalk had been educated and had scored his first triumphs as virtuoso and composer.[26] French obituaries understandably focused on the composer's early works, which had won praise from such deep-dyed Parisian culture-makers as Victor Hugo and Theophile Gautier.

Two of Gottschalk's other sisters were in London at the time, so it fell to them to inform the British press. Even though Gottschalk had never performed in England, his works were well known there, and the *Morning Post* anticipated a fresh burst of interest in them following his death.[27] By contrast, the *Illustrated London News* was dismissive of the composer, referring archly to his "elegant drawing-room pieces for [piano]."[28] In the same vein, the *Orchestra* acknowledged Gottschalk's genius but scarcely paused on his music before going on to stress his charity, kindness, and "freedom from ridiculous vanity."[29]

Gottschalk's entire career can be seen as a rearguard action against Germany's growing ascendancy in music. It is therefore no surprise that both the musical and general press of that country ignored his death. The news reached Berlin nonetheless, and a young American pianist studying there recorded her sorrow in a letter:

> I was dreadfully sorry to hear of poor Gottschalk's death . . . but what a romantic way to die!—to fall senseless at his instrument, while he was playing *La Morte!!*. It was very strange.
>
> If anything more is in the papers about him you must send it to me, for the infatuation that I and 99,999 other American girls once felt for him still lingers in my breast![30]

By April 1870 the news reached the Russian capital of St. Petersburg. "The sadness that consumes the Rio public has, of course, been echoed in our old Europe as well," wrote one critic. "Who does not know his compositions?"[31]

The first inkling of Gottschalk's death to reach North American readers was on January 21, 1870, the morning after the Rio mail steamer arrived in New York. The *Tribune, Herald,* and *New York Times* all printed obituaries on that day, the *Times* confirming that it had been widely expected that the composer would soon be returning to his homeland. Newspapers in Boston, where Gottschalk had experienced his first crushing defeat, picked up the story from the New York press and reported it dryly.[32] Philadelphians learned about Gottschalk's death through a factual letter sent by Henri Préalle in Rio to the composer's friend and executor, Charles Vezin, who then shared it with the local press.[33] Nowhere did the death cause more general sorrow than in Gottschalk's home town of New Orleans, which received the news via Havana. The French-language newspaper *L'Abeille* reminisced nostalgically about Moreau's triumphal return to the Crescent City from France seventeen years earlier.[34]

In no time the North American press also picked up every rumor buzzing about in Rio. Firmin Moras's claim that the composer had died from a blow with a sandbag gained particularly wide distribution, beginning with the *New York Tribune.* From there the story spread rapidly across the country and even back to South America, where it was reprinted in the popular Buenos Aires newspaper *La Tribuna* on September 22, 1871.[35]

Far more damaging was a long essay, nominally a eulogy to Gottschalk, that appeared in the *New York World.*[36] From the time he returned to New York from France in 1853 down to his final departure from the United States in disgrace in 1865, Gottschalk had always been a bone of contention among critics. The stakes were high, since he epitomized aspects of an emerging American culture that some loved and others loathed. Now, in death, he was again in the middle of this cross-fire.

The anonymous writer from the *World* began mildly enough, acknowledging Gottschalk's ability to "[take] captive the multitude. His was the temperament and the eloquence that they needed and could respond to." This said, the "eulogist" proceeded to tear into his subject as the personal embodiment of all that was wrong in American life. Gottschalk "was the possessor of the sacred fire in some degree," he conceded, but in the end produced nothing more than

> all sorts of dainty and effeminate caprices, *morceaux*, and fantasies for such as had keen parlor sensibilities. Born to the warmer soil of the South, [Gottschalk] was . . . attuned to the culture of Paris to full utterance.

Now the *World*'s critic was at full stride. How sad, he continued,

> that flattery soon converted [Gottschalk] . . . from an Apollo to an Adonis. He lounged listlessly onto the platform, snuffed up the incense of applause, and sat down at his instrument with a dreamy, languid grace that was accounted irresistible. Something of the same voluptuous charm was evoked from the piano.

The eulogist's goal was to reveal Gottschalk as a lightweight. "Poems, dreams, passions came at [Gottschalk's] bidding in brilliant flashes," he admitted, "but in none was there any of the lasting refulgence of higher poetry." Gottschalk, in short, exalted "the passion of the creature, [but] never the aspiration of the soul." Finishing off his lifeless victim, the eulogist attacked Gottschalk's character, denouncing him for "taking pride in the conquests of the *roué.*" Summarizing a generation of gossip, the *World*'s critic concluded piously that "Gottschalk's career points afresh the old and ever lasting moral that under all true Art must lie morality."

Pro-Gottschalk forces in New York did not long remain silent in the face of this attack.[37] The controversial *Orpheonist and Philharmonic Journal* set the tone for many other commentators when it declared that Gottschalk "was one of the few original and remarkable artists of this century."[38] But it fell to Henry Clapp Jr., friend of Walt Whitman, patron of Mark Twain, and former editor of the *Leader*, to pen a direct response to the *World*.[39] Knowing that others would defend Gottschalk's music, the critic whom a generation of New Yorkers knew as the "King of Bohemia" concentrated on the man. Alternatively flippant and sentimental, Clapp touched appreciatively on everything from Gottschalk's fluency in four languages "to his gifts as writer and raconteur." He then focused on the question of Gottschalk's character:

> He was more than generous to both friend and foes; his charities were without limit or stint; he always had an open heart and an open hand for his brother

artists; he was devoted to the last drop of his blood to his family; he was passionately fond of children; he never prostituted his art to base purposes; he loved his country best in her darkest hour; his devotion to truth in every department of art and science was an absolute worship; and, finally, I never heard him speak ill of any human being.[40]

One would never suspect that Clapp and the *World* were writing about the same person. But this polarization was typical of Gottschalk's fate, for as eulogies and posthumous criticism multiplied, the actual man and music receded from view. As this happened, Gottschalk ceased to be a reality and became instead an abstract principle.

Yet for the time being, the physical remains and earthly possessions of Moreau Gottschalk still existed in Rio, and these had to be attended to. This proved to be no easy matter, for at the very time the obituaries were appearing, an extraordinarily messy fight developed over Gottschalk's estate.

The difficulties began the moment Brazilian courts tried to untangle the composer's debts. In order to repay Gottschalk's many creditors, the acting American consul, Mr. Henry W. Milford, had tried to assemble all his possessions. To do this he called on the help of Gottschalk's former secretary and valet, Firmin Moras. Milford, who was desperately ill at the time, wanted only to settle the matter as quickly as possible.[41] He was ready to accept at face value Moras's assurance that Gottschalk's worldly effects consisted only of "clothing, twenty-three bound volumes, a quantity of pamphlets and music, one album, several trifling articles of gold and silver, and three pianos."[42] Nor did he question Moras when the latter assured him that he had turned over these objects to the court.

Moras, however, had duped Milford, and with good reason. Gottschalk, it turned out, had failed to pay his valet's salary for 1869. On his deathbed he had dictated a will, witnessed by Gottschalk's doctor and an unknown but suspiciously named "Mr. Moreau,"[43] leaving Moras what was owed him and also a further two years of salary as a kind of severance pay. Moras, however, was convinced that Gottschalk's cash-hungry sisters would cheat him of these payments, and he therefore held back from the court many of the jewels and medals that had been bestowed on the virtuoso. While promising Milford he would deliver them to Gottschalk's sisters in Europe, he intended actually to hold onto them until he was paid. Among these treasures was a bejeweled sixteen-ounce medal of solid gold awarded him by citizens of New Orleans in 1853.

While this was taking place at the American consulate, Gottschalk's friend Henri Préalle reported on the composer's death to sisters Clara and Celestine, as well as to Gottschalk's executor, businessman Charles

Vezin of Philadelphia.[44] Both Vezin and the sisters assumed that Gottschalk had left behind a considerable estate. Vezin had in his possession a signed will made by Gottschalk in 1855 which enumerated an impressive list of jewels already in hand by that time.[45] Moreau had supported Clara and her five siblings in good style for seventeen years, and they, too, blithely assumed he had died rich, which was definitely not the case. To complicate matters further, Gottschalk left his sisters no information about Vezin's role as executor. Thus, within months of Gottschalk's death, two competing powers of attorney were en route to Rio.

Now the good-hearted Préalle gave the valet money to go to London to plead his case with the sisters. Checking into the posh Charing Cross Hotel, Moras scandalized Clara by demanding not only his pay but her power of attorney.[46] When she refused to give either, he sailed back to Rio and instituted a suit against Vezin and the estate.[47] Meanwhile, however, nearly all the property had been sold at auction by the Orphans (probate) Court on March 26, 1870.[48]

Gottschalk's manuscripts suffered a similar fate. The twenty-three volumes of music and other papers had been purchased at auction by the Rio publishing house of Narciso, Arthur Napoleão & Cia. The firm had every intention of capitalizing on their publication,[49] which was to be supervised by pianist Arthur Napoleão, the proprietor.[50] What Arthur Napoleão did not know is that Gottschalk had designated the Cuban composer and pianist Nicolás Ruiz Espadero as his literary executor. To make matters worse, neither Napoleão nor Espadero was aware that Gottschalk was under exclusive contract with the New York firm of William Hall & Son, which now believed it owned all his unpublished works and took steps to claim them.

By now these claims, the powers of attorney from Clara Gottschalk and Vezin, and lawyers representing Firmin Moras were all present in Rio.[51] In the midst of this mounting chaos, the United States government entered the case. Back in December 1869 Henri Préalle had dutifully written Gottschalk's first cousin, Congressman Leonard Myers of Philadelphia, to inform him of the composer's death. When Myers learned of the various claims being advanced, he immediately wrote Secretary of State Hamilton Fish to ask him to intervene. Fish, not knowing that Gottschalk's possessions had already been sold and that Firmin had absconded with the remaining jewels, ordered the U.S. consul in Rio to take steps to have all property returned to the family.[52]

Now the action shifted back to Firmin Moras and Vezin. Confident that Vezin was holding back and aware that the Philadelphia will was about to be probated, Firmin wrote Vezin an abusive and threatening letter setting a deadline for payment in full. Then he set his terms: "If after three months the money has not been paid me, the body will be seized for the whole amount that the will states, and this will be published in all the newspapers of the United States, Europe and Rio, along with the copy of the [deathbed] will." Like blackmailers everywhere, Moras claimed he wanted to avoid a scandal. But he could not let Vezin forget that he had been treated "like a *dog*." And hence he repeated his demand: "For the family's honor, send the money as soon as possible because if by some misfortune it does not arrive in three months the body will be seized."[53] Vezin failed to meet the deadline. Moras, however, had not succeeded in capturing Gottschalk's coffin from the São João Baptista Cemetery. Having played every card in his hand, the valet therefore absconded with nearly all of the remaining jewels and medals. No one connected with Gottschalk ever saw him or the medals again.

Vezin, meanwhile, had his own problems. Gottschalk had described him as "my best friend,"[54] and the Philadelphia business community knew him as a respected importer, sportsman, and socialite. But as a Philadelphia reporter later learned, he had been neglecting his business, was "living pretty high," and as a result was greatly over-extended.[55] In desperation, Vezin borrowed against his own firm, bankrupting it, and then swindled money from a large estate entrusted to his care.

Moving quickly, Vezin took passage from New York to Rio in hopes of saving himself with the help of Gottschalk's purported fortune.[56] Hard on Vezin's heels came a Philadelphia attorney bearing an indictment from a Pennsylvania court. And not long after the attorney came a further letter from Secretary of State Fish demanding Vezin's extradition. It took no time at all for Vezin to discover that his friend's estate was insignificant and that his few possessions had already been sold. Now Vezin, too, had played his last card and had no choice but to answer for his crimes or flee the courts. He chose to flee, probably to Portugal,[57] where he disappeared forever.

It took two more years for the dust finally to settle. Neither William Hall & Son nor Espadero got the manuscripts, which remained in Rio with the firm of Napoleão & Cia. Some found their way back to the United States in the 1960s. Most remain lost to this day. Clara eventually came to Rio and, after meeting with the Emperor, finally accepted the fact that her brother had been sending all his earnings to her and her sisters, saving nothing for himself.

The entire episode attests to the quality of confused desperation that permeated Gottschalk's practical affairs. He may have been the first American composer or performer acclaimed on three continents, but his life was a constant improvisation, a jumbled struggle for survival. A good bourgeois, Moreau worked tirelessly to put his affairs in order. In the end he failed.

The coffin was opened a final time to allow the touring American soprano Carlotta Patti to bid farewell to her old colleague. Then the body was shipped to New York aboard the steamer *Merrimack*. Henri Préalle complained bitterly at being charged the same as for a living person but, loyal to the end, paid the passage with his own money.[58]

Over the preceding months various memorial concerts had been held in Manhattan. Some were benefits to assist Gottschalk's sisters, while others had no other purpose than to enrich the opportunists who mounted them.[59] Now all parties joined to organize a grand funeral mass at the Church of St. Stephen on East 28th Street. It was rainy and raw on the morning of October 3 as the brightly painted three-aisled Gothic sanctuary filled to overflowing. Sisters Celestine, Augusta, Clara, and Blanche had all arrived from Europe, and most of the stars of New York's artistic and social firmament were there as well.[60] A mass of flowers covered the bier, the floral effusion being surmounted with a crown, wreath, and cross—all courtesy of William Hall & Son and Chickering & Sons. Eight pallbearers wearing white scarves seated the guests. Among the pallbearers was Charles Vezin, whose swindling scandal had not yet broken, along with Charles Francis Chickering and Thomas Hall, sons of Gottschalk's piano maker and publisher, respectively.

A double octet performed ("mutilated," claimed the *Orpheonist*) a vocal transcription of the composer's tear-jerker *The Last Hope*. The organist then played ("horribly macerated," grumbled the irascible *Orpheonist*) Gottschalk's *Pensée poétique*. After this the fifty singers of Berge's Choral Union performed a requiem mass by Cherubini, once the director of the Paris Conservatoire where Gottschalk had been denied admission.[61] The organist closed the service with his own rendition of Gottschalk's lachrymose *Morte!!*. Never mind that the Spanish title, *She Is Dead!!*, referred to a woman rather than to Gottschalk himself.[62] The mourners assumed that Gottschalk, like Mozart, had written his own requiem and were nearly all in tears as they filed out of St. Stephen Church.

On the steep steps, Gottschalk's casket joined the casket of his brother Edward, who had died in 1863 and was now to be reburied next to Moreau in bucolic Greenwood Cemetery in Brooklyn. There, surrounded by a substantial cast iron railing ornamented with lyres, was a marble pedestal surmounted by a seven-foot tall marble angel. She held a book, upon whose pages were graven the names of six of Gottschalk's best loved compositions. At the angel's feet rested a marble lyre with its broken strings.[63] And on a stone slab positioned in front of the pedestal were carved the words "L. M. Gottschalk—*Morte.*"

For a few years after the funeral soulful New Yorkers made pilgrimages to this cultural shrine, leaving flowers and poems. Eventually the grave fell into disrepair. The angel was toppled from her pedestal, and the lyre fence crumbled. Eroded by time, even Gottschalk's engraved name gradually grew illegible and finally disappeared.

Chapter Two

🧬 Origins

THE saga that concluded with the death of Gottschalk in Rio had begun four decades earlier, in the most southward-looking city of the United States. On May 8, 1829, Louis Moreau Gottschalk was born in New Orleans. No birth certificate was issued. Not until a year and a half had passed did the infant enter recorded history, and then under peculiar and foreboding circumstances.

On the night before Christmas Eve, 1830, a Philadelphia businessman named Arnold Myers accompanied his brother-in-law's young wife to a ball in New Orleans. Seventeen-year-old Aimée Bruslé Gottschalk had scarcely left her home since the birth of Louis Moreau, her first child. Her reappearance in society was not going well. There were dancing and games but Myers noted that Aimée took no part in them. Her husband, Edward Gottschalk, was nowhere to be seen. Nearly twice her age and a Londoner by birth, he may have been put off by the frivolity of the young French-speaking crowd. Or he may have avoided the party for some other reason. His absence only deepened Aimée's gloom.

Arnold Myers reported on all this to his wife in Philadelphia. He observed that other guests snubbed Aimée Gottschalk and that she was very sensitive to this. Myers was sure that she would not accept any more invitations. "She is extremely diffident," he noted, "much more than I should have expected in a French woman."[1]

Myers, a Jew, had come south to attend the baptism of his nephew, Louis Moreau Gottschalk. He did not record his impression of the ceremony, which took place at St. Louis Cathedral on the Place d'Arms, but he took smug pride in his own ability to chatter in Italian with the presiding priest, the Abbé Moni. Yet there was no gaiety in the air. The baptism of young Moreau, as he was to be called, had been delayed a year and a half.[2] During the intervening period Aimée had given premature birth to a second child, who had died within days.[3] This misfortune, in turn, had been hastened by even more traumatic events in the young mother's life.

She and Edward Gottschalk had been married in 1828, when Aimée was only fifteen.[4] The wedding at St. Louis Cathedral had brought together leaders of two very different worlds. Witnesses for the bride included James Pitot, author, businessman, and former mayor of New Orleans,[5] and the revered Louis Marie-Elizabeth Moreau-Lislet, a jurist, co-author of the Louisiana Civil Code, and a great uncle of the bride. On the groom's side was Samuel Hermann, a wealthy German-born commission merchant, merchant banker, and slave trader. Like his young friend Edward Gottschalk, Hermann was Jewish by birth and had married a Catholic.[6] Both wives were Louisiana-born and of French descent, hence "Creoles." With Hermann stood Thomas Franklin, a Yankee immigrant who had amassed a fortune in real estate.

Anyone present would have recognized this as a cross-section of New Orleans's diverse elite and could have assumed the young couple would soon take their place among them. The Bruslés in particular had reason to rejoice at the marriage. With eight children, Theodat-Camille Bruslé and Alixe-Josephine Deynault Bruslé could provide their daughter with a dowry consisting of only a bed, an armoire, some linens, and a few jewels.[7] Theodat-Camille had gone broke six years earlier, and the memory of this disaster lingered on, especially with his wife who, to satisfy creditors, had undergone the humiliation of renouncing her community assets in the marriage.[8] Now the Bruslés had reason to expect that their daughter's happy union would save the girl from a like fate.

A month after the wedding, Edward Gottschalk's firm of Gottschalk, Reimers and Co. declared bankruptcy.[9] Its debts were staggering and spread as far afield as Hamburg, Germany.[10] To settle them, Edward sold whatever assets he could, including both land and slaves.[11] He even went to his mulatto mistress and persuaded her to let him resell land and slaves he had signed over to her.[12] It is hard to conceive a more thorough humiliation for Aimée than to be saved financially by her husband's mistress. And yet the rescue failed. Weeks later, Aimée Bruslé Gottschalk, like her mother before her, renounced her meager part in the community assets she shared with Edward.[13]

This tale of woe is sharply at odds with Moreau Gottschalk's own description of his childhood in his *Notes of a Pianist:*

> From my birth I had always lived in affluence—thanks to the successful speculations entered into by my father. Certain of being able to rely upon him, I quietly permitted myself to follow those pursuits in which I anticipated only pleasure and enjoyment.[14]

It also clashes with reminiscences, written in the depths of the Civil War, of a New Year's day in his young life:

> I saw, one by one, a child's memories rise before me—my father's hearth, our family's happiness, the throbbings of that unspeakable joy which, while one still lingers in the Aurora of his life, is wakened by those magic words "Christmas"—"New Year."[15]

There were joyful Christmases in the Gottschalk household, to be sure, with toy swords, tin soldiers, and a domestic crèche adorned with fresh flowers. But the myth of an idyllic childhood perpetuated by both Moreau and his relentlessly positive sister Clara is far from the reality.

Perhaps it is inevitable that the childhood of America's greatest romantic composer should have been so richly embroidered with myth. Musical friends in Paris later claimed that Gottschalk had been raised in a tropical Arcadia, a romanticized America akin to that described by the French poet Chateaubriand or by Longfellow in *Evangeline*.[16] This fanciful notion spread to America and then back to England, where it was reported:

> The Gottschalk family inhabited an isolated country-seat on the shore of Lake Ponchartrain. The first impressions of youth must have exercised a powerful influence on the romantic imagination of the future composer. The mysterious noises of the forest, the Aeolian harmonies, the poetry of a savage life, formed the heart and spirit of the artist and made a decided impression on him.[17]

In reality, the Gottschalks owned not a "country-seat" but a modest wooden house, and it was located not on the shores of Lake Ponchartrain but in the seaside spa of Pass Christian, a summer watering place frequented by New Orleanians and planters from Mississippi and Louisiana. To be sure, yachting was already popular there, as were genteel garden parties beneath the live oaks.[18] But the Gottschalks' home was unpretentious, and the few dispirited Indians still about were traders, the rest of their numbers having been banished by the state of Mississippi in 1830.[19]

Nor were the Gottschalks here merely to enjoy their "country-seat." Edward Gottschalk had bought the house in Pass Christian after losing his New Orleans residence through bankruptcy. He briefly moved the family there in 1832 in order to escape an epidemic of cholera raging in New Orleans, a plague so devastating that corpses were piled up like timber at the cemetery gates.[20]

It was during this brief exile that young Moreau evinced his first interest in music, by bobbing up and down to his mother's piano playing. One hagiographer has the three-year-old tot already playing operatic arias by ear.[21] Moreau's own claims do not go beyond *Hail, Columbia*, which he picked out with one finger. One day as he was doing this, an Indian stopped by the house. After the boy finished playing, the Indian strode to the keyboard and crashed down on it with both hands, exclaiming triumphantly "I never tried before and I make more noise than he."[22] This boast came to symbolize for Gottschalk the American infatuation with volume and bigness, at the expense of delicacy and sentiment.

These various incidents suffice to underscore the complexity, and at the same time the importance, of Moreau Gottschalk's early years. As much as any artist before him, he took inspiration from his childhood experiences. He drew not merely on the external aspects of his early life but also on its enduring psychological legacy. This legacy was defined by Moreau's attempts to come to grips with the starkly juxtaposed worlds of Edward Gottschalk and of Aimée Bruslé Gottschalk. The composer scarcely mentioned either his father or mother in his later writings, and both were dead by his twenty-seventh year. But their respective lives and worlds constituted the benchmarks of Moreau's mental world. So compelling was the "problem" of Gottschalk's split heritage that he came to perceive all American life in terms of the polarity symbolized by his mother and father.

As late as Bach's time, most European composers sprang from musicians' families, with the others coming generally from equally humble non-musical backgrounds. All this changed in the romantic era.[23] Berlioz's father was a highly literate physician, the fathers of both Liszt and Saint-Saëns were civil servants, and Schumann's father was a moderately prosperous publisher. Though born on the geographical fringes of European culture, Moreau Gottschalk fitted this pattern, his father being a solidly middle class businessman.

The romantic era also saw for the first time the appearance in Europe's musical mainstream of Jewish composers. Felix Mendelssohn and Giacomo Meyerbeer (born Jakob Liebmann Beer) were but the best known of several. Gottschalk's rise was part of this shift. If the boy's impulse and inclination toward music traces to the influence of Aimée Bruslé, it was Edward Gottschalk who channeled young Moreau into the profession of virtuoso pianist and composer.

A further trait of many fathers of romantic artists is that they tend to vanish from sight. Romantics, after all, see themselves as heroic loners and are generally disinclined to dwell on their antecedents, especially when the fathers are earnest bourgeois. Even among fathers of romantic composers, however, Edward Gottschalk stands out as a man without qualities. Moreau mentions him only twice in his lengthy *Notes of a Pianist*, first, in order to attribute to him a business acumen which he conspicuously lacked and, second, to report his father's ill-considered prejudice against P. T. Barnum as a manager.[24] Moreau's sister Clara recalled her father in only two sentences. She observed that "although kind, [he] was what is called strict, and brought up [Moreau] in the most elevated ideas, and never permitted him the indulgence of any weakness." Also, she credited her father with being "of great reputed wealth, much esteemed as a gentleman of fine culture, and remarkable as a linguist—he spoke eight or nine languages."[25]

The daguerreotypes of Edward Gottschalk are less flattering. These reveal a black-haired, hatchet-faced man, glassy eyed behind pince-nez, and with tightly pursed lips. A caricature published in a Parisian daily portrays him as a crabbed and stooped drudge.[26]

If this were the whole picture, Edward Gottschalk could be safely consigned to the oblivion reserved for fathers of romantic artists. But during his lifetime this pale and cold figure significantly shaped his son's career, and after his death he continued to cast a deep shadow over his son's life. Moreau never openly rebelled against Edward Gottschalk. Even after the father's death, his son continued to submit to the fate his father had prepared for him—clear evidence of the father's defining importance.

Legal documents in the notarial archives of New Orleans confirm that Edward Gottschalk was born in London in 1795. His father was Lazer (Lazarus) ben Gottschalk Levi, and his mother was Jane Harris Gottschalk.[27] In spite of their Anglicized name, the Harrises were German Jewish immigrants to England, Jane Harris's first name actually being Shinah, from the German-Yiddish adjective "beautiful" *(schöne).*[28]

Who were the Gottschalks? No firm information on Edward Gottschalk's family has yet come to light. It is not even known where in London they lived. But the various branches of the Harris family were all enrolled in the same Westminister synagogue as the renowned scholar Jacob Hart, who was known as Rabbi Gottschalk (ca. 1745–1814).[29] This grammarian and philosopher wrote widely on subjects as diverse as Aristotle, Newton, and Tom Paine.

Rabbi Gottschalk's Hebrew name was not Jacob Hart but Eliakim ben Abraham. "Eliakim" in Hebrew means "God's fool." A *Schalk* in German is, in fact, a jester or fool. Hence Gottschalk. Eliakim ben Abraham traced his family originally to Eisenstadt, Hungary, the same town in which Haydn spent so many years in the service of his patron Prince Esterházy.[30]

There is evidence, albeit inconclusive, that suggests that Edward Gottschalk was the grandson of this erudite Jew with three names. Eliakim ben Abraham had one son, Eliezer or Lazarus.[31] The Hebrew name of Edward's father was Lezer ben Gottschalk Levi, or "Eliezer, son of

Gottschalk."[32] In daily life he used the German name of Gottschalk, possibly out of deference to his distinguished father. He could just as well have taken the English name Hart, which was obviously used in the family. It is surely no accident that among Edward Gottschalk's business associates in New Orleans were Nathan and Moses J. Hart, and also Hart Schiff.

A possible fly in this genealogical ointment is Moreau Gottschalk's report to several friends that he was of Danish descent.[33] But this is consistent with the fact that his father is said to have studied at Leipzig, an obvious choice of university for an assimilated Jew from the Baltic area.[34] Also, Edward Gottschalk is known to have had close business ties with Bremen and Hamburg, natural contacts for a businessman hailing from the North Sea—Baltic region.[35]

These facts in no way contradict the idea of Moreau Gottschalk's descent from Eliakim ben Abraham, whose cultural world was strongly German and who himself had ties with the Danish court synagogue. This fragile skein of evidence suggests that the family of Edward Gottschalk arose in Central Europe but by his father's generation—that of Moreau's grandfather—was based in England, even as it maintained close ties with northern Germany and the Baltic region.

This cultural-geographic perspective gains in interest in light of Moreau's pronounced antipathy to Northern Europe. He spoke three European languages fluently, but German was not among them. He never traveled to Germany, even though he had a loyal German publisher, nor did he ever perform in England, even though virtuosos from Haydn to Paganini considered that country an especially lucrative field for concertizing. Practical reasons for this avoidance can be found, yet none is really convincing. One is left suspecting that Moreau's coolness toward Germany and England had deeper roots: specifically, that he perceived those two countries somehow as his father's environment, not his own, and that he could openly oppose attitudes and values to which he silently objected in his father by rejecting any association with these two countries.

This possibility gains credence in the context of Moreau's attitude toward his Jewish heritage. Edward Gottschalk, like so many London Jews of his generation, did not practice his religion and was thoroughly assimilated into the Christian society around him.[36] Like other upwardly mobile London Jews, Edward gladly rejected his heritage in favor of a solid niche in middle-class life. In this, too, he shared the assimilationist ideal of North German Jewry and bears comparison with Mendelssohn's father in Leipzig and with Meyerbeer's father in Berlin.

Notwithstanding this, Moreau Gottschalk's environment in New Orleans had a Jewish cast. Once established there, Edward Gottschalk immediately sought out Jewish businessmen like Samuel Hermann and Hart Schiff and entered into many deals with them. His partner, John Peter Reimers, was also an assimilated Jew.[37] Inevitably, these men were frequent visitors in the Gottschalk home, as were such English-Jewish Gottschalk uncles as James, George, and Joseph Victor.

When the first Jewish temple was formed in New Orleans, Edward Gottschalk was listed among the contributors, even though he did not join. Later, he subscribed to the *Occident and American Jewish Advocate*, the leading magazine for American Jews at the time.[38] Given all these Jewish elements in the Gottschalk home, it is not surprising that when Moreau and his brother Edward Jr. traveled to Cuba, young Edward noted in his account book the start of the Jewish New Year, and when Moreau toured in the Antilles, he did not hesitate to make contact with leaders of the local Jewish communities.[39]

Yet Moreau took no pride in his Jewishness. In his mind, to revert to a Jewish environment was to sink backwards. One of his sisters, Augusta, later moved to England and, financially strapped, accepted work in a London Jewish household. "I don't like the idea of seeing Augusta in such a humble condition as a governess of children in a Jewish family," he complained to his sister Clara. "It is not right to leave [her] like this."[40] Such statements are rare, to be sure, but they reveal the gulf separating Gottschalk from the Jewish heritage represented by his father.

For all Moreau Gottschalk's efforts to distance himself from his Jewish forebears, he nonetheless accepted two of Judaism's most important tenets. First, he gave generously and usually anonymously to every conceivable charity. Throughout his life he was a soft touch, handing away tens of thousands of dollars, even when he himself was living from hand to mouth. His first public concert in New Orleans was to benefit a struggling violinist, while his final series of performances in Rio de Janeiro benefited schools and hospitals in the Brazil capital.[41]

Some of this generosity must surely be attributed to Gottschalk's Catholicism and to his lifelong loyalty to Freemasonry, which also demands philanthropy of its members. In part, too, it was simply the common practice among leading performers at the time. When Paganini once refused to give a charity concert in London, he was roundly criticized by the British press for his stinginess.[42] But above all it must be traced to Edward Gottschalk and to his family's heritage of Judaism, which strongly enjoined philanthropy on the faithful.

A second and even more important legacy from Edward Gottschalk to his Catholic son Moreau was the duty to provide. Orthodox Judaism is patriarchal, and its ethics are saturated with the paternal duty to family. This obligation is explicit in the Jewish marriage contract, stated in the wedding service, and repeated in family Sabbath prayers. For all his way-wardness, Edward Gottschalk tried to honor this obligation and took pains to inculcate it in his eldest son. "When Moreau shall have brothers and sisters," he told the five-year-old boy, "Papa counts upon his working for them, and [you] must think beforehand that they will have a father in Moreau."[43]

Even before his father's death, Moreau was called on to apply this maxim. And from then to his own death, he toiled unceasingly to provide for his widowed mother and six siblings. In the fullest sense, "they had a father in Moreau." But that was just the problem. Edward Gottschalk had inculcated in his son the duty to provide for family yet he himself, due at first to financial reverses and then to his early death, fell short as the head of his family. By the very standard he derived from his family's Jewish heritage, Edward Gottschalk was a failure. Hence the son's dis-taste for his father's worlds of England and Germany and his coolness toward the faith of his forefathers.

Why had Edward Gottschalk emigrated to America?[44] He left no ac-count of his motives, but one thing is certain: he did not flee religious persecution. These were years in which English Jews were moving rap-idly toward real emancipation, a process that reached its culmination with the election of Benjamin Disraeli as prime minister.[45] Rather, Ed-ward Gottschalk was seeking economic advancement and was perhaps even responding to an advertisement promoting Jewish emigration that appeared in the London press about the time he left for Louisiana.[46]

Nearly all Edward Gottschalk's many brothers and sisters emigrated with him. In 1822 older brother George had arrived in New Orleans from Germany.[47] James arrived several years later and joined Edward's firm as a junior partner.[48] In 1836 Dr. Joseph Victor Gottschalk arrived from Pyr-itz in East Prussia and offered his services to the public as "Physician, Surgeon, Occultist, & Accoucheur."[49] Sister Clara also came and promptly married a Jew from Bremen, Peter Gildemeister.[50] Yet another sister, Ade-laide, settled in Philadelphia and married a member of the large Jewish community there, Henry Seeligson;[51] also in Philadelphia lived sister Fleurette and her husband, Arnold Myers. At least two members of the Harris family also settled in New Orleans, making a grand total of six Gottschalk relatives there besides Edward.[52] Edward was the only one of his siblings to marry outside the faith.

Throughout the 1820s Edward Gottschalk engaged in trade with the North German entrepôt of Hamburg. He bought and sold commodities, traded in currencies, and speculated in downtown New Orleans real es-tate. He also emerged as an active slave trader, as evidenced by numer-ous transactions recorded in the notarial archives.[53] A number of other

Jewish immigrant merchants also participated in this traffic, which was an accepted occupation among white New Orleanians in the 1820s. The social status of slave trader at this time was not inferior to that of other merchants.[54]

Slave trading was a clear example of Edward Gottschalk's rapid assimilation to his new environment, but it was not the only one. Another example involved his private life. New Orleans was unique in North America in the size and wealth of its population of free African-Americans. Usually mulatto, these "free people of color"—les *gens de couleurs libre*, in the words of Moreau-Lislet's Civil Code—were at liberty to acquire property and enter the professions. Many grew rich, and some even owned slaves and plantations. Catholic, French-speaking and proud, these free people of color were briefly to publish their own literary journal, *Les Cenelles*, and found their own Philharmonic Society. The 1820s and 1830s were their golden age.[55]

Distanced both from the slave population and the whites, members of the free mulatto population lived lives of ambiguity. If their daughters were free to own real estate, plantations, and even slaves, those same daughters were frequently placed out with wealthy white men as mistresses. The fabulous Bernard Mandeville-Marigny, a leader of the French population and a *bon vivant* who invented the game of craps, maintained such a "quadroon." So did Judah H. Touro, patriarch of the city's growing Jewish community and New Orleans's greatest philanthropist. So, also, did Edward Gottschalk. Judith Françoise Rubio (or Robio or Roubio) was a mere sixteen when she became Edward Gottschalk's mistress in 1822.[56] New Orleans–born and the daughter of a coach and harness maker,[57] Judith Rubio descended from a family that had almost certainly fled from Saint-Domingue after the slave insurrections there. Over the next decade she was to grow wealthy through the beneficence of Edward Gottschalk, who not only gave her a house and servants but placed many of his own assets, including slaves, in her name in order to avoid creditors.[58] Significantly, these transactions continued after Gottschalk's marriage to Aimée Bruslé in 1828. Judith Rubio, who signed her last will and testament with an "X," became, in effect, Edward Gottschalk's business partner.

And also the mother of his children. Beginning with William in 1822, the Rubio-Gottschalk union produced two sons and two daughters. Edward Gottschalk named his mulatto daughters after his own sisters. His last child by Judith Rubio was Alcide, born in 1833, five years after his marriage and four years after the birth of Moreau Gottschalk.[59] There is no evidence to support the claim that Alcide was born to a different father.

Edward's union with a free woman of color was no secret to the New

Orleans business community or to his own relatives. Jewish businessman Jacob Hart sold slaves to Judith with promissory notes signed by Edward.[60] And brother George Gottschalk was present as witness when Judith dictated her will. Nor did Edward fail as a provider for his five mulatto children. He served in the capacity of tutor and legal guardian to these offspring after Judith's death in 1834, at the age of twenty-eight. His Rubio daughter Fleurette was sufficiently well-off to buy a slave and to send her daughter to a boarding school in Ohio.[61]

And so the question arises, was Moreau Gottschalk aware of the existence of his five mulatto half brothers and sisters? When Edward's legal family was living on Rampart Street between Bienville and Conti, Judith Rubio was on Bienville between Dauphine and Burgundy, three blocks away. Later, when Edward's legal family was domiciled on Esplanade Avenue at Royal Street, several members of the Rubio clan were living on the opposite corner. After Judith's death it was Edward, as executor, who advertised the sale of her property in the local press.[62] It is therefore inconceivable that Judith Rubio's existence and that of her Gottschalk family were unknown to young Moreau. Yet he never wrote or spoke of them, nor did he in any way acknowledge them during any of his return visits to his home town.

By 1828 Edward Gottschalk was solidly established in New Orleans. He had recently started his own firm and was making money in real estate, commodities, currency trading, and slaves. Judith Rubio and her brood were comfortably cared for and conveniently at hand. It was at this moment that he chose to take a wife, Aimée-Marie Bruslé, the fifteen-year-old daughter of Theodat-Camille Bruslé and Alixe-Josephine Deynault (or D'Eynaut or Deynaud).[63] His choice perfectly fit the profile of a wife for an ambitious young outsider in New Orleans.

Catholic and French in culture and language—she never learned to read English[64]—Aimée Bruslé represented to this newcomer the white Creole establishment of New Orleans. That old Mayor Pitot and the revered Uncle Moreau-Lislet stood as witnesses for the bride spoke for itself. And the fact that she was Catholic and he a non-practicing Jew? No problem. Years before, Hart Shiff had married Marguerite Basilique Chessé in St. Louis Cathedral, and Judah P. Benjamin was soon to marry Natalie Saint-Martin in that hallowed shrine as well.[65] To be sure, all three were marriages of convenience, and each of the Creole wives soon tired of both her husband and New Orleans and fled to Paris. Yet such marriages were in fashion, for the simple reason that they provided legitimacy for the husband and money for the wife.

Many years later, Moreau Gottschalk's sister Clara smugly confided to a New Orleans correspondent about the aristocratic origins of the Bruslé family, telling him airily that "the old Creoles were too lazy to say that *de* which prefixed noble French family names."[66] Elsewhere, Clara described how her brother was introduced into Parisian society by his grand-aunt, the Marquise de la Grange, a cultivated aristocrat.[67] Moreau himself referred to his great-grandfather as the "Comte de Bruslé."[68] Marquises, counts, the best Parisian salons—it all sounds very grand, or so Clara believed. Whether from modesty or skepticism, however, Moreau was usually more diffident. In fact, his Bruslé ancestors and their destroyed world were for him more a source of terror than of pride.

The village of Petite Rivière d'Artibonite lies squarely in the middle of Haiti, once the French colony of Saint-Domingue. Petite Rivière is a verdant island of deep green palms and banana trees slightly elevated above the surrounding ocean of sugar cane. On both sides of the Artibonite plain are huge mountains stretching west to the port town of Saint-Marc. Egrets stride about in the deep grass between the large brick Catholic church and the manse next door. In the late eighteenth century this was France's richest colony and the source of lucre so vast that it reshaped Europe's economy clear to the Urals. Described by one expert as "one of the most astonishing phenomena in the history of imperialism," Saint-Domingue in general and Petite Rivière in particular supplied half of Europe with tropical produce.[69]

The economy of Saint-Domingue in the eighteenth century was based on slavery, with chattels outnumbering the white masters ten to one. Between these two races was a third caste, the mulattos. These were people of mixed blood, French in language and culture, legally free, but fully subordinate to the whites. The interaction among these three castes was intense and daily, and each felt the cultural influence of the others. But their interests were fundamentally antagonistic, which accounted for the social instability that always existed even under the placid surface of the colony's life.

To control this volatile tropical money machine the French crown set up in Saint-Domingue a powerful civil administration backed by a large army. Moreau Gottschalk's great-grandfather Joseph-Antoine Bruslé was born in New Orleans in 1726 and went to seek his fortune on the island in the 1750s.[70] At first, he grew coffee in the mountain valleys or *mornes* near Grande-Rivière du Nord, but he eventually took a job as commandant of police in Petite Rivière d'Artibonite.[71] The post was an important and lucrative one, and he received a title for it. But he was not among the great planters of Saint-Domingue, nor was he one of the high French nobility who built their wealth on the fecund island. Antoine-Bruslé was, in fact, a *petit blanc*.

As representatives of the French crown, however, the Bruslés were prominent members of society in Petite Rivière. Over two generations their outlook and habits were molded by the distinctive environment there. A refugee from this lost world, Médéric-Louis-Elie Moreau de Saint-Méry, left a vivid description of it.[72] Leaving sugar production in the hands of their white overseers, members of the elite devoted themselves to the island's conservative politics and to a profligate social life. Few were interested in books, but they all pursued music, theater, and dancing with a passion. The fifteen-hundred-seat theater at the capital of Cap Françoise (now Cap Haitiens) brought the latest hits from Paris, and mulatto orchestras in smaller towns like Petite Rivière flavored French dance tunes with an Afro-Caribbean beat.

The French women of Saint-Domingue were poorly educated and strong-willed; Moreau de Saint-Méry called them childish.[73] But they were highly musical, as virtually every visitor attested. Wealthy beyond measure, they were also spendthrifts, as were their husbands. Indeed, by 1789 this pleasure-seeking island was deeply in debt.[74] This indebtedness gave an aura of fraudulence to the life of the colony and caused some of the more realistic residents to curse the place as an abode of the damned.[75]

Separated by a generation from this world, Aimée Bruslé Gottschalk nonetheless inherited many of its salient characteristics. Tutored by her uncle Moreau-Lislet, she was not uneducated.[76] But she was a willful spendthrift, childish, and indulgent both toward herself and toward her children. Like a Creole grandee in Saint-Domingue, she never considered herself wholly at home in New Orleans and used the first opportunity to flee to a Paris she had never known.

Given all this, it is no wonder that Moreau developed a theory that "women, even the most virtuous, will never have the judgment to know how to bring up their sons. I would be worthless and parasitic today," he wrote, "if my father had not had the courage to get me away from the family."[77] He viewed his mother as hopeless in all practical matters and condescended to her in the frequent letters he wrote her.

Notwithstanding these blunt views, Gottschalk was strongly attached to his mother, and that attachment exerted a direct influence on his outlook. His impulse for music had come from her, and from her also came the French language and Catholic faith that were so much a part of his orientation. Most important, he found his mother's ancestral world darkly fascinating, and that fascination profoundly colored his artistic imagination.

At age twenty-eight Moreau Gottschalk found himself sailing past the Haitian coast en route to St. Thomas. It was night, and as the other passengers slept, Moreau went up on deck and contemplated the desolate mountains of the former Saint-Domingue. "Everything, and more espe-

cially the name of Saint-Domingue, seemed to speak to my imagination
. . . ," he recalled. "My recollections [were] drawn . . . by a mysterious
affinity."[78]

This "mysterious affinity" pertained to the gory rebellion of the 1790s,
that destroyed the French colony and caused the murder or emigration
of nearly all its white inhabitants. It started in 1793 when Jacobins in
Paris declared the end of slavery throughout France and its possessions,
at which point the whites and mulattos of Saint-Domingue together appealed for help to Great Britain in the hope that English rule would lead
to the restoration of the slave economy that had sustained them. By 1794
British troops were in control of the entire center of Saint-Domingue,
including Petite Rivière. Joseph-Antoine Bruslé, Moreau Gottschalk's
great-grandfather, became a captain in the British army. This brief episode ended when bands of freed slaves under their feared leader Biassou
launched a massacre of both whites and mulattos.[79] Joseph-Antoine
Bruslé perished in the ensuing fighting, his brothers were put to death,
and their daughters died after "the most horrible outrages."[80] These were
the great aunts of Moreau Gottschalk. Eventually the brilliant general
Toussaint L'Ouverture, a former slave, drove both the British and their
French and mulatto allies from the island. Among the few to escape was
Moreau Gottschalk's grandfather Théodat-Camille Bruslé, son of Joseph-
Antoine, and several members of the Deynault family of Petite Rivière,
including Joséphine-Alix, Moreau's grandmother. They were all among the
twelve hundred whites and mulattos and sixteen hundred slaves who arrived in Kingston, Jamaica, at the end of 1793.[81]

Viewing the looming and dark mountains of Haiti from the deck of his
ship, Moreau Gottschalk mulled over this grim history. "Can anyone not
be astonished that the mere name of Saint-Domingue wakens somber
memories?" he asked. "Our dwelling burned, our properties devastated,
our fortunes annihilated—such were the first effects of that war between
two races who had in common only that implacable hatred which each
nourished for the other. . . . But," he asked, "can anyone be astonished
at the retaliation exercised by the Negroes on their old masters? What
cause, moreover, [could be] more legitimate than that of this people, rising in their agony in one grand effort to reconquer their unacknowledged
rights and their rank in humanity?"[82]

Toussaint L'Ouverture, who achieved the final victory over the Bruslés
and the Deynaults, was not a person whom the Gottschalk family had
reason to hold in high regard. Yet Moreau's great-uncle Moreau-Lislet had
actually served this African-American general as a secretary after Toussaint L'Ouverture's victory and held him in the highest respect thereafter.[83] Thanks probably to Moreau-Lislet, Toussaint emerged in Moreau

Gottschalk's mind as "the enthusiastic liberator of a race that nineteen centuries of Christianity had not yet been able to free from the yoke of its miseries."[84]

It was in Kingston, Jamaica, that Moreau Gottschalk's grandfather married Joséphine-Alix Deynault.[85] Initially, the British on Jamaica gave a warm welcome to the refugees from Saint-Domingue and treated them as allies. However, the refugees soon wore out their welcome. Finally, the British royal governor in 1804 arranged for the free passage of the entire group, including whites, mulattos, and slaves, either to Guadeloupe or the United States. Thousands sailed for Philadelphia and Charleston. The Bruslés and Deynaults, along with many others, chose New Orleans.[86] Besides being Catholic and French-speaking, New Orleans had the added attraction of being in a slave state, the sugar economy of which strongly resembled that of Saint-Domingue before the revolution.[87] Paradoxically, these pro-British émigrés from Saint Domingue, including Théodat-Camille Bruslé and several Deynault in-laws, were to be crucial to Andrew Jackson's victory over the British at the Battle of New Orleans in 1815.[88]

For two generations before the arrival of the French refugees from Saint-Domingue, New Orleans had been a provincial outpost of Spain, its population divided among French, Spanish, and a smattering of Yankees. The ten thousand refugees arriving from Saint-Domingue doubled the number of inhabitants and transformed New Orleans into a French city until they were in turn overwhelmed by waves of Yankee immigrants who arrived during young Moreau's childhood years.[89] Mulattos came as well, and both whites and mulattos brought slaves, who formed a third of New Orleans's population by 1810.

The immigrants of all races brought their culture with them. Their music and dancing enlivened the city, while their leaders—men like Moreau-Lislet—shaped its laws. One of the few bookstores in town was run by one of the refugees, Gaston Bruslé, a great-uncle of Moreau Gottschalk. Intellectual life also flourished in the Masonic lodges that the immigrants established, among them L'Étoile Polaire No. 5, to which Théodat-Camille Bruslé belonged until he went bankrupt.[90]

Whatever their pretensions to culture, many of the Creole immigrants had a hard time economically. After he and his family arrived in 1804–05, Théodat-Camille Bruslé found work as a customs inspector.[91] Both the Bruslés and Deynaults brought household slaves with them and traded freely in slaves thereafter.[92] Once he had amassed some capital, Bruslé purchased a large bakery on Chartres Street, along with the eleven slaves needed to run it.[93] The business turned out to be a disaster. One slave, Philippe, got a hernia; a second tried to run away and was sentenced to work on a chain gang; and a third, chief baker Asa, became paralyzed and had to quit work. In 1823 Bruslé declared bankruptcy.[94] His debts were staggering, including $42,190 owed to Moreau-Lislet alone. This is the point at which his wife renounced her community assets, the same humiliation that circumstances forced upon her daughter, Aimée, seven years later.

In a series of novels published in the late nineteenth century, New Orleans author George Washington Cable painted a highly romanticized picture of the white Creole elite from Saint-Domingue. Their leaders undeniably prospered and held sufficient political power to force a temporary stand-off with the incoming Yankees.[95] But while a few *grand blancs* flourished, the Bruslés' standing in society steadily sank. With at least eight children, they had many mouths to feed.[96] Merely to recover from the bankruptcy would have required the work of years. So when young Edward Gottschalk of London appeared on the scene, he was looked upon as a godsend. He seemed rich, was well educated, and could speak French. Above all, he was not a crude Yankee, and he expressed his readiness to have the children of his marriage raised as Catholics.

Unfortunately, marriage to Edward Gottschalk did not check Aimée Bruslé's downward slide in society. First there was Edward's bankruptcy in the months after the birth of their son Moreau. On the heels of this misfortune, Aimée was forced to renounce her community rights in the marriage and also to accept the fact that she was being rescued financially in part through the sale of slaves owned by her husband's mulatto mistress.

Once he came to terms with his creditors, Edward Gottschalk immediately began borrowing again in order to purchase real estate, hoping to settle the many claims against him through highly leveraged deals. New Orleans was experiencing the greatest land boom in its history, and he wanted to be a part of it. First, in April 1831, he bought for himself and his family a house on Rampart Street.[97] Then he proceeded to acquire large holdings elsewhere in the city and in the nearby town of Carrollton.[98] He also traded actively in slaves, turning over his "property" rapidly in order to ride the crest of the economic boom.[99]

Had everything worked as planned, Edward would have paid off his debts and built the kind of fortune that friends like Samuel Hermann had amassed. But this was not to be. By the spring of 1833 it was clear that once again Edward was badly over-extended and was in urgent need of cash. Once again he set about to liquidate every possible asset, beginning with those in his wife's name, in hopes of keeping his creditors at bay until his major investments would begin to pay off. The situation grew more desperate by the day. On March 20, 1833, Edward's financial house of cards collapsed. On that day the *New Orleans Bee* carried an announcement that Edward Gottschalk was leaving the country and was selling seven slaves and his residence at 88 Rampart Street, along with all its contents. Indeed, the detailed listing of the Gottschalk's household furnishings published in the *Bee* was itself an exquisite humiliation for Aimée. There were beds, cradles, clocks and sideboards, card tables, looking glasses, "elegant English chandeliers," cut glass, carpets, and rugs. As all the world could see, during the brief interval between financial crises, the Gottschalks had lived well. Also listed were "a superb harp" and "a second hand elegant piano of German manufacture [and] three new ones."[100] Thus were Aimée's musical aspirations placed on the auction block, along with everything else she owned.

Nor did the situation improve after this crash sale. By the following August twenty-one-year-old Aimée followed her husband into bankruptcy.[101] Some of the thirty-nine creditors held debts incurred by Aimée's shopping sprees. Most of the debts, however, arose from Edward's effort to raise capital in his wife's name. Consequently, Aimée was forced to sell off even the meager household effects she had assembled since the auction.[102] After this last sale the Gottschalk family moved to a tiny cottage, still standing, at the corner of Royal Street and Esplanade Avenue.

When they left Saint-Domingue, the Bruslés had brought with them Sally, a slave of about ten years of age. Many émigrés had emancipated their imported slaves, but the Bruslés could not afford this act of benevolence and instead kept Sally as a chattel.[103] Moreau later described her as "la Négresse Congo," but it is unclear whether this is a general reference to Sally's roots or evidence that she had actually been born in Africa.[104] Sally had served the family in Jamaica and had been nurse to the Bruslé children in New Orleans. She later became Moreau Gottschalk's nurse and, with his Grandmother Bruslé (née Deynault), one of the few sources of continuity in his young life. Now, over fifty, "sickly and subject to rheumatic pains," she, too, was put up for auction.[105] Uncle George Gottschalk's offer to purchase Sally in his nephew Moreau Gottschalk's name was almost certainly made in order to satisfy the pleadings of the young boy, who would otherwise have lost his beloved nurse.[106]

As required by Louisiana's Civil Code, a dryly factual record of the sale of Moreau's nurse was filed in the archive of the notary public, Mr. Carlile Pollock. Unstated in the sale price of $283.50 is the fact that this Sally, together with Grandmother Bruslé, served as a living link between the Bruslés' lost world in Saint-Domingue and young Moreau. Together, these old women, one white and one African-American, had regaled him with the Creole legends and lore of Saint-Domingue as well as with terrifying tales of the bloody slave revolt both had miraculously survived. Moreau recalled a typical scene:

> We would listen by the trembling fire on the hearth, under the coals of which Sally, the old Negress, baked her sweet potatoes, to the recital of this terrible Negro insurrection. She was the same old Sally who, while listening all the time [to Grandmother Bruslé], spoke in a low voice to a portrait of Napoleon hung above the fireplace, which she obstinately believed was bewitched. . . . I was without any doubt Sally's favorite, to judge by the stories with which she filled my head. I was not tired of listening for the hundredth time to the marvelous adventures Compé Bouqui (the clown of the Negroes) and the knavery of Compé Lapin, whose type represents the Punchinello of Europe.[107]

Sally and Grandmother Bruslé formed a unique team. Taking turns, they passed on the lore of Haiti and South Louisiana, the Grimm's fairy tales, as it were, of the Creole world. From time to time Sally would interrupt Josephine-Alixe Bruslé's narrative to exorcise a *Zombi*. "Shivering with fright," Moreau recalled, "we narrowed our circle around my grandmother, who, after crossing herself and scolding Sally, took up her story where she had left off."[108]

Moreau Gottschalk literally owned this Sally until she was transferred once more to the care of Grandmother Bruslé. Both Sally and Grandmother Bruslé survived into the 1850s, living links with a world more vivid to Moreau than his own ill-starred environment.

By the time of Moreau Gottschalk's fifth birthday his family had settled into a more stable existence. They shared a four-storied house, still standing at 518 Conti Street, with several Bruslé relatives,[109] and Edward Gottschalk returned to his ceaseless, but now more profitable, speculation in slaves and land. The family grew with the birth of Celestine in 1833, Edward Jr. in 1836, Clara in 1837, Augusta in 1840, and Blanche in 1842. The expanded family also attained a measure of creature comfort, although the shadow of the two earlier bankruptcies continued to hang over the family in the form of onerous debt payments.

By the measure of their day, both Aimée and Edward Gottschalk were failures. Down to the time she left for Paris, Aimée never enjoyed the carefree life of music, dancing, and social soirées she considered her birthright. Edward, for his part, failed to attain the wealth and standing he had thought would be his when he departed London for New Orleans. Worse, he failed to meet the very Jewish ideal of father-provider that he preached so relentlessly to his eldest son. Thus did Moreau Gottschalk grow up in a world of failed hopes and dreams deferred.

Chapter Three

❧ Young Gottschalk and Musical Democracy in New Orleans

E DWARD Gottschalk's improved circumstances continued even through the financial panic of 1837, which closed fourteen New Orleans banks and devastated many local families. The city did not fully recover until 1842, but Gottschalk managed to keep his head above water this time. During these years there were several deaths in the family, including two of Moreau's uncles, Charles Bruslé and Dr. Joseph Victor Gottschalk.[1] But even these did not disrupt an environment that was now more favorable for a young person's education than anything Edward and Aimée Gottschalk had been able to provide heretofore.

To be sure, there were still moments of dark terror, and these left an indelible impression on Moreau. A quarter century later he still recalled being thrilled at his grandmother's chilling tales of the escaped slave John Squier, nicknamed Bras Coupé ("Broken Arm"), who adroitly eluded his would-be captors for months as the entire populace of New Orleans followed the adventure. Rumors spread throughout the superstitious old city that bullets flattened against Bras Coupé's chest and that his glance cast a spell. Eight-year-old Moreau knew the full details of Bras Coupé's folkloric life and may even have been among the thousands who viewed his body when it was exhibited on the Place d'Arms in 1837.[2]

Three years earlier, when Moreau was but five, an even grislier episode in race relations touched the Gottschalk household directly. A wealthy but demented Creole lady named Delphine La Laurie maintained a much admired residence on Royal Street. One day in April 1834, fire broke out in the attic of this structure. Firemen and city officials burst in to save the building and its inhabitants. In the process of their rescue mission they discovered seven manacled slaves under the eaves, along with vile instruments of torture their owner had used upon them. Madame La Laurie fled, and the outraged townspeople ransacked her home.[3]

Madame La Laurie's oppression of her slaves instantly entered the lore of New Orleans. For the Gottschalks it was no mere legend, however, for the witness who filed the most detailed deposition on the La Laurie affair was Judge J. F. Canonge, who rented a house from Aimée Gottschalk,[4] and one of the two witnesses to Canonge's statement was Edward Gottschalk.[5]

The terror and fright other American romantics experienced at second hand by reading the stories of Edgar Allen Poe or E. T. A. Hoffmann came to Moreau directly from his immediate environment. He was fascinated by the music of the complex and biracial world into which he was born. Yet this fascination had a darker side, as is suggested by his later decision to set to music a poem entitled *Le Mancenillier*, the name of a sweet and enticing tropical plant that is fatal to anyone who consumes it.

Balancing these sinister tales was a serious Catholic upbringing from Abbé Blanc and other members of the local clergy. Many contemporary visitors and not a few later writers dismissed New Orleans's Catholicism as hedonistic and over-forgiving.[6] Yet a Northern-born Protestant clergyman who knew well the Catholic hierarchy of Louisiana in the period of Moreau's childhood flatly rejected this characterization. On the contrary, he considered the New Orleans clergy he knew to be "models of clerical wisdom, decorum, and propriety" and praised their "spotless moral life." Indeed, he concluded, Catholicism in New Orleans was "infinitely superior to any Protestant denomination in its provision of money and charity for the poor."[7] Moreau never rejected his solid grounding in this world of New Orleans Catholicism. It provided him a standard against which he measured both Yankee Protestantism and the corruption of the Catholic Church in South America.

If his Catholic upbringing traced to Aimée Gottschalk, Moreau's studies at an English-speaking private school reflected his father's preference. George W. Harby had come to New Orleans from Charleston, South Carolina, and in 1833 founded an "academy" on Tivoli (now Lee) Circle.[8] At the time Moreau studied there, Harby's Academy offered courses in orthography, penmanship, reading, arithmetic, history, geography, and grammar.[9] Thanks to this, by the time he departed for Paris at age twelve, Moreau had already received a thorough English-language education of the same type that propertied Americans elsewhere would have known. He had also been tutored in French by a native instructor, M. Mauroy.[10] If Moreau returned from Paris with a slight French accent, as some of his New England detractors loved to point out, he was nonetheless a native speaker of English who had received five years of education in a premier American school.

Moreau's experience at Harby's Academy opened to him a world at once broader and less threatening than that of his family. In later years he was to become a champion of education as a liberating force. Not once, however, did he speak of the family as the primary unit in society, nor did he ever marry and start a family of his own. Given his experience of childhood in a crisis-ridden family, this is scarcely surprising.

It was Edward Gottschalk who pushed Moreau to excel in music.[11] For this purpose he engaged F. J. Narcisse Letellier, a tenor at the Théâtre d'Orléans, composer, and in his spare time a "professor of music."[12] A Parisian with family still in the French capital, Letellier brought his young piano student along rapidly. When Moreau was seven, Letellier is said to have invited him to play the organ at the St. Louis Cathedral during mass, while he himself worked the pedals and stops.[13] Letellier may also have introduced Moreau to composition, as he himself was composing and publishing romances during the time he was teaching young Gottschalk.[14] Moreau also took violin lessons from a Frenchman named Elie, who played in the orchestra at the Théâtre d'Orléans.[15]

To this point, there was nothing exceptional about Moreau Gottschalk's musical upbringing. He was, in fact, well on the way to becoming yet another foot soldier in the army of child prodigies that was invading the American concert stage in the 1830s. Every city had its own juvenile geniuses. Baltimorians, for example, thrilled to young Martin Goodall, who dressed in knee-pants and played Mendelssohn, and to the neonatal pianist Josephine Branson, who made her stage debut at the age of four.[16]

What saved Moreau Gottschalk from this fate and set him instead on a course that would change the shape of American music? Aside from his own inborn talent, he was shaped from the earliest age by a cultural environment in New Orleans that was second to none in the Americas with respect to the quantity, quality, and diversity of music performed there. The *Bee* did not exaggerate when it boasted that "the little musical enthusiasm prevailing in the United States is nearly entirely concentrated in New Orleans."[17] Far from being on the "exotic periphery," as musicologist Gilbert Chase claimed, Gottschalk's home town was, in the 1830s, the focal point of music in America.

It is hard today to grasp the sheer vitality of musical life in the Crescent City during the period of Gottschalk's boyhood. With a population of only sixty thousand, New Orleans supported several full-time theaters and major halls, each staffed with resident orchestras and performers, and a half dozen dance halls, which called nightly on the services of yet more musicians. Several music stores sold instruments and published large numbers of compositions by local composers. A triangular touring circuit embracing New Orleans, Havana, and New York brought artists from every part of Europe. Fiddlers and banjo-pickers drawn from the bustling American West appeared on street corners, in the city's saloons, and, slightly later, in minstrel theaters; the Catholic churches supported choirs and organists; and the garrison bands of local U.S. Army units produced martial music to fill any moments of silence that may accidentally have opened.[18]

Up North, what little music that was to be heard was confined to six days each week, leaving the Sabbath wrapped in deathly quiet except for hymn singing. In the theaters, ballrooms, and public squares of New Orleans, by contrast, secular music poured forth on the Sabbath as well, to the horror of virtually every visiting puritan but to the delight of guests from the Continent. It is doubtful that there existed a city of comparable size anywhere that was more single-mindedly dedicated to music than New Orleans.

This remarkable effervescence presented three striking and distinctive features: first, the city was madly devoted to opera, and especially to the grand and ebulliently lyrical operas of contemporary France and Italy; second, popular, folk, and dance music poured forth from every segment of the population, whether frontiersmen from the West, native-born Louisiana Creoles, both white and black, or new immigrants; and, third, both the sophisticated operatic performances and the folksier music of the dance-halls were accessible to the entire population, rich and poor, white and black. Together, these features made for what was, by any measure, the most stunning manifestation of Jacksonian democracy in the realm of culture to be found anywhere in America. Each of these three characteristics left an indelible mark on Moreau Gottschalk.

New Orleans boasted two permanent opera companies before any other city in the United States had even one. In the five years leading up to Moreau Gottschalk's departure for Paris in 1841, the French company at the Théâtre d'Orléans offered 364 performances of sixty-five operas by twenty-seven composers.[19] In a single week in 1836—the year Moreau was first taken to the opera—New Orleanians could attend fourteen different performances of nine operas by four different companies, "two [of them] unsurpassed in the United States."[20] Over the entire decade, New Orleans audiences heard more American premieres than the rest of the country combined, and more new operas were written in New Orleans than anywhere else in the New World. When an Italian company arrived in New Orleans in 1837, the local *Picayune* could state flatly, "We have now, in this place, what no city in America, and few cities in the world can boast of, strong companies in the English, French, and Italian languages, and what is more they are all extremely well patronized."[21] Moreau was eight years old at the time.

Public support was essential to the success of opera in New Orleans, for all performances were produced on a purely commercial basis. If the twenty-five thousand whites and fifteen thousand free people of color did not buy tickets, a production would die. Thus Moreau Gottschalk grew up in an environment in which artists assumed they must respond to the public's taste and in which the public sensed its own controlling influence over the arts. However rough on performers, these attitudes nonetheless represented Jacksonian democracy in action.

Marketing was important. The plots of new operas were published in the press, and special productions were mounted to attract children and amateurs.[22] Even the halls were designed to impress and delight the public. The St. Charles Theater, for example, built when Moreau was six, was the largest in the United States and featured a two-ton chandelier. It provided a special section for free people of color and, in the upper gallery, ample seating for slaves. Operatic music thus permeated the whole society, and it was not uncommon to hear African-American workers whistling Italian arias on the street.[23]

In the world of New Orleans opera and classical music the color line separating whites from free people of color was far weaker than in society as a whole. Edmond Dédé (1827–1903) was the son of a free Afro-Caribbean band master from Saint-Domingue and was studying under the conductor of the St. Charles Theater orchestra in the years Gottschalk took lessons from Letellier. Dédé, too, completed his studies in Paris. Unlike Moreau, he settled in France, finding a permanent position in Bordeaux as conductor of the municipal orchestra there.[24] He returned only once to New Orleans, in 1893, when he appeared on a program with Basile Barès and W. J. Nickerson, later "professor" to Jelly Roll Morton.[25] Yet another pianist and contemporary of Gottschalk was Lucien Lambert (ca. 1828–96). A free African-American, Lambert studied piano in Paris. Lambert knew Moreau as a boy and enjoyed a friendly rivalry with him. Later, he identified himself as a "protégé de M. Gottschalk."[26] Their paths crossed again in Brazil at the end of Gottschalk's life, when Lambert assisted in several Gottschalk concerts and then served as a pallbearer at his funeral.[27]

Opera in New Orleans was the music of democracy, permeating all levels of society. Public balls were frequent and open to absolutely anyone who could pay the price of admission.[28] The orchestras that played at these balls adapted arias from popular operas, much the way Broadway hit tunes later provided themes for jazz musicians. It is appropriate that Gottschalk's formal debut occurred in a ballroom and that his program featured operatic fantasies.

New Orleanians' passion for opera brought leading European talents to the banks of the Mississippi. Eugène-Prosper Prévost (1809–72) had been a colleague of Berlioz at the Conservatoire in Paris before settling in New Orleans as director of the Théâtre d'Orléans. Moreau was nine at the time. Another arrival was Jean-Baptiste-Louis Guiraud (1803–ca. 1864), who had beaten Berlioz for the coveted Prix de Rome. His son Ernest, born in 1837, quickly absorbed the city's operatic atmosphere and at age fifteen composed and produced a complete opera of his own, *Le Roi David*. He, too, was sent to Paris for study, but he never returned. Ernest Guiraud later composed the recitatives of Bizet's *Carmen*, completed the orchestration of Offenbach's *Tales of Hoffman*, and, as a professor at the Paris Conservatoire, taught such luminaries as Claude Debussy (1837–92).[29]

The two-way traffic with Paris occasioned by New Orleans's unquenchable thirst for opera drew all the city's musicians into its orbit. Paul Emile Johns (ca. 1798–1860) owned a New Orleans music store in the 1830s and published an *Album Louisianais* during Moreau's childhood. Other aria-like songs by Johns were issued in Paris by Camille Pleyel, a piano manufacturer, publisher, and future patron of Gottschalk.

Among Moreau Gottschalk's compositions were to be thirty-one fantasies on themes from operas by Méhul, Verdi, Thomas, Rossini, Donizetti, Bellini, Weber, Wagner, Gounod, Mendelssohn and Flotow. Many of Gottschalk's closest musical friends were to be opera singers, and, like most virtuosos of his era, he included fantasies, transcriptions, or free improvisations on operatic arias in virtually every one of his concerts. Beyond this, he himself was to compose three operas, as well as a shorter operatic work in a Spanish genre.[30] Even Gottschalk piano pieces with no obvious relation to opera reveal the influence of the romantic stage in their emphasis on emotional impact at the expense of formal structure and in their overall vocal and lyric quality.

Throughout his life Gottschalk retained the utter present-mindedness that characterized the musical public of New Orleans. The very concept of a "classic" was unknown there. Practically the only earlier composer revered in New Orleans during Moreau's childhood was Étienne Henri Méhul (1763–1817), whose opera *Le Jeune Henri* (1797) provided themes for one of Gottschalk's most enduringly popular fantasies. Gottschalk also absorbed his native city's preference for Italian and French composers, as opposed to German. The one exception to this bias was Weber's *Der Freischütz*, which New Orleans audiences knew as *Robin des Bois*. Far more to the local taste were the operas of Bellini, Donizetti, Rossini,

Meyerbeer, and, above all, Daniel-François Auber (1782–1871).[31] Gottschalk came to admire all of these with the exception of Auber, whose graceful comic operas held no interest for him at all. Parisians claimed the only emotion Auber knew was boredom, which may account for Gottschalk's indifference to his music.[32]

Far more stirring for Moreau were the grand musical dramas of Giacomo Meyerbeer, and especially his stupendously popular opera of 1831, *Robert le Diable*. This opera, with its Gothic plot, supernatural interventions, and fantastic stage machinery, took New Orleans by storm in 1835, when both the English and French companies competed to produce the American premiere.[33] In the end, *Robert le Diable* became the most widely performed opera in New Orleans, and probably in the United States as a whole.

Aimée Gottschalk adored this opera and played the aria *Grâce* on the piano for her son.[34] She took young Moreau to a performance of *Robert le Diable* when he was seven, and he sat entranced. Later he claimed that the Meyerbeer opera "filled [his] early years with ineffable joy" and referred to its author as his "beloved and illustrious master."[35]

Scarcely had Meyerbeer's masterpiece been staged in Paris than Chopin composed a fantasy for piano and cello based on its main themes. Franz Liszt followed with his own intricate and demanding version, while Beethoven's pupil Carl Czerny weighed in with yet another fantasy.[36] Gottschalk was to join this group, for he often used arias from *Robert le Diable* as themes for improvisations. Meyerbeer's *Les Huguenots* also hit the New Orleans stage with what Berlioz had described as the opera's "thundering discharge of lyric electricity."[37] Again, Gottschalk swallowed the work whole. A quarter century later he was still improvising on what he called the "eternally beautiful" aria *Bénédiction des poignards* from this Meyerbeer opera. When Meyerbeer died, Moreau penned a moving obituary for the *Home Journal* of New York.

Gottschalk was inspired directly by Meyerbeer's method of harmonization. Musicologist Leann F. Logsdon has shown how much Gottschalk owed to Meyerbeer.[38] The use of secondary dominant chords, diminished triads, and progressions by thirds are no mere technical devices enabling Gottschalk to shift smoothly from major to minor or back. Rather, they are an important part of the quintessential Gottschalk sound and among the elements to which the peculiar emotional impact of his compositions can be traced.

Alongside this world of opera, New Orleans boasted a diverse band of street corner virtuosos, minstrel entertainers, fiddlers playing for dancing, and ordinary people singing songs of distant times and places. No less than the world of opera, this realm of untutored musicians was accessible to all and enjoyed by everyone. Musical segregation by class or race was utterly impossible in a city where peoples' homes were acoustically wide open to the streets for most of the year.

Did young Moreau hear Thomas D. "Daddy" Rice, father of American minstrelsy, perform *Jump Jim Crow* between acts of *Robert le Diable* at the Camp Street Theater?[39] Did he hear the beloved street vendor Old Corn Meal, who in 1837 sang at the St. Charles Theater in what was possibly the first appearance by an African-American musician on the highbrow American stage?[40] Did Moreau see blackface dancer Master Diamond perform his double-shuffle on street corners or on the New Orleans stage?[41] And what about the banjo virtuoso Picayune Butler, who was playing on New Orleans streets during Moreau's childhood? These were all among the inescapable elements of New Orleans's cultural scene during those years.

Yet it was not these public performers, with their distinctly North American music, who left the deepest impression on the aspiring pianist and composer. By far the most important musical legacy that Moreau Gottschalk received from his New Orleans childhood was Creole melodies. By the time he departed for France at age twelve, Moreau's memory was richly stocked with Creole songs that were later to inspire his best work as a composer and win him undying fame. The role of these Creole melodies in his oeuvre was analogous to the Polish airs young Chopin brought from Warsaw to Paris, and their impact on later music was, if anything, greater.

Where was Gottschalk exposed to songs like *Le Belle Lolotte*, which provided the theme for *La Savane*, op. 3, or *Chanson de Lizette*, which is the first theme of *Le Mancenillier*, op. 11, *En avan' Grenadie*, which is the theme for *Le Bananier*, op. 5, or *Quan' patate la cuite*, well known as the main theme of Gottschalk's *Bamboula*, op. 2?[42] The most common explanation is that such tunes were ubiquitous in New Orleans, the inescapable background music for life there at the time. This argument usually focuses on young Moreau's supposed contact with Sunday afternoon public dances held by slaves on Congo Square on Rampart Street. It has often been argued that through contact with Congo Square Moreau was exposed not only to the specific tunes he later used in his own compositions but also to a living African cultural memory, which he appropriated as his own.[43] Gottschalk's biographer Vernon Loggins made this claim in 1958.[44] The argument is logical enough since public dances featuring slave musicians playing Afro-Caribbean drums are known to have been held on Congo Square in the early nineteenth century and since the Gottschalks are known to have lived nearby on Rampart Street. To clinch his case, Loggins even portrays young Moreau dancing on the gallery of his family house on Rampart Street to the exotic sounds floating down the street from Congo Square.

Thanks to Loggins, the link between Gottschalk's most famous works and Congo Square has entered the general literature. The sole authority to question it has been musicologist Gilbert Chase, who pronounced the supposition that Gottschalk had "lifted" his *Bamboula* from Congo Square "farfetched."[45] But Chase's was a solo voice. Some have gone so far as to charge Gottschalk with stealing the music of Congo Square and profiting from it while its true African-American authors remained poor and anonymous.

Before accepting such charges as valid, it would be well to take a closer look at the assumptions upon which they are based.

The devil dwells in the details. The Gottschalks lived on Rampart Street only between April 1831 and March 1833, and half of that time the family spent in Pass Christian avoiding cholera. Six or eight months in the life of a two-year-old hardly seems enough time in which to form an exhaustive knowledge of the several dozen melodies that Loggins and others claim Moreau appropriated from Congo Square. Another inconvenient detail is that the Gottschalk residence at 88 Rampart Street was over a half mile distant from Congo Square, too far for the melodies of songs to carry. Of course, the young boy could have been taken to Congo Square by his nurse, a common practice a generation earlier, if not in the 1830s.[46] But did this happen, and was it at Congo Square that the infant Moreau accumulated his rich collection of Creole melodies?

Congo Square derived its name not from some public belief that African dances were held there, as is generally assumed, but from a controversial "Congo Circus" organized by a Signore Gaetano from Havana in 1816 and open only to whites.[47] Following the wave of immigrants from Saint-Domingue, African-Americans held Sunday dances at Congo Square for several years. Among the dancers during the earliest years were at least some first generation slaves from Africa. However, by the second decade of the nineteenth century assimilation had progressed far. African music and dances were dying out, and their place was taken by West Indian *contradanzas* and by popular American melodies of various types. By the 1820s the assemblies at Congo Square, though raucous and picturesque, were sufficiently altered for them to have been called "balls" without irony.[48] By the 1830s even these activities were sharply on the decline. It is thus extremely unlikely, not to say impossible, that Congo Square was the source of young Moreau's detailed knowledge of Creole lyrics and songs, even if he spent much time there and remembered it all, for which there is not a shred of evidence.

How, then, did the purported Congo Square theory become so intimate a part of the Gottschalk legend? The first mention of this link appears in a short promotional pamphlet on Gottschalk issued in Philadelphia in 1853 by a New Hampshire–born lawyer named Edward Henry Durell. "H.D.," as he identified himself on the cover, had spent several years in New Orleans after 1837 and had published a small volume on the lore of that city.[49] He had followed Moreau's rise to prominence and in his promotional booklet stated that one could see dances like the Bamboula performed on "the public squares in the lower portions of the city." Durell does not, however, affirm that he himself actually witnessed the exotic scenes he describes, nor does he state or imply that this was Gottschalk's source.[50]

This was left to novelist George Washington Cable, who in the early 1880s was commissioned by the *Century Magazine* to do a series of articles on Creole music. This was an era in which "traditions" were being invented throughout Europe and America—mass-produced, in fact—and Cable used the opportunity created by the editors of the *Century* to manufacture some traditions for New Orleans.[51] The first of his articles appeared in February 1886 and was entitled "The Dance in Place Congo." Cable had picked up stories of wild dancing on that spot from New Orleans old-timers but was unable to derive from his informants anything concrete about either the dances or the music accompanying them. Lacking direct evidence and convinced that he had in hand something truly exotic, Cable turned to descriptions of slave dances on Saint-Domingue a half century earlier contained in Médéric Moreau de Saint-Méry's *Déscription topographique . . . de l'Isle Saint-Domingue*, published in Philadelphia in 1797–98, and to the same author's *De la danse*, issued on Parma in 1801.[52] Moreau de Saint Méry's accounts are colorful, to be sure, but they pertain to the world of Aimée Gottschalk's Bruslé forebears, and not to New Orleans of the 1830s. This meant nothing to Cable, however, who blithely pasted them into his description of Congo Square without acknowledging his chronological and geographical slight of hand.

But what about the songs? Again, Cable could glean no specific evidence from his New Orleans informants. Stymied in his own effort to find the Creole exotica expected by his New York editors, Cable did the next best thing: he contacted Moreau Gottschalk's sister Clara Gottschalk Peterson.[53] This was no accident, for Cable's very interest in Creole songs had been stimulated in the first place by Moreau Gottschalk's music. Cable realized that the Gottschalks knew these songs as well as or better than anyone else and was not particular from what source they had derived them, so long as he could use them for his article on Congo Square. To his credit, Cable never failed to acknowledge his indebtedness to Gottschalk and Clara when he spoke about the subject of Creole music during his later lecture tours with Mark Twain. But he failed to note that these songs had no known connection with Congo Square.[54]

It was this collection of evidence, deriving first from Moreau de Saint-Méry's books on Saint-Domingue in the eighteenth century and second from Clara Gottschalk, that provided the core of Cable's article on "The Dance on Place Congo." And it is this article, in turn, on which virtually every writer, including Loggins, relies to support the claim that Gottschalk's music was inspired by Congo Square. If there was any exploitation in the situation, it was not in Gottschalk's use of songs from Congo Square but in Cable's appropriation of songs from Moreau Gottschalk to flesh out his mythological image of Congo Square as a dissemination point for West Indian and African culture in New Orleans.

Cable in turn had been pushed to this thesis by Lafcadio Hearn, the Greco-Irish wanderer, writer, and proto-anthropologist who served as associate editor of the *New Orleans Item* while Cable was writing his essays. Hearn, a fanatical Gottschalk devotee, had urged his friend Cable to borrow heavily from the New Orleans composer, whom he described elsewhere as the "alchemist" and "magician" who had extracted the musical perfume from the flowers of the Antilles.[55] Initially, Hearn had been searching for direct African holdovers in the culture of New Orleans. He eventually concluded that this formulation was wrong and that the immediate source of what he considered exotic in the music and culture of New Orleans was not indigenous at all but had been brought there from the West Indies.[56]

If a two-year-old Moreau did not learn his Creole songs by hanging on the fence of Congo Square as a spectator, where did he acquire his thorough knowledge of this music? The answer is that young Gottschalk learned these songs in his own home. Neither he, his sister Clara, nor anyone else with direct knowledge of the Gottschalk family ever claimed otherwise. Thanks to two natives of Saint-Domingue, his Grandmother Bruslé and his African-American nurse Sally, he was exposed to these songs from earliest childhood. His sisters sang them,[57] and he learned to play them on the piano. Indeed, the music of old Saint-Domingue formed an essential element of the Gottschalks' family life. The Gottschalks were not unique in this respect, as Cable acknowledged. In presenting the song *Ah, Suzette,* Cable himself noted that it was from a "[white] Creole drawing-room in the rue Esplanade that we draw the following, so familiar to all Creole ears."[58] But the music of Saint-Domingue was a constant and vital presence in the Gottschalk's family circle.

Thus Moreau Gottschalk drew upon a French- and African-tinged Caribbean folk music that was part of his own family's immediate world. It is impossible to determine the extent to which this had become part of some generalized legacy in New Orleans. But Gottschalk knew it because it was part of the Bruslé family's heritage and was still perpetuated around their hearth three decades after they arrived from Saint-Domingue via Jamaica. No other musician seems to have had a more thorough knowledge of these songs, and none was more deeply influenced by them. Indeed, many are known today because Gottschalk alone preserved them.

As the economy of New Orleans recovered from the Panic of 1837, society also revived. As this happened, a string of illustrious visitors came to town and added excitement to young Moreau's life. Among them was "America" (actually Helena) Vespucci, a self-proclaimed descendant of America's namesake. Moreau was among the crowd that cheered this adventuress when she appeared on the balcony of the St. Louis Hotel in 1839.[59] Then came Andrew Jackson in January 1840, to commemorate the twenty-fifth anniversary of the Battle of New Orleans by laying the cornerstone of a monument in his honor on Jackson Square. By virtue of the fact that Grandfather Bruslé and several uncles had fought by Jackson's side in 1815, Moreau was outfitted in a bright uniform and included in the party that received "Old Hickory" at the St. Louis Hotel.[60]

The ardor with which New Orleanians welcomed Jackson reflected the fact that the city was becoming more self-consciously American. Moreau thrilled to the parades of local militia, who looked for all the world like members of an operatic chorus in their gaudy uniforms.[61] Impresario James Caldwell of the St. Charles Theater offered a prize for the best variations on *Hail, Columbia* and *Yankee Doodle*, patriotic airs upon which Moreau would frequently improvise later.[62] It was at this time, too, that a local Native American Party began to gain political ascendance over the Creole and foreign elements.

Amidst this wave of American nationalism, Felix Miolan, concertmaster of the Théâtre d'Orléans and a friend of Moreau's teacher Narcisse Letellier, pleaded with Edward Gottschalk to allow his son to appear in a concert the violinist was arranging to benefit himself. Edward agreed, but refused to let Miolan scoop a more formal debut for his son, insisting instead that Moreau be identified on the program simply as "young X, a Creole."[63] The performance was set for May 21, 1840, at the new St. Charles Hotel, the largest hostelry in America and just completed by Anglo-Saxon New Orleanians in order to upstage the St. Louis Hotel, deep in the French Quarter. Moreau appeared four times on the program, three of them as an accompanist in chamber groups. During the same week the celebrated ballerina Fanny Elssler was performing in *La Sylphide* at the Théâtre d'Orléans. Her show-stopper, interpolated into the ballet, was a spicy Latin dance entitled *La Cachucha*. Moreau made his solo debut by performing a series of variations on this hit tune, much to the audience's delight.[64]

Even before the Miolan benefit, the identity of "young X" was well known around town. Prodigies were everywhere in demand, and nowhere more so than in the Royal Street home of Gabriel and Jeanne Boyer. Mr. Boyer ran a "Day and Boarding School for Young Gentlemen" on Conti Street, while his wife was a "professor of music" in whose salon gathered both local and visiting musicians.[65] Moreau began playing weekly at the Boyers', gaining valuable experience and also meeting visiting musical luminaries.[66]

Soon Letellier and Madam Boyer agreed that Moreau had learned all he could in New Orleans and that he should continue his studies in Paris. Edward Gottschalk readily assented.[67] In an effort to pay for this venture, and also to capitalize on the popularity of "young X," Mr. Gottschalk arranged a farewell concert to benefit his son. Knowing that study in Paris would have more appeal to local Creoles than to Yankees living across Canal Street, Edward Gottschalk rented the ballroom of the St. Louis Hotel, engaged the full orchestra and soloists from the Théâtre d'Orléans, and appealed to the French consul, M. David, to serve as honorary patron for the event.[68] The press built up the concert as the debut of "the first Creole to dedicate himself to an artistic career."[69] In the same spirit of Francophone pride, the *Daily Picayune* reported that on the evening of the concert the St. Louis ballroom "glittered with Creole beauty." Door receipts were close to six hundred dollars, an impressive harvest.[70]

The two-part program was one of those mixed salads that delighted the nineteenth-century public. Each part began with an overture from an Auber opera, included both string and horn solos, and featured Moreau in the roles of both accompanist and soloist. Significantly, his major solos were variations on operatic themes, the first from Donizetti's *Anna Bolena* and the finale a chorus from Meyerbeer's *Il Crocciato in Egitto* as transcribed by the Parisian virtuoso and piano manufacturer Henri Herz.

Warmed by the spectacle of a slender eleven-year-old playing bravura variations on familiar themes, the audience cheered appreciatively. When the French consul presented Moreau with an immense wreath, the young virtuoso modestly turned to Aimée Gottschalk, who was sitting near the stage, and said, "Mama, it's for you!" Again, the audience roared its approval.

Aimée Gottschalk desperately feared the departure of her eldest child, so the family kept her ignorant of the precise time of his debarkation for Paris. Edward booked passage on the ship *Taglioni*, appropriately named for Marie Taglioni, the great Italian ballerina and star of the Paris opera.

Advertised as an "A-1 and fast sailing packet ship having handsome accommodations," the *Taglioni* had the added advantage of having an old friend of Edward Gottschalk's, Captain Rogers, at the helm. The Taglioni set sail on Saturday, May 1, 1841.[71] The passage to Le Havre was uneventful for Moreau, but back at home Aimée Gottschalk fell into so deep a depression that the family feared for her life.

Thus closed the New Orleans phase of Moreau Gottschalk's upbringing. Spanning barely a dozen years, it nonetheless exerted so decisive an influence on his later life that even a decade spent in Europe failed to dilute its impact. Thereafter he never spent more than a few weeks at a time in his home town, and when the United States split apart in Civil War Gottschalk sided with the Union, against his native city and region. Yet to the end he remained a New Orleanian of the 1830s. He combined in himself the city's seemingly incompatible strains of cultures tracing to North America, Southern Europe, the Caribbean, and Africa. Like other New Orleanians of his day, he was addicted to opera and to democracy in the arts; and like them, too, he was by temperament exuberant but tinged with the sadder tones that lurked just under the surface of life in the sugar-growing régions of the Caribbean with their economics based on slavery.

Gottschalk always considered New Orleans his home, and when he would encounter fellow New Orleanians in St. Louis, Virginia City, or Acapulco, he would seize upon them as soul mates. This practice serves to underscore the fact that from the day of his departure from the United States in his twelfth year, Gottschalk felt himself to be perpetually in exile from his New Orleans home, an uprooted wanderer in the best romantic tradition.

Chapter Four

❧ A Creole in Paris

EDWARD Gottschalk had arranged for his son to attend a private
boarding school in Paris run by a Monsieur and Madame Dussert.[1]
Once Moreau arrived in the French capital, he therefore headed directly
to the Dusserts' apartment at 74 rue de Clichy.

The solidly bourgeois five-story building in which the Dusserts resided
still stands at the corner of rue Ballu. Henri Murger, author of the book
La Vie de Bohème that gave bohemianism its name, was to live nearby at
number 30 rue de Clichy, yet the area was far from being the haunt of
artists.[2] Only a few doors away were the headquarters of the British Bible
Society and beyond that the Maison du Protestantisme Français. Throughout his teenage years Moreau was to live in this island of earnest respectability just up the hill toward Montmartre from the vast Église de la Trin-
ité, then under construction.

Paris of the early 1840s brings to mind images of a debauched young
Baudelaire squandering his family's fortune at his residence on the Île de
Saint-Louis; of audiences at the Théâtre Français spellbound by the terri-
fying intensity of the young Jewish actress Rachel; and of George Sand
looming with her cigar over a fragile and ailing Chopin in the salon of the
Princess de la Muscova. All this in fact took place, but it was set against
the background of a far more conventional, even bland, society.

Paris was growing stolidly bourgeois. Sturdy apartment houses like
those on rue de Clichy were rising everywhere in the city of nearly a
million, and railroad lines were being extended from the remote provinces into the heart of Paris. Bankers, not bohemians, were in charge, and
over them reigned the unlikely King Louis Philippe, the monarch who
wore a felt hat instead of a crown and who carried a homely umbrella
instead of a scepter.[3] Never mind that huge and corrupt monopolies were
spreading through the economy, or that the Parliament continually

pressed Louis Philippe for the sweeping electoral reforms that were so badly needed. The Paris at which Moreau arrived was solidly respectable. And more than slightly vulgar. Snuff had been replaced by cigars; high-bodiced and delicate Empire dresses had given way to ponderous and over-ornamented brocade gowns.

No sooner had Moreau arrived at the Dusserts' than the twelve-year-old and his parents began a remarkable and revealing correspondence. Written in French, the letters were sent through Captain Rogers and other travelers. Some of the letters were lost, including those carried by members of the Schiff family of New Orleans, who were shipwrecked off Jamaica.[4] Yet the letters that survive provide invaluable glimpses into Moreau's personal and professional world, as well as insights into a skein of family relationships that was heavy with expectations and fears, triumphs and anxieties.[5]

Madame Dussert quickly established herself as a second mother to Moreau, as he announced to his parents in a long letter of June 8, 1842.[6] Wasting no time before showing off her prodigy in society, she took him to a masqued ball dressed as Louis XIV. His description of the event is not lacking in vanity:

> I had a sky blue velvet jacket with embroidery of silver braid, short britches of deep purple velvet with buttons the whole length of the trousers and silk braid, white silk stockings, and small shoes *à la* Louis XIV with blue rosettes.

Naturally, Moreau was called on to play the piano. A few days later we find him at another soirée being applauded madly for his performance of "a big piece from *William Tell.*"

For one such salon appearance Moreau was honored with an "Order of the Four Emperors of Germany and of the Lion of Holstein-Limbourg."[7] Over the years he was to collect many such medals and never failed to wear them on his lapel when he performed. He knew that the worth of these honors lay not in the gold and jewels they contained but in their ability to impress. Deep in the interior of Peru a merchant was once so awed by Moreau's Spanish medals that he offered the pianist hospitality and a piano purely on their account.[8]

Before Moreau departed from New Orleans, Aimée had importuned her son to contact a "Countess de la Grange," an aristocrat and friend of the arts who Aimée hoped would help her son. Variously described as a distant relative and (more likely) as a friend of Bruslé relatives, the Marquise de la Grange lived in the solid old Faubourg Saint-Germain and was among those aristocrats from the earlier regime who had been relegated to the sidelines by the rise of Louis Philippe.[9] Some months after his arrival in Paris the boy reminded his mother that she had forgotten to give him the Marquise de la Grange's address. In practically the same breath, however, he went on to explain his disinterest in currying favor with the rich. "Dear Mama," he wrote, "Don't think that Madame [sic.] de la Grange's acquaintance would be of great use to me, for the more I know the more I see how much egotism there is in Paris, as well as in all the other big cities." Then, with a sense of responsibility almost chilling in a thirteen-year-old, he stated, "I definitely expect that in two years and perhaps less I shall be earning a living on my own."[10]

For all his protestations against his mother's social climbing, Moreau was delighted when M. Dussert took him to meet the renowned pianist and composer Sigismund Thalberg. Liszt, Chopin, and Thalberg were the reigning virtuoso pianists of Europe. "Imagine my joy," Moreau wrote, "when I finished playing and Thalberg took my hand and said to M. Dussert 'This child is surprising! He now needs lessons in composition, for I can see from here what he will become.'" Appealing to his father, Moreau declared, "I think, Dear Papa, that [Thalberg] is right, for if I knew how to put my ideas into music I would do so very quickly. But first I must learn composition."[11]

At the height of all this activity Moreau came down with the measles and spent several months recuperating with relatives of Madame Dussert's at the village of Remilly, near Sedan. Far from being preoccupied with his own condition, however, Moreau used his letters home to inquire about his sisters, to comment on the likenesses on a family portrait sent him from Conti Street, and to thank his parents for sending boxes of guavas and yams in syrup, which arrived rotten. Amidst these family trivia, he also reported with unsettling insight, "I learned with much pleasure, mingled with fear, that Mama is pregnant."

The parents' side of the correspondence is no less revealing. In one businesslike letter Edward Gottschalk informed Moreau that he could cope with all his son's expenses and reported in detail on both family and neighbors.[12] He also forwarded from Moreau's Uncle James Gottschalk a copy of the Declaration of Independence and several books about the United States, "desirous that you should never forget that you are American." Aimée struck the same patriotic note when reporting on the admirable moderation exercised by the New Orleans police department during a bank riot in the spring of 1842. "You can bask in the glory of being an American," she effused. "Would you believe it, my friend, the riot was caused only by Germans, French, and Spanish? Not one American! [Ours] is the first nation of the world."[13]

Aimée Gottschalk's letters in her native French lack all punctuation and are riddled with grammatical mistakes. She reported on yellow fever epidemics in New Orleans, shared with Moreau her impression that business there was in a slump, and ended with a plea: "My dear child, forgive your mother, who isn't writing cheerful things . . . but I am waiting for letters from you to cheer me up." Over and over she exhorted him to stand straight, stop biting his fingernails (a lifelong problem), and to "satisfy these around you" by behaving well. More to the point, she urged Moreau repeatedly to seek help from the rich. "I am so angry," she wrote, "that [a visiting uncle] did not take you with him to [the city of] Nancy. He found there some extremely rich relatives who have no children. In this world it is sometimes necessary to gain the patronage of rich people."[14]

The weight of the burden placed on Moreau's shoulders by his mother's expectations must have been enormous. "If you love your mother, you must study twice as hard as you have to," she wrote.[15] "Think of your parents," she counseled him. "We put all our happiness in your future. Be mindful of that, and out of gratitude you will not allow yourself those moments of indolence that take hold of you."[16]

This mood of financial and personal anxiety surfaced also in Edward's letters, even as he assured the boy that all was well:

> Continue, my son, to study hard in order to create a destiny for yourself. Not only so that you will be independent, but also to replace me at your mother's side if I die, and to be the father of your brothers and sisters.[17]

Thirteen-year-old Moreau addressed these fears and the duties to which they gave rise by announcing to his parents that he would soon be self-supporting. He also sidestepped all entanglements with rich relatives. Consciously or unconsciously, the boy understood that the only way out for him was to become truly independent. But how? Moreau Gottschalk endeavored to free himself from further parental pressures not by rebelling against them but by shouldering the burdens they implied. This is a common response among older children in a family, of course, but it was also adroit, in that the objective of the strategy was not to acquiesce in new forms of dependence but to achieve personal freedom. The price proved to be very high in the long run, however, entailing nothing less than a lifetime of toil. But neither in his family life nor in his music was Moreau Gottschalk a rebel.

Reciprocating for the amateurish family portrait sent him by his parents, Moreau arranged in the autumn of 1842 for his own portrait to be painted and sent back to New Orleans. With the help probably of the Dusserts, he located a painter, J. Berville, whose studio was in the aristocratic rue de la Chaussee d'Antin. Berville's portrait reveals a handsomely dressed but reticent boy with a wise half smile on his lips. Reflecting Moreau's new-found interest in composition, it depicts him with his right arm resting on a musical manuscript and with a quill pen in his hand.[18]

When Letellier and Edward Gottschalk sent Moreau to Paris, their clear intention had been for him to study at the famed Conservatoire, which was then in its heyday. Soon after Moreau's arrival, M. Dussert took him around to Pierre Zimmerman (1785–1853), then head of the piano department and one of the founders of the French school of playing. The teacher of composers César Franck, Charles-Valentin Alkan, and other leaders of French music, Zimmerman was the Conservatoire's one-man admissions office for piano students. He was also the gatekeeper for musicians who aspired to receive the coveted Prix de Rome.

In these years the statutes of the Conservatoire contained a clause banning foreigners from admission. Eighteen years earlier this provision had been invoked to prevent Franz Liszt from matriculating. Since then it had been enforced only irregularly. When the director of the Conservatoire first rejected the young cellist and future composer from Cologne, Jacques Offenbach, Offenbach's father pleaded and argued so relentlessly that the boy was admitted.[19] Victor-Eugène Macarty, the mixed-race offspring of a prominent Louisiana planter and a slave, applied to the Conservatoire a year before Gottschalk and was accepted in the voice department, even though he was not French and was over age to boot.[20]

Neither of these exceptions had been made by Zimmerman, however. When young Gottschalk arrived at the door of the piano department's head, Zimmerman rejected him without an audition, stating bluntly, "L'Amérique n'état qu'un pays de machines à vapeur" ("America is only a land of steam engines").[21]

The Dusserts next took Moreau to the German-born pianist Charles Hallé, who, at age twenty-one, was making a name for himself in the French capital. He was a friend of Berlioz and later distinguished himself as a conductor in Manchester, England. Hallé was known to the Gottschalk family because his new wife, Désirée Smith de Rilieu, was a New Orleans native and friend of Moreau's great-uncle Gaston Bruslé.[22] The Hallés' apartment on rue de l'Arcade was most welcoming to Moreau, not only because Hallé himself was an amiable man but because the servants there were all freed slaves from New Orleans.[23] Unfortunately, the popular Hallé was on the road performing as often as he was in Paris, and within a year the Dusserts were once again looking for a pianist to teach Moreau.

Given the extraordinary status of pianos and pianists in Paris of the 1840s, the choice of a teacher gained hugely in importance. Statistics tell part of the story. About this time the French capital had sixty thousand pianos and one hundred thousand persons who could play them.[24] Assuming that half the population consisted of workers and tradespeople and a third of the remainder were under ten or over fifty years of age, this meant that fully a third of the youth and young adults of Paris were banging away on fortepianos. Never before or since did the piano attain such dizzy heights of popularity as it did in the French capital between 1835 and 1848.[25]

With its ability to play both *forte* and *piano*, the instrument was the perfect vehicle for expressing the emotions of romanticism. It could reproduce in an engaging fashion virtually any music, from operatic arias to the latest popular romance. Unlike the violin, the piano had a steep learning curve, so that even beginners could produce credible sounds in a short while. The piano was also a highly visible possession, signifying by its mere presence in a home the high tone of its owners. Finally, the piano was also a sophisticated piece of technology. An innovative Frenchman, Sébastian Érard, had developed an ingenious "double escapement action" that facilitated dizzying speed in performance. Ignace Pleyel, also a Parisian, had figured out how to manufacture pianos with unheard-of efficiency.

The same Parisians who played or heard the piano at home constituted a ready audience for concerts, much the way amateur tennis players flock to professional tournaments today. Hector Berlioz reported on "an avalanche" of concerts in Paris,[26] many of them sponsored by leading piano manufacturers to promote their wares and held at Salle Érard or Salle Pleyel. The more brilliant and dramatic the performer the better for everyone, and so a new artistic type appeared: the virtuoso.

By no means could every fine player become a virtuoso. Johann Hummel was a stunning performer but possessed none of the qualities of the showman. Gottschalk, who heard Hummel in these years, recalled how singularly disappointing it was for audiences to see "a fat man with a bourgeois face and an awkward gait, wearing a long landlord's coat, with a black skullcap that he never took off even in his concerts."[27] Liszt considered that Charles-Valentin Alkan had the finest technique of any pianist he ever heard, yet Alkan was not cut out for virtuoso status on account of his morbid shyness.[28] To be a virtuoso was to be a Napoleonic hero in a bourgeois age. The virtuoso's life was itself a flamboyant work of art. Naturally, the virtuoso did not merely play music but interpreted it.[29] He was a man of spontaneity and feelings who turned his back on rigorously structured sonatas in favor of "fantasies," "romances," "meditations," and "grand caprices." Thus he was the antithesis of the rational and predictable businessman who dominated economic life.

The great Paganini provided the archetype for piano virtuosos through his satanic wizardry on the violin. Paganini had awed Chopin and inspired

Liszt to pursue a virtuoso career. To be sure, there was an element of pure hokum in Paganini's show-stoppers, as, for example, his left-hand pizzicato and his performances on a single string. Yet the French public loved it and created a lucrative market for Paganinis of every instrument. "The piano virtuosos come to Paris every year like swarms of locusts," wrote the German poet Heinrich Heine, "less to gain money than to make a name for themselves here, which will help them all the more to a rich pecuniary harvest in other countries."[30]

Of all the virtuosos who flocked to Paris, three stood out above the rest: Frederic Chopin, Franz Liszt, and Sigismund Thalberg. A French-Pole, Austrian-Hungarian, and German, respectively, these three outsiders to Paris took the city by storm and achieved an eminence as artists and a notoriety as people that were unequaled by anyone except Paganini himself. During Moreau Gottschalk's student years, these three split the public into partisan factions.

Much later, Moreau penned his impressions of these giants, as well as lesser stars, in a Spanish-language essay published in Havana and awkwardly entitled "Music, the Piano, and Pianists." In this long and chatty reflection on his youth, Gottschalk particularly emphasized Chopin's contribution. Moreau heard Chopin perform in a private salon and was impressed by his overall delicacy, reserve, and sensitivity. Directly or indirectly, Moreau acquired Chopin's *bel canto* style of phrasing. From Chopin he may also have derived his *legato* execution and his inventive approach to fingering, even though he was not as addicted to *rubato* as was the Polish master. Chopin's pioneering use of the pedal probably also influenced Gottschalk, for later American reviewers often noted his mastery in this area.

Was Moreau aware of the parallels between his own life and Chopin's? The sternly rationalist father from Western Europe (in Chopin's case France) who married a sensuous Catholic native of his adopted country; the marriage that produced a son who embraced the mother's world and its music and then magically transformed that music for the enjoyment of a cosmopolitan audience—all this closely anticipates Gottschalk's life.

Moreau almost certainly heard Liszt at one of his public concerts in the spring of 1844.[31] It is not clear whether the two actually met, the evidence on this point being contradictory.[32] However, Gottschalk viewed Liszt with deep skepticism. Calling him the "Alcibiades of the piano," he considered Liszt to be "devoured by a thirst for glory" and dismissed his compositions as containing the "most incomprehensible, most extravagant literary-musical formulas that one can imagine."[33] Conceding Liszt's "volcanic intelligence," Moreau nonetheless ridiculed what he considered to be Liszt's grotesque affectations:

> [Liszt's] long hair, the new banner around which the sacred battalion of romantic pianists rallied, came to be the symbol of the art for his numerous adepts. There was no romantic who did not wear his hair long and there are today some who have none of Liszt's talent except the hair!

Gottschalk also assailed Liszt's manner at the keyboard:

> When Liszt played, the movement of his head, his arms, the contractions of his enormous fingers, made him seem like a fakir in the throes of an ecstatic convulsion, ever leaning backwards, eyes closed, the mouth tense, shaking his immense locks, ever hurling himself upon the keyboard like a wild beast over its prey, flooding it with the surge of his hair, which, tangled with his fingers on the suffering keys, seemed to be struggling like the ancient python, in the embrace of an invisible god.[34]

Finally, Gottschalk judged Liszt's composition with extreme severity. Unwilling to acknowledge Liszt's harmonic innovations, which had such an impact on Wagner, Gottschalk refused to see in Liszt's music anything but the work of an egocentric stunt man:

> In [them] we see the constant effort of one seeking to hide the sterility and triviality of his ideas beneath a mantle of the unusual, the eccentric, and the obscure. He invents nothing. Intoxicated by the facility of his fingers, he piles up difficulty upon difficulty as if he wished only to defy other pianists.

In spite of such tirades, Moreau retained more than a few traces of Liszt's influence, notably his capacity for a fierce *sforzando* when necessary. He also borrowed Liszt's innovation of giving solo piano concerts, a practice which Gottschalk was among the first to introduce to America.

Sigismund Thalberg was the polar opposite of Liszt. Where Liszt was all storm and stress, Thalberg was "statuesque," in the words of Gottschalk's teacher Hallé.[35] The musical statue that was Thalberg was largely self-carved. All Europe believed that he was the illegitimate son of an Austrian prince and that he was immensely rich. Thalberg never disabused people of this version of his genealogy, but it was utterly false. His birth certificate shows that he was the legitimate son of two solid German burghers from Frankfurt. Thalberg's image of himself as aristocrat embodied the same search for identity as the half-French Chopin's assertion of himself as a bearer of Polish culture, or the quest by the non-Hungarian speaking and Austrian-born Liszt (originally List) for a Magyar identity.[36] Unfortunately, Thalberg's assumed identity as an Austrian aristocrat was far less fertile musically than Chopin's or Liszt's more nationalistic self-definition. Most of his compositions were operatic transcriptions. Even though he often transcribed his material into new keys, modified the rhythms, and introduced new harmonies—all techniques later used by Gottschalk—Thalberg's final products were invariably somewhat vacuous.[37]

The one area in which Thalberg achieved unparalleled distinction was in his execution at the keyboard. Here is Gottschalk's description of Thalberg's playing:

> The modern piano began . . . with Thalberg. He gave the instrument the stamp of his serene, majestic, and elegant talent. He brought many orchestral effects to the piano, bringing out at one time three, four, or more parts, and differentiating each of them with heretofore unknown shades of color. Inspired by the harp, he invented the so-called "arpeggio" effect, which has been so abused, and which consists of surrounding the melody with a brilliant group of notes which cover it without concealing it, like a light, transparent veil.[38]

Like everyone else, Gottschalk believed the legend of Thalberg's background. Unlike much of the public, however, he blamed it for Thalberg's shortcomings:

> His talent seems to have been impregnated with the atmosphere of this courtly and artificial life: pompous, noble, elegant, it is at times a little cold, and seems to disdain transports of passion as signs of weakness incompatible with the serene majesty of the Beautiful. Greater abandon is called for, even at the expense of Thalberg's marvelous perfection.

It was inevitable that Liszt and Thalberg would come into frontal conflict, which occurred during a highly publicized series of musical duels culminating in a debacle for Thalberg at the apartment of art patroness Princess Belgiojoso.[39] Young Gottschalk picked up every detail of this keyboard combat from the gossip of the day and came down on the side of Thalberg. His grounds for this judgment were non-musical. Liszt, he believed, had defamed his rival in anonymous and mean-spirited letters to the Geneva press.

Of what Charles Hallé called the "three mighty heroes" of the piano, Moreau placed Chopin first. After him came Thalberg, "whose legacy is the foundation on which nearly all those who are composing for the piano, or think they are doing so, build. Indeed," wrote Gottschalk, "it has become very difficult for a young pianist-composer to preserve his originality in the midst of the resulting mania for plagiarizing [Thalberg's technique]."[40]

Gottschalk's education in Paris took place just after the decisive battles in the war of piano virtuosos. He admired the combatants' skills and devoted many years to building his own mastery of the instrument. Even though he perceived clearly the sham and pretense of the Paris virtuosos, within a decade Moreau Gottschalk was himself to become the principal bearer of their school of virtuosity in America.

This, then, was the intense and fiercely competitive world of the piano in Paris at the time the Dusserts set out to find Moreau a teacher. The three giants were out of the question since Thalberg was endlessly touring, Liszt was in the midst of an affair with the Countess Marie d'Agoult, and Chopin took as pupils mainly well-heeled young ladies from the Faubourg Saint-Germain. And so Dussert went to the teacher whom Chopin himself had first approached after arriving in Paris, Frédéric-Guillaume Kalkbrenner (1784–1849), the dean of Parisian instructors in piano.

German-born but a resident of Paris since his tenth year, Kalkbrenner ran what amounted to a factory for virtuosos. A composer of mercifully forgotten works, Kalkbrenner's one claim to fame was his ability to engender the light, sensuous touch that differentiated the Parisian school of piano from the more brilliant playing of the Viennese and Germans. Besides writing a ponderous *Méthode* for piano, Kalkbrenner had also developed a clumsy apparatus for developing his stroking or caressing (*carezzando*) touch. The *guide-mains* or "hand guide" was nothing more than a rail placed above the keys on which the student would rest his hands.[41] Yet it was unquestionably effective as a pedagogical tool.

Colossally vain, Kalkbrenner had rejected Hallé as a pupil and told Chopin it would take three years to straighten out his technique.[42] There was no denying that Kalkbrenner could develop a limpid technique that was "polished as a billiard ball," as one cynic observed,[43] yet there was also no denying that he was one of the most obnoxious people in Paris. Gottschalk later recalled an anecdote about Kalkbrenner's effort to pass off his nine-year-old son Tuturo as a great improviser. "On being presented to the Duchess d'Orleans, Tuturo sat down at the piano to improvise. For a few measures the young prodigy did rather well, but suddenly he grew confused, began fumbling, and then stopped, screaming 'Father, I've forgotten the rest!' "[44] Gottschalk also spoke of Kalkbrenner's "soporific vacuity."[45]

In the end, Kalkbrenner did not himself take on Moreau as a student but passed him to his top disciple, Camille Stamaty (1811–70). Moreau came to revere this man and flourished under his training.[46] Deeply Catholic and a generous donor to all charities, Stamaty had been raised in Italy, where his Greek-born father served as a minor French diplomat. Through lessons with Mendelssohn he had developed a love for Bach and Mozart, but he did not pass this on to Gottschalk.[47] Among Stamaty's other students was young Camille Saint-Saëns, who had been his pupil since age seven.[48] Saint-Saëns had only praise for the Kalkbrenner-Stamaty method, like Gottschalk, but was critical of his emphasis on a continuous and monotonous legato, and his "mania for continual *expressivo* used with no discrimination."

With Stamaty's help, Moreau finally found a teacher of composition in the person of Pierre Maleden (1806–?). Although Moreau left no record of his studies with Maleden, it is clear that he had found a most stimulating professor. Saint-Saëns, whom Stamaty also placed under Maleden's care, described him as

> thin and long haired, a kind and timid soul, but an incomparable teacher. He had gone to Germany in his youth to study with a certain Gottfried Weber, the inventor of a system which Maleden brought back with him and perfected. He made it a wonderful tool with which to get to the depths of music—a light for the darkest corners. In this system the chords are not considered in and for themselves—as fifths, sixths, sevenths—but in relation to the pitch of the scale on which they appear.[49]

Moreau later claimed that harmony was "a science I knew before I had learned it."[50] But it is evident that Maleden's unorthodox approach to tonality stimulated Gottschalk's interest in harmonic coloration and his venturesome approach to chromaticism.

While Moreau's musical training was proceeding, the Dusserts did not neglect his general education. First in the *pension* (where the other boys called him "the Millionaire")[51] and then with private tutors, he was fed a steady diet of improving activities and uplifting books down to his sixteenth year. To confirm Moreau's standing as a young gentleman, the Dusserts sent him to master fencing under the renowned Grisier and to learn equestrian skills from the master horseman Pelier.[52] He also studied Italian to the point that he could read Petrarch and Machiavelli in the original. Moreau never visited Italy, but he later used the language daily in his contacts with Italian singers and drew librettos for his operas from texts by Italian writers. His sister Clara claimed he also studied Latin and Greek,[53] but there is not a hint of this in anything he wrote.

When Moreau traveled to South America in 1865 he had in his bags the *Dictionnaire universel d'histoire et de géographie* published by the Paris professor Marie-Nicolas Bouillet in 1842.[54] From this and other sources he gained a reasonable knowledge of European history, which he fleshed out over the years with readings in historical novels. When, for example, he chose the tumultuous life of France's King Charles IX as a subject for an opera, he drew on Prosper Merimée's gore-filled novel on that monarch, published in 1829.[55] Of political economy, mathematics, science, or technology there is not the slightest trace in Gottschalk's formal education. The keen interest he developed later in social and political issues derived from personal experience rather than from his studies in Paris. He was, after all, being prepared to be an artist and gentleman, not a politician or banker.

The one area in which Moreau's education was beyond reproach was literature. Not only was he exposed both to classical and modern writers, but he absorbed his readings to the point that they inspired many of his compositions and informed the way he viewed the world. Many years later he found himself walking along the shore of the Saint Lawrence River watching the tumultuous waves, a scene that called to his mind Alfred de Musset's *Ballad to the Moon*.[56] The sight of a motley band of soldiers from various lands in Washington during the Civil War brought to his mind Schiller's play *Wallenstein*.[57] Recuperating in a remote Cuban plantation from a bout of yellow fever, he observed that French *littérateurs* Joseph Méry or Théophile Gautier "would have gone mad in contemplating this paradise, in which only an Eve was wanting."[58] Introspective by nature, Gottschalk perceived experience through the eyes of his favorite authors. The world of letters was no less real to him than that of daily life.

Cervantes, Montaigne, and Chateaubriand were his frequently cited companions, as were modern writers like E. T. A. Hoffmann, Poe, and Dumas. Gottschalk was addicted to the ribald comic novels of Charles-Paul de Kock (1794–1871) and also sought out the bitingly witty novels of Alphonse Karr (1808–90). He came to admire Hawthorne, Irving, and other American writers as well, but they were never close to his heart. Of English authors, he respected Thackeray and Tennyson, but Dickens bored him.

As a true child of the romantic age, Gottschalk worshipped at the altar of Poetry from childhood on. Friends testified that he was an adept memorizer who had committed to heart whole books, among them Boileau's ponderous *L'Art poétique*.[59] One of his first compositions was inspired by poems attributed to the Scottish bard Ossian, the same literary forgeries that had inspired Mendelssohn. A single line by Victor Hugo gave rise to Gottschalk's composition *Reflets du passé*, while Hugo's poem *L'Extase* from *Les Orientales* provided the text for Gottschalk's piano composition of the same title (op. 62). For his *Pensez à moi* he mined a poem by Alfred de Musset.

Even though Gottschalk himself penned verse for several of his songs, he more commonly took inspiration from others. The two poets who sparked Gottschalk's musical imagination most directly were both deep-dyed French romantics, Alphonse-Marie-Louis de Lamartine (1790–1869) and Charles-Hubert Millevoye (1782–1816). Lamartine's *Méditations poétiques* were constantly in his travel bag, and he drew upon them for such piano compositions as *Solitude* (*L'Isolement*, op. 65). Beyond any direct borrowings from Lamartine, Moreau found in this worldly French poet the mirror of his own *mal du siècle* melancholy—gloomy, gentle, and lyrical, but never leading to rebellion.

Even more important to Gottschalk was Charles-Hubert Millevoye, who anticipated a century of consumptive outpourings in European literature before his own premature death from tuberculosis. Gottschalk's disturbingly sinister composition on the fatal West Indian bush *Le Mancenillier* is based on a poem by Millevoye, as was his elegiac nocturne *La Chute des feuilles* (op. 42, *The Fall of Leaves*). Only weeks before his death Gottschalk was still quoting Millevoye, whose works he had first encountered as a student in Paris a quarter century earlier.[60]

Moreau's education was by no means confined to formal studies. During his student years he was a frequent visitor at Paris art galleries and developed an enduring interest in painting and sculpture. He had little or no contact with the many Americans who had flocked to Paris to study at the École des Beaux Arts, but he became a familiar with the academic paintings of Paul Delaroche, the sculpture of Danton, and miniatures by Isabey.[61] This youthful grounding led him later to form ties with several American artists, notably the American landscape painter Frederic Edwin Church.

Moreau avidly attended concerts. Besides hearing the piano titans, he apparently attended several monster concerts organized by Hector Berlioz. Notwithstanding his later fame, Berlioz in these years was a harried composer with a disastrous marriage and little income beyond that which he received as librarian of the Conservatoire. The great Paganini had recognized Berlioz as a kindred virtuoso and granted him twenty thousand francs, but Berlioz had long since spent this. Now he was trying to propel himself before the Paris public by any means possible in order to win a conductorship.[62] His method for achieving this goal was to organize what he called "music festivals" involving hundreds of musicians. In the late spring of 1844 a World Exposition of Industrial Products was just closing in Paris, and the huge pavilion was available. Working from dawn to dusk, Berlioz threw together a "festival" of five hundred choristers and 480 instrumentalists.[63] The grand monster concert closed with a resounding *Hymne à la France* that Berlioz had composed for the occasion. The following spring Berlioz was at it again, this time with a festival of four concerts held at the Cirque Olympique and culminating in an original *Marche triomphale.*[64]

Neither festival earned much money, and both left Berlioz exhausted, verging on collapse. They left an indelible impression on one young member of the public, however, as evidenced by the fact that Gottschalk later organized his own festivals on the pattern of those mounted by Berlioz and Berlioz's French imitators. Indeed, the last major performance of his life was just such a monster concert, held in Rio de Janeiro. In this area, as in others, the mature Gottschalk continued to be powerfully influenced by impressions from his early boyhood.

The spring of 1845 brought a tide of American exotica to Paris. First came P. T. Barnum with his Lilliputian wonder, General Tom Thumb. King Louis Philippe received "Général Tom Pouce" at court, the impressionable French went wild, and Barnum had to hire a cab to haul the bags of silver home each night after the performance.[65] Amidst this furor, the American Western painter George Catlin showed up with four hundred paintings of Native American life and eight tons of artifacts, including wigwams, tomahawks, and buffalo robes. The stars of his entourage were Little Wolf and a band of painted and feathered Iowa Indians, who were promptly invited to perform, complete with war whoops, at the Tuileries Palace.[66]

Moreau Gottschalk was among the gawking spectators for both of these shows but was unimpressed to the point of ridicule. Not so the Parisian public, in whom Tom Thumb and Catlin stimulated a curiosity about all things American that had not been seen since the publication of Alexis de Tocqueville's *Democracy in America* a decade earlier. It was at this moment that Moreau's teacher Stamaty decided to present his young student to the musical public at a "non-paying" debut concert. Thanks to Moreau's performances at private salons, rumors regarding the American's talent were widespread and interest was high. The concert was set for April 2, 1845, at the Salle Pleyel at 20 rue de Rochechouart, not far from rue de Clichy on the approach to Montmartre. Stamaty's teacher, Kalkbrenner, held stock in Pleyel et Cie, and Camille Pleyel himself had just become a Chevalier in the Légion d'Honneur, adding luster to the piano maker and his concert hall. Pleyel's patronage assured that the entire musical elite of Paris would be in attendance for Moreau's debut.

Théophile Tilmant, conductor at the Théâtre Italien, was engaged to conduct the orchestra, and he in turn hired as assisting artists Chopin's friend, the cellist Auguste Franchomme, the baritone Jean Geraldy, and others. Invitations from "Young Moreau Gottschalk of New Orleans" were printed and sent out to leading musicians, critics, and friends of Pleyel's.[67]

Participating in the preparations was Aimée Gottschalk, who had arrived the previous autumn with little Celestine, Clara, Augustine, Blanche, and Edward Jr.[68] As early as 1843 Aimée had wanted to join her son in Paris but had been constrained by the fact that her husband was not free to go with her. In the end, she came without Edward, who stayed behind gave up the Conti Street house and sold several slaves, one of whom had been registered in Moreau's name.[69]

Moreau arranged for his sisters and brother to sit in the front row, but Aimée retreated to an obscure corner of the concert hall in order to observe.[70] They were not the only Americans in the audience, as many others of Moreau's countrymen had flocked to hear the unlikely phenomenon of "un jeune américain, qui a un talent musical."[71] Also there was Moreau's first Paris teacher, Charles Hallé, who had returned briefly to Paris in order to give several concerts.[72] More important for Moreau's future was the presence of Chopin (weak from consumption), Thalberg, the conductor Habeneck, the aged composer Auber, and even crusty Professor Zimmerman from the Conservatoire.[73] Liszt was away from Paris with the Countess d'Agoult, and Berlioz was in Burgundy, but virtually every other Parisian musical luminary was present among the overflow crowd.

Stamaty had calculated Moreau's program perfectly. As a tribute to Chopin, he led off with the Pole's Concerto in E Minor. Then, in a nod to the other two lions of the piano, Moreau performed Thalberg's fantasy on themes from Rossini's *Semiramide* and concluded with Liszt's dramatic fantasy on themes from Meyerbeer's *Robert le Diable*. With these selections Stamaty challenged the public to compare his pupil with the greatest virtuosos of the day.

The tactic succeeded, and at the end of the concert Moreau was crowned with a wreath of oak leaves, amidst rousing applause.[74] Thalberg congratulated Moreau afterwards, and Chopin himself appeared backstage to congratulate the young American. It was a symbolic moment, with the Old World acknowledging the New World in one of those scenes so beloved by monumental painters of the nineteenth century.

Inevitably, no one quite agreed on what Chopin actually said to the boy. Gottschalk's first biographer has him exclaiming simply, "Bien, mon enfant, bien, très bien; donnez moi encore la main" ("Good, my child, good, very good; let me shake your hand once more.")[75] Gottschalk's zealous French publisher, however, claimed that Chopin added "Embrassez-moi, encore, encore!"[76] Moreau's adoring sister Clara did the publisher one better by having Chopin place his hands on Moreau's head and declare, "Je vous prédis que vous serez le roi des pianistes" ("I predict that you will become the king of pianists").[77]

The lofty Kalkbrenner did not deign to appear backstage, but Moreau betook himself the next day to the master's apartment on the rue Saint Lazare in order to thank him for attending. Kalkbrenner unbent a bit and declared that Moreau, as a pupil of Stamaty, was therefore his own musical grandchild. Then, with majestic condescension, he asked:

> For God's sake, who advised you to play such music? Chopin! I hardly pardon you; but Liszt and Thalberg, what rhapsodies! Why did you not play one of my pieces?[78]

Parisian critics rarely covered debut concerts, but they made an exception in this case. The *Revue et gazette musicale de Paris* thought that the Chopin concerto did not adequately show off Moreau's talent but that his execution of the pieces by Liszt and Thalberg revealed his "brilliant qualities," which lacked only the force and confidence age brings.[79] The *Ménestrel* confidently placed Moreau "in the first rank of our virtuosos." These judgments reached New Orleans within weeks, and *Le Courrier de la Louisiane* promptly reprinted them, adding flourishes of its own.[80] Nor did the New Orleans press neglect the fact that invitations to the concert had mentioned Moreau's native city by name. "A Creole," it noted, "[Moreau] desired that New Orleans should partake of his first success."

Chapter Five

✖ *Bamboula* and the Louisiana Quartet

T HE late 1840s were not auspicious years for the musical life of Paris. Early in 1846 the French economy went into a tailspin. This recession spelled doom for the Orleanist monarchy, which never recovered from the shock. It hit the concert-going public as well, with the result that Franz Liszt abandoned the French capital and resumed his ceaseless touring, this time to Hungary and the Balkans. Henri Herz took off for America in hopes of tapping new markets there.[1] Unfortunately for Hector Berlioz, it was just now, in December 1846, that he premiered his *Damnation de Faust* at the Opéra Comique. The hall was half empty and his much awaited work bombed with those few members of the public who braved the winter slush.[2]

However unfavorable for more established musicians, the post-1846 economic slump benefited young Moreau Gottschalk. Had the recession not occurred he would doubtless have charged ahead immediately to make his second Paris debut at a paying concert. Instead, he held off until November 1847 before making a trial appearance before a paying public, meanwhile devoting himself to the further study of composition. These two and a half years between his Salle Pleyel debut and his first paying concert were essential to his growth as a composer.

When finally he emerged to offer another concert, Moreau chose the provincial city of Sedan for the event.[3] Thalberg graciously attended and praised his young friend, but the expected professional debut in Paris was held off for another two years. The concert offered at Salle Pleyel in 1849 marked the end of Moreau's apprenticeship and the beginning of a career of relentless concertizing that stretched, with only brief interruptions, down to his death.

Moreau's acquaintance with the concert world deepened during these last years of his apprenticeship. He appeared from time to time at fashionable salons, and he himself continued to be an inveterate concert-goer. Through Paganini's star pupil Camillo Sivori he glimpsed at second-hand the musical and dramatic fireworks that had defined virtuosity for all Europe. The colorful Norwegian violinist Ole Bull, who later emigrated to America, showed how the folk songs of northern lands could furnish material for virtuosic display. The Belgian violinist Henri Vieuxtemps provided the young American yet another model of the performer-composer.[4] In the months before the debut of Berlioz's *Faust*, Moreau also assisted in several large concerts the composer hastily organized at the handsome old Théâtre Italien.[5] For someone of Gottschalk's taste, this theater near the Passage Choiseul was a kind of shrine, for it was there he first heard such renowned singers as Carlotta Grisi, Marietta Alboni, and Henriette Sontag, all of whom he later encountered in America.

Moving deftly among highbrow salons and the major theaters and concert halls, the seventeen-year-old Moreau became quite a man-about-town. Over the next few years he was to become acquainted with what Parisians dubbed in English the city's "high-life," which centered around the Boulevard des Italiens and such temples of *gourmandise* as the Maison Dorée and Les Frères Provençaux.[6]

Amidst these pleasant rounds, Moreau sat for his portrait at the studio of Luigi Rubio. Moreau's choice of this Neapolitan painter reveals the extent to which the young American aspired to follow in Chopin's footsteps. Rubio's mistress and later wife, Vera de Kologrivoff, was a Russian aristocrat, who happened also to be one of Chopin's top pupils. Through her, Rubio gained a commission to paint the composer's portrait. The resulting image of the melancholy and emaciated Pole created such a stir in Paris that it was natural that the aspiring Chopinian from New Orleans should seek out the same painter.[7]

Rubio's portrait of Gottschalk is lost, but a lithograph of it produced a few years later shows a delicate, almost effeminate young man dominated by a fashion-plate coiffure and an expanse of starched white waistcoat.[8] This dandified image is in sharp contrast to a daguerreotype of Moreau at this time, which reveals him as far from ethereal and even a bit robust, and with a slightly apprehensive but at the same time self-possessed look in his eyes.[9] Comparing the two, one cannot help but ask which is more true to life, the dandified image or the more forthright physical reality? The answer is that each reflects faithfully a side of Moreau's character, which was in fact divided. That bifurcation, moreover, closely resembles the outer circumstances of the young man's life, and specifically his parents' evolving relationship to each other.

Since arriving in Paris in 1844, Aimée Gottschalk had dedicated herself to tearing away the veil of gloom that was the legacy of her parents'
and husband's bankruptcies. Moreau, of course, was to be the instrument
of her emancipation. No sooner had her son made his successful debut
than the thirty-two-year-old mother of six stepped out into Parisian society. Then in 1846 she made a brief return visit to New Orleans and to her
husband. From this renewed contact with Edward Gottschalk a seventh
child, Gaston, was born later in the year.

Just before sailing for America Aimée had sat for a large and opulent
portrait by the fashionable painter V. de Jonquières. The striking canvas
shows Aimée with a large jewel in her hair and wearing a rich, dark gown
with deep décolleté. Amidst these period clichés Aimée Gottschalk herself stands out arrestingly, with her large hazel eyes, round chin and soft
mouth, the very picture of self-indulgent and benign sensuousness.[10]

This portrait of Aimée Gottschalk corresponds precisely to the Rubio
portrait of Moreau in its depiction of a person dedicated to a sybaritic
life. Paris was not cheap, however, and Moreau was yet to contribute
meaningfully to the family coffers, as he had boasted he would soon do.
Edward Gottschalk, now living alone in rented rooms at Tremé and Canal
streets in New Orleans, had to pay the piper. By selling slaves and taking
out loans to cover his ever more risky investments in uptown New Orleans real estate, he tried to stave off disaster. Moreau's sober and apprehensive look in the surviving daguerreotype is therefore quite understandable, given the perilousness of his father's situation.

As early as his fifteenth year, Moreau was fully aware of his family's
impending ruin. Years later he wrote his brothers and sisters:

> I preached in the desert for four or five years, from 1844 to 1852. With the
> irresponsible carelessness which [my mother] inherited from the country
> where she had always lived [i.e., Saint-Domingue], and from the education
> Father had given her, she spent two-hundred-eighty-five thousand francs!! This
> figure came from our poor Father. Two-hundred-eighty-five thousand francs—
> in other words, a fortune. Father meekly approved all this, which I can under-
> stand, without at the same time excusing all of Mother's spending. He hid the
> condition of his business from her instead of telling her the truth. He con-
> firmed her belief that he could afford all her extravagance, and meanwhile
> resorted to the ruinous practice of borrowing. This meant pushing back, while
> at the same time expanding, the abyss which one day it would be irrevocably
> necessary to cross.[11]

Unable at this time to afford a visit to his family in Paris, Edward
Gottschalk continued to send off money and, to Moreau, even a gold
watch chain and two rocking chairs. But soon the strain of his situation
began to tell on Edward's health as he complained of inflammation of the
bladder, attacks of cholera, and severe spells of unspecified sickness.[12]

Concern over the looming crisis doubtless figured in Moreau's decision to offer a first paying concert at Sedan, near Madame Dussert's family home. Such concerns also must have prompted Aimée finally to open a *pension* for young girls at 10 rue des Filles de Calvaire. The large unornamented building still stands, with shops on the ground floor and two floors of comfortable rooms above. Located in the Marais district, the *pension* was well situated to attract daughters of the wealthy families living in the nearby mansions surrounding the Place des Vosges. There is no evidence, however, that this enterprise in any way alleviated the family's financial problems. Moreau meanwhile moved to less expensive quarters at 2 rue Thèrese in the Batignolle district.

Spinning in the social whirl of Paris and at the same time sensing impending disaster, Moreau in his own life had replicated the combination of opulent sensuousness and utter impermanence that his Bruslé forebears had experienced in Saint-Domingue and his own immediate family had known in New Orleans. It is surely not stretching the point to detect a trace of this tension also in Gottschalk's music. Nor is it surprising that someone whose emotional world was defined by the two poles of sensuousness and doom would have preferred to express himself through intense works of brief compass rather than in longer and more emotionally diverse compositions.

His performing career temporarily in abeyance, Moreau focused all his energies on composition. This was the easier since his piano teacher, Stamaty, had in 1846 yielded to his strong Christian impulse and retreated into a monastery in Rome. Moreau's lessons in composition with Maleden continued, however, and by 1848 he reached his first flowering as a composer.

As early as his thirteenth year Moreau had written an *Étude*, now lost, and, in the following year or so, a *Polka de salon* and a *Valse de salon*, both of which he printed privately as gifts for friends. The *Polka de salon* survives as op. 1 and is notable only as a piece of feverish juvenilia, generously peppered with notes to show off both the budding composer and the aspiring virtuoso. A *Polka de concert* followed, and then a very graceful mazurka entitled *Souvenir des Ardennes*.[13] This was followed by a whole series of mazurkas over the following years, two of which were published together under the title *Colliers d'or* (op. 6).[14] These mazurkas, not to mention the several polkas of these years, attest to the strong influence exercised by Chopin's works on young Moreau's imagination. For now, he wanted nothing more than to place himself in the shadow of the great Pole who had shaken his hand after the Salle Pleyel concert.

Even though several of these works of Moreau's apprentice years are not lacking in charm, they are mere exercises. Progressing to a *Grande*

Étude de concert and a *Grande Valse de concert,* they reflect Pierre Maleden's pedagogy more than Moreau's own sensibility.[15] They did bring Gottschalk a degree of fame, however. In the summer of 1846 he made a walking tour in the Vosges Mountains north of Strasbourg. While passing through a small Alsatian town he was stopped by a gendarme who demanded his passport, which Moreau had mislaid. Vainly attempting to identify himself, he noticed another gendarme scanning a number of *La France musicale* in which his composition *Colliers d'or* was prominently advertised. Fortunately, the mayor of the village had two daughters, both of whom played the piano. When Moreau offered to perform the advertised piece for these two young ladies, the mayor accepted, and he was soon released.[16]

Besides preparing him for later compositions, these early works by the young Gottschalk confirmed him as a pianist in the mold of Liszt and Chopin, one who would perform mainly his own compositions rather than those of other composers. To be sure, works by Chopin, Onslow, Liszt, and Mendelssohn were in his repertoire, but a concert by Gottschalk meant mainly music by Gottschalk.

By 1847 the reign of Louis Philippe seemed stricken with senility. The economy was floundering, and labor was daily becoming more restive. Worse, a regime devoted to the maintenance of the happy medium, *le juste milieu,* no longer engaged the public's interest. "France is bored," proclaimed the poet and politician Lamartine.[17] In a quintessentially Parisian form of protest, the intellegentsia assuaged this boredom at large banquets at which speaker after speaker flayed the government of Louis Philippe. Finally, on February 24 the King abdicated, a republic was proclaimed, and Lamartine himself took over as head of the Provisional Government.

To this point it was all very exciting. As one wag put it, a writer long known as the unofficial "Minister of Ideas" now had his chance to rule France.[18] But more was afoot. No sooner did the King abdicate than the Parisian mob sacked the Tuileries palace, laborers established National Workshops, and socialists organized huge demonstrations under their freshly unfurled red flags. When Lamartine tried to repress the National Workshops in June 1848, insurrection exploded across the French capital. At this moment Karl Marx, a Parisian by adoption, penned his *Communist Manifesto,* in which he exhorted, "Workers of the world, unite!" A revolution that began with noble and even poetic sentiments ended in a bloodbath.

The Revolution of 1848 brought a tide of republicanism in the arts. The Opéra was renamed the Théâtre de la Nation and the Théâtre-Français became the Théâtre de la République. A newspaper sponsored a competition for a new national anthem, and a General Association of Artists and Musicians issued ringing declarations to whomever would listen.[19] Soon, however, the rising turmoil brought disaster. Theaters and concert halls closed down, and performers lost their livelihood. Adolphe Adam, the composer of exquisite ballet music, went bankrupt. The ailing Chopin left for England. Gottschalk's old teacher Hallé also crossed the channel to escape the mounting confusion, while Liszt, having abandoned Paris in 1847, now decided to make his home permanently in Weimar.

How did the nineteen-year-old Gottschalk greet the Revolution of 1848? Alone among the better-known musicians of Paris, he was born in a republic and was bound to welcome the fall of the July Monarchy. Besides, his natural sense of philanthropy gave him a sympathy for the downtrodden. His sister recalled his encounter at this time with a young French army recruit who was in tears over the punishment he would receive for having torn his new uniform.[20] Moreau took the soldier to a tailor and had the uniform repaired. Such attitudes, along with the fact that he was not yet dependent on ticket sales for his livelihood, prompted Moreau to stay in Paris through the bloody June Days and watch the revolution unfold.

During these months his career took an important leap forward when he was invited to perform at the salon of the newspaper magnate and power broker Émile Girardin (1806–81) and his wife, the novelist Delphine Gay (1805–55). Back in 1836 Girardin, then a young stockbroker, had stunned Paris by founding a newspaper, *La Presse*, priced at just half the cost of the next cheapest paper in France. This entrepreneurial coup earned Girardin a fortune and enabled him thereafter to indulge his taste for political intrigue, flamboyant mistresses, and whatever was *à la mode* in culture. He and his erstwhile wife, one of the most brilliant and admired women of Paris, cohabited in a columned mansion in the rue de Chaillot, out near the Bois de Boulogne, where Girardin had once killed a man in a duel. Here Madame Girardin presided over one of the era's most influential salons, a gathering that served as the point of tangency between the world of power and the world of ideas. When in February 1848 Émile Girardin bluntly informed King Louis Philippe that he should abdicate, the Saturday salon at the rue de Chaillot became virtually the weekend seat of government. It was precisely at this moment that Moreau Gottschalk, flushed with the success of his first published compositions and his well-received performances at the eminent salons recently vacated by Chopin, was invited to appear there.

Moreau later characterized the assembled throng at Girardin's as "an extraordinarily heterogeneous society."[21] He described Lamartine, poet and president, "leaning elegantly against the marble mantelpiece, resting his head on one of his beautiful hands, which by one of those failings common in great men, it pleased him to show off." There, too, were Prince Jerome Bonaparte, back from his exile in New Jersey and beyond; the poet Victor Hugo, with his "titanic head"; and also the *basso* Luigi Lablache, "the fattest man and the most subtle spirit ever known." The romantic poet and critic Théophile Gautier was seated at a table and drawing caricatures of other guests with a crayon. Finally, just as Moreau sat down at the piano to perform, novelist Alexandre Dumas burst into the room pushing forward his daughter and proclaiming loudly, "Ladies and gentlemen, here is my best work."

We know nothing of Gottschalk's several appearances at Girardin's except what Gottschalk himself wrote. One thing is clear: with these appearances at the rue de Chaillot Gottschalk had arrived at the same pinnacle of Parisian life on which Chopin, Liszt, and Thalberg had earlier stood.

When the bloody June Days exploded, Moreau's naive faith in the revolution evaporated. Henceforth, he viewed it as "the terrible insurrection which made Paris a slaughterhouse."[22] Long after most other musicians had fled the capital, Moreau now also wanted to escape. The man who made possible the Gottschalk family's departure from Paris was France's leading doctor, a pioneer in toxicology and forensic medicine, Matthieu Joseph Orfila (1787–1853).[23] Besides his scientific pursuits, Orfila was a discriminating musical amateur whose wife hosted one of the city's most high-toned musical salons. Alone among Parisian salons, the Orfilas' did not permit guests to enter while a musician was performing, and both hostess and host would invariably seat themselves directly by the pianist as a mark of their appreciation of the performer's artistry.[24]

Not only did Moreau perform at the Orfilas' salon, but he became a regular guest at Dr. Orfila's table. It must have been an unusual sight: the nineteen-year-old American discoursing on topical subjects with France's leading scientists and men of letters. Also among the guests from time to time was the vain Kalkbrenner, whose surprise at the presence there of the young Louisianian was surpassed only by the eagerness with which Moreau collected and later recorded gossip whispered around the table about the pompous professor from the Conservatoire.

Gottschalk, viewing the demise of the stillborn republic with sadness and disgust, wanted to escape from Paris. The onset of a cholera epidemic only made more urgent his desire to leave. At one of Dr. Orfila's dinners he had met Dr. Eugene Woillez, director of a large psychiatric hospital at Clermont-sur-l'Oise, situated on the new rail line an hour's distance north of Paris. Woillez invited Moreau to spend the summer at his home in this pleasant Picardy town surmounted by its ancient castle and the fourteenth-century Church of Saint-Samson. Gottschalk eagerly accepted and ended up spending the rest of the year 1848 there. These months in Clermont-sur-l'Oise were to be one of the most productive periods in his life.

Woillez lived in a comfortable home inside the high walls of the sprawling asylum, which covered nearly as much territory as the town itself. Housing nine hundred inmates of both sexes, it was a monument to that era's most idealistic thinking about the insane. The Centre Psychiatrique assumed that inmates were rational but beset by unreason, which could be cured through moral treatment and the establishment of a harmonious style of life. More like a utopian colony than a madhouse, it featured formal and informal gardens, promenades, and a family-type life. Its founders accepted Rousseauean notions of human perfectibility and believed that such a state could be achieved through a regimen based on liberty.[25]

Woillez was a polymath. In addition to running the huge asylum, he established the region's first system of public hygiene, published large volumes on the antiquities of Picardy, and illustrated all his writings with his own drawings.[26] A republican, in August 1848 he issued his own engraving of the local *fête de la fraternité* at which Moreau was doubtless present. He was also a tolerably good singer and had a small organ in his home.[27] Through his influence (and probably Gottschalk's as well) the town's first musical competition was held early in 1849.[28]

Caught up in the enthusiasms of his host, Moreau wrote a mass, unfortunately now lost, for the asylum church. For the first performance he invited a few artists from Paris and also several of the more docile inmates:

> I was struck with the bearing of the latter, and [asked] my friend to repeat the experiment and extend the number of invitations. The result was so favorable that we were soon able to form in the chapel a choir from among the patients of both sexes, who rehearsed on Saturday the hymns and chants that they were to sing at mass on Sunday.[29]

As this choir developed, Moreau noticed among the spectators an unshaven and filthy priest. Upon inquiring, he learned that this patient was a "raving lunatic who was getting more and more intractable every day." But the priest wanted to join the choir, and Gottschalk permitted him to do so. The new chorister soon became a regular participant; his raving subsided, and his personal hygiene improved.

From this experiment in music therapy Gottschalk concluded that music did not merely entertain but was in fact a moral agent, capable of curing and uplifting people. For the rest of his life he never passed up an opportunity to inspect a mental asylum.[30]

At Clermont-sur-l'Oise Moreau found a serene and supportive environment in which he was free to compose music without the need to meet social obligations or satisfy demands that he perform. Coming at the end of his apprenticeship and after the stimulation of the revolutionary days in Paris, this half-year interlude was a godsend. Gottschalk lost some time to a brief bout with typhoid fever, but otherwise the nineteen-year-old used this precious opportunity to the fullest. Indeed, it was in these months at the home of Dr. Woillez that Moreau Gottschalk found his identity as an American composer and broke new paths that anticipated developments in the music of his native land a half century later. It was fitting, therefore, that the four pieces that flowed from his inspiration in Clermont-sur-l'Oise—*Bamboula, La Savane, Le Bananier,* and *Le Mancenillier*—were all published over the name "Gottschalk of Louisiana," by which he was thereafter known throughout Europe.

Down to the crucial final step, the path to the first work in this Louisiana quartet, *Bamboula*, can be traced with some precision. The nineteenth century's revolt against the Enlightenment provides the context. In the previous century, truth had been sought in the universal, or at least in what seemed universal to enlightened Europeans. From biology to theology this produced systems that were at once grand and forbidding, in that they embraced all known phenomena of a given type but at the same time belittled what was particular or exceptional—that is, what each of us perceives as real in our own daily lives. With regard to social life, Humanity was everything. The peculiarities of any single community or ethnic group were of little consequence.

The nineteenth century's reaction against this was strong, involving an enthusiastic embrace of the non-universal, the specific, the unique. In music this meant the exultation of all that was vernacular, national, or local—the stranger the better. Chopin may have been a universal genius, but in his day he was revered for having revealed the "truth" of authentic Polish music. Like the popular nineteenth-century genre paintings to which it corresponded, such "national" music was built not on abstract themes but on specific motifs, which the composer incorporated wholesale into his work.

Besides its embrace of melodies that were local and specific, romanticism in music sought out the exotic as an end in itself. As the critic Gautier expressed it in an essay on Gottschalk, "what pleases us in music, as in all other things, is novelty."[31] At one level, this fascination with the exotic was yet another manifestation of Lamartine's quip that "France is bored." At another level, it bluntly repudiated the stolid *juste milieu* of the reigning bourgeoisie by contrasting it to the elemental vitality of exotic cultures. Gottschalk acknowledged this when he credited Liszt for founding "his unrestrained school upon the ruins of the old routine."[32]

Where were Parisians to find these exotic realms of authenticity? Earlier, composers like Étienne-Nicolas Mehul had responded enthusiastically to the rough-hewn grandeur they found described in the forged Scottish epic *Ossian*. More recently, a few artists had discovered similar "authenticity" in their own back yard, among the French peasantry. Thus the Salon of 1847 featured folksy genre paintings by Jean-François Millet (1814–75), Gustave Courbet (1819–77), and Rosa Bonheur (1822–99).

Far more popular among Parisians, however, were representations of the exotic and undeniably authentic world of Arab North Africa. Victor Hugo's *Orientales*, Eugéne Delacroix's watercolors of Algeria, and Félicien David's compositions *Le Harem* and *L'Egyptienne* all embodied this new cultural "find." The fact that thousands of French soldiers and officers spent the 1840s conquering Algeria left many of their compatriots with romantic notions about heroic Arabs akin to the feelings of some citizens of the United States toward the native Americans of their continent. On a popular level, this new fashion created an instant market for bombast like Leopold de Meyer's barn-burner *Marche marocaine*, not to mention the notorious can-can, which filtered back to Paris from Algiers in this period.[33]

In the years before 1848 Moreau Gottschalk covered every stop on this path. Not only did he compose the first version of his *Ossian* ballades (op. 4), but he rewrote his early *Polka de salon* (op. 1) as a *Danse ossianique* (op. 12). In its final version this piece has absolutely nothing "Ossianic" about it. In fact, it is a good if emotionally light salute to Chopin, but with one difference. If the bass line were changed to a habanera rhythm or if it were syncopated, the piece as a whole would be transformed into a jaunty Caribbean dance. A year later Gottschalk made this leap, albeit in another composition. For now, he wrote *Le Lai du dernier ménestrel* in the same pseudo-Scottish vein.[34] Still seeking the authentic and exotic in the storied North, he penned a *Marche scandinave*, now lost.

The next stop on Gottschalk's musical odyssey was the French countryside. Two compositions, entitled *La Moissonneuse (The Reaper)* and *La Glaneuse (The Gleaner)* memorialize the same rural scenes that were to attract the attention of French romantic realist painters. Gottschalk may have been inspired by early paintings by Rosa Bonheur, whose work he knew,[35] but it is worth noting that he anticipated Millet's treatment of the theme of gleaners by eight years. Both of Gottschalk's "peasant" pieces are mazurkas, not French folk songs. The one point of interest in the rather gaudy *La Moissonneuse*—no copy of *La Glaneuse* survives—is that it begins with the same type of cadence that Gottschalk used shortly afterwards in both *Bamboula* and *Le Bananier.*

Tracking the same route laid out by French romantics, Gottschalk then touched base briefly in the Arab world. As early as 1847 we find him improvising on the immensely popular French army marching song *Partant pour la Syrie*, a theme that engaged his interest over two decades. Shortly after his return to Paris from Clermont-sur-l'Oise he also composed a piano solo, now lost, based on the aria *Fatma* from the orientalizing opera *Le Caïd* by his friend Ambroise Thomas.[36]

All these pieces attest more to young Gottschalk's knowledge of French literature and painting than to his skills as a musical ethnographer. None contains more than the vaguest hint of the specific *melos* that the various ethnographic titles lead one to expect. On this important point Gottschalk had struck out. His compositions so far were competent and undeniably popular, but he was yet to find an idiom that both responded to the French interest in the exotic and gave him a distinct musical voice. Having searched in vain outside of himself, he had no choice but to look inward.

America had long been an object of curiosity for the French. Back in the 1790s the arch-romantic François René Chateaubriand had traveled to the New World in hopes of discovering the Northwest Passage. Although he failed at this, his evocative writings on the American wilderness sparked the French imagination. Neither Alexis de Tocqueville's clinical *Democracy in America* nor the decidedly bad paintings on American themes by artists from the United States exhibited at the Paris salons in the 1840s dispelled this aura of the exotic.[37]

The French singled out Louisiana for what they believed were its especially exotic qualities. In the eighteenth century the Abbé Prévost had published *Manon Lescaut*, the tragic tale—later a ballet by Halévy and then an opera by Auber—of a French girl sent to Louisiana in the early eighteenth century. France's lost colony on America's southern coast continued in Gottschalk's day to stir Parisian imaginations.

Still more did Saint-Domingue, where so many prominent French families had made their fortune and met their ruin. In the spring of 1848 the campaign to abolish slavery in France's remaining West Indian colonies finally succeeded, and Lamartine's Provisional Government extended full French citizenship to all former slaves in Guadeloupe and Martinique. Naturally, Parisians were more than a little curious about the culture of their new fellow citizens in the West Indies and rushed to the Théâtre de la République to hear actors declaim Lamartine's poem on the black Bonaparte of Haiti, Toussaint L'Ouverture.[38]

Strangely, this wave of interest in America generally and in France's present and past colonies in the Caribbean in particular found little resonance in music. True, Adolphe Adam had written a ballet based on *The Last of the Mohicans*, and Félicien David had composed a symphony entitled *Christophe Colomb* (1847). But neither evoked anything specific about the music of the New World, which remained a silent realm.

The one exception, and an interesting one, was a work of the Polish composer and pianist Jules (Júlian) Fontana (1810–65), Chopin's close friend and musical executor. Back in 1842 Fontana had crossed the Atlantic in order to pursue a concert career; he eventually spent half a dozen years in Havana. While there he wrote two fantasias on local themes. The first of these was entitled *La Havanne: Fantaisie sur des motifs américains et espagnoles*, in which he included a *Chanson de nègres de l'île de Cuba*.[39] Fontana's material was promising, but he worked it out in a bland, academic manner; even the syncopations, which he introduced in a section entitled *La Ley brava*, were bloodless. While it marked the debut of Afro-Caribbean syncopations in classical music, Fontana's fantasy caused not the slightest stir in Paris or elsewhere and was apparently unknown even to Gottschalk. If Moreau was to explore the syncopated music of the New World as a genre source, he would have to forge out on his own, as a pioneer.

What led Gottschalk to embrace musical themes from his own early life in Louisiana? Since nearly a half century was to pass before Anton Dvořák urged students at his American Conservatory in New York to take the same step, and still longer before Charles Ives turned for inspiration to the music of his Connecticut childhood, the question is worth asking. Moreau himself left no clues, but an answer comes from his sister Clara. While reflecting her usual confusion on dates, her account of the immediate inspiration for *Bamboula* is so specific that it is hard to dismiss as a mere figment of her imagination:

> Moreau was stricken down with typhoid fever. During the delirium which accompanies this fever he was seen to wave his hands, which those around him supposed to be symptoms of the delirium; but during his convalescence, which was very slow, he one day got up and wrote out *Bamboula*, which he said had been running in his brain during his illness.[40]

At another time he might not have acted on the impulse of a delirious recollection. However, he was in the home of a renowned psychiatrist, who viewed delirium and insanity of all sorts as objects of study and treatment rather than of fear. It is quite likely that Moreau received encouragement from the musical Dr. Woillez to develop the melodic inspiration that had seized him.

The folk or popular song that burned in Moreau's memory was *Quan'*
patate la cuite.[41] This simple melody, in all likelihood recalled from his
Grandmother Bruslé and from his nurse Sally, was quite separate from
the evocative name Gottschalk assigned the piece, *Bamboula.*

Why *Bamboula*, the name of a deep-voiced Afro-Caribbean drum?[42] It
would have been silly to give the piece the folk song's title in Creole
dialect, which referred to nothing more than grilling potatoes in the fire.
Nor was the piece merely an elaboration of the Creole song, since
Gottschalk introduced several further themes and virtually recomposed
the principal melody. Given this, Moreau decided to give the work not
an ethnographic name but a catchy genre title, which would flag it as a
sophisticated fantasy evoking all that the word *bamboula* signified in
France. The very title thus indicates that *Bamboula* was intended as a
self-conscious work of art rather than a piece of ethnographic reporting.

In this regard Gottschalk presents a contrast with Franz Liszt, who
was reworking his gypsy songs into "Hungarian" fantasies at the same
moment. For the worldly Liszt, the untutored gypsy musicians of Central
Europe were an exotic alternative to the world in which he moved, noble
savages unspoiled by civilization but with much to teach it.[43] For
Gottschalk, by contrast, the Creole airs did not conjure up some primitive
"other" but were a living voice from deep within his own receding past.
For all his later interest in folk songs, Moreau showed little interest in
the people who created and transmitted them. Let his audience treat
Bamboula and other Creole pieces as exotica. For Moreau they bore the
stamp of the viscerally familiar, of loss, of nostalgia.

Bamboula was organized around three sections, as so many later
Gottschalk pieces were to be. The second theme was an imaginatively
reworked and transposed version of the main theme, but the third, based
on a series of off-beat syncopations, is probably original to Gottschalk.
Beginning with the strong cadence with which he introduces the piece, it
is clear that this would be no mere transcription of a folk tune. *Bamboula*
is an exuberant and brilliant showpiece, with constantly shifting moods
and tonalities and with virtuoso passages throughout.

Hard on the heels of *Bamboula* came *La Savane*, the second Creole
genre piece, this one based on the song *Lolotte pov'piti Lolotte*. Known
by various names throughout the West Indies, this melody was unre-
corded until Gottschalk included it in his composition. It closely resembles the well-known *Skip to My Lou*, which probably derived from it. But
Gottschalk took only a portion of the original melody and broke it down
into colorful variations, in the course of which he repeats phrases, modulates, and substitutes chords at will. Most significant, he slows down the
tempo and shifts into the minor, thus transforming an airy and light-

spirited melody into a dark and brooding chant, preserving only enough of the innocence of the original to impart a haunting and truly sinister quality to the piece. As with *Bamboula,* he in fact recomposed the material so that it corresponded not to some remote ethnic original but to his personal emotional and artistic vision.[44] Announced for publication shortly after *Bamboula,*[45] *La Savane* was even in its title another genre painting, an example of the "poetic music" that offered a vital alternative to classical forms.[46]

Later, after he had left Clermont-sur-l'Oise, Gottschalk announced yet a third Creole fantasy, this one based on the well-known march-like song *En avan' Grenadie.*[47] Again, Moreau built a genre painting around this slight theme, entitling it *Le Bananier, chanson nègre.* This time, what one Gottschalk scholar calls the "artistic metamorphosis" begins the moment the theme is stated, for Gottschalk shortened it from ten to eight measures. By displacing accents, modulating keys, and generously applying color through the use of his "signature" chords—diminished sevenths and augmented sixths—Gottschalk created a little gem, utterly simple at first, but rising eventually to sweeping runs and surging rhythms.

In an effect that was to amaze audiences, Gottschalk leads off *Le Bananier* with what Americans a century later would call a "hoochie-koochie" figure in the left hand. It sounds for all the world as if he was setting the stage for the entry of a belly dancer, which in fact may be close to the truth. Nationalistic Americans might detect in this an echo of Caribbean drums—again, that Congo Square myth—but it more likely draws on the Algerian Casbah, as interpreted by returning French troops and popular Parisian entertainers.

The fourth in the series of Gottschalk's Creole compositions, entitled *Le Mancenillier,* was not written until two years later and not published until April 1851.[48] Like the other three, the title is a genre reference, a *mancenillier* or *manchineel* being a tropical tree that produces small apple-like fruits that are dangerously poisonous. Sap and even raindrops falling from a mancenillier can cause scarring blisters. Unlike the other three Creole pieces, the title of *Le Mancenillier* has a literary caste, for it refers to a voluptuous poem of the same name by Charles-Hubert Millevoye.[49]

Like *Bamboula* but unlike *La Savane, Le Mancenillier* is built on three distinct themes. This time, however, all three are actual folk songs. Thanks to the diligence of musicologist John G. Doyle, these have been identified as *Chanson de Lizette,* an eight-bar melody from Saint-Domingue; *Ou som souroucou* ("What's the matter that you drink so much water?"), a black Creole melody later documented in New Orleans; and either *Ma mourri* from Louisiana or the related *Tant sirop est doux* from Martinique.[50] Characteristically, Gottschalk reshaped all three melodies, although to varying degrees, the third being the most extensively recrafted so as to fit the dramatic needs of the composition.

Le Mancenillier is true program music. Millevoye's poem tells of a beautiful island girl, Zarina, who is in love with the good Zephaldi but is courted by the fierce King Nélusko, whose advances she cannot resist. Resigned to her fate, she prepares for her night with King Nélusko by sitting under the mancenillier tree. At the last moment she is rescued by Zephaldi.

The three musical themes of *Le Mancenillier* correspond to the stages of Zarina's scrape with death. First comes the pensive *Chanson de Lizette*, which is introduced with a somber bass cadence "da-da-da-*dum-dum*." Then, in an abrupt reverse, Gottschalk describes Zarina beneath the mancenillier with the sweetly sunny and innocent melody *Ou som souroucou.* Finally, her salvation by Zephaldi is celebrated with *Ma mourri*, which is not unlike the main theme of *Bamboula.* This brief narrative gem is introduced with a dark melody of Gottschalk's own composition which functions much like an overture. With the third "festival" theme of *Ma mourri*, Gottschalk cuts loose with complex tonalities and modulations; these lead to a long coda (printed in the original Paris edition but excluded from later American versions), which serves as a kind of finale to the mini-opera.

The haunting *Le Mancenillier* is at once the most faithfully authentic of the four Creole pieces and the most studiously "artistic." *Chanson de Lizette* was known to Moreau from childhood, when Clara and his other sisters sang it in harmony.[51] The piano piece lovingly preserves the original mood. By contrast, Moreau had never seen a mancenillier, as the tree is not found in Louisiana. The idea of using it as a metaphor for the aura of fatalism and death that hangs over the tropics came to Gottschalk through his readings of romantic poetry. This same dark undertone had sounded in the three earlier Creole pieces, but in *Le Mancenillier* it is explicit in the very title.

It is probably this sinister quality, unexpectedly interwoven with lilting tropical melodies, that accounts for the peculiar fascination all four of Gottschalk's Creole pieces exercise. The blending of erotic and ecstatic folk dance with brooding and even morbid themes gave rise to a distinctive and compellingly "tropical" strain of lyricism heretofore unexpressed in European music or culture generally. It was a potent compound, but one whose full potential was not to be realized for another three quarters of a century with the advent of jazz. Together, these four "Creole" pieces created a sensation, not only in Paris but in Europe generally. Here, finally, was something exciting and new, an exuberant leap beyond the *juste milieu.*

There is no doubt that Gottschalk's brilliant execution added to the impact of these compositions. *La France musicale* described his performance of *Bamboula* in some detail:

> The pianist vigorously attacks the Creole song. Then follows a second motif. . . . The accompaniment he makes very *staccato.* The middle theme, played languidly, contrasts in a strange, but deliciously poetic way, with the bass, which continues energetically to make the rhythm.
>
> On the third melody, in B flat, comes a variation with a *crescendo fortissimo,* and directly afterwards the same motif in B flat reappears and disappears. Hardly is it finished when the *rentrée* is made by a dazzling run, which I can only compare to a cascade of pearls. . . . After this follow variations in triplets, made with wonderful lightness.[52]

An American reported that Gottschalk performed all his Louisiana pieces "with absolute rhythmic accuracy. This clear definition . . . contributed more than anything else to the fascination which he always exerted over his audience."[53] This contrasted with Chopin, whose strict rhythm was confined to his left hand.[54]

For all the brilliance of Gottschalk's performance, the impact of these four Louisiana pieces reached far beyond those who heard him play them. Beethoven's former pupil Karl Czerny was intrigued by *Le Bananier* to the point that he made a four-hand arrangement of it.[55] Jacques Offenbach rescored *Le Bananier* for cello, and Leon Reynier transcribed it for violin. The young Bizet henceforth included these Gottschalk compositions in his solo repertoire, as did the great pianist Alexandre Goria, to whom Gottschalk dedicated *Le Bananier,* and also the piano virtuosos Alfred Jaël and Josef Wieniewski. Other artists performed these pieces as far afield as Uruguay.[56] In far-off St. Petersburg the Russian chemist and composer Borodin took the trouble to copy out *Le Bananier* by hand and borrowed a number of phrases from it for use in his own *Polovtsian Dances* in the opera *Prince Igor.*[57]

The deeper impact of Gottschalk's Creole compositions was not fully evident until the twentieth century. As critic Harold C. Schonberg has pointed out, Darius Milhaud's *Scaramouche* (composed in 1939) and his *Saudades do Brazil* (1920–21) "are not really too different in concept from Gottschalk's . . . *Le Bananier.*"[58] The many "classical" composers of the twentieth century who have used jazz, tangos, and Caribbean and Afro-American rhythms to enrich their musical palette all owe a debt to these pioneering compositions by Gottschalk.

 Celebrity

MOREAU did not return to Paris until the early weeks of 1849. When he arrived back in the capital *La France musicale* acknowledged that he was still unknown to the larger public but that his compositions, "which he performs with rare delicacy," represented a brilliant continuation of the "poetic school of Chopin."[1]

The republic of 1848 was by now only a memory, Prince Louis Napoleon having defeated Lamartine in elections for the presidency and begun his comic opera ascent to his grandfather's imperial throne. Gottschalk had no use for the aspiring emperor for he believed that this new Napoleon had gained his position through nothing more than his resonant name and his dashing appearance on horseback.[2]

During the first months after his return to Paris, Moreau was welcomed into the most prestigious musical salons and is reported to have participated in a concert at the Opéra Comique on February 9, 1849.[3] One of the salons at which Moreau performed was that of the elderly Countess Marie-Elizabeth de Flavigny, the mother of Liszt's mistress Marie d'Agoult.[4] The German-born Countess de Flavigny, who maintained one of the most highly regarded musical salons of Paris, became Gottschalk's loyal supporter and patron.[5]

Far more important in the long run was Moreau's contact with María de las Mercedes Santa Cruz y Montalvo, the Countess Merlín (1789–1852).[6] Even the ambitious Madame Girardin acknowledged, "It is impossible to appreciate too highly the influence that the salon of the Countess Merlín exerted upon the musical society of Paris."[7] Merlín herself was a singer who, Gottschalk later recalled, "in spite of her advanced age . . . sang nonetheless with a passion, enthusiasm, and a style that put in the shade the talents of more than one singer of renown."[8] Rossini had heard his music performed at Countess Merlín's salon on rue Berlin, and it was there that Meyerbeer, Bellini, and Donizetti found a sympathetic audience long before the public had acclaimed their music.[9]

Besides her role as a musical king-maker, Countess Merlín was also the Caribbean world's unofficial ambassador to France. Born in Havana, she opened her doors to all notable visitors from the West Indies and vigorously patronized all musicians and writers from the islands. It was natural, therefore, that she should have sought out Moreau the instant his *Bamboula* was first heard and that she would ask him to perform this work repeatedly before her guests.[10] Thanks to Countess Merlín's broad tastes, her salon also provided an opportunity for Moreau to show his skills more generally, and he recalled having performed works by Bach for her guests.[11]

Catapulted into Paris from Countess Merlín's salon, *Bamboula* rapidly took on a life of its own. Long before it appeared in print, *La France musicale* effused:

> The *Bamboula* is at its height. One must have lived under the burning sky from whence the Creole draws his melody; one must be impregnated with these eccentric chants, which are little dramas in action; in a word, one must be a Creole, as composer and executant, in order to feel and make others understand the whole originality of *Bamboula*.
>
> We have discovered this Creole composer; an American composer, *bon Dieu!* Yes, indeed, and a pianist composer and player of the highest order, who as yet is only known to the aristocratic salons of Paris, but whose name will soon make a great noise.[12]

At age nineteen, Moreau was yet to appear before a paying public. To rectify this and to take advantage of what was obviously a good business opportunity, Camille Pleyel proposed a public performance for April 17, 1849. Salle Pleyel was packed, and the audience listened politely as Gottschalk played the Andante from Beethoven's "Moonlight Sonata" and participated in a reading of a sextet by Onslow. Interest picked up when he turned to a Chopinian *Mazurka* of his own, but it was *Bamboula* that the public awaited. By the time Moreau unexpectedly returned to the principal theme and then the brief finale, the entire audience was on its feet cheering loudly. *La France musicale* claimed Moreau's success that evening surpassed anything France had seen for years, and concluded that "Gottschalk is henceforth placed in the ranks of the best performers and of the most renowned composers for the piano."[13]

With exquisite timing, *Bamboula* appeared in print at the Bureau Central de Musique in the same week of the concert. Then, a few months after this stunning debut, Chopin died. Moreau was out of town for the funeral, but his mother was among the enormous crowd at the Madeleine, where Chopin's body lay in state. Back at Pleyel's hall after the funeral, everyone was musing on who could replace the beloved genius. Camille Pleyel, whose pianos Chopin had preferred, declared flatly, "Gottschalk is the only one who can fill Chopin's place."[14]

Even before these events, signs of acceptance in the highest musical circles were evident. Professor Marmontel of the Conservatoire had invited Moreau to appear on a matinee program to highlight his own best pupils.[15] Later, Marmontel went so far as to list *Bamboula* as one of the set pieces for his students' mid-year examination and invited the composer to serve as one of the judges. Thus Moreau Gottschalk, who had earlier been rejected by the Conservatoire, now sat with the man who had rejected him, Professor Pierre Zimmerman, as they graded Conservatoire students on how well they performed a composition by the rejectee.[16]

Berlioz, too, came into further contact with the young American. While bantering one day, Berlioz challenged Gottschalk to play all the arias of Meyerbeer's *Le Prophète* in their correct key and order. Moreau succeeded.[17] Another time when Berlioz's cousin Jules showed an interest in organ building, the composer contacted Moreau and asked him for a letter of introduction for Jules to use if he went to the United States to try his hand at organ building there.[18]

It was in the weeks following the Pleyel concert that Moreau brought forth his *La Savane*.[19] Its impact was less flamboyant than that of *Bamboula*, yet it added a new level to the general excitement surrounding Moreau. Moving beyond the salons, he appeared at recitals of fashionable piano teachers and at popular Parisian locales like the Baths of Tivoli.[20] The pace was exhausting, however. Fatigue, combined with the danger posed by a renewed epidemic of cholera that had already struck down Kalkbrenner, soon drove Moreau from Paris. After contemplating a tour to London, he settled on Le Havre, where he refused public concerts and devoted himself mainly to composing.[21]

Except for the summer vacation in Le Havre, Moreau's whereabouts until mid-December were a mystery. And not just to the modern biographer. *La France musicale*, edited by the Escudier brothers, Gottschalk's friends and publishers, reported on November 4 that he had been sick for some time. A week later it retracted this report, claiming instead that Moreau had been visiting the country homes of various friends.[22] About the same time his mother wrote him—unfortunately, his address is lost—asking, "Are you not planning to come back? It is time. Everyone here is saying all kinds of things, this and that, that you have found a lover who is keeping you there, and indeed all kinds of other things. It is time to come back."[23] If the rumors were false, Moreau did nothing to dispel them. Evidently, he did not feel the slightest obligation to explain whether he was recovering from illness, dallying with an unknown lover, or simply seeking solitude.

The one thing of which we may be sure is that Moreau composed much music during these months. It was probably at this time that Moreau wrote (or completed) *Le Bananier*, since he began programming it in concerts immediately after he returned to Paris in December 1849.[24] By the time he returned to Paris he also had in hand an elaborate and highly original composition based loosely on the hunting music from Méhul's opera *Le Jeune Henri*. As an example of program music at its best, Gottschalk's fantasy on *La Chasse du jeune Henri* (op. 10) surpasses Méhul's original in the vividness of its narrative, its carefully crafted transitions, and its startling effects. This piece marks Gottschalk's entry into the world of operatic fantasies—"transcriptions" is too demeaning a term. These were the free variations on well-known themes that provided flexible vehicles for nearly every leading composer of the day.[25] Also in this idiom was Gottschalk's *Caprice élégant*, based on an aria from Ambroise Thomas's opera *Le Songe d'une nuit d'Été.*[26]

During the second half of 1849, Gottschalk planned a trip to Spain. Over the previous half dozen years Spain had become a major point of pilgrimage for French romantics in search of exotica. Trend-setting Théophile Gautier had just been to this outpost of the strange and colorful and had published a popular book on his wanderings there.[27] Liszt, too, had spent a winter on the Iberian peninsula.[28] So convinced was Jacques Offenbach of his profound sympathy for Spain that he did not even bother going there before composing a *Grande Scène espagnole.*[29]

It is possible that it was through Countess Mérlin or the Marquis d'Albucenza that Moreau gained an invitation from Queen Isabel II to perform in Madrid.[30] At any rate, Moreau had taken care to dedicate *Bamboula* to the Spanish queen. For good measure he dedicated *La Savane* to Queen Mary II of Portugal on the assumption that a side trip to Lisbon was likely. Had it not been for the possibility of resuming his lucrative concertizing in Paris during the spring of 1850 Gottschalk would undoubtedly have left immediately for Spain.[31]

The 1850 season began with a bang when Gottschalk and the violinist Max-Mayer teamed up for "a veritable musical tournament" on January 11. On this program he unveiled a new mazurka, *Fatma*, a completely reworked version of his *Ossian* ballades, and *Le Bananier*, which was encored. So excited was the audience that it demanded more and began loudly entreating the two artists to perform selections from Rossini's *William Tell.* With no prior preparation, Max-Mayer and Gottschalk impro-

vised a long fantasy on themes from Rossini's opera; when the audience
thundered for yet more, Max-Mayer produced his own new *Fantasia alla
Polacca*, to which Gottschalk improvised an accompaniment.[32]

A month later Gottschalk repeated this triumph at the Salle Érard,
home base of the renowned Érard pianos so beloved by Liszt.[33] By now
Bananier fever was raging everywhere, even eclipsing the previous year's
Bamboula-mania. The audience at Érard's cheered for five minutes after
Moreau performed *Le Bananier*. Soon virtually every pianist in Paris was
performing the piece. A journalist asserted, "It has been a long time since
we have seen such a success as has been attained by *[Le Bananier,]
Bamboula*, and *La Savane*. . . . To find a comparable example, one
would have to reach back to the successes of Chopin's first works."[34] On
one evening alone *Le Bananier* was programmed simultaneously at three
different concerts around town.[35]

Appearing with Gottschalk at the Salle Érard concert was Jacques Offenbach, at the time still a struggling cellist and unheralded composer.
The son of a Jewish cantor, Offenbach had changed his name from Levy
in order to sidestep possible anti-Semitism in the French capital. Gawky
behind huge eyeglasses, he exuded what one American called a "perilous
malignancy."[36] Within months, however, Offenbach was to be offered the
baton at the Comédie Française, thus launching his career in operetta.
Meanwhile, he and Gottschalk appeared together frequently, and Moreau
composed a duet for the two of them.[37]

The rest of the spring was consumed with a dizzy round of concerts.
In various combinations with Offenbach, pianist Alexandre Goria, harpist
Félix Godefroid, soprano Henriette Sontag, and others, Gottschalk appeared in a concert for the blind, recitals at the Conservatoire, a benefit
for an Italian actress, and all the major private salons.[38] He was now what
today would be called a "hot property," and every major piano manufacturer was bidding for his endorsement. In addition to several further concerts at Pleyel's and the performance at Salle Érard, he appeared at the
hall owned by the virtuoso and manufacturer Henri Herz in a concert
attended by Louis Napoleon.[39]

In these many performances Gottschalk unleashed his entire arsenal
of new compositions. While *Le Bananier* rose to new heights of popularity with its publication and republication through pirated editions, *La
Chasse du jeune Henri*, *Fatma*, and the *Ossian* ballades also aroused
much interest. Moreau even found time to compose his own adaptations
of two engaging lyrics by the harpist Godefroid, *Le Rêve* (*The Dream*,
now lost), and *Danse des sylphes* (op. 86).[40] The pace was wearing,
though, and by late spring the press was reporting that Gottschalk was
ill.[41] Suddenly, in the second week of June 1850, he abruptly departed for

Switzerland, where, as he announced, he intended to relax for the summer.[42]

This, at least, is what Moreau told the public. But when a policeman at Dijon detained Gottschalk because he had (again) forgotten his passport, he found in the pianist's baggage a general letter of introduction from Érard. Moreau was stopped again at Rousses for having no passport, at which time he produced a carton containing one hundred photographs of himself and showed the police that these fit the description of him just published in a Paris magazine known to the gendarmes.[43] It turned out, too, that Érard had conveniently sent with Gottschalk the splendid concert grand that had just won first prize at the Paris Exposition.[44] In spite of claims by *La France musicale* that "in going to Switzerland Gottschalk had nothing else in mind than to find some rest,"[45] he clearly intended to test himself before a non-French audience.

Moreau was exhausted even before he was incapacitated for several weeks en route by food poisoning. He finally arrived at the castle at Grandson in the Swiss canton of Vaud, where he spent another month resting and writing.[46] The picturesque twelfth-century castle was now leased by Henri Frédéric Perret, who had spent many years in New Orleans, married a Creole there, and formed a friendship with the Bruslés.[47] While recovering at this fabled spot Moreau arranged for two concerts in Lausanne and received a deputation from Geneva inviting him to appear there in August.[48]

By accepting these offers Gottschalk unwittingly placed himself on the fringe of political controversy. The United States and Switzerland had yet to sign an agreement covering the rights of their citizens to travel in each other's country. At the time of Gottschalk's arrival, the American minister was reviewing a draft agreement, but it specifically excluded Jews from the free travel extended to other Americans.[49] Though Catholic by faith, Gottschalk was an ethnic Jew and, given his name, ran the danger of being treated as such by Swiss law. Fortunately, Moreau's fame enabled him to sidestep the problem. He arrived at Geneva in late July and settled at the comfortable new Hôtel du Rhône, overlooking the Grand Quai.[50]

The successful nineteenth-century composer-virtuoso required the tactical skills of a general. To conquer a new city, for example, he did not begin with a frontal assault on the main concert hall but by first developing local allies and patrons. By the end of July the Geneva press was reporting that "Mr. Godschack" had appeared in a number of local homes and had been judged "a veritable marvel": "His performance . . . is something between Liszt and Thalberg . . . and his American melodies were enthusiastically received."[51]

At length, seemingly in response to a groundswell of demand, Moreau "permitted" himself to appear in concert at the Casino on August 7. A full orchestra was on hand, as was the German-born violinist and conductor Julius Eichberg (1824–93). Moreau described Eichberg, who later emigrated to America, as "an excellent man, distinguished violinist, and graceful composer."[52] It was through Eichberg's help that Geneva now opened its doors to the touring American.

Tickets to the Casino were grabbed up the moment they went on sale, and a hundred additional tickets had to be printed.[53] At the concert Gottschalk played a selection of his recent works, including a one-piano version of *La Chasse du jeune Henri* and a new set of variations, now lost, on Bellini's *La Sonnambula*.[54] To close the evening, he and Eichberg drove the Swiss audience to distraction with an extended set of daring and brilliant variations on themes from Rossini's *William Tell*. Some of these may initially have been borrowed from the Parisian violin-piano team of de Bériot and Osbourne.[55] Evidently, in the months since he and violinist Max-Mayer had improvised this production, Moreau had fully developed his own version and had written it out. Recast again for two pianos and then solo piano, Gottschalk's *William Tell* fantasy was to be the cornerstone of practically every remaining concert he gave in Switzerland.[56]

The Calvinists of Geneva abandoned their reserve and pelted the visitor with flowers in such profusion that he could not hold them all. The press hailed "the universality of his talent, and his execution now fiery and passionate, now fresh and dreamy."[57] However, a more cautious note also sounded when one reviewer dismissed the Louisiana pieces as "no more than sparkling trifles" and judged the concert "inconclusive."[58] This began what was to be a lifelong jousting between Gottschalk and Protestant champions of "serious" music, a battle that pitted the austere values of Northern Europe against the brighter sensibilities of Paris, Louisiana, and the West Indies.

Gottschalk made no concession to this criticism. After a brief trip back to France to close the season at the Casino in Aix-les-Bains,[59] he returned to a second Geneva concert at which he offered, in addition to his own works, only the familiar Onslow *Sextet* and Weber's *Perpetual Motion*.[60] He and Eichberg again performed their variations on *William Tell*. Demand for tickets was so great that two hundred additional seats had to be packed onto the stage. The critics fell silent.

Using the oldest ploy in the book, Moreau had announced that his second concert would be the last before he departed for Madrid.[61] When finally he "relented," the Geneva press claimed it was a victory for free Helvetia over tyrannical Spain.[62] The next concert was set for September

11, and this time Moreau threw a sop to the classicists by programming a Beethoven piano sonata and a violin sonata by Mendelssohn.[63] As usual, he performed several of his Louisiana pieces, and their "artless" simplicity led the *Journal de Genève* to proclaim Moreau both "child and master."[64] It might have added "showman," for at this third Geneva concert Gottschalk pulled out a new *Caprice and Variations* (op. 89) on *Carnival of Venice.* Anticipating generations of American town bandsmen down to Sousa's era, he framed this as a flamboyant show-stopper. A later reviewer described the *Carnival of Venice* variations as "filled with the most original and daring caprices, many played on a single hand."[65] So trite did this numbing trick-piece become for later generations that it is hard to imagine the electrifying effect it must have had on these first audiences in Geneva. At any rate, Gottschalk seems not to have written it down, no doubt because of his frequently expressed view that to write out such a work would invite others to steal it, and also because of his overall disdain for formalizing what were, in reality, inspired improvisations. The posthumous version that survives is from the hand of his Cuban friend and chronicler Nicolás Ruiz Espadero.[66]

Following the usual ritual for touring virtuosos, Gottschalk next offered a concert to benefit the poor. After managing to garner half the wealthy of Geneva as patrons for the event, he was disquieted to learn that a touring violinist from Rome had scheduled a concert for the same evening as his. Caught in a bind, Moreau wrote a letter to this Signor Farina, asking him to postpone his debut and offering his own services to Farina on another date if he would do so. When Farina consented, Moreau went out of his way to promote the Italian's concert, an act of benevolence that benefited both musicians.[67] In the same spirit, Moreau scheduled a further performance to benefit the victims of the Revolution of 1848 in Krakow, Poland.[68]

At his benefit for the poor, Gottschalk tried to meet the expectations of every faction in his audience. This resulted in a truly bizarre program. A Beethoven sonata was paired with the *Carnival of Venice*, a trio by Mayseder stood opposite *Le Bananier*, and Liszt's two-piano fantasy on themes from Bellini's *Norma* was complemented by *Jankee Dootle (sic).*[69] The unlikely program carried the day, however, no doubt encouraging in Moreau the false hope that he could be all things to all people. Not until he reached America was he disabused of this misperception.

The high point of these concerts was the premiere of a new and elaborate set of variations on *God Save the Queen* (op. 41). Under the title *America* this later became a Gottschalk favorite in the United States, where Gottschalk published it with a dedication to Anton Rubinstein. All too easily dismissed by highbrows as simply another potboiler, *God Save the Queen* in fact contains intriguingly recomposed slow passages as well as bracing moments in the spirit of Chopin.

Why should Moreau have composed variations on *God Save the Queen* for a Swiss audience? Certainly not out of affection for the British. When an Englishman approached him on the street in Geneva and offered a guinea to serenade his ailing wife for an hour, Gottschalk reacted with righteous indignation.[70] The reason he wrote this complex elaboration of the British anthem is that the same tune served as the national hymn of Switzerland. Besides pleasing his local hosts, a set of variations on *God Save the Queen* was a good item for an itinerant virtuoso to have in his repertoire, for the same melody served as the national anthem of at least seven of the states of Germany, as well as several Scandinavian countries.[71]

Prior to his first Geneva concert, Gottschalk received a message at the Hôtel du Rhône informing him that the aged Russian Grand Duchess Anna Fedorovna, aunt of Britain's Queen Victoria, would be in attendance that evening. For her and her suite he reserved the first row of boxes, which were furnished with divans and cushions of red velvet. During the intermission the Grand Duchess's chamberlain, Baron Vaucher, introduced Moreau to his royal fan, who promptly invited him to visit her at her home on the lake outside Geneva.[72] Gottschalk traveled to Frontenex, where the Grand Duchess resided in a converted outbuilding of a large estate, La Grande Boissière.[73] The site was spectacular, with Mont Blanc visible to the east and the Jura Mountains to the west. Here the Grand Duchess maintained a miniature court.

German-born Anna Fedorovna (1781–1860) had been divorced from Tsar Nicholas I's brother, Konstantin. Once the hope of Russian liberals, Konstantin had proven a disastrous and impotent husband to Anna. The Tsar was all too glad for her to depart for Switzerland, provided she stayed out of politics. Now she lived quietly with "Baron" Vaucher, in reality the Swiss son of a dentist-surgeon, who was known to be thoroughly dishonest and was the subject of much local gossip.[74]

In this worldly but pathetic nest of gentlefolk, the Grand Duchess quizzed Moreau on American politics and inquired about the "great American statesman" Barnum.[75] This combination of ignorance and condescension, which Moreau increasingly observed in Europeans, contributed to his growing patriotism as an American.

Down to his departure from Switzerland, Gottschalk spent much time at La Petite Boissière. Grand Duchess Anna lavished gifts on him, among them a huge pearl surrounded by diamonds.[76] Moreau was greatly impressed by the cultivated and serious attitude toward music which prevailed at this retreat, and especially by one Baron de Bock, who regaled him with long tales of his friendship with the composer Weber.[77] De Bock stimulated Moreau's already keen admiration for this composer. This resulted in a piano adaptation of Weber's *Invitation to the Waltz*, only a fragment of which is preserved, a four-hand fantasy on the overture to the opera *Oberon*, a scoring of Weber's *Concertstück* for piano and string quartet, and, at the end of his life, a set of variations on Weber's *La Dernière pensée*.[78]

To the Grand Duchess Moreau dedicated his reworked *Ossian* ballades (op. 12) and an elaborate *Grande Fantaisie triomphale* (op. 84) based on themes from Verdi's opera *I Lombardi*. Gottschalk had almost surely been present at the premiere of this opera (retitled *Jérusalem*) in Paris in 1847 and probably knew the variations on the famous trio published by his friend the pianist Alexandre Goria.[79] Moreau's three-part elaboration is certainly no masterpiece, but it includes competent examples of virtually every device that gave popularity to the genre of operatic fantasies.

Predictably, given the politics of the situation, the patronage of Grand Duchess Anna produced invitations neither to London nor St. Petersburg, even though a New York paper had already announced that Gottschalk would soon be off to Russia at the invitation of the Tsar.[80] By late October 1850 Moreau departed Geneva for Lausanne. With him was the lucky Farina, who was joined by local musicians from each town they passed through. Eichberg, who was unable to leave Geneva, published an essay on Moreau in the Lausanne press that amounted to a free advertisement.[81] Both concerts at the Lausanne Casino were mobbed. Steamers from neighboring cities on the lake brought the curious, who thronged to hear Gottschalk in spite of the excessively high ticket price.[82]

Aside from a Mendelssohn violin sonata, the concerts repeated those in Geneva, yet their success was, if anything, greater. *Le Nouvelliste vaudois* tried every adjective in the book, calling Moreau "*pyramidal, phenomenal*, raving, et cetera, et cetera, but we give up on these words for they seem to us less than we wish to say."[83] Interestingly, what appealed particularly to the Lausanne public was not Moreau's pyrotechnics but the "sadness and simplicity" of his American pieces, "songs which bring tears to our eyes."[84] The critic detected this same note of sadness in Gottschalk's face, which he found "very pale, his eyes cast down. His physiognomy expresses melancholy," declared the critic, "and there is in all his features a trace of pain and sadness."

In honor of their guest, the people of Lausanne organized a large banquet, at which they declaimed poetic confessions declaring that "We could spend our lives listening to you, Gottschalk. . . . We love you."[85] Two concerts in Neuchâtel produced the same effect, only this time the locals organized a ball in Moreau's honor. At the town of Vevey on November 13, Moreau prudently announced a benefit for the local hospital.[86] He did the same at Yverdun, where he gave two concerts.[87] These acts of philanthropy promptly entered the Gottschalk folklore, and by the time he had returned to the United States the wing added to the nursing home at Yverdun through his generosity had grown into an entire facility.[88]

These final concerts in Switzerland, including a last performance in Geneva in honor of his friend Eichberg,[89] provided Gottschalk with a staggeringly unrealistic introduction to the demanding world of touring. Returning to Paris via Grandson, Moreau had the satisfaction of reading a Swiss writer's statement that, "as an artist, he leaves us a unique and ineffable remembrance; as a man, he has gained our hearts."[90] Another prayed "that God may watch over him for the sake of his numerous admirers and . . . his mother and her young family, in which he takes the place of a father."[91] Such accolades made the life of a touring virtuoso appear to him as a grand procession from one group of adoring fans to the next, with convenient stops at storybook castles and banquets with royalty, all accompanied by unimaginable financial rewards. Life was really splendidly simple. Deceptively so, for even in Europe this idyll was becoming a rarity. In America it had no bearing on reality whatsoever.

La France musicale announced Moreau's return to the French capital on January 12, 1851. "Never," it glowed, "have we seen such enthusiasm for an artist as met Gottschalk in Switzerland." Parisian readers were prepared to accept this with a knowing leer. Some while earlier the pianist and critic Oscar Comettant had written rather maliciously in the *Siècle* that Gottschalk had surpassed even Jenny Lind, for she had never been abducted. After a concert in Switzerland, Comettant confided, Gottschalk had been waylaid by "a young, beautiful, and robust Geneva woman." Pouncing on him at the stage door, she had "covered the pianist with flowers and, quickly wrapping him in a large coat, lifted him up and swept him off to the bewilderment of all." Comettant, who later claimed that Gottschalk was actually a Frenchman with no American element in his makeup, coyly admitted that "we do not know if this news is exact, but we print it just as we heard it."[92]

This typified the adulation and sensationalism that greeted Moreau on his return to Paris. Fortunately, he had a full month before beginning a series of four concerts on February 26. During this time he participated in a few recitals, including one in which he played on a square piano by Érard as an advertising ploy.[93] Instead of presenting major concerts, he devoted himself to catching up on his family's affairs, polishing up his new compositions, and composing several new works. Among the latter was an *étude dramatique* called *Mazeppa*, after the wild and fiery Ukrainian Cossack of the seventeenth century. Nominally based on Byron's poem by that name, *Mazeppa* was built around themes by Joseph Quidant that had been dedicated to Gottschalk himself. Gottschalk's version was in fact a tribute to Franz Liszt, renowned as the "musical Mazeppa," who had unwittingly provided inspiration for the entire Swiss tour. In acknowledgment of this, Moreau dedicated the piece to the great virtuoso. It is a pity this composition is lost, as it was described by a European reviewer as being particularly dramatic in character and by Gottschalk's Cuban friend Espadero as of "immense beauty" and "full of ingenious mechanism" that required "a capable interpreter."[94]

More important were three new pieces from Gottschalk's pen: an etude entitled *La Mélancolie* based on a melody by the harpist Félix Godefroid, a nocturne entitled *La Chute des feuilles* (op. 42), and *Le Mancenillier*, the fourth and last of the Louisiana quartet. All three are on elegiac themes, reflecting the melancholia first observed in Moreau by the critic in Lausanne. Notwithstanding Moreau's somber state of mind, he plunged into a fresh round of concertizing, scheduling a series of four performances at the newly opened Bonne Nouvelle Hall near the Porte Saint-Denis.[95] He also planned performances at Professor Marmontel's salon and at the Collège Louis le Grand.[96]

Amidst all this concertizing, a devastating fire broke out at the Pleyel piano factory on March 25, 1851.[97] Hundreds of Pleyel craftsmen were thrown out of work, and Gottschalk's old patron was nearly bankrupted. Moving quickly, Moreau organized a benefit for the unemployed workers and enlisted other artists to assist him. This workers' relief concert was a marketing triumph, for it enabled Moreau to make a pitch directly to every well-heeled Parisian he had ever met. At the concert itself he performed fourteen times, and at the end a delegation of Pleyel factory workers mounted the stage to present him with an enormous bouquet.[98] In one stroke Moreau had reached out to both capital and labor, thus symbolically effecting the social reconciliation of which most Frenchmen only dreamed.

Adolphe Adam, composer of *Les Sylphides* and dozens of other ballets and operas, covered the Pleyel concert for *L'Assemblé nationale* and watched wide-eyed as the audience demanded four encores in a row. Adam concluded:

> Mr. Gottschalk has become the man *à la mode*, the indispensable pianist. . . . The secret of his unheard-of success is that he is an *entertaining* performer. The combination of this noun and adjective may be surprising, yet never has such an alliance of two words been more justified. Mr. Gottschalk's music has all the grace of Chopin but with more arresting forms; he is less magisterial than Thalberg but has perhaps more warmth; he is less severe than Prudent

yet plays with more grace and elegance. For the best way to please is not to want to please too long.[99]

Adam's panegyric was but one voice in an outpouring of praise that surpassed anything Paris had seen for years. Léon Escudier led the way in March when he declared Gottschalk to be "admirable, marvelous, immense. Since Liszt fell silent, I know of no other person more worthy of being carried triumphantly into the world of arts than he. . . . Gottschalk is now on the throne."[100] Such hyperbole was understandable since Escudier was both Moreau's publisher and friend. It was not expected from Escudier's chief rival, however, the high-toned *Revue et gazette musicale*, which pronounced Gottschalk "prodigious," as well as "indefatigable and charming."[101] Paolo Fiorentino, the often acerbic and much feared judge of music for the *Constitutionnel* and *Corsaire*, sounded the same note:

> As soon as he finishes, the audience yells "Encore!," and he starts again with perfect grace. If inspiration strikes, instead of repeating the previous piece he plays a new one more charming than the first. The public again cries "Encore!" with gusto. . . . I would not dare to analyze so original a talent as his, so poetic and so marvelous.[102]

Or again from Fiorentino, a few weeks later:

> This year's favorite in the salons, concerts, and public and private gatherings is Gottschalk. . . . He has in his countenance and talent an indescribable note of melancholy, as well as the grace of Chopin. His compositions are distinctive, original, and charming, and are generally of a coquettish brevity. His execution displays finish, brilliance, neatness, rapidity, and stunning zest. Just as he seems to drench you with a soft melody of almost imperceptible finesse, his fingers unleash a storm of notes with admirable force and sonority. . . . Gottschalk's talent is of a high and serious nature. He possesses honest and true inspiration, the reflection of an intimate and vividly felt poetry.[103]

Taxile Delord of *Le Charivari* had also watched the parade of virtuosos with a cynical eye. Gottschalk, he concluded, was different. Liszt and Thalberg had once been his rivals, but, Delord asserted, "if Mr. Gottschalk . . . works seriously and does not take his future success for granted, he will be . . . a true master in his own right."[104]

Even Oscar Comettant, who had started the nonsense about Moreau's abduction in Geneva, mustered praise for the Salle Bonne Nouvelle concerts:

> In his most recent concert [Gottschalk] showed himself to be as agile in performing the Beethoven sonata . . . as he was original in his new pieces, particularly *Le Mancenillier*, which I prefer even to *Le Bananier*. Gottschalk is American, and he has brought from his native land songs full of melancholy, charm, and originality, and he has appropriated them by completing them, embroidering them with his imagination into spontaneous pictures.[105]

Even more given to irony was the critic Théophile Gautier, but in writing about Gottschalk he abandoned his usual posture:

> It is more difficult than one can imagine to leave the beaten path and pitch one's tent separately from [those of Liszt, Prudent, and Thalberg]. Mr. Gottschalk, still very young, has been able to acquire the originality that escapes so many others thanks to solid studies and then to having allowed himself to wander adventurously in the aromatic savannas of his country, whence he brings us perfumes and colors. . . . All his songs of the New World have an originality that is full of melancholy, energy, and suaveness and which carry you deep into fantasy and dreams.[106]

No Frenchman revered Beethoven more deeply than did Hector Berlioz, and like other reviewers he praised Gottschalk's performance of the Master's work. Then he turned to the American's own compositions:

> Mr. Gottschalk is of that small number who possess all the diverse elements that endow a pianist with sovereign powers, all the faculties that can surround one with irresistible prestige. He is an accomplished musician who knows precisely how far a fantasy can be carried. He knows the limit beyond which rhythmic liberties produce nothing but disorder and confusion, and he never crosses that limit. He phrases soft melodies with perfect grace and has mastered the keyboard's delicate traits. With regard to deftness, spirit, surprise, *brio*, and originality, his playing dazzles and shocks. Yet the childish naiveté of his smiling caprices and the charming simplicity with which he renders simple things seem to emanate from a second personality. In the presence of a musically civilized public Mr. Gottschalk's success is immense.[107]

Capping these encomia was an essay by Victor Hugo, whose romantic outpourings in *Hernani* had once driven old academicians to trembling and outrage but who now, square-jawed and responsible, was bitterly opposing Prince Louis Napoleon in his drive to become emperor. Hugo characterized Gottschalk as "not only a great pianist, for which we acknowledge him, but also a thinker who nourishes sweet dreams, a poet, and a competent and eloquent orator who can enrapture and move audiences."[108]

To be sure, a few critics needled Moreau, but he could afford to dismiss them politely. When one of them, who was blind, persisted in ridiculing the Creole names of his compositions, friends of Gottschalk urged him to call the man to account. One evening Moreau encountered his foe as the two of them were leaving a concert. As they met at the top of the stairs, Gottschalk took the blind man's arm and led him to the door. When the critic asked to whom he was indebted, Moreau simply gave his name and left.[109] No wonder, as one writer noted, "rivals were reduced to calling Moreau 'Monsieur Bamboula' for want of a better way to attack him."[110]

Gottschalk was in truth a celebrity, and he began behaving like one.

He sat in a box at the opéra with the writer and pianist Madame Mennechet de Barival, to whom he had dedicated *Le Mancenillier* and who,
conveniently, had penned adulatory reviews about Moreau's "ardent and
fertile imagination" and "exquisite taste."[111] He put in appearances at
Lord Tudor's fashionable salon off the Champs-Elysées,[112] and he claimed
diplomat and writer Count Salvandy as a friend. Was there a place for
Americans in Moreau's social rounds? A French writer commented that
Americans came to Paris "resolved to make as much noise as possible.
. . . And they dress ridiculously."[113] It is therefore no surprise that Mo-
reau steered clear of what was called Paris's "Yankeedoodledom."[114]

The one American who entered Gottschalk's world was Boston-born
George F. Root (1820–95), who was in France on a sabbatical from his
duties as music teacher at a fashionable New York school for girls. Later
the composer of the hugely popular Civil War song *Battle Cry of Freedom*, Root was a pious Protestant who taught at Manhattan's Spingler
(popularly dubbed "Spinster") Institute connected with the Church of the
Puritans. In spite of all this, he and Moreau hit it off, and when Root
asked his friend to give lessons to a young girl from his school,
Gottschalk obliged.[115] The girl was Mary Alice Ives, daughter of a Presbyterian minister from Vermont. Much later she became one of Gottschalk's
most loyal admirers and his biographer.

As a young celebrity, Moreau sat many times for his portrait with such
fashionable painters as Blanc Alophe, Nanteuil, and Colliere.[116] Unfortunately, all these canvasses are lost. A cartoon of Gottschalk by the celebrated satirist and photographer Nadar reveals nothing. The best insight
into Moreau's appearance at this time is a print by Eugéne Battaile done
in 1850 at the peek of the *Le Bananier* craze. There he sits, with a look
of phlegmatic insouciance on his face, his hair carefully curled forward.
What a shame not to know the color of the long, sleek-waisted jacket.
Was it peach? Buff blue? These were the very years when the word *chic*
was coined, and Moreau embodied it to the nines.[117] Arsène Houssaye,
man-about-Paris and memoirist, later blessed the city for having
"deprovincialized" him.[118] Gottschalk had completed his own process of
deprovincialization before his twenty-second year.

In fact, Moreau bordered on *le dandysme*, the combination of ironic
panache and fatuous narcissism made famous by the Anglo-Frenchman
Count Alfred d'Orsay.[119] This is what the Battaile print exhibits to a fault.
One of the more despicable affectations of the Parisian dandy was to
secure the services of a personal groom or "tiger," a diminutive fellow
who would pad along a few steps behind as the dandy made his daily
rounds.[120] Later, when Gottschalk reached Spain, he, too, procured a "tiger" in the person of an Andalusian child named Ramón.

Gottschalk was in danger of becoming ridiculous. Yet he did not cross the line. For one thing, the hectic pace of his life prevented him from lounging away evenings at places like the Café de Paris on the Boulevarde des Italiens. Nor, evidently, did he bother to explore Paris's fabled *demi-monde*, with its *lorettes* and *grisettes*. Bohemia was not foreign to him, as he later showed clearly when he participated in America's first avant-garde circles. But for now Moreau was otherwise occupied, and too much the insider to play at being an outsider. Besides, he was not wholly lacking in American moralism. Years later he said that anyone who succumbed completely to self-indulgence and trivia "would have to be a fool or a Parisian, which are practically synonymous as far as I'm concerned." [121]

Even if he was not a full-blown dandy, Moreau adored the social and musical life of Paris, and through it he made contact with many people who were to play important roles in his later life in America. Pasquale Brignoli (1824–84), a gifted Neapolitan tenor and ardent womanizer, had just taken Paris by storm. "I love him and he loves me," Moreau later declared.[122] Through Brignoli he met soprano Anna de la Grange, with whom he later toured in America. He also encountered Chopin's Polish friend Jules Fontana and a host of visiting artists from every corner of Latin America with whom he was later associated.

Offsetting the influence of Parisian high-life was Gottschalk's now habitual introspection. This was manifest in a friendship that developed with the Reverend Adolphe Monod (1802–56), a Swiss Calvinist prominent in the Protestant church of France.[123] Moreau was a frequent visitor at Monod's home, and they maintained a close bond for years. Moreau's spiritual searching led him also to join a Masonic lodge at this time. While Freemasonry never replaced Gottschalk's Catholic faith, it certainly appealed to the optimistic side of his nature and to his philanthropic spirit.[124]

Whatever benefits derived from Moreau's immense popularity in Paris and from his diverse associations in the French capital, they did not solve the question of his future. Many a musician, after all, had basked briefly in the adulation of the Parisian public, only to sink back into a lifetime of obscurity. Moreau had yet to face the most basic career decisions. His very success had enabled him to postpone them, but delay was now becoming more difficult.

Was he still an American, and should he return home? Berlioz had assumed Gottschalk would eventually return to the United States a conquering hero. A few newspapers in New York and New Orleans had followed his career with interest, but to most Americans the young Louisianian remained utterly unknown.[125] Or, alternatively, should he stay in France or Europe and attempt to make a career there?

Beyond this, Moreau had yet to face the question of whether he was to be primarily a composer, a virtuoso pianist, or something else. The decision was starkly practical. There is evidence that Gottschalk was planning an "American concerto" at this time, but even ten successful concertos would not necessarily provide him a living.[126] It was one thing for Rossini to have amassed a small fortune through his operas and then, at age thirty-seven, receive a lifetime annuity from the French government for having done so.[127] More typical was Adolphe Adam, who each year for decades had turned out two or three operas and ballets but scarcely eked out a living and was forever worrying about his finances.[128] Berlioz proclaimed bluntly that "to be a composer in Paris one must rely entirely on oneself. . . . One must be content with mutilated, incomplete, uncertain, and more or less imperfect performances, for want of rehearsals for which one cannot pay; inconvenient and uncomfortable rooms; and annoyances of all sorts."[129]

Gottschalk's one advantage as a composer was that his works could be marketed to a broad public. This, however, required a publisher who was an effective promoter and at the same time honest and loyal. Since copyrights were as yet virtually unenforceable, it was too much to expect a publisher to meet all three of these conditions. Back in 1849 Moreau had signed a publishing contract with the brothers Léon and Marie Escudier (1821–81 and 1819–80). Berlioz, whom the Escudiers also published, probably tipped them off about Gottschalk.[130] The Escudiers promoted their stable of composers on the pages *La France musicale*, which they owned. They also arranged joint publication agreements with Schott in Germany and with Riccordi in Milan.

The drawback was that the Escudiers were notoriously tightfisted. After selling two thousand copies of *Le Bananier* in a few months, they refused to increase Moreau's commission by a sou. While Gottschalk was in Geneva, he therefore made contact with a Lyon publisher named Benacci, who had previously come to Paris in hopes of buying rights to any piece that Gottschalk would make available to him.[131] Benacci offered ten thousand francs outright for the copyright to *Bamboula* and *Le Bananier*. The Escudiers retorted that "if [he] were to offer us sixty thousand, we should refuse it."[132] When Moreau sold the *Danse des ombres* to Benacci, the Escudiers were understandably peeved and began giving their friend the cold shoulder.[133] Meanwhile, pirated editions abounded, and Gottschalk began peddling separate works to publishers in Spain and France, including several who worked initially under the Escudiers' very nose in the French capital.[134]

Many composers in Paris supplemented their earnings through journalism. Under the impact of the marketing innovations introduced by Girardin, circulation to all the leading Paris papers soared during the 1840s. Ferociously competitive, editors were willing to pay large sums for stories and *feuilletons* by favorite authors. Liszt cashed in on this, as did Berlioz, but at the price of resentment and self-loathing. Declared Berlioz: "Everlastingly to write *feuilletons* for one's bread! To write nothings about nothings! To bestow lukewarm praise on insupportable insipidities! . . . This indeed is the lowest depth of degradation!"[135] Later, Gottschalk was to pursue precisely such a literary career. For now, though, journalism was not an option for an American in Paris.

This left open only the path of touring virtuoso. The concertizing artist in mid-nineteenth-century Europe faced a crisis of patronage. His choice was between a waning royal and aristocratic patronage and a commercial concert business that was as yet barely developed. Hence virtuosos were compelled simultaneously to grovel before official patrons and to humiliate themselves before newspaper editors who could publicize their concerts. "It is hardly believable," wrote Heinrich Heine, "how abasingly [composers] beg in the newspaper offices for the tiniest handout of praise, how they bend and squirm."[136] Later, Gottschalk was to become adept at this sordid art, but for the time being he concentrated on royal patrons.

Emperor Dom Pedro II of Brazil visited Paris in 1849 and made the rounds of the musical salons. At one of these he met Gottschalk whom he rewarded with some modest support.[137] Shortly thereafter Moreau sent him this self-abasing letter:

> Sire,
> My status as an American, in addition to the enlightened protection Your Majesty sees fit to grant to the Arts, gives me the courage to present Your Majesty with my latest composition.
> The award which the Conservatoire gave me and the reception that my composition has received from the public during my last concerts in Paris, though I ascribed both more to Your Majesty's beloved name than to my own merit, nevertheless give me the hope that Your Majesty will see fit to grant me a title, which is the object of my ambition and which I have always aspired to deserve: the title of Knight of an Order of Your Majesty.
> Of Your Majesty,
>> Sire, [I am] the most obedient, the most
>> devoted, and most respectful servant,
>> Louis Moreau Gottschalk of Louisiana,
>> Composer of *Bamboula, La Savane, Études,*
>> etc.
> Paris, September 28, 1849[138]

Twenty years later this letter bore fruit when, in the last year of his life, Gottschalk visited Brazil and received Dom Pedro II's patronage. For now, however, none of his appeals for royal patronage paid off, with the one exception of Isabel II of Spain. With no alternative, Moreau decided to make his long-delayed tour of the Iberian peninsula, an expedition that was to confirm his calling as a traveling virtuoso.

Over the years, comfortably employed historians have been quick to dismiss Moreau Gottschalk as "merely" a virtuoso, as if he had prostituted his true calling in favor of keyboard pyrotechnics and musical hucksterism. How much better, they imply, had Gottschalk settled down in some quiet place and dedicated his life to composition. Gottschalk, they would have us believe, was not really "serious."

Impelled by this smug line of reasoning, some critics relegate Gottschalk to the role of a charming warm-up act before the emergence of America's "real" composers—Edward MacDowell, Charles Ives, etc. But Ives, it should be remembered, could afford to indulge his formidable genius because, as a successful insurance executive, he functioned as his own patron. And MacDowell could develop his more modest gifts from the comfort of America's first endowed chair of composition, at Columbia University. It is revealing that, prior to receiving his chair at Columbia, MacDowell had abandoned all hope of pursuing a career as composer and had reconciled himself to what he considered the "lesser" status of a performing pianist. He had little choice in this, his biographer tells us, "if he was to meet financial obligations, secure more piano pupils, and gain an audience for his compositions."[139]

This occurred thirty years after Gottschalk's career decision. Now, in 1851, the twenty-two-year-old star faced a future without the slightest sign of regular support from any quarter and with the sure knowledge that his family's finances had long since eroded disastrously.

Chapter Seven

✖ The Siege of Spain

G OTTSCHALK'S Swiss triumphs owed much to the fact that Franco-phone Swiss had followed faithfully the Parisian press and were curious about the new star from Louisiana even before he arrived in their midst.

By contrast, the number of educated Spaniards who cared a whit about the latest cultural fads in Paris was small. Even if upper class Spanish women aped French fashions, their tastes lagged behind Paris by at least a year. New developments in the fine arts and music took still longer to cross the Pyrenees, which meant that Moreau himself had somehow to create a market for his concerts. He knew that royal patronage would help, so he dedicated *Bamboula* to Queen Isabel II. But not even a queen could order her subjects to attend concerts and buy tickets to them. In order to fill the house, one had to fan public interest with a campaign of publicity.

Enter Eugéne Gouffier, Parisian journalist, "secretary" to Moreau Gottschalk, and, in effect, his promoter, advance man, and manager. Gouffier left Paris for Bordeaux ten days before his artist and settled into the Hotel de France to book halls and generate articles in the press.[1] In Gouffier's luggage were copies of all the most extravagant reviews from Paris and Geneva. A typical Bordeaux journalist reported coyly that "a copy of the *Journal de Debats* recently fell into our hands" and proceeded to transcribe Hector Berlioz's review as if he himself had dug it out of the library.[2]

Journalistic ethics being as loose then as now, paragraphs from Parisian reviews were often interposed into the accounts of concerts that local reviewers were too lazy to attend. Gouffier did not discourage this practice. He also told his fellow journalists whatever they wanted to hear. In commercial-minded Bordeaux, for example, he spread word that Moreau was "the son of one of the wealthiest and most opulent bankers in New York."[3] In Spain Gouffier conjured up other qualities as needed, thus enhancing the Gottschalk myth. At one point in Valladolid, Gouffier's activities in behalf of his client extended to spreading disinformation in order to suppress a potential scandal.

In fairness to Gouffier, his task was less than thankless. For most concerts Gottschalk himself was the presenter, which meant that Gouffier had not only to print up tickets but also to announce their availability in the press and sell them. To prove he was doing his job, Gouffier collected every notice that appeared in the press. Moreau later pasted them all into scrapbooks. Some of these pieces reveal the frustrations with his boss that Gouffier experienced. Arriving in Bordeaux, for example, he announced a concert for sometime between May 15 and 20.[4] Backtracking, Gouffier then announced on the sixteenth that Moreau would not arrive until the twentieth.[5] Moreau did not appear until May 24, however, by which time many of the Bordelaise were leaving for the summer.[6]

Moreau charmed the locals at several Bordeaux salons, including one where he played steadily for three hours.[7] Then he offered a full concert at the Grand Théâtre and another in the main hall of the Bordeaux prefecture.[8] To top these off, Gottschalk joined with a local soprano and violinist to present a soirée at the home of a wealthy merchant. "At 2:30 in the morning," the local paper reported, "he was still at the piano, applauded, surrounded, celebrated. They showed him no mercy."[9]

Reviews of these Bordeaux concerts for the first time ranked Gottschalk higher even than Liszt and Thalberg. "He does not imitate anyone," wrote one; "his playing is neither that of Liszt nor Thalberg. It is still better—that of Gottschalk."[10] This expansive view was partly the result of the Bordelaise hearing practically for the first time an all-piano concert in which the performer played exclusively his own works. Some criticized him for this, but others argued that this was "like reproaching him for having a double genius, for inventing and executing, for being head and hands all at once. . . . Molière performed only his own comedies before Louis XIV. The people are now king, and for them Gottschalk performs only his own music."[11]

As in Paris, a cult of personality began to form around the young American:

> Picture a pale young man with somewhat unkempt hair, classical features, a distinguished manner, and hands the likes of which one seldom sees. It's Gottschalk. Never will a more pure or brilliant talent charm our ear, tempering the audacity and fire of Liszt with the melodic sentiments of the German masters.[12]

Moreau's announcement that he intended to give a concert for the poor at the Grand Théâtre raised his standing still higher. "Honor to the great artist," sang the local press, "who knows how to combine a large talent with a big heart!"[13]

Then, without offering the public the slightest explanation, Gottschalk disappeared for a month. The reason for this interruption is that his father had unexpectedly arrived in Paris. Moreau rushed there to see him. Two years earlier Edward Gottschalk had reported to his brother-in-law that his family was still in Paris and that "the expense of keeping them there has been so great that I have never been able to pay them a visit."[14] Now, thanks to having moved to a modest room in the home of an Italian family in New Orleans, Edward Gottschalk had saved enough to make the journey.

A long letter on his Paris visit that Edward wrote to his brother-in-law in Philadelphia exudes a pathetic pride in each of his children and in his wife, who was now "a complete Parisian lady."[15] Accepting his fate, Edward Gottschalk made no reference to finances. The only discordant note, in fact, was his mention that Aimée had been bedridden for most of the time Moreau was in Switzerland and had so spoiled Edward Jr. that "for the quiet of the family" he had to be taken back to New Orleans. "A new burden upon me," noted the father.

During his ten days in Paris Moreau took his father around to all the salons, where, in Edward's words, "your humble servant was introduced by his son, who appeared proud of his father, for a better son does not exist." After one such performance, wrote Papa Gottschalk, "the ladies were in an ecstatic state and the men so enthused that they lifted him out of his chair to hug and kiss him. One Spaniard kissed his hands with a frenzy as [if] he were a beautiful girl, [and] another kissed the skirt of his coat." Whenever Gottschalk was practicing at home, hundreds of people would gather on the street below to hear him play.

In the same letter Edward Gottschalk provided a unique description of Moreau's method of composition:

> It is curious to see him compose. He sits at his piano and plays for a quarter of an hour, speaking with any number of persons all the time, when suddenly he gets up and puts a few notes in writing; it is a new idea that has struck him. Thus he has sheets of [notes] carefully preserved and whenever he is in the mood he works them out.

Even though Edward Gottschalk was not able to discover any failing or vice in his son, he nonetheless bemoaned what he considered Moreau's lack of business acumen:

> To my sorrow, I must confess that I fear he will be long before he can realize
> a fortune, [for] he is too cozy and too charitable, and is foolishly lavish in his
> charities and attachments, which the captains of industry know how to ex-
> ploit. Nor has he sufficient firmness in his contracts. Thus, he sold his *Le
> Bananier* for two hundred fifty francs. The firm made thirty thousand francs
> out of it and has to reprint it perhaps for the tenth time. . . . I hope experi-
> ence and my advice will correct such matters a little.

Closing his report from Paris, Edward Gottschalk described a visit
from the wife of the vice-regent of the Russian-ruled part of Poland, who
simply invited herself and her two small children to Gottschalk's rooms
for a private concert. After he played for this willful lady, Moreau received a diamond pin from one of her children and an invitation to perform in Russia, where, she said, "the court shall be open to you." Papa
Gottschalk saw this as an opportunity not to be missed and advised his
son to head for Russia as soon as possible. "Unfortunately," Edward confided to his brother-in-law, "[Moreau] has the galling habit of all great
artists, [in that] he is led away by his feelings and if he is pleased in a
place [he] remains there, forgetting the future."

Rushing back to Bordeaux, Moreau finally fulfilled his promise to give
a benefit concert for the poor.[16] And none too soon, for many there had
assumed the promise broken. The Bordeaux public had also been bombarded with letters from a singer who claimed Gottschalk had broken his
promise to allow her to appear with him in public.[17] At this concert he
joined a local pianist, Emile Forgues, in performing a two-piano version
of his *Jérusalem* fantasy, which he had composed since his return from
Paris. After the concert the Bishop of Bordeaux gave a huge banquet in
his honor, and the local Saint Cecilia Society honored him with membership.[18]

Gottschalk and his entourage (which also included a piano tuner)
gave a similar charity concert in Libourne and then proceeded to the
town of Pau, which was almost empty due to the summer diaspora.[19]
Unwilling to concede the slightest defeat, Gouffier booked two concerts
in the lounge of the small hotel and assembled a crowd that greeted Moreau with a "thunder of enthusiasm."[20]

At Tarbes Moreau performed at the Church of Saint-Jean and at the
hall of the local philharmonic society. The party then moved on via Bayonne to Biarritz, Gottschalk's last stop in France.[21] By now, nearly every
story in the press apologized for the brevity of the composer's visit, explaining that he was eagerly awaited in both Spain and Portugal.

This was a typical piece of hyperbole by Gouffier. In fact, there is not
the slightest evidence that the touring American was eagerly awaited in
either country, or that anyone besides a few bureaucrats at the Spanish

court had any idea he was coming. In the end, it took three months before the first major concert hall in Madrid was opened to Gottschalk, and he had to abandon all hope of touring in Portugal. On the other side of the ledger, Moreau was received so warmly in Spain that he stayed there fully two years. Besides emerging as a fluent speaker and writer of Spanish, he entered into more intimate contacts with Spanish life and music than any romantic composer before him, with the possible exception of the Russian Mikhail Glinka.

The entire Spanish venture reflected the influence of Liszt on Gottschalk's image of himself as composer and virtuoso. However, Liszt's tour of the Iberian peninsula in 1844–45 had been less extensive than Gottschalk's, has included fewer performances, and had a far more blatantly commercial air: Liszt brought with him the son of the Marseilles piano manufacturer Louis Boisselot in order to peddle instruments.[22] More important, the impact of Spain on Liszt's music was comparatively slight, as evidenced by the fact that he waited nearly two decades to complete his *Rhapsodie espagnole*. By contrast, Moreau plunged into Spain like an American college student on his junior year abroad. While not uncritical of the country—he later ridiculed the false pride of the Spaniards[23]—Moreau carefully studied Spain's popular music and incorporated it into a score of works composed during these two years and afterwards.

Gottschalk and his party crossed into Spain in time to present a first concert at Saint Sebastian on September 23, 1851.[24] Moving quickly along the coast, they reached the Basque capital of Bilbao on the steep banks of the winding Nervion River. There he gave three concerts in the municipal theater. The last, to benefit the local hospital, produced the same outpouring from Bilbao's mayor as the poor relief concert had evoked in Bordeaux.[25]

En route to Madrid Gottschalk stopped briefly at Burgos, with its huge, pale yellow cathedral. News of this brief stop was reported as far afield as the Lisbon press, clear proof that Gouffier was now actively preparing to extend the tour to Portugal.[26] Before departing for Madrid, Moreau visited the cathedral, with its gruesome relics, the first of many encounters with Spanish Catholicism that was to leave him bitterly cynical toward Spanish-born priests wherever he encountered them.[27]

The trip to Madrid was, in this last period before the advent of railroads in Spain, excruciatingly difficult. Gottschalk trundled along on a mule-driven cart that also carried two of Mr. Érard's grand pianos. Théophile Gautier, describing this same trip a few years earlier, wrote of "the dusty mud-built villages, mostly in ruins"; of the meals consisting only of a few *garbanzos*, "which rattled in our stomachs like shots in a tambourine"; and of the "antediluvian" mule-drawn vehicles.[28] After passing through the desolate plateau of yellow sand and lead-gray rocks surrounding Madrid, Gottschalk arrived in the Spanish capital on October 23, a week after Gouffier, who had already taken up residence at the Calle de la Montera.

Gouffier had placed announcements on Moreau's arrival in every Madrid paper. Stripped of their ad-man clichés, these notices reveal two vexing problems facing the touring virtuoso. First, he had zero name recognition, no small concern in a country in whose language the word *Gottschalk* is unpronounceable. Within weeks the Madrid press had celebrated the arrival of Gothshalk, Gottschat, Gostchalck, Golschalk, Godatchak, Gosttchal, and Glotshalke. In one masterly headline, *La Nación* exposed the depth of the identity problem by announcing the arrival of "El Violinista Ottschalk."[29] Sheer tenacity on Gouffier's part eventually overcame this obstacle, but not without creating other difficulties. As curiosity mounted, pirated editions of Gottschalk's music hit the shops.[30]

A second problem was more serious. Liszt had been invited to Spain by the Liceo Artístico y Literario of the capital. Moreau had hoped to one-up the Hungarian by gaining royal patronage. This had been the goal of his dedication of *Bamboula* to Queen Isabel II and, apparently, of representations in Gottschalk's behalf by the Grand Duchess Anna. No sooner did Moreau arrive in Madrid than he penned a long letter to the Grand Duchess's friend de Bock, in which he breezily announced that he was momentarily awaiting a letter from the Queen Mother granting him entry into the palace and that "any day now the young Queen will summon me, even though her condition [Isabel was pregnant] prevents any official reception."[31] In the expectation of an early summons to the Court, Moreau refused all other engagements, both public and private.

Unfortunately, if Gottschalk was unknown to the public, his identity as an American was by now all too well known in the Spanish government, which was locked in serious conflict with the United States at precisely this moment. So grave was this diplomatic confrontation that it was out of the question for the Queen to receive socially any American citizen. Had Moreau, as a son of New Orleans, somehow arranged to appear before the public he would have been in danger of physical assault. No wonder that Gouffier promptly issued further announcements declaring that the American would not appear before a Madrid audience and that he was, in fact, merely pausing briefly en route to Portugal.[32]

Spain was the United States' only real enemy. Besides embodying principles of monarchy that were antithetical to the new republic, Spain owned Cuba, which had long been coveted by expansionists in the United States. Every president from Jefferson to Buchanan had expressed a desire to annex the island, and interest in buying Cuba only grew over time, especially among slave-owners in the South.

By the late 1840s this hope had come to nothing, so a combination of American expansionists and Cuban nationalists under General Narciso López decided simply to conquer the island. They mounted three unsuccessful expeditions, all of them comprised of "filibusters" recruited among the freebooters of New Orleans.[33] In the last of these, a force of 450 men set sail from the Crescent City but was driven off course and ran aground near Havana. Several hundred of the American filibusters were captured, and López himself was executed on September 1, 1851.

It was Gottschalk's misfortune that news of these events reached Madrid only weeks before his arrival there. Spaniards were indignant. As the United States minister in Madrid reported on September 18, "a portion of the public here is very violent and abusive in its language, even advising and threatening a declaration of war against the United States."[34]

There was worse to come. On September 10 the newspaper *La España* reported a further insult to Spanish honor that had taken place in Moreau's home town. Late in August 1851 the steamer *Crescent City* had arrived in New Orleans from Havana bearing news that López's expeditionary force of Louisiana filibusters had been captured. Rumor in New Orleans had it that the filibusters had been betrayed by the local Spanish consul, Juan Laborde. A large mob of New Orleanians attacked and sacked the Spanish consulate and would doubtless have lynched Laborde had he not fled.

These further indignities hit Madrid like a bomb. *El Clamór pública* railed against the "cowardly insults" perpetrated in New Orleans. It vowed: "If we are destined by Providence to the cruel ordeal of losing this precious reminder of our former greatness . . . [let us] fight like good men, and fall like heroes."[35] On top of all this the aggrieved Spanish consul, Laborde, arrived in Madrid from New Orleans and began further whipping up anti-American sentiment just as several hundred captured filibusters, most of them United States citizens, arrived in Spain as prisoners.[36]

Even these grave problems might have been surmounted had the Spanish government not been in a mood to put the worst possible interpretation on everything. The young Isabel II owed her throne to the most reactionary circles in the Spanish army and was ever ready to do their bidding.[37] It would have been unthinkable for her to receive Gottschalk so long as this crisis continued. Moreau, underestimating its seriousness, turned to the Queen's mother, the Dowager Maria Cristina, and her live-in favorite, the Duke of Riansares y Tarancón, to whom he presented introductions. Riansares received him cordially.[38] But as an old soldier himself and a certified reactionary, he could offer Gottschalk no better advice than to present himself to Isabel and the Spanish public not as an American but as a Frenchman. Moreau flatly refused to do this and therefore had either to wait until the crisis passed or leave Spain.

During this period of idleness, Moreau frequented the famous cafés of Madrid, squalid in appearance but featuring refreshments superior to anything in Paris and authentic Spanish music of every description.[39] Glinka, during his Spanish sojourn, had searched out local singers and guitarists and recorded their songs in his notebook.[40] These notes provided the basis for his *Capriccio brillante*. Gottschalk, too, plunged into the music of Madrid's cafes, improvising with local pianists and, as a journalist noted, "listening enthusiastically to whatever pieces our compatriots play, especially the *jota [aragonesa]*."[41] Court circles later criticized him for hanging around bars, but those casual evenings in Madrid yielded material for several compositions both published and unpublished.[42] They also gave rise to a brief affair with a singer named Carmen, from the Café Suizo. Unfortunately for Gottschalk, Carmen had another admirer as well, a tenacious medical student who waited three months to get his revenge.[43]

Meanwhile, at Riansares's suggestion Moreau wrote directly to the Queen, setting forth his readiness to perform, but only as a U.S. citizen.[44] She did not respond, for he was still *persona non grata* and would remain so for several more weeks. By mid-November, however, Spain's foreign minister, the Marquis de Miraflores, had concluded that tensions with Washington were at a dangerous peak. In an attempt to calm the waters he arranged for several of the American prisoners in Spain to be released.[45]

As part of the same effort to step back from armed conflict, Queen Isabel II invited Gottschalk to give a private performance for her and her family at the Palacio Real. That this was part of the diplomatic maneuvering and not a response to Gottschalk's appeal is clear from the fact that the invitation was timed to coincide with the first pardons. The Spanish government was moving fast in its campaign of conciliation. Gottschalk received the invitation on the afternoon of November 17, the same day he was to appear![46]

It is hard to imagine a more pitiful band of royalty than the Bourbons for whom Moreau performed that night. The arch-reactionary Riansares was there, and also his consort, the Dowager Maria Cristina, known throughout Spain as La Ladrona ("the Thief") for having pocketed four hundred thousand pounds of poor-relief money.[47] Also present was the effeminate and impotent King Francisco d'Assisi, probably the one sincere music lover in the room. In an amazingly cynical move, the Orleanist government in France had demanded that sixteen-year-old Isabel marry this Bourbon heir as a means of guaranteeing that no member of the Bourbon line would ever claim the Spanish throne. Forced into this loathsome situation, Isabel had reacted by indulging in a life of scandalous adultery mixed with extreme piety. A string of lovers produced a string of babies, the second of whom was about to be born.

This, then, is a group portrait of the Spanish royalty who greeted Gottschalk upon his arrival at the Palacio Real on the evening of November 17, 1851. Moreau's own description of the soirée was contained in a letter to his father written two days later.[48]

The evening began when the King's pianist came for the American and escorted him from the hotel to the palace. Marshaled into one antechamber after another, Moreau finally was presented to the royal family. The French-born King immediately won Gottschalk's sympathy with his amiable and courteous deportment. The Queen, whom Gottschalk generously described as "very tall and stout," stationed herself beside Moreau's chair as he and the court pianist played a duet. Then followed *Le Bananier*, which the King professed to play frequently himself, *Danse ossianique*, and *Moissonneuse*. Again, the King took the conversational lead. Confessing that while the latter piece was "poetry itself," he averred that, since "the only pianists we admire here are those who perform acrobatic feats on their instrument," it would not be appreciated in Spain.

Finally, Isabel II herself requested *Bamboula*, which Gottschalk had dedicated to her. After some further conversation, the evening concluded. The King stood in the doorway of the salon waving to his American guest as he took his leave through a series of four chambers. Moreau explained to his father, "This is considered to be the most polite compliment the king can pay to a visitor, but it is rather troublesome as it obliges one to retire backwards."

News that Gottschalk had appeared at the palace reverberated in the Madrid press.[49] The next day Moreau received an invitation—addressed to "Mr. Golzak"—to a ball sponsored by the Dowager Queen.[50] Gottschalk arrived in full dress and was conspicuously in evidence as he danced the polka with the Countess of Casa Valencia, whom the Queen had designated to be his partner. Isabel II, immobilized by the last stages of pregnancy, watched from an elevated throne, the rest of her family arrayed at her side like *putti* on a baroque fountain.

The government's desire to calm the political waters was now clear to all, so Gottschalk was received throughout the capital. Over the following weeks he was heard at four aristocratic salons, in the process creating immense interest as a pianist whom the Queen herself had judged to be better than Liszt. Pressure for a public performance mounted.

Yet several more weeks passed before he appeared at the Coliseo del
Circo, the same former circus building on the Plaza del Rey where Liszt
had performed. There may have been problems finding a hall, but more
serious political impediments still remained. After all, several hundred
American prisoners still languished in Isabel's jails, and no satisfactory
apology for their deeds had been received from Washington.

Fortunately, Secretary of State Daniel Webster had written a letter to
the Spanish minister in Washington apologizing for the mob attack on the
Spanish Consulate in New Orleans. In a tactful concession to Spanish
sensibilities, Webster even paid honor to the Spanish flag that had been
desecrated on Lafayette Square, noting the many lands over which it had
waved in glory. Received in Madrid in early December, this letter struck
just the right note with the Spanish government, and Isabel's foreign minister decided that the American secretary of state had removed the last
impediments to an honorable settlement. On December 11 Count Miraflores informed the American minister that on the next day Isabel II
would pardon all American prisoners held in Spain and Cuba.[51] Within
twenty-four hours Gottschalk made his public debut at the first of two
concerts in the Coliseo del Circo.

Hastily organized, the Madrid concerts of December 13 and 17, 1851,
established Gottschalk's enormous popularity in Spain both as an artist
and as an accidental symbol of Spanish-American reconciliation.[52] However, both concerts were plagued with serious problems. To showcase
the young American, organizers placed his Érard grand in the middle of
the hall surrounded by the audience, leaving the orchestra somehow to
coordinate its exertions from the stage some distance away. Due to the
suddenness with which the diplomatic crisis had been resolved, the orchestra was unrehearsed. Scarcely had Gottschalk commenced playing
Emile Prudent's fantasy Le Bois than he began furiously gesticulating
with both hands and feet to get the ensemble back on tempo. The second
pianist, normally the principal cellist in the orchestra, was also flying
blind, and throughout the Jérusalem fantasy Moreau signaled him desperately in an attempt to keep the duet from falling apart.

None of this bothered the audience, which responded with shouts for
encores and a barrage of wreaths. This, in spite of what one German
visitor considered the highly critical attitude of Madrid concert-goers generally.[53] The enthusiasm may have been caused in part by the several
new works which Moreau premiered on those evenings. At the first concert Gottschalk offered a Gran galop de bravura, based on themes from
Joseph Quidant's setting of the Mazeppa story. Some years later
Gottschalk published this as the Tournament Galop, a true barn-burner,
the finale of which is marked "tutta la forza possible, Molto animato

grandioso."[54] At the second concert Gottschalk introduced a new operatic fantasy entitled *Souvenirs de Bellini,* based on themes from *I Puritani, La Sonnambula,* and *Norma.* Although Moreau had worked with some of these same materials earlier, Gottschalk scholar Clyde W. Brockett has argued that these variations warrant classification as a new and autonomous work.[55] One reviewer hailed the fantasy as a "most perfect expression of Italian music."[56]

More important than either of these was a new *Capricho español* introduced at the second concert. Recently rediscovered in the Spanish national library by Brockett, this pioneering work revealed the fruits of Moreau's "research" into Spanish music conducted in the cafés of Madrid. Here Moreau introduced several typically Spanish dances, including a *caña,* a *fandango,* a *jaleo* from Jerez (and with it a *cachucha,* known to Moreau since New Orleans days), and the famous *jota* from Aragón.[57] The Madrid audience went crazy over this musical bow to their country by an American, a tribute that paralleled Daniel Webster's salute to the Spanish flag published only days before. But *Capricho español* was no mere documentary presentation of Spanish music, for Gottschalk had freely recomposed his material, extending phrases at will, dropping whole sections of pieces, and interposing original melodies of his own. And for the first time in European classical music, he attempted to replicate the sound of a Spanish guitar, a technique that he was to bring to fruition in *The Banjo.* He thus accomplished for Spanish music the same transformation that he had achieved in his earlier Creole pieces. Both Glinka and Liszt had used the *jota,* but neither went as far as Gottschalk in celebrating the specific textures of the Spanish dance.

The two concerts at the Coliseo del Circo launched Gottschalk's Spanish career. After spending the Christmas holidays in the capital, he departed in early January for Valladolid, northwest of Madrid. Though renowned as Columbus's last home and the place where Cervantes wrote part of *Don Quixote,* Valladolid was now a ramshackle and depopulated city dreaming of past glories.[58] Its one virtue was that the king's sister, the Infanta Maria Josefa, resided there with her husband, the Governor of Old Castile. The Queen had written ahead to ensure that Gottschalk would receive a warm welcome.

Crowds awaited Gottschalk's arrival at the hotel, and a delegation of uniformed students welcomed the American hero. Scarcely had Moreau unpacked when the Governor himself arrived to pay his respects and to offer Gottschalk the use of his carriage. Two days later, and apparently before they had heard him play a note, the musicians of Valladolid honored Moreau with a serenade, which was followed by a grand banquet hosted by the Governor and attended by every dignitary in town who valued his job. The Governor's wife, Maria Josefa, had baked a cake for the occasion, "kneading it with her own hands."[59] The next day Maria Josefa received Gottschalk at her residence. He arrived with a new composition, entitled *Infanta Doña Josefa Waltz*, dedicated to his hostess and scored for four hands.[60] In quick order Moreau then offered three public concerts. After the third, held at the Teatro de la Comedia, he returned to his hotel only to discover that the entire theater orchestra had preceded him there. Alighting from the Governor's carriage, he found the dusty path to the hotel door completely covered with the cloaks of the orchestra members.[61]

This mad round of adulation came to a crashing end on or about January 25, 1852. Within two days Gottschalk's secretary, Gouffier, had placed a bland announcement in the Madrid press indicating that Moreau had accidentally broken the little finger of his right hand and was convalescing. When the Madrid newspaper *La España* reported that the finger might have to be amputated, some suspected that Gouffier had deliberately underreported the incident.[62] Gouffier then put out a further announcement explaining that the injury had taken place while Gottschalk was climbing out of his coach.[63]

In reality, both of Gouffier's announcements were efforts at damage control. Far more colorful explanations of Gottschalk's mishap were already making the rounds. The mildest of these claimed Gottschalk broke his finger while arm wrestling *("pulseando")* with a friend,[64] but others referred darkly to some "disgrace."[65] Gouffier redoubled his efforts to peddle the coach story, with all its studied vagueness.

Since Moreau enjoyed royal patronage, the press suddenly found it best to drop the issue just as it was getting hot.[66] Years later, Moreau's sister Clara felt obliged to clear up the lingering rumors about Gottschalk's little finger. Claiming that she had heard this version from Moreau himself, she explained that the finger had been broken when the King's pianist, overcome by jealousy, slammed the coach door on Moreau's hand. "By this stratagem [the King's pianist hoped] to disable Gottschalk forever after," she wrote.[67] The trouble with this second effort at damage control is that after allegedly committing this perfidious act against Gottschalk, the court pianist, Juan María Güelbenzu (1819–86), went on to participate happily in at least one further concert with the American.

Moreau himself gave a quite different version to Léon Escudier in Paris and, separately, to his biographer Luís Fors in Buenos Aires. In his memoirs, Escudier reports that after one of his concerts Gottschalk had been approached by an unknown medical student, who grabbed his right hand as if to shake it but then deliberately twisted it to the point of breaking several bones.[68] Fors, who did not know Escudier's book, provides a similar account, with one telling addition. The medical student, he asserts, was the same one whom Moreau had offended back in November by his attentions to the café singer Carmen.[69]

Threatened with the loss of a finger, Moreau promptly canceled a planned return to Burgos and spent the next several months recovering. Convalescing amidst admirers on every side, Gottschalk seems to have abandoned his natural modesty. It was then that he picked up a young urchin named Ramón and transformed him into his personal houseboy *cum* valet. The eight-year-old had no known family and was living on the streets by making and selling wax figurines of bulls. Moreau cleaned him up and outfitted him in an Andalusian costume. Thanks to his new patron, Ramón eventually was able to present his figurines to the Queen of Spain, to whom Moreau introduced him as a "fellow artist." Later he would travel to the New World with Moreau and eventually serve as a valet to a Confederate general from New Orleans, P. T. G. Beauregard.[70]

In the same blush of youthful vanity, Moreau accepted an invitation from the Count of Pierra, Gentleman of the Chamber and Colonel of the Farnesio Regiment, to review the entire garrison of Valladolid.[71] It must have created a curious impression among the soldiers to be inspected by a twenty-three-year-old pianist who hailed from a country that only weeks before was Spain's worst enemy and who had never shot a gun, let alone served in an army.

This could all be dismissed as silly had Moreau not managed to turn his new status with the Spanish officers corps into a musical opportunity. This happened because he realized that one key to Spain was its army, with all its blustery heroics and theater-set grandeur. Not only was the army the chief prop for Isabel's throne, but in the popular mind it symbolized the nation as well. Gottschalk therefore conceived a grand fantasy based on the army's marching song and national anthem, the *Marcha real*. Soon this blossomed into a far larger work, his most expansive to date, entitled *Siege of Saragossa (El Sitio de Zaragoza)*.

The nineteenth century was the great age of story-telling. Not only did magazines serialize long novels, but galleries were hung with story-paintings, and dance companies performed story-ballets. Narrative music, of course, was nothing new; witness the story-line or "program" underlying Beethoven's *Pastoral* Symphony. But for narrative so vivid that no one could miss it, nothing beat a battle piece. Beethoven had tried his hand at this popular medium with his *Wellington's Victory Overture*. However, it fell to the Bohemian Franz Kotzwara (ca. 1750–91) to define the genre with his immensely popular *The Battle of Prague*.[72]

Gottschalk's choice of the siege of Saragossa as a theme for his battle piece was exceedingly clever. This campaign had occurred in 1808 when one of Napoleon's retreating armies attempted to seize the city of Saragossa (Zaragoza) and thereby prevent the collapse of French rule on the Iberian peninsula. In the end, the French forces prevailed, but only after a ruinous siege in which the Spanish troops and especially the townspeople put up an intrepid defense.

The siege of Saragossa entered the political mythology of Spain as a symbol of the unity of Crown, army, and people. By Isabel's day the national euphoria had vanished. The country was wracked by discord, military juntas were dictating policy to the Crown, and the bloated imperial court impoverished ordinary Spaniards. Yet the myth of Saragossa lived on. Precisely because the myth drew people's minds away from the sordid realities, it grew ever more important to official Spain.

Gottschalk called his *Siege of Saragossa* a "Symphony for Ten Pianos." Such multi-piano extravaganzas had been around for decades, as often as not giving rise to ridicule since few composers could resist the temptation to keep each instrument in constant *fortissimo* action. To avoid this, Gottschalk marshaled his ivory warriors at times with such understatement as to arouse criticism from those wanting more fire and brimstone.[73]

Unfortunately, the full score of this work is lost, and the surviving reduction for a single piano remains unpublished.[74] However, from this and from a detailed description of the full work printed in the Madrid press, it is clear that the *Siege of Saragossa* was built around the national *Marcha real* and the popular multi-strain dance *La Jota aragonesa*.

The "story" opens with cascades of descending chromatic octaves evoking the din and chaos of the siege. Then, after hints of various melodies, the *Marcha real* appears, quietly and in a minor key, as if to suggest the army's desperation in face of the besiegers. After another flare-up of fighting, the *Marcha real* sounds again, this time intricately interwoven with the *Jota*, symbolizing the appearance of the armed townspeople themselves among the defenders. Eventually this blossoms into a fullblown treatment of the *Jota*, then a renewal of the bombardment, with descending octaves, and then a finale consisting of a fugue-like treatment of the *Marcha real* with the sound of clarion trumpets in the treble.

At least three aspects of this grandiose narrative piece merit special notice. First, Gottschalk not only presented the *Jota* with great faithfulness, but he created around it a free fantasy no less textured and diverse than Glinka's *Capriccio brillant* of 1845 or Liszt's *Rhapsodie espagnole* of a decade later. Moreau himself was evidently delighted with the results, for he immediately proceeded to develop it further into a bravura concert piece rich with dramatic transpositions and guitar-like motifs. With evident pride he dedicated the first published version to his old teacher from New Orleans, François Letellier.[75]

Second, in order to underscore the unity of army and citizenry, Gottschalk sounded the *Marcha real* and the *Jota* simultaneously. This presented a formidable challenge to his performers, for the *Marcha real* is in march time while the *Jota* is in three-quarter time. The effect was stunning. It enabled the listener not only to "read" the narrative but to capture the psychology of the scene as well. More than half a century later Charles Ives employed the same technique of aural painting to represent the exuberant cacophony of two brass bands passing on the street during a Fourth of July parade in New England.

Third, in his finale Gottschalk recomposed the *Marcha real* into a grand canon, symbolizing the merging of citizenry and army in their common struggle.

By the time Moreau completed the *Siege of Saragossa*, his finger had healed and he was ready to perform again.[76] Isabel II had meanwhile given birth to a daughter. Discreetly passing over the question of paternity, her ministers proposed to honor the infant by raising a public subscription to establish several hospitals. Learning of this, Moreau dedicated the profits from one of the Valladolid concerts to this cause, as a result of which the Governor of Old Castile sponsored the pianist for a Spanish knighthood. The King, however, blocked his receipt of the Order of St. John of Jerusalem, arguing that this title could not be conferred upon a foreign national. This was technically correct, but the fact that the King intervened personally, rather than through a minister, suggests that Moreau's links with the court were beginning to unravel. Everyone saved face, however, when a few months later Gottschalk was knighted with the Order of Isabel Católica, which he proudly wore to the end of his life.[77]

Around the middle of May 1852, Moreau returned to Madrid, eager to perform his *Siege of Saragossa* before the public there. The political mood was far more favorable than when he had arrived the previous autumn. During the winter a priest with an old grudge against the crown had tried unsuccessfully to assassinate Isabel as she emerged from the Royal Chapel. The American minister immediately sent a warm letter to the Spanish government in which he spoke of the priest as the sole perfidious man in all of Spain, "a soil remarkable for loyalty and charity."[78] This expression of sympathy strengthened Gottschalk's hand, and he immediately set about arranging a series of four concerts at the large Teatro del Principe. The premiere of the *Siege of Saragossa* was set for the first evening in the series, on June 13. The press build-up was impressive, and even before the great event the Circulo Filarmonico had designated the American a member.[79]

On Sunday, June 13, the Teatro del Principe was packed with "all of the aristocracy of Madrid."[80] It must also have looked like a military review, given the number of Spanish army officers who turned out to hear the *Siege of Saragossa*. The program was dense with Gottschalk favorites, including the *Danse ossianique*, which only days before had been performed locally by a full military band. The second half of the program began with the public premiere of Gottschalk's new waltz for two pianos, *Vallisolitana*. The composer was accompanied by J. G. Miralles, a musician known to all night-stalking Madrid swells as the pianist from the Café de la Esmeralda. The local press had only days before revealed that Gottschalk had been frequenting the Esmeralda and sitting in with Miralles as they improvised together on Spanish popular tunes.[81] Now the two were on stage together for the biggest piano fest in Spanish history. After Moreau galloped through his *Carnival of Venice*, Miralles reappeared as one of Gottschalk's nine aides-de-camp. Identically clad, this battalion of pianists marched onto the stage to launch the *Siege of Saragossa*. "The applause burst upon us like the roar of water," wrote Moreau to his mother.[82]

The pianists had scarcely begun the first section when the audience erupted into applause. The second part was encored, and when the two thousand strings of the ten pianos reverberated with the *Marcha real*, the entire audience rose to its feet. The Minister of Agriculture, bursting with patriotic ardor, roared, "Long live the Queen!" Gottschalk had to repeat the entire work.

After the concert a procession of fans accompanied Moreau to his rooms. Two regimental brass bands were already there, playing Gottschalk's *Danse ossianique* as an immense crowd formed on the illuminated street. Moreau made a brief speech in Spanish, which he called "not so bad for a first effort,"[83] after which the crowd lifted him up bodily and passed him about amidst revelry that lasted until three in the morning.

Three further concerts followed, including a benefit for a fellow musician and another in support of the ladies' auxiliary of a parish church.[84] These various repetitions of the *Siege of Saragossa* transformed Moreau into a local culture hero, as the Royal Academy of Arts rushed to enroll him as an honorary member.[85] Gottschalk did not pause to bask in this adulation. Probably at Gouffier's urging, he sent a ticket for the second concert to the renowned bullfighter and celebrity Don José Redondo y Dominguez, known as El Chiclanero.[86] We do not know if the great

Chiclanero attended the concert, let alone if he stayed to the end, but he responded to the invitation by sending Gottschalk a sword used by his own teacher, the legendary bullfighter Francisco Montes. In a letter accompanying the sword, he modestly pleaded for the American to send him his autograph in return.[87] Gouffier, earning every centime of his pay, promptly gloated to the local press about this gift.[88]

As the torrid July heat finally descended on Madrid, Gottschalk left the capital for La Granga ("the Farm") de San Ildefonso, the flamboyantly rococo summer palace of the Bourbons near Segovia, to which the entire court retired each summer. Earlier, Moreau had informed the press that he would leave soon for England. Then he changed his announced destination to Lisbon, only to depart in early August for the ancient Moorish province of Andalusia, far to the south.[89] The last four months of Gottschalk's Spanish sojourn were devoted to visits of varying lengths to Córdoba, Seville, and the Atlantic ports of Cádiz and San Lúcar de Barrameda.

To set out in early August for this sweltering region was folly, but Moreau was evidently keen to check off every point on Liszt's tour of 1844–45 and, if possible, outdo his Hungarian predecessor in each city. In certain outward details Gottschalk's trip closely resembled that of Liszt. At Córdoba, for example, the archbishop presented him with a collection of his "pastoral verses," just as he had Liszt.[90] At Seville Moreau chose as assisting pianist one Eugenio Gómez (1802–71), organist at the cavernous Gothic cathedral, who had presented a dozen of his compositions to Liszt for criticism.[91] A Paris paper reported that Gottschalk performed ten times in Córdoba and that a benefit concert there raised four thousand francs.[92] Thanks to this, the archbishop feted him at a lavish banquet, and the city elders saluted him, just as they had Liszt.[93]

The chronology of these months is confused, but one thing is clear: that Moreau continued to compose new works based on what he was hearing around him. It was in Córdoba, for example, that he created his one venture into what today would be called flamenco music, his intense but extremely simple *Chanson du gitano*.[94] Gottschalk was not the first Parisian visitor to be fascinated by the gypsies *(gitanos)* of Córdoba, and particularly by their women, of whom Gautier wrote, "They sell amulets, tell fortunes, and follow the suspicious callings inherent to the women of their race."[95] He was the first, however, to transform their songs into art music.

En route to Córdoba Gottschalk had passed through the western edge of the bleak La Mancha country and heard its driving, strangely syncopated dance music. Some years later he issued an intriguing evocation of this obsessively rhythmic sound in his sparkling *Manchega* (op. 38).[96]

Whether acting on his own inspiration or under the influence of Cuban music, he transformed the original three-quarter time into six-eight time, producing a throbbing polyrhythmic beat. This muscular concoction contrasts sharply with Gottschalk's purely "classical" *Pensée poétique*, composed at the same time in a competent but tame Chopinian mode.

Moving westward down the Guadalquivir valley, Gottschalk arrived by late September in the former Moorish center and capital of the West Indies trade, Seville. Here he found not only a stark and whitewashed vision of old Spain but also a city where women wore their *mantillas* with dresses cut to Paris fashions, and where men smoked cigars from the huge State Cigar factory, where Bizet's Carmen was said to have been employed.[97]

Gottschalk took time to play the tourist as he inspected on horseback the Roman ruins at nearby Italica.[98] Here, too, he composed a stylish *Minuit à Seville* (op. 30). More than his other Spanish pieces, this caprice exudes a vocal or operatic air. It is a good Chopinian mazurka, but with an Iberian beat. Underpinning the melody is a guitar-like bass figure, which, as Brockett has pointed out, represents a clever transformation of a typical bolero rhythm.[99] While in Seville, Moreau also reworked the *Capricho español* from his second Madrid concert and transformed it into what was virtually a new piece, *Souvenirs d'Andalousie.*[100] Both works were premiered almost immediately, thanks to the patronage of the Duchess de Montpensier, the Queen's sister, who resided in Seville.

The Infanta Luisa and her husband, the French-born Duc de Montpensier, were scarcely older than Gottschalk, both were music lovers, and Luisa, like her sister, was pregnant. Herein lay a serious problem for Gottschalk. Seven years earlier the French king had maneuvered successfully to marry off Isabel to the impotent Francisco and her sister Luisa to his own son, the Duc de Montpensier. The lusty Isabel had endangered this tidy scheme by enlisting Guard officers to sire two daughters, thus creating a full-blown diplomatic crisis that threatened the future of the entire Bourbon dynasty. If either were to be recognized as legitimate, Bourbon hopes in Spain would die; if not, then the crown would pass to the offspring of the ardently pro-French Duke and Duchess de Montpensier. Thus international intrigue rendered the two sisters rivals.

Moreau seemed blithely oblivious to this conflict. Not only did he make his Seville debut at Montpensier's Saint Telmo Palace (he received a set of diamond buttons for his efforts),[101] but he then proceeded to San Lúcar de Barrameda on the Atlantic coast, where he was the guest of the Duke and Duchess at their summer residence. Here, near the port that had launched Magellan on his trip around the globe, Gottschalk could reminisce about the Revolution of 1848 with the son and daughter-in-law of the deposed French king. During this seaside visit he also hastily composed a *Valse pour deux pianos*, never published, of which he was very proud.[102]

After a further pair of concerts at Cádiz, with its narrow streets and massive ramparts pounded by the Atlantic, Moreau returned once more to Seville, where he again mounted his Spanish war-horse, the *Siege of Saragossa*, for one final and thunderously successful assault on the Andalusian public. Then, with a total absence of fanfare, he took a steamer back down the Guadalquivir to Cádiz and on November 29, 1852, set sail on the French ship *Isabel* via Gibraltar for Marseilles.[103]

The departure was disconcertingly abrupt. For once, however, Gottschalk's Spanish-born biographer Luís Fors cites no amorous adventure or scandal as the cause, blandly noting instead that Moreau had received word that his father was expecting him in New York.[104] However, the notorious dancer and courtesan Lola Montez later referred in public lectures to the fact that a Madrid belle who later became the Empress Eugenie of France "evinced a great admiration for the celebrated Pianist" and introduced him into Spanish society.[105] Gottschalk's publisher Escudier wrote that Gottschalk actually became involved with this Countess de Teba, while a London magazine, in a story published a decade after the composer's death, claimed that he had been asked to leave Spain after he carried off the heart of an infanta.[106]

Sorting out this confusion, it is quite possible that Isabel II, upon learning of Moreau's close relationship with the Duke and Duchess de Montpensier, revoked her patronage and asked for his departure. This is mere speculation, however. What is certain is that during the autumn of 1852 relations between Spain and the United States had again taken a sudden turn for the worse. The Madrid government was convinced that the United States was once more discriminating against Spanish ships in its ports.[107] In retaliation, Isabel's captain-general in Cuba had refused to allow the United States Mail Steamship Company's ship *Crescent City* to land in Havana. By October 1852 the *Crescent City* affair had reignited anti-Spanish sentiment in New Orleans and elsewhere. A fresh brigade was being raised in anticipation of war with Spain, and the cry "Action! Action!! Action!!!" sounded in the American press.[108]

On top of this, the "red-hot republican" Pierre Soulé, Edward Gottschalk's old friend, had just been named American minister in Madrid. Soulé made no secret of his hostility to the Spanish monarchy and of his passionate desire to annex Cuba. By the time he arrived in Madrid there already existed "a vast amount of prejudice against him."[109] Soulé's presence alone was reason enough for Isabel's government to want to distance itself once more from Americans. Thus ended the brief flowering of amity between Spain and the United States that Moreau Gottschalk had symbolized.

Driven by these various motives, Moreau abandoned all thought of a tour of Portugal and rushed back instead to Paris. Little Ramón was with him, and when the *Isabel* put in briefly at the dusty Mediterranean port of Almería the boy suddenly froze with fright. "Señor," he moaned, "I know the houses; it is here where my father beat me so much. . . . For the love of God, Señor, do not let me return."[110] Unfortunately for Gottschalk, locals recognized the child at once, a crowd formed, and its angry leaders demanded that Gottschalk return Ramón to his father.

It turned out that Ramón Sr. was close at hand, in a ground-floor cell of the local jail, within earshot of the crowd. He was awaiting a sentence of death by garroting, i.e., strangulation, for having murdered a customs inspector while carrying out a smuggling operation. Caught between the pleas of poor Ramón and the mob's mounting demand that the "Englishman" be jailed for kidnapping, Gottschalk wisely sought help from the town's magistrate. Fortunately, this gentleman had heard Moreau perform in Madrid and had no desire to jail him. Instead, the magistrate referred the matter to the boy's father.

Asked if he would authorize his son's adoption by the "rich Englishman," Ramón Sr. dolefully shouted through the bars, "My son Ramón, the child of my loins! Jesús María! Virgen del Carmen! Abandon him to an Englishman? You cannot think of it, Señor Corregidor!" The crowd concurred, but when Moreau climbed a stone and quietly placed three dollars in the condemned man's hands, Ramón Sr. consented to the adoption, and the crowd burst into applause. Shouting *"Viva el Inglés!"* the throng led Ramón and Gottschalk in triumph back to their awaiting ship.[111]

There was no time for Moreau to dally in Paris, for the steamer *Humboldt*, on which his father had booked passage for him, was set to depart on December 27.[112] It is probable, however, that Moreau paused long enough to dash off a short composition entitled *Le Reveil de l'aigle* in honor of the newly proclaimed Emperor Napoleon III.[113] This was a prudent move. Berlioz had predicted that the young composer would return to his native land a conquering hero, and this was doubtless Moreau's hope. Nonetheless, he needed a fall-back position, and a piece dedicated to the new ruler of France could serve that end.

During the few days he spent in Paris, Moreau bade good-bye to patrons and associates and gathered his close friends and family for a final soirée at his home. His mother, Aimée, was there, as were his sisters

Clara, Celestine, and Augustine, as well as his younger brother Gaston, now only five years old. Aimée's health had grown yet more frail, and in spite of being only thirty-nine years old, she must have had intimations that she would never see her son again. Indeed, this proved to be the case. When Moreau finally boarded the boat-train for Le Havre, he parted forever from his mother and sisters. Then, as the *Humboldt* steamed out of the harbor and into the wintry English Channel, Moreau glanced back at Europe for the last time.

Chapter Eight

🎕 "Financial Music" and Democracy

W HY did Moreau Gottschalk return to America in 1853? In all likelihood because he had no ready alternative. France held few attractions, for the newly crowned Napoleon III had yet to clarify his views on
patronage of the arts. England was no more inviting. In spite of having
written and performed his sensational variations on *God Save the Queen*,
Gottschalk received no invitation to cross the channel. And for all her
enthusiasm toward the young virtuoso, the Russian Grand Duchess Anna
had long since burned her bridges in St. Petersburg and could open no
doors for him there. Nor, finally, did Gottschalk have allies in Germany
who could help him.

Given all this, Edward Gottschalk probably advised his son to return
to America. Moreau was known throughout Europe as "Gottschalk of
Louisiana," yet he had not set foot there for a decade. It was time to
do so.

The United States had changed fundamentally during Moreau's absence. A fresh boom had stimulated urban life, ribbon-like networks of
canals had been built linking remote cities, and railroad lines were being
extended at a furious pace. Inexpensive construction techniques involving
mill-cut lumber and mass-produced nails enabled the ordinary American
family to house itself better than most Europeans.

When Moreau sailed for Europe in 1842, the entire Northeast was still
feeling the aftershocks of the great movement of Christian revivalism.
The renowned evangelist Charles Grandison Finney had even planted his
flag on Broadway, where rich industrialists built him a tabernacle. Now,
that fervor had died down, and the tabernacle was a concert hall. Secular
crusades filled the gap left by a waning revivalism. Temperance cam-

paigns, efforts to abolish slavery, and movements in behalf of women's rights were all flourishing, at least within those areas from Vermont to northern Ohio where the flame of evangelism had earlier burned. Even in these regions, however, a more settled life had replaced the old agitation of spirit. To be sure, Americans were competing to set up new businesses and streaming westward to open the frontier. But their houses had taken on a more homey look. Even the most modest new dwellings had a "parlor," and these were increasingly dominated by ponderous pianos, the high altars of a new cult of domesticity. Leisure was still limited, but its use had already become an issue separating the moralists from those who sought more earthly pleasures.

The spread and secularization of leisure was visible in the concert halls, opera houses, and assembly rooms that sprouted up in every city. Even small towns like Utica, New York, or Toledo, Ohio, could boast of newly built auditoriums. Some of these were paid for by civic or philanthropic groups. Others were joint-stock companies owned by a few dozen investors. But most were built by entrepreneurs on borrowed money, which they intended to pay back with box office receipts. Their task was difficult, however, for tickets were generally fifty cents each, yet a year's subscription to a newspaper like the *Boston True Flag* cost a mere two dollars.[1]

To attract an audience, managers scoured the land for talent. Resident performing groups were unheard of except in the largest cities, so local theater managers depended on touring groups, which proliferated with the spread of steamboats and railroads. During the decade of the 1840s hundreds of modestly staffed theatrical companies, minstrel troops, and opera companies arose, not to mention bell-ringers, family choirs, magicians, yodelers, and trained animals. As these performers traipsed from town to town they gradually worked out the most cost-effective routes, creating circuits that wound up and down the Eastern seaboard, reached westward to St. Louis, and extended down the Mississippi to New Orleans.

These circuits bypassed most of the South, for the simple reason that railroad construction lagged there. The fact that most of the Old South was rarely visited by the major touring troupes caused its cultural tastes gradually to diverge from those of the rest of the country. This cultural split anticipated political events. During seven months in 1850 Congress had bitterly debated the spread of slavery to new territories. Thanks to deft work by Senator Henry Clay of Kentucky, a grand "Compromise of 1850" was reached, enabling the North and South to coexist politically for nearly a decade more. But even as this happened, the entertainment industry had moved far down the path toward disunion.

Railroads and steamboats made possible the tours of countless performers who moved like gypsies among the hundreds of concert halls
dotting the American landscape. The key to success for any touring musician was the small band of New York–based impresarios who appeared
on the scene in the late 1840s. Included among these men were some of
the greatest charlatans, blowhards, and geniuses of their age. But theirs
was no chicken-and-egg relation to the great musicians of their era: in
America, the impresarios came first. It was they who did most to create
the musical world to which Gottschalk returned.

Impresarios had long been a fixture of European musical life. Berlioz,
who despised impresarios for their "insipid, prudent stupidity,"[2] functioned with some success as his own manager and publicity agent. In
America, where distances were greater and touring circuits in endless
flux, the agent or impresario was a necessity. In spite of this, most musicians hated them, and even the impresarios themselves viewed each other
as hucksters. One of the best of their number admitted that it was all but
impossible "to arrive at a due recognition of the various rascalities of the
American musical agent."[3] The artist's agent, he claimed, worked like a
boa constrictor, enveloping his musician-victim in his coils.[4]

Gottschalk came to share this negative view. The artist, he wrote, "is
a piece of merchandise, which the *impresario* has purchased, and which
he shows off to the best advantage according to his own taste and
views."[5] Elsewhere he commented that "The artist, once thus sold, no
longer belongs to himself, but becomes the property of the impresario,
who endeavors as he sees fit, to heighten its value."[6]

However unsavory or unloved, the impresarios and managers provided essential services to aspiring artists. Most of those at the lower
reaches of the field were American natives, since they knew well the local
theater managers who hired talent. But except for P. T. Barnum, all of
the top impresarios were foreign born, since at that level the key skill
was to gain the confidence of the great performers, who were themselves
most often of European birth.

At the time of Gottschalk's return, three European impresarios dominated the field. For sheer brashness and go-for-broke boldness they had
no equal until Barnum appeared on the scene in 1850 with Jenny Lind.
Far more knowledgeable about music than Barnum, they shared his zeal
for self-promotion, to the point that it was often unclear whether the star
of an announced extravaganza was the artist or the impresario. It was
Gottschalk's fate to toil as a collaborator or competitor with all three of
these men.

The least extravagant of the trio was Maurice Strakosch, who had
once spent a few weeks in St. Petersburg and thereafter styled himself

"Pianist to the Emperor of Russia." Born in 1827 in the Austrian garrison city of Lemberg (now Lviv, Ukraine), Strakosch studied piano and composition in Vienna, toured Europe as a virtuoso, and settled briefly in Paris. There, according to his grossly immodest third-person memoirs, he frequented the salons of Gottschalk's patron Girardin and other grandees.[7] The Revolution of 1848 drove Strakosch to what he hoped would be the American bonanza. New Yorkers turned out for his frequent piano concerts between 1849 and 1851 but judged his technique flawed.[8] So, after marrying the Italian-born soprano Amalia Patti (and thus linking himself to a musical dynasty later associated with Gottschalk) he settled down to a career in opera management. Extravagant promises made during frequent trips to Europe landed him some major talents, whom he and his non-musician brother Max tried desperately to keep out of the clutches of rival impresarios.

Seemingly ubiquitous, the Strakosch brothers swooped down on every major city in North America and the Caribbean, offering evenings of opera or piano and peddling Maurice's mass-produced polkas. Maurice Strakosch's system of managing, a rival claimed, "was to invent the most extravagant and exaggerated puffs for his star, and thus to center the attention, or rather the curiosity, of the public on one particular artist and, by ignoring the rest of his company, not to raise great expectations for his other artists."[9] In the end, this system did not pay off. By 1860 Maurice gave up the battle and returned to Europe, where he eventually capitalized on the greatest star of the century, Adelina Patti. His brother Max stayed behind and focused his restless energies on promoting the career of Moreau Gottschalk.

With his departure Maurice conceded defeat to his cousin Max Maretzek—"Maretzek the Magnificent," as he was always called.[10] Born in 1821 at Brno in the Austrian province of Moravia, Maretzek's career had already included stints in Paris and London before he arrived in New York in 1848. As both composer (of several operas) and conductor, Maretzek had known all the right people in Paris, including not only Berlioz, Chopin, and Liszt, but also Karl Marx and the extravagant impresario and conductor Louis-Antoine Jullien. Together, these links transformed a talented musician into a fabulous showman committed to bringing music to the masses and to making a profit doing so. Handsome, witty, and impeccably groomed, Maretzek was a street fighter who, from the day he took over the Academy of Music, saw his task in military terms. He spoke of "vanquishing" the Italian operatic opposition, "leaving . . . the battleground," and "constantly working to outflank [a rival] or his agents."[11] No act of vengeance was too expensive or too petty for him.

"Maretzek the Magnificent" never claimed Gottschalk as one of his stars, yet the impresario was to be a recurrent factor in Moreau's career. Most of the young virtuoso's closest musical friends came from Maretzek's stable of talent; Maretzek invested in a major Gottschalk project in Havana; and at one crucial point Maretzek was to bail Gottschalk out of a serious mess.

Not even this degree of cooperation ever existed between Gottschalk and the third great impresario. Bernard Ullmann, in fact, was to be Gottschalk's managerial nemesis. Like Strakosch and Maretzek, he hailed from the Austrian Empire, having been born in Budapest. Ullmann was not lacking in artistic judgment and is credited with bringing to America Henriette Sontag, the cigar-smoking ("to improve her voice") soprano Beethoven had chosen for the premiere of his Ninth Symphony.[12]

Diminutive in stature and fiercely aggressive in business, Ullmann would stop at nothing to promote his current stars, and he bribed the press in a particularly shameless manner. At the conclusion of Madame Sontag's 1853 tour, Ullmann presented her husband with a bill for $6,701.32 to cover the cost of "advertising." The *Musical World* claimed Ullmann's bribes for this tour totaled fifteen thousand dollars.[13] No wonder a critic called Ullmann "one of that pestilence of musical brokers . . . who waylay foreign artists on or before their arrival here, and represent *their* experience . . . as indispensable to their success in guarding them against Yankee craft and imposition."[14]

No impresario surpassed Ullmann in his readiness to employ sensational or tacky tricks to promote an artist. Who but Ullmann would advertise a concert lighted by precisely one thousand candles?[15] Who but Ullmann would conceive a *hommage à Washington* with five orchestras, soloists, and a choir of eighteen hundred?[16] In such projects Ullmann revealed his boundless cynicism. Strakosch was puzzled by the New World and Maretzek challenged by it. But Ullmann heartily despised America and had the poor judgment to spell out his contempt in a Spanish-language book published in Havana—and promptly publicized in New York by Maretzek.[17]

By 1853 these three impresarios held dominion over the operatic and concert life of America's big cities. They fought like scorpions in a bottle but also conspired together to drive up prices or to destroy concert hall managers who resisted them. Until Maurice Strakosch insisted on keeping a base in New York, they were even scheming to divide the entire hemisphere into spheres of influence.[18]

On their opportunism, at least, these three outlandish entrepreneurs were disarmingly candid. For example, when Ullmann was in New Orleans with one of his pianists he was received by the Gottschalks' friends the Soulés. When Mrs. Soulé pressed the impresario on what type of music his artists played, Ullmann replied bluntly, "Financial music."[19]

For all their hokum and hucksterism, these impresarios were among the first purveyors of high culture to realize that America was a democracy. Wealthy Whigs may have had a powerful voice in Congress, but in the concert house Jacksonian democrats were ascendant. The new impresarios accepted this reality and labored to attract ticket-buying customers rather than subsidies from rich patrons. Performers complained bitterly about them, but Max Maretzek was right in arguing that the impresario was as much the artist's slave as vice versa.[20]

In 1850 these grand impresarios all became honor students of the most uninhibited huckster of all, Phineas T. Barnum. Until then, Barnum's stable of stars had still been confined to woolly horses, mermaids, and elephants. By propelling the Swedish soprano Jenny Lind onto the stage of New York's Castle Garden in September of that year, he invaded the highbrows' world, and American culture was never to be the same again. For the first time, all the arts of mass promotion were concentrated on what had until now been a diversion for the few. His sales campaign for the "Swedish Nightingale" called for her to reach down to the American citizen through various ploys and for common Americans to look up to her—by reaching for their wallets. "When people expect to get 'something for nothing,' " Barnum pronounced, "they are sure to be cheated, and generally deserve to be."[21]

Barnum presented Lind in such a way as to pander to the public's every prejudice. He had her declare her intention of presenting her patriotic audiences with a great "American national song." At a time when most people assumed opera singers lived lewd and lascivious lives, he assured the public that Lind had forsworn Italian opera.[22] Naturally, he intimated, the chaste Miss Lind shuddered with horror at the bawdy French and even refused to sing in that country, reserving her aesthetic favors for the morally pure Americans. Was it irrelevant that both the French and Italians were Catholic? Barnum missed no chance to remind the public that he was presenting a *Protestant* singer who loathed popery—this at a time of unprecedented anti-Catholic and nativist sentiment throughout the American North. Fortunately for Barnum, Jenny Lind's sentiments on all these points were heartfelt. She really was a bigot.[23]

Lind had barely begun her two-year American tour when the European-born impresarios began capitalizing on her success. Maretzek resolved to out-Barnum Barnum with his own star import, appropriately named Teresa Parodi. Other prominent aspirants for Lind's scepter were Marietta Alboni, Giulia Grisi, and Beethoven's protégée, soprano Henriette Sontag. The public responded warmly to each of these imported divas. As the star system took ever deeper root, America was rocked by salvo after salvo of visiting geniuses, among them the brilliant and bizarre Swedish violinist Ole Bull,[24] William Vincent Wallace (dubbed the "Irish Paganini"), and Paganini's own disciple, Sivori. Needless to say, each of them was touted as a virtuoso, a friend of American democracy, a paragon of morality, and an intimate of the American greats.

Pianists figured prominently among the flood of virtuosity that preceded Gottschalk's arrival from Europe. American manufacturers had been turning out well-built instruments for a decade, doubling the number of pianos per inhabitant. Nine thousand instruments were produced in 1852 alone, and the number soared thereafter.[25] As a New York paper observed some years later,

> From the God-like composer, who is almost lost to human view on the heaven-piercing summit of his Art, down to the humblest worshipper at Music's shrine, all alike find the piano a resource, a strength, a refuge.[26]

Maurice Strakosch had been among the first wave of piano virtuosos in the late 1840s, as was Chopin's friend Jules Fontana. For all their skill, both were found wanting by the American public. The first imported pianist to satisfy the public's craving for raw keyboard brilliance was an Austrian, Leopold de Meyer (1816–83), who was billed as the "Lion Pianist" and even the "Monster Pianist."[27] De Meyer had gained fame in Europe for his *Marche marocaine*, a piece of exotica that anticipated the cancan. Arriving in 1845, he displayed a dazzling, full-armed technique and a bulbous physique, which he showed to best advantage by wearing trousers with broad stripes like those on mattress ticking. De Meyer also understood the role of American women as opinion-makers in the arts, and when bouquets were tossed to him he never failed to gather them up and offer them to the most beautiful ladies in the house.[28] In several areas de Meyer even anticipated Barnum. He was the first visiting artist to discover the advantages of private performances for journalists prior to his public debut in a city, and his use of *Yankee Doodle* as an encore played directly to Americans' patriotic sentiment. When Gottschalk exploited both devices seven years later, he was on well-trodden ground.

De Meyer's rival was yet another Austrian, Henri Herz, who became known in America as the "Vulcan Pianist" and churned out his own variations on *Yankee Doodle* and *Hail, Columbia*. These exertions reflect the fact that he had fallen into the managerial clutches of Bernard Ullmann. Herz had sailed to America in 1846 hoping to make some money concertizing and to promote the pianos he had been successfully manufacturing in Paris.

Herz gained so much notoriety that Barnum showed up at one of his New York concerts and proposed that he join the Jenny Lind tour as accompanist. The genius of humbug confided that he planned to promote the singer as a genuine angel descended from Heaven. Herz impertinently asked if Barnum intended to advertise him as one of the cherubim. When Barnum retorted that one angel was enough for any troupe, Herz lost interest and instead joined forces with Bernard Ullmann.[29]

By the time of Gottschalk's arrival in New York in 1853, American audiences had endured a seven-year plague of heavily promoted European divas and thundering pianists. Inevitably, a reaction set in. Critics honed their knives at the first mention of the word *virtuoso*, with pianists coming in for the unkindest treatment. An unknown Long Island poet named Walt Whitman complained in verse about the "glib piano," and less acute listeners began staying away from keyboard performances in droves.[30] Only three dozen concerts involving piano in any form were presented in New York in any one year between 1850 and 1853. By comparison, there were anywhere from 80 to 120 operatic performances annually.[31]

The only pianist to gain the public's sympathy was the "small, unpretending, pale-faced man" Alfred Jaëll (1832–82), who arrived from Austria under Maretzek's aegis in 1851. Jaëll was immediately acknowledged as "the foremost pianist who has visited this country."[32] At his debut concert he performed, among other works, Gottschalk's *Le Bananier*, advertised as "a Negro song."[33] The *New York Times* gratefully acknowledged in Jaëll's playing the absence of those "labored effects . . . which grated the sensitive ear of the listener to de Meyer."[34]

In addition to rebelling against pounding virtuosity and against the piano as a solo instrument, Americans also took umbrage at what seemed like the locust-cloud of foreigners. When a native-born church singer named Emma Gillingham Bostwick emerged from semi-retirement to give some concerts in New York in 1851, a large contingent of down-town merchants turned out to cheer her.[35] Mrs. Bostwick's success proved beyond a doubt that Americans were finally ready to listen to home-grown talent. This was asserted with great vehemence by a Brooklyn-born pianist and violinist named George F. Bristow. A composer of vast ambition and respectable talent, Bristow had written a *Concert Overture*, op. 3, which became the first work by an American to be performed by the New York Philharmonic, in 1847. When that same orchestra refused to devote more than a public rehearsal to his next symphony, Bristow exploded.[36] With a flurry of petulant letters and more furious public outbursts, he declared what was to become a sustained war by New York–based "Americanists" against Europe's dominion over the New World's musical life.

Taken together, the dramatic developments in American music on the eve of Moreau Gottschalk's return created a challenging situation. The United States was by now a rich land, but with none of the cultivated grandees who still paid the bills for musicians in Europe. In their place was a mass audience, receptive to culture but empowered by democracy to expect artists to take cues from them rather than vice versa. A tribe of resourceful and cutthroat impresarios read the public's tastes and transformed them into orders, which they issued to composers and performers.

Out of this arose the beginnings of the music business in America. Responsive to the public, this new industry was not above pandering to it by programming what Bernard Ullmann had dubbed "financial music." Often this was pure trash. Yet before accepting Ullmann's crass judgment as final, it is worth recalling that he was a European who had not spent one day in a democratic society until he stepped off the ship in Manhattan. The tragedy is that many Americans, especially some Bostonians, shared his low estimation of the public's taste.

When Moreau Gottschalk left France, he knew little or nothing of these developments. Unconsciously at first, and later consciously, this young man of twenty-four years had to wrestle with the tension between his country's aspiration to democracy in art and mere "financial music." Over the years he would discover that the two were interrelated in ways the foreign impresarios did not perceive and his own Paris education had not prepared him to comprehend. To his good fortune, however, Gottschalk had spent his earliest years in a part of the United States where the relationship between musician and public had been posed in terms that were less categorical and less hostile to the audience's democratic instincts. During Moreau's American years (1853–65) he called on that New Orleans experience and developed a path-breaking approach that responded to the public without condescending to it.

Chapter Nine

✂ New York Debut

AFTER a fifteen day passage, the *Humboldt* steamed into New York harbor on January 10, 1853. It had made a fueling stop in Cowes, which was the closest Gottschalk ever got to England. The ship's manifest listed Moreau's profession as "pianist" but failed to mention Ramón's presence, suggesting that Gottschalk considered the lad his servant rather than his ward.[1] In the baggage was the splendid grand piano which Camille Pleyel had presented him in Paris.[2]

Waiting on the pier were Gottschalk's father and his brother Edward, who for several weeks had been busily making arrangements for Moreau's arrival. One must wonder how Moreau's impoverished father viewed Ramón, who stepped off the gangplank dressed smartly in an Andalusian costume.[3] Edward Gottschalk's expenditures on his son's career had already been enormous, and he now faced the biggest outlays yet to cover publicity for the debut, not to mention the cost of housing the party of four at the pricey Irving House on Chambers Street.

But prospects were good. New York was booming, with a population of more than half a million and evidence of new construction on every side. Brick and brownstone row houses were rising everywhere, and the first Paris-style Mansard roof had been built on a merchant's palace only months before.[4] Even a casual look at such a metropolis would have encouraged Edward Gottschalk to think that his outlays would eventually pay solid dividends.

Within days Moreau had acquainted himself with Broadway, the bustling heart of New York's cultural and theatrical life. Here, in the blocks running north to Houston Street, were concentrated nearly all of the best hotels, many of the largest churches, and the grandest concert hall and opera theater in town. Most had been constructed over the half decade prior to Gottschalk's arrival. Among the most impressive new structures were the Metropolitan Hotel (1852), Wallack's Theatre (1852–53), Washington Hall (1851), and Metropolitan Hall (1851). A few blocks uptown at Union Square the vast Academy of Music was under construction.[5] And at the busiest block on Broadway stood P. T. Barnum's gaudy museum, festooned with banners and with a six-piece brass band blazing away all day long on a balcony high above the street. Notwithstanding the competing tumult of horse-drawn coaches on flagstone, the exhalations of this ensemble were audible for blocks.[6]

This ten-block section of Broadway may have constituted the cultural heart of New York and even the United States, but few visitors from abroad were prepared for what they encountered there. True, cultural institutions abounded. Besides the theaters and churches there were the National Academy of Design, the Lyceum of Natural History, and the American Art Union. But in mid-century America the realm of culture could not be separated from the earthier life of society as a whole. The sound of Barnum's band, for example, penetrated to the very rooms of the Philharmonic Society.

And worse. The sidewalks of Broadway teemed with street vendors, curb-stone merchants, and lamp-post dealers peddling everything from newspapers to medicine.[7] There were also more than two thousand gambling saloons in the city. Centering on Broadway, these establishments were ubiquitous but unmarked, generally relegated to the upper stories of buildings. The game of faro had already made its debut at the saloons, but cards, dice, and roulette were equally popular.

Crime also abounded in this environment. The police were few and still un-uniformed. Brawls occurred daily and often ended in stabbings. Muggings and garrotings, too, were common, especially of successful gamblers and flush-looking theater-goers. This is scarcely surprising, since the most wretched tenement housing stood cheek by jowl with the brownstone Italianate mansions.[8]

Amazingly, cultural life thrived in this yeasty environment and was significantly colored by it. Like the city itself, the performing arts of New York presented indescribable contrasts, bewildering diversities, and an eclecticism such as only a booming and chaotic entrepôt could offer. "Broadway," observed a contemporary, "represents the national life—the energy, the anxiety, the bustle . . . of the republic at large."[9] Just as millionaires and beggars, poets and pawnbrokers, all rubbed shoulders along the sidewalks outside Broadway theaters, so also did Beethoven and bawdy ballads, Schiller and slapstick, appear together on programs within. High culture did not yet seek for itself a separate realm.

Opera continued to dominate the public's interest. Only months before Gottschalk's arrival, soprano Henriette Sontag had participated in an outrageously over-promoted monster concert organized by the irrepressible Ullmann. The prospectus alone, wrote one critic, "for impudent, ridiculous humbug throws all quack medicine advertisements completely in the shade." [10] This extravaganza was but one assault in the ongoing warfare between Sontag and her rival, Marietta Alboni. These two divas split fashionable society into two factions and assured that every performance of either would be a sell-out. So long as the contending impresarios were able to pump up the public's interest in this battle of the divas, anyone else performing locally had to take the back seat. Gottschalk's debut concert a month later had to begin an hour early so the audience could rush off in time to hear Madame Sontag in Donizetti's *La Figlia del reggimento* at Niblo's Garden.

When P. T. Barnum initially exhibited his Lilliputian Tom Thumb in Boston, he advised his agent there to "first introduce him to some tip-top families or have them come in and see him on the first day while I am there." [11] Moreau's first task in New York was to meet "tip-top" people, and especially the press. To this end, his father arranged a private soirée at their rooms at the Irving House. Early in the evening of January 17 a small group of "artists, connoisseurs, and members of the press" assembled.[12] Although the local *Courrier des États-Unis* had informed Manhattan's French community of Gottschalk's arrival, no one knew what to expect that evening. Among those lounging on sofas or sitting in easy chairs was George William Curtis, later a close ally of Gottschalk's most relentless critic but now quite enthralled by him. He recalled that Gottschalk

> was truly pleasing. He was young, simple, and modest. His face had that glazed vagueness which it still has, and was inscrutable. That is, it was impossible to tell if it was a natural masque which it was in vain to study, or if it were merely dullness. The general impression was of a boy who had been kept very constantly at severe practice of the piano, and knew little else.[13]

After running his hands over the keyboard, Moreau launched into a grand polonaise by Chopin, delivering it with masterly precision. Curtis called it "a thoroughly appreciative and respectful performance without niggling or affectation of any kind." Then came a full hour of mazurkas, preludes, waltzes, sonatas, and nocturnes, all by Chopin. Those who had expected to hear merely a prodigious athlete were astonished. Moreau then glided into his *Bamboula* and wound up with his bravura *Carnival of Venice.*

Such private hearings were considered off the record, but James Gordon Bennett of the *New York Herald* could not restrain himself. For the first time, he wrote, a pianist made the instrument sing and imparted to it the fluidity of a violin. Praising Moreau's performance of "touching melodies" from his own pen, Bennett asserted that the young American combined the sublimity and grandeur of Thalberg with the beauty and finish of Liszt. The soirée was a success.

As an encore, Moreau served up what the *Evening Mirror* called "a magnificent apostrophe to our national airs."[14] As Moreau told the group, he intended to develop these into a grand work incorporating a number of well-known American themes, to be scored for ten pianos. Evidently, he had already decided to write for Americans a piece akin to his immensely successful *Siege of Saragossa*.

Barnum's further advice to his Boston agent regarding Tom Thumb was "fail not to *circulate documents*,"[15] that is, biographical sketches and publicity material. Among editors present at the private soirée was Baron Régis de Trobriand of the *Courrier des États-Unis*. A French aristocrat and amateur baritone who could always be called upon to sing at parties, Trobriand was the first to transplant the French journalistic essay or *feuilleton* to America. Having already met Gottschalk and his mother in Paris,[16] Trobriand immediately put himself forward as Moreau's champion and assigned one of his staff, Paul Arpin, to write a biography of the American composer. Arpin plunged eagerly into his task and within days had turned out a sixty-four page biography, complete with testimonials from leading Frenchmen and a list of his works.[17] Serialized in the *Courrier* on February 2–4, it was published as a separate volume only days later.

Another prominent critic present at the soirée, Henry C. Watson of the *Mirror*, translated Arpin's book into English.[18] Watson, also an amateur singer and would-be composer, was among the growing band of outspoken Francophiles in New York's cultural world. Extremely combative, he had tried to destroy the Philharmonic at its birth and had even dared to criticize the chaste Jenny Lind. Over the years, no other critic surpassed Watson in his loyal and steadfast support of Gottschalk.

Just as Arpin was churning out his biography, the New York lawyer Edward Henry Durell (1810–87) rushed into print a second account of Moreau's career. Durell had attended Harvard, read law, and moved to the Crescent City in 1837, just in time to watch young Moreau's rise to fame. Using the pseudonym H. Didimus, he had authored a volume on New Orleans. Probably at the urging of Edward Gottschalk, he wrote a long essay entitled "L. M. Gottschalk," which appeared first in *Graham's Magazine* and then separately as a pamphlet.[19]

Two other prominent critics who attended Moreau's Irving House soirée were Richard Storrs Willis and his older brother, Nathaniel Parker Willis. Richard, who had studied music in Frankfurt, was an ardent Ger-

manophile, sometime composer, and regular music critic for the *Albion.*
Sharply different from Moreau in temperament and taste, Richard Storrs
Willis was nonetheless drawn to his young compatriot and consistently
backed his career, as did Nathaniel.

Handsome and worldly, N. P. Willis had started his career in Boston
but fled to New York to escape what he considered to be the New England city's oppressively moralistic atmosphere.[20] A gifted essayist and
poet on topical themes, Willis was even considered by one contemporary
to be "by all odds, the most popular American author."[21] For all his talent,
however, Nathanial Willis squandered his energy by playing the role of
Manhattan's premier *bon vivant.* In 1850 he seduced the wife of the renowned actor Edwin Forrest, who reciprocated by assaulting him with
his cane on Washington Square.[22] This led in turn to the most celebrated
divorce case of the day. Such shenanigans claimed more and more of
Willis's attention and caused him in the end to be remembered as "one of
the greatest of small men."[23]

Even though Willis was abandoning New York at the time he met Moreau, it was he who introduced the young musician to the city's leading
literary and artistic salon, presided over by the poet Anne Lynch. Describing herself as "mentally in the condition of a bottle of champagne which
has been well shaken,"[24] this well-connected but unconventional lady was
the Madame Girardin of Manhattan, and her salon was the best place for
someone like Moreau to make his social debut.

But where should he make his debut as pianist and composer? The
best tactic was to begin in a small room and then, if successful, shift to
a larger auditorium for later performances. The smaller auditoriums of
Broadway were still too big, however, and lacking in intimacy. So for the
February 4 debut the Gottschalks booked a small concert hall known as
Niblo's Saloon. In the 1850s the Broadway area was dotted with so-called
concert saloons. A contemporary reported that these rough establishments provided "a low order of music . . . as a cover to the real character
of the place."[25] Most, in fact, were little more than brothels. An exception
was the concert room built by caterer and impresario William Niblo on
the southeast corner of Broadway at Prince Street, adjacent to the mammoth new Metropolitan Hotel. Originally part of a suburban pleasure garden, Niblo's Saloon was now linked with the grand theater that Niblo had
built in 1849 to house operatic productions.[26] It was quite acceptable for
a properly escorted lady to go to Niblo's, and its proximity to the opera
theater in which Madame Sontag was holding forth made it the perfect
spot for the debut.

Besides reserving Niblo's, Moreau and his father had to engage an
auxiliary pianist and also to find someone to organize and lead the or-

chestra. Ordinarily, these tasks would have fallen to the impresario. Strakosch was on tour, however, and both Ullmann and Maretzek were up to their ears in the great battle of the divas. Eager to pinch pennies and ever confident in his powers as a businessman, Edward Gottschalk himself took on the role of impresario.

Happily, the brilliant Irish musician William Vincent Wallace (1812–65) was in town.[27] This colorful violinist and composer had farmed in Australia, concertized in Paris, and nearly been blown up in a steamboat wreck on the Ohio. Berlioz considered him a genuine eccentric.[28] He was now happily married in New York but had not bothered to divorce his first wife in England. Wallace volunteered to hire and lead the orchestra. Moreau was grateful, and only much later did he criticize Wallace for plagiarizing his music.[29]

Also on hand to serve as assisting pianist was the English-born Richard Hoffman (1831–1909), a pillar in New York musical life since the time he had been hired as an assisting artist for Jenny Lind's concerts. As a boy, Hoffman had worked the stops for the organist at the premiere of Mendelssohn's *Elijah*, the composer himself giving orders as to which stops to pull. Later he studied in Paris under Kalkbrenner. He and Moreau immediately became friends. Moreau particularly admired Hoffman as "a conscientious artist, a perfect musician, a distinguished and modest man."[30]

With the hall booked and Wallace and Hoffman hired, everything was ready for the young American's debut. But was Moreau really American? The French pianist and critic Oscar Comettant, who had preceded him to New York, insisted that "Gottschalk has nothing American about him except the fact of his birth; he is French in spirit, heart, taste, and habits."[31] By contrast, James Gordon Bennett of the *Herald* had already waved the flag in announcing Moreau as that "young *American* artist,"[32] while the *Daily Mirror* firmly proclaimed him "decidedly American in manner, sympathy, and enthusiasm—though he has been abroad for eleven years."[33]

The new star's relation to American life and culture was no trivial matter. At the very time of Gottschalk's return from France, the question of the United States' national identity in music was being debated in New York with an intensity that surpassed all previous discussion of the subject since the nation's founding. By purest coincidence, Gottschalk's debut at Niblo's Saloon occurred within days of the culmination of this polemic.

The instigator of this grand debate was one of the most talented and perplexing figures ever to appear in the world of American music, the "compulsive iconoclast" William Henry Fry (1813–64).[34] A journalist by profession and composer by avocation, Fry had only recently returned from a six-year stint as the *New York Tribune's* correspondent in Paris. Fry had gone to France in hopes of getting his opera *Leonora* staged there, and by this means proving his talents to a skeptical American public. The Paris Opera scarcely looked at Fry's score, however, which caused him to view Europe with even greater resentment than he showed toward his native land.

By the time he got back to New York, Fry was a ticking time-bomb of fierce opinions on music, culture, and politics. No wilting flower, he rented the cavernous Metropolitan Hall and hired the entire Philharmonic Orchestra, as well as various choirs, soloists on diverse instruments, a corps of Italian operatic stars, and a military band. Thus armed, Fry announced a course of lectures, complete with musical illustrations, on the "Science and Art of Music" from the beginning of time down to 1853.[35] Here, for the first time in America, was an exposition of "curious and rare music of all ages and countries," a comprehensive history of world music.[36]

Fry's main concern, however, was the fate of music in the United States. As early as 1840 he had asserted his belief that "this country must produce geniuses in every department of art and science, superior of the greatest in ancient or modern times."[37] Now he reiterated and adorned this point, supplementing it with round denunciations of everyone and everything in American music, excepting only himself.

Notwithstanding such bitterness, which reached pathological depths, Fry's main message regarding the United States was positive. As the *Tribune* reported three days before Gottschalk's arrival in New York, Fry argued that America's democratic institutions fostered more progress in art in ten years than other countries could achieve in a century.[38] And however bleak the picture at present, America's music was destined both to attain the highest artistic quality and to achieve mass popularity.[39]

Here, finally, was a resounding declaration of the United States' independence in the arts. As Richard Storrs Willis put it, Fry had used his remarkable command of vitriol and abuse to say "more bold, manly, searching, audacious, and *American* things concerning Art than have ever before been said in America."[40]

For all the enthusiasm of the moment, there were ominous signs as well, unsettling notes that Moreau and his father could not afford to ignore. On the one hand, up in Boston an influential music journal edited by John Sullivan Dwight decried Fry's iconoclastic attitude toward European composers in general and Beethoven in particular. Was it necessary, Dwight asked, to tear down this rich tradition "merely in order that we may appreciate the symphonies, operas, cantatas, *Bananiers*, etc., of our native aspirants?"[41] In other words, if Fry claimed that to be an American one had to embrace the music of Gottschalk, Mr. Dwight objected.

As Fry was completing his lectures, Gottschalk fell ill, probably from anxiety over his impending debut.[42] The concert, originally set for February 4, had to be postponed to the eleventh. Since the orchestra was unavailable for that date, Gottschalk engaged the outspoken George F. Bristow as an additional accompanist, joining flautist John Kyle, tenor John Fraser, soprano Rose DeVries, and Richard Hoffman. The new date also meant that Gottschalk had to go head-to-head not only with Sontag next door at Niblo's Garden but also with the American premiere of Shakespeare's *Midsummer Night's Dream*, with Mendelssohn's music, at Burton's Theater.[43]

Using every ploy to fire the public's interest, Moreau announced days before the debut that he had just received a letter from the Grand Duchess of Russia inviting him to perform at the court of St. Petersburg.[44] A good move, to be sure, but it only focused the question of how the American public would receive the first of their fellow countrymen to have been given what the *Albion* called "the stamp of European approbation."[45] The answer came at Niblo's Saloon, which was fitted out with a special platform on which stood Gottschalk's Pleyel and two grands from the firm of Chickering & Sons in Boston.[46] The hall was packed with what the *Herald* called "one of the most refined and fashionable audiences that ever assembled at any concert room in this city."[47] Among those in attendance were ex-president Martin Van Buren and the eleven-year-old French violin prodigy Paul Julien.

The program opened with a flute solo, after which Gottschalk performed his fantasia on themes from Mehul's *Le Jeune Henri*. Following a Scottish song, Moreau and Hoffman returned with the thundering *Jérusalem* fantasy, after which Mme. DeVries sang an aria by Verdi. Gottschalk closed the first half with Liszt's setting of the sextet from *Lucia de Lammermoor*. After a further round of Scottish ballads by Frazier, Moreau launched into his three "poetic caprices," the mazurka *La Moissonneuse*, (op. 8), *Danse ossianique*, (op. 12), and *Le Bananier* (op. 5). Although Gottschalk's Louisiana compositions were already popular in the United States and were in the repertoire of several touring artists, this was the first time the public had heard any piece in this genre played as it was intended to be. After another aria by Mme. DeVries, Moreau and Hoffman returned with a newly composed (but now lost) *Valse di bravura* for two pianos. Gottschalk completed the program with his show-stopping *Grand Caprice and Variations* on *The Carnival of Venice*.

From the moment Moreau stepped onto the platform the audience went wild. It heartily approved of his "youthful and modest appearance, his pale and intellectual cast of countenance,"[48] and cheered him even before he struck the first note. No sooner did he wind up his first piece than cries of "Bravo" were heard, ladies waved their handkerchiefs, and the entire audience rose in delight. "Never since Jenny Lind's concerts was any other artist received with such enthusiasm as the young American pianist," wrote the *Herald.*[49] Another witness spoke of the "frenzy of enthusiasm" that greeted Moreau, adding that Gottschalk was "the only pianist we have yet heard who can electrify and inflame an assembly."[50] So excited was the public that it frequently exploded with applause in the midst of the performance. At the conclusion of the concert several ladies rushed forward to be introduced to the pianist.[51]

This reception was the more impressive in light of the public's general weariness with touring piano virtuosos. The *Times,* for example, had only recently declared the piano a poor concert instrument,[52] while the *Courier and Enquirer* confessed that the public regarded the piano "as an intolerable bore."[53]

The critics' response was equally positive, although more nuanced. All agreed that Gottschalk had no superior anywhere as a virtuoso, but there was disagreement about both his musicality and that of the public who applauded him. Richard Grant White of the *Courier and Enquirer* praised the "dash, glitter, and quaint conceits" of Moreau's playing and acknowledged that he could annihilate any difficulty."[54] But he went on to express regret "that so much stupendous and wonderful labor produced so little music" and scolded the audience for falling for it. By contrast, Richard Storrs Willis had nothing but praise for Gottschalk's artistry and noted that his playing was "precisely of the kind which most palpably hits the popular taste."[55] Clearly, those critics who accepted the public's values were delighted by Gottschalk, while those who rejected the public's taste as vulgar blamed him for his popularity.

Those who praised Gottschalk took pains to claim him as the New World's answer to the old, "a fine young American gentleman," in the words of Richard Storrs Willis.[56] With tub-thumping national spirit, Willis compared Moreau to the yacht *America,* which had won the first America's Cup race in 1851. William Henry Fry declared Moreau to be "a superlatively great artist . . . [who from] a national point of view stands alone. Who compares with him? No one."[57] Then, in an intriguing aside, Fry contrasted young Moreau with all past American stereotypes—Leatherstocking, Franklin, and Davy Crockett—and concluded that he represented a new kind of "splendid artistic model." Thanks to Gottschalk, Fry exulted, "it is now acceptable for Americans to range beyond the earnest traditional professions and embrace a career in Art."

Entering dangerous territory, Fry went on to contrast Gottschalk's vital new works with those by such dead fogies as Haydn and Beethoven.[58] With this step, he launched an early salvo in what was to grow into a full-blown war between partisans of *Le Bananier* and of Beethoven. With his unerring sense for what would most offend his opponents, Fry announced that "if we must signalize any one of [Moreau's] pieces, his Creole melodies [*Le Bananier*, etc.] are admirably beautiful."[59]

Taken together, the reviews of Gottschalk's debut were extraordinarily positive. Most agreed with the *Home Journal's* judgment of the February 11 event: "We mention the date, because we are convinced that the musical history of the country will require that it should be preserved."[60]

Six days later the critics had a second chance to hear Moreau when he appeared at Niblo's Garden on one of Sontag's off-nights. This time he had the benefit of Wallace and the orchestra, and Madame Sontag herself was present, *sans* cigar but applauding enthusiastically.[61] Moreau played two sections of Weber's *Concertstück*, chosen, no doubt, to establish his credentials with the Beethovenites. Seymour of the *Times*, however, was "astonished [but] not delighted."[62] Strangely, he identified the problem as Gottschalk's emphasis on "the letter of the composer rather than the spirit." Richard Hoffman gave a more plausible explanation for what was evidently a flawed performance. In his anxiety, Moreau had bitten his fingernails so badly that his fingers were bleeding. Unable to execute Weber's glissandos, he substituted improvisations that spoiled the performance.[63]

Gottschalk and Hoffman repeated the *Jérusalem* fantasy to better effect, but *Bamboula*, *La Savane*, and *Le Bananier* again produced the most discussion. By now Seymour was sinking into dyspepsia and dismissed *Bamboula* as "neither brilliant, imaginative, or even difficult."[64] Richard Grant White acknowledged the "quaint, pretty rhythm" of *Bamboula* but, in a telling reaction to the work's syncopation, found himself unable to excuse "so much irregularity and caprice."[65] For Seymour and White, *Bamboula* was simply too eccentric, too American.

This was precisely the quality that attracted the otherwise cosmopolitan Charles Burkhardt of the highbrow *Albion*. Singling out *La Savane*, *Le Bananier*, and *Bamboula*, Burkhardt hailed Gottschalk as "an American player and composer [and] the originator of a new school":

> We believe his compositions and playing—pure, national, and classical—will have a happy effect on the rising generation, and be the foundation of a school, at once legitimate, and characteristic. His *Bamboula*, *Le Bananier*, etc., are truly original specimens of a new and delightful, a purely American, or if you please Southern, Creole school, the Gottschalk School, as it may yet be called.[66]

Horror of horrors! Fry's views on the future of American music were contagious, and Gottschalk's music their carrier. As if accepting his new role, Moreau improvised an encore with no precedent in the annals of American musical nationalism. In 1853 Americans still considered *Yankee Doodle* the most evocative of their national tunes, like the *Marseilles* for the French. Herz and Maurice Strakosch had both exploited it for encores. Gottschalk, however, did them one better by combining it contrapuntally with *Hail, Columbia.*[67] As his right hand beat out *Yankee Doodle* in the treble, the left produced a sonorous *Hail, Columbia* in the bass. This encore unleashed a "perfect *furore,*" as the *Herald* reported.[68] Gottschalk was pleased with the device, too, and used it a decade later in his sensational *The Union.*

For all the public's enthusiasm, these debut concerts were a financial disaster for the Gottschalks. Rent was due on the hall, and pay was owed to orchestral musicians and supporting singers. Receipts covered less than half the expenses, and the resulting deficit reached twenty-four hundred dollars.[69] Moreau himself called the second concert "a fiasco." It was well and good for the lithographic firm of Nagel & Weingartner to issue a large print of Moreau and for the young hero to be idolized at post-debut performances at Anne Lynch's salon.[70] But Edward Gottschalk was now broke, and he had already been having "all the trouble in the world" paying for his wife Aimée's expenses in Paris, as he told her in a letter.[71]

Just as Mr. Gottschalk was totaling his losses, P. T. Barnum approached Moreau with a stupendous offer. In exchange for three years' exclusive rights, Barnum would pay Gottschalk twenty thousand dollars annually. Suddenly Moreau beheld the prospect of repaying all his and his father's debts and achieving financial independence for the family. For Moreau personally it meant the long-term possibility of devoting himself to composing and to concertizing only when he wanted to. But in a fateful move, Edward Gottschalk intervened and refused Barnum outright.[72]

Reflecting later on his father's decision, Moreau referred only to Barnum's reputation as a huckster. "My father," he wrote, "had his prejudices (unjust) against Barnum, in whom he obstinately insisted in seeing only a showman of learned beasts."[73] Was Edward Gottschalk wrong in this? As judicious a businessman as Henri Herz had also refused Barnum. And Richard Hoffman had surely related to the Gottschalks how Barnum, after hiring him as accompanist to Jenny Lind, canceled his place on the tour at the last minute. Hoffman nearly sued. Against this background it is not surprising that the fastidious Edward Gottschalk refused to allow his son to sign with an impresario whose "properties" at the time included a petrified horseman, living reptiles, and the "child tamer of leopards, aged seven."

Whatever Mr. Gottschalk's rationale, his decision had important consequences for his son. It is no exaggeration to say that the decision prevented Moreau from becoming America's first full-time composer. Yet financial security might have had negative effects. It is unlikely, for
example, that Gottschalk would have remained so responsive to public
taste had he had Barnum's money in the bank. He might not have spent
what proved to be the artistically fruitful year of 1854 in Cuba and might
even have returned to France.

Only days after rejecting the Barnum offer, Moreau signed with another manager, William F. Brough, an Irish-born singer and actor who had
shifted to management shortly after his arrival in the United States in
1834. Brough had successfully managed diva Marietta Alboni's engagements but was now free for a period to take Moreau on a tour to the
South.[74] Although a seasoned impresario, Brough did not over-exert himself in Moreau's behalf. His passive and careless management suggests
that he viewed the Gottschalk tour simply as a filler between more important assignments.

Prior to his departure for New Orleans, Moreau traveled to Philadelphia for two appearances at the recently enlarged Musical Fund Hall.[75] In
spite of its austere Quaker past, Philadelphia boasted a rich musical life
ranging from a hundred-member Musical Fund Orchestra to Sam San-
ford's new minstrel theater, where Cool White held forth.[76]

It was in Philadelphia that Gottschalk met his uncle Arnold Myers for
the first time, and also his cousin and contemporary Leonard Myers
(1827–1905), a sympathetic and responsible young lawyer and later member of Congress. Through Leonard, in turn, he was introduced to the
lively Charles Vezin, an importer of millinery and a socialite whom the
papers called "fast-living Charlie." The two became close friends.[77]

A preview performance aroused the interest of the local press, which
hailed Moreau as "an honor to America"[78] and someone who had demonstrated his patriotism in the face of slights by arrogant Spaniards.[79] The
two concerts offered by Moreau and his troupe were well received, the
high point being the premiere on March 3 of a new *Fragment of the Symphony, "The Battle of Bunker Hill."*[80]

This piece, which eventually metamorphosed into a war-horse for ten
pianos, is easily dismissed as a facile stepchild of Gottschalk's *Siege of
Saragossa*, with American airs plugged in for the Spanish. Since *The Battle of Bunker Hill* is lost, it is impossible to determine the extent of Moreau's borrowing from himself. However, there were good reasons for
him to approach *The Battle of Bunker Hill* as a fresh challenge. He was,
after all, eager to establish his credentials as a truly American composer,
and not simply a Louisiana regionalist or Franco-Spanish import. More-

over, the United States' recent Mexican War against Spain had given rise to flag-waving pieces that associated a Spanish tinge in music with the enemy's forces.[81] This alone would have disqualified most of the *Siege of Saragossa*. Gottschalk faced competition as well. The seventy-fifth anniversary of the Battle of Bunker Hill, celebrated in 1851, had given rise to a well-publicized "descriptive symphony" by the New York Philharmonic violinist Simon Knaebel. For his *Battle of Bunker Hill*, Knaebel sent two full orchestras into the field. Representing American and British armies, the opposed ensembles played music depicting everything from the digging of fortifications to the final bloody combat.[82] With so formidable a rival as this, Gottschalk could not afford merely to rework his old Spanish material. He therefore started fresh, constructing his *Bunker Hill* around the juxtaposition of *God Save the Queen* and *Hail, Columbia*, the United States' unofficial national anthem.

The Philadelphia concerts completed, Moreau's father and brother departed for New Orleans. Brough's touring troupe, consisting of Moreau, baritone Herman Feitlinger, and soprano Rose DeVries, set out for the West and South. After crossing the mountains by stagecoach, they boarded an Ohio River steamboat and headed directly to Cincinnati. Evidence of Brough's carelessness was immediately evident. Cincinnati in 1853 was the Queen City of the West, the boisterous center of American expansionism. Its riverfront teemed with traffic, and its opera houses and minstrel theaters were packed. Unlike New York, it professed "great excitement in pianos," with no fewer than eight firms advertising their wares in the local press.[83] Yet Gottschalk swept through town with but one concert, and that one neither advertised nor reviewed.[84]

The troupe then proceeded to Louisville, where it offered two hastily arranged concerts. In the second of these, on March 19, Moreau presented a second part of his proposed "grand national symphony," here entitled *National Glory*. This extended work, now lost, became a regular feature of his programs for years. In Boston it was named *American Reminiscences*, and in Cuba as *Recuerdos de mi patra (sic)*. A reworked and shortened version was issued in 1859 as *Columbia, caprice américaine*, (op. 34). It stood directly in the line of descent from Gottschalk's operatic fantasies, except that it was built not on melodies by Verdi or Donizetti but on tunes by America's own Stephen Foster. *Old Folks at Home* was there; so was *O! Susanna*, and probably also the just-published *My Old Kentucky Home, Good Night.*[85]

Gottschalk was not the first "serious" composer to be enchanted by Foster's melodies. Both Henri Herz and William Vincent Wallace had issued "brilliant variations" on *O! Susanna.*[86] But for these foreign-born musicians Foster's melodies were merely musical flags, the external emblems or trademarks of the United States. Gottschalk viewed Foster as an authentic American bard, and he seized upon Foster's melodies as evocative raw material for the new American music he was creating. It is intriguing to speculate on what would have happened had the two met, for there is a natural affinity in their music. But their paths never crossed, even though Gottschalk and Foster were both in New York in January 1853, and even though Gottschalk visited several times at the home of one of Foster's relatives.[87]

When Gottschalk performed his rhapsody on Foster melodies in Louisville, the Western audience responded with shouts and hog calls.[88] Up to this moment, Gottschalk's musical evocations of America had been confined to patriotic airs and up-tempo melodies. Now he discovered that a rough-hewn Western audience could respond also to sentimental music of the heart.

On March 22 the Brough troupe set sail on the *Belle Key* for New Orleans. Whatever excitement Moreau felt at returning home after more than a decade's absence was more than matched by the enthusiasm of his proud fellow townspeople. Forewarned by telegram of Moreau's arrival, a large crowd consisting of the city authorities, a deputation of Masons, musicians from the several theater orchestras, and three or four thousand well-wishers assembled at the crowded levee. After waiting several hours in vain, they received a further telegram announcing that a steamer headed toward New Orleans had exploded. A murmur ran through the crowd. From mouth to mouth flew the question: "Was it the *Belle Key?*" Soon the question turned into a statement, and sorrow swept the city. Under heavy penalty, people were forbidden to speak of the news on the street, lest Moreau's Grandmother Bruslé learn of it and die of shock.

Meanwhile, Moreau was peacefully sailing toward New Orleans, the *Belle Key* having been delayed by nothing more serious than a storm. Arriving late in the evening, he went to the home of his aging grandmother who, in good New Orleans fashion, was still at the theater. "My old negroes," he reported, "old friends of my childhood, taking me in their arms, throwing themselves at my feet, gave me the most touching spectacle of affection."[89]

The Crescent City had been transformed since Moreau's departure. Its population had more than doubled to 150,000, a fifth of whom were free people of color or slaves. In 1852 the city's English-speaking and Protestant population broke the faltering grip of the French-speaking Creoles and took control of the city government. Increasingly, the old rivals made common cause against the new Irish immigrants who flooded the city. A mood of militant nationalism was felt, and the arrival of young Gottschalk, a native son who represented the union of French- and

English-speaking populations, provided the perfect opportunity for it to be expressed.[90]

The madness began on Moreau's second night, when the entire orchestra of the St. Charles Theater serenaded him at his rooms in the vast new St. Charles Hotel, with its dome modeled after the Panthéon in Paris. Moreau invited the musicians to his rooms, where he reciprocated with a serenade of his own. The next day he assembled the press for a second impromptu concert. The journalists judged his playing "stupendous."[91]

The one group that did not pay homage to Gottschalk were leaders of the city's free people of color. Several years earlier they had beseeched the touring Henri Herz to perform for them in a special concert, for which they were prepared to pay his usual fee. Herz was ready to consent when his manager, the notorious Ullmann, flatly refused.[92] Whether mindful of this rebuff or sensitive to the fact that Moreau himself did not acknowledge his four mulatto half brothers and sisters among their number, they did not repeat their appeal.

Two nights later the city's Masons offered a grand banquet in Moreau's honor at their Perfect Union Lodge on Rampart Street. Placide Canonge produced a long volley of applause when he recited in French a lengthy panegyric *To Gottschalk*. Nearly airborne from eloquence, Canonge concluded:

> O, brilliant poet, whom glory eternalizes,
> You walk today in the promised land.
> Walk, then, o miracle of Art,
> Walk, and your sweet country follows you with its gaze
> . . .
> The angel who once watched over your cradle
> Kneels still by your piano.[93]

Whether Moreau was moved or amused by this outpouring is not known. Years later, however, he was still quoting with glee another masterpiece by a New Orleans bard, this one in English:

> I could sit entranced and drink,
> And feel the mellow music sink,
> Deep, deep in my bosoms core,
> Til liquefied, I feel nothing more;
> My soul all wrapt up in ecstasy,
> And my frame in numb catalepsy.[94]

In the last days before his first concert, Moreau performed at the Boyers' salon and paid visits to old well-wishers, including Archbishop Blanc. In all his rounds he was accompanied by his proud teacher, François Letellier, and by his father, nearly crushed by troubles but for the moment beaming radiantly.[95]

Starting on April 6 and extending through May 17, Gottschalk offered New Orleanians a series of ten concerts, interrupted by two in Mobile, Alabama, on April 20 and 22. Most were held at the new Odd Fellows' Hall, an imposing structure recalling the Temple of Diana at Ephesus and symbolizing the new power of the Anglo-Saxon elite. Two were held at the Théâtre d'Orléans and included the theater's orchestra, and the last was held at the Mechanics' Institute Hall. Herman Feitlinger sang in several, but Gottschalk was careful to enlist local talent both as singers and as assisting pianists. Tickets to the first concert were a staggering two dollars, while the price of admission even to the final performance for workmen at the Mechanics' Institute Hall was a dollar. Most performances were sold out.[96]

Brough or Moreau had decided to present the native son as a national artist rather than as a purely local figure. Accordingly, the opening concert on April 6 featured a second performance of *National Glory*, here described as "a fragment from the symphony *Battle of Bunker Hill*."[97] The piece's ending was greeted by a shower of flowers and thunderous applause. When the tumult failed to subside, Moreau stepped forward and addressed the audience. Speaking in French, he stated that he had intended his *National Glory* as a *profession de foi*. Whatever fame he may have achieved elsewhere, declared Moreau, he had never forgotten, nor could he ever forget, that he was an American to the bottom of his heart. If it had been his good fortune to contribute in some slight degree to American art and American superiority, this would be his greatest reward.

The speech produced a further ovation and shower of bouquets.[98] "He is just too wonderful," effused a Crescent City belle to her sister. "I cannot tell you how divinely he plays—such execution, such power & at times such extreme delicacy of touch. . . . I don't believe I can enjoy hearing the piano played by anyone else again." Besides, she concluded, he had "large dreamy blue eyes & beautiful smile & the most perfect teeth I ever saw."[99]

Sticking to the tactic of emphasizing national over regional themes, Moreau held back the New Orleans premiere of *Bamboula* until the third concert. The audience came armed for the great event.[100] As Moreau finished the last bass notes, what one attendee described as "a perfect avalanche of bouquets" rained down on him, "hitting him on the head, on the back, on both sides; falling on the piano, under it, all over it, and all over the stage, like a tremendous hail storm, literally compelling him to beat a hasty retreat into the anteroom."[101] Returning the next morning, the same witness reported that the stage had been pelted with over 370 bouquets, "some of them huge."

Following the concerts in Mobile, Moreau shifted his venue to the

Théâtre d'Orléans. As if anticipating criticism that he ignored the classics, he performed Weber's *Concertstück* and added two movements of Beethoven's "Kreutzer Sonata" to the sixth concert for good measure.[102] Balancing these were a new (and now lost) *Memories of Bellini* and two Spanish works, *La Jota aragonesa* and a *Fandango*, the latter apparently written specifically for these performances.[103]

The next two concerts, both for charity, produced further innovations. For the seventh, held on May 11, Gottschalk published a list of twenty-six works, all but four of them his own, from which the audience could select the program. Three of these had never been performed before and one of them, entitled *Moripont*, has eluded Gottschalk bibliographers to now.[104] Both of these works were performed at the eighth concert on May 11.[105] On that occasion the mayor of New Orleans, Mr. A. D. Crossman, speaking on behalf of a committee made up of the leading Yankee and Creole citizens, acknowledged Moreau's "character as a gentleman and talent as an artist" and presented him with a medal of solid gold weighing sixteen ounces and inscribed on the one side with Gottschalk's bust in profile and on the reverse with the words "à L. M. Gottschalk, ses Compatriotes de la Nouvelle Orléans, 11 mai 1853".[106] Not to be outdone, the ladies of the city presented him at his concluding concert with "a crown, a pin, and a ring in diamonds, all of a great worth."[107]

Thus honored and feted, Moreau embarked on May 18 on the steamboat *Magnolia*. Over the previous seven weeks he had achieved both the musical and financial success that had eluded him in New York. He had performed his operatic fantasias, Creole caprices, and Spanish works. He had premiered four new compositions and established himself as a distinctly American voice in his country's musical life. He had begun paying back the debts incurred in New York and had even offered a benefit concert for his bumbling manager, Mr. Brough. Unfortunately, this marked the high point of Moreau's first return to the United States.

Chapter Ten

✖ Defeat in New England

GOTTSCHALK'S spring 1853 tour was in trouble from the start. To help his destitute father, he had given his entire earnings to Edward Gottschalk, leaving only twenty dollars for himself.[1] Also pinching pennies, William Brough had booked the troupe's passage north on one of the oldest and slowest steamers on the Mississippi.[2] Moreau had brought along his younger brother Edward Jr., who dutifully recorded every stop on the tedious journey in an account book. The schedule was absurd. Why did Brough book two performances in tiny Natchez and none in booming St. Louis? Why did he mount a full performance in minuscule New Albany, Indiana, and then give but one concert in Cincinnati? Why did he later bypass the Ohio capital at Columbus but give a full-blown concert in the village of Wellington, Ohio, which was not even incorporated as a town?[3]

Brough's task was difficult, for wherever he took the troupe he had to contend with other touring artists. Max Strakosch and the eleven-year-old singing wonder Adelina Patti left Cincinnati just as Gottschalk arrived. The European dancer and seductress Lola Montez was scheduled at Cincinnati's National Theater opposite Moreau's concert at Smith & Nixon's Hall. And no sooner did the Brough troupe depart Cincinnati than the boy violinist Paul Julien and soprano Amalia Patti Strakosch, Adelina's sister and Max's wife, swept in. Competition was fierce, and Brough failed to claim the territory by booking ahead.

Moreau realized that his concerts were a failure but did not understand the cause. In a letter to a Spanish friend he described Brough as

> a perfect gentleman who knows that whole United States step by step and the press of the whole Union. He goes three or four hundred leagues ahead of me and handles the publicity, etc. Then my secretary follows a few days after him, engages lodgings, and does all that relates to the material side of the concert.

> Finally I arrive with the business manager, two singers, and an accompanist. My secretary leaves me then and goes to the nearest city where he picks up the instructions that my general agent has left all along the route.[4]

Considering that Moreau's "secretary" is none other than seventeen-year-old Edward, and that half the stops show every sign of being improvisations on Brough's part, it is clear that Moreau was either naive or overly eager to impress his European friend.

Brough continued to promote Moreau as an all-American artist and harbinger of a new "classical" American music. At Louisville, where Moreau gave a benefit concert on board the steamer *Shotwell* for the local orphan asylum, the New Orleanian was touted as "proud of his country."[5] At Cincinnati, where the public was seeking to raise thirty thousand dollars to buy Hiram Powers's sculpture, *America*, a long story in the *Enquirer* entitled "The Nationality of Gottschalk" reported that he possessed a "true pride of country and a proper manner of manifesting this feeling."[6] Following the concert, the same paper judged that Moreau was as good as any composer alive and announced that "we are proud to record that this genius is American."

The rest of May and June 1853 became a blur, with concerts in Buffalo and practically every smaller town in up-state New York. The only moments of relief were a brief inspection of Niagara Falls and tea with the aging America Vespucci, whom Moreau had seen when she presented herself to a New Orleans public fourteen years earlier and who was now established at a forlorn island of Parisian culture on an isolated property near Ogdensburg.[7] By the end of June Gottschalk and Herman Feitlinger were at Samson Street Hall in Philadelphia, after which the tour disbanded.[8]

In Philadelphia Moreau contacted the publisher J. E. Gould, who agreed to issue three of his works immediately. Moreau then joined his Myers cousins for several weeks at the resort of Cape May, New Jersey, where he carried out this commission. A glistening *polka de salon* entitled *The Water Sprite (La Naïade)* op. 27, also appeared, with a dedication to a Philadelphia flame, Miss Mary J. Smith. Another polka, entitled *Forest Glade*, op. 25, bore a dedication to Leonard Myers.

Moreau composed *Forest Glade* on a Sunday. Just as he sat down at the piano to work on it a violent thunderstorm burst out. At the first flash of lightning a delegation of frightened and indignant Protestant ladies came pounding on his door. Seeing in the storm unmistakable evidence of divine wrath, they demanded that he cease profaning the Sabbath with his music.[9] Moreau complied, but the incident confirmed a resentment against Protestant moralizing that was to grow ever stronger with the coming years.

No such problems existed at the chic spa of Saratoga Springs, New York, to which Gottschalk retired for the rest of the summer. Situated only a few hours north of Manhattan along the new train line, Saratoga Springs was already established as America's premier watering place and a magnet for worldly visitors from New York business houses, Southern plantations, and points between. Saratoga was also popular among wealthy Cubans, and a *contradanza* entitled *Saratoga cubano* had just been published in Havana. The most fashionable merchants and *modistes* of New York moved their shops to Saratoga each summer, as did chic portraitists and photographers. Here an ex-prizefighter like hard-drinking John Morrissey could sport about in a white linen suit and with a huge diamond on his finger, confident that his political sins with the notorious Plug Uglies gang would be disregarded.[10] At the same time Nathaniel Parker Willis decried the exclusiveness "exercised so insultingly and tyrannically at American watering places."[11] Saratoga, in short, catered to both parvenus and patricians.

The focus of all this activity was the alkaline, sulphur, and carbonated springs that promised to "correct vitiated secretions and so renovate health."[12] Rambling hotels with immense wooden galleries for seeing and being seen stood adjacent to each spring. The Congress Hall and Union Hotel faced each other on stately Broadway and were the focal point of both curative and social activity.

This first summer Gottschalk stayed not at one of these grand establishments but at the slightly more modest United States Hotel, paying for his room and board by giving a concert in the ballroom on August 22.[13] But if he was lionized socially, the praise did not translate into further concerts, and so he proceeded to Saratoga's only rival as a resort, Newport, Rhode Island, where he performed three times.[14] None of these summer concerts proved of much use financially. With no prospects of further performances, Gottschalk devoted himself to composing.

It is all but impossible to reconstruct the full list of compositions that flowed from Moreau's pen that summer of 1853. He himself listed nearly a dozen pieces, most of them short and published posthumously, if at all.[15] His one major project seems to have been to fill out the collection of ballades he had begun with the two early *Ossian* pieces and continued with *La Savane* (subtitled *Ballade créole*). In the eight ballades that survive, Gottschalk reveals himself as a faithful Chopinian, relying on gentle lyricism to sustain the multi-strain forms. The best of them, including the Ballade in A-flat Major, are delightfully simple yet sprinkled with splendid and idiomatic dashes of color in the right hand and characteristic elements of chromaticism in the left.[16]

The most enduring fruit of this bucolic summer was Gottschalk's striking and highly original piece of Americana, *The Banjo*. For the six months since his return from Europe Moreau had been experimenting with the American themes that bombarded him from every side. Beginning with national airs, he moved on to the hugely popular songs of Stephen Foster, and from there to the sound of that most characteristically American instrument, the banjo. Tracing its origin to West Africa, a simple banjo-type instrument had been popular among African-American musicians for centuries.[17] In the nineteenth century this prototype merged with European guitar-type instruments and picked up additional strings, the fifth producing the kind of drone common in Scotch-Irish music.[18] This led to a period of intensive development by manufacturers, with the result that by the 1840s the banjo had become a virtuoso instrument that was popular among all segments of the population. Stephen Foster's lyrics for his 1848 *O! Susanna* celebrated the fact that Americans moved westward with banjos on their knee.

Banjo-mania exploded with full force in the early 1850s. Christy's Minstrels made hay in 1851 with Foster's raucous *Ring, Ring de Banjo*, which inspired legions of imitators, among them Harriet Beecher Stowe, who penned words for *While I My Banjo Play*. There was even an Ohio River showboat named *Banjo*.[19] Classical musicians were not blind to this craze. Maurice Strakosch composed a "characteristic caprice" in imitation of the banjo, which he performed in New Orleans to great acclaim only weeks before Moreau arrived there.[20] Later, an enthusiastic critic from the New York newspaper the *Albion* hailed this work as a "first fruit of the 'Gottschalk School'," but the belittling *Times* found "nothing especially sublime" about it.[21] Either way, the banjo could not be ignored.

Gottschalk would have heard banjo music from earliest childhood. One of the country's most famous black virtuosos, West Indian–born Picayune Butler, was playing for tips on New Orleans street corners throughout Moreau's childhood. Butler meanwhile had moved to New York and was playing on Broadway at the time of Gottschalk's return. Whether or not Gottschalk heard Butler, he knew the traditional African-American banjo so well that his *The Banjo* is today considered a prime source of how it sounded.[22] He would also have heard many of the thousands of white players, amateur and professional, who had made the banjo a national instrument by the 1850s. Particularly important to him were the blackface minstrel performers who were transforming banjo technique by adding guitar-style strumming and new elements of virtuosity. Gottschalk not only heard the most renowned of these groups, Buckley's Serenaders, but wrote a review for the *Morning Times* of a concert that featured leader George Swayne Buckley (1829–79), the first banjoist to play in the guitar style.[23] He also heard other minstrel players, which

led one contemporary critic to state categorically that *The Banjo* was
Gottschalk's tribute to the playing of Thomas Vaughn, the virtuoso banjo
player from Christie and Wood's Minstrels.[24] Whether or not this is the
case, the uproarious final measures of *The Banjo* clearly depict this
strumming technique in full force.

Gottschalk's *The Banjo* (more accurately, *The Banjo I* and *The Banjo
II*, since he produced two quite different variants of the piece) differs
from virtually every other work in the same vein in two important respects. First, Gottschalk sought to evoke not merely the general mood of
banjo playing but its specific musical textures. He rejected the approach
of romantic genre painters who were content to depict their subject ex-
ternally. Instead, he emerged as a realist intent on conveying his subject
in all its specifics, down to the pentatonic chords, the African-American
frailing ("plunk-briing, plunk-briing") method of plucking, and the Irish-
derived "weakened beat" syncopations.[25] Second, he sought to go beyond
the presentation of ethno-musicological specifics to create a self-
conscious work of art that stands squarely in the tradition of European
classicism. The composition was carefully structured to rise in intensity
and culminate in a virtuosic finale. At key points in the more elaborate
version Gottschalk relieved the crescendo with a melodic bridge based
on Foster's 1850 minstrel song *Camptown Races.*[26] Never before had
Gottschalk achieved a more effective overall architecture.

Moreau did not perform the original *The Banjo* (op. 82) for another
four months and did not allow it to be published until a completely revised version (op. 15) was in hand a year later. The first version, misla-
beled as *Banjo II*, did not appear until after his death. As revised, however, *The Banjo* created a sensation and was promptly copied by other
composers.[27] Its very success threw down the gauntlet to champions of
European classicism. As a Sacramento paper observed, *The Banjo* was "a
remarkable imitation and therefore called clap-trap music by the classical."[28] Some of Gottschalk's highbrow friends apologized for his vulgar
lapse.[29] But the public loved it. Indeed, one of the most widely sold self-
instruction books for banjo paid tribute to Gottschalk (ludicrously mis-
identified as M. Thalberg) in its preface: "The fact of the eminent pianist
and composer [Gottschalk] having long directed a share of his study to
the development of [the banjo's] capabilities is conclusive proof as to its
real merits."[30]

A mere ten days after Gottschalk departed New Orleans on the *Magnolia*, an Irish laborer died there of yellow fever.[31] By late August 1853
three hundred people were perishing daily from the disease.[32] Learning
of this, Moreau rushed back to New York from Newport and hastily organized a benefit concert for the relief of his fellow townspeople.[33] Mo-

reau's appearances at Saratoga Springs and Newport had stimulated the public's interest in him as an artist, and to this was now added respect for him as a humanitarian.

Clear evidence that he had attained the status of a public figure was the speed with which newspapers disseminated a rumor that he planned to marry. Reports that Moreau was to wed a wealthy Philadelphian— possibly the Mary J. Smith to whom he dedicated *The Water Sprite*— originated in New York musical circles on September 12 and spread rapidly by telegraph to papers in Philadelphia, Baltimore, Hartford, Boston, and Newark.[34] This rumor was almost certainly false, since Moreau continued to garner dinner invitations from other young ladies in New York.[35] But it left no doubt that he was in the public's eye and that a successful autumn season could make him the first native-born American to become a matinee idol.

This did not happen. Indeed, over the next months Gottschalk's career all but collapsed, reaching a low ebb from which he barely recovered. Many factors contributed to this, but the most important ones were set in motion by the untimely appearance in America of Louis-Antoine Jullien (1812–60), an orchestra leader at once so gifted and so extravagantly colorful that he totally eclipsed the more reserved Gottschalk. Due to Jullien, Gottschalk lost his manager, was closed out of New York, and was forced to embark on what proved to be a ruinous tour of New England.

Jullien was, to say the least, controversial. One leading American called him "the musical charlatan of all ages," while another judged him "a versatile genius."[36] Berlioz characterized him as "a man accustomed to appeal always to the childish instincts of the crowd and to succeed by the most stupid means,"[37] but Boston's most austere musical journal found him fascinating. After a solid musical training in France, Jullien had fled to England in 1838 to escape creditors.[38] In London he founded the renowned Promenade Concerts at Covent Garden and Drury Lane, thus creating the tradition of "pops concerts" that continues to this day.

Jullien's enormous popularity rested on two pillars. First, he was a consummate showman. He made sure his orchestra included the world's biggest drum and a trombone the size of a steamer's smokestack. Second, Jullien hired the very best musicians, drilled them to perfection, and performed flawlessly a vast repertoire ranging from the classics to his own hugely popular quadrilles. All this cost money, however, and by 1849 London police had arrested Jullien for insolvency.

Jullien relaunched his career when he and his orchestra made their debut at New York's Castle Garden on August 29, 1853. Appearing almost nightly, the Jullien orchestra began a run of over one hundred concerts, smothering all other performers in town. By November Jullien "had the whole field," reported *Dwight's Journal of Music.*[39] Worse, Jullien hired William Brough as his assistant manager. Even though this arrangement had been made much earlier, it left Gottschalk with neither impresario nor engagements at the start of the fall season.

Moreau never commented on the blow he suffered at the hands of Louis-Antoine Jullien. He pondered its lessons, however. Judging by his subsequent actions, Gottschalk derived four conclusions from Jullien's conquest of America. First, his interest broadened to embrace composing and conducting for orchestra. When William Henry Fry compared the Jullien orchestra with the Parthenon,[40] he reflected the general view that orchestral music represented the pinnacle of musical achievement. Second, Jullien provided additional inspiration for Gottschalk's many later music festivals. Moreau never stooped to some of Jullien's more outrageous ploys, but the democratic notion that the public would open its heart and pocketbook to grandly staged festivals captured Moreau's imagination.

Third, Jullien strengthened Gottschalk's instinctive belief that high culture and popular culture were compatible and could even reinforce one another. The highbrow *Dwight's Journal of Music* may have denounced Jullien as a humbug, but it also devoted four laudatory articles to him in a single issue.[41] Finally, Jullien confirmed Gottschalk's interest in creating an American national music. The great showman had dedicated original works to every nation he visited. A New Orleans critic wrote of Jullien and his *American Quadrille:* "He has roused patriotic feelings which seem to slumber amongst us. He has done more by fifteen minutes of his weird enchantment to awaken the American idea, . . . to place us face-to-face with the grandeur of our country, . . . than all the orators, or writers, or artists of the world could effect."[42]

Amidst the Jullien hysteria, Gottschalk undertook a third New York performance at Niblo's Saloon on October 13. Foolishly acting as his own manager, Moreau failed to advertise, forgot to order printed programs, over-charged the public, and, except for *American Reminiscences,* programmed the same pieces he had played the previous spring.[43] Nevertheless, the reviews were positive, and some even thought he had eclipsed his previous efforts. The balance sheet told a different story. Fully two-thirds of the tickets went unsold, leaving a painful deficit.[44]

Working hastily to correct his error, Moreau made contact with a minor New England–based impresario named F. B. Helmsmuller, long the manager of the Germania orchestra but recently fired by Bernard Ullmann. Angered at being dismissed, Helmsmuller leaked to the press that Ullmann had regularly ordered him to bribe critics.[45] Helmsmuller's role in this scandal revealed him as even sleazier than Ullmann himself, but

Gottschalk was desperate. Quickly engaging the Welsh harpist Aptomas (Thomas Thomas, 1829–1913) and the beautiful young New York soprano Henriette Behrend, Gottschalk departed on a New England tour thrown together for him by Helmsmuller.

The effects of poor planning were felt immediately. Members of the troupe had never appeared on the same stage together until they performed at Brewster Hall in New Haven. Rather than surmount this problem by warming up in more small towns, Helmsmuller took his artists directly from New Haven to Boston. Having only recently proven his skills at manipulating the press, he then inexplicably neglected to send publicity material ahead to the Massachusetts capital. In yet another gaffe, he failed to arrange for Gottschalk to host local journalists at his hotel. As a result of these various lapses the first concert was actively touted in only one paper, *Gleason's Pictorial Drawing-Room Companion.*[46] This did more harm than good in some quarters, since *Gleason's* was known to be no fan of some of Boston's most highly regarded political activists and had even branded the local abolitionist William Lloyd Garrison a "fanatic."[47]

Helmsmuller aside, self-righteous Boston was the wrong city to approach so casually. Mark Twain later remarked that a Boston audience meant "four thousand critics."[48] True, the city did not lack a common touch or even vulgarity. Ordway's Minstrels were already popular there,[49] and when Jenny Lind came to town a local actor named Ossian Dodge, known for his imitations of birds, sheep, and guinea hens, offered $640 for a single ticket.[50] But whatever the reality, Boston's cultural elite preferred to see their city as a bastion of morality and high-mindedness. Thus they banned smoking on the city's sidewalks and confined cigars to a "smokers' circle" on the Common.[51] Other self-appointed protectors of virtue made sure that the waltz, which they judged lascivious, was kept out of town until long after it was being danced elsewhere in America.[52]

At the moment of Gottschalk's arrival, earnest members of Boston's elite were immersed in two great crusades. Many of those who circulated between Beacon Hill and Harvard Yard were convinced that public taste was plummeting and that it was their duty to rescue it. They blamed the uneducated and boozing Irish Catholics and vowed to lift the lamp of culture amidst the darkness created by these new immigrants. Music was an important focus of their effort. Soon a host of new institutions had been created to elevate the public's musical taste.[53] The Boston Academy of Music took as its mission nothing less than to stamp out boorishness.[54] An anonymous writer in the *North American Review* groaned that America's own music gratified only "a vulgar and depraved taste" and vowed to dedicate himself to the noble cause of making people more virtuous.[55]

Needless to say, Bostonians of this stripe had loathed the opera company from New Orleans's Théâtre d'Orléans when it came to town a generation earlier. Reviewers found its performances "too Frenchified" and the language "a gabble." New Orleanians responded to this insult with "laughter and pity," suggesting that "a cock fight would be more to the taste of Bostonians than the French opera."[56] Proper Boston, in return, judged New Orleans and France as enemies of Good Taste and moral cesspools to boot.

Boston's second crusade was against slavery. Historians may debate whether the city's abolitionists hastened the end of human bondage in the United States or so polarized North and South as to ensure that the Civil War would be the century's bloodiest. The abolitionists themselves harbored no such doubts. Several times in the period immediately preceding Gottschalk's arrival, abolitionist bands broke into courtrooms and jails to snatch fugitive slaves from Southern owners who had come to reclaim them. Harriet Beecher Stowe had just described this process in her hit novel *Uncle Tom's Cabin.* Unfortunately for Moreau, Stowe had made sure that her worst sinner, Simon Legree, was from Louisiana. Then, in a striking example of fiction anticipating reality, only three days before Gottschalk's first concert at Music Hall, the Boston press issued feverish reports on a real New Orleans woman, a Mrs. McClenathan, who had gone to court in Boston in order to keep possession of a slave girl who was traveling with her and her children.[57] In the face of all this, who could doubt that Moreau was an emissary from the Devil himself?

The first concert was set for October 18, 1853, at Music Hall, which stood at the end of Hamilton Place just opposite Park Street Church. Built in 1852 "after a year of study of European concert Halls,"[58] this plain auditorium was intended as a shrine for classical music. It seated two thousand. In a clear misjudgment, Helmsmuller set the price of admission too high. Three papers complained about this. As the *Commonwealth* explained, "no solo performer, even of the highest reputation, can attract a paying audience at one dollar." [59] This, along with Helmsmuller's failure to place the usual puff pieces in the press, resulted in a meager audience that barely filled the front rows. All the critics showed up, however. The *Post* noticed "many of our first musical critics and performers present,"[60] while the *Evening Transcript* declared that "a more critical and discriminating audience was never before gathered together in our city to pass their judgment upon the merit of a performer."[61]

In a city immunized against vanity, Moreau's modest demeanor earned approval. "He gives no ostentatious indication of self-satisfaction," wrote the *Courier*, "but proceeds to his work as an artist feeling the worth of his profession."[62] As he moved through his program the small audience applauded enthusiastically. The *Post* went so far as to say that Gottschalk was "rapturously received and his performance elicited the warmest encomiums."[63] Another indicated that the public was "highly gratified";[64] while the critic for a third reported that "we all agreed . . . that Gottschalk had laid claims to be considered at the head of his art."[65]

So far so good. But if all could agree that Gottschalk's technique was unsurpassed, opinions differed widely on his compositions. Some were positive. The *Daily Evening Transcript* characterized Gottschalk's music as "entirely original" and praised the "piquant novelty of his style." In a backhanded acknowledgment of his use of syncopation, it also alluded to "the abruptness of his transitions, the oddity of his accentuation, and particularly [the] lack of repose, which is evident in all his performances."[66]

What the *Transcript* hailed as "piquant," the *Commonwealth* found to be "the veriest trash that was ever offered to a Boston audience."[67] Let Gottschalk be "enthusiastically applauded," intoned the *Commonwealth*. His "poetic caprices *La Savane* and *Le Bananier* had in them much more of caprice than of poetry," and his *American Reminiscences* were "only reminiscences of the *Old Folks at Home*, which appeared in vague, scarcely recognizable forms at the beginning of the fantasia. . . . Relief was experienced when the work ended." *Dwight's Musical Journal* shared this harsh judgment of the *American Reminiscences*, calling the piece "trivial and insulting." Thankfully, this critic left before Moreau ended the evening with an improvisation on *Yankee Doodle*.[68]

For the second concert Helmsmuller cut the ticket price to fifty cents. Even this failed to improve attendance. As a sop to critics who had rejected his Louisiana compositions, Gottschalk added to the program classical works by Beethoven, Onslow, and Liszt and performed only the most European of his own works. Indeed, his performance of Liszt's *Lucia* transcription unleashed "a burst of applause, of acknowledged mastery, of appreciated greatness."[69] However, most reviewers simply ignored this second performance.

An hour before this concert began, a telegram from his Uncle George Gottschalk in New Orleans informed Moreau that his father was on the verge of death.[70] This could not have come as news to Gottschalk, since Uncle George had kept him apprised of his father's waning health since August and he himself had written several letters to his mother in Paris preparing her for the inevitable.[71] Even at the first concert observers had noted Moreau's "listless manner and apparent inattention."[72] The telegram from New Orleans nearly destroyed the second. Edward Gottschalk did not actually die until two days after the performance,[73] but Helmsmuller informed the audience that Moreau had just lost his father. "I might have put off the concert," Gottschalk recalled, "but the expenses had been incurred; the least delay would have augmented my [financial] loss. I thought of those to whom I had become the only prop; I drove back my despair and played."[74]

The losses were crippling. The first concert grossed only one hundred dollars, and the second yielded forty-nine dollars.[75] After paying his supporting musicians Moreau was once more broke, without money even to pay his hotel bill.[76] Gottschalk had hit rock bottom.

Then, as if by some miracle, the hotel bill was settled, train tickets were purchased, and within days the troupe was performing before two hundred people at Westminster Hall in Providence. Amazingly, it seems not to have occurred to Moreau to inquire into what had caused this turnabout. Only a year later did he learn that a prominent Boston piano manufacturer had quietly loaned three hundred dollars to Helmsmuller in order to save the young artist's career.[77] By the time Gottschalk heard about this good-hearted act, his benefactor, Jonas Chickering, had died.

This was not the first time Jonas Chickering (1798–1853) had shown such generosity. Over the years he had financed the European education of several young American musicians and had rescued Boston's Handel and Haydn Society from financial collapse.[78] Moreau was deeply grateful for Chickering's patronage. He dedicated his *Réponds moi* to Mrs. Chickering and remained a loyal champion of Chickering pianos throughout his life. Up to now, Moreau had been associated with the Paris piano builders Pleyel and Érard. In switching to Chickering's instruments he was prompted by more than personal gratitude. Naturally, Moreau wanted to be associated in advertisements with a list of Chickering artists that eventually came to include Sigismund Thalberg, Louis-Adolphe Jullien, Maurice Strakosch, and Leopold de Meyer.[79] On the other hand, the Chickerings not only paid Gottschalk for his testimonials but gave him a commission on all instruments he sold. In effect, Moreau Gottschalk the performer became a traveling piano salesman for Chickering as well.

Beyond this, Chickering pianos were ideally suited to Gottschalk's professional needs. The great challenge to piano makers since Mozart's day had been to build an instrument capable of producing a powerful tone yet strong enough to withstand the immense string tension necessary to create such volume. In 1843 Jonas Chickering patented an iron frame with built-in bracer bars.[80] With this invention Chickering transformed piano making. By Gottschalk's day he employed two hundred workmen who produced a thousand instruments a year, a ninth of the country's total production.[81] Pianist and fellow instrument maker Henri Herz felt that Chickering pianos lacked the combination of power and sweetness characteristic of the finest French instruments but conceded that they were at least the equal of the best English pianos.[82] They also were phenomenally durable, which was particularly important for a touring artist like Gottschalk.

In spite of Jonas Chickering's timely aid, Moreau's New England tour went from bad to worse. And no wonder, since Helmsmuller continued to mismanage the operation. Thus, the troupe appeared four times in Providence, three times in New Haven, and twice each in Worcester, Massachusetts, and Hartford, Connecticut. Having failed both to book sequentially in each city and to do the necessary promotion, Helmsmuller had no choice but to move his musicians every day, hop-scotching among these cities by train.[83] The musicians were soon exhausted. After reading Gottschalk's bad reviews from Boston, Henriette Behrend demanded that she be given top billing and quit the tour when this was denied her.[84] Helmsmuller grew desperate, as is evident by the fact that he even impressed Moreau's lackadaisical brother Edward into service. In his notebook Edward recorded that in New Haven there were "posters numerous and well stuck up," and listed the newspapers in which ads were supposed to appear.[85] But they did not.

These most recent programs reflected the impact of Moreau's double drubbing in Boston. For the first several performances he avoided entirely his Louisiana- and American-oriented works. Later, however, he recovered and introduced a new impromptu based on the popular song *Home, Sweet Home*, as well as an otherwise unknown *A Night Among the Gypsies in Andalusia*.[86] The hall was full for this performance in Providence,[87] but such moments were few. At Hartford barely two hundred tickets were sold, and for a New Bedford concert the total fell to 127. Deducting for advertising, the printing of programs and handbills, licenses, freight charges, and ticket sellers, the profits on these three performances ranged from \$84.27 on down to \$24.12.[88] Even these totals did not include payments to assisting artists and Helmsmuller's own fee. No wonder that by the time Gottschalk arrived back in New York on November 14 he was deep in the hole.[89]

Gottschalk's accumulated debts since his return from Europe had reached the enormous sum of sixteen thousand dollars.[90] He hoped to start recouping these losses at concerts booked in cities a few hours distant from Manhattan but these performances only worsened the situation.[91] Moreau's friends had no doubt that Helmsmuller was swindling him.[92]

Amidst this deepening crisis, Gottschalk found time to assist at the New York debut of a fellow Creole from New Orleans, pianist Gabrielle de la Motte, on November 19. Conceding that she was "very young, very pretty, and very *spirituelle*," the press advised her against a soloist's career.[93] After this concert Gottschalk had no further bookings. He tried to join various touring troupes but their ranks were full. In desperation Moreau offered himself as accompanist to the violinist Ole Bull but was rejected.[94] The situation grew worse by the day. Moreau had borrowed heavily from George Henriques, a New York lawyer who had spent years in New Orleans and been close to the Gottschalk family. This debt could not be ignored. But neither could Gottschalk ignore the fact that he had nothing but a few old summer clothes as winter approached.

Then there was his family in Paris. Aimée must have been consoled to know that before he died her late husband had accepted baptism into the Catholic Church.[95] But she, too, was broke. Moreau wrote advising her to sell all her furniture, "keeping only what is absolutely necessary," and to move immediately to the home of friends in the town of Tarbes in the Hautes Pyrénées. "Do not waste time thinking," he advised her. "Go find an auctioneer."[96]

Observing all this, Moreau's usually frivolous younger brother Edward wrote to his cousin Leonard Myers: "My opinion is that [Moreau] cannot live any further upon his profession. He will return here without a cent. . . . What a bad position is ours!!"[97] A friend was convinced that Moreau was on the verge of suicide.[98]

After briefly entertaining the possibility of returning to France, the Gottschalk brothers set sail for New Orleans on December 17, 1853.[99] Word of Moreau's financial plight had preceded him there.[100] Within three weeks of his arrival on December 31, 1853, friends had organized two subscription concerts in his behalf, to be held on February 1 and 3, 1854.[101] During the intervening weeks he attended to family matters and again devoted himself to composition. While still in Europe he had written a *Marche funèbre*, which remained unpublished. He now did a second version memorializing his father, a dolorous and touching piece in which unexpected chord progressions impart freshness to what are otherwise clichéd funereal motifs.[102] He may also have written *Le Chant du martyr* at this time. While this is a somewhat soupy tear-jerker, and the *Marche funèbre* is not much better, they both reveal that Gottschalk was beginning to embrace the current of sentimentalism so popular at the time.

At the first concert at Mechanics' Hall Moreau led off with *Remembrances of Home*, yet another variant on his Foster fantasia. This was followed by the premiere of *The Banjo*, not in the form best known today but in the earlier version, known as *The Banjo II*. Both of these works were mere preludes to the feature of the evening, the premiere of Gottschalk's *Grand National Symphony for Ten Pianos, Bunker Hill*.[103] Mustering an army of the best pianists in town, Moreau led them through all the phases of the great battle. Since the work is lost, a description from the local French press must suffice:

After a most harmonious introduction, the music announces that the combat has started, and we hear two songs that clash, *God Save the Queen* and *Yankee Doodle.* Then the two armies increase their firing, the action heats up, but always, over the voice of the cannon, the gun shot, the cries of the dying, we hear those two exciting airs from the respective camps. . . . Soon sheer noise dominates: We sense that death has accomplished its work, that destiny has made its pronouncement. So a victory chant rises, and five pianos sing *Hail, Columbia,* while five others respond with *Yankee Doodle.*[104]

The large audience loved it and demanded that Moreau repeat it at the second concert. The critics also hailed *Bunker Hill,* although the *Courrier de la Louisiane* felt compelled to explain rather defensively that "this composition has nothing to do with charlatanism."[105]

Profits from these performances may have enabled Moreau to pay back part of his debts, but they fell far short of what he needed. Although life insurance companies were already operating in New Orleans, Edward Gottschalk Sr. had taken out no coverage. This left Moreau with absolutely no resources at the very time he became sole provider for his mother, two brothers, and four sisters.

Legends abound about Gottschalk's heroic efforts to pay off his father's debts at this time. All these reports are probably apocryphal. Had he actually repaid these debts, Louisiana law would have required him to notarize each payment. But there is no evidence in the voluminous notarial archives that Moreau did anything at this time to settle his father's debts. A second legend has Moreau emancipating his slaves, an act one biographer called "one of the fairest jewels in his crown."[106] Moreau himself wrote that "my horror of slavery made me emancipate . . . three slaves that belonged to me."[107] The only possible slaves to whom he might have been referring were Sally, his old nurse, her children, Adele and Jules, and Adele's daughter, Marie, a minor. These had never belonged to Moreau, and when his father broke up the household he had transferred them to the care of the Bruslé family. Edward Gottschalk must certainly be credited with a certain humanitarianism in keeping Sally and her daughters in the family. Far from emancipating them, however, he seems to have used the sale to settle a debt to the Bruslés.[108] Moreau was never in the picture.

Moreau did not pay his father's debts at the time because he was broke. He could not emancipate or sell slaves because he owned none. In fact, by February 1854 he had no resources at all, lending credence to impresario Max Maretzek's sweeping assertion that "beyond a doubt a really creative genius in Poetry, Music, Painting, or Sculpture must starve in America."[109]

With his father's death, twenty-four-year-old Moreau Gottschalk became the sole provider for seven dependents, six of whom were living in the most expensive city in Europe. Neither his Catholic faith, the Jewish ethos of his upbringing, nor the Louisiana Civil Code, with its emphasis on the family unit, would have permitted him to shirk this responsibility. Yet there is not the slightest doubt that Gottschalk willingly assumed this burden. These new responsibilities, however, had a profound effect on his life, for they left him permanently preoccupied with money. Even if he tried to relax for a few weeks or briefly withdrew from the world in order to compose music, he still had to continue forwarding regular payments to Paris. This brute fact strongly affected Gottschalk's personal and artistic life.

With the second performance of his *Bunker Hill* on February 3, 1854, Gottschalk exhausted his possibilities in New Orleans. Both Ole Bull and Henriette Sontag were arriving in town shortly, and by the time they finished their concerts Lent would commence. With no ready alternative, Gottschalk booked passage for Cuba.

Chapter Eleven

✕ Mr. Dwight's Crusade

MOREAU Gottschalk's first American tour was a financial disaster, but it was not lack of money alone that impelled him to spend the next year in Cuba. During his brief Boston sojourn he encountered something quite new in his career that was far more devastating than the indifference of audiences. There, on the pages of *Dwight's Journal of Music and Art*, he was subjected for the first time in his life to withering criticism.

Unaccustomed to anything but praise, Moreau was profoundly shaken. He responded with a curious mixture of passivity and aggression. The passivity took the form of a personal boycott of Boston that he continued for nearly a decade. He refused even to look at *Dwight's Journal of Music*, turning his back with visceral disgust when others read it in his presence. The aggression sounded in Gottschalk's characterization of Dwight's paper as "the reservoir of every little bilious envy, of every irritating impertinence, of all sickly spleen which, under the form of anonymous correspondence, gives the writer the small comfort of injuring all those who give umbrage to their mediocrity."[1] For nearly a decade Moreau never missed an opportunity to savage the journal that had attacked him.

Scarcely had Moreau arrived in New York from France than *Dwight's* began finding fault with him.[2] First, *Dwight's* correspondent in New York ignored Moreau's debut concerts there. Then, when a Boston publisher issued one of Gottschalk's *Ossian* ballades, *Dwight's* wrote archly, "We shall see how much of Ossian there is in the young Creole's fancies."[3] Then, at the time of the first Boston concert, *Dwight's* groused about "the extravagant fame and the peculiar kind of enthusiasm which preceded the arrival of the New Orleans virtuoso, announced in the bills always as 'the great American pianist.' "[4] Finally, in its review of the Boston concert, the journal tore into Gottschalk's compositions with a vehemence never before seen on its pages:

> Some [of these pieces] we had heard from other players, and by their triviality were forced to feel that either these belied him, or that it was by sheer professional puffery that [Gottschalk] had been so long proclaimed the peer of Liszt and Thalberg and even Chopin; Gottschalk's *Bananiers* and *Danses Ossianiques* bear no more comparison [with the works of these composers] than the lightest magazine verses with the inspired lyrics of the great bards.

Dwight's acknowledged Gottschalk's playing to be "the most clear and crisp and beautiful that we have ever known." But then it once more attacked his compositions:

> Could a more trivial and insulting string of musical rigmarole have been offered to an audience of earnest music-lovers than *American Reminiscences* to begin with! These consisted of a thin and feeble preluding, . . . followed at last by fragmentary and odd *allusions* to *Old Folks at Home* and then by that homely tune, (which seems to be a sort of catching, melodic *itch* of the times) fully developed, and then varied in divers difficult and astounding ways. . . . also *O! Susanna* (if we remember rightly) in the same fashion.[5]

The heart of Dwight's attack fairly brimmed with Boston's own sense of cultural inferiority vis-à-vis Europe. Gottschalk's sins, Dwight charged, were that he refused to play the classics and that his own compositions quoted too generously from lowbrow American popular music of the day. Moreau was stunned by this unexpected assault, and especially the notion that a twenty-four-year-old American composer should perform not his own works but those of dead Europeans. To this moment he had lived in a world in which a repertoire by living composers was considered normal, in which audiences welcomed composers who performed their own works, and in which folk and popular themes often appeared in the concert hall, without giving rise to pretentious debates over whether or not they constituted Art. Now, in democratic America of all places, he was charged with disrespect for the past, with failure to bow down before the artistic throne of Europe, and with having insulted Boston by introducing popular and patriotic tunes into compositions he performed there.

Rather than get angry, Gottschalk got even. For the second Boston concert he had announced that he would play several more of his own compositions. At the actual performance, however, he substituted for one of his own announced pieces a "classical" work, probably a *Bagatelle* by Beethoven. *Dwight's* took the bait,[6] judging the American's creations to be far inferior to Chopin's mazurkas, let alone to pieces by the great Weber. Thus Moreau doubly humiliated *Dwight's*, which not only failed to identify the Beethoven piece but pronounced it inferior to works by a lesser master.

This juicy trick was not original with Gottschalk. Liszt had pulled the same stunt some years before, a fact well known to Gottschalk's teacher Charles Hallé.[7] Whatever its genealogy, the hoax passed unacknowledged, in the best tradition of practical joking. The closest Gottschalk came to admitting to it was a newspaper article in which he decried listeners who emote over a Beethoven symphony because someone instructed them that the author was great and the work sublime, but would fall asleep over the same symphony if they had not been so informed.[8] In spite of Gottschalk's silence at the time, word of the hoax spread, eventually reaching even a contributor to *Dwight's*, who related it in his memoirs.[9]

Aside from its entertainment value, why should this protracted feud between Gottschalk and a Boston critic still concern us? First, because this confrontation did more than anything else to make Gottschalk conscious of aspects of his own outlook that he had heretofore taken for granted. Second, the protracted conflict eventually touched on an extraordinary range of issues, among them the nature of art and music, the value of the European heritage in America, the role of cultural hierarchies in a democracy, and, above all, the character of American music and civilization.

Gottschalk's stance on such issues provides a key for positioning him among the conflicting cultural currents of his native country. It also reveals much about American life more broadly, since Gottschalk and Dwight represented a basic polarity that had emerged within the nation by 1853. To some extent, these rival ideals were symbolized by Boston and New Orleans, the home towns of the two contenders. But even by the 1850s each of these opposing perspectives had strong partisans elsewhere throughout the country. The struggle thus reveals the extent to which Victorian America had already ceased to be a cultural monolith, if ever it had been one.

John Sullivan Dwight, the founder of the journal that bore his name, was born in Boston in 1813, sixteen years before Gottschalk. He did not take up any musical instrument until age fifteen and remained throughout his life a weak amateur player of the flute and piano. The curriculum at Harvard had no place for music when Dwight studied there, nor was there one at the Divinity School to which Dwight shifted after completing his undergraduate studies. Dwight and his friends eventually changed all this when they founded the Harvard Musical Association. But the future "dictator of musical Boston" went to his grave with no formal training in music theory or composition. Nor could he have heard much classical music growing up, for in spite of the concerts mounted by the Handel and Haydn Society and a few other amateur groups, the range of European music performed in Boston before mid-century was limited, far narrower, for example, than in New Orleans, New York, or Philadelphia.

For all his professed love of music, young Dwight's deepest concern was to emancipate himself from the Protestant Christianity to which he had earlier intended to devote his life. He had abandoned strict Calvinism for Harvard's new Unitarian faith. But this failed to inspire him, and for all his good intentions, the aspiring pastor proved a dismal failure in the pulpit.[10]

The young minister's preaching career reached this pathetic end because he could not find in the highly intellectual Unitarian faith any of the emotional warmth he was seeking. Instead, he joined many other former Boston puritans who fled into the warm, lofty, and eminently safe world of German literature and philosophy.

When social reformer George Ripley approached him to translate a volume of Goethe's minor verse, Dwight eagerly accepted. Continuing his self-emancipation, Dwight abandoned the pulpit and joined Ripley and his wife when they set up Brook Farm. Here, not far from Boston, more than one hundred Unitarians, Transcendentalists, and other seekers after a new faith established a commune based (or so they thought) on the communitarian theories of the French utopian Charles Fourier.[11] Central to Fourier's program was the belief that human beings could fully liberate their passions—sexual as well as psychological—and yet maintain a spirit of community. Dwight stopped well short of this. But he resonated to Fourier's interest in music, and at Brook Farm he embraced this new calling.

Over several years, the former clergyman penned essays on music for the farm's weekly, *The Harbinger*, and devised pioneering programs of music education for children. But as he pursued this new cause, Dwight revealed in startling ways that he remained at heart a judgmental puritan. He set about fixing labels of Good or Evil on every work of music and behaving for all the world like one of those puritan divines on whom he had earlier turned his back.

Dwight founded his *Journal of Music* in 1852 in order to uplift the public. Those who sought enlightenment from Dwight were few, however. Under his editorship the number of subscribers never rose above one thousand and usually remained at five hundred.[12] In spite of this, *Dwight's* set a new standard in America for thoughtful if tendentious writing on music. Thanks to Dwight's generally high standards, he attracted contributions from many talented writers, including Alexander Wheelock Thayer, whose majestic biography of Beethoven later became a model for musical scholarship on both sides of the Atlantic. Dwight himself wrote insightful essays on Bach, Handel, and all those other German composers whom he accepted as part of the great canon.

At the heart of Dwight's view, and underlying his conflict with

Gottschalk, was the notion that music is "the language of natural religion,"[13] that it is "the highest outward symbol of what is the most deep and holy."[14] Starting with this view of music as "the Christian Art *par excellence*,"[15] he moved on to embrace music itself as a new religion. In Europe this attitude produced what Berlioz called "musical Protestantism" and contemptuously dismissed as "a cross-grained, jealous and intolerant worship."[16] In a New England still recovering from two centuries of Puritanism, this new faith revealed itself as narrow, self-righteous, and sectarian.

Under Dwight's influence this ersatz religion of music became thoroughly secularized. The goal was no longer to attain holiness through music but to achieve "culture."[17] To have bad taste in music was to commit a secular sin, and it rendered one not merely unholy but uncultured. Thus Dwight's new faith evolved finally into a kind of social bigotry.

What defined this faith? Christians had their Bible, but Dwight clutched his Beethoven.[18] Others, of course, had admired Beethoven. But to Dwight and those who would make of art something sacred, Beethoven's oeuvre was Holy Writ. When the Harvard Musical Association built Boston's Music Hall it furnished the stage with a large statue of Beethoven, as if to remind both audience and performer of the eternal standard against which each performance should be measured. Woe unto the concert artist who failed to perform Beethoven, and eternal damnation to anyone who treated the Master with disrespect.

Gottschalk sinned on both counts. True, his repertoire included the *Sonata pathetique* and several other works by the Master.[19] He even recommended to students that they practice several pages of Beethoven sonatas daily,[20] and he frequently entertained friends at home by playing those works.[21] Yet Gottschalk rarely programmed Beethoven in public. Worse, he stubbornly defended his decision to perform mainly his own music, arguing that when people bought a ticket to a reading by Thackeray they expected him to read his own novels, and not the works of Shakespeare.[22] "Besides," he said, "there are plenty of pianists who can play [classical] music as well or better than I, but none of them can play my music half as well as I can."[23] To cap it off, Gottschalk belittled Beethoven as a composer for the piano, arguing that the titan from Bonn had never grasped the piano's full potentialities and failed to write idiomatically for it. Never mind that as pro-Beethoven a pianist as Boston-born William Mason agreed with him on this point. In making it, Gottschalk had crossed the line to perdition.[24]

Once having erred, Gottschalk proceeded to fall ever deeper into heresy. For Dwight, the ideal performer would be an all-but-invisible person who merely transmits the Great Work to the audience. Such an artist would perform with no "show or effect," so that "the composition is before you, pure and clear, . . . as a musician hears it in his mind in reading it from notes."[25] The inevitable next step was for members of the audience to bring the score into the concert hall. In Dwight's Boston, score-reading became a mark of culture. Gottschalk loathed the practice. When he noticed a member of the audience following the printed music at a performance in Worcester, Massachusetts, he ranted that "of all the absurdities practiced by the Anglo-Saxon race in matters of art, this is what makes me suffer the most."[26]

Gottschalk, the romantic, assumed the uniqueness of each performer and performance. Dwight cleaved to the literal text, which he considered immutable. Dwight eventually found his ideal performer in the clinically precise German virtuoso Sigismund Thalberg. Revealing all his biases in one sentence, Dwight once described Thalberg as "a modest, quiet, self-possessed, well-bred, middle-aged English-looking gentleman, making his way across the stage as quietly as if he were the stillest retired scholar in the audience seeking his way to a seat."[27] This curious description makes it clear that for Dwight the ideal performer would look for all the world like a Protestant clergyman seated at the keyboard. The task of such a performer was simply to present faithfully the musical Scriptures and to live a life worthy of that calling. Whoever would instead impose his own interpretation on Beethoven or, worse, reject Beethoven in favor of his own compositions would be like the Catholic priest who denies his parishioners access to the Scriptures while adorning himself with costly robes and living a dissolute life.

In condemning all interpretation and virtuosity in music, Dwight adopted the arguments and even the language of New England's nineteenth-century crusade against Catholicism. He translated the prevalent denunciations of priestly vanity, neglect of Holy Writ, and popish decadence into the world of music. Whole paragraphs of Dwight's attacks on Gottschalk could have been interposed with little change onto the pages of Theophilus Fisk's nasty anti-Catholic tract *Priestcraft Unmasqued*, which was all the rage during Dwight's years at Harvard's Divinity School.[28]

Gottschalk responded to such dogmatism with arguments that were no less one-sided than Dwight's. While respecting the moral life, he acknowledged that an artist's private character may sometimes be "unworthy of the sentiments that his writings inspire."[29] Asked Gottschalk: "Should we reject the works of Poe because he was a drunkard, or Victor Hugo because he was no model of conjugal fidelity? Or Rembrandt because he was a miser?"[30] Absolutely not, Gottschalk claimed, for the artist lives through his work, even as he himself dies away.

Increasingly, Dwight became an embattled man. His conflicts with Gottschalk receded to the status of mere skirmishes in his larger war over how the American public chose to use its leisure. Americans at mid-century enjoyed more free time than ever before. To Dwight's disgust, most devoted it to enjoyments and pleasures of the most diverse sort. The newspapers listed whole columns of dances, while audiences flocked to the countless minstrel troupes that were touring the land. Dwight, who persisted in the Calvinist belief that most of humanity was by nature depraved, cast himself into the role of moral paragon holding back this flood of sybarites. His objective was simple: to reclaim free time from the morass of sensuality into which it had fallen and to rededicate it instead to the new god Culture. In other words, Dwight sought to sacralize the emerging world of leisure.[31]

Gottschalk saw Dwight's campaign as an effort to create a full week of Protestant Sundays. He opposed Dwight's effort to impose a single standard of taste and reveled instead in eclecticism, which he considered to embody the essence of the era. Knowing that reputable theaters might interrupt a dramatization of Sir Walter Scott's *Ivanhoe* with a boxing match—this actually occurred in Cincinnati[32]—he designed his programs to accommodate Americans' love of diversity and their fascination with unlikely contrasts. He would have accepted as praise the observation of a Toronto paper that he chose works that were "very diverse in their character, so that even the interest of the unlearned never flagged."[33] Making a full-blown doctrine of this, Gottschalk maintained:

> those whose taste is not eclectic have no more right to govern criticism than a man with a jaundice or green spectacles to decide upon the coloring of a picture. I admire the beautiful wherever I find it, never bothering myself to demand its passport.[34]

For Dwight, the "passport" of a work of music or of a performer provided a key to its character, with those originating in Northern Europe being at a decided advantage. It was the Dwightians of America who had embraced the chaste and pious Swede Jenny Lind during her celebrated tour.[35] In doing so, they implied that the purer North, epitomized by Lind, would save humanity from the sinful South, epitomized by Italian opera. Here again, Dwight transferred Protestantism's old war against Catholicism into the world of music, with the "spiritual" sounds of Lutheran Germany battling the libidinous wails of popish France or Italy.[36] As stated by Dwight's correspondent in Chicago, W. S. B. Mathews, "Italian opera is based rather upon sensual or intellectual appreciation than upon spiritual grounds."[37] New York prudes sought a court order to close down performances of *La Traviata* because they judged its libretto to be "lewd and licentious."[38] In Boston they tried to rewrite the ending of *Rigoletto.*[39]

Gottschalk, as a Southern Catholic who adored Italian opera, epitomized the enemy. Attacking him, Dwight struck a blow against all that Gottschalk stood for, as if he could thereby rescue Boston and all America from its slide into depravity. Back in New York, however, there was usually someone on the spot who was eager to strike back. Walt Whitman, for one, championed Italian opera as serving "the good old cause, the great idea, the progress and freedom of the race."[40] In Boston, by contrast, Gottschalk had to face the musical puritans alone. With no one else to defend him, he himself struck back furiously:

> Oh, the bogus *savans!* . . . Their intolerant and hypocritical devotion, the exclusive homage with which they vow to the great dead, are only a cloak beneath which they hide their own envious mediocrity. . . . Self-anointed hierarchs of taste, they find convenient shelter behind the names of two or three classic dead men. . . . Had I to choose between the art-indifferentism of the masses and the bogus enthusiasm of these pretentious fools, I would not hesitate one moment to accept the former, so great is my horror of the latter.[41]

Underlying Dwight's eagerness to uplift his fellow Americans was his belief that they had no real culture or music of their own. The typical American, he claimed,

> makes little music at home, or at most only on the Sabbath day. During the week his melodies are unheard. He does not go to his labors singing to himself along the road. Our people work in silence, like convicts in a Penitentiary.[42]

If America as a whole lay under a cultural shadow, the South represented inky blackness. Dwight claimed that the American South was incapable of producing "anything like Art or the love of it among a people semi-barbarous through willful rejection of the cornerstone of civilization, which is freedom."[43] To Dwight, African-Americans of the South were "the only musical population of this country." But even this qualified compliment was rich with condescension, for Dwight shared the prejudice of most correct-thinking Boston abolitionists that blacks were "the simple children of Africa" and were "inferior to the white race in reason and intellect."[44]

Dwight contrasted America's bleak cultural landscape to that of Germany. When a prominent Leipzig musical journal praised Dwight's sycophantic efforts, Dwight responded in words rich in idolatry and self-promotion, speaking of an emerging "Anglo-Saxon solidarity" in music.[45]

Had Gottschalk not existed, Dwight would have had to invent him, for he represented the precise antithesis of all his own views. Not only was Gottschalk Catholic, Southern, and pro-French, but he adored Italian opera and blithely incorporated into his compositions folk songs, African-American rhythms, and "claptrap" by Stephen Foster. Worst of all, more and more of his fellow citizens seemed eager to accept this decadence as quintessentially American! When a New York paper extolled "our own *American* pet, *Gottschalk* . . . the wonderful, electric, fascinating *Gottschalk*," Dwight asked: "Does not that beat all the high-falutin' puff you ever read?"[46]

Gottschalk's response to Dwight's Germanophilia and anti-Americanism was, to say the least, less than dignified, on the same low level as Chopin's remark that "these Germans are terrible people; they know nothing at all about music."[47] Yet Gottschalk was not alone in this view. His friend George F. Bristow once suggested that Dwight and company "pack back to Germany and enjoy the police and bayonets and aristocratic kicks and cuffs of that land, where an artist is a serf to a nobleman."[48] This was mild compared with Gottschalk's lunges for the jugular. Of the typical German musician in America he wrote:

> His hair is uncombed, as becomes all men of genius who respect themselves a little. He professes a particular esteem for beer, and seeks in it (without excluding other stimulants) his inspirations.[49]

Encountering a glasses-wearing German, he inquired

> whether the Germans who are to become musicians are born with little gold spectacles, just as others are born with a wart on the nose, or whether this parasite is developed and grows in proportion as they plunge into the depths of the science of harmony.[50]

Moving beyond Germans Gottschalk ranted incessantly against Anglo-Saxons in general, and especially their obtuseness with respect to music. In part these were the natural reactions of a Southerner to New England. Under Dwight's barbs, and probably goaded by unacknowledged feelings of hostility directed against his own Anglo-German father, Gottschalk descended to the same level of ethnic stereotyping as his opponent.

Looming over all the other differences that divided Gottschalk and John Sullivan Dwight were their opposing views on democracy. It is paradoxical that Moreau Gottschalk, the Paris-trained Catholic from New Orleans, should emerge as a champion of American democracy in a battle with John Sullivan Dwight, who held aloft the banner of Harvard, Boston, and Emerson.

Curiously, neither one had displayed any set opinions on this issue until their encounter in 1853. Gottschalk, of course, had observed the new "democracy" on the streets of Paris during the Revolution of 1848, but otherwise he had had neither intellectual nor practical experience with it. It was the controversy with Dwight that forced him to address the question of his political identity as an American. Dwight, during his Brook Farm years, had benign thoughts of reform, although without really doing anything about it. Only through his conflicts with Gottschalk and other musicians who courted acceptance by the American public did Dwight at last define his views on democracy.

Gottschalk's eclectic programming, with its frank appeal to the tastes of the democratic public, evoked Dwight's horror. Reports on the behavior of a youthful audience at a Philharmonic concert in New York triggered the deeper fears underlying Dwight's concern. The crowd had been large and voluble but quite unresponsive to a masterpiece by Beethoven. This led Dwight to charge that the Philharmonic pandered to the vulgar masses. Any institution taking so populist an approach, he claimed, was doomed. "It is better," Dwight concluded, "that only a few hundreds or ever so small a circle of persons in each large community learn to appreciate and love the masterworks of genius, than that none at all should."[51]

After studying more closely the lives of Handel and Haydn, Dwight came to realize that even in Germany there existed only an "appreciative few."[52] By such steps he lost all interest in a mass audience and came to reject democracy.[53] Here again Dwight, who had thrown Calvinism out the front door, welcomed it in at the back door in the form of a secularized doctrine of the Elect. Earlier, he had hoped a cultured elite would use its moral authority to exercise stewardship over the masses. Later, as a new generation of wealthy Boston manufacturers came to the fore, Dwight conceived the possibility of a new marriage of wealth (the industrialists') and virtue (his own).[54] This fusion of wealth and virtue gave rise to the ideal of the "Boston Brahmin" to whom the benighted American public was supposed to look for culture and enlightenment.

The link of money and culture was to prove a potent combination, for it provided a solid financial underpinning for Dwight's concept of a sacralized culture.[55] This new support freed at least a few musicians from the need to pay court to the vulgar (paying) public.

Is it any wonder that Gottschalk rejected all this? After all, he did not have the slightest prospect of benefiting from the largesse of the new Brahmins, who were safely in Dwight's anti-democratic camp. Moreau may have had good friends among the wealthy, but no rich businessman except old Jonas Chickering ever stepped forward as his patron. Lacking well-heeled backers, Gottschalk became a democrat as much by necessity as by choice. Over the years, however, he made a virtue of this necessity. More than any American musician before him, he consciously embraced democracy in the sphere of culture, as well as in government.

The final paradox of Moreau Gottschalk's confrontation with John Sullivan Dwight is that he eventually came to appreciate his opponent's views and even to some extent share them. Writing in 1861, he castigated those who composed or performed only for the market, and decried the tendency of public taste to descend to the lowest common denominator.[56] A few years later he inveighed against audiences who saw music merely as a "fashionable luxury." Writing for the mouthpiece of Boston Brahminism, the *Atlantic Monthly*, he even declaimed on music as "the privileged instrument of a moral and civilizing influence."[57]

For all this, Gottschalk stopped well short of Dwight's undemocratic notion of the Elect. Instead, he continued to hope that all people possess an innate sense of artistic excellence. But if such an inborn proclivity to culture exists, he believed that it was to be found "among the majority even of civilized men only in the state of germ or embryo. To be developed, [this aesthetic sense] has to be carefully cultivated; to be perfected it requires a special education."[58] It was on this basis that Gottschalk, like Dwight before him, eventually became an outspoken champion of public education.

Growing public acceptance of his own music even caused Gottschalk to soften some of his old ethnic and regional prejudices. As music-loving German immigrants came to comprise an ever larger part of his audience, he ceased his vitriolic fulminations against that people.[59] Angered by his younger brother Gaston's mindless Francophilia, Gottschalk came also to recognize the shallow, pleasure-seeking side of French life.

Wonder of wonders, Gottschalk even embraced Dwight's home town, Boston. By this time, in the early 1860s, Boston had long since embraced Gottschalk. Longfellow paid him court, and an admiring Oliver Wendell Holmes dined with him. As Gottschalk left Boston after a particularly warm visit in December 1864, he wrote

> Adieu, Boston! You are stiff, pedantic, exclusive (Mr. D. [i.e., Dwight] is its oracle)! Your enemies say that you are cold and morose. For myself, I say that you are intelligent, literary, polished. . . . Besides, I love pedantry and vanity when they engender such results as the great organ [at Musical Hall] and the bronze statue of Beethoven in the library.[60]

John Sullivan Dwight must have rolled his eyes in wonder.

Chapter Twelve

✖ An Untimely Visit to Cuba, 1854

W HEN Gottschalk embarked for Cuba on the American-flag steamer *Crescent City*, he left behind his Spanish-born valet, Ramón, now English-speaking and without the Andalusian costume that had helped him cut such a figure in Manhattan a year earlier. Besides the fact that it was silly for a starving pianist to be acting the part of a Parisian dandy, Gottschalk's rather exploitative arrangement with the nine-year old was bound to offend the sensibilities of Americans. Ramón's departure into the care of a New Orleans family was one of several signs marking the start of a new and more American phase of Gottschalk's life.

Boarding the *Crescent City* with Gottschalk was his brother Edward, now seventeen years old. Moreau looked on Edward as his auxiliary pianist and personal assistant and blithely assumed that Edward relished this role. But Edward saw himself as a student of the military arts and as a rising specialist on the navies of the world. In his bag was an account book in which he was supposed to have recorded the tour's finances. He filled it instead with sketches of ships at anchor and lists of warships of the European fleets, complete with the number of cannons carried by each.[1]

Edward, with his boyish enthusiasm for war, must have been delighted with what he learned of the story of their own ship, the *Crescent City*. Two years earlier, it was this ship the Spanish captain-general in Havana had seized during the saber rattling that led to the termination of Moreau's tour of Spain. Now this same vessel carried Gottschalk into the narrow entrance of Havana's harbor. It skirted the heavily armed Fort Cabaña on the right and, on the left, the looming Morro Castle, built atop a formidable rock and bristling with more cannon. Beyond lay the spot where Columbus landed (incongruously marked by a miniature temple), and finally the sixteenth century Plaza de Armas, at once smaller and more darkly oppressive than the similarly named square in New Orleans.

Gottschalk took all this in and noted also the yellow, green, red, and white houses beyond. Now, finally, he was in the tropics, the Caribbean world of which his native New Orleans was only the northernmost and increasingly Yankee-dominated outpost. Even the excruciating torture inflicted by Spanish customs clerks barely fazed him. He knew that at this moment Havana ranked among the world's wealthiest cities and that touring musicians of every description had thrived there. Why should he not succeed in Havana as well? Queen Isabel II herself had provided him with a letter of introduction to her captain-general.[2] The Spanish monarch had also honored him with an imperial decoration, making him one of only 298 knights of the Crown in the entire New World.[3] Though he served as his own manager and promoter, Gottschalk could not have been better prepared to take the Cuban capital by storm.

But all these auspicious signs proved useless. Far from extending a warm welcome to the visiting American, official Havana held him at arm's length for a month. The reason was simple. Spain and the United States were again locked in conflict over Cuba, and this tension mounted nearly to an explosion during the very days following Gottschalk's landing on February 14.

The elements of this clash were the same as during Gottschalk's Spanish sojourn, only worse. Several weeks after Spain seized the *Crescent City* in September 1852, Franklin Pierce was elected president of the United States, having campaigned on a plank that included the annexation of Cuba. No sooner had Pierce appointed the New Orleans firebrand Pierre Soulé as minister in Madrid than Soulé began issuing provocative threats against Spain and then an ultimatum demanding the release of the *Crescent City*.[4] As tactless as he was self-confident, Soulé tried to persuade Pierce that the United States should simply buy Cuba. To ensure that Queen Isabel would be willing to sell, Soulé applied pressure on her through her arch-enemies, the Spanish liberals. This tactic backfired. By the summer of 1853 it was clear that Isabel would not sell. Soulé therefore switched course and issued blunt calls for a revolution in Cuba, to be led by Cuban planters hostile to Spain and with armed support from American filibusters. In July President Pierce personally recruited one John Quitman, a Southern adventurer, to organize an armed force to carry out Soulé's scheme.[5]

Gottschalk would have followed the American minister's wild projects with the interest of a personal friend. During his months in New Orleans, Gottschalk could scarcely have missed seeing the highly visible efforts by Quitman's agents to recruit and train four thousand troops to be sent to conquer the island.[6]

Spain viewed with alarm these efforts to seize her last remaining possession in the Americas. The situation of Isabel's government was the more grave because it faced not one but three enemies: first, the North Americans who wanted to annex Cuba; second, the Cuban sugar planters who championed this goal as a way to protect the system of slavery on which their prosperity was based; and third, Great Britain, which had freed the slaves in its own Caribbean colonies and was now eager to spread emancipation to Cuba in order to drive up the cost of producing sugar on that island and thereby render British sugar competitive once more.

Confronted by these forces, Isabel's government took extreme measures. It abolished the slave trade and freed all slaves imported to Cuba after 1835. In a step which Cuban planters promptly branded "Africanization," it also permitted intermarriage between the races and allowed the importation of free black labor to Cuba. With these bold strokes Madrid put Cuba's arrogant planters on the defensive and transformed Great Britain from an enemy to an ally in Spain's effort to keep Cuba out of the clutches of the United States.

To implement these laws, Isabel named a tough new captain-general, the Marques Juan de la Pezuela, who was installed at the palace on the Plaza de Armas on December 3, 1853.[7] This military man was determined to demonstrate that Spain would no longer allow herself to be pushed around by the North American colossus. With no regard for subtlety, Pezuela seized another American steamer, the *Black Warrior*, on the trumped-up grounds that its captain had misrepresented its cargo on the manifest he submitted to Spanish customs agents in Havana.[8] Pezuela played this risky card just twelve days after Gottschalk's arrival in Havana.

Amidst such provocations and counter-provocations, it is no wonder that the captain-general was in no mood to welcome a twenty-five-year-old touring pianist, even if he came armed with a Spanish knighthood and a letter of introduction from the Queen. Indeed, one must wonder what prompted the young New Orleanian to make a trip to Cuba at the precise moment when the press of the Crescent City was screaming for the annexation of the island; when buildings throughout New Orleans were plastered with posters recruiting volunteers to carry out that task; and when the Louisiana legislature was voting fiery resolutions attacking Pezuela as a tyrant.

In all this, Gottschalk demonstrated a remarkable indifference, if not obtuseness, toward political realities. Surely, he had no grounds for surprise when Pezuela forced him to cool his heels in Havana. Yet in Gottschalk's defense, one might note that in the 1850s it was not as clear as in our century that art must submit to the demands of politics.

Gottschalk, at any rate, acted as if music were above politics, or at least separate from them. And within two months the captain-general dropped his opposition and allowed the young American to perform in public.

During long hours on the voyage from New Orleans, Moreau and Edward had gotten to know a tall, red-bearded Italian fellow passenger, the Count de Cassato, and his traveling companion, Count de Malaperta, two aging cronies who were touring the world for culture and pleasure. As Italians, the counts naturally were interested in music. Disembarking in Havana, they wasted no time in finding a piano in order to hear their young friend play.[9] They found their way to the narrow Calle Obrapía and followed it west five blocks to a music emporium owned by the Edelmann family.

Whatever impression Gottschalk made on the genial Italians, he stunned Carlos Edelmann, one of the store's proprietors, and the several other onlookers who wandered in while he was playing.[10] Edelmann, himself an accomplished pianist, promptly arranged an informal soirée for his North American guest on the following evening, to which he invited several dozen local pianists and enthusiasts. To ensure that his unexpected catch did not slip into the hands of rival music dealers, of which there were several, Edelmann also offered the Gottschalk brothers lodging in a third-floor apartment above the shop's second building at the corner of Calle Aguiar.[11] Gottschalk declined, however, taking rooms instead with a Miss Laffenandine at the high price of two dollars a day.[12]

The speed and adroitness with which Carlos Edelmann brought Gottschalk under his entrepreneurial wing says much about the dynamic musical life of the Cuban capital. That there was any cultural life there at all may seem surprising, for Cuba in 1854 was virtually under military dictatorship. All political decisions flowed from the captain-general and, ultimately, the throne. Official actions were backed by a garrison twice the size of the entire United States army at the time.[13] Since the government owned the major newspapers, its control over the press was absolute. The Catholic faith was compulsory for residents and newcomers alike. And censorship was so thorough that the word *liberta* in Bellini's *I Puritani* was replaced with the woman's name *Lealta*.[14]

These draconian measures were intended to assure that the Cuban planter-grandees entertained no frivolous thoughts of independence from Spain and that their 375,000 slaves also stayed safely in line. It mattered little that such a regime stifled literature and other writing.[15] The goal of this harsh system was to maintain control, not to nurture a tropical Athens.

Paradoxically, these very conditions fostered musical life in Havana, much the way similarly repressive politics had encouraged musical activity in Hapsburg Vienna. Music was "safe" and provided risk-free diversion and entertainment. The brothers Carlos and Ernesto Edelmann turned this paradox of despotism to their pecuniary advantage.

Other factors also worked to their benefit, notably the close cultural ties that existed between Havana and the Paris of Chopin and Liszt. French was the language of culture in the salons of old Havana, and French visitors could expect to be greeted with all the obsequies that are the mark of true provincialism. French culture in fact served as an anti-dote to the severity of Spanish rule. The Havanese elite made regular pilgrimages to Paris, whence they brought back whatever tastes reigned in the French capital. The piano being the centerpiece of salon life in the Faubourg Saint-Germain, it naturally assumed the same status in Havana. The Edelmanns served this cult of musical Francophilia as dutiful sex-tons and benefited richly.

The ease with which the brothers Edelmann assembled the musical elite of Havana to hear Gottschalk reflects the intimacy of that city of narrow streets and the village-like atmosphere that coexisted with these cosmopolitan dreams. Still more, it attests to the Edelmanns' personal authority in Havana's musical world. They held court in the ground-floor room of their shop at No. 12 Obrapía, between Calle de Cuba and San Ignacio. Book-lined walls and traditional Havanese stained glass in the transom windows made it seem less a hall of commerce than a private salon. The fact that Mozart had had words of praise for the Edelmanns' grandfather, a Strasbourg musician guillotined during the French Revolu-tion, only heightened the family's standing, as did the fact that the father of Carlos and Ernesto, the Paris Conservatoire–trained Juan Federico (born Johann Friedrich, 1795–1848), had taught several of the most tal-ented pianists who assembled for Gottschalk's soirée.[16]

The impromptu recital at Edelmann's passed splendidly, with Gottschalk being nearly asphyxiated by the enthusiastic crowd.[17] The contrast with his reception in Boston was dramatic. There, non-musicians had brought to bear a ponderous moralism, while here skilled performers pursued music simply for the joy of it. There the emphasis had been on criticism, here on appreciation. In Boston individualism prevailed. At the Edelmanns' the arrival of new talent was welcomed as a gain for the entire group.

Probably no other city in the hemisphere could boast so many first-rate pianists as Havana. Together, these Cuban pianists constituted a kind of fraternity or mutual admiration society. Gottschalk felt at home in their milieu and was in turn accepted as a full member of the lodge. Cuban writers who have chronicled the story of their island's music are right to treat Gottschalk as one of their own, a full participant in, and contributor to, the national culture.[18]

Among the nearly two-score pianists associated with Gottschalk in Cuba, one stood out for his cosmopolitan talent, brooding eccentricity, and intimacy with Gottschalk: Nicolás Ruiz Espadero (1832–90).[19] Their first meeting was as unusual as their friendship. Carlos Edelmann was walking with his American guest along the Calle de Obisbo when they passed a music store owned by a Spaniard named Maristany. Stopping out front, Gottschalk was stunned to hear someone inside playing his own music brilliantly. When Gottschalk asked who it was, Edelmann replied, "Espadero!"

Edelmann and Gottschalk entered the store and approached the pianist. "Do you know who this gentlemen is?" asked Edelmann. Espadero, who had never seen a picture of the American and did not realize he was in town, examined Edelmann's guest and calmly replied, "Gottschalk." After a frenzy of handshakes, Gottschalk sat at the piano and played his *Forest Glade*, to Espadero's delight.[20]

A print of Espadero dating from this period shows him as a keen-eyed young man with a neatly trimmed full beard. A somewhat later portrait preserved in the Museo de la Música in Havana shows a lean-faced man with wispy side whiskers and an intense but abstracted look. The latter reveals Espadero's strange personality more faithfully than the former. "His existence," wrote the musicologist Alejo Carpentier, "was a long romantic dream populated with distant images having very little to do with the realities right outside his own windows."[21]

An extreme introvert, Espadero had been educated entirely at the family's home at 854 Calle de Cuba. His father was a wealthy journalist and co-founder of *El Patriot Americana*, a liberal weekly that championed freedom of the press, the abolition of slavery, and democracy. The elder Espadero wanted his son to pursue a career in law or the civil service rather than music. Espadero's mother, the daughter of a wealthy Spanish officer, spent dreamy hours at the piano and did not object when her son Nicolás put a blanket over the instrument so he could play beyond the strict time limits laid down by his father.

Only with the death of the elder Espadero was the sixteen-year-old able to pursue his true vocation. Henceforth, Nicolás lived through music. He became a recluse in his family home, where he survived for forty years with little but a piano, paper for compositions, and cats beyond number. Relieved of financial pressure by a substantial inheritance, Espadero never took employment, taught only a few students, and rarely ventured beyond his house except to play on the pianos of local music dealers in the early evening hours, which is what he was doing when Gottschalk encountered him. Up to that day he had performed in public only once.

For all his reclusiveness, Espadero was anything but provincial. He had absorbed the music of Havana itself but recast it into the language of Chopin, Liszt, and Gottschalk. Espadero never left the island of Cuba, yet his compositions are the most "European" of his generation. Indeed, his colleagues viewed him as more French than Cuban. When Chopin's close friend Jules Fontana arrived in Havana, it was the young Espadero of all the Havana pianists who most sought him out and formed the most enduring friendship with him.[22] On both sides of the Atlantic Espadero was acknowledged as the most professional Cuban composer of his generation, and the most original in either Spain or Cuba in the nineteenth century. A confirmed romantic, he believed that feeling is everything in art, and form secondary.[23] The very titles of his compositions reflect this stress on feeling: *Tarantella furiosa*, *Vals satanico*, etc.

The friendship between Espadero and Gottschalk represented the attractions of opposite personalities. Yet as musicians they shared much in common, and each was to inspire the other to some of his finest works. No sooner had they met than Gottschalk recruited Espadero to appear with him in one of his public concerts. Within days he had also recruited Espadero's teacher, Fernando Aristi (1828–88). Born a year before Gottschalk, Aristi had studied piano with the elder Edelmann up to the time he was sent to Paris in 1842. There, unlike Gottschalk, he managed to get lessons directly from the haughty Kalkbrenner, with whom he studied until his return to Havana in 1848. It is quite possible that Aristi and Gottschalk actually met in Paris. Yet by 1853 their fates were diverging, for while Havana appreciated its own talents, it did not idolize them or even support them well. After his return, Aristi devoted himself mainly to teaching and hosting musical evenings at his home on Calle del Tulipán.[24]

The third pianist recruited by Gottschalk was the Cuban-born Pablo Desvernine (1823–1910). Like Aristi, Desvernine studied under the elder Edelmann, who prepared him for the inevitable pilgrimage to Paris and to Kalkbrenner's factory for aspiring virtuosos. Desvernine and Aristi were paired from the outset. Each had a French-born parent—Aristi's mother and Desvernine's father—and they were often invited to perform at the same Parisian salons. In 1846 they teamed up for a musical expedition to Spain, where, like Gottschalk four years later, they performed for Isabel II. Neither royal honors nor promises of future engagements in Europe ensued, however, so Desvernine returned to Cuba.

Some years later Desvernine was to move to New York, where he had relatives on his mother's side. There he attracted a host of pupils and entered the musical history of the United States as the teacher of the composer Edward MacDowell. At the time Gottschalk met him, Desvernine was living quietly in Havana composing operatic fantasies, serving as organist in the church of San Felipe, and contributing to literary and musical journals.[25] His close friend was the Cuban romantic poet Rafael María Mendive (1821–86), whom Longfellow had translated.[26] Through Desvernine Gottschalk also met Mendive, who penned a poem in his honor and who for many years was to remain one of his most appreciative admirers in Cuba.

The day after Gottschalk arrived on the *Crescent City*, the French violin prodigy Paul Julien gave a major concert in Havana.[27] Two weeks later the local press was still reporting coyly:

> All the "officianados" are wondering when Gottschalk will start his concerts. All we know is that right now he is looking for a place to perform. Unfortunately, he cannot use any of our theaters because of obvious reasons.[28]

Closed out by international politics from the major halls, Gottschalk confined himself to appearances at local salons. The most important of these was hosted by Onofre Morejón y Arango, secretary of the Liceo Artístico y Literario de La Habana, a high-toned organization where Havana's cultured bourgeoisie could gain respite from the city's ceaseless socializing.[29] The Liceo's home near the Plaza de Armas was small, but Gottschalk could appear there without causing an international incident and could even charge admission. The date was set for March 13, 1854.[30] Gottschalk announced that Desvernine and Aristi would join him for the event, as would the violinist Silvano Boudet (1828–63), a composer from Santiago de Cuba specializing in masses and dance music.[31]

Gottschalk's program opened with him and Desvernine galloping through the fantasy *Jérusalem* and ended with Gottschalk's own *Carnival of Venice*. It was a safe beginning, the only surprises—and very important ones—being a set of variations on Stephen Foster's *Old Folks at Home* and an impromptu, "composed expressly for tonight," on the Cuban popular song *El Cocoyé*.[32] The "massive audience" responded with "fierce" applause, endless curtain calls, and standing ovations. The press—Pezuela's official press—outdid itself in the extravagant metaphors it conjured up to praise the North American artist. "His left hand is outrageous," wrote one paper:

> When playing fast, his fingers seem to be motivated by electricity. It is as if they were provided with double fingertips made of iron, allowing him to produce strong sounds, like waves hitting each other. At other times, they produce soft quiet dulcet sounds like those of the tranquil sea or a softly running stream.[33]

Behind all the rhetorical flourishes, one understands that the audience was duly impressed by the virtuosity of this "Paganini of the piano" but more deeply moved by his ability to evoke specific images and convey narratives through music. Rafael Mendive appreciated this when he published an ode *To Goltschalk (sic)* the next day.[34] The Havana public had found something refreshingly different in Gottschalk and rushed to buy the engraving of him (shown with neither of his later trademarks, mustache and droopy eyelids) published in the leading cultural journal.

The one piece that "stole the audience's heart" and produced a standing ovation at the Liceo concert was Gottschalk's impromptu on *El Cocoyé*.[35] And no wonder, for *El Cocoyé* was far and away the most popular melody among all segments of the Cuban population during the middle of the nineteenth century. The tune originated among the Afro-Cuban carnival organizations of Santiago de Cuba and was thought to have been brought there from Saint-Domingue.[36] In the 1830s a Spanish regimental bandsman, José Casamitjana, picked up the tune from the mulatto singer María de la O and arranged it for his Cataluña Regiment band. Soon it was to be heard at Santiago's fashionable Café La Venus. By 1847 Laureano Fuentes, leader of a popular dance orchestra, rearranged it and published it as part of a *Potpourri cubano*. Several composers also arranged it as a *contradanza* for piano, among them Pablo Desvernine, whose *El Cucuyé (sic)*, published by Edelmann, was almost certainly the source of Gottschalk's inspiration.

In his characteristic fashion, Gottschalk not only took over this beloved melody but recomposed it. In the process he created a ferociously demanding virtuoso piece, varied in content and compact in structure.[37] Just as he had done in his *Bamboula*, Gottschalk began his *Cocoyé* with a drum beat in the bass, a bow to the Afro-Cuban folk origin of the tune. After this almost violent cadence, he plunged into the melody, accompanying it with a "*de*-dum-de-*dum*-dum" syncopation that anticipates ragtime, rather than with the more sedate Havana ("habanera") rhythm ("*dum*-de-*dum*-dum") later used by Bizet in *Carmen*. Two further themes followed, both based on folk melodies, and each more gentle than the one before. By the time Gottschalk launched into the rousing coda the Liceo audience was on its feet.

With *El Cocoyé* Gottschalk synthesized the spirit of Saint-Domingue and the earthy street festivals of Santiago de Cuba with the disciplined virtuosity revered at the Liceo. More than any composer before him, Gottschalk in *El Cocoyé* brought together the island's popular and high cultures, and the Cubans loved it.

The swelling demand for a second concert posed the same diplomatic problems that had forced the first to take place at the Liceo rather than at a more commodious hall. This time luck favored Gottschalk. Three days after the Liceo concert Captain-General Pezuela released the *Black Warrior*.[38] Immediately after this the official press announced a second concert by the "incredible pianist," to be held at the Teatro de Villanueva on March 25.[39] This was a crudely built round structure perfect for the Havana circus, which regularly performed there, but miserable for concerts. Touring Spanish light opera *(zarzuela)* companies used it because the rent was cheap. For solo artists the Villanueva was pure punishment. It rained the night of Gottschalk's appearance, which made matters still worse, yet the hall was nearly full. *El Cocoyé* was again heard, as was *Le Bananier*, which the Havana public recognized as similar in spirit. A *Souvenir de la Luisiane* caused little notice, but the Havanese went crazy over the *Siege of Saragossa*, played by an army of ten pianists, including Aristi, Desvernine, Espadero, Carlos Edelmann, and brother Edward.[40] What particularly struck the critics was the way Gottschalk interwove original pieces with Spanish national songs, as well as the passages in which the *Marcha real* and the *Jota aragonesa* were played simultaneously over the accompanying roar of simulated cannon fire. That the anthem was performed by a citizen of the United States, and a Southerner at that, did not hurt Gottschalk's popularity with members of the Spanish garrison in attendance.

Having twice proven himself before the Havana public, Gottschalk was now ready to assault the local Olympus, the Gran Teatro Tacón. This splendid opera theater had been erected in 1839 under the then captain-general, Miguel Tacón y Torrens, a true despot yet a city builder of genius, who adorned Havana with many public buildings and promenades. Money for the grand theater, with its five tiers of seats and enormous crystal chandelier, came from the fabulously corrupt Don Francisco Marty. Reputedly more wealthy than the king of Naples, Marty had built his fortune on the three pillars of slave trading, a royal monopoly on fishing in Cuba, and gambling houses. The aristocracy of Havana found this shady *parvenu* distasteful and at first refused to attend operas at his giant hall. In an act that must rank high in the annals of revenge, Marty simply locked the doors and over several weeks ordered his company to perform for himself and a handful of friends, who sat in solitary splendor. The public finally capitulated but Marty did not allow it to enter until all of the boxes had been booked for the season.[41]

This bizarre incident indicates the Havana public's keen taste for opera at the time of Gottschalk's visit. Marty's Tacón company was up to the challenge, and when it visited New York in 1850 it presented what were by general agreement the best performances ever seen in the United States. The Tacón was also a center of Havana's social life. The Paseo

Isabel II on which it stood had just been constructed as a twelve-block-long tropical version of a Parisian boulevard. Following the route of the old walls of Havana, this Paseo was the site of evening strolls and carriage rides by the wealthy in their graceful one-horse *volantes*. Immediately in front of the theater stood a statue of Gottschalk's patron, Isabel II, and a park in which the captain-general's band performed each evening in what local Creoles called the "poor man's opera." To succeed at the fourteen hundred seat Gran Teatro de Tacón was to succeed in all Cuba.[42]

Catholic Havana reveled in Sunday entertainments of all kinds, and when Gottschalk stepped before the forty-foot proscenium of the Tacón on Sunday, April 2, he looked out on a full house. By popular demand, he repeated his ten-piano version of the *Siege of Saragossa*, carefully remembering later to present each of his assisting pianists with a silver matchbox.[43] The pianist also programmed his flashy *Carnival of Venice* and a muscular eight-handed version of *William Tell*. Then, since this concert had been announced as Gottschalk's last in Cuba, he closed it with a three-part salute to the island.

First, he offered a newly composed *Adiós a Cuba*, described in the program as a "*capricho* on Cuban national airs."[44] It is a pity this work is lost, for the audience was so thrilled with it that it interrupted the performance several times with prolonged applause and shouts of "Bravo."[45] Evidently, *Adiós a Cuba* was a sustained improvisation building not only on Cuban tunes but on what Gottschalk described to a local journalist as "a potpourri of Cuban rhythms."[46] Unfortunately, the composer never chose to publish this work, and his usual shorthand manuscript was not among those that survived after his death.

El Cocoyé again brought down the house and prepared the audience for the third Cuban piece, which was a new composition based on the phenomenally popular song *María de la O*.[47] Long a fixture of Carnival celebrations in Santiago, the singer María de la O had acquired legendary fame throughout the island. Among the street processions in Havana's Carnival in 1853 had been a figure representing the renowned Afro-Cuban woman from Santiago, accompanied by several dozen masqued blacks, a brass band from the local garrison, and masqueraded horsemen. By the time Gottschalk picked up the tune, both María de la O and the melody celebrating her would have been known to every Cuban. Gottschalk's composition based on this melody is lost but, like *El Cocoyé*, it drew stormy applause from audiences across the island.

In later years Gottschalk was often the butt of criticism on account of his manager's habit of announcing multiple "farewell concerts" and then not leaving. But the Tacón concert was the genuine article for the simple

The funeral procession, Rio de Janeiro, 19 December 1869. *A Vida Fluminense,* 25 December 1869.

North America, South America, and Europe mourn the death of Gottschalk. *A Vida Fluminense,* 25 December 1869.

The grave of Gottschalk, Green Wood Cemetery, Brooklyn, New York. Fors, *Gottschalk.*

Gottschalk's wayward executor, Charles "Fast Charlie" Vezin of Philadelphia. Glover Collection.

Edward Gottschalk, father of the composer. Glover Collection.

518 Conti Street (left) in New Orleans, where Gottschalk lived 1834–42. The Historic New Orleans Collection.

House on Esplanade Avenue at Royal Street, New Orleans, where the Gottschalks lived, 1833–34. Photo by the author.

The Saint-Louis Hotel, where Moreau Gottschalk made his debut. Robert C. Reinders, *End of an Era*, New Orleans, 1964, no. 153.

Virtuoso Sigismund Thalberg at the time of Gottschalk's arrival in Paris. New York Public Library.

Portrait of Moreau by J. Berville, ca. 1843. Courtesy of Carmen D. Valentino.

Portrait of Aimée Bruslé Gottschalk, ca. 1847. Lilly Glover, New Jersey.

Three virtuosos: Gottschalk, Prudent, and "Listz," by Nadar. Reprinted in *La Nation Argentina*, 8 June 1867. Gottschalk Collection, New York Public Library.

Cartoon of Edward Gottschalk, Paris, 1851. Free Library of Philadelphia.

Jacques Offenbach, at the time he and Gottschalk were performing together, 1850. S. Kracauer, *Offenbach in Paris*, New York, 1938.

Home of Dr. Eugene Woillez, Clermont-sur-l'Oise, where Gottschalk wrote *Bamboula*. Dr. Claude Teillet, Société archéologique et historique, Clermont-sur-l'Oise.

à sa Majesté

ISABELLE II,

Reine des Espagnes.

BAMBOULA

Danse des Negres.

Fantaisie

POUR

PIANO

PAR

L.M. GOTTSCHALK,

de la Louisiane.

A.V.

Op: 2.   Prix: 9.!

Paris, Editeur, LÉON ESCUDIER, rue de Choiseul, 21

Title page to first Paris edition of *Bamboula*. Collection of the author.

Moreau Gottschalk in Paris, 1852. Offergeld Collection.

Print of Gottschalk in 1850 by Eugène Battaille. Free Library of Philadelphia.

Broadway in the season of
Gottschalk's arrival. New-York
Historical Society.

Niblo's Saloon in 1853. *Gleason's
Pictorial Drawing-Room Companion*, 1853, Offergeld Collection.

Moreau Gottschalk in New York, 1853. Free
Library of Philadelphia.

Richard Hoffman, Gottschalk's
assisting pianist and friend. New
York Public Library.

Print by Nagel & Weingärtner N.Y.

Gottschalk at the time of his New York debut, 1853. Gottschalk Collection,
New York Public Library.

John Sullivan Dwight, Gottschalk's nemesis. Harvard University Archives.

Gottschalk's confidant, Nicolás Ruiz Espadero. Museo de la Música, Havana.

Gran Teatro de Tacón, Havana. Samuel Hazard, *Cuba with Pen and Pencil*, Hartford, 1871, p. 61.

Manuel Saumell, composer of *contradanzas*. Museo de la Música, Havana.

Teatro Principal, Puerto Principe, Cuba, scene of several Gottschalk triumphs. Museo de la Música, Havana.

The Union Hotel, Saratoga Springs. *Frank Leslie's Illustrated Newspaper*, 28 May 1870.

Title Page to *The Last Hope*, subtitled "Religious Meditation." Collection of the author.

Edward Gottschalk, Jr., at the time of the Cuban tour. Glover Collection.

Cover page to *The Banjo*. Collection of the author.

Gottschalk's patron General José Antonio Páez of New Granada (Venezuela). Glover Collection.

George Henriques, Gottschalk's landlord and protector. Glover Collection.

Gottschalk at Saratoga Springs, 1855. Gottschalk Collection, New York Public Library.

Gottschalk with George Warren at Saratoga, 1864. Gottschalk Collection, New York Public Library.

Dodworth's Hall, New York. New-York Historical Society.

Gottschalk at Saratoga. Glover Collection.

Gottschalk and Adelina Patti in New York,
January, 1857. Gottschalk Collection,
New York Public Library.

Anna de la Grange in 1856. New York Public Library.

reason that the artist, acting as his own manager, had failed to land any further bookings. The ever hospitable Onofre de Marejon extended an invitation to play at his fashionable soirées,[48] but they were no substitute for paying concerts, especially when money had to be forwarded monthly to Paris and when bills at Miss Laffenandine's boarding house were mounting. In spite of the public's enthusiasm at all three of his Havana concerts, Gottschalk had by now realized that the paying public's first love was opera, not piano music, and that for all the city's fabulous wealth, its concert-goers were unwilling to spend much money unless something truly sensational was offered. P. T. Barnum had learned this to his regret, when the Havanese attacked him as a "Yankee pirate" for over-pricing the tickets to Jenny Lind's concerts at the Tacón. Barnum's reply to those complainers was "that there was not enough money on the is-land of Cuba to induce me to consent to it."[49]

Added to this was the onset of Lent, which for forty days gave the entire island of Cuba a solemnity comparable to Sunday in Boston. As if this were not enough, during the month of April the Quitman expedition was preparing to launch its invasion from New Orleans.[50] A sympathetic Cuban wrote a poem to Gottschalk declaring:

> Our nations are enemies
> For high political reasons,
> Though we were friends earlier.
> Why must our hearts be this way? . . .
> More than your friend, I am your brother.[51]

Even with such allies, the idea of touring in the interior at this moment was problematic due to mounting instability there. As part of his policy of Afri-canization, Captain General Pezuela was organizing freed slaves into militia units and setting up free schools for the liberated children of slaves, even though similar schools had never been provided for whites. When violence broke out, Pezuela's government forbade whites to bear arms.

Gottschalk and his brother had no choice but to hang around Havana. Moreau caught up on his correspondence and played a few small-scale concerts in the ballroom at the nearby town of La Regla, as well as a benefit at the Liceo for the violinist Silvano Boudet, soon to depart for Paris.[52] In addition to repeating the Cuban works from the Tacón concert, Gottschalk introduced at the Boudet benefit a new piece, *El Deseo*, de-scribed as a "zapateo Cubano."[53] Immediately after these events the com-poser probably made an unpublicized trip to the Western tobacco-growing region of Vuelta de Abajos, for he returned with a *Recuerdo de la Vuelta de Abajo*, now lost, which included several more Cuban songs and a dance, the *zapateado*.[54]

For several weeks after this, Gottschalk vanished from the pages of the Cuban press, probably a reflection of the captain-general's hardened line. Only on May 20 did Gottschalk surface again, this time with an announcement in the *Diario de la Marina* that he intended to sell his Pleyel piano and depart forthwith for Europe![55] It mattered little that the Cuban press again began printing poetic tributes to the visiting virtuoso, or that a portrait bust of him was being exhibited in the capital.[56] Gottschalk was nearly broke.

On May 8 the political crisis began to lift. President Pierce, having fanned the flames of annexation, suddenly pulled back, claiming now to prefer that the island be bought rather than conquered by arms. Isabel II, sensing that the main effect of Pezuela's efforts so far was to expand the number of Cuban planters seeking U.S. statehood, recalled her captain-general. Just at this moment Gottschalk received an invitation from the Philharmonic Society (Sociédad Filarmónica) in the booming port city of Matanzas.

Situated just over fifty miles east of Havana, Matanzas in the 1850s was Cuba's second city in terms of commerce and wealth.[57] Ringed by hills to the south and picturesquely situated between the San Juan and Yumurí rivers, Matanzas was very compact except for the new "Versailles" district of mansions near the railroad station. Until recently its social life had been dominated by French, British, and American residents, many of them sugar planters or entrepreneurs. Now the Spanish and Creole element was coming to the fore. These people dominated the local Philharmonic Society and were eager to welcome any artist who had been well-received by their rival city, Havana.

Whether because Gottschalk had no manager or because the Matanzans were inefficient, planning for the concert was a mess. Havana papers reported on plans for two or three concerts to be offered early in May.[58] Each fell through. Not until May 21 did the first one take place.[59]

As if settling in for a full series, Gottschalk carefully recruited local talent, this time an extraordinary eighteen-year-old mulatto violinist named José White.[60] That Matanzas had nurtured this virtuoso says much about the town, as does the fact that until Gottschalk's arrival White was virtually unknown beyond the banks of the Yumurí. Gottschalk helped send the young man to the Paris Conservatoire, where in quick order he won first prize and earned warm praise from Rossini.[61] Fifteen years later White was appointed director of the Imperial Conservatory in Rio de Janeiro and was able to thank his old sponsor personally when Gottschalk arrived in Brazil.

Not even the combined virtuosity of White and Gottschalk moved the Matanzans, however. The frustrated reviewer for *La Aurora del Yumurí* bemoaned his townspeople's lack of interest in the classical program offered that night and their obvious preference for "trained dog shows and monkeys."[62] He might also have pointed to the ads for Barnum's "Swiss [actually English] Bell-Ringers," who outdrew Gottschalk. Or he might have noted the excitement surrounding the appearance in Matanzas of the Zarzuela de Robreño company, which proffered one-act programs from Spain mixing light operetta and vaudeville. Gottschalk and White's program mixing chamber music and European light classics could not hold a candle to this.

Yet if the Matanzans were cool to what they considered "serious" music from Northern Europe, they were by no means indifferent to music as such. Their Philharmonic Society dated from 1829,[63] and at the time of Gottschalk's visit the wealthy Dr. Ambrosio Sauto was collecting money to build one of the finest opera theaters in the New World. The problem was that Matanzans considered piano fantasies based on *William Tell* or *Carnival of Venice* to be alien works. Italian opera was closer to their taste, but closer still was the home-grown dance music to be heard almost nightly at the many balls held in the city. Indeed, the fundamental activity of the Philharmonic Society was not to enlighten the public with works by foreign masters but to organize these balls.[64] It was thus a mark of respect for Matanzans to organize a grand dance in Gottschalk's honor and also to hold an improvised ball on the deck of the Spanish warship *Isabel II*.[65]

All Cuba shared this passion for dancing and for the enchanting music it inspired. No visitor to Cuba failed to note this, some with delight, others with disgust. During his several visits to Cuba Gottschalk experienced directly this love of dancing and formed close ties with many of the artists who wrote the most popular dance music. It was inevitable that Cuban dance music left its mark on many of his compositions, as it must also have influenced his style of performance.

In broadest perspective, the nineteenth-century mania for social dancing was common to the entire Caribbean, as well as to New Orleans and large sections of South America. Dancing tied these regions into a single cultural zone. Cuban dancers seized upon every new step emanating from Europe, whether the waltz, polka, lancers, schottische, or quadrille. They also enjoyed home-grown dances such as the rustic *zapateo* or *zapateado*. However, one dance took hold in the 1820s and gained such absolute hegemony for a generation that it left an indelible stamp on Cuban music as a whole. This was the *contradanza*. Originally the humble English "country dance" and gallicized to the more noble *contredanse*, this square dance for two couples reached Cuba via Spain. Each *contradanza* consisted of two repeated strains, making four dance segments, the moods of which shifted back and forth from elegant formality to the most sensuous lyricism. The figures had been imported from Paris and Madrid, but once in the Caribbean they had been transformed by dancers of all races and classes.[66]

An English visitor to one of the more proper balls found the local *contradanza* to be "unrivaled for its grace and elegance anywhere."[67] Had this tourist, Sir James E. Alexander, visited one of the many public dance halls he would surely have added "sensuousness." The rhythms of the Cuban *contradanza* exuded sensuousness. In early years the most common form was either the *habanera* or a smoother variant, "*de*-de-de-*dum*-dum."[68] As the dancing grew more vivacious, the music incorporated Afro-Caribbean syncopation in the form used by Gottschalk in *El Cocoyé*. The result was a remarkable synthesis, in which general European, Spanish, and Afro-Cuban elements merged into a new form far richer than any of its composite parts.

In the decade before Gottschalk's arrival, a veritable *contradanza* industry arose in Cuba. The Edelmann firm published hundreds of *contra-danzas* whose topical titles celebrated every political event of the day.[69] There were pro-U.S.-statehood pieces like *La Filabustera* or *Viva Lopez* and anti-statehood works like *Viva Cuba!*. They appeared in prodigious numbers and defined a main current of Cuban music for several generations.

The performance of *contradanzas* at balls held in private homes or public halls provided a steady source of income for the pianists of Havana. Gottschalk's highbrow friends Aristi, Desvernine, and Espadero were not too proud to compose brilliant *contradanzas*, as did many others, including the gifted Afro-Cuban musician Tomás Buelta y Flores. Over the years virtually every major Cuban composer was to dedicate at least one *contradanza* to Gottschalk. Luigi Arditi, a broad-gauged composer of orchestral works and operas, dedicated no fewer than six to his "fellow artists in general and to a well-known one who is among us in particular."[70] Gottschalk, in turn, composed at least seven *contradanzas*, dedicating them to his pianist-composer friends. New ones are still turning up in Cuban archives.[71]

There was but one absolute master of the island's *contradanza*, the self-effacing Manuel Saumell (1817–70), who could rightly be called the Schubert of Cuba.[72] It was Saumell above all who introduced Gottschalk to the elegant and sensuous subtleties of the *contradanza*. And it is Saumell who stands at the head of the genealogy of lyrical, syncopated music that extends through Gottschalk to a host of late-nineteenth-century Cuban masters and thence to Scott Joplin, Jelly Roll Morton, Artie Matthews, and other creators of American ragtime. We may smile when the Cuban writer Natalio Galan compares the meeting of Saumell and Gottschalk with the meeting of Socrates and Plato or of Buxtehüde and Bach, but he at least appreciated the significance of the moment.[73]

Lanky, balding, and wearing mutton-chop whiskers, Saumell was anything but imposing. But for years he was the one member of the Liceo who could always be called upon at the last moment to arrange a program or accompany a singer. Unlike the wealthy Espadero, Saumell had to earn a living, which he did by playing piano at the many dances the elite of Havana held in their homes. In his mild way Saumell aspired to more. He played Beethoven trios with gusto, performed on cello and organ as well as piano, and composed chamber music of considerable charm. In 1839, just three years after the Russian Mikhail Glinka wrote his pioneering "national" opera, *A Life for the Tsar*, Saumell penned a true Cuban opera, *Antonelli*, the first national work composed in the Americas. Unfortunately, local impresarios merely yawned at the thought of an opera on sixteenth-century Cuba. So *Antonelli* was never performed.

Groping for a path between his aspirations and necessity, Saumell turned to composing *contradanzas*. Like Schubert with his songs, Saumell produced them by the dozen, dedicating *contradanzas* to his friends and to such visiting piano luminaries as Henri Herz from Paris, Maurice Strakosch from New York, and Jules Fontana from Warsaw. To Gottschalk he dedicated *La Luisiana*, one of his best, *Dice que no*, and later a *Recuerdos de Gottschalk*.[74]

Saumell's *contradanzas* are gems in miniature. Adhering strictly to the two-part form, they span a broad emotional range, from the martial to the coquettish, from the nostalgic to the earthy. In their lyricism and utter simplicity the Saumell *contradanzas* evoke the mood of the best Viennese country dances. At the same time, anyone who has ever enjoyed a rag by Scott Joplin will immediately sense the many ways in which Saumell anticipated the great composer from Texarkana. The Saumell-Joplin link may be direct, via Gottschalk, or through later Cuban composers, whose works filtered into the United States in original form or through Mexican or North American copies. Whatever the route, it is undeniable that many chord progressions, bass lines, and even melodic devices employed by Saumell and Gottschalk recur later in Joplin's music.

It is above all in his use of syncopation that Saumell anticipated American ragtime. Gottschalk, of course, had long since used the Afro-Caribbean *cinquillo* in his Creole pieces, the "*de*-dum-de-*dum*-dum" syncopation heard in *Bamboula*. From Saumell he gained a more subtle use of syncopation and a new appreciation of the virtues of simplicity. *El Cocoyé* was a show-off piece, the kind of work Liszt might have written had he been Creole instead of Hungarian. In most of Gottschalk's many subsequent works from the Antilles he muted his natural urge toward virtuosity, with the result that a more subtle and emotionally textured spirit could prevail. Perhaps this shift reflects merely the inevitable seduction by Caribbean languor of an ambitious North American. But it surely owes a debt to the gentle, syncopated lyricism of the Cuban *contradanza* and to the master of that form, Manuel Saumell.

Toasted, feted, but poorly remunerated, Gottschalk left Matanzas for Cárdenas, the rival port city twenty-five miles to the east. Called "the American City," Cárdenas prospered from the huge sugar plantations inland from it and reflected the tastes of the American merchants who dominated the town. When a Yankee artist from Connecticut came through in search of tropical exotica he concluded: "I can not, at this moment, recollect any one inducement to the traveler to visit [Cárdenas], unless he is in the sugar and molasses line."[75] Gottschalk loved the town, however, later calling it "a charming city whose memory is connected to the best recollections of my trip to Cuba."[76]

Gottschalk performed in Cárdenas, but the visit as a whole was more social than artistic.[77] In fact, this was the direction his whole expedition was taking. Back in Havana by the end of May, he plunged into more socializing. The visiting Admiral Duquesne held a dinner in his honor, at which this dignitary quizzed the American on the danger of Indian raids in St. Louis.[78] Gottschalk himself announced a concert at which he intended to give a present to the incoming governor-general. Instead he suddenly disappeared, unaccountably racing across the island to visit the town of Güines.[79] Returning to Havana, he again announced his farewell concert and again left town, this time to the lovely hill town of Trinidad on the southern coast. When Moreau finally returned to Havana in early July the official press observed without a trace of irony that "in Trinidad Gottschalk was praised in spite of not presenting any concert there."[80] Then, having promised the Havanese a concert for six weeks and having also announced his intention of honoring the captain-general, the young American abruptly left town once more, this time for the eastern port town of Cienfuegos, with the intention of offering recitals "upon the request of the most important families in town."[81]

Why all this confusion? First, there was the fierce tropical heat. The *Gaceta de la Habana* doubted that Gottschalk would be "strong enough to wage victorious battle against the heat and the absence of many families who have left for the summer."[82] The sole purpose of the flight to Güines was to cool off. Second, as a manager, Gottschalk was a rank amateur. Following the European custom, he looked for patrons rather than contracts. He accepted hospitality in Trinidad (possibly at the home of a wealthy American resident named Baker) but returned when he got no bookings with "sufficient remuneration."[83] Third, Gottschalk was again broke and whatever progress he had made in paying off his father's debts, his family in Paris remained destitute. His mother was living by selling off her jewelry. By early autumn she was so far behind on her rent payments that some of her furniture would be claimed to meet the debt.[84] Learning of this, Moreau sent off nearly all of the 2,550 francs he had taken in at the Gran Tacón concert to help his mother in Paris.

Desperate, Gottschalk placed almost daily announcements in the *Diario de la Marina* suggesting that he might be willing to sell his magnificent Pleyel. He reminded readers that the instrument came "from one of the leading manufacturers in the world, who employs no fewer than 450 workers."[85] But there were no takers.

Having reached a professional impasse, Gottschalk commiserated with his friend Espadero and his cats. Espadero responded with a gently morose *contradanza*, which Edelmann published under the title *La Melancolia.*[86] Just at this moment the invitation arrived from Cienfuegos, 120 miles away on the southern coast. Gottschalk was offered a paying concert if he would agree to perform a second concert to benefit the local Charity Hospital.[87] With no alternative, he accepted at once.

By now his brother Edward had become a burden on Moreau. This good-natured teenager had appeared in only one concert, had been of no help whatsoever as manager-accountant, and, with his fragile health, was suffering from the heat. Before departing for Cienfuegos, Gottschalk therefore arranged for Edward to take passage aboard Captain Rollins's steamer *Isabel* via Key West and Charleston for Philadelphia, where he remained with his Myers cousins until his return to France in early 1857. As Moreau plunged into the sweltering Cuban interior, Edward was noting in his account book the name of a Parisian *eau de toilette* and the address of the New York importer where he could obtain it.[88]

In Cienfuegos Cubans finally opened to Gottschalk their pocketbooks as well as their hearts. The hall was packed long before the eight o'clock curtain and no one left before the last encore at eleven-thirty. Along with pieces he had popularized in Havana, the visitor performed his *The Banjo* (first version) and a new *Recuerdos de Cuba*, probably a development of his *Adiós a Cuba* from a month earlier.[89] The next day he performed again for the Philharmonic Society, which gave a luncheon that evolved into a dance that ran through the evening. Cienfuegos embraced Gottschalk and Gottschalk, as the Havana press rhapsodized, fell for Cienfuegos, "especially the feminine part."[90] When it was all over the young people of the town accompanied their guest to dockside, where he departed on the steamer *Tayaba*. Changing ships in Santa Cruz, he arrived in Santiago de Cuba on July 22, 1854.

In all his travels to date, Moreau Gottschalk had never encountered a place that touched his personal and musical identity more directly than Santiago. Guidebooks of the day noted Santiago's wealth, which derived from sugar, mahogany, the large copper mines nearby, and international trade. Tourists were charmed by its hilly streets rising from the bay, its ancient cathedral, and its shops, where Parisian goods could be bought more cheaply than in New York.[91] For Gottschalk, as he settled into the Commerce Hotel, Santiago presented very different features. Situated only 130 miles across the Windward Passage from Saint-Domingue, Santiago de Cuba had received a large contingent of émigrés fleeing the bloody revolution on that island. Some twenty-five thousand white, mulatto, and black refugees had poured in by 1808. Thanks to the agricultural skills of these newcomers, eastern Cuba's production of coffee, tobacco, and cotton soared, and the lucrative sugar industry came into being. They also brought their French language and Creole dialect, identical to what Gottschalk had learned at home.[92] Above all, the immigrants from Saint-Domingue brought their music and dances.

By coincidence, Gottschalk arrived at the very moment Santiago was throwing itself into its annual three-day festival, a religious event accompanied by an explosion of balls, wild street dancing, and madcap parades involving the entire population, both black and white. Since the local press had been crowing about Moreau for a week before he actually stepped off the ship *Almendares*, the Philharmonic Society had doubtlessly invited him to its ball on August 24.

On the same day as the ball Gottschalk encountered a rollicking street aggregation of Creole-speaking blacks who were to seize his imagination: the Tumba Francesa.[93] Founded by free black and mulatto refugees from Saint-Domingue, this informal ensemble came together on Sundays throughout the year to sing and dance to music produced on a variety of Afro-Caribbean drums of a type *(tumba francesa)* unique to Saint-Domingue. Some of the drums were so big that the players placed them sideways on the ground and sat astride them. Others were smaller and had bells on them. Traceable to the Bantus and Carabali of West Africa, these had evolved in Saint-Domingue and Santiago into the *boku* and other forms found nowhere else.

The music of the Tumba Francesa society derived mainly from old French and Spanish sources, but its members wrote their own tunes as well. *El Cocoyé* was their best-known melody, and the singer María de la O had actually been associated with the group. The dances, too, were

European *contradanzas*, quadrilles, polkas, and lancers, as filtered through steamy nights on the great sugar island to the east. The rhythms, however, showed the direct influence of the African *cinquillo*, the "*de*-dum-de-*dum*-dum" cadence that vitalizes and transforms any four-beat melody under which it is placed. And it was these rhythms that gave the group its characteristic sound.

Listening to the Tumba Francesa, Moreau Gottschalk arrived at the very heart of the musical culture that had inspired his compositions from childhood on. Quite by accident he had traced it backwards from the music of Louisiana's immigrants from Saint-Domingue to the *contradanzas* of Havana and Matanzas, and thence to its root source in the remarkable cultural synthesis that was Santiago. This contact was to add a fresh rhythmic vitality to his compositions and push them further in a direction that anticipated ragtime by half a century.

Gottschalk gave four concerts at the Teatro de Centro in Santiago, beginning on August 29. This time Gottschalk had provided the local press with old reviews from Spain, and the pre-concert build-up was excellent.[94] Moreover, the Philharmonic Society sponsored the concerts, and this organization had the reputation locally as a social club, certainly an advantage in Carnival season.[95]

On the eve of the first concert Gottschalk wrote a friend: "If I am not successful tomorrow I can blame only my lack of talent."[96] As usual, he had recruited local talent, this time the violinist and composer Laureano Fuentes and two blind pianists, Fedrico Jiraudy and Isidoro Garcia Meton.[97] Even though the performance had to compete with the lure of the Zarzuela de Robreño, it was a success. A local poet proclaimed to Gottschalk:

> Your fingers can make converts
> Of indifferent souls.
> Fame has granted you crowns
> Of everlasting laurels.[98]

The next concert included a new fantasy, now lost, on four Cuban themes, *La Sombra, El Zapateo, María de la O,* and *El Cocoyé.*[99]

The Philharmonic Society was so pleased with these performances that it presented the young Cubanophile with a handsomely inscribed diploma of membership "por su talento artístico."[100] More noteworthy, a farmer from nearby Limones sent the following to the local paper:

> Señor Editor:
>   Please be so kind as to deliver to Mr. Gochac *[sic]* this gift of tobacco from my farm is a memento from one of his most passionate admirers.
>   I would be most pleased if he were to compose a little dance for my wife,

in return for which I would send him tobacco twisted by my wife herself. I
will come by his house for it in around four days.

Your servant,
Raphaél el Montuño[101]

By now Gottschalk was being treated practically as a native. He took
on several students and played informally in the salons of Santiago notables. He had finally managed to sell his Pleyel, and this greatly eased his
financial pressures, although not without anguish. "I am truly afflicted by
this separation," he wrote a friend, "and am jealous of the person who,
with a few miserable ounces of gold, gained the right to mistreat a most
loyal and obedient friend of mine."[102]

In early October the local press reported happily that "the great pianist . . . still remains in town, much to the pleasure of his friends and
admirers."[103] Not until the end of the month did he depart, having by then
spent six weeks without a major concert.

What had been occupying Gottschalk's time? Doubtless, he devoted
many days to composing. Even allowing for the many Cuban works that
he performed before this date, there remain a number that would have to
have been composed during these weeks.[104] The free time also provided
an opportunity for him to revise several manuscripts for publication by
Edelmann in Havana.

But he had more on his mind. In a letter to his mother written two
years later, Gottschalk tells how he was befriended in Santiago by a family of immigrants from Saint-Domingue, the D'Espaignes. Here is his own
account:

> The D'Espaigne family took a great liking to me. This was shared by their only
> daughter, Mlle. Mathilde D'Espaigne, age sixteen. They gave me to understand
> that the poor child expected the usual outcome of her romance, that is to say,
> marriage. She was terribly rich; I had nothing. I let the family know of my
> susceptibility and of my scruples. They kept after me so much that I gave my
> word. We became engaged. She was very beautiful but so young and ignorant
> of the world that I placed this condition. I wanted her to see the world and
> live with other young people for at least a year. If her love for me (love which
> touched on idolatry) could survive such a test, then I would be convinced of
> the sincerity and depth of her feelings. Also, I must add that for all her beauty
> I had more friendship for her than love. The trial was too much for her. After
> having written to me every day for six months and also after a little negligence
> or laziness on my part in answering her burning and naive epistles, she took
> her revenge on my neglect and chose as an instrument of her revenge a hand-
> some colonel, heavily bearded and quite well-furnished with dollars. The mar-
> riage took place last month, I think. Thus ended my romance.[105]

In other words, Gottschalk managed to get himself engaged to a sixteen-
year-old girl—not itself exceptional in those days—and then to place con-

ditions on her without having accepted any reciprocal obligations on his side. Once back in the United States he cooled to the arrangement, and Mathilde D'Espaigne eventually married someone else.

What is curious about this revelation—the nearest Gottschalk ever came to speaking about his intimate relations with women—is that it was made in a letter to his mother. He was by then the sole source of support for her and his siblings, having assumed his father's role. The obvious reason for which Gottschalk never married, and one which he himself acknowledged, is that he was convinced that financial responsibilities to his family prevented him from taking on additional obligations. Even though he claimed that the D'Espaignes were "terribly rich," it is almost certain that they were merely musicians like himself and that Mathilde's father was Rubén Despaigne, a violinist.[106] In addition to his anxieties over money, did Moreau then simply lose interest in Mathilde and back away from what he had apparently viewed as a mere flirtation? This fits with what later became the popular image of Gottschalk's casual relations with women. Alternatively, did he draw back from this engagement because, having stepped into his father's shoes, he felt that marriage was an act of infidelity to his mother and to his family? Or finally, was there in Gottschalk some unacknowledged uncertainty concerning his sexual identity that drove him, on the one hand, to endless flirtatious relationships with women but, on the other hand, caused him in the end to draw back each time? Any combination of these factors may help explain the complexities of Moreau's emotional world, as well as the aura of lyric melancholy that hovered over him throughout his life.

Whatever deeper motives impelled him to breaking off the engagement, Gottschalk's behavior was reprehensible. Not only did he jilt a minor, but he did so in such a way as to transfer responsibility for the break from himself to the girl. In this and subsequent relations with women Gottschalk showed himself to be self-centered and even self-indulgent, even as he justified his behavior in terms of devotion to familial duty or other high-minded impulses.

Beyond such personal matters, political events conspired to keep Gottschalk in Santiago. Once President Pierce cooled to the idea of an immediate invasion of Cuba, he asked Soulé to meet with other American diplomats in Europe to coordinate a plan for purchasing the island. Soulé, however, was once more stirring up a revolution against Isabel II among the liberals of Madrid. When he and his fellow diplomats assembled at the Belgian town of Ostend, he put aside the President's request for a plan to buy the island and instead produced a plan of action more aggressive than anything under consideration in Washington. Pierce was furious and wasted no time in repudiating Soulé and asking for his resignation.

But the damage was done. By the time a copy of the "Ostend Manifesto" reached Washington on November 4, 1854, American policy toward Cuba was once again in turmoil.

Even though Pierce had given up on acquiring Cuba, the Democrats were still eager to promote American ascendance in the Gulf of Mexico. And at the very time Gottschalk was playing the Spanish anthem in Santiago as part of his *Siege of Saragossa,* Quitman and his ten thousand troops remained poised to attack. Their goal was to assassinate the new Spanish captain-general and transform Cuba into the thirty-second state.[107] Rumors of these intrigues flooded Havana and reached Santiago just as the new captain-general arrived there for a state visit in mid-October. Under the circumstances, Gottschalk was well advised to stay quietly in the provinces until the crisis passed.

On November 7 the pianist *sans* piano arrived in the town of Puerto Príncipe (today Camagüay), an ancient city of torturously narrow and unpaved streets that served as the capital for the eastern region of Cuba.[108] Gottschalk was plunged into gloom:

> I have been in this *necropolis* for eight days. . . . Seeing the desolate aspect of the streets, the dullness of the inhabitants, and the muteness of its public places, it is easier to believe this to be a *campo santo* than a city of forty thousand flesh and blood inhabitants endowed with vital warmth and movement.[109]

Just as Gottschalk was writing off Puerto Príncipe, emissaries from the town came to say that they would take charge of all arrangements for a concert in the local Gran Teatro if he would only stay and perform. Gottschalk yielded to their pleas. That evening he was serenaded by the orchestra of the local Academia de San Fernando, and the Governor invited him to dine. As Puerto Príncipe warmed to Gottschalk, he warmed to Puerto Príncipe, now hailing it as a place which "conceals a *tropical* enthusiasm for art."[110]

The local paper characterized the concerts of December 4 and 11, 1854, as "grandiose, poetic, melancholy, capricious, brilliant, and dominated by [Gottschalk's] genius, which made torrents of harmonies break forth from the keyboard."[111]

These performances yielded a bumper crop of versified hyperbole.[112] The reason for this, aside from gratitude to the great visitor for having momentarily broken the reigning torpor, is that in Puerto Príncipe Gottschalk had premiered three extended works based on local themes. Unfortunately, his *Camagüay Fantasy,* the *Caprichos sobre danses de Puerto-Príncipe,* and his *Recuerdos de Puerto-Príncipe* are all lost. Not even the composer's usual shorthand sketches survive, but the local paper reported that all three compositions were applauded frenetically, especially when Gottschalk quoted the locally popular tune *La Caringa.*[113]

On shipboard from Cienfuegos to Santiago Gottschalk had played chess with a young French-speaking officer, José Angelet, who served as the Spanish military governor in the small town (more accurately, village) of San Juan de los Remedios. Angelet had spoken tantalizingly of the town's renowned crab dishes and urged the composer to visit him. By late January Gottschalk showed up in what he nicknamed "Crabopolis" *(Cangrejopolis)* to enjoy the cuisine and perform for the local philharmonic society. Cuban hospitality reached a high point in Remedios when, following the performance, a full mixed choir arose to sing a hymn to the "Artist of the Century, Gottschalk!" composed by none other than the military governor himself. Beautiful nymphs, laurel wreaths, and Apollo himself were invoked, and disparaging lines were published about the transitory fame of Liszt, Chopin, and Thalberg.[114] Following the performance of this small-town cantata, a young girl dressed in blue appeared on the stage carrying a torch and wreath of laurels, followed by two other girls who crowned the pianist. A dinner followed, and then a dance, which was judged "one of the biggest events the town of Remedios has ever known."[115]

Before returning to Cárdenas, Havana, and the status of mere mortal, Gottschalk paid an official call on the Bishop of Remedios, who had missed the concert. Notwithstanding the fact that only a few weeks before he had written that the faith of the Archbishop of Santiago never seemed to him more than "a decent mask to cover imbecility and hypocrisy," Gottschalk obligingly offered to perform at mass in Remedios and set to work composing several pieces for the occasion. At least three hymns, a religious fantasy, a *Rex altissime,* and a *Pange linguae* for male voices were premiered at a mass attended by a crowd of six hundred that spilled out of the cathedral and onto the plaza. None of these works is preserved or even mentioned in the existing literature on the composer.[116]

On February 13, 1855, the well-traveled pianist finally reached Havana, where he lay bedridden with fever for several days. By now he had played out the role of the "good American." Concern over a possible invasion by Quitman's forces was high, and the captain-general had imposed a temporary state of emergency. In spite of this, the official press regretted that Gottschalk had announced his intention to depart and bemoaned the fact that he would not give a farewell concert, "for reasons . . . known to the priest alone."[117] Implying a comparison to Quitman, the *Diario de la Marina* observed that "the celebrated pianist has run through the interior of the island like a conqueror, but his conquests were limited to specific hearts and to the general affection of inhabitants of the cities he visited."[118]

Where could Gottschalk go now? From Remedios he had written to his mother that he intended to go to Mexico and Peru as soon as he had earned enough money for the passage.[119] Rumors were abroad in Santiago that he intended to visit Mexico and that friends there would introduce the composer to General Santa Anna, the Mexican hero (or, to Americans, villain) of the Alamo.[120] In Havana, by contrast, people thought the young American was heading to Europe.[121]

Whatever his earlier plans may have been, once in the Cuban capital Gottschalk resolved to return at once to New Orleans. As soon as his fever subsided and he had settled all outstanding publishing matters with the Edelmanns, Gottschalk raced around town saying his farewells, then boarded an English steamer bound for Mobile and New Orleans. It was February 23, 1855.

Chapter Thirteen

🎼 Last Hopes, Dying Poets

AMONG the pieces to emerge from Gottschalk's pen during his visit to Santiago de Cuba was a brief melody that for better or worse, was to change his life. The tune stands out among scores of other slow ballads of the day on account of its three-quarter time and its long crescendo culminating in a pianissimo ending, like an operatic aria. Once back in New York, he gave his publisher, Firth Pond & Co., a couple of scraps of manuscript paper on which he had sketched out the piece.[1] The publisher consented to issue it, but *The Last Hope* did not sell well. Within a year Firth Pond & Co. sold its entire back list of Gottschalk imprints to the firm of William Hall & Son. For an additional fifty dollars it also threw in *The Last Hope*.

Hall had some difficulty getting Gottschalk's revised version of the piece into print.[2] Once it hit the music stores, however, the composition was a success.[3] Orders poured in, and Hall could scarcely satisfy the demand. Audiences who in 1853 had wanted only pyrotechnics at *fortissimo* volume now demanded that Gottschalk play this melancholy air at every concert. Soon *The Last Hope* began to dog Gottschalk mercilessly. He admitted that "even my paternal love for *The Last Hope* has succumbed under the terrible necessity of meeting it at every step, of playing it every evening, and hearing it played every day."[4] When he deleted it from the program in a small Wisconsin town, someone passed up a note from the audience asking, "Will Mr. Gottschalk oblige *thirty-six* young ladies who have studied *The Last Hope* by playing said piece?" Soon he abandoned himself to fate and accepted the fact that *The Last Hope* was "one among other inevitable afflictions of my life."[5]

Little did Gottschalk suspect how high this tide would rise. In 1856 he had related a colorful version of the story behind *The Last Hope* in a letter to his friend Gustave Chouquet in Paris. Chouquet published the account in *La France musicale*, whence it filtered back to America.[6] When the lugubrious tale began appearing as a preface to new editions of the piece, it drove sales to yet greater heights.

Gottschalk's version of the story is pure melodrama. While he was in Santiago de Cuba he had met an elderly woman who took a maternal interest in the young pianist. Suffering from a terminal illness, the lady pleaded with Gottschalk to play for her on the piano during her last hours: "Have pity, my dear Moreau, and play for me a little melody, an *última esperanza*." Gottschalk did, and the lady died contented. This tale spread quickly across the land and was even telegraphed from town to town before Gottschalk's concerts, but not without florid elaborations.[7]

Just after the Civil War, Hubert Platt Main, later the wealthy author of no fewer than one thousand hymns, found himself working for a religious publishing house in Cincinnati. A zealous fan of Gottschalk and particularly of *The Last Hope*, the young Main began stalking his idol from concert to concert.[8] Even before now *The Last Hope* had been described in printed editions as a "Religious Meditation." Lest anyone miss the point, the title page invariably featured a bucolic scene bathed in rays of the setting sun and surmounted by a shimmering cross. Main's contribution to this pious confection was to dig up some verses by a British Presbyterian that fit exactly the meter of *The Last Hope* and to publish the two as a hymn, now entitled *Gottschalk*.

Thanks to Hubert Platt Main, tens of thousands of Protestant hymnals henceforth contained pious lucubrations written by, and bearing the name of, a Jewish-Catholic widely known to contemporaries for his amorous adventures. Charles Ives, who doubtless learned the hymn in the choir loft of his father's church in Danbury, Connecticut, was to quote the melody of *The Last Hope* in his setting of Psalm 90. For generations *The Last Hope* remained one of America's best-known melodies, issued in endless editions and published widely throughout the Americas and Europe as well.[9] A historian of popular music has called it "the most popular and most performed solo piano piece published in America during the nineteenth century."[10]

Throughout the rest of his career Gottschalk wrote many more pieces in a deeply sentimental vein. George Upton, a friend and fellow pianist, argued that "all his music was either sensuous or sentimental."[11] Whether measured by his output in this vein or the stupefying quantities in which the public bought up his musical melancholia, Gottschalk must be considered at least in part a sentimentalist.

The very titles of some of his works are an invitation to tears: *The Dying Poet; O Loving Heart, Trust On! Day Is Past and Over; Tremolo;*

The Dying Swan; and *Morte!!*. Such pieces established Gottschalk's persona in Victorian America. Along with his heavy-lidded and soulful eyes, they confirmed his bona fides as a Man of Feeling. Gottschalk understood this full well and tested new pieces in this genre by the effect they had on his audiences' tear ducts. Not without pride he reported to his publisher that when he played *Morte!!* in South America "a great many women have had hysterics and weep over it."[12]

After his return from Havana in 1855 he focused his energies on composing works in a sentimental vein. Not only did he back away from Creole lore, but he took no further interest in the Stephen Foster songs that had so intrigued him after his return from Europe. He also turned a deaf ear to other forms of regional folk music he encountered on his travels. Both the Ohio River ports and the old Erie Canal towns of upstate New York were teeming with living folk songs during the very years Gottschalk visited them.[13] Yet they made no impression on him.

In this turn away from folk sources and toward a new music of sensibility—read "tear-jerkers"—Gottschalk was participating in a broad movement in American music and culture. From the settled East Coast to the rough-and-ready frontier, mid-century Americans were redirecting their musical attention inward, to the heart. Not so many years earlier, any song with a lively tune and slapstick lyrics found a ready audience. For a decade Americans reveled in a swaggering, tobacco-spitting, hitch-up-your-pants-and-sing kind of music. No one captured this mood better than Stephen Foster. It found its epitome in the nonsense lines of his *Camptown Races* and in the jocular cadences of the *Glendy Burke*, named for a fast new steamboat. Above all it resonated in his *O! Susanna*, the battle cry of those fighting the wilderness on the Western frontier.

Then, in one of those sudden shifts typical of popular music, Americans began calling for the exact opposite qualities. They wanted music that was serious rather than bantering, reflective rather than extroverted, refined rather than bawdy. Strange to say, the very minstrel companies that had fanned the earlier fad now popularized this new sensibility. Christy's Minstrels showed the way by presenting dozens of new slow-tempo songs whose lyrics often reached subterranean depths of pathos.[14] The narrator of Christy's *Good News from Home*, for example, had

> No father's near to guide me now,
> No mother's tear to soothe my brow,
> No sister's voice on mine ear,
> No brother's smile to give me cheer.

Then there was *Lilly Dale* (for which Thalberg wrote variations), along with its post-mortem sequel, *The Grave of Lilly Dale*. Edgar Allen Poe once declared that the most poetical theme was the death of a fair young woman. *Lilly Dale* and dozens of other songs capitalized on this truth.

This opened a vast field for opportunists. W. H. Curry, author of *The Grave of Lilly Dale*, showed his commercial acumen when he lifted the meter of Foster's *Old Kentucky Home* for a doleful tune of his own. Gottschalk's friend George F. Root also revealed an understanding of the marketplace when he capitalized on Foster's fame with his mortuary melody, *The Old Folks Are Gone*. It would be a mistake, however, to see only opportunism in this boom. Foster took great pride in sentimental ballads such as his *Old Folks at Home* and *Massa's in de Cold, Cold Ground*.[15]

By the time Gottschalk returned from Cuba the demand for sentimental ballads seemed unquenchable. Publishers sought them out from whomever would provide them and issued them in prodigious numbers. In an age when America still sang, these works were performed around the family piano and crooned 'neath the elms on town squares everywhere. In the process they became fixtures of the aural life of most Americans down to the second quarter of the twentieth century.

Composers and would-be composers zeroed in on this new market, thus creating the predecessor of Tin Pan Alley. Henry Russell, who wrote the music for *Woodman, Spare That Tree*, boasted of having composed and published over eight hundred songs during his career.[16] The German-born Charles Grobe of Baltimore left even Russell in the shade with a life's work that ended with op. 1348.[17] It is true that Grobe's output included pieces in many genres, but he more than held his own in the competition to moisten handkerchiefs.

When Americans could not meet the demand, others rushed to the rescue. Englishman Henry Bishop, the first composer to be knighted in Great Britain, had composed a simple melody that languished until an American writer's poem, *Home, Sweet Home*, was attached to it.[18] *Home, Sweet Home* had been played and sung for a generation before it entered Gottschalk's repertoire in a series of variations. Six months before his death Moreau was still performing this work.[19]

The all-time champion among composers of sentimental ballads scarcely traveled beyond her native Warsaw. Thekla von Badarzewska-Baranowska (1834–61) was a one-work composer, but that one composition, *A Maiden's Prayer*, achieved what a learned German critic has called "the most extraordinary and at the same time the most trivial success in the history of the piano."[20] Like Gottschalk's *The Last Hope*, Foster's *Old Folks at Home*, and Bishop's *Home, Sweet Home*, von Badarzewska-Baranowska's *A Maiden's Prayer* became a standard tool for anyone seeking to touch the sensibilities of Americans through music.

This tidal wave of mid-nineteenth century sensibility has fared but poorly at the hands of critics and musicologists. The merest mention of these simple but beloved ballads causes most learned commentators to unleash a bristling arsenal of negative adjectives: banal, simplistic, moralistic, synthetic, bombastic, lachrymose, bathetic, cynical, etc. Composer Robert Schumann coined the dismissive term "salon music" to describe such pieces and the term caught on also in highbrow American circles.

But the pejorative "salon music" is not the most damaging epithet attached to these pieces. Even more devastating is the charge that sentimental music was "genteel,"[21] that is, the music of a repressive bourgeoisie whose members sought at any cost to distance themselves from the life and folk culture of the un-genteel "masses."

It goes without saying that Gottschalk was, and is, the butt of much criticism along these lines.[22] One modern critic has found Gottschalk's ballads "quaint, even comic, and we play them, if at all, with an indulgent smile."[23] The same critic, it might be noted, berated Stephen Foster because he "succumbed to the Genteel Tradition; drank himself into ill health; and died in a New York slum."[24]

Underlying these summary judgments is a cluster of closely related but unstated biases. First among these is simple embarrassment. Anyone alive in the silent film era knew it was Gottschalk's *The Dying Poet* that pianists invariably cranked out to accompany that tender moment just before the heroine was tied to the railroad tracks. Hence even Harold Schonberg, otherwise one of Gottschalk's most discerning champions, found the "drawing room *morceaux* embarrassingly sentimental. We can smile at these."[25]

At a deeper level, *The Last Hope* and Gottschalk's other soulful ballads must be dismissed by anyone who is convinced that the rather prim Victorian environment to which most nineteenth-century Americans aspired was emotionally barren. During most of the twentieth century such a view was common among members of America's cultural avant-garde. *Bamboula*, of course, was just fine, because it is "a pianistic arrangement of an authentic [read "proletarian"] New Orleans dance."[26] But sentimental ballads were bad, for they lack, in the words of one critic, "the genuine emotion, the organic vitality, . . . of, for example, the old folk ballads."[27]

Do such works as *The Last Hope* possess any redeeming qualities? Or do they instead represent a lapse in Gottschalk's art? Or, yet again, are they pieces Gottschalk himself did not take seriously but churned out simply because the market was there?

This last hypothesis found a strong partisan in Gottschalk's early biographer Luis Ricardo Fors. According to Fors:

> Avaricious editors obliged him to compose against his will and contrary to the
> impulses of his good taste and his talent. He wrote these under burlesque
> pseudonyms or completely vulgar names but the editors, always thirsty for
> maximum profit . . . published these imperfect compositions over the author's
> actual name.[28]

Octavia Hensel, another early biographer, quoted a letter from the composer to make the same case:

> I think so little of these compositions that I do not care to attach my name to
> them. But Ditson [his publisher] will take them with a *nom de plume.*[29]

The trouble with these statements is that they refer not to the works
of ponderous sentimentality that are under discussion but to dance pieces
like *Hurrah Galop, Fairy Land Schottische,* and *Love and Chivalry,* all
of far lower emotional valence.[30]

There is no question, however, that the composer despised most of
the maudlin treacle that filled the music shops. He loathed them because
their melodies were so atrocious "as to produce in one the same effect
that the Venus de Milo would [if she were] dressed up like Punch."[31]
Above all, he despised "that detestable musical thing so touching to lymphatic and sentimental girls," *The Maiden's Prayer.* "It is a loathsome
drug," he wrote, "which is sold everywhere, and sells better than Drake's
Plantation Bitters. It is an epidemic which spares no one."[32]

The vehemence with which Gottschalk attacked such effusions bears
emphasis. In a Havana journal he tore into "those sentimental trashy
pieces which . . . threaten to obliterate the last vestiges of the pure and
serious art which the great masters bequeathed to us."[33]

Either Gottschalk was a hypocrite in condemning such melodies or
he sincerely believed that such compositions as his *The Last Hope* and
Ricordati were of an entirely different character. There is much evidence
indicating that Gottschalk took these works quite seriously. He warmly
encouraged singer Clara Brinkerhoff when she proposed wedding *The
Last Hope* to the words of a Protestant hymn. She was left in no doubt
that his encouragement stemmed from the genuine religious sentiments
he attached to the ballad.[34] Similarly, there is not a trace of cynicism in
Gottschalk's characterization of his *Ricordati* as "a dreamy character and
full of pathos."[35]

For all his Parisian irony, Moreau inhabited the same emotional world
as Stephen Foster, Henry Russell, and, yes, even Mlle. Bardazewska. Many
anecdotes reflect this. Once, after the death of his mother, he played at a
private home in New York. A child approached him saying, "When you
play, I hear the angels sing which Mama tells me 'bout." Gottschalk lifted

the child and whispered to him, "Tell me about the angels. I haven't any mama now to tell me."[36]

Art and culture are peculiarly subtle thermometers of a community's life. During the years in which Gottschalk became the country's premier purveyor of music of the heart, the United States was swept up in a whirlwind of change. Hundreds of miles of steel rails were being laid each month. Forests were being hacked down to provide ties for the rails and wood for the locomotives. Ranks of new farmers poured on to all this freshly stripped land. They quickly built new homes, using a new method of construction, the "balloon frame," whose very name breathes the transience and impermanence that was the hallmark of the new life. Never in history had it been easier for masses of people to move and change their lives, and never in history had more chosen to do so.

Stephen Foster had spent several years trying to be an accountant at the very eye of the storm, the teeming waterfront of Cincinnati, Queen City of the West. The male audiences at Christy's Minstrels could hear all their own bravado echoed in the chorus of his *O! Susanna*. But all this transience and flux had another side, which was the very opposite of these men's swagger. The revolution that opened the West also engendered the anguish of separation and loss. *My Old Kentucky Home* drew tears precisely because none of the social forces or technologies that drove people away from their places of birth ever drew them back. Separation and loss were the more painful because the raw new settlements and towns offered so little in the way of consolation and solace.

In an earlier day Americans might have borne the resulting sorrows in stoic silence. Now they burned to sing about them. Twenty years earlier the flames of Christian revival had erupted in upstate New York and fanned across the country. Suddenly, it became acceptable, even desirable, for a person to express profound emotions outwardly in song.[37] Inevitably, the religious fires burned down to a glow, but the readiness of ordinary Americans to ventilate their innermost feelings in song remained.

Gottschalk, raised in a boom town in the home of an immigrant father, separated from his family during crucial pre-adolescent years, touched by several deaths in his immediate family, and doomed by his performing career to a life of ceaseless travel, had direct experience of the feelings of separation and loss that moved ordinary Americans. Up until his first Cuban visit, however, Moreau had not considered the emotions of a person's daily life as fit sources of inspiration for his own music.[38]

It was to Nicolás Ruiz Espadero to whom he owed a change of heart. "It was much by our advice," recalled Espadero, "that he undertook to express in music the 'sentiment' of the circumstances in which, at various times, he found himself."[39]

It was not enough simply to hear *The Last Hope*, however. People wanted also to visualize it. Hence they pressed the composer to tell them the circumstances of its composition so they could translate it into visual images. Gottschalk's public also demanded to know the story of his *Berceuse, Morte!!*, and many other sentimental works. "Music is not properly one of the representative arts," wrote the *Buffalo Daily Courier*, "and yet Gottschalk almost makes it such. He has caught up and expressed [the subject of each piece] as perfectly as a painter might."[40]

What kind of "painter" was Gottschalk? Nearly all of his sentimental pieces represent vignettes taken from daily life and are precise analogues in music to the genre paintings of the day. The narrative expressed by *The Last Hope* and by the painting *First Grief* (1860), by Gottschalk's friend Erastus Dow Palmer, are closely related. *The Banjo* has parallels in the paintings of William Sidney Mount. Sometimes a given theme was expressed first in painting, as when the American landscapist Asher B. Durand did his oil *Woodland Glen* a year before Gottschalk used the same theme in *Forest Glade*. At other times a musical version came first, as when Gottschalk's *The Gleaner* (*La Glaneuse*, 1848) anticipated Millet's 1857 canvas on the same subject. Whether his composition preceded or followed the related painting, contemporaries generally understood that Gottschalk's music was linked closely with genre painting, and several writers discussed the relationship in detail.[41]

Whatever the medium, these genre pieces scored highest when they stated or implied a whole narrative. Harriet Beecher Stowe's *Uncle Tom's Cabin* gained impact precisely because it read like an album of heart-rending sketches or a cycle of lachrymose songs. Gottschalk's *Pastorella e cavalliere*[42] also delighted audiences because it enabled them to "read" its narrative. Toronto's *Daily Globe* presented its readers with a blow-by-blow account of this brief work, in which the banal theme of farm girl and city slicker is elevated to the status of Art.[43] Audiences for such works clearly saw all life as a sequence of emotion-laden vignettes and asked the artist to stop time momentarily so they could relish fully the pathos of it all.

To translate this into solo piano music called for a good lyric sense, the ability to expand the emotional range of a melody through variations that did not smother it, and a balancing of the unexpected and the familiar that comes about only through careful craftsmanship. Gottschalk's worst efforts in the sentimental and narrative genre lack these qualities and are dismal. His best sentimental works, however, demonstrate a subtle mastery of all these elements.

A successful ballad had to have a melody that was unaffected, simple, and compelling. Occasionally, Gottschalk would work with "found" melodies. In the case of *Berceuse*, for example, he took over the French lullaby *Fais dodo, mon bébé* or its Louisiana variant, *Fais dodo, Colas.*[44] More often, however, the melodies were his own. A few, like *O Loving Heart, Trust On*, are awkward. The very best, however, offer elegant and soaring lyrical structures. Even one of the composer's harshest contemporary critics, George T. Ferris, conceded that his melodic inventions were "brilliant, charming, tender, melodious, [and] full of captivating excellence."[45] Sometimes, as in the lovely *Illusions perdues*, they have a Latin tinge, while at other times, as in *Solitude*, they have more of a Chopinesque character.

Virtually all the more successful melodies rise steadily through the first dozen bars or so, even shifting from minor to major tonalities in the process, only to fall off at the end in a kind of sigh. The musicologist John Godfrey Doyle has identified the characteristic chord progressions that Gottschalk employed to give color to the melody of *The Last Hope*. His use of chromatic passing tones and augmented sixth chords, for example, became a Gottschalk signature, appearing in many works down to *Tremolo*, written only months before his death. Wagner used similar chord patterns in the opening bars of the prelude to *Tristan und Isolde.*[46]

Ornamentation and variations further enhance the texture of Gottschalk ballads and extend their emotional range. The elegant filigree ornaments in *Ricordati* refresh the melody just when it might otherwise have flagged, while the unexpected introduction of a sixth chord in *Berceuse* briefly imparts to that piece a Debussy-like color.

Such nuances enabled the composer to introduce his own sorrowful or bemused commentary on the melody, as if to remind listeners that they are hearing self-consciously created art and not mere folk music. Contributing to the same end were the introductions and codas with which the composer would surround a work. The left-hand arpeggio at the beginning of *Solitude* accomplishes this perfectly, as does the introduction to *Illusions perdues*. *The Last Hope* remained a concert favorite in part because of the daringly chromatic introductions the composer would improvise for it.

These various qualities all provide some basis for distinguishing among Gottschalk's various works of "sensibility" and between Gottschalk's productions in this vein and the mass of tear-jerkers produced by his contemporaries. Yet even when this is done, one is still left wondering whether the composer was not guilty of precisely the fault with which he often charged others, namely, of resorting to patterns, formulae, and clichés.

Gottschalk himself clearly did not believe that he was trafficking in stereotypes. Yet the fact remains that repetition of various sorts—call them "clichés"—abound in his more meditative pieces. At one level this may be seen as a flaw, just as it is in the works of even the best writers of German *Lieder*. However, it may also be inherent to the theme of loss and longing. Beneath the title of the published version of *Ricordati* the composer placed an epigraph from Dante's *Divine Comedy:* "There is no greater pain than to recall, out of one's sorrow, a happier time." The process of recollection or reminiscence, which is itself a process of repetition, provides the sole point of fixity in a world of flux.

But wait! Did not the composer himself identify the public for *The Last Hope* as "lymphatic girls" and students at female academies in Wisconsin? If this is so, then surely such talk of an audience for sentimental ballads made up of mature men and women who had actually experienced feelings of loss and death is beside the point.

Among the mass publications to hail the composer-pianist was *Godey's Lady's Book*.[47] Were it not for one fact, this would seem to support the view that the audience for Gottschalk's sentimental works consisted mainly of young girls. But *Godey's* aimed not at the youth market but at young mothers. Thus, when editor Sarah Josepha Hale organized a campaign to establish Thanksgiving as a national holiday, it was younger mothers, not teenage girls, whom she sought to mobilize.[48]

The generation of mothers who read *Godey's* in the mid-1850s were putting American domesticity on an entirely new basis. They affirmed romantic love between freely chosen partners rather than the old patriarchal domination. In child-rearing they favored affection over repression and often had fewer children in order to foster this.[49] Through their influence American homes became cozier, with warmly carpeted rooms in which members might find time to rest and reflect, both in company and alone. In short, the innovating younger mothers of the 1850s were transforming American life by making it more open to sensibility and emotion. It was they who championed Gottschalk to their daughters, not vice versa.

The implication of this is that women, not men, were the main arbiters of culture in Gottschalk's America. Max Maretzek had no doubt that this was the case:

> Up to this very day, the male portion of society visit only in such houses, and patronize such artists and productions as the ladies, in this respect very decidedly the better half of them, have thought proper to seal with their approbation and declare "fashionable."[50]

Elsewhere, Maretzek was even more blunt: "Indeed," he wrote, "beyond the principal cities, it is the ladies alone that patronize and love the Arts."[51]

Where were the men while their wives were ventilating their newly emancipated emotions? The stock answer is that they were at the office, grubbing money. Maretzek was complaining that few men were pace-setters in music and fewer still used their new money to support that art. Only later, when the founding and supporting of symphony orchestras became a matter of civic pride, did the men come on the scene.

Given this, it is the more surprising to discover that the audience for sentimental ballads included large numbers of men. It was men who flocked to the minstrel shows to hear lachrymose lyrics about a wilting Jeannie or an expiring Nellie. Even Abe Lincoln was notoriously vulnerable to such popular ballads and their lyrics about the fading beauty of roses or the singing of nightingales.[52]

Thus it comes as no surprise that when Gottschalk toured the rough-hewn and bawdy mining camps of California and Nevada he included in his repertoire *The Last Rose of Summer, The Last Hope, The Dying Poet, Murmures éoliens,* and his *Home, Sweet Home* variations. Among a San Francisco audience that might have included Mark Twain, "the delicate touch of Gottschalk created a sensation."[53] A reviewer for the *Daily Alta California* wrote, "Here is the true poetry of music, combining as [Gottschalk] does sentiment and delicacy."[54] The heartfelt response of another San Francisco audience to *The Last Hope* and *The Dying Poet* was due, one critic claimed, to the fact that all those present were "imagining words of their own."[55] At a performance of *Home, Sweet Home* at still another California concert, many tough-looking miners among the all-male audience broke down in sobs because the piece caused their minds "to wander back to the spot of their birth."[56]

For all his finely cut New York tail coats, aloof manner, and love of royal medals, Moeau Gottschalk understood all this from the outset. Returning to America in 1853, he realized that even in that hectic era millions of ordinary Americans were capturing moments for reflection and that these were opening up to them new vistas of emotional fulfillment. Gottschalk's works of "sensibility" were in tune with this mood and thus touched a vast audience of anonymous and by no means exclusively genteel women and men.[57]

The critic Robert Offergeld perceived this well and linked Gottschalk with a new "music of democratic sociability."[58] Arthur Loesser, who explored the social history of the piano, appreciated the democratic character of *The Last Hope:* "By the rarefied monastic standards of latter-day highbrows, *Last Hope* ranks as trash," wrote Loesser. "However," he continued, "if there is value in something because it has given satisfaction to a great many people for a long time, then *The Last Hope* must count as an important piece of music."[59]

Chapter Fourteen

❧ Taking Root in New York, 1855

MOREAU Gottschalk returned to New Orleans early on February 28, 1855, for what turned out to be his final visit to his home town. The local French press welcomed the city's "delicious talent" with open arms, complaining that he had "allowed himself to be seduced too long by the luxuriant nature of Cuba."[1] The English-language *Daily Picayune* effused over the "talented young artist of whom this . . . city has so much reason to be proud."[2]

Anyone in the linguistically divided city who bothered to read both papers would have sensed at once that something was amiss. Both reported that Gottschalk's visit would be brief and that he was heading abroad at once. But whereas the English press announced that he was departing for South America, the *Courrier de la Louisiane* chided him for his plan to return to Paris.[3] Both versions were wrong, however, for Gottschalk had no idea what his next move should be.

As usual, the young man whom the *Courrier* called a "superior artist" was flat broke, and without a piano to boot. His Gottschalk and Bruslé relatives doubtless saluted him for having assumed the support of his mother and six siblings in Paris. Thus reminded both of his obligations and of his inability to meet them, Moreau reacted instinctively and threw himself into work. In quick order he arranged a "farewell" concert at the Odd Fellows' Hall, agreed to play a benefit for the outgoing manager of the Théâtre d'Orléans,[4] signed up to perform between the acts of a Rossini opera, and then scheduled still another final concert, again at the Odd Fellows' Hall. He also sold himself as entertainment for a ladies' handicraft fair held at the St. Charles Hotel;[5] made two flying trips to Mobile; gave lessons; and arranged for a local publisher to issue a *Caprice espagnole* (an elaboration of his *La Jota aragonesa*), the *Jérusalem* fantasy, *Danse des sylphes*, and *Bunker Hill*.[6]

The first Odd Fellows performance was judged an unprecedented success.[7] There, on March 13, he gave the American premiere of *The Last Hope* and also *María de la O*. As Gottschalk played *The Last Hope*, a New Orleans lady observed,

> His head was slightly bowed, and I'm sure his eyes were closed. . . . I was crying so when he came to the end that I felt ashamed of myself. Then after I looked about and saw that nearly everybody else was crying also, I felt better.[8]

Regarding *María de la O*, the program declared provocatively that it was "an African dance and air as heard one night by Mr. Gottschalk in the woods of Santiago performed by a band of runaway Negroes."[9] At this concert the composer also brought out a new solo, *American Sketches*, dedicated to the firemen of New Orleans and featuring variations on a fire company march, complete with fire bells and a nod to Jullien's *Fireman's Quadrille*. Yet a third premiere that evening was a two-piano *Grande Fantaisie de bravura* on themes from the operas *Norma* and *Sonnambula*. At the final concert he focused on his newly published compositions, adding only *El Cocoyé* and a group of his earliest Creole pieces.[10]

Climaxing this frenetic round of concertizing was one of the more bizarre adventures of Gottschalk's career. For some days an aeronaut named Godard had been making balloon ascensions from central New Orleans. Either at Godard's initiative or his own, Gottschalk climbed into the wicker gondola late in the afternoon of March 26.[11] The balloon rose above the gathered crowd and headed north over the grounds of a soap factory. The cooling air brought it down after a mere six minutes, however, and it descended directly on the tracks of the Pontchartrain Railroad, the anchor chord nearly grazing the locomotive that happened to chug by at just this moment. In the nick of time Godard jettisoned enough ballast that he and the composer could land safely.

Inspired by this adventure, Gottschalk went back for a second ride on Palm Sunday, April 1, this time bringing on board a small keyboard instrument called a harmonicon.[12] Alerted by advertisements, a multitude of spectators assembled and a brass band was holding forth as Gottschalk soared heavenward. With him was the adoring Ernest Canonge, who had declaimed the dozen stanzas of French verse honoring Moreau at the banquet during the composer's first return to New Orleans in 1853. As the balloon began to rise, the band fell silent. Once aloft, Gottschalk found inspiration in the circular horizon and shifting light. Then, as the Gulf of Mexico came into view, Moreau improvised ecstatically on the harmonicon. Once more the soap factory loomed up, however, and so did the tracks and even the passing locomotive of the Pontchartrain Railroad. Fortunately, the aeronauts again escaped without injury. The resulting composition, *Pensée poétique*, is a lyrical reverie that modulates from minor to major in such a way as to suggest the surmounting of earth-bound concerns.[13]

This adventure provided the perfect build-up to Gottschalk's final New Orleans concert, held a week later at the Théâtre d'Orléans. Assisted by the entire operatic corps, Gottschalk repeated highlights from his previous concerts but for some reason withheld his new aeronautical composition.[14]

Immediately afterwards the pianist succumbed to fatigue and illness and remained bedridden for six weeks. Only as the fierce summer heat descended on New Orleans during the second week of June did his doctor allow him to leave his bed, and then only on the condition that he head north immediately in order to take ocean baths. Thanking his public through the press and making only the most cursory farewells, Moreau departed New Orleans and set his sights for New York.[15]

There is no evidence that Gottschalk ever took the sea baths. Instead, he stopped briefly in Manhattan and then proceeded at once to the spa at Trenton Falls near Utica, New York. Described by Nathaniel Parker Willis as "the most *enjoyably beautiful* spot among the resorts of romantic scenery in our country,"[16] Trenton Falls was a popular stopping point for tourists en route to Niagara. Gottschalk could recuperate there and cover his costs by playing in the salon of the rural tourist hotel. He also composed a new piece, a brilliant *caprice de concert* for piano entitled *Printemps d'amour.*[17] After giving several concerts in neighboring towns of upstate New York, he spent August in Saratoga Springs and then returned to Manhattan.

Once in New York City he was taken into the home of Mr. George Henriques, the lawyer who had known the Gottschalk family in New Orleans twenty years earlier and who was now living with his wife and daughter at 149 West 14th Street.[18] Here Moreau found the supportive father and loving family he had not known since his eleventh year. To Gottschalk, Henriques was

> the best man in the world. He has a heart of gold. He loves me beyond all expression, to the extent that he cannot go to bed if I am out, even if he had to stay at the window until 2 or 3 o'clock in the morning.[19]

For his part, the kindly Henriques, a gray-bearded man with a bemused look, dedicated a photograph of himself in Moreau's album "to my dear son [from] one who always loves you" signing it "your adopted father."[20]

To have found a secure island in the heart of Manhattan was a particular boon, given the uncertainties that beset Gottschalk on every side. True, both the political and economic environments were favorable. The

Cuban crisis had passed, and President Franklin Pierce had pushed through the Kansas-Nebraska Act, dividing new territories between free and slave states. This was too clever by half, though, for it led to bloody fighting in Kansas and to tough new laws against fugitive slaves elsewhere in the Midwest. All this came later. For now, business was booming in New York, and no one had the slightest premonition that a major crash would occur within two years.

Gottschalk's problem was that he arrived in the East with no bookings and no manager, and at a time when most of the autumn's concerts had already been arranged. He moved at once to find an impresario. His search turned up no one but M. D. S. Bookstaver, one of the lesser lights in the world of concert management. Bookstaver set to work at once, but with little hope that he could reap a bounty of engagements. Meanwhile, the inevitable lead time before the first performances left the pianist with several free months. His first task, and one to which he turned at once, was to get his compositions into print so that profits on their sales could make up for lost concert revenues.

Up to now Moreau had had a serious business relationship with only one publisher, the Parisian firm owned by the Escudier brothers. They in turn arranged for further editions in Germany and Italy. This arrangement with the Escudiers had not prevented Gottschalk from sending pieces from time to time to several other publishers in France, Spain, and Russia. After returning to America, Gottschalk had fallen into the habit of giving his works to whatever publisher was closest at hand. By 1855 these included Edelmann in Havana, Philip Werlein's firm in New Orleans, Gould & Co. in Philadelphia, and, above all, Firth Pond & Co. in New York.

This house is remembered today mainly for its notoriously tight-fisted dealings with Stephen Foster. English-born John Firth, seizing on the minstrel craze when it first appeared, had published Henry Russell's hit *Woodman, Spare That Tree* and arranged for exclusive rights to Stephen Foster's songs.[21] This made him America's most successful musical publisher by far. So when in late 1853 he advanced the twenty-four-year-old New Orleanian two hundred dollars for a *caprice religieux* and a second work, he had reason to expect timely delivery by a grateful composer.

Moreau failed to meet Firth's deadline. Angered, the publisher turned to Gottschalk's friend and patron Henriques with a demand that he either get Gottschalk (who was now in Cuba) to deliver the music or himself repay Firth Pond & Co. half of the two-hundred-dollar advance.[22] The fact that *Chant du martyr* (subtitled *Grand caprice religieux*) was not published until the early 1860s confirms that Gottschalk let down Henriquez as well as Firth. He may have intended *The Last Hope* as a kind of consolation payment, but this did not mollify Firth, who was by now eager to divest himself of a composer who had proven neither popular nor reliable. In the late spring of 1855 he therefore sold his entire interest in Gottschalk to his former partner John Hall, also of New York. It was "General" John Hall more than anyone else who launched Gottschalk's American career.

John Firth had gotten his start in the music business as an apprentice to a New York flute maker. Among his fellow apprentices was John Hall, a native of Tarrytown, New York. Born in 1796, Hall fought in the War of 1812 and subsequently rose to the rank of brigadier general in the volunteer state militia. Henceforth he was known simply as "the General." Military accolades opened to Hall a public career. He briefly read law and held various elective offices before setting his sights on making money. Since he and Firth were now brothers-in-law, it was an easy step for them to go into business together as Firth & Hall. They were joined by Sylvanus Pond, a New Englander, who headed the instrumental side of the business.

The company thrived until 1847, when Hall, along with his son James, withdrew to set up their own publishing house of William Hall & Son at the corner of Broadway and Park Place. His shop quickly became the city's premier rendezvous point for musicians of all stripes, and especially pianists. It did not hurt that tickets to most New York concerts were also dispensed there. Like the Escudiers' shop in Paris or the Edelmanns' in Havana, Hall's was virtually a social center. Gottschalk whiled away many hours there, as did his musical disciples.[23]

The firm of Hall & Son entered the music business just as Americans were flooding the U.S. copyright office with new compositions. In 1854 alone, 650 new titles were submitted for registration.[24] Until 1855 the works of European composers were judged to be better than compositions by Americans and therefore worth their moderately higher prices. On January 1, 1855, General Hall stunned the music world by doubling his price on all European works. With this bold stroke the United States' premier publisher enacted what amounted to a protective tariff to benefit America's composers.[25]

Only months after this, Hall bought out all the Gottschalk works formerly owned by Firth Pond & Co., including *The Last Hope*. Gottschalk took an immediate liking to Hall, who treated him as a talented if somewhat wayward son. He also came to appreciate the General as a quintessential Yankee:

> The *adaptability* of the Yankee is wonderful. . . . My music publisher, Hall,
> was first a lawyer, afterwards, by turn, a dealer in furniture, manufacturer of

guitars, music publisher, piano manufacturer, member of Congress, etc. . . . I ought to add that through all these numerous changes he has merited the esteem of his fellow citizens by the incorruptible honesty of his dealings and the uprightness of his mind.[26]

No copy of Gottschalk's September 18, 1855, contract with Hall has survived, but it apparently obligated the composer to deliver a half dozen new works annually for five years. Initially Hall purchased flat rights to a composition.[27] Later, when he realized that Gottschalk's concerts were the best form of advertisement, he gave the composer a royalty as well. On his side, Gottschalk promised to include pieces issued by Hall in all his programs. This very practical consideration goes far toward explaining the repetitious nature of many of Gottschalk's programs. His concerts, like the tours of popular music stars today, which are directed toward the sale of recordings and videos, were above all a means of promoting the sale of sheet music.

Under pressure to meet his new contract, Gottschalk in quick order wrote out *The Banjo* (op. 15), *Marche de nuit, La Jota aragonesa,* and several other pieces.[28] No sooner were these works completed than he shipped copies to the Escudiers in Paris and to Schott in Mainz.[29] Meanwhile, he contacted the publishing house of Gould & Co. in Philadelphia and entered into a separate contract with the provision, unusual for that day, of a straight ten percent on gross sales. Gottschalk shrewdly realized that sales would suffer if the music was too difficult for amateurs or if it was printed too small. He therefore produced a number of simpler pieces and adopted the pen names of "Oscar Litti" and "Paul Ernest" for use on them. He also badgered Gould into putting no more than twenty-two measures per page. "The larger the measures the clearer the music is to the eye and the better will be its sales," he explained.[30]

Meanwhile, the prospects for engagements in the immediate future remained poor. The theaters were full, but piano concerts remained under the cloud that had enveloped them since the early 1850s. Worse, in Gottschalk's absence a new Viennese import named Gustave Satter (1832–79) had laid claim to first place among Manhattan pianists.[31] If the piano scene was bleak, the state of opera was abysmal. In spite of its resonant name, the Academy of Music was a purely commercial venture and a singularly unsuccessful one at that. When an earlier management team fell on its face, the irrepressible violinist Ole Bull, fresh from the collapse of his effort to establish a Norwegian colony in Pennsylvania, leased the Academy in partnership with Max Maretzek and Maurice Strakosch. Bull's offer of a thousand-dollar prize for the best opera by an American composer on a strictly American subject would seem to have been a perfect opening for Gottschalk. But at the very time when

Gottschalk might have taken advantage of this opportunity it vanished in thin air, as did Bull's operatic season, for he was again broke and his investors were howling.[32] By contrast, the burlesques of operas offered by Buckley's Serenaders, White's Serenaders, and other companies of black face minstrels drew full houses with full wallets.

With the public cool toward pianists and several of the more energetic impresarios tied up in wrangling over the Academy of Music, Gottschalk's prospects were bleak. He could not even present himself as an exotic from Paris, as that niche in the theatrical market was being filled by the larger-than-life personality of Rachel, the passionate tragedienne who had driven Parisian audiences to delirium with her husky-voiced renditions of the French classics.

Thus thwarted, Gottschalk did the next best thing and took on piano students. Most were young females who had been vaccinated against professional-level achievement by their parents' low expectations of them. But there were also several serious professionals of Moreau's own age. Tall, blond-haired Harry Sanderson was a leader among this group. Here was someone as true-blue American as any of those who cheered Buckley's Serenaders, yet he was a dedicated pianist and eager to compete with the imports. Unfortunately, it was Sanderson who founded the tradition of treating Gottschalk's compositions as if they were calisthenics designed to show off the performer's arm muscles. Eventually his penchant for thunderous effects reached the point where Gottschalk dismissed him as a "monster."[33]

Another of Gottschalk's American disciples, T. Franklin Bassford, surpassed even Sanderson in his eagerness to remake himself in his teacher's image. No sooner did his teacher gain popularity with his *Marche de nuit* than Bassford gave forth with a *Marche du matin*.[34] Soon this Gottschalk clone was sporting a drooping mustache, fancy kid gloves and an affected Creole-French accent.

When not busy guiding these students, Gottschalk had time to broaden his contacts in the New York musical world. Alfred Boucher, for example, was a music teacher whose house at 22 West 11th Street was a gathering place for many performers and impresarios. Moreau became a frequent visitor at soirées there, and his younger brother Gaston later married the Bouchers' daughter. It was probably at the Bouchers' that Gottschalk met Maurice Strakosch, the Austrian-born pianist and self-promoter, and his brother Max, later Gottschalk's manager. Through the brothers Strakosch Moreau came into contact with the Patti family, a large and grandly talented tribe of singers and violinists who launched the counter-assault that first put Americans on the opera stages of Europe. During the summer and autumn of 1855 Moreau also renewed his friendship with the tenor Pasquale Brignoli, whom he had known in Paris and who was now part of the aggregation at the Academy of Music. The American-born soprano Clara Brinkerhoff was still another musician who entered the composer's social orbit during 1855.[35]

No friendship formed by Gottschalk in this period was more unlikely than that with pianist William Mason. The son of hymnologist Lowell Mason, who epitomized the dour approach to music-making that Gottschalk contemptuously ascribed to Protestantism, Mason pursued his piano studies in Berlin and Leipzig rather than Paris. When Mason returned, Dwight hailed him as the first American to play genuine "classical" music on the piano and seized every opportunity to promote him at Gottschalk's expense.[36]

Mason's brief contact with Liszt, Schumann, and Brahms had broadened the sympathies of the young Bostonian.[37] Now he looked with worshipful eyes upon all those bright spirits who were creating new music and winning praise for doing so. Gottschalk and he were in many respects opposites, yet Mason was fascinated by Moreau and became his lifelong friend.

All these contacts reflect the extent to which musicians themselves, if not yet the public, accepted Gottschalk as a rising leader in the American musical world. Further evidence of this was his election to honorary membership in the New York Philharmonic Society.[38] A favorable vote had not been assured. Oscar Comettant was in New York at the time and reported that "one of the most envenomed opponents of [Gottschalk's] nomination was Mr. Schaffenberg [*sic*], a sterile musician and dull and monotonous pianist." William Scharfenberg (1819–95) was a German-born pianist who had studied with the great Hummel. A founding member of the Philharmonic, he had taken a strong dislike to Gottschalk when he first appeared at Niblo's Saloon in 1853 and never relented thereafter. That Scharfenberg was motivated by insecurity and envy is suggested by Comettant's further observation:

> The members of [the Philharmonic] play the works of Beethoven passably well for persons who have not heard them performed by the good orchestras of Germany or especially by the orchestra . . . of the Paris Conservatory. But tell them at New York that their Philharmonic Society is not the best of its kind in the world, and you will be eaten alive.[39]

In the end, Gottschalk was elected.

Recognition by his professional peers brought benefits to Moreau. At an exhibition of American manufacturers held in the autumn of 1855 he joined Mason on a committee to evaluate American pianos. They awarded the prize to an unknown manufacturer from Varick Street, a "Mr.

Steinway, . . . of whom we have never before heard, and no wonder, as he does not advertise."[40]

Teaching and the preparation of manuscripts for publication kept Gottschalk busy through the autumn but did not prevent him from having an extensive social life. Since he had only recently returned from Cuba, it was natural that members of Manhattan's large Hispanic colony would have sought him out. As early as July 1855, Cuban and other Latin American notables feted the American and offered rhymed toasts to his muse.[41] Among those present was General José Rufino Echenique, president of Peru from 1851 to his overthrow by revolution in 1854.[42] The deposed Echenique took an interest in Gottschalk and invited him to visit his country.

Even closer to Gottschalk was José Antonio Páez, once a colleague of the great Bolívar and a hero of Venezuelan independence. Twice president of his country, Páez had been the first to advocate freedom for the black race throughout the Americas. Courtly and generous, this self-made man had once captured a dangerous enemy and then taken the man into his home as a guest.[43] Now, in exile, he was the toast of New York.[44] Gottschalk confessed to his sister Clara that he admired Páez immensely. They exchanged portraits, and Gottschalk dedicated to Páez his *Marche de nuit* (op. 17), which memorialized the general's guerrilla-style campaign against Spanish rule. With the exception of the fine harmonies in the introduction and trio, *Marche de nuit* is among Gottschalk's more colorless pieces. Moreau liked it, however, considering it to be "the least bad of everything I've composed."[45] The public was even more positive, ordering five thousand copies of the sheet music even before it appeared in Hall's shop.[46]

By mid-century, New York was a hive of specialized activity. A Manhattan hatter, for example, was more likely to be acquainted with fellow hatters around town than with a neighbor in another line down the block. In spite of such specialization, the cultural life of the metropolis was remarkably integrated, both horizontally and vertically. Prominent painters mixed easily with acclaimed opera stars, and poets with artists. Similarly, hacks and highbrows interacted incessantly, as did journeyman portraitists and the galleries' reigning masters. Such cross-contact was fostered by the fact that artists at every level were producing for the market. Manhattan audiences included not a few snobs, like the lawyer and aficionado of music George Templeton Strong. But such people did not yet dominate, with the result that artists in most fields still directed their appeal to the hearts and pocketbooks of the general public at large.

Moreau Gottschalk was sociable by nature.[47] From his years in Paris he retained a lively interest in literature and the arts which he fully indulged in New York. The friendships he formed with painters and writers were at least as important to him as his links in the world of music.

Following a concert at Albany in the autumn of 1855 Moreau met sculptor Erastus Dow Palmer. By year's end he considered this native-born talent his "eminent, amiable, and sympathetic friend."[48] Palmer's white marble *Indian Girl*, like Gottschalk's Creole pieces, stood out not only for its American theme but for its being clothed in "American" rather than classical dress. Americans were excited to discover in Palmer a local talent who, like Gottschalk, had mastered classical technique but then cast off the yoke of Europe.[49]

In the audience at the same concert at Albany was George William Warren (1828–1902), pianist and organist at the local St. Peter's Church. Robust and full-bearded, Warren stood in the same solid Yankee tradition as Lowell Mason, even to the point of editing a major Protestant hymnal, *Warren's Hymns and Tunes*. Yet while he and Gottschalk stood on opposite sides of many fault lines running through American life, Warren was drawn at once to the composer from New Orleans. "I then heard him for the first time," Warren recalled, "and succumbed at once. It was love at first sight—love for the man, his genius, his most extraordinary playing, and the utter (inner) simplicity of character, which I discovered at a glance."[50]

Gottschalk reciprocated this affection. As he had done with Espadero, he collaborated with Warren on compositions, especially after the latter became organist at St. Thomas Church in Brooklyn.[51]

Gottschalk and Warren shared an unbounded enthusiasm for the paintings of an American contemporary, Frederic Edwin Church. Raised in affluence in Hartford, Connecticut, Church had studied art with Thomas Cole, founder of the Hudson River school of landscape painting. Church emerged on the New York scene just at the time of Gottschalk's return from Europe. These two romantics were eventually brought together by their common passion for the American tropics. Church was among those many New Englanders who were groping for a spiritually warmer environment than that provided by Calvinism.[52] A first trip to Ecuador in 1855 had whetted his taste for this sensuous and exuberantly tropical alternative to his own measured world.

After attending a Gottschalk concert in the winter of 1855–56, Church understood at once that his Creole contemporary embodied in music everything he himself had been seeking in art and life. He therefore approached George Warren and asked for an introduction.[53] Warren had already regaled Church with glowing accounts of his pianist friend and had praised Church to Gottschalk. And in truth, the seven-foot canvasses that became Church's trademark were visual versions of the "monster concerts" Gottschalk was to produce all over Latin America. Church's enormous yet meticulously rendered views of Niagara or his depictions of the ominous Cotopaxi volcano stunned audiences in the same way as had Gottschalk's thunderous *Bunker Hill* or his brooding Caribbean fantasies. Both artists were matinee idols, and both at heart were populists, with no trace of condescension toward their audiences.[54]

Several years after the painter and composer first met, Church joined an expedition by ship to the Arctic. He returned with a series of enormous paintings depicting icebergs in an eerie yet warmly luminous glow. Several contemporary critics drew a direct parallel between this "message" and what Gottschalk was doing in his compositions:

> In pondering over the sad mystery of these Icebergs, we float down again to Tropical Seas and Islands; and as we linger under the shade of palm and banana tree, the rude chant of the Negro strikes the ear in the grotesque and characteristic framework of *Le Bananier,* the plaintive melody of *La Savane.* . . . With an insensibility to these influences, there can be but little sympathy or appreciation of the works of Mr. Gottschalk. . . . Where else in the United States can we look for a spontaneous gush of melody? . . . [Not to} the old Puritan element, [with] its savage intent to annihilate the aesthetic part of man's nature under the deadening dominion of its own Blue Laws.[55]

And so the three Yankees—Erastus Dow, George Warren, and Frederic Edwin Church—were all drawn to Gottschalk as a living symbol of the warmer emotions they sought to infuse into their art and as an artist who had preceded them in embracing American themes. Church's meeting with Gottschalk confirmed the new direction in his life, and when Gottschalk eventually left New York for the Caribbean, Church sailed for South America to create his most important canvasses. Before departing, however, Church gave his friend a landscape, "a little masterpiece."[56] Gottschalk, in addition to dedicating a further *Mazurka poétique* to Church,[57] paid tribute to him as "the most gifted artist that I know, the most sensitive to music, the most modest man, and, finally, one of the rare illustrious men whom I actually like."[58]

During Gottschalk's first visit to New York in 1853, the suave Nathaniel Parker Willis had taken him to Anne Lynch's literary salon at her home on 37th Street, a few doors west of Fifth Avenue. By the time Gottschalk returned from Cuba, Miss Lynch's soirées had become self-consciously highbrow, and Gottschalk avoided them.[59] Instead, he was drawn to the extraordinary figure of Henry Clapp Jr. and to the circle of irreverent young writers and wits gathered around him.

At Clapp's death twenty years later, obituaries recalled him as the "King of Bohemia." He held this title by default, for he was the United States' first true bohemian. By common consent he was also the wittiest

man on the North American continent. It was Clapp who described his
fellow journalist Horace Greeley as "a self-made man that worships his
creator."[60] Of poet and fellow bohemian George Arnold he said, "He can
be true to more women than any man I ever knew." And when a San
Francisco impresario wired humorist Artemus Ward to ask, "What will
you take for forty nights in California?" Clapp suggested the reply,
"Brandy and water."[61]

Such quips were perfectly suited to the informal and brief journalistic
essay known in French as a *feuilleton* and popularized throughout Europe over the previous decades. Clapp was among the first to introduce
this form into the United States. His pointed barbs assured for "Figaro"
(his pen name) a small but fiercely loyal readership. They also assured
him a long list of detractors. Prominent among his enemies was William
Dean Howells, later a distinguished novelist but now merely an Ohio
newspaperman in search of the East's culture. Clapp showed up late for
his meeting with the budding writer. Howells found "Figaro"

> a man of such open and avowed cynicism that he may have been, for all I
> know, a kindly optimist at heart. . . . He walked up and down his room saying
> what lurid things he would directly do if anyone accused him of respectability,
> so that he might disabuse the minds of all witnesses.[62]

For all this, Howells had to confess a "fascination for [Clapp] which I
could not disown, in spite of my inner disgust."

Moreau Gottschalk felt the same fascination toward Clapp but with
none of the disgust. Here was a conversational virtuoso whose sharp-
edged assaults on convention gave Gottschalk a language to express his
own private qualms about the life around him. He greatly valued his
friendship with Clapp and stayed in touch with him through letters (alas,
now lost) when he was on concert tour.[63]

Henry Clapp had been born to staunch Yankee parents on Nantucket
in 1814. Touched by the great spiritual revival of the 1830s, Clapp became
an ardent evangelical Christian, an abolitionist, and a foe of the demon
Drink. As editor of the Lynn, Massachusetts, paper, he waxed so intem-
perate in the cause of temperance that he was briefly jailed for it.[64]

Up to this point Henry Clapp's career had certain parallels with that
of John Sullivan Dwight. The main difference was that Clapp was a more
ardent Christian, a more passionate abolitionist, and more militant in the
cause of temperance. He also became a more doctrinaire follower of
François Charles Fourier. Dwight perceived in the French eccentric nothing more than a general affirmation of secular art and the life of feeling.
Clapp, by contrast, responded to the utopian's summons to emancipate
the passions and his flat rejection of authority in all things including art.

With a convert's zeal he turned his back on evangelical piety and lashed out at Boston and all it stood for. In the ultimate act of apostasy he moved to Paris, the locus of evil, and plunged headlong into *la vie bohème.*

Clapp soon developed an acute appreciation for genuine talent, no matter how unconventional. In the year he met Gottschalk, Clapp became the unflagging champion of Walt Whitman, whose *Leaves of Grass* had just appeared in print. Whitman shared Clapp's great love of France and sprinkled his letters with French expressions learned during a brief residence in New Orleans.[65] Whitman also loved music, by which he meant not the "classical" repertoire but "Italia's peerless compositions," that is, the Italian operas so beloved by democratic America.[66] Such feelings brought Whitman close not only to Clapp and his circle but to Gottschalk's world. He admired Gottschalk's close friend Brignoli and expostulated on the tenor's "perfect singing voice" with its "tremulous, manly timbre!"[67]

Clapp's appeal to Moreau Gottschalk was based on his savage antipathy to puritan sanctimony, his boundless love of the French language, and his vision of a democratic United States free of the hypocrisy of highbrow Good Taste. Through Clapp, Gottschalk discovered that there were other Americans who shared his own views on these matters. When Gottschalk first met Henry Clapp in 1855 his bohemian literary circle was only beginning to coalesce. Several key members joined later, including artists George H. Boughton, Wilson Fisk, and Sol Eytinge Jr., Dickens's favorite illustrator; and many of the group, including Clapp himself, did not really come into their own until the late 1850s, by which time Gottschalk was once more out of the country.

These young writers and artists opened new horizons to Gottschalk. Dirt poor and struggling, they lived by and for the popular press. They lavished on their sketches, essays, and reviews a rigor rarely before seen in American journalism. As one of them later recalled, "unmerciful chaff pursued the perpetrator of any piece of writing that impressed those persons as trite, conventional, artificial, laboriously solemn, or insincere."[68] Thanks to Henry Clapp and his circle, Moreau Gottschalk became not only a confirmed democrat and champion of young American art but a writer as well. In time this became his third profession, along with composing and performing on the piano.

These artistic and literary contacts brought Gottschalk long-term benefits, but did not solve his immediate problems. Each month during the autumn of 1855 he sent his mother fourteen hundred francs, or about four thousand dollars in today's currency.[69] In spite of his hope to cover these costs from lessons, he was steadily depleting his savings from New

Orleans.[70] Prospects for an upturn were bleak. A flock of unknown pianists had descended upon New York, more than satisfying the public's limited interest. Besides Oscar Comettant from Paris there was Narcisso Lopez Jr., son of the general of Cuban fame, who attracted an audience the *Times* described as consisting "for the most part of fierce looking but diminutive Spaniards."[71]

More serious competition was offered by the six chamber music matinees announced by William Mason and cellist Carl Bergmann in late November 1855.[72] Besides presenting the New York premiere of a trio by "Mr. Brahms,"[73] the first concert in this series featured on violin the twenty-year-old German-born Theodore Thomas, who later founded the Chicago Symphony Orchestra.[74] In a separate initiative, Theodore Eisfeld was offering evening chamber music performances of a strictly classical repertoire. Even though it took several years for such concerts to catch on, they doubtless skimmed the audience for anything Gottschalk might have done.

As if this were not enough, the tragedienne Rachel had begun her performances on September 3 and continued them through the autumn. As seven thousand dollars poured in on opening night, her brother and manager reported that "the administrative moneybags are swelling delightfully."[75] But ticket sales dropped by half the second night and continued to plummet thereafter. Gottschalk, however, was convinced she was netting truly vast sums and this depressed him mightily.[76] On top of all this, the irrepressible Jullien had again swept into town with his monster concerts and *The Fireman's Quadrille.*

The best his manager could do was to book Gottschalk into Fulton Hall in Lancaster, Pennsylvania, on November 2. Moreau regaled the audience with several fantasias and *Bunker Hill,* described as "a fragment of the great National Symphony." Unfortunately, he had to divide the take with a hapless soprano, Miss Annie Spinola.[77] Among the audience was Newton Lightner, brother-in-law of Stephen Foster.[78] Lightner and his friends petitioned Moreau to offer a second concert, which Moreau himself arranged some weeks later in connection with a performance in Baltimore, also booked without his manager's help.[79]

So completely did Bookstaver fail as manager that Moreau turned to his cousin Leonard Myers for help in organizing a pair of concerts in Philadelphia. Just at this moment a long letter arrived from Hector Berlioz in Paris.[80] Whatever encouragement Berlioz gave his young American friend, Gottschalk ruled out a return to Europe. This was only prudent, since as many as eight pianists were offering recitals each night in Paris at the time.[81]

When Gottschalk arrived in Philadelphia on November 12, his spirits sank still further. The city was a frozen Arctic with ice-breakers needed to cut a passage for the Camden ferry.[82] To Moreau's utter disgust he found that his brother Edward, who had been sponging off the Myerses for a year, had done nothing either to promote his career as a pianist or to find other employment. "His profession is smoking and being filthy in his clothes," Moreau reported to his mother. "Perseverance? He has never had it and never will."[83]

Few of the local papers had been contacted regarding the virtuoso's arrival, and fewer still had been persuaded that they should cover Moreau's concerts at the Musical Fund Hall. Instead, the press was full of ads for concerts by some half dozen brass bands and for Rachel's impending arrival on November 19.[84]

Gottschalk's glum mood is reflected in the *Pennsylvania Inquirer*'s announcement that the Philadelphia concerts would be the composer's last "previous to leaving his native country. . . . It may be for years and it may be forever." Acknowledging that Gottschalk had been far more warmly received in Europe than America, the *Inquirer* concluded on a more cheerful note, saying that "his countrymen will, no doubt, be eager to testify their national interest in the man, as well as the great musical genius."[85]

The concerts were indeed well received, and Edward managed not to disgrace himself as assisting artist. But the press hardly noticed, and after Gottschalk had sent his earnings off to Paris he was once again broke. By the time he showed up for a concert in Baltimore he was not only without cash but his bank account in New York was down to the last five dollars. In desperation he drew twenty dollars on General Hall's account with a promise to repay the debt promptly.[86]

Having struck out in the East and with no prospects in Paris, Gottschalk's last hope was California. Jenny Lind's former tour manager, Le Grand Smith proposed a round of concerts in the American El Dorado, and Moreau eagerly accepted. Plans were finalized, but two hours before the departure time Smith broke his leg, thus closing this final avenue of escape from the blind alley in which Gottschalk found himself. It was scant consolation that the ship on which he was to have sailed to California sank en route to the West.[87]

Chapter Fifteen

American Triumph: The
Dodworth's Hall Concerts and
the Great Non-Battle with
Thalberg

ALMOST three years after returning to the United States, Gottschalk had yet to break through to the larger public as he had done in France, Switzerland, Spain, and Cuba. His mood was down, and as the year 1855 waned his depression deepened. These months were by no means wasted, however, as he worked deep into the night preparing manuscripts for publication under his new contract with General Hall. By mid-November the first fruits of this effort emerged in print.

When he played some of these compositions for Hall, the publisher asked, "Why do you not give a concert to make them known?" "*Ma foi,*" Gottschalk replied, "it is a luxury that my means no longer permit me!" "Bah! I will pay you $100 for a piano concert at Dodworth's Rooms," responded the General.[1] The date was set for December 20, 1855. The place was Dodworth's Hall, a 580-seat room on Broadway at 11th Street.

This concert was carefully planned to relaunch a career that had foundered badly since February 1853. Advertisements appeared in the *New York Times*, the *Herald*, and other leading papers. A drum beat of longer articles whipped up enthusiasm for over a month before the event itself. The stuffy *Albion* began these on November 17, announcing:

> Gottschalk is in New York! We knew not where he was, and sighed for him, when we accidentally encountered him the other evening. Our delight at the encounter was great, for Gottschalk is not only in our eyes one of the most

marvelous pianists of the present epoch, but he is also a composer of the first rank, a man possessing both head and heart, a poet, a genuine poet! Since Chopin, we know of no one so capable of filling his place as Gottschalk.[2]

The *Courrier des États-Unis* announced in faltering English, "[Gottschalk] will finally break, in favor of the New York public, his too long silence in which he had closed himself up."[3] In the last week before the concert it was trumpeted as a must event for the several thousand New Yorkers who numbered themselves among the ultra-elite.[4]

Hall deliberately excluded the public by reserving three hundred seats for the press and select musicians.[5] The remaining tickets were sold at once, and at the last minute Hall offered the public two hundred more tickets for which no seats were available. These, too, were snapped up. By the time Gottschalk sat down at the Chickering piano, the aisles were packed and the audience filled the stage. Many ladies had to stand the whole evening. Thanks to General Hall and to Gottschalk's prolonged absence from the public eye, the first Dodworth concert was a triumph before the first note sounded, truly a "veritable artistic ceremony."[6]

Here was a double rarity in New York and America generally: a full evening of piano music, and most of it by a single American composer. The evening opened with Gottschalk and the Bohemian-born Karl Wels playing the composer's two-piano *Italian Glories*, a fantasia on themes from Bellini's operas *Norma*, *Lucrezia*, and *Sonnambula*. Gottschalk then followed with a fragment from his new *Fantasia on Themes from Lucia*. Both of these introductory pieces were bravura exercises in typical opera fantasy style, in which the familiar operatic themes were ornamented with dizzying unbroken runs and unexpected chord progressions. Then followed one of the *Ossian* ballades and *Marche de nuit*, which *Leslie's* reviewer judged to be "an exquisite reverie—sad, tender, and thoughtful."[7] The first part of the program concluded with an unidentified mazurka by Gottschalk and *The Banjo*, which was encored amidst tumultuous applause.

The second half of the program opened with another bow to Europe in the form of Onslow's E-minor sonata for four hands, for which Gottschalk was joined by his old friend Richard Hoffman. "There has never been such duet playing in America," rhapsodized Henry Watson.[8] But the real sensation of the evening was *The Last Hope*. The *New York Times* reviewer, in what Gottschalk considered "one of the most excellent articles I have ever had in my life,"[9] expressed particular admiration for *The Last Hope*, describing it as a "lamentation of decided Hebrew character."[10] Indeed, the *Times* review was nothing short of ecstatic at

those zephyr-like tremolos; those perfectly spiritual *arpeggios*, leaping up to heaven like a flame from the altar; those passionate combinations struggling for mastery like man's desires.

The only sour note was sounded by Theodore Hagen, writing in the *Review & Gazette*. He acknowledged that Moreau could play anything he wished. "Why not, then, for his own sake and that of a better art than the one which his fantasias present, play something of the serious masters?" Apparently Mozart, Chopin, and Onslow did not count in this category. Yet even Hagen was struck by *The Banjo*, admitting that Gottschalk's "nervous touch, his dashing, daring playing, his restless melodic phrasing . . . created really interesting pictures . . . of Southern life and Negro enjoyments [rooted in] the soil and, at least, the traditions of its people."[11] Surprisingly, Hagen also approved of the *Marche de nuit*, finding that it revealed "a real artistic feeling, elevation of mind, and some noble phrasing," which he went so far as to compare with Chopin.

The first Dodworth's Hall concert hit like a thunderbolt. The battalion of pianists in attendance judged it a triumph and paid their respects to the composer at his residence the next day. Even though Gottschalk cleared only $150,[12] he left the hall with the public clamoring for more. A second concert was immediately scheduled for the following week. When the night arrived the hall was packed yet more tightly, this time entirely with paying customers. Hagen's call for a more "classical" repertoire had clearly stung Gottschalk, who programmed two movements of Beethoven's "Kreutzer Sonata" for violin and piano, as well as Weber's *Concertstück*, a Gottschalk favorite. A last-minute substitution denied Hagen his Beethoven, but no one else missed it. Other works from the first concert were repeated, with the addition of the *Jérusalem* fantasy and a new work, *Danse des sylphes*, a clever reworking of Dieudonné Felix Godefroid's popular piece for harp.

One of the very few complaints came from the *Evening Post*, which groused that Gottschalk's ubiquity in the program was "wearisome."[13] The unanimous enthusiasm of every other critic and especially of the broader public suggests that the *Evening Post*'s critic may have been sore at having had to pay for his ticket. Far more typical was the *Spirit of the Times*, which declared that "for depth of feeling, liquidity of touch, marvels of execution, easy accomplishment of great difficulties, and variety of tone, [Gottschalk's] performances are, in our estimation, unrivaled." The *Marche de nuit* alone "entitled [Gottschalk] to a place among the best classic music executives and authors."[14]

With the second soirée at Dodworth's Hall, Gottschalk banished all thought of leaving America. Suddenly he found himself at the very apex of Manhattan's music world, with critics and public both clamoring for him to continue his innovative concert programs. Happily, Dodworth's Hall was available. All New York knew the Dodworth family, who had emigrated from England earlier in the century and established themselves as brass band leaders, dance instructors, and concert organizers. The location of their hall on Broadway next to Grace Church suggested just the right mixture of entertainment and culture. And its acoustics were superb. Moreau and General Hall therefore took immediate steps to transform the experimental Dodworth's Hall concerts into a full series.

By the time they finally ended in June 1856, Gottschalk's programs were the longest cycle of concerts ever heard in the New World. They had attracted a far larger audience for chamber-scale performances than anyone had even dreamed possible. They generated for serious music a social prestige associated heretofore only with opera. And they established the first and, for many years, the very best platform for the performance of new American music. Until the Dodworth's Hall concerts, no American composer had ever achieved a fraction of the public acclaim and critical acceptance that Gottschalk gained in those months. Gottschalk's success created a new standard for music written and performed by Americans, for Americans.

Before continuing the cycle of concerts, Moreau had to make a brief trip to Washington, Baltimore, and Philadelphia, in order to fulfill obligations entered into by his impresario, Bookstaver. The bitter cold that had plagued Moreau in Philadelphia in November continued through these first days of 1856, only now it was worsened by huge snowfalls, which left ten-foot mounds of snow in Manhattan and more to the south. The concerts were of little note, but the return trip from Baltimore to Philadelphia was a nightmare that brought lasting consequences. Ordinarily, this leg of the journey would have required five hours. This time snowdrifts engulfed the train three hours from Wilmington, Delaware. The engineer detached the locomotive in order to seek help and was soon stuck in another drift. A fresh snowstorm completely buried the cars, and the huddled passengers were soon freezing, without fuel or water. They grew hungry, "children wept, the women cried lamentably, the conductor swore like an Irishman."[15] Gottschalk climbed to the roof of a wagon and waited until he spied a sleigh a quarter mile away. He climbed into the sleigh with several other passengers, including a red-faced and potbellied man who took up nearly all the space. After five minutes the sleigh overturned, depositing its passengers into a five-foot drift. Moreau ended up face down in the snow with the obese man squarely on his back, "struggling, screaming, whining, and pushing me further down with each of his efforts." Finally the driver disentangled them and they reached Chester, Pennsylvania, where the innkeeper regaled them with frozen apples and sarsaparilla.

Eventually the passengers were rescued and Gottschalk reached New York. However, one of his trunks containing musical manuscripts never caught up with him. Gottschalk was notoriously careless with his manuscripts. Since his music was largely improvisational in character, he rarely set down more than shorthand notes on a given piece unless required to do so by a publisher. We will never know what was lost in that snowbound trunk, but it probably included recent compositions, drafts of early works, and materials for the subsequently abandoned *American Concerto*. Singer Clara Brinkerhoff claimed that it also contained parts of a lost opera.[16]

Returning to New York, Gottschalk encountered the most animated concert scene in years. A usually dour critic confessed, "The concert season of the present winter seems to be as lively and active as that of last year was barren and lifeless. There is a complete rush amongst our artists, or those who bear this name, to exhibit their talents and abilities."[17] The unprecedented triumph of Gottschalk's first soirées had carried three messages to performers and their managers. First, it told them that New Yorkers might be willing to pay as much as a dollar a seat for chamber music or even solo performances. Second, it suggested that it might be easier to market an entire series than single programs. Third, it wiped away the prejudice against piano concerts that had existed since the invasion of Henri Herz, Leopold de Meyer, and the other imports of the 1840s. Now every pianist wanted to preside over his own soirées. News of this situation even reached Europe. By year's end the most celebrated pianist on the Continent, Sigismund Thalberg, would be in New York trying to capitalize on Gottschalk's triumph.

The Mason-Bergmann chamber music matinees resumed on February 26, 1856, with works by Beethoven, Bach, and Rubinstein. Gottschalk's nemesis, William Scharfenberg, participated in these. Carl Bergmann of the Philharmonic also assembled a pick-up orchestra to present little-known classical works in a series of ten weekly "sacred" concerts, so named because they were held on Sunday evenings. Still a third series consisted of piano music performed by George Washbourn Morgan.

As organist of Grace Church, Morgan had only to walk next door to hear Gottschalk's Dodworth's Hall soirées. Convinced that he could do as well as the New Orleansian, he announced his own series at Dodworth's Hall to begin on January 8, 1856.[18] Gottschalk's secret, he thought, lay in his strong persona. Morgan therefore dispensed with assisting artists and put himself forward as announcer and musicologist-in-residence. Noting Hagen's criticism of Gottschalk for playing too few of the "classics," Morgan dished up a heavy diet of Beethoven. Unfortunately, Hagen himself ridiculed Morgan's verbal introductions,[19] while others found fault with Morgan's readings of Chopin and the romantics.[20]

Meanwhile, Gottschalk's star continued to rise. As Richard Storrs Willis put it:

> Public appreciation seems finally attending to Gottschalk (it has taken a some-
> what stupid while to do so). He is fast growing into his proper sphere . . . as
> one of the first living pianists.[21]

Gottschalk was the man of the hour. Unlike his competitors, he provided music "calculated for both the lovers of more severely classical, and those who affect music of a more popular character," wrote the *Atlas*.[22]

The third soirée took place on January 25, and except for short selections from Weber, Beethoven, and Liszt, it presented only music by Gottschalk. It was an evening of premieres, opening with a new Gottschalk fantasy on the finale of *Lucrezia Borgia* and progressing to a poignant new sentimental ballad, sharply etched and stated with great simplicity, *Solitude*.[23] Then came another premiere, this time a "valse poétique" entitled *Sospiro*. Gottschalk took pride in what he called the "exquisite details of harmony" in this graceful waltz in D-flat.[24] A fourth New York premiere was *Souvenirs d'Andalousie*, a collection of Spanish themes now codified into a single work and featuring a fandango. Continuing in a Hispanic vein, Gottschalk also presented *El Cocoyé* for the first time in New York.

The third concert at Dodworth's Hall was such a success that invitations to appear elsewhere soon poured in. His manager, Bookstaver, therefore opened a second front with a series of soirées at Polytechnic Hall in Brooklyn.[25] More important, Gottschalk was emboldened to plan a pioneering all-Spanish program for his fourth soirée, on February 4. In probably the first complete evening of "ethnic" music ever offered in the United States, Gottschalk presented a two-part program, the first devoted to his Spanish compositions and the second to his Cuban works. While advertised in both the Spanish and French press, the program was promoted above all for American audiences, who turned out in force. It was a cold night, but many Spaniards also showed up, announcing their presence with "guttural and accentuated cries," as non-Spaniards in the house noted with condescension.[26] The audience was edified by the Spanish and Cuban pieces but wanted above all to hear Gottschalk's latest hits. Rearranging the program, he obliged with *The Last Hope* and his brilliant fantasy on themes from Donizetti's *La Figlia del reggimento*, concluding amidst a thunder of applause with *The Banjo*.[27]

After a discreet interval to enable the phenomenal young violinist Paul Julien to play two farewell concerts at Niblo's Saloon,[28] Gottschalk announced his fifth soirée for February 14. *Marche de nuit* and *The Last Hope* were now in print and selling like hotcakes. Eager to cash in on both his music sales and the Dodworth bonanza, Moreau placed an announcement in the *New York Times* informing his public that he was "unavoidably obliged to postpone his departure to Lima for six or eight weeks."[29] During this period he intended to "accede to the requests of numerous friends and receive a limited number of pupils on the piano-forte."

The fifth concert at Dodworth's Hall included assisting pianist Karl Wels and the prodigiously talented Welsh harpist Aptomas. Here Moreau offered up, in addition to *Bamboula* and his *Carnival of Venice*, several new works in an unapologetically romantic genre. First came the pre-miere of *Chant du soldat*, subtitled *Grand caprice du concert*. An ex-tended "story" piece, *Chant du soldat* embodied that mixture of bravado and sentiment with which Americans were to march to war a few years later. Written in rondo form as a set of variations, it immediately found favor with the public, as did the more sentimental work premiered that evening, *Rayons d'azur*, a complex polka in six sharps subtitled "Shades of Evening."[30]

As the series at Dodworth's Hall progressed, Gottschalk plunged ever more confidently into new or neglected compositions of his own, as well as works by other composers. In the sixth concert he gave the American premiere of Liszt's recent transcription of the *Benediction* and *Sermon* from Berlioz's opera *Benvenuto Cellini*. He evidently maneuvered through the Lisztian intricacies superbly, yet "Gamma," writing in the An-glophile weekly *Albion*, ruled that "Mr. Gottschalk should borrow only from himself."[31] Now that he had begun reaching into recent Parisian classics, Gottschalk was not to be deterred. The same night he performed Chopin's *Scherzo* op. 31. On February 23 the Philharmonic's conductor, Theodore Eisfeld, invited Gottschalk to repeat both the Liszt and Chopin works in one of his own chamber music concerts. Here, as Watson pointed out in *Leslie's*, Moreau was playing before an audience "not . . . specially convened to listen to him, but one accustomed for years to con-sider and scrutinize works of the highest character and performances of the topmost merit."[32] The *New York Times* judged the Chopin piece to have been performed "in a superb manner" and was "a little astonished at Mr. Gottschalk's courage in attacking [*Benvenuto Cellini*] after the fa-tigue of Chopin's lengthy *Scherzo*."[33] The audience called Moreau back twice. "There is no doubt about one thing," concluded the *Times*. "Mr. Gottschalk is the rage. It is no slight thing to be doubly encored by the critical audience of Eisfeld's soirées."

Not everyone joined in the applause. Among the lovers of chamber music assembled there were all the deep-dyed Dwightians of Manhattan, among them the censorious Hagen of *Gazette & Review* and, sitting icily with his wife Ellen, the lawyer and musical dilettante George Templeton Strong. Genuinely susceptible to good music, Strong had long since fallen into the habit of recording in his diary his Jehovah-like judgments of every concert he attended. For Strong, as for Dwight, Good Music was a new faith, to be promoted through mission work. Propagating Haydn masses was for him a "missionary movement, to proclaim to our music-loving friends who sit in Darkness and the shadow of Donizetti a musical revelation beyond their dreams."[34] Anti-French, anti-Italian, anti-Catholic, anti-opera, anti–new music, and anti-American in music, Strong was an anti-Semite to boot. At the Eisfeld soirée Strong positively squirmed with indignation:

> Gottschalk (with an order in his buttonhole) gave an unfortunate piano fit with a hysterical scherzo of Chopin's. He was honored with a double encore, and played first a sledge hammer *Fantasia* [Liszt's transcription of *Benvenuto Cellini*], which may have been meant to depict the bombardment of Sebastopol . . . [The second encore was *The Last Hope*,] the subject of which was manifestly this: "The Traveler having gone to sleep in the depths of a tropical forest, is gradually awakened by ants and other bugs crawling over him."

Strong subjected himself to further misery at Gottschalk's seventh soirée at Dodworth's Hall on February 28. Hundreds had bought tickets for the previous concert, only to be denied entry at the door. In spite of efforts to limit the number of tickets issued to the size of the room, the audience this night was still larger.[35] Strong groused about the "absurd crowd, idiotic excitement, infinite bother in getting seats for the ladies."[36] Gottschalk's program seemed deliberately calculated to goad Strong:

> Any blacksmith excels this wretched, diminutive, Jewish-looking coxcomb in strength of muscle; many mechanics could surpass his nicety and quickness of manipulation, and there was nothing in his performance save his combination of a coal heaver's vigor with an artisan's dexterity. . . . [The audience] applauded accordingly, instead of rising like one man and one woman in kicking him out of the concert room as a profane puppy desecrating a noble art.[37]

Mr. Strong notwithstanding, the enthusiasm for Gottschalk's Dodworth soirées continued to mount. By the eleventh, two hundred more seats had been added to the hall.[38] Down to the end of the series, on June 7, the entire stage was packed with seats, and benches were added to the rear of the hall. Throngs of ladies in crinoline were to be seen standing on these throughout the performances.

If anything, the programming grew more idiosyncratic as the series progressed. Among works that Moreau premiered were the mazurka *La Scintilla; Priére du soir*, based on an aria from Ambroise Thomas's opera *Le Songe d'une nuit d'été; Galop di bravura* for two pianos;[39] *Esquisse* (possibly the same as *Esquisses créoles*, now lost); and *Ricordati*, subtitled *Méditations (Yearning Romance).*[40] In addition to these compositions of his own, Gottschalk branched out to include works by Schubert, Schumann, Henselt, Prudent, Thalberg, and his old Paris friend Alexandre Goria. More important, he used the remaining concerts in the Dodworth series to introduce compositions by many of his American (or Americanized) friends and collaborators, including William Mason *(Étude, Silver Spring)*, William Vincent Wallace *(Second Polka de concert)*, Karl Wels *(Airs from Il Trovatore)*, and Aptomas *(Scotch Melodies; Study and Imitation of Mandolin)*. At a time when few American composers could get a hearing for their works anywhere, Moreau Gottschalk used several of his concerts at Dodworth's Hall to showcase the compositions of others.

After the thirteenth soirée (April 10) an announcement appearing in all major papers reported that only three more concerts would be held that spring.[41] This was true only in the narrowest sense. Beginning with the Brooklyn soirée in January, Gottschalk had taken his series to Newark, Albany, and Philadelphia. Moreover, he transformed several benefits for fellow musicians into extensions of his own programs. Thus on February 29 he was scheduled to play two pieces in a benefit involving members of the tragedienne Rachel's company but ended up performing four works.[42] The same happened when the soprano E. Patania and pianist Karl Wels gave recitals in May.[43]

Together, the concerts at Dodworth's Hall achieved for Gottschalk a degree of popular acceptance never before accorded an American performer or composer. "Gottschalk is the rage among the music people at present," wrote the *Atlas*. "His genius, too long obscured by . . . extreme modesty, is now the wonder and admiration of the world of Harmony."[44] The *Atlas* concluded, "This modest and excellent artist is at last appreciated in this metropolis as he should be."[45]

Extravagant notices like these, and others too numerous to count, makes one all the more curious about the nature of Gottschalk's success. Was it because the season was slow, or because the alternatives were so dull? It is true that such musicians as William Mason and Theodore Thomas were less colorful than Gottschalk. Many years later Offenbach wrote of Thomas's spiritless performances and his ridiculous conducting style, which made him look "like a huge bird about to take its flight."[46] But the absence of more engaging competitors was more the effect of Gottschalk's success than the cause. As the *Courrier des États-Unis* noted, "the [Dodworth] concerts are so well received that we do not have any other musical festivals."[47]

A second explanation emphasizes Gottschalk's personality, and especially his status as a sex symbol among the younger women. Diego de Vivo, who later served Moreau as an assistant tour manager, wrote admiringly of his "brown hair, small build, his mustache over a smiling mouth, his lovely, dreamy eyes. His was the most charming personality of any among the artists whom I have known."[48] The females in his audience responded to this.

Such fans were particularly numerous at schools for young ladies. One of the wits in Clapp's bohemian circle lampooned this in a poem about *The Finishing School*, where

> Receptions were given each week on a Wednesday,—
> Which day by the school was entitled "The Men's Day,"
> Because on such date young New York was allowed
> To visit *en masse* that ingenious crowd,
> When they talk threadbare nothings and flat shilly-shally,
> Of Gottschalk's mustache, or Signora Vestvali.[49]

After one of the concerts at Dodworth's Hall, Gottschalk inadvertently left a glove on the piano; one of his female admirers recovered the glove and distributed it in fragments among some fifty fervent fans. The *World* reported that "the true loyalists adopted rose-colored hats as a sign of allegiance, and we recall a concert given in the Academy of Music in which the first-class boxes seemed to be a veritable garden of roses which undulated with the delicious breath of music by our inspired friend."[50] No wonder a Hartford paper attacked Gottschalk as the "Adonis of the concert-room" and as a "ninny."[51]

In this context, it is worth pointing out that young people in general, and young women in particular, dominated not only Gottschalk's audiences at Dodworth's Hall but the audiences for nearly all performances in mid-nineteenth-century America except theater and minstrel shows. They even made up the solid core of the Philharmonic's audience. Of a Philharmonic evening in 1856 one critic wrote:

> It was crammed, jammed, steaming hot, noisy, and uncomfortable. . . . the entire youthful population was present. All the ladies . . . were under eighteen years of age, and all their male accompaniment . . . twenty or twenty-one. Those are the recognized Philharmonic ages.[52]

This is relevant but does not explain the exceptional appeal Gottschalk exercised over his young audiences. Many, no doubt, were intrigued by the element of pure showmanship. Here was something new for practical Americans: a compatriot bent over the keyboard in a dreamy state, lost to the world. Was this humbug? P. T. Barnum had discovered an amazing feature of American character, namely, its guileless fascination with new sensations, on the one hand, and its keen readiness to expose each fresh wonder as humbug, on the other.[53] A Chicago paper applied the humbug test to Gottschalk and pronounced itself satisfied:

> We do not believe this is studied art or affectation; we have watched him closely and, whether soaring grandly into the thunders of the *crescendo* or

> floating away in the faintest *pianissimo*, he gives not the faintest sign of any-
> thing like a realization of his surroundings.[54]

One aspect of Gottschalk's performance never failed to capture the
attention of American audiences, to the point that it became an essential
part of what later vaudevillians would have called his *shtik*. This was the
doeskin gloves he invariably wore when he arrived on stage and then
removed with studied deliberation, as the wide-eyed audience looked on.
Fellow pianist Richard Hoffman recalled this as "often a very amusing episode":

> His deliberation, his perfect indifference to the waiting audience was thor-
> oughly manifest, as he slowly drew [his gloves] off, one finger at a time, bow-
> ing and smiling meanwhile to the familiar faces in the front rows. Finally dis-
> posing of them, he would manipulate his hands until they were quite limber,
> then preludize until his mood prompted him to begin his selection on the
> program.[55]

Compare this description with Liszt performing before three thousand
people in St. Petersburg: "Liszt mounted the platform, and pulling his doeskin gloves from his shapely white hands, tossed them carelessly on the
floor."[56] Gottschalk himself claimed that there were practical reasons for
appropriating this Lisztian touch. As he explained to a fellow performer:

> I never commence till I feel at ease. I make myself deliberate, and keep my
> head cool. I walk in very leisurely, I salute very moderately, I begin to take off
> my gloves as if I had come on for that purpose. Then I glance around in hopes
> of seeing an inspiring face, or at least a friendly one, so that my spirit may be
> in consonance with the music I am going to play, even if I am not in the
> mood.[57]

Another friend, George Upton, argued that the fussing over gloves "was
not an affectation, as many thought. He said it gave him time to compose
himself and get at ease."[58]

Whatever practical concerns may have prompted Gottschalk's glove
ritual, the gloves themselves had an entirely different valence in America
than in Europe. Under the pressure of Jacksonian democracy, distinctions
in American dress had begun to disappear.[59] That arbiter of taste Nathaniel Parker Willis acknowledged the politics of what he called the "hostility
to white gloves."[60] Gloves were a symbol of highbrow Culture. The flamboyant conductor Louis-Antoine Jullien used gloves to symbolize Beethoven's lofty status as an artist. Whenever he performed a work by Beethoven, a servant would walk on stage with a silver tray on which rested a
jeweled baton and white kid gloves, which Jullien would put away again
once he had finished conducting the Master's work.[61]

The gloves were, equally, a defiant symbol of romantic manhood, a
slap in the face to those American men at mid-century who affected a

stolid probity in dress, attiring themselves in what a cynic called "the inky habiliments of woe."[62] When the Hungarian patriot Louis Kossuth came to America in 1851 he took the country by storm, particularly its female part. Mr. Willis understood why:

> That [Kossuth] dresses picturesquely in furs and velvet, wears *light kid gloves* [emphasis added] and a mustache . . . may be disparagements among the men—but not among the ladies.[63]

And so Gottschalk, too, with his gloves and mustache, challenged the bland taste of the American businessman. His very dress presented an alternative to "the inky habiliments of woe" favored by the rising commercial class, just as his music challenged their Northern austerity with Southern warmth.

Taken together, these elements of manner, presentation, and dress turned each Gottschalk concert into a show. But they by no means suffice to explain the man's immense popularity among the serious musical public and among the critics. Part of the answer, of course, lies with the sheer appeal of Gottschalk's compositions. Moreau also had a knack for combining his works into engaging programs. Most of his performances began with a rousing curtain-raiser, followed by a cluster of ballads or sentimental pieces, the first part then concluding with an operatic fantasy. The second half invariably opened with another rouser, after which the assisting artist would play or sing. This led without further solos to the finale, which all but guaranteed that Gottschalk would be recalled for one or more encores, usually drawn from his American or Caribbean repertoires.

The sheer range and diversity of Gottschalk's programs appealed to audiences. Through him, Americans enjoyed the lyrical essence of opera without the tedious plots. He also exposed them for the first time to the syncopated rhythms of south Louisiana and the Caribbean that were to overwhelm American popular culture a half century later. And along the way, the public at a Gottschalk concert also encountered Chopin, Onslow, and even Beethoven. In short, he offered something for everyone.

Above all, Gottschalk's unprecedented success was due to his performance style, which virtually every listener, friend or foe, acknowledged to be uniquely his own. Richard Storrs Willis, called his style "*sui generis* . . . His fluency of style is remarkable, even in these days of remarkable pianoforte fluency. The instrument talks, *breathes* under his hand."[64] The *New York Times* raved over the "luxury of this new quality of sound" that Gottschalk elicited.[65] Another observer spoke of the "maddening fascination of [Gottschalk's] playing."[66]

Hundreds of reviews written during Gottschalk's career attempted to explain this "maddening fascination." Invariably, they mentioned Gottschalk's clarity of touch. A Cincinnati reviewer reported, "Every note is distinct, a crystal of sound, as well defined amid the mass as a diamond among ten thousand equally brilliant and sparkling."[67] Another Midwestern reviewer claimed, "He has evoked new effects from the instrument that none other has dreamt of."[68] Fellow pianist Richard Hoffman recalled, "He was possessed of a ringing, scintillating touch, which joined to a poetic charm of expression, seemed to sway the emotions of his audience with almost hypnotic power."[69]

One thing is clear: Gottschalk stood outside the Liszt tradition of thundering virtuosity. True, a Chicago reviewer could speak of the fact that "the strength and elasticity of his wrist and fore-arm are enormous, and apparently beyond the reach of fatigue." But that same reviewer then rhapsodized, "Nothing can exceed the distinctness of his scale, the evenness and limpidity of his trills, single and double, the smoothness with which his fingers travel over thirds and sixths, or the agile willingness of wrists in octaves."[70] In San Francisco it was "the delicate touch of Gottschalk [that] created a sensation."[71]

The *New York Times*, contrasting Gottschalk's style to that of all of the muscle-bound virtuosos, reported:

> His playing is full of inner meaning and suggestiveness. All his wonderful mechanical skill and dexterity are kept in the background by the strong and impalpable force of a predominant idea.[72]

When a *New York Times* reviewer referred to "the striking peculiarity of Mr. Gottschalk's playing," he was alluding above all to the fact that "the instrument became *vocal* under his touch."[73] This vocal quality accounted for the fact that "all his best thoughts are uttered in a language of his own." A Detroit reviewer focused on how Gottschalk "succeeded in imparting a peculiar *singing* character to his melodies."[74] George Warren, who was intrigued by Gottschalk's technique, recalled that "his playing was often most solemn and religious, when the hammer could not be heard against the string, and the whole thing was organ-toned."[75] A Cincinnati reviewer made the same point when he said that "he can accomplish better than any pianist living that most difficult of all feats, making the piano *sing*."[76]

There was one further quality essential to Gottschalk's sustained popularity: Moreau Gottschalk was an inveterate and inspired improviser. As a Chicago reviewer observed:

> The charm of Gottschalk's playing is, that he rarely interprets the same piece twice in precisely the same manner. The main features, of course, are there; but the finer shades of sentiment and feeling depend upon the mood of the

composer. We have often heard the same piece rendered by Gottschalk a second time with far more delicate tints and exquisite coloring than upon the
first occasion.[77]

In the same vein, the *New York Times* spoke of "an originality so strikingly manifest that it is always as much a matter of uncertainty to himself
as of doubt to those who are listening to him, what novelty or rendering
he may choose to introduce in the piece of his own composition which
he may be singing to his hearers on the instrument."[78]

It is fashionable today to contrast the improvisational character of
jazz to the formalized note-reading of "classical" music. Gottschalk was
as much an improviser as any twentieth-century jazz musician. That he
wrote down his compositions at all speaks more to the profitability of
sheet music sales in that era than to any preference he had for formal
composition over improvisation. At any rate, it was Gottschalk who introduced spontaneity into American classical music, and it was with
Gottschalk's death that such spontaneity went into eclipse again for several generations.

The concerts at Dodworth's Hall left Gottschalk flush for the first time
in his life. He was living comfortably at 149 West 14th Street and sending
large remittances to his family in Paris.[79] He even drew up a will.[80] Witnessed by George Henriques and two other New Yorkers, the will provided for all Moreau's assets to go to his mother. As executor, he named
his friend Charles Vezin of Philadelphia. The bond between these two had
became cemented since their first meeting.[81] That Vezin would in the end
turn out to have a disreputable side could not have been further from
Moreau's understanding of the man.

Moreau took steps also to cash in on his newfound role as social lion.
Through his association with Henry Clapp and his bohemian circle, Moreau had begun to take an interest in writing. Two of his greatest heroes
in Paris, Liszt and Berlioz, had pursued parallel careers as journalists,
Berlioz in particular having lived as much by his mordant pen as by his
compositions. Gottschalk had already ventured into the realm of criticism
when in November 1855 he published a lengthy review of the New York
premiere of Meyerbeer's opera *Le Prophéte.*[82] Some months later he was
approached by the *Morning Times* to do a column of art criticism and
gossip under the heading "Crotchets and Quavers."[83] Moreau accepted
and, in the tradition of Clapp's bohemians, adopted the pen name "Seven
Octaves."

In the several columns he wrote before being swept up in a fresh
round of concertizing, "Seven Octaves" dispensed wit and judgments in
many areas. Regarding New York architecture, he asked, "Why do they
not put some little finish to the side walls?" He pronounced the organ at

St. Paul's Church "miserably out of order." And he declared the violin playing of "Frederick Buckley of Buckley's Minstrels "a great deal too good for the audience." "Seven Octaves" even had the audacity to review—favorably—his own concerts with Anna de la Grange. With touching modesty he revealed, "Gottschalk played as only he can play."[84]

Gottschalk also covered the theatrical scene, an intriguing detail in light of his later affair with the actress Ada Clare. Most interesting, however, were his thoughtful observations on current painting and sculpture. He devoted particular attention to recent work by his friend Erastus Dow Palmer, "the immortal Palmer." Characteristically, Gottschalk's intent was to decipher the program of each work of sculpture, that is, to make explicit the narrative underlying the work.

A year later "Seven Octaves" re-emerged as a composer. Meanwhile, Gottschalk's spreading activity extended to his involvement in the creation of the first organization devoted to the performance of music composed in the United States.[85] The New York American Music Association was founded in the spring of 1856 amidst the enthusiasm of the Dodworth boom. It was the brainchild of two people, Charles Jerome Hopkins and George Frederick Bristow, both of whom had serious grudges against the New York musical establishment.

Hopkins, the son of the Episcopal bishop of Vermont, had studied chemistry in Burlington before bringing his talents to the New York music scene. When no one rushed to recognize his skills on viola, trombone, piano, organ, or cello, let alone his gifts as a composer, he settled for a post as organist at a church in Yonkers.[86] Bristow was a composer, violinist, and polemicist who shared William Henry Fry's paranoid belief in a European conspiracy against American music. Even though he himself was a founding member and director of the Philharmonic Society, Bristow accused the Philharmonic of systematically working for the extinction of American Music. With snide malice he asked, "Is there a Philharmonic Society in Germany for the encouragement solely of American music?"[87] In a complete rage, Bristow resigned from the Philharmonic's board and announced that he would form a new and truly *American* philharmonic society in New York.

Their shared resentments brought Hopkins and Bristow together. Their object, as reported by *Dwight's Journal of Music*, was "the fostering of native talent and the production of native musical works."[88] They proclaimed: "It is the opinion of many, and it has been often asserted, more especially by foreigners, that America can boast of no classical music."[89] Bristow and Hopkin proposed to disprove this.

The first concert passed almost without notice in February 1856.[90] The second concert, held at the Stuyvesant Institute on April 3, drew more attention.[91] Candido Berti, a Gottschalk disciple and assisting pianist at several of the soirées at Dodworth's Hall, performed a Gottschalk piece, while Gottschalk's friend, soprano Clara Brinkerhoff, performed a song by T. Franklin Bassford, the Gottschalk look-alike. At mid-point in the evening an electric thrill ran through the hall when Gottschalk himself showed up unannounced. The audience refused to allow the program to proceed until he performed his spare, moody, and curiously dissonant new song *Alone* with Mrs. Brinkerhoff. Again the audience clamored for more, until Gottschalk satisfied it by playing *The Last Hope*.[92]

The New York American Music Association struggled on for another year and a half before expiring. The Association had made its point, however, even though nearly a century was to pass before the public accepted it. And its most successful soirée was dominated by Gottschalk and the circle of young musicians who had formed around him.

The series at Dodworth's Hall completed, Gottschalk turned his attention to the hinterland. Following the pattern laid down by Paganini and Liszt, he expected that news of his success in the artistic capital would precede him into the countryside and thereby guarantee him good audiences in secondary centers. Again, Bookstaver served as his agent. Doubtful that provincials would abide a full evening of piano music, he and Moreau searched for a singer to broaden the program. They were lucky to be able to team up with the exquisite Anna de la Grange. Three years older than Gottschalk, de la Grange had inspired both Rossini and Donizetti to write for her.[93] Moreover, she could sing in five languages, including Hungarian, which had caused an elated Budapest public to dub her "Queen of the Hungarians."[94] Along the way she had married a Russian baron and acquired more than a few pets. Indeed, Americans noted that she traveled with "quite a menagerie, including three dogs, a parrot, a mocking bird, and a husband, all docile and well-trained."[95]

The indefatigable Bernard Ullmann had brought "Madame la Baronesse de la Grange" from Europe to star in his Niblo's Garden company, with which he hoped to trump Maretzek's crew at the Academy of Music. There was nothing genteel about this battle of opera companies, and before it was over Ullmann had threatened Maretzek with a revolver and de la Grange feared for her life.[96] By the late spring of 1856 de la Grange was available to tour with Gottschalk. They joined forces for the first time at the Academy of Music in Philadelphia in April. Encores turned the evening into a marathon in which de la Grange sang eight pieces and Gottschalk performed eleven.[97] They then proceeded to Baltimore, Albany, and Newark, New Jersey. De la Grange joined Gottschalk for his sixteenth and final soirée at Dodworth's Hall on June 7, with Gottschalk reciprocating for a huge concert at Niblo's Saloon a few days later, which was advertised as de la Grange's farewell concert before departing for Cuba, Europe, and beyond.[98]

De la Grange, it seems, had adopted Gottschalk's habit of celebrating premature and multiple *concerts d'adieu*. Her departure—for Havana— did not take place for another four months. Meanwhile, she and Gottschalk concertized throughout the Northeast and Canada. This tour proved either that musical fashions still spread slowly in 1856 or that Bookstaver was an incompetent manager. The local press in Syracuse did not know if Gottschalk was a soprano or contralto and expected de la Grange to play the flute.[99] The press in Utica received no advance notices either and therefore disposed of a successful concert there with a few trite phrases.[100]

The pace picked up as they proceeded through Binghamton, Troy, Oswego, Buffalo, Rochester, Watertown, and Ogdensburg. By the time the company reached Montreal Bookstaver had managed to send enough biographical material to convince the press that de la Grange, at least, was "Française de naissance et de coeur."[101] Thanks to this, the pair gave four concerts and were serenaded at their hotel, where Gottschalk's room was invaded by zealous fans.

The balance sheet did not reflect this enthusiasm. Anticipating Gottschalk's arrival, a shrewd businessman had booked every Montreal theater. Before allowing Gottschalk and de la Grange to perform there, he extorted half of their profits from them.[102] This was but the first of many experiences that confirmed Gottschalk's profound dislike of Canada and Canadians. It did not help that in Toronto a loose roof tile landed on Gottschalk's head while he was strolling.[103] Justified or not, Gottschalk's distaste focused on French Canadians. To his mother he reported, "Only French is spoken there and the way of life is what it must have been in Louisiana sixty years ago. The clergy is still prominent in all the splendor of its ignorance and stupidity. . . . This explains the dilapidated condition of the houses and mines."[104]

It must have been a relief for Gottschalk and de la Grange to arrive in Saratoga Springs, with its throngs of admiring New Yorkers. After only a few days there, however, they pushed on to Newport, where Brignoli was summering. All three found rooms in the rambling Ocean House and set about at once to conquer the local salons. Down to the end of August they offered "grand concerts" and "musical festivals" almost nightly.[105]

This seaside idyll ended when the two operatic stars were summoned back to New York for what turned out to be de la Grange's last appearances in Manhattan before leaving for Havana. Gottschalk, too, headed back to Manhattan, where many expected him to resume his popular soirées.[106] But the success of the series at Dodworth's Hall had not been

lost on Bernard Ullmann. Word got around that in August he had sailed
for Europe with the purpose of signing up Sigismund Thalberg. Sensing a
head-on collision at the keyboard, Gottschalk held back with his soirées,
giving only occasional solo recitals and appearing instead with Anna de
la Grange whenever her schedule permitted. This further collaboration
resulted in Gottschalk's writing a *Grande Valse poétique concertante* for
voice and piano, which they premiered at a Musical Fund Society concert
in Philadelphia on October 14.[107] Highly praised at the time, this work
was never published and is now lost.

More important than these occasional performances was Gottschalk's
decision to launch a "Conservatory of Music." The previous spring he had
marketed a dozen hour-long lessons of group instruction at sixty dollars—an unheard-of price at the time. Howls arose from as far away as
Boston, where Mr. Dwight called the rate an outrage.[108] But the program
was so successful that Moreau repeated it in the autumn, using the Descombes Piano Studios at 766 Broadway.[109] Now he had yet bolder plans
afoot. In mid-September Gottschalk placed advertisements in all the leading papers inviting students to sign up for his "conservatory," which offered "practical and theoretical instruction on the piano, after the plan of
the Conservatory of Paris."[110] Never mind that Gottschalk had never studied at said institution. His plan was for courses of eight two-hour lessons
for eight students at a time. At twenty dollars per student, this enabled
him to gross $160 for sixteen hours of work. Considering that concert
audiences at the small halls outside New York City rarely paid more than
fifty cents per seat, Gottschalk's *conservatoire de piano* was bound to be
more lucrative than touring. Such calculations led the *New York Times*
to call teaching "the only 'way to wealth' for a pianist in America."[111] It
was indeed, and Gottschalk prospered. His "conservatory" was America's first.

While Gottschalk was thus engaged, a fresh wave of excitement began
swelling in New York over the impending arrival of Sigismund Thalberg.
Except for Liszt, this most widely traveled virtuoso was universally acknowledged as the greatest pianist of the age. At forty-four, Thalberg was
no longer the young swell whom Parisians had once compared with
Chopin. But he had polished to a high sheen his renowned "three-handed"
feat of surrounding a melody with arpeggios. His repertoire of operatic
fantasies had also grown with the years and now numbered over sixty.
The poet Heinrich Heine called his playing "gentlemanly."[112] His dress
was equally refined and understated. Chopin had it right when he observed that Thalberg "takes tenths as easily as I octaves, [and] has diamond shirt-studs."[113]

Ullmann prepared well for the arrival of his virtuoso on the steamship

Africa on October 2. The *Herald* crowed about Thalberg's impeccable English.[114] Up in Boston, Dwight reminded readers that Thalberg, as a student of Beethoven's student Czerny, stood in the direct line of apostolic succession.[115] Only cynics dared call Thalberg "Old Arpeggio"[116] or note that his repertoire in America consisted of scarcely more than a dozen pieces.[117]

Thrilled New Yorkers quickly divided into pro-Thalberg and pro-Gottschalk camps. They eagerly awaited what they expected to be the piano duel of the century, pitting Europe against America, age against youth, classicism against romanticism. But neither warrior joined the battle. Thalberg, after all, had welcomed the thirteen-year-old Gottschalk to Paris in 1842 and had attended "Master Moreau's" first paying concert in Sedan in 1847. When he arrived in New York now he went directly to 14th Street to renew this friendship. Moreau found him a "good fellow" and "still the same, although a little older. He is beginning to show his age."[118] Thanks to Thalberg's cordiality and diplomacy, Gottschalk happily attended Thalberg's debut concert, genially cheering his old ally.[119] The shrewd Ullmann, sensing that collaboration could be more lucrative than rivalry, engaged Gottschalk to join Thalberg for the sixth and seventh concerts in the series.

The public went wild over their performances of Thalberg's four-hand fantasia on themes from *Norma*. "To add Gottschalk to Thalberg," gushed critic Richard Grant White, "is indeed 'to make honey a sauce to sugar.'"[120] These two concerts alone grossed a staggering three thousand dollars. Recognizing their mutual advantage, the two virtuosos agreed that Gottschalk would perform in four more Thalberg concerts and that Thalberg would make guest appearances in two major Gottschalk performances. Gottschalk immediately reported the deal to the Escudiers and *La France musicale*.[121]

From the very first outing it was clear the joint concerts were a huge success—so much so, in fact, that the two virtuosos added appearances in Baltimore and at Music Fund Hall in Philadelphia.[122] But in spite of the reigning spirit of collaboration, the public was not to be deterred from viewing the joint concerts as a duel. The battle raged furiously through the salons of New York. "Rival forces attack each other at the opera and at morning visits," reported the *Sunday Times*. "Not even the election campaign was half as bitter as this strife, which divides families and separates sets. Engagements are broken off, because the lover persists that Gottschalk's eyes have a greenish tinge; I have lost more than one invitation for not avowing myself an open adherent of Thalberg."[123]

What did the critics say? Thalberg's extraordinary ease and fluency at the keyboard earned him glowing reviews. The *Herald* judged his playing to be "art in its most classical form." [124] The *Times* fell down in awe before this "middle-aged gentleman, wonderfully like a fox-hunting squire of Merry England," and judged him unequivocally "the greatest pianist we have ever had in America." [125] *Atlas* pronounced Thalberg "the king of pianists." [126]

Several reviewers used praise for Thalberg to score points against Gottschalk. *Atlas*, for example, declared:

> We can't refrain from expressing our pleasure in Mr. Thalberg's manner upon the stage, and the fact of his discarding the catch-notice customs of most pianists—namely, excessive clutching of the hands, tearing off with exhausting efforts white kid gloves, smiling, frowning, glaring, at the audience.[127]

George Templeton Strong, who had persuaded himself that Thalberg, too, was Jewish, nevertheless found it "refreshing to observe the absence of affectation, pretension, and claptrap in all the man does." [128] Hagen of the *Review & Gazette* was even more blunt: "The performance . . . served admirably to show Thalberg's great excellencies . . . [as contrasted with] Mr. Gottschalk's peculiar qualities." [129]

The praise for Thalberg was not without qualification. *Dwight's Journal of Music* reported that "he played like a machine with a soul," [130] while *Atlas* admitted that "there is no mystery in [Thalberg's] music." [131] Gradually the critics came to appreciate that Thalberg and Gottschalk represented sharply different ideals. The *Sunday Times* drew the contrast between "the one [who is] all genius, the other [who is] all art; the one [who is] young, impassioned, irregular, fitful—the other [who is] middle-aged, calm, unimpassioned, but omniscient and omnipotent as far as his piano is concerned. Gottschalk surprises, moves, entrances; Thalberg diffuses serene pleasure, and performs most unheard of feats with perfect ease." [132] Prima donna Clara Louise Kellogg drew the same comparison:

> Thalberg was marvelously perfect as to his methods; but it was Gottschalk who could "play the birds off the trees and the heart out of your breast," as the Irish say. Thalberg's work was, if I may put it so, mental; Gottschalk's was temperamental.[133]

No wonder the *Atlas* thought Thalberg foolish to have courted Gottschalk: "We do not think Lord Byron would have allowed Shelley to perform similar services to him." [134] Some thought Thalberg served to heighten Gottschalk's standing, while all agreed Moreau lost nothing by the comparison.[135] The *Times* concluded at the end of the concert series that it was Gottschalk who had "met with a success here never before equaled by an instrumentalist." [136]

Gottschalk more than held his own with the critics yet was trounced by Ullmann's brazen skill as a promoter. Typical was a series of matinees he organized after Gottschalk's departure. Having noted New Yorkers' respect for Thalberg's "aristocratic" style, Ullmann organized matinee concerts at which liveried black servants served cakes and chocolate during intermission. To ensure that the unwashed would be excluded, Ullmann announced he would issue tickets only to those with a "correct" address.[137] "Of course, the consistently democratic sneer at this sort of thing," wrote one critic, "but everybody, *sans culottes* and all, want to be present on these delightful occasions."[138]

Ullmann than moved to seize the democratic high ground, first by dragging Thalberg out to Grammar School Number 11, and then by setting up an extravaganza at which Thalberg played for a crowd consisting of deputations of fifty girls from each school in the city, the entire Board of Education, and a gaggle of clergymen.[139] In short, Ullmann smothered Gottschalk from both sides, snobbism and democracy.

Long before Thalberg's arrival, Gottschalk had declared his intention to leave for New Orleans and then Cuba late in November.[140] He postponed the date in part to fulfill an unexpectedly busy concert season. Among these dates was a concert at the Brooklyn Athenaeum on October 14, at which he programmed for the first time a *Grande Marche solennelle*, subtitled "a fragment from the Concerto in F." This is almost certainly the same composition he published as *Apothéose* (op. 29) and dedicated to King Leopold I of Belgium.[141] Purely classical and with elements reminiscent of both Chopin and Schumann, this long and tedious work is one of the few in Gottschalk's oeuvre to suffer from overly bland thematic material. The concerto of which it was a part is lost, if ever it existed.

The proposed tour of Cuba was postponed also to accommodate the schedule of young Adelina Patti, who had just signed up to make the tour with Gottschalk. At thirteen, the youngest Patti sister had already been performing for six years and was known to audiences throughout the United States.[142] Both Adelina's parents were noted singers, Donizetti having written a part especially for her mother. In 1845 the family had emigrated to New York where Salvatore Patti, Adelina's father, tried his hand at being an impresario. When this venture went sour the elder Pattis, nearly destitute, placed all their hopes in the musical talents of their children.

They could not have made a better move, for theirs was arguably the most talented musical family in American history. Leaving aside three siblings by Signora Patti's first marriage, there were Amalia, a capable mezzo who married Maurice Strakosch; Carlotta, a fine pianist whose beautiful soprano voice was channeled into a triumphant concert career when lameness in one leg kept her from the opera stage; Adelina; and her handsome younger brother Carlo, who boasted virtuosic skills on the violin.

Plans for a tour of Cuba were solidly in place by early December,[143] so Gottschalk scheduled his New York farewell for December 26. No sooner was this decided than Moreau received word from Paris that his mother had been seized with apoplexy and died on November 2.[144] Uncertain about his sisters' and brothers' fate, he briefly considered sailing for France. However, when his sister Clara confirmed that they could continue to live with the kind and solidly bourgeois Maurigy family, he put away these thoughts and concentrated instead on the approaching tour of the West Indies.

The farewell concert at Niblo's Saloon on December 26 built into a landmark event. Thalberg had already agreed to join Moreau, and since he was to depart shortly thereafter for New England, it became a joint *concert d'adieu*.[145] To top it off, Gottschalk announced that he and Thalberg would premier a new *Grand Duo di bravura* on Verdi's *Il Trovatore*, an opera that had been all the rage since its New York premiere in 1855. As the finale of the two virtuosos' New York season, this show-stopper offered thunder, lightning, and a hailstorm of arpeggios and tremolos culminating in the "Anvil Chorus." "An extraordinary production," declared the *Times*.[146] In a seismographic report on the piece, Richard Hoffman announced that it produced "the most prodigious volume of tone I ever heard from the piano," especially the "remarkable double shake which Thalberg played in the middle of the piano, while Gottschalk was flying all over the keyboard."[147]

In the best Gottschalkian tradition of farewell concerts, he and Thalberg repeated their muscular feat three nights later at the Brooklyn Atheneum, after which Thalberg finally departed for Boston.[148] Gottschalk's last pre-departure duties consisted of a benefit for his ne'er-do-well manager, Bookstaver, and a benefit for Moreau himself organized by his friends in Brooklyn.[149] More important was his first and only appearance with the New York Philharmonic, which took place on January 10, 1857.

For the first time in its history the Philharmonic had had a successful season. The invitation to the American-born "honorary member" therefore had a celebratory quality about it. Inevitably, Gottschalk programmed his new grand duo on *Il Trovatore*, which he performed with a newly arrived Thalberg pupil named Émile Guyon. He also played the first movement of Adolf Henselt's Concerto in F Minor (op. 16), a work rarely performed because of its reputedly insurmountable difficulty. Seymour of the *Times* had only praise for Gottschalk's delicate reading of this finger-breaker, but the performance was so understated that even Dwight's reviewer complained that Moreau had been smothered by the orchestra.[150] Then came the inevitable barb: "Whenever I hear [Gottschalk]," wrote *Dwight's*, "I regret anew that such high power should be thrown upon the music (music indeed!) to which he almost entire confines himself." Theodore Hagen of the *Review and Gazette* was even less generous, faulting Gottschalk for taking uncounted liberties with Henselt's text and for freely substituting his own version of the score whenever he felt so inclined.[151]

With these concerts behind him, Gottschalk rushed to complete his planning for Havana. He and Adelina paid a visit to Charles D. Friedrichs's photographic studio on Broadway to sit for promotional pictures and *cartes de visite.*[152] He booked passage for France for his worrisome brother Edward and assembled a packet of manuscripts to be delivered to Léon Escudier for publication.[153] To his uncle Arnold Myers in Philadelphia he shipped several cases containing music, posters, engravings, and the landscape Frederic Church had given him.[154] In the midst of these activities Moreau fell sick, had to back out of a last concert with Eisfeld, and forgot to write a letter of introduction to Thalberg for Church.[155] At length, he set sail for Havana in late January, along with Adelina Patti and her father Salvatore.

Chapter Sixteen

 Ada Clare

MOREAU'S departure for the West Indies was timely. His mother's death had freed her remaining resources for the support of his siblings. Brother Edward was now a grown man who could serve *in loco parentis* in Paris. Thalberg's American tour promised to be a long one, so it was pointless for Gottschalk to mount a concert tour in his wake. And by early 1857 the economy was already beginning to show the first signs of a panic that would eventually batter the entertainment industry along with manufacturing and trade.

In many respects, the public mood was souring. New Yorkers were excited that construction work on Central Park was about to begin but could not ignore the sharp rise in street violence downtown. Brawling toughs organized into gangs with names like the Dead Rabbits and the Five Pointers were threatening law-abiding citizens, who began arming themselves with revolvers. The Supreme Court was soon to rule on the much publicized Dred Scott case, which would reopen the question of fugitive slaves in the North and thereby fan sectional conflict. Five years earlier a footloose and happy country had sung *O! Susanna* and *Old Folks at Home*. Soon the public mood would find expression in martial airs like *The Battle Cry of Freedom*.

All of this helps explain why Gottschalk might have decided on a concert tour of the Caribbean in 1857. But it does not explain why he stayed away from the United States for five long years. Since the Dodworth's Hall concerts, he had become a celebrity who was welcomed in the best venues and could command the highest ticket prices. Why, then, should he have abandoned the United States for so much longer than was required for the usual concert tour to Havana? Clearly, some further consideration dominated Gottschalk's thinking.

The missing factor is that Moreau had just survived a harrowing crisis in a tortured relationship with the young actress and writer Ada Clare (1834–74). This liaison, which extended over three and a half years, was marked by greater intimacy and complexity than any other of Moreau's several attachments with women. It was an unfortunate affair from the start. Ada Clare missed no opportunity to air every aspect of her relation to the composer in the press. Thanks to her exertions, their affair became the talk of the town and left Gottschalk with a reputation that he would never live down.

It is all but impossible to determine just what took place between the twenty-seven-year-old musician and the twenty-two-year-old aspiring writer and actress. There is not a word about the affair in any of Gottschalk's surviving letters or notebooks. Either he chose silence, as seems probable, or his sister Clara managed to purge such references as she organized his papers after his death. Hence only Ada's side of the story is at hand, and even her account is mute on one of the most crucial points, namely, whether Moreau Gottschalk was indeed the father of Aubrey Clare, Ada's son.

The problem is that Aubrey's birth, like thousands at the time, was not registered. Later documents furnish him with a birth date, but their evidence is contradictory, with one setting it in 1857 and another fixing it in 1859. The earlier date would permit Gottschalk's paternity, while an 1859 birth would rule it out since he was by then in the Caribbean. Ada herself put down the date 1859 in three different census returns. Aubrey, however, reported his birth date as 1857.[1]

Nearly all of Ada's acquaintances accepted the 1857 date, and only two evinced the slightest doubt regarding Gottschalk's paternity. One was the illustrator and satirist Thomas Butler Gunn (1826–?). Even though he dismissed Clare as someone interested solely in fame, the English-born Gunn followed every detail of her life with interest. In his diary for 1859 he recorded the rumor that Aubrey had indeed been born in Paris, "the result of a liaison with a young Frenchman." Then, six months later, he picked up a further report, namely, "that Ada Clare's child was fathered by Gottschalk's brother [i.e., Edward]; both men had a liaison with her."[2] Years later another writer who frequented Clapp's soirées published the same accusation against Edward Gottschalk Jr., stating that he "did not want to use up all the available adjectives on an unworthy father, whose only claim to fame was that he was the pianist's brother."[3]

Nothing that is known of Gottschalk's brother Edward would rule out this possibility, but it poorly fits the facts of Ada Clare's life. Well into her supposed pregnancy she was still performing on the stage, filling such roles as that of handmaiden to the Egyptian queen in *Antony and Cleopatra*. Granted that Ada may herself have rebelled against the prevailing practice of pre-natal confinement and that her pregnancy may have been concealed by a voluminous Victorian dress, it is highly unlikely that a theater director would knowingly have accepted a pregnant woman for the role of a young girl.[4]

Among those who contradicted the claims of Edward Jr.'s paternity was Ada's most intimate friend and companion, the pioneer feminist and ardent social reformer Marie Stevens Howland. Of Aubrey Clare she wrote:

> I always supposed [he] was the son of Louis Gottschalk. [Ada] never in her frequent talks of him did anything to destroy my illusion, if it were one. She was crazily enamored [of Gottschalk] as all her friends knew. . . . How *unlikely* that the father of Aubrey should be any other; especially as [Ada's] business in life at the time was running after Gottschalk.[5]

Walt Whitman, who knew Ada well, had no doubts that Gottschalk was Aubrey's father, nor did Henry Clapp Jr.[6]

Even as a child, Aubrey had definite views on the matter. A friend once overheard Ada asking the boy, "Who is your father?" Aubrey replied, "Oh, Gottschalk's my father." "What makes you think so?" retorted Ada. To this Aubrey replied, "Oh, don't you know that whenever we are in the same city with him he sends me tickets for all his concerts? And then he gave me a suit of soldiers clothes, just because I wanted them, and a sword and a gun and ever so many other things. I'm sure he is my father."[7]

At the time of this dialogue, mother and son were in California, where Ada was writing a featured column for the *Golden Era* and trying to re-launch her stage career. As a single mother she traveled alone with her son, never apologizing for her status or even explaining it. This was a bold sally in Civil War–era America, and Ada carried it off with apparent aplomb. Not so poor Aubrey, who as a boy expressed bewilderment and anger over his fate by pounding nails into pianos.[8] He went on to live an aimless life, working as a cigar seller and clerk during intervals in a lack-luster career on the stage. Marie Howland remembered him as "a good low comedian and a scoundrel."[9]

Who was the woman who spent a significant part of her young life chasing Gottschalk, probably bore a child by him, and later wrote a novel detailing their failed relationship? She once described her own life as "the focus of dullness" and ridiculed herself as "presenting many salient points for satire."[10] Nothing could be further from the truth. Born to a wealthy South Carolina family, this high-spirited young woman emancipated herself by fleeing to Greenwich Village. By age twenty-four she was the acknowledged "Queen of Bohemia," as Gottschalk's close friend Henry

Clapp Jr. was the King. Her life may have been "earnest but fruitless,"[11] as one friend claimed, but it was anything but dull. On the rebound from her disastrous affair with Gottschalk she worked to transform herself into an archetypal "new woman," plunging headlong into one professional or personal adventure after another in ever more desperate efforts to assert her independence and autonomy. Even her death at age thirty-nine was unconventional, or, more precisely, gruesome and horrible. A month after being bitten in the face by a lap dog in the grubby office of a Manhattan theatrical agent, she dissolved into raving while on stage at a playhouse in Albany. After enduring days of agony she died, either of rabies or from the massive doses of chloroform administered by her doctors.[12]

Novelist William Dean Howells avowed that "[Ada Clare's] fate, pathetic at all times, out-tragedies almost any other in the history of letters."[13] Walt Whitman, who considered Ada one of his "sturdiest defenders [and] upholders," wrote simply, "Poor, poor, Ada Clare—I have been inexpressibly shocked by the horrible & sudden close of her gay, easy, sunny free, loose, but *not un-good* life."[14]

Like Gottschalk, Ada Clare was a Southerner, but unlike him, she descended from old, rooted families on both her father's and her mother's side. She was born Ada McElhenney in Charleston, South Carolina. Most of her first years were spent either in the city or at her family's cotton plantation on Toogoodoo Creek, some thirty-five miles down the coast from Charleston. Unlike the Gottschalks and the Bruslés, there were no bankruptcies among the McElhenneys, thrifty Scottish Presbyterians all.[15] Not only did they prosper, but the male members of the family participated in a cultural world that assumed that service to the larger community was a sacred duty. A second cousin of Ada's father was Senator John C. Calhoun, the South's most keen-witted and fiery statesman.[16]

In Ada's generation this tradition of civic responsibility turned inward, producing men of letters rather than statesmen. Paul Hamilton Hayne, a first cousin who was partly raised under the same roof as Ada, was a poet who later gained recognition as an essayist on Southern topics.[17] Ada was to serve her literary apprenticeship under Hayne.[18]

From an early age, she demonstrated a keen desire to join the exciting intellectual world in which the menfolk of her family moved. As a child she rough-housed with Paul Hayne and the other boys, "climbing trees, riding horses bare back, swimming in the open stream, and paddling leaky boats."[19] In due course, however, she found herself being channeled into activities more appropriate to a Victorian girlhood, emerging as an accomplished and attractive young woman who possessed all the interests and arts needed to flourish in Charleston society. But she loathed the process by which she had been broken from tomboy to lady. Looking back on her girlhood from the age of thirty, Ada complained bitterly of having been "brought up in the old girl-slaughtering style."[20]

At age fourteen Ada was left an orphan. From this moment to the time she fled from her family and Charleston in 1854, she was the ward of her maternal grandfather, Hugh Wilson. In the Wilson home Ada was exposed to two contradictory influences. On the one hand, Wilson was an immensely rich cotton planter who presided over several plantations and three hundred slaves and reveled in the life of a rural grandee. On the other hand, Wilson was a stern moralist and strict disciplinarian who grounded his actions in the austere doctrines of Old School Presbyterianism. Ada McElhenney, spoiled and willful thanks to a life of privileged luxury, rebelled against her grandfather's control.

In the summer of 1853 an entourage consisting of Ada, two other single women, a chaperone, and several servants settled into the United States Hotel at Saratoga Springs, the very establishment at which Moreau Gottschalk was staying. Ada threw herself with abandon into the frivolous social whirl of the great spa. As if taking her cues from the plot of a sentimental novel, she fell desperately in love with the seemingly carefree pianist, four years her elder and the polar opposite of all she loathed in her familiar world. Through Gottschalk, she could for the first time see the possibility of attaining both of the qualities most notably lacking in her life up to now: intimacy and autonomy. Only later did it become clear that they were, for Ada, contradictory goals.

A year and a half later, she audaciously published a detailed and barely disguised account of her passion for Moreau in the *Charleston College Magazine*. The essay, entitled "The Rationale of Watering Places," must have exploded in the proper old city like a bomb. In Ada's third-person description of her romance with Gottschalk, an innocent young woman falls head over heels for an older man who, in the end, proves "fickle and inconstant."[21] She loves him nonetheless: "A furious tornado, sweeping over the burning tropics, would have agitated her soul less than a single sigh which he breathed across her cheek."

In her essay, Ada dwelt less on the object of her love than on the transformation it brought about in herself. Through it, she was lifted above the earnest Presbyterians and frivolous cynics of her native Charleston and freed to be herself. Yet in spite of the tender feelings she professed for Gottschalk, she was coming to despise men in general, for having "ordained that a woman's entire sphere shall be to love." This said, Ada closed the essay by describing how the spa's band played "some of Gottschalk's strongest music, the wild creations of that still wilder spirit[;] . . . its notes seem to re-echo the tones of his own indescribable voice and to bear the reflex of [Gottschalk's] own sad but wildering eyes."

Even a less strait-laced guardian than Grandpa Wilson might have been shocked by Ada's carryings-on at Saratoga that season. The following year she pleaded with her grandfather to be allowed to return, but he flatly refused, citing her "imprudence" of the previous summer.[22] Ada was not so easily deterred. She managed to pilfer several hundred dollars of donations collected by her grandfather from the citizens of South Carolina in order to build a monument to John C. Calhoun in Charleston. With this money in her purse she took passage on a ship to New York. Then, with a good Presbyterian sense of justice, Ada promised her lawyer that she would pay interest on the "loan" until she had repaid the principal in full.

At the time Ada McElhenney fled to Manhattan in July 1854, Gottschalk was busy concertizing in the Cuban provinces. He was on her mind, however, and many years later the son of her cousin Paul Hayne declared categorically that she had gone to New York "under the spell of an infatuation for a musician."[23] Once there, she wanted the world, and certainly all of Charleston, to know that she was in love and that she had become an authority on the subject.[24]

Ada sent what she later described as a "charming article on Gottschalk" to an unidentified national women's magazine. Publishing it, the editors added their own laconic introduction: "We have received the following poetical notice of the pianist Gottschalk," they wrote. "It contains, in the midst of all its juvenility and crudeness, an amount of eloquence and passionate intellectuality which surprises us. It is evidently the work of a young, enthusiastic girl with an over-sensitive nature. *We hope she has a mother.*"[25]

By now, Ada was immersed in Alfred Lord Tennyson's newly published book-length poem entitled *The Princess*, an amusing tale about higher education for women. The heroine of Tennyson's farce is Princess Ida, who turns her back on marriage in order to found a university for women. When Ida's prince discovers that his fiancée has done this, warfare breaks out between the sexes. The prince soon falls wounded, however, and when Princess Ida nurses him back to health, they fall in love and marry.

Ada McElhenney, in an essay on *The Princess*, passionately defended both emotional freedom and higher education for women.[26] "Every true woman would sacrifice to her love the most brilliant position on earth," she admitted, yet the capacity to love could not be taken as a pretext for denying women their independence in the intellectual sphere. Women had to be freed from all forms of involuntary dependence on men, which Ada saw as no different than a dog's dependence upon his master.

These parting shots effectively foreclosed the possibility of Ada's easy return to Charleston and her past. Making the break complete, she submitted the same essay to the *National Era,* an abolitionist journal published in Washington, D. C. Two years earlier, this magazine had introduced Harriet Beecher Stowe's *Uncle Tom's Cabin* to the public in serialized form. Now, with this essay by a twenty-year-old woman from a slave-holding South Carolina family, it cast its lot also with the feminist cause.[27]

The essay on *The Princess* assured Ada a warm reception in the New York literary world. At Anne Lynch's salon Ada met "all the notorieties which the city affords." To a Charleston confidant Ada gloated, "I am lionized to an extent that you could not believe."[28] Ada's feminist essay on *The Princess* also paved the way for her entry into more avant-garde circles. Soon she had made friends with New Hampshire–born Marie Stevens (later Howland) and Massachusetts-born Annie Ballard, who boarded with Marie Stevens on Bleecker Street.[29] Both were associated also with the notorious Steven Pearl Andrews. An ardent follower of Fourier, Andrews regularly assembled a motley crowd of perfumed coquettes, bloomerites, and champions of free love at what he called "the Club," a meeting room above Taylor's Saloon at 555 Broadway.[30] Among Andrews's regulars was Gottschalk's friend, Henry Clapp Jr. Muck-raking journalists stalked Andrews's unconventional coterie.[31] At length the police raided Andrews on October 18, 1855. It fell to poor Clapp to defend them in court, but since he was himself perceived as part of the problem, his defense was unpersuasive.

Moreau did not return to the United States until March 1855. Meanwhile, Ada had turned twenty-one and was bombarding her family lawyer in Charleston with letters demanding access to the principal of her inheritance. Charles Dickens had only recently published his *Bleak House,* with its wearying account of suits and counter-suits over family properties. At the center of Dickens's web was the orphaned Miss Ada Clare, described by Dickens as "such a beautiful young creature."[32] Ada McElhenney easily discovered herself in Dickens's forlorn heroine, and from this moment Ada McElhenney became Ada Clare.[33]

By now Ada aspired to fame as both writer and actress. With her newly secured fortune she could afford drama lessons,[34] and by August 1855 she was ready to make her debut in an amateur production in New York. On stage Ada was visually stunning.[35] But her voice proved weak, and her acting skills were modest at best. The debut was a failure. Word of this stumble reached Ada's cousin Paul Hayne, who rejoiced that her father had not lived to see his daughter on the boards.[36]

It is possible that Ada Clare had made contact with Gottschalk in the summer of 1855 while he was at the Trenton Falls spa in New York state, and his mazurka *Printemps d'amour* (op. 40), with its ragtime-like syncopations, may have been intended as a present to her. Whether or not this is the case, they were definitely in direct contact with one another by autumn. With few concert bookings on his schedule, Moreau had ample time to spend with Ada. He was also writing occasional theater reviews, which he signed "Seven Octaves." These were written in a gossipy style wholly uncharacteristic of Gottschalk but very much recalling Ada Clare and the light-hearted members of Henry Clapp's circle. One can assume that Moreau and Ada were attending performances together during these months and that she stood over his shoulder as he wrote his reviews.

Down to Gottschalk's electrifying Dodworth's Hall concerts, his relationship with Ada Clare remained casual. Broke and contemplating a tour of California in order to recoup his fortunes, Moreau had other things on his mind. Yet he was strongly attracted to this vital and exuberant fellow Southerner. For all his independence, Gottschalk until now had never experienced intimacy or even affection in the normal sense. Now both were his without conditions.

The sudden surge in Gottschalk's popularity following the concerts at Dodworth's Hall coincided with Ada's full emergence as a New York "personality." To be sure, her further appearances with the amateur troupe had been notably unsuccessful, to the point that even the *Atlas* dismissed the entire company as "third-rate stock players."[37] But by the spring of 1856 actress and impresario Laura Keene had engaged Ada as an ingenue at her newly opened theater on Broadway. Since Laura Keene specialized in tableaux as well as plays, she could use Ada for her petite beauty, without calling on her meager skills as an actress.[38]

Thus, just as Moreau was being lionized by the public, Ada, too, became a popular figure on Broadway, where portraits and daguerreotypes of her were exhibited in the windows of several commercial establishments. Gottschalk and Ada Clare formed a mutual admiration society and soon became lovers as well, apparently in April and May 1856. It was probably during these months that Aubrey was conceived, in which case he would have been born early the next year, at the time of Moreau's friendly rivalry with Sigismund Thalberg.

Ada's relationship to Gottschalk presents striking parallels to George Sand's with Chopin and Countess Marie d'Agoult's with Liszt. Like Sand's affair with Chopin, Ada Clare's with Gottschalk took place fully in the public glare. Like Countess d'Agoult's liaison with Liszt, Ada's with Gottschalk produced an illegitimate offspring. Finally, just as George Sand had written a novel to vent her anger at having lost Chopin, so Ada Clare later dissected her brief season with Gottschalk in a scathing novel, *Only a Woman's Heart.*

Neither Gottschalk nor Ada Clare could possibly have been blind to these similarities. There was one fundamental difference, however. Whereas Chopin and Liszt had carried on their amorous affairs in the permissive salons of Paris, Gottschalk's was played out in the more strait-laced environment of the United States. In such a world, Ada Clare's dramatic affair with Gottschalk offended just about everyone.

The idyll with Ada Clare lasted only through June 1856. Moreau's series at Dodworth's Hall had made him the city's culture hero of the moment, while Ada's appearances at Laura Keene's Theatre and her follow-up performances at Wallack's Summer Garden in a cloak-and-dagger thriller, *The Phantom*, sustained her notoriety into the summer.[39] Then Ada dropped from sight. Even her allies on the staff of the *Atlas*, normally eager to chronicle her every move, fell silent about her until November 2. On that day the English poet and former Anglican clergyman William Bennett ("Zavarr Wilmshurst") issued a poem entitled *To Ada Clare*. In a few lines he announced that Ada had "dared her destiny" and "strayed thru dread infinity" and was now "lost."[40]

If her friends' assumption regarding the paternity of Ada's child was true, she was now seven months pregnant. Whether Ada sought marriage is unknown, but Moreau flatly refused to play the role of Liszt to this would-be Countess d'Agoult. Once more, then, he formed a liaison with a young woman and then suddenly drew back from any commitment. His mercurial behavior cannot be excused. Perhaps, though, he felt that if he allowed himself to love Ada Clare he would somehow imperil his role as caregiver to his family. Or perhaps his hasty retreat was based on some deeper fears, whether about Ada or himself. At any rate, he abandoned her. Bennett, a close friend and admirer of Ada, was quite justified in asserting that by the standards of the larger community she was indeed "lost."

Powerless to affect the situation, Ada nonetheless embarked on a desperate campaign to win back Gottschalk. Her stratagem centered around what she wrongly believed to be the piano "duel" between Moreau and Sigismund Thalberg. Ada had read the enormous build-up to Thalberg's arrival in the press and sensed that the presence of the German virtuoso would divide Manhattan society into pro-Gottschalk and pro-Thalberg camps. Not being in touch with Moreau, she did not appreciate the mutual regard that linked them. Blind to this, Ada forayed onto the pages of the *Atlas* with a series of nasty satirical attacks on Moreau's rival.

Ada signed her articles "Alastor," after Shelley's poem of that name. Subtitled "The Spirit of Solitude," *Alastor* was written when the twenty-three-year-old Shelley thought he was dying. Having isolated himself in contemplation of the universe, Shelley's Poet in *Alastor* realizes the need to find an earthly object of his love. When he fails, he dies in disappointment. As Shelley wrote, "the Poet's self-centered seclusion was avenged by the furies of an irresistible passion pursuing him to speedy ruin."[41] Once more using literature as a mirror for her own fate, Ada Clare appropriated Alastor as her latest pseudonym.

Alastor's first assault on Thalberg, published on November 16, depicted him as a fop. "The Pianist King" was so convinced of his appeal to the public, she wrote, that he posted seventeen policeman around the concert hall to manage the crowd. "Employed to the latest moment in making his invincible toilet," the Pianist King then ascended the stage:

> Angels and ministers of grace! He stands for three seconds motionless with horror; the audience consisted of nine of the deadliest heads the city could furnish, and one crusty old man—very old and remarkably crusty—a sexton by profession.

After Thalberg's next concert she accused him of giving away nineteen hundred tickets and of programming pieces by Gottschalk in order to draw a crowd. "The audience," she reported, "was extremely select—the nine sisters Gamp were there, with their lidless, dragon eyes of a virulent blue."[42] Ada also reported that Thalberg "was obliged to employ three errand boys to arouse from profound slumber each individual in the room."

Alastor went on to accuse Thalberg of trying to "out-Gottschalk Gottschalk," but to no avail:

> When thou wast dreaming that the audience made a rustling sound only in turning over the leaves of thy sweet biography in order to discover what developments of thy infancy had foreshadowed such after ability, why—why didst thou raise thine eyes to behold them—*horible dictu!*—drawing out from their capacious pockets night-caps and gowns, and patent-folding pillows?

A week later Alastor struck again in a front-page essay entitled "Brewers of Small Beer."[43] She began with an incoherent attack on those critics who had lauded Thalberg, calling their praise the "hallelujahs of flunkies" and singling out one such critic as a "leadhead." Then she launched into a bizarre narrative in which she described how she had constructed a mechanical pianist who was taking the city by storm. At first it seemed that this ventriloquist dummy was intended to represent Thalberg. By the following week's episode, entitled "The Automaton Pianist," it was clear that she was now speaking about Gottschalk.

From this moment on, Thalberg dropped out of the picture, and Alastor aimed her guns squarely at her former lover. Over the next five weeks Alastor alternately abused and implored Gottschalk, all the while railing against her own wretched fate.

What had happened? Evidently, at some point in the last half of November 1856, Moreau made clear to Ada that he would neither acknowledge the child she was carrying nor ever again be her lover. By this time, too, Moreau had publicly announced his plan to tour Cuba and had scheduled his farewell concert with Thalberg for December 26. This plunged Ada Clare into despair.

Even though direct evidence is lacking, it is possible that Ada understood Moreau far more deeply than he may have wished. She could not have been unaware that he was captive to the sense of responsibility his father had nurtured in him and that all warmer emotions in his life were associated with his mother, and hence with irresponsibility and selfishness. Ada may well have deliberately become pregnant in a conscious attempt to get Gottschalk to extend this sense of responsibility to herself. When Moreau drew back, Ada responded first with denial, then anger, and finally despair bordering on madness.

Her article "The Automaton Pianist" described the musical automaton Alastor herself had created, "Mr. Narcissis Medoro Adonis Hyperion."[44] "My adored nightingale," she wrote, "that is to say the Automaton," arrived at the next concert arrayed in his best clothes. After kissing her creation, Alastor seated him at the piano, and the concert commenced, with Gottschalk purportedly in the audience to observe his mechanical likeness.

> Alas! I had kissed him so vehemently upon the eyes, that I had driven them out of their sockets half an inch into his head, and so slipped off the wire that connected them with the *smile*. . . . I drew what is scientifically called the collapse wire, and so caused his face to droop upon his hands. The audience, feeling this to be a heart-rending display of the artist's melting his soul into tears, were at first brooded over by a death-hush, and there arose a faint sound of weeping, without distinction of sex. . . . Gottschalk, one of the first to break into sobs, was finally borne out in a swoon.

At this point, Alastor succeeded in rewiring the Automaton's eyes. Thus revived, he played "his great fantasia, *In Memory of a Fool*, dedicated to Miss Ada Clare."

In her next article, entitled "Whips and Scorns of Time,"[45] Alastor addressed herself squarely to Gottschalk as the lover who had spurned her. She reviewed the story of her childhood in South Carolina and recalled the recklessness of her first days in New York and how Moreau had encouraged her as a writer. Now, defeated and in despair, she addressed him directly: "Dear friend, how changed am I. One would scarcely know me. . . . These limbs of mine . . . writhe with only the convulsions of a parting life."

Two days after Moreau's farewell concert with Thalberg, Alastor published yet another article, "The Pangs of Despised Love," filled with utter despair:[46]

> Let me tell you how you despise [me]. . . . [Yet] this one whom you so love to fling your sneers upon . . . cannot turn upon you, were the power of all the world put into her hands.

Then, in an apparent and chilling reference to her pregnancy, she described her heart as "a ship laden with a precious burden, God-bound to a distant land."

To this point, Ada's mounting anguish had been expressed in the conventions of mid-nineteenth-century drama. The next article by Alastor appeared on January 4, 1857, three days before Gottschalk's appearance with the Philharmonic Society. With this essay, entitled "Ada Clare on Suicide," she stepped out from behind her pen name and brought the series to a terrible finale.[47]

By now, Ada's thoughts were less on Gottschalk than on the ridicule to which she felt she was being subjected. How could she escape such ignominious attacks and declare her freedom? She mulled over the possibility of fleeing into "that most hideous of all vices, mental and bodily prostitution." Still seeking the possibilities open to men, she next considered suicide. She praised Greeks and Romans for their manly acceptance of suicide and asked whether women were not also entitled to take this heroic step, especially if it could lead to their freedom? Ada Clare had first-hand knowledge of people who were driven by unrequited love to take their own lives.[48] Two years earlier she had rejected the advances of a young English poet, who finally killed himself by drinking prussic acid.[49] Now it was Ada's turn to die by her own hand.

At the last moment she drew back from her decision. In a final article, which was published on the day of Gottschalk's Philharmonic appearance, she acknowledged that she suffered from "mental disease" and announced that suicide would not be her fate. "I say to myself, my poor Ada, that this is a short play and you may as well see the end of it. It is not courage that is demanded of you, but patience."[50] It was probably only days after writing this that Ada Clare gave birth to her son, Aubrey.

How did Gottschalk react to Ada Clare's very public outbursts of rage and despair, sustained over two months? Prudently, he made no public response. Nor, apparently, was there even private contact between him and Ada during the three months prior to his departure for Havana. Theatrical and literary New York was like a village, though. The public at his last few concerts must have been abuzz with the scandal, and news of it would surely have reached the Manhattan-based impresarios who would have booked any further tours for Moreau in the United States. Not even the huge success of the series at Dodworth's Hall could have neutralized the impact of such damaging reports as these. In the end, Moreau saw the professional path before him completely blocked by an impediment of his own making. Hence his decision to flee the country.

The deeper consequences of his encounter with Ada Clare were soon evident in Gottschalk's conduct. Never again did he risk even the degree of intimacy with a woman that he had experienced with Ada Clare. Instead, he directed all his energies toward fulfilling his responsibilities toward his brothers and sister, meanwhile conveniently ignoring his responsibilities toward his own child, if Aubrey Clare was indeed his son. Along the way there were many flirtations, especially with very young women, but these were a poor surrogate for what was absent in his life in the wake of the Ada Clare affair. To the extent that his emotional life found expression at all, it was through his music and writing.

By the time Ada's series reached its dramatic climax, Moreau was busy with his farewell appearance in Brooklyn with Thalberg. On January 18 Ada set sail for Paris.[51] She was alone, presumably having placed the baby in the care of a nurse, as was common practice for propertied women in the slave-owning South. Moreau and the Patti family soon departed New York. By the time Gottschalk and his party reached Havana, Ada Clare was ensconced in the Faubourg Saint-Germaine, where she remained, except for a brief return visit to New York, for nearly two years.

Chapter Seventeen

✕ Souvenir de Porto Rico

BEGINNING in December 1856, Havana was abuzz with news of Gottschalk's return. Or was it the great Thalberg who was coming?[1] No one was quite sure, but interest was high. When finally Gottschalk arrived with the Pattis on the steamer *Quaker City*, it was indeed news. Within two days of their arrival on February 12 it was reported that the celebrities would appear at the Gran Teatro Tacón.[2]

Moreau was rhapsodic to be back. "The sky, the air, the flowers, the fruits, are full of music to me," he effused.[3] The contrast with his mood only weeks earlier could not have been greater. Even though he had more than held his own in the contest with Thalberg, the episode had depressed him. So did the music business as a whole, which, he charged, reflected America's "love of the almighty dollar."[4] And the rather shoddy episode with Ada Clare had also taken its toll. Relieved of these burdens by the sights, sounds, and smells of Havana, Gottschalk felt a deep euphoria.

He settled into the Legrand Hotel, exhausted.[5] Rumors that he suffered from consumption circulated in New York.[6] Havana, of course, was the perfect place to spend a few winter months before returning renewed to the United States.[7] But whatever he told friends, Moreau was contemplating a more protracted trip, and one he intended to document in detail. He had brought from New York a box of notebooks in which he began jotting down impressions of people and of his surroundings. These small, leather-bound volumes became his intimate companions, a "kind of silent confidant, which has the immense advantage over everybody I encounter on the road of listening to me without compelling me to make myself hoarse in replying. Moreover, [they] listen without interrupting."[8]

Did Moreau see these notebooks as his private diary? Not at all. Far from being a medium for Anglo-Saxon confessional writing, the notebooks were a self-conscious literary effort intended eventually for publication. Hence their wealth of details on the places he visited and their silence on Ada Clare and every other topic Moreau considered personal.

Gottschalk had many mentors as he turned to travel writing. He surely knew of Berlioz's book on his travels in Germany and Italy.[9] There was also the popular American travel writer Bayard Taylor, who moved in the same Manhattan literary circles as Gottschalk. Even if he was criticized for "traveling farther and seeing less than anyone alive,"[10] Taylor was enjoying immense success at the time of Gottschalk's New York sojourn and provided a ready model. Whoever his teachers, the student learned fast. Initially, Moreau's travel notes were designed for the readers of *La France musicale.* Gradually, however, they gained a wider following, and within a few years they were regularly reprinted in newspapers in New York, Milan, Mainz, St. Petersburg, and even Boston.

Over the coming months Moreau abandoned any lingering thoughts of an early return to the United States. He eventually prolonged his stay in the Caribbean to five years. Much later, he referred sheepishly to this period as "years foolishly spent, thrown to the wind, as if life were infinite, and youth eternal." In words calculated to offend the more puritanical readers of the *Atlantic Monthly,* in which they were published, he spoke about how he had

> roamed at random under the blue skies of the tropics, indolently permitting myself to be carried away by chance, giving a concert wherever I found a piano, sleeping wherever the night overtook me.[11]

For all Moreau's talk about these as "lost years," they in fact constituted the most fruitful period of his life. For the first and last time in his career he lived the life of a composer, thus fulfilling the dream he had had at age thirteen when he had sat for the portrait of himself with pen and music paper, but no piano. Indeed, many of Gottschalk's most significant and enduring pieces were composed precisely during these "lost years."

No less, it was in this period that he reached full maturity as a writer, observer on the arts, and thinker on the relation between culture and politics. Up to now he had been an optimistic populist, assuming that the only distinction in music or art that really counted was between good and bad. During his long Caribbean interlude he began to revise this faith by admitting the existence of differing cultural levels in society.

Four days after arriving in Havana, Moreau received a summons from Captain-General José Concha to give a command performance at his fortress-like palace on the Plaza de Armas. In sharp contrast to his first visit to Cuba, Moreau was now very much *persona grata.* Concha received him cordially in his Parisian-style drawing room on the second floor and gave him his personal endorsement and support.

To appear at the Gran Teatro Tacón, however, required more even than Concha's backing, for that house had been occupied for several months by the irrepressible impresario Max Maretzek and his Italian opera troupe.[12] Anna de la Grange was there, as was Brignoli.[13] Maretzek had no interest in Gottschalk since he did not manage him, but claimed to have discovered Adelina Patti when her father took the seven-year-old for an audition in 1849. This led him to schedule a Gottschalk-Patti concert for February 20, 1857.

The Tacón concert was enlivened by Moreau's performance, with his friend Nicolás Espadero, of the bravura transcription of Verdi's *Il Trovatore* that he had composed for himself and Thalberg. He ended with the crowd-pleaser *El Cocoyé*.[14] Maretzek could not deliver another night of the great hall, so Patti and Gottschalk had to content themselves with a second performance wedged between the acts of a comedy a week later.[15] Between the two appearances they raced off to the booming sugar ports of Matanzas and Cárdenas for lucrative appearances before local merchants and planters, many of them from the United States.

Once the initial enthusiasm that greeted the performances had passed, Havana proved to be a waste of time. "Our city," confessed one critic, "is quite dormant when it comes to the 'divine art.'"[16] So the artists took to the road, crossing Cuba to Surgidero de Batabano and then traveling by boat to the port of Cienfuegos, eighteen hours to the east.[17] A benefit concert for the local hospital there led to a grand ball in Gottschalk's honor, attended by "all the beautiful black eyes of the world."[18] The party then forged inland by cart and horseback to the town of Santa Clara. The town's young people greeted them on the road with white Andalusian horses, which Gottschalk and the Pattis mounted for their triumphal entry into the provincial center.

Unfortunately, they faced competition from one Colonel Wood, who was delighting Santa Clarans with his circus and freak show.[19] The local barber, shaving Moreau, inquired if he were an artist, adding that if he was, he was also a thief. After several such encounters, Gottschalk began speaking with frank cynicism about the audience. What could a mere pianist do before a public that preferred sword-swallowers and tightrope walkers? All the worse if that pianist "had never taken a perilous leap on a horse, and had no desire to have an anvil placed on his stomach—all of which constitute the *non-plus ultra* of the artistic ideal in these countries of the sun."[20]

This dyspepsia may have been heightened by the capriciousness of Adelina, whom Gottschalk discovered to be a spoiled child. Papa Patti and Moreau were constantly assaulted by waves of admirers "who had been burned by the flame of the big black eyes of our little Latin girl."[21] Anonymous letters, bouquets, and gifts flooded in, and it fell to her father and Moreau to put up a barrier to such "volcanic effusions."

In spite of his growing doubts as to Adelina's character, Gottschalk composed (or adapted) three solos for the fourteen-year-old who would later be the world's most renowned soprano. Unfortunately, neither his *Chant des oiseaux* for soprano, flute, and piano, his *Valse poétique* for soprano and orchestra, nor his vocal variations on the *Carnival of Venice* survives.

Following this misadventure, the trio returned to Havana and embarked immediately by steamer along the northern coast to Puerto Príncipe, scene of Gottschalk's greatest triumphs in 1854. Once more the entire town turned out, and after the third performance the local Philharmonic Society staged a grand march accompanied by soldiers bearing torches. To a tune from a French comic opera the townspeople sang the refrain "Oh! Oh! Oh!, How handsome is our Moreau, as he sits at his pianó! Moreau! Moreau! Moreau! Glory to Gottschalk! [pronounced "Gotschó"]."[22] Wallowing in the moment, Moreau strutted along, blowing kisses to the crowd.

In spite of its ups and downs, the tour of rural Cuba afforded Moreau the opportunity once more to hear both the local folk music and the *contradanzas* played by both white and Afro-Cuban dance orchestras. In several letters to his family he wrote enthusiastically about the scenes of provincial life he encountered. He continued to absorb musical impressions after reaching Santiago, on Cuba's eastern tip. There, in late April, he met his old friend from 1854, organist and composer Silvano Boudet, and drew him and several of his students into a series of three concerts.[23]

The strain of travel finally caught up with Moreau in Santiago, and for three weeks in early May he lay sick with an intestinal disorder, probably dysentery. Soon every doctor, pharmacist, and veterinarian in town hovered over his bed, all expecting the worst.[24] News of this misfortune quickly reached Havana and from there was disseminated over the newly laid telegraph lines to the United States.[25] Several Cuban papers printed detailed reports on the death of "el Genio de la Música." One offered its readers a free lithograph of the deceased, while another, in the notorious Santa Clara, offered its funeral homage to the *"bard of the tropics."*[26] Touched by these gestures, Gottschalk obligingly consented to remain dead for several days. Then he swung into action, sending written proof of his continued existence to any papers that would print it.

After three more concerts for the Philharmonic Society in Santiago, Moreau and the Pattis returned to Havana. All three were in low spirits,

Moreau due to the lingering effects of his illness and the Pattis because Adelina's aunt, the celebrated soprano Clotilde Barili Thorn, was dying of consumption in nearby Matanzas. Even though the public expected a farewell concert, the party quietly boarded the steamer *Solent* and on June 10 departed for St. Thomas in the Danish West Indies.[27]

One morning during a chilling rain at sea, Moreau found himself above deck at daybreak, leaning on a bulwark and contemplating the barren landscape of Haiti.[28] The high mountains stood out in desolate profile, and he recalled the melancholy tales from this island told him long ago by his grandmother and his nurse, Sally. It was at this moment that Moreau felt drawn to this brooding tropical world on the horizon by "a mysterious affinity."[29] Over the next two years this sense of connectedness with the French Antilles gave Moreau a feeling of home that he had not known since first leaving New Orleans.

Soon after this, the ship put into the Haitian capital of Port-au-Prince for a brief stop.[30] The illiterate Emperor Faustin was waging a murderous war against neighboring Santo Domingo at the time, so the only people prepared to receive Gottschalk were the handful of local liberals, nearly all of whom were Freemasons. After performing for his fellow Masons, Gottschalk rejoined his party, and proceeded at once to St. Thomas.

The plan was to stop on St. Thomas only as long as was necessary to catch the steamer *Isabel* for New Granada, now Venezuela. Moreau's friend General José Antonio Páez had provided him with all the introductions in Caracas that he could need, so Gottschalk's expectations for a South American trip were high. In St. Thomas, however, he learned that civil war had broken out in Venezuela. Páez had already left New York for his homeland, where he took control of the situation and established himself as a virtual dictator.[31] Travel to New Granada was out of the question for the time being, so Gottschalk and the Pattis paused at St. Thomas until July 12.

Fortunately, Moreau's other South American friend, General Echenique of Peru, had sent a letter of introduction to the local Danish governor, who immediately sought out his famous visitors. The Governor received them at a banquet that included the Mexican General Santa Anna. Within days those who had met Gottschalk at this event had raised a subscription of fifteen hundred dollars for him to give three concerts in the ballroom of the Commercial Hotel in Charlotte Amalie.[32]

It was an unlikely time for such gatherings, since yellow fever was raging on the island of Saint Thomas. Indeed, ten people who arrived on the *Solent* with Gottschalk had already succumbed to the disease.[33] Nonetheless, the concerts went forward and attracted the largest audience ever assembled on St. Thomas. It was here that Moreau premiered his *Chant des oiseaux* as a piano solo, without the soprano part that he added later. It is likely that at this time Gottschalk also met Charles (now Carlos) Allard, a prize-winning flautist from the Paris Conservatoire who had for several years been living in Ponce, Puerto Rico. The two became fast friends. Allard joined the tour and continued to travel with Gottschalk for more than a year after the Pattis left.

In their last performance on St. Thomas, Adelina sang *Home, Sweet Home*, with which the peripatetic diva was to close all her concerts over the next half century. The audience at Charlotte Amalie responded by presenting the artists with three-foot bouquets of red and white camellias.[34]

His health recovered and his purse refilled, Moreau spent a further week relaxing, often in the company of a cousin, Rachel Gottschalk, who was then resident there. He also found time to tour St. Thomas on horseback. After the wilds of provincial Cuba, he was charmed by this tidy and bourgeois Danish entrepôt, with its painted wooden houses that reminded him of toys from Nuremberg.[35] The Afro-Caribbean population, emancipated a decade earlier, impressed him as "remarkably handsome and clean," and he reveled in the prevailing atmosphere of "happiness and self-satisfaction."[36]

With their South American venture suspended, Moreau and the Pattis were left adrift. The United States was in the grip of the Panic of 1857 and offered no immediate prospects. They had heard too many tales of disastrous musical tours of Mexico to consider that an option, and so the three took passage for San Juan, Puerto Rico. Their arrival was noted in the San Juan press on July 14.[37]

Superficially, this looks like another ill-timed and ill-planned trip on Gottschalk's part. July and August in Puerto Rico were times to escape the heat, not for concert-going. The summer and autumn of 1857 were particularly unfavorable, for yellow fever was claiming many victims in Puerto Rico's main urban centers, as it had on Saint Thomas. Gottschalk, moreover, still felt the effects of his recent illness and needed a rest. Papa Patti, mindful of the danger of straining his daughter's voice, wanted also to declare a moratorium on performances. Yet only after offering two concerts in San Juan and being honored at a ball did the three retire from the public. They accepted an invitation to spend time at a plantation in the Puerto Rican countryside while Carlos Allard returned to his home in Puerto Rico's second city and cultural capital, Ponce.[38]

For a month or so Gottschalk and the Pattis settled comfortably at Plazuela, a vast sugar-producing domain thirty miles west of San Juan near the village of Barceloneta. Even though only a seventh of Puerto Rico's population consisted of slaves, the great sugar plantations along the northern and western coasts were all based on chattel labor. Among these plantations, none was more up-to-date in its technology than Plazuela.[39] Here was a sprawling complex of purging houses, drying houses, sugar mills, furnaces, huge roller presses, vats, vacuum pans, and packing houses.

Bustling and modern Plazuela was an unlikely spot at which to seek rest and serenity, let alone draw inspiration from the music of untouched folk cultures. Yet Gottschalk achieved both here. At Plazuela he found respite from the life of a nomad virtuoso and for once concentrated on composing, drawing on local musical idioms and also on musical notions that had been developing in his mind for years. Moreau credited this good fortune to his English-born host and hostess, who took him into their family.[40] Cornelio Kortright (Cornelius Cartwright) had developed Plazuela over forty years and now in his old age lived there happily with his wife, a talented singer.[41] French poetry, informal musicales, and dramatic readings all flourished in the Kortrights' comfortable mansion.

The music Gottschalk composed at Plazuela falls into a wide range of levels and genres but is all marked by its accessibility to the kind of cultivated but unpretentious people who gathered in the Kortrights' salon. Much is lost, but several important pieces found their way into print, while others were preserved in various forms, including the pages of a manuscript workbook Moreau kept over several years during his Caribbean hegira.[42]

Since Gottschalk still held out hope of visiting his friend General Páez in Venezuela, a first task at Plazuela was to prepare several compositions celebrating that soldier's life. He thus prepared for publication the *Marche de nuit* (op. 17) that he had composed in New York. After opening with a *pianissimo* in the left hand, this piece lumbers through a *misterioso* passage until it suddenly breaks into a sprightly and strangely inappropriate march more like the walk-around in an old-fashioned dancing class than anything suggesting an army on night maneuvers. *Chant du soldat* (op. 23), which was completed at Plazuela, is of an entirely different quality. Here Moreau shifts back and forth between a gently nostalgic lyric and a call to arms. For all its sentimentality, this musical essay comes across as authentic, no doubt because its alternation between regimentation and repose mirrored the tension between the public and private realms that existed in Gottschalk's own life.

A second task facing Moreau was to fulfill long-delayed commissions for work to be published under the pen names "Oscar Litti," "Seven Octaves," "A.B.C.," and "Paul Ernest." Gottschalk had conjured up several of these pseudonyms at the time he signed his contract with the Philadelphia publisher Gould. Other publishers soon began issuing these off-brand Gottschalk pieces. A solid tradition holds that pieces by all these Oscar Littis and Paul Ernests were a scam, Gottschalk's cynical vehicle for fathering lucrative musical offspring without acknowledging his paternity. His biographer Fors wrote that these were all "light compositions which avaricious editors forced him to compose against his will and against the impulses of his good taste and talent."[43]

This is not the whole story. Gottschalk took professional pride in these pieces. He berated his publishers for errors in typesetting them and for printing them with more than his specified number of measures per page.[44] Nor did he reject such compositions as illegitimate offspring. He said of a *Valse de concert* issued under the name Paul Ernest that it was "very brilliant" and that he "found it pretty and I am sure it will be very popular." He actually dedicated a Paul Ernest *Polka* "to my friend Gottschalk,"[45] scarcely the act of one who was ashamed of the composition. The immensely popular *The Dying Poet* appeared first as a piece by "Seven Octaves," but in later editions Moreau proudly identified it as "composed and performed with immense success by L. M. Gottschalk (Seven Octaves)."

To some extent, Gottschalk's use of various pen names merely followed a literary fad in the 1850s and 1860s. "Mark Twain" was the best known of these, but there were also "Orpheus C. Kerr" ("Office Seeker"), "Petroleum Nasby," and "Ada Clare." Beyond this, it should be noted that Gottschalk's pseudonymous pieces in nearly every case constituted far simpler arrangements of his compositions than what he himself would have performed before the public or issued under his own name. Indeed, his press kit in the 1860s identified works by Oscar Litti and Paul Ernest as Gottschalk's "easier pieces."[46] In a clever effort to acknowledge this bifurcation in the musical marketplace, Moreau once prevailed on his Havana publisher Edelmann to issue a broadside of a *contradanza* with simpler and more difficult versions printed on the same page.[47]

Along with composing a sheaf of lighter pieces at Plazuela, Gottschalk also turned to more substantial compositions. One, particularly intriguing, is *La Tulipe de Brabant*, which is not so much as mentioned in existing bibliographies of his works. Moreau described this as "my best work and the most serious. I have completed it with much care [and] it produces a marvelous effect before a civilized audience."[48] Since he sent the manuscript to Escudier for publication, it is possible that *La Tulipe de Brabant* may someday turn up in some Paris archive. For now it remains lost.

At Plazuela Gottschalk also wrote out a publishable version of his extended *Grande Marche solennelle*, subtitled *Apothéose*. Composed during the previous year, this march shows the influence of Mendelssohn, Wagner, Rossini, and Gottschalk's own *Siege of Saragossa*.

The last and most significant group of compositions from Plazuela were those drawing on Caribbean motifs. Since his arrival in Cuba, Moreau's concert schedule, while busy, had enough gaps to leave time for social life. In the Caribbean this meant attending dances where local ensembles performed music, often of local origin. While Gottschalk left no record of visiting suburban dance pavilions like the Glorieta de Puentes Grandes outside Havana, he almost certainly did so, for the music popular at such spots resonates in his compositions. At the Glorieta one could hear Feliciano Ramos's famed Orquesta de la Unión, which bridged the lowbrow and highbrow musical tastes of Havana, or La Flor de Cuba.[49] In San Juan and at Plazuela he doubtless heard other local ensembles playing the ubiquitous Puerto Rican *danza*, a local variant of the Caribbean-wide *contradanza* and ancestor of the *bomba* and other twentieth-century Puerto Rican dances.[50]

In Havana, Santiago, and San Juan he would also have heard military bands. In their informal concerts on public squares, these brass ensembles played not only marches but also *fandangos, tiranas, boleros, seguidillas,* and other local music.[51] Beyond this, Plazuela, with its large slave population, would have been one of the best places on the island to hear rural Afro-Caribbean performers. And finally, the subsistence farmers of the Puerto Rican interior, the *jíbaros*, had their own distinctive music, which Gottschalk saluted in his compositions from Plazuela. Firm evidence is lacking on precisely when and where Gottschalk heard all these vernacular musics, but the torrent of compositions that poured from his pen between 1857 and 1859 leaves no doubt that he had gained a close knowledge of them all.

It is fortunate that both of the known "Caribbean" pieces dating from Plazuela are preserved, for they are of exceptional beauty and interest. *Danza* (op. 33) is one of Gottschalk's most delightful compositions. Preserving the A-B *contradanza* form, this sparkling and mercurial concert piece constantly shifts mood from bright to dark and bright again. Key changes, moves in and out of the minor, and inventive chord shifts render this simple piece constantly interesting. It contains syncopations that startlingly anticipate ragtime, as well as a brief three-beat habanera accompanying figure later used widely in jazz.

The second "Caribbean" piece from Plazuela, *Souvenir de Porto Rico* (op. 31), bears the subtitle *Marche des Gibaros,* referring to the rustic peasants of the island. A Puerto Rican enthusiast, Emilio Pasarell, later claimed that the simple theme was derived not from folklore directly but from a symphony composed by his own ancestor, Manuel Pasarell y Mila de la Rosa.[52] Whether or not this is the case, and there exists not a shred of corroborating evidence, both Gottschalk's and Pasarell's themes derive from the Puerto Rican song *Si me dan pasteles, les dénmelos calientes,* a chant-like melody sung by strolling bands of musicians during the Puerto Rican Christmas season.[53]

In form, *Souvenir de Porto Rico* resembles the *Pilgrims Chorus* from Berlioz's *Herold in Italy* in that it depicts the sound of itinerant musicians as it comes into earshot, rises to a peak, and then fades away. The *marcha* itself is in a minor key and darkly sinister, its eight-measure refrain relieved by a bridge of the same length in the major. Like *Bamboula* and *El Cocoyé,* Souvenir de Porto Rico begins with a firm cadence in the bass, but unlike them, it also closes with a cadence. Syncopations based on the Afro-Caribbean *tresillo* and *cinquillo* rhythms ("*da*-dum-da-*dum, da*-dum" and "da-da-*dum*-da-*dum*") lighten the ponderous theme, which builds to an extraordinary climax in which Gottschalk introduces syncopations more arresting than any others to be heard in composed music before the age of ragtime and jazz. The effect is monumental.

After the sustained stay at Plazuela, a caravan consisting of Gottschalk, the Pattis, a maid, two servants, a guide, several horses, and two mules carrying trunks set out via Arecibo for Mayagüez, on the western tip of Puerto Rico. They were a sight to behold. Moreau wore a straw hat, inside of which he had placed large, moist leaves to cool himself. A poncho of tar-covered cloth stretched to his feet. High boots from a San Juan cobbler reached to his belt, which was festooned with a pair of horse pistols. Papa Patti had by now grown a flowing white beard, which made the party of travelers appear yet more exotic.[54] They arrived in Mayagüez early in October.

It was probably while visiting at a plantation near Mayagüez that Gottschalk and the Pattis met a planter named Rios and his seventeen-year-old son. Both hailed from Humacao on the other end of the island and were guests in Mayagüez. The son wasted no time falling in love with Adelina and in due course proposed to her.[55] Moreau was convinced nothing would come of this, for he considered Adelina "too selfish to love, too spoiled to be lovable, and too coquettish to be loving."[56] But such advances were unacceptable to the single-minded Salvatore Patti, who quickly pulled his daughter away in order to resume the musical tour. At a pair of concerts before leaving Mayagüez, Gottschalk played his finished versions of *Chant du soldat* and *Marche solennelle.* Live doves with gilded plumage and adorned with ribbons descended on the stage, and then the entire party proceeded to a huge banquet.[57]

Proceeding hastily down the southwest coast of Puerto Rico, the artists performed in Cabo Rojo and then headed east to Ponce on the southern coast. Gottschalk was to spend three lively and productive months in this port town. He was quite at home in such world centers as Paris and

New York, but his best creative work occurred in more modest surroundings—places like Clermont-sur-l'Oise, Valladolid, and Ponce. More worldly and cosmopolitan than any other American artist of the day, Gottschalk was at the same time among the first bards in the Americas to celebrate peoples and places distant from the great cities. His months in Ponce epitomized his openness to such cultural decentralization and populism.

Situated on the narrow coastal plain, Ponce had grown to be a modern commercial center through the marketing of coffee and sugar. Neoclassical brick homes were replacing the old balconied Spanish houses. The foreign consuls domiciled there helped support the Teatro de Ponce, a privately run concert hall built of wood. Local dressmakers would stand outside the Teatro with sketchbooks poised to copy the latest designs from abroad worn by local ladies of fashion. Transcribers from the local publishing house of Bazar Otero did the same for the music they heard within the hall.[58]

For all its aspirations, little Ponce remained an easy-going Caribbean town. People of modest means were at home in the theater, especially in the upper ring, called the "Chicken Roost" *(Gallinero)*. Public dances were frequent and so well attended that a tax on them provided enough money to pave sidewalks throughout the town. Since the Spanish government required that the music played at the balls be registered at the Casa Alcaldia, we know what tunes were in vogue that season. Local composers took the prize, with Gottschalk's friend Charles Allard vying with Ponce band leader Gregorio Ledesma for popularity.[59] As soon as he arrived in Ponce, Gottschalk looked up Allard; soon he drew Ledesma into his concert programs as well.

The fact that Moreau so quickly identified the two most popular composers in town shows how adept he was at ferreting out local talent. It is certain that he attended balls and heard the local *orquestas típicas*, combinations of cornet, clarinet, trombone, violin, and various rhythm instruments.[60] Such groups, like their counterparts in Havana, were musical transformers, bringing to bear their "classical" techniques on rougher folk music and introducing popular tunes and rhythms into cultivated dance music. They were also the carriers of the local dance music tradition.[61]

Within weeks Moreau had composed a Puerto Rican *danza*, entitled *Las Ponceñas*, and also a *contradanza*, which he called *Tennessee* after a steamer that plied the New York–Ponce run. He later performed this composition in the United States but never published it, and it is lost.[62] Contrary to his usual practice, Gottschalk boldly announced a series of four concerts stretching from November 11 through December 1, 1857, offering a discount for those who subscribed to all four.[63] By the holiday season Gottschalk-mania was high, with the American vice-consul Jorge Lhose throwing a huge party in his honor. Seizing the moment, Moreau then announced his intention of organizing a "grand festival" of Puerto Rican music, to be held on January 7, 1858.

Gottschalk's familiarity with large orchestral endeavors dated to his fifteenth year, when Berlioz mounted several highly publicized *concerts monstres* in Paris. Later, the ornate productions mounted by Louis-Antoine Jullien in New York so thoroughly dominated the Manhattan scene that Moreau was forced to undertake his disastrous New England tour of 1853. These lessons had not been lost on him, and he now endeavored to lead a grand festival of his own. He designed it to appeal equally to Ponce's highbrows and to denizens of the "Chicken Roost."

Over the years, Gottschalk was to put together more than half a dozen such "festivals." He became forever identified with these grandomaniac productions, providing grist for those eager to dismiss him as a mere showman. At a time when newspapers ballyhooed "monster ships" and "monster steam presses," any musician who mounted "monster concerts" was ready prey for sophisticated critics. But there was more method than madness in these festivals.

With one exception, all were staged in Latin countries. Not one was held in the United States, and with good reason. Moreau conceived such festivals specifically as a means of reaching Spanish American audiences. His whole trip through Cuba and Puerto Rico had reinforced his earlier impression of Spaniards as a people puffed up with national pride. Two days before his Ponce festival he complained to his brother how the Spanish there were "formidable in their recognition of the superiority of the Spanish race":

> They read two or three pages about the conquest of Mexico written two centuries ago and feed themselves on the victories of Charles V. . . . They end up convinced that the universe has its eyes riveted on them, that England is jealous of them, that France covets them, and that all the rest of Europe, which they call small fry, is stealing their poetry, music, and wisdom. . . . As for Americans, they simply dismiss them as barbarians.[64]

For a foreign musician to reach such a people, Gottschalk concluded, he had to appeal to their sense of *gloria*, and this, he believed, was bound up with their love of their army. Gottschalk reasoned that he could co-opt this sense of *gloria* by bringing the grandly attired Spanish military bands onto his own concert stage. Only in the last three years of his life did he give these festivals a different orientation.

The Grand Festival at Ponce involved a mere forty musicians from the local garrison. People came by horseback from afar to hear the program, however, which was devoted almost entirely to Puerto Rican music. Adelina Patti, a capable pianist, performed an unidentified Puerto Rican composition by Gottschalk.[65] The composer, Patti, and Allard then performed the *Chant des oiseaux*, the one non–Puerto Rican work of the evening. Following this, the band played a larger instrumental version of Gottschalk's *contradanza*, *La Ponceña*, the first orchestral work from his pen to be performed in public. The high point of the evening was the "magnificent triumphal march," *La Puertorriqueña*, an extended work built on Puerto Rican themes that brought the audience to its feet. And no wonder. In addition to the brass band and two pianos played by four pianists, Moreau brought forth violinists and an entire battalion of rhythm players. For the first time in a European-type band or orchestra, Moreau introduced eight maraca players and eight musicians performing on the güiros, the grooved gourds rubbed by a stick that provide the distinctive clicking in much Afro-Caribbean music. This innovation introduced in a work now regrettably lost stands at the head of more than a century of symphonic and orchestral music evoking Latin rhythms and timbres.

Even though the Grand Festival in Ponce included only forty musicians, Moreau was exhausted by the effort of composing all the music and organizing all the ensembles. After a final concert to benefit flautist Charles Allard, he fell ill and was, as he said, "nailed to [my] bed for five weeks." He described his illness as "my old malady, irritation and inflammation of the intestines." In all probability Moreau experienced a second flare-up of the dysentery he had contracted in Cuba.

However serious the disease, the cure was worse. Moreau reported to his uncle:

> I was bled several times, had about fifty leeches applied to me, had cupping glasses put on, and was inserted into boiling baths. They tormented and tortured my poor carcass under the pretext of driving out the illness that had taken up lodging in my body.[66]

Following a further month of recovery, Gottschalk made several excursions around Puerto Rico. On one such trek he visited the picturesque hill town of Barranquitas. The Ponce concerts had stirred so much commotion that even in this remote village the locals demanded a performance. This led, according to one account, to a bizarre adventure.[67] The organizers eventually found an ancient piano, which Moreau himself had to tune. The only place suitable for a concert was the local inn, which at the time was monopolized by an invalid, a wealthy foreigner who chose precisely this moment to die. Since Gottschalk had to leave almost the next day, his hosts had no alternative but to organize the concert in the salon where the deceased still lay in his coffin. To hide this inconvenient presence, they built a platform over the wooden coffin and lifted the piano onto it.

The concert came off without a hitch. Gottschalk played some local tunes and dances and even introduced a new piece, *Marlborough, s'en va t'en guerre.*[68] As he played, Gottschalk glanced several times to his feet, and each time he did so his music grew more and more sad. Suddenly, with a great crash the entire platform collapsed, taking Gottschalk's piano down with it. The audience was thrown into pandemonium. One of the guests climbed into the rubble and announced, "He's dead!" With this, he pulled out a body—not Gottschalk's, however, but the foreigner's. Eventually the virtuoso himself climbed out of the mass of lumber, intact and smiling, amidst general relief.

Following this picaresque adventure, Moreau traveled north to the capital at San Juan, hoping to build on his success at Ponce. The city was originally formed around the large military base and arsenal but now boasted a thriving commercial center as well. Symbols of San Juan's broadened cultural life were its Philharmonic Society, founded in 1832, and the handsome municipal theater (now Teatro Tapia) recently built on the sloping Plaza de Santiago just under the walls of the huge castle of San Cristóbal. Here, on May 16, 1858, Gottschalk gave the first of several San Juan concerts.

These were apparently a success, although not to such an extent that Gottschalk could avoid reducing prices in order to compete with a visiting *zarzuela* company. The situation looked promising, however, and before the end of the month the San Juan press was speaking of a projected monster concert for 250 musicians. Similar reports, obviously emanating from Gottschalk himself, appeared in *La France musicale* and referred to the monster concerts as an accomplished fact.[69] Notices appearing in the New Orleans press also reported that a two-hundred foot-stage had been constructed and that the "army of musicians" had fulfilled all expectations.[70]

No program for this second and expanded Puerto Rican monster concert has yet turned up, nor are there reviews that confirm that it actually took place as planned. If it did, one can assume that the program included several lost Puerto Rican compositions, including Moreau's new *La Puertorriqueña*, an orchestral version of *Las Ponceñas*, and a *Valse di bravura por Orchestra militaire.*[71]

By mid-July Gottschalk, Allard, and the Pattis had concluded their performances. Whether because he had bookings in the United States or because he realized Moreau's further plans were vague to the extreme, Papa Patti withdrew Adelina from the rest of the tour. Soon after the last event, Salvatore Patti and his daughter departed by steamer for New York. The parting was amicable and paved the way for many further years of Gottschalk's collaboration with members of the Patti family. Adelina soon launched her half-century reign as opera's greatest diva.

This concluded the first leg of Gottschalk's Caribbean hegira.[72] The trip had begun purposefully enough, but with each passing month it had assumed more the character of an improvisation than a deliberately planned tour. Except for the burst of activity connected with the festivals in Ponce and San Juan, the tempo had gradually slowed and the stops grew longer and more frequent. The tropical climate demanded this, but other factors were at work as well.

Since age six or seven, Moreau had been tied to a piano, first as student and then as a virtuoso. Only at Clermont-sur-l'Oise, during his forced idleness at Valladolid, and in a few summer vacations had he been able to focus on composing, and even then he had to turn out works for piano, to the neglect of orchestral compositions. The year in Puerto Rico opened this new horizon to him.

His many compositions for both piano and military band show that Gottschalk was by no means idle during his Puerto Rican sojourn. On the contrary, he had never been more active musically. Over the next year and a half he was to continue along these new directions as he composed innovative orchestral pieces and worked on at least three operas, not to mention a sheaf of further works for piano. By the end of 1859 it appeared certain that Moreau Gottschalk was transcending the role of composer-virtuoso and was on the verge of entering more expansive realms of composition and performance.

Chapter Eighteen

✕ Matouba: Nights in the Tropics

THE length of Gottschalk's Puerto Rican sojourn had been determined by events in the civil war then raging in his real destination, New Granada, as Venezuela was then known. As long as the fighting lasted, a visit by touring artists was out of the question. His presumed host in Venezuela, General Páez, was not only involved directly in the combat but had now proclaimed himself dictator. Only in early July of 1858 did it appear that the Venezuelan crisis was subsiding, and it was then that Gottschalk departed for Caracas via Kingston, Jamaica.[1] With him was flautist Charles Allard, who gave up his teaching in Ponce to join the tour to South America. As supporting artist, Allard received barely a fifth of total receipts.[2]

At Jamaica Gottschalk and Allard learned that their trip to South America had again to be postponed due to renewed fighting there. While they lingered in Jamaica, Moreau explored the town of Kingston. Years later he told his friend Fors of a chance visit he made to a Protestant chapel there. The minister was trying to raise money to aid the families of drowned sailors and was holding a service for this purpose just when Gottschalk dropped in. Moreau at once took over the wheezing organ and began improvising. Gradually the chapel filled with worshippers and spectators. Gottschalk then took his hat and passed it from pew to pew, collecting donations.[3] The *Song of the Orphans (Canto des huerfanos)* that he played that day was never written down and is lost.

Foiled in their hope of reaching the Venezuelan coast from the north, Gottschalk and Allard sailed east by steam packet to Barbados, hoping to cross from there via Trinidad to the South American mainland in order to enter New Granada from the east.[4] Moreau took an instant dislike to Barbados, which seemed to him to possess every English vice and no English virtues. To his uncle Arnold Myers he poured out his contempt for the Protestant Bible Societies there, the widespread drunkenness, the public's disinterest in art, and the virulent attacks on the United States that he heard on every side.[5] He also railed against the "insolent conceit" of the free black population on the island. "However liberal you may be," he confided, "you would have all the trouble in the world containing your indignation."

After a single concert at the Union Hotel, he and Allard departed at once for Port-of-Spain, Trinidad. Here, again, he derided the contempt that English residents showed toward artists, and he took gleeful delight at the sight of a local French-speaking Afro-Caribbean who insulted a redcoat on the street by singing a French army marching song at the top of his voice.[6] For all his criticism of Trinidad's English rulers, Gottschalk delighted in the French-speaking Creole society there, both white and black, and through contact with them he even warmed to the local English. He stayed in Trinidad long enough to give six concerts at the Council Chambers and to be honored by a grand ball held by the British governor. Along the way he reversed his earlier hasty judgments. By the time he left, Gottschalk had reciprocated by feting the British governor at an "impromptu reunion of gentlemen friends," was speaking enthusiastically of "English dignity," and was performing endless variations on the Anglo-American hit *Home, Sweet Home.* He had also made contact with the local English-speaking Jewish community, whose members received him warmly.[7]

Unfortunately, matters in the South American mainland had again taken a turn for the worse. Páez' forces held only the westernmost part of the country. Sensing a possible break-up of New Granada, the British and French had sent in their fleets and threatened to bombard Caracas. Gottschalk and Allard, having already sailed back and forth more than two thousand miles in hopes of reaching Caracas safely, once more had to delay their final crossing to the South American mainland.[8] This created a scheduling problem, for by now the list of alternative concert sites had shrunk almost to nothing. With little choice, the touring artists set out for Georgetown, British Guiana, around the middle of September 1858.

A paucity of evidence regarding Gottschalk's whereabouts over the next several months has led to fantastic legends about a supposed trip to war-torn Caracas and his discovery there of the four-year-old *Wunderkind* Teresa Carreño, who would later become his student and a world-famed virtuoso.[9] In *Notes of a Pianist,* however, Moreau refers only to travels in "the Guianas and the shores of Pará," while in a letter several years later he wrote of travels to British Guiana, Demerara, and Dutch Guiana.[10] This suggests that he divided his time between Georgetown in present-day Guyana and Paramaribo, now in Surinam. At the time, both towns were forgotten backwaters. Even though an exhaustive search of local archives has failed to produce any confirmation of Gottschalk and Allard's presence there, it was apparently in these forlorn places that the two artists whiled away several months, hoping that New Granada would soon be pacified so that General Páez could receive them. This never happened. Except for the friendship Gottschalk formed with the American businessman Francis Jay Herron (1837–1902), later a Union general during the Civil War, the period was wholly uneventful.[11]

Finally conceding defeat in the effort to get to Caracas, Gottschalk and Allard thought briefly of heading south to Brazil. But when they heard reports that cholera was raging in Rio de Janeiro, they abandoned all hope of further travels in South America. Retracing their route north, they steamed to the only centers of culture in the Caribbean that Moreau had not already touched in his travels, namely, the islands of Martinique and Guadeloupe.

Gottschalk was to spend more than a year in these tropical colonies of France. In the absence of more concrete information, Moreau's retrospective account of this year published in the *Atlantic Monthly* has stood unchallenged, with all its studied vagueness. As a consequence, the period has been treated as a *tabula rasa*, to be filled by whatever strikes the biographer's fancy.[12]

Examined more closely, the year 1859 emerges not as a "lost" period but as an important turning point in Gottschalk's life. He arrived on Martinique as a no-longer-young virtuoso and composer, aged twenty-nine, whose career had been floundering since his departure from New York. When he departed, he was as a thirty-year-old composer with a trunk full of operatic and orchestral works and plans for many more. If the months surrounding Moreau's thirtieth birthday were exceptionally productive, they were also extremely happy, a time in which he once more experienced, as he wrote, "all the joys that I had not experienced since I left my family."[13] And no wonder, since these serenely beautiful isles presented in living form the same Creole French culture that had, in its waning days in Louisiana, suffused Moreau's New Orleans childhood. Here were the roots of that "mysterious affinity" that he had first sensed in the West Indies while sailing past Haiti a year earlier. In some deep sense, Gottschalk had come home.

This magical suspension of time no doubt began the moment Moreau realized that for once he had no schedule to meet and no urgent need to make one. Freed from such anxieties, he could enjoy the indigo sea and the deep violet sunsets as he sailed northward to Martinique. On Martinique's rugged northwest coast he caught sight of the brooding mass of volcanic Mount Pelée, and on its seaward flank the city of Saint-Pierre. Some years later Gottschalk's literary disciple Lafcadio Hearn called this "the quaintest, queerest, and the prettiest withal, among West Indian cities: all stone-built and stone-flagged, with very narrow streets, wooden or zinc awnings . . . The architecture is quite old . . . and it reminds one a great deal of that characterizing the antiquated French quarter of New Orleans."[14] Moreau was also entranced by the Creole dialect, the cuisine, and even the dress of the diverse population:

> Nothing is more animated than the narrow, hilly, and bustling streets [of St. Pierre]. There the traditional mulatto women dance and sing to the accompaniment of the *bamboule*, in a display that is so effaced with us [in New Orleans] that it can only be found in books. I could not give you an idea of the piquant effect of these costumes, of these very colonial manners, of this ease, of these primitive ways. Except for the poisonous snakes, which are abundant and which, like the Minotaur, impose an annual tribute on the population, it is a little paradise on earth. The women, when they are not frightened, are charming.[15]

Martinique and Guadeloupe fed Moreau's deep sense of longing, that ineffable nostalgia that permeates Gottschalk's Creole pieces and links him inextricably with the other great American lyric voice of his generation, Stephen Foster. The Creole civilization of the French West Indies was a culture in decline. The former prosperity manifest in Saint-Pierre's grand public buildings and its three-storied opera house had been based on sugar plantations operated with slave labor. The Revolution of 1848 had brought about the abolition of slavery in France's colonies. This, along with the eclipse of the windmill-driven sugar-processing plants in favor of steam power and the spread of beets as a source of inexpensive sugar, was gradually choking off the source of wealth in Martinique and Guadeloupe. Decay was already evident in the peeling walls and faded paint of buildings on both islands. Yet, as often happens, the economic decline coincided with a brief cultural effervescence.

The people of Saint-Pierre were crazy about music. Scarcely had Gottschalk arrived in the city than he was besieged by requests for piano lessons. He penned a long letter to Léon Escudier, later printed in *La France musicale*, pleading for him to recruit Parisian musicians who would emigrate there.[16] "Save me," Moreau wrote, "from these respectable fathers adorned with charming daughters who, in defiance of common sense, drone the keyboard from morning to night." He also made a strong pitch to attract a comic opera company, which the local public demanded "with might and main," and to which it was prepared to grant a monthly subsidy of fifteen hundred francs.[17]

During the Christmas season of 1858 Gottschalk presented two "grand musical fetes" in Saint-Pierre. As in San Juan, he mobilized the local army band, in this case the musicians of the First Infantry Regiment stationed in Fort-de-France. He also composed for the occasion a new work for military band and orchestra entitled *Gueydon Canal* in honor of a public works project named for the outgoing governor of the island, Comte Louis-Henri Gueydon. Purportedly evoking "the local color as derived from a variety of sources," this composition, lost even to bibliographers, may still be resting in some French military archive.[18]

At the end of February Moreau and Allard joined forces with local violinists and singers to present a farewell concert.[19] As in previous concerts on Martinique, Gottschalk indulged in several improvisations, which led one reviewer to remark on his "subjective and personal" style.[20]

Early in 1859 a family of Italian opera singers named Busatti arrived in Saint-Pierre from Caracas. They brought nauseating tales of the civil war there, including reports of drunken soldiers killing women and children in the streets simply for amusement. The Busattis' grim reports appalled Gottschalk, who finally acknowledged to himself that the notion of touring in General Páez's homeland had been an "insane idea."[21] In other respects as well the arrival of the Busattis left a powerful impression on Moreau. He was struck by their musical daughter, with her "foreign black eyes filled with fire." To her, no doubt, was dedicated *Jeune fille aux yeux noirs*, a lost work for piano.[22]

Gottschalk had heard no other major singer besides Adelina Patti since his departure from Havana two year earlier. However imperfect the Busattis' rendering of arias from Rossini and Verdi, they rekindled his love for opera. In short order he had proffered a *Grande Fantaisie de concert* (op. 68) based on Donizetti's *La Favorita*, as well as other variations on Verdi's *Macbeth* and on *I Puritani* and *Cantilène* by Bellini.[23] In opera Moreau now found what he believed to be his true vocation.

A curious piano solo that Gottschalk characterized as "a little sentimental drama" provides evidence on his new direction. *Pastorella e cavalliere* (op. 32) or *The Young Shepherdess and the Knight*[24] tells the story of a village maiden who rejects the advances of a gallant knight and then plays a rustic song as he rides off in confusion. In spite of some banality toward the beginning, this piece, composed in Guadeloupe, contains an impressive second section and an interlude that would have warranted full orchestration. His delightful *Esceñas campestras cubanas*, composed in Havana, develops a similarly brief and naive narrative into a fully orchestrated operetta in one act.

The notion of writing a full opera did not suddenly descend upon Gottschalk in 1859. Clara Brinkerhoff claimed that Moreau had written an opera prior to his second departure for the Caribbean and that the manuscript had been among those papers lost during the great Maryland snowstorm in January 1856.[25] The *Grande Valse poétique concertante*, written for soprano Anna de la Grange later that spring, may well have been a reconstructed fragment from this work.[26] Regarding the identity of this lost opera, there exists no direct evidence and only one hint. During the time of Gottschalk's visit to Madrid, a minor Spanish writer named Antonio Camino published a novel entitled *Isaura, ó La Venganza de una muder*, dedicated to Isabel II.[27] Gottschalk himself referred to the fact that he was working on an opera entitled *Isaura di Salerno* in Martinique and Guadeloupe, and obituaries published in Brazil at the time of his death reported that he had completed an opera named *Izaura* and hoped to produce it in Europe.[28] Is it possible that Moreau had come across Camino's novel in Madrid and transposed the setting to a town more appropriate for an Italian opera? Could the resulting opera have been the work that he lost on the train in 1856? Did he doggedly return to the same project in 1859, plugging away on it thereafter until his death a decade later?

By the time Gottschalk reached Havana again in 1860 he had in hand also two acts of another opera, this one entitled *Amalia Warden*.[29] All that survives is Act I of the libretto, dated 1860.[30] Given the hectic schedule Moreau followed after returning to Havana, it is all but certain that he composed the two acts of this opera during his sabbatical in Guadeloupe and Martinique. In this case, the subject matter and origins are known.

Back in 1833 the Parisian composer Daniel François Auber had composed a five-act opera entitled *Gustave III, ou Le Bal masqué*. The libretto by Augustin Eugène Scribe told of an actual happening at the court of Sweden in 1792. The King, Gustave III, was in love with one Amelia, wife of a courtier named Ankerström. Convinced that his wife had betrayed him, Ankerström murdered the King at a masqued ball, only to discover later that Amelia was innocent.[31] Auber's work was in the repertoire of the Paris Opera throughout Gottschalk's residence in France, and the budding composer presumably saw it there. At some later point—probably in Havana in 1857—he dug up a poem in French based either on the original story or on the text by Scribe. Gottschalk modified this text to serve as a libretto and had it translated into Italian by his friend, the baritone Alessandro Lorenzana.[32]

What Gottschalk did not realize is that several other composers had also taken an interest in the dramatic incident. As early as 1840 Bellini had planned his own opera on the subject. Then, in the autumn of 1857, while Moreau was in Cuba, Giuseppe Verdi had begun work on what was to become his opera *Un Ballo in Maschera (The Masqued Ball)*.[33] On

February 17, 1859, within months of the day Gottschalk began work on his own version, Verdi's opera was premiered in Rome. Gottschalk had been scooped. For the time being, however, he remained ignorant of this and blithely continued to work on his own opera *Amalia Warden.*

While Gottschalk was sojourning in Saint-Pierre during the spring of 1859, his publisher Hall forwarded to him a letter from Bernard Ullmann offering a six-month contract for seventy-two hundred dollars, all costs included.[34] Mistrustful of the slippery impresario, Moreau demanded that he be paid half the amount in advance. Confident that Ullmann would agree, he then asked Léon Escudier to publish a notice in *La France musicale* that he would be undertaking a six-month tour in the United States and then return to France.[35] Meanwhile, a number of suspicious fires had broken out in Saint-Pierre. The French governor, suspecting arson, imposed martial law on the entire island of Martinique, closing all theaters and cafés each evening at 9:00 p.m.[36] Gottschalk therefore decided to cross over to Guadeloupe, 120 miles to the north, and to take Allard with him. For the next half year Moreau was out of touch with Ullmann, and the American tour faded like a tropical sunset.

The first stop on Guadeloupe was the town of Le Moule, a small sugar port on the eastern coast built around a horseshoe-shaped harbor adjoining the placid Ravine Gardel. Belying its small population, Le Moule boasted stone warehouses at portside for sugar, a handsome park, houses indistinguishable from those in New Orleans, and a just-completed stone church that would have been at home in Renaissance Rome. Grand plantation houses like Château Murat sprinkled the nearby countryside, and adjoining them stood decaying windmills, emblems of a fading technology.

Guided by some sixth sense, Gottschalk found his way to this genteel Creole society in decline. Since there was no concert hall in Le Moule, a rich sugar merchant simply removed the interior walls of his house, and there Moreau and Allard gave three concerts.[37]

After several further performances at Point-à-Pitre, the capital of Guadeloupe, Gottschalk and Allard moved on to the old town of Basse-Terre on the island's southwest coast.[38] Here, along the narrow band between forested mountains and the rocky coast, they found yet another antique version of New Orleans, split by the Rivière aux Herbes and dominated by the massive Fort Saint-Charles. Long stagnant, Basse-Terre nonetheless boasted a cathedral, the comfortable Hotel Célánire, and even a music store. The local public enthusiastically welcomed Gottschalk and Allard on June 12, when they delivered the first of what turned out to be twelve concerts. Here Gottschalk premiered his new fantasies on Donizetti's *La Favorita* and developed further his transcriptions from Verdi's

Macbeth and Bellini's *Cantilène.*[39] He also offered piano lessons at the outrageous rate of forty francs an hour, which he smugly reported to readers of *La France musicale.*[40]

The culmination of Gottschalk's conquest of tiny Basse-Terre occurred on July 10, 1859, at a grand ecclesiastical festival. During the day, the local St. Joseph Convent celebrated first communion for the two hundred girls studying in its school. An immense crowd assembled in the chapel and surrounding park to hear Moreau perform a long improvisation on the organ during mass. Later, the bishops of Trinidad, Martinique, Dominica, and Basse-Terre assembled in full regalia for a grand open-air procession, with church bells ringing and troops of the entire garrison drawn up in ranks. That night, after performing at a ball held by the French governor, Gottschalk offered a benefit concert at the Synodal Hall adjoining the bishop's residence. A plain wooden structure with classical ornaments, this grandly named room was no bigger than the Parisian salons at which Moreau had so often appeared. The four bishops were seated on a wooden dais built at one end, and an audience of 150 clergymen and seminarians packed the room to bursting. At this concert, which a local reviewer claimed "never has, nor ever will have, an equal," Gottschalk for the first time performed a "fragment of a new symphony" entitled *La Nuit des tropiques (A Night in the Tropics).*[41]

What was this work Moreau tested on the assembled clerics at Basse-Terre? Not so much as mentioned before that evening, what was probably then still an incomplete sketch grew within a few months into a fully scored symphony in two movements.

The composition of *La Nuit des tropiques* is bound up with one of the most obscure but important creative periods in the composer's life. For a span of time estimated by various writers as a few summer months in 1859 up to a year or more, Gottschalk was at Matouba, a remote and mountainous spot in Guadeloupe. It was at Matouba that he completed and scored the first movement of *La Nuit des tropiques* and composed a great number of other works, published and unpublished.[42]

Gottschalk's productivity at Matouba has never been in doubt. Rather, it is the nature of the place and Gottschalk's state of mind while there that are uncertain. Assumptions on these issues became major building blocks of the Gottschalk legend. Even while he was at Matouba, the New York press characterized Moreau as "dallying in the fragrant islands of the West Indies."[43] Marguerite Aymar, a New York friend, reported later that he spent a full year "in the grand solitude of the highest peak of the mountains of Guadeloupe, with no living soul near him save one faithful servant."[44]

Gottschalk himself helped create the romantic legend of his Matouba

idyll with two essays, one issued in France just after he left Guadeloupe
and a second that was published in the *Atlantic Monthly* in 1865.[45] These
evocative sketches reveal Gottschalk as an arch-romantic, a wanderer
from civilization's path. To *La France musicale* he reported:

> I am writing to you from the bottom of the Matouba gorge, near the old La
> Soufrière volcano, the highest in the Antilles. I am alone in the face of a verita-
> ble chaos of smoking mountains, rivers that seem to climb toward their
> source, trees that push their roots upward, precipices, tempests, the most
> complete solitude, Neapolitan evenings following terrible thunderstorms last-
> ing an hour, with no neighbors, an eternal silence, and nothing but the im-
> mense harmony of a continuous landscape having as its figured bass the din
> of the Rivièr Rouge, which flows at the bottom of a precipice behind my dwell-
> ing. Here there is an antediluvian Negro, one-armed and stammering, who pre-
> pares Caribbean viands for me. . . . I am here inspired.

For the *Atlantic Monthly* he developed the picture more fully:

> Seized with a profound disgust with the world and with myself, tired, discour-
> aged, suspicious of men (and of women as well), I hastened to hide in the
> wilds on the extinguished volcano of N––, where I lived for many months like
> a cenobite . . .
>
> Perched upon the edge of a crater, on the very top of the mountain, my
> cabin overlooked the whole country. The rock on which it was built hung over
> a precipice whose depths were concealed by cacti, convolvulses, and bam-
> boos. The person who had preceded me here had surrounded this lower
> ground with a parapet and had built a terrace on the same level as the bed-
> room. He had requested to be buried there, and at night from my bed I could
> see the white tombstone in the moonlight a few steps from my window. Every
> evening I moved my piano out upon the terrace, and there, in view of the most
> beautiful scenery in the world, which was bathed by the serene and limpid
> atmosphere of the tropics, I played *for myself alone* everything that the scene
> open before me inspired.
>
> And what a scene! . . . Before me sixty miles of country whose magic
> perspective is rendered more marvelous by the transparency of the atmo-
> sphere. . . . Behind me was a rock on which broke a torrent of melted snow
> which, turned from its course, leaped with a desperate bound, and engulfed
> itself in the depths of the precipice that gaped under my window.

Having painted this vast canvas, Moreau then proceeded to regale the
earnest readers of the *Atlantic Monthly* with generalizations about his
half decade in the tropics:

> I again began to live according to the customs of these primitive countries,
> which, if they are not strictly virtuous, are nonetheless terribly attractive. I
> saw again those beautiful *trigueñas*, with red lips and brown bosoms, ignorant
> of evil, sinning with frankness, without fearing the bitterness of remorse. All
> this is frightfully immoral, I know, but life in the savannas of the tropics, in
> the midst of a half civilized and voluptuous race, cannot be that of a London
> cockney, a Parisian idler, or an American Presbyterian. . . . The moralists, I

well know, condemn all this; and they are right. But poetry is often in antagonism with virtue.[46]

Rounding out his picture, Gottschalk introduced his sole companion besides his cook, the man who played the role of loyal Friday to this Robinson Crusoe from New Orleans. He was

> a poor fool I had met on a small island and who attached himself to me, followed me everywhere, and loved me with that absurd and touching constancy which one meets only in dogs and madmen. My friend, whose folly was quiet and inoffensive, believed himself to be the *greatest genius in the world.* He suffered, he said, from a gigantic and monstrous tooth (and it was only by this that I recognized that he was insane, the other symptoms being found among too many individuals to be considered as an abnormal trait of the human mind)—a monstrous tooth that periodically increased and threatened to encroach upon his whole jaw. . . . In the midst of this intellectual ruin, only one thing survived—his love for music. He played the violin, and—a singular thing—although insane, he understood nothing of the Music of the Future [e.g., Wagner]![47]

His contemporaris lapped up this romantic gruel, not suspecting that it might have contained at least an element of fantasy designed purely to shock them, *épater le bourgeois.* A modern skeptic, by contrast, quick to detect every sign of the artist fabricating his own persona, may hesitate to accept the possibility that Gottschalk's account had any objective basis at all.

The reality is more interesting than either. On the one hand, the composer sought out and found a retreat remarkably similar in most respects to what he later described in the published accounts. On the other hand, Gottschalk worked like a romantic painter to intensify the most dramatic elements of the scene, to suppress banal aspects that were present, and to ascribe to himself a languorous and reflective mood when in fact he was working with single-minded intensity.

Gottschalk's account of the physical setting at Matouba is accurate in all details but one. Far from being perched on the edge of a crater, the village of Matouba is several miles distant from "Napoleon," the highest of the mountain La Soufrière's several craters.[48] Even today the tropical forests and deep gorge teem with parakeets and grossquits. However, Matouba is only four miles from Basse-Terre and in Gottschalk's day could be reached in an afternoon. Matouba itself boasted several country houses owned by Basse-Terre merchants, including the one loaned to Gottschalk.[49] It was not uncommon for the owners of such retreats to be buried *in situ,* and several such terraces with tombstones still stand in the region.

As to Gottschalk's madman Friday, this was Firmin Moras, a mulatto educated by his European father to read Voltaire and Rousseau and to play the violin.[50] Pursuing an interest in music therapy that dated from his stay in Clermont-sur-l'Oise, Moreau made Moras's mental recovery his personal cause. The cure was successful, and Firmin Moras became Gottschalk's paid valet and factotum, remaining with him until the composer's death.

With several interruptions for concerts and lessons in Basse-Terre, Gottschalk remained at Matouba through most of July and August 1859. Far from wallowing in *far niente*, however, he produced an impressive outpouring of new compositions. Three simple dance pieces published under the name "Seven Octaves" lead off the list, two of them—*Love and Chivalry* and *Fairy Land*—being in the form of schottisches and the third being a *galop de concert* entitled *Hurrah Galop*. Signaling his pride in these pieces, the composer included on the published edition of *Fairy Land* a dedication "To My Dear Friend L. M. Gottschalk."

The second group of compositions written at Matouba and Saint-Pierre can all be considered "classical" to the extent they are in the Old World dance genres that had become the stock in trade for composers since Chopin. In actuality, these more European pieces all display the same characteristic features of Gottschalk's style that are evident in his Caribbean works, just as the latter, conversely, are thoroughly "European" in that they apply tested classical methods to the exposition of folk material.

The mazurka *Jeunesse* is an airy and transparent piece, but the Mazurka in F, is of an entirely different order. Pensive and dark at first, it moves to a striking romantic arabesque pattern, which, as Richard Jackson has pointed out, anticipates a principal theme in Rimskii-Korsakov's opera *The Golden Cockerel* of almost a half century later.[51] Less successful is a flashy but shallow concert mazurka, *Polonia* (op. 43), which pays tribute to Chopin more in its name than content, as Gottschalk himself admitted.[52]

A series of études and romances also emerged about this time. A list of Gottschalk compositions published during his lifetime included the etude *Rome*,[53] the *Étude pour un main*, and also the *Études de concert*, all of which are lost. Of the three romances reported to have been written in this period only the *Romance* in E-flat major survives.[54] A mere sixty measures, this slight but attractive composition contained more of the chromaticism evident in *Mazurk (sic)*, unusual seventh chords, and a strikingly dissonant eleventh chord that holds the lyric in suspension for two beats. In its understated way, *Romance* utilizes harmonies that sound throughout Wagner's *Tristan*.

More ambitious in plan but trivial in its realization is *Murmures éo-*

liens (op. 46), a Lisztian effort to capture the sound of an aeolian harp vibrating in the soft evening breeze.[55] Even careful construction fails to sustain the slight melodic line. Perhaps Gottschalk's *Paulina*, a serenade for male voice, and his *Andante* for violin and piano were more interesting works in the same vein, but they are lost.[56]

Two pieces from Matouba were intended as celebrations of national feeling. By now his friend General Páez was emerging as the victor in the civil war in New Granada. In a letter sent to Gottschalk at Basse-Terre, Páez requested a triumphant march to be played when he reviewed his entire army at the city of Barcelona. Gottschalk expedited to him a piece entitled *La Bataille de Carabovo*, of which he was very proud. Now lost, this march may still rest in some Caracas archive.[57] Quite different in character was *Columbia* (op. 34), subtitled *Caprice américain*, a rambunctious transformation of Stephen Foster's *My Old Kentucky Home*. Gottschalk stripped Foster's ballad of all sentimentality, leaving it "devoid of nostalgia and magnolias," in John Godfrey Doyle's apt phrase.[58] Outfitted with a new middle section replacing the passage "Weep no more my lady . . . ," Moreau's boisterous romp suggests a banjo and dancing. After a surprisingly cheerful minor passage, it arrives at the final phrase which, repeated several times with rising tempo and virtuosity, culminates in a grand cadenza.

A third major group of compositions from Matouba and Saint-Pierre drew on the indigenous rhythms of the French Antilles and Cuba. Gottschalk had first mined this rich lode in his four Louisiana pieces of 1849–51. During his 1854 tour of Cuba he returned to it again, this time making contact with the local *contradanza* tradition. *El Cocoyé* and other surviving pieces from that year are not without interest but are marred by a display of virtuosity that had been intended, no doubt, to impress the fraternity of Cuban pianists who gathered at Edelmann's. Only when he arrived in Puerto Rico three years later did Gottschalk return to a more searching look at Creole music. His *Souvenir de Porto Rico, Las Ponceñas*, and *contradanzas*, written at Plazuela or Ponce, represent the beginnings of a new fascination that reached full flower at Matouba and Saint-Pierre. Gottschalk's Latin-tinged compositions of this period represent a landmark in the music of the Americas.

In light of the fact that Gottschalk had not set foot in Cuba for more than two years, the prominence of Cuban themes in these pieces is surprising. One is explicitly titled *Danse cubaine*, and nearly all employ the habanera rhythm. In all of them, too, the *cinquillo* rhythm is prominent, whether in its basic form or in its endless variations.

Several features set off these Caribbean works from their predecessors in Gottschalk's oeuvre. At some points they exhibit daring chord structures similar to those found in more classical compositions of the same period. Another distinction is that Gottschalk had so completely mastered the melodic language of the region that he could now free himself entirely from specific prototypes and create his own themes. In the published editions of several of these compositions Gottschalk included an editorial note boasting that the melodies were original. Speaking in the third person, he went on to explain that "Chopin, as is well known, transferred the national traits of Poland to his mazurkas and polonaises, and Mr. Gottschalk has endeavored to reproduce in [his] works . . . the characteristic traits of the dances of the West Indies."[59]

Even though he used original material in these pieces, Gottschalk took pains to ensure that others would play them in such a way as to preserve the distinctive relation of melody and rhythm that defines all Caribbean dances. In the published version of several of the Matouba compositions he provided instructions on how to make the melody sing while maintaining the *staccato* accompaniment in the left hand.[60] Such instructions anticipate Scott Joplin's similar instructions on how to perform his rags for piano.

Ojos criollos (op. 37), written in Saint-Pierre and labeled a *Danse Cubaine*, is a pure *contradanza* arranged for two or four hands.[61] Its rhythmic pattern presages that of many American cakewalks, including the evergreen *At a Georgia Camp Meeting*. It also contains an intriguing offbeat passage that directly anticipates jazz of the 1920s. This wonderful piece, which achieved immense popularity, provides in its many variations a splendid insight into how the simple Cuban *contradanza* was actually performed.

Souvenirs de la Havane (op. 39) is also a *contradanza*, but one elaborated into a virtuosic concert piece complete with a Creole version of Thalberg's "three-hand" style. The moody introduction bursts into a highly syncopated major section that is notable for the way Gottschalk's characteristic "perfume" of nostalgia emerges in the very midst of all the exuberance.

Another Cuban dance, *Réponds-moi! (Dí qui sí)*, was definitely composed at Matouba and is one of Gottschalk's brightest and most sassy *contradanzas*. At the same time, it is an art piece featuring bursts of virtuosic display. In view of this delightful gem, it is all the more regrettable that a further group of *danzas* composed at this time, as well as a *Marcha de los Caribes*,[62] a *Fantaisie sur des airs martiniquais*, and a *Souvenirs des Antilles*, were either never written down or were lost.[63]

Overshadowing these miniature delights is the most important product of Gottschalk's Matouba period, *La Nuit des tropiques*, subtitled *Symphonie romantique*.[64] As much as any other composition by

Gottschalk, the *Symphonie romantique* claims an important place in the history of music in the Americas. The Cuban writer Alejo Carpentier pointed out that Gottschalk was the first composer to employ Afro-Cuban instruments in his compositions, anticipating his successors by some sixty years.[65] This two-movement work is at once a sophisticated symphonic poem in the tradition of Berlioz and a raucous dance, conjuring up a Cuban festival. Simultaneously highbrow and lowbrow, it defies simple categorization by cultural level. Even its instrumentation, combining the latest valved brass instruments from Paris and primitive Caribbean drums, traditional European strings and Spanish folk instruments, reflects a boldly innovative approach to culture. Exuding the sensibility of one who was both a musical aesthete and a musical populist, *La Nuit des tropiques* blends Parisian elegance with American democracy.

Gottschalk never programmed this composition in his native land, nor was it published or performed in any form for nearly a century following Gottschalk's death. More recently, a series of mediocre recordings based on poorly reconstructed versions of the original score have obscured its strengths and amplified its shortcomings.

Gottschalk's *Symphonie romantique* is no symphony at all in the classical sense but a free-form poem based on subject matter and musical materials drawn from the Americas. Its name *La Nuit des tropiques* refers only to the first movement, an andante in six-eight time. The second movement, *Une Fête sous les tropiques*, is an allegro-moderato subtitled *Fiesta criolla*. Both movements are grand in scale, calling for several hundred musicians. Yet for all this, the symphony is a very simple work, as is understandable for the first full orchestral score written by a composer who had heretofore concentrated almost exclusively on the piano. While not lacking in subtlety, Gottschalk's symphony has overall a delightfully naive quality as compared with the intricate scores of his European contemporaries.

The first movement, *La Nuit des tropiques*, probably derived its name from the symphonic ode entitled *Christophe Colomb* by the French composer Félicien David. The second movement of David's elaborate work was entitled *Une nuit des tropiques*. Gottschalk almost certainly heard this performed at the Opéra Comique when it was premiered there in 1847.[66]

The mood of a tropical night was well described by Lafcadio Hearn, who traveled on Gottschalk's heels to Guadeloupe in search of the seed grounds of Creole culture. His description precisely fits Matouba:

> In these tropical latitudes Night does seem "to fall,"—to descend over the many-peaked lands: It appears to rise up, like an exhilation, from the ground.

The coast-lines darken first;—then the slopes and the lower hills and valleys become shadowed;—then, very swiftly, the gloom mounts to the heights, whose very loftiest peak may remain glowing like a volcano at its tip for several minutes after the rest of the island is veiled in blackness and all the stars are out.[67]

Gottschalk, with his keen audio-visual sense, attempted to portray such a scene much the way his artist friend Frederic Edwin Church did in his great canvas *Morning in the Tropics,* painted the previous year.[68]

La Nuit des tropiques has a narrative program. It begins with a serene night in the Antilles, into which rolls and crashes a mighty thunderstorm. Gradually this subsides, leaving in its wake once more a shimmering and peaceful tropical world. The three main themes, each expressed first in the key of E-flat major, correspond to these phases. But the strength of Gottschalk's composition lies not in these themes but in the way he manipulated them. He devoted more than half of the movement to sophisticated developmental passages that pass through multiple modulations and shift frequently from major to minor. Along the way he incorporated a rich array of augmented sixth chords, diminished sevenths, and secondary dominants that would have been more at home in a Wagnerian opera than in any work by an American to date. And for the storm passage he unleashed a mighty barrage of trombones, horns, euphoniums, tubas, trumpets, cornets, and ophicleides, the raspy and guttural bass horns so favored by Berlioz.

Following the storm section, Gottschalk introduced a grandly serene melody played on the most unlikely instrument, the piston-valved cornet *(cornet à piston)* first exploited by Berlioz in his *Symphonie fantastique.* In the second Havana performance of the symphony he enhanced this poignant aria by adding long chords played by six "harmoniflautas." This now extinct Spanish popular instrument produced sounds akin to a bass harmonica and must have imparted to the work a rich hum suggestive of languid night sounds.

If the first movement brings to mind a romantic landscape by Church, the second movement, *Une Fête sous les tropiques,* is a fast, action-filled genre painting depicting a Creole festival. Long before Bizet and Saint-Saëns began toying with habanera motifs, Gottschalk drew a riot of Caribbean rhythms into his composition. Not only did he employ nearly a dozen variations on the syncopated *cinquilla* rhythm, but he often set several of them against each other, employing in this task woodwinds and brasses as well as rhythm instruments. Again he slid from key to key, modulating through a half dozen tonalities as he moved among his several themes. In the midst of this exuberant display, he imposed a bizarre fugue passage before returning to the finale.

The great innovation of this *Fiesta criolla* movement is the scoring for Cuban rhythm instruments, including maracas and güiros. Complementing these popular instruments, essential to Caribbean popular music but never before employed in symphonic ensembles, was a veritable army of drums. Along with European timpani, snare drums, and bass drums, Gottschalk called for a battalion of Afro-Cuban drums of various sizes and depths. This multi-cultural innovation electrified the Havana audience when the symphony was premiered there in February 1860. It would have been even more daring in Paris, where up to this time no composer had ventured further in the use of folk instruments than Berlioz and Bizet, who had employed the *tambourin provençal*.

During the last week in August 1859, Gottschalk quit Matouba and sailed from Basse-Terre back to Martinique. He arrived at the capital of Fort-de-France just in time to participate in festivities surrounding the dedication of a new monument to the Empress Josephine, who had been born nearby at Trois Islets. The governors of the colonies of France, Denmark, and Great Britain all assembled at Fort-de-France, along with hundreds of soldiers and thousands of visitors from throughout Martinique.[69] The city was a madhouse and quite inadequate to house the thousands of visitors. Moreau spent the first night of the celebration on the floor under the bar of a local pub, wedged between several English officers and under constant attack by ants. The next night he abandoned all thought of sleeping and walked the town, examining the Josephine statue by Debret that still stands in the Savane park.

On the final day the Governor presented a grand ball and concert. Eight hundred guests were invited, and fifteen hundred showed up, many drawn by the knowledge that Gottschalk had been contracted to perform at the lordly fee of twelve hundred dollars. Most of his program was unexceptional. Moreau concluded with a solo version of his *Siege of Saragossa*. As the battle raged, he happened to glance into the hall, where he noticed a red-faced English major, snoring loudly. Diverting from his score, he launched boldly into *God Save the Queen*, which propelled the poor major to his feet. No sooner did he begin cheering than Gottschalk played simultaneously the French national march, *Partant pour la Syrie*, at which point the Gallic part of the audience sprang from its chairs and applauded wildly.

Returning to his beloved Saint-Pierre, Gottschalk spent his last two months in the French Antilles composing and being feted by friends. At one banquet a local Creole named de Pezin rose to declaim verses dedicated to the guest from Louisiana. He spoke of Gottschalk's Creole elegies, his syncopated melodies accompanied by the sound of the *tamtam*, and, above all, of his celebration of "our flowers, our fields, our woods, our winds, our hurricanes, . . . and of the diaphanous tropical night, where the summer breeze sighs while weeping in mysterious veils." [70]

After a final concert at which he played his most recent compositions from Matouba, Gottschalk departed with Allard and Firmin Moras. A huge crowd accompanied them to the wharf.[71] The local governor had placed his official yacht at the disposal of his guests, and it now carried them via Saint-Barthélemy to St. Thomas, where local residents presented Gottschalk with an elaborately tooled cigar case. The party proceeded thence to Puerto Rico, where Allard parted company in order to return to Ponce. The English steamer *Trent* then carried Gottschalk and Moras on the last leg of their journey, and on November 26, 1859, they arrived once more at Havana.

Chapter Nineteen

🕸 Havana Twilight

SCARCELY had Gottschalk settled into a rented apartment at 470 Calle Aguiar in Havana's dense and bustling old quarter than he was beset by his many friends from previous visits. The loyal Espadero came to see him, as did the violinist José White, just back from Paris, the poet Rafael Mendive, and many others. Gottschalk's photo album rapidly filled with *cartes de visite* of dapper men and chic women, all taken at Charles D. Friedrichs's fashionable studios in Calle de Habana.[1] On December 17, 1859, New York's *Musical World* had clamored for Gottschalk to return at once to the United States, but he scarcely gave it a thought.

Gottschalk's admirers arranged for him to perform at the Liceo Artístico y Literario, and within days they had sold four hundred tickets.[2] Then he fell ill and spent a week with three doctors hovering over him.[3] The Liceo concert, finally held on December 22, brought together José White, Espadero, and a number of singers from Max Maretzek's operatic company, then in Havana. The great Maretzek himself attended, as did publisher Carlos Edelmann, who provided two Érard pianos.[4] The Havana audience heard nearly an entire program of Gottschalk's newest Caribbean works and was delighted.

A few weeks later the same musicians reassembled for a second performance at the Liceo. On this evening Gottschalk presented a *Gran Galop de Bravura* for two pianos based on a theme by the French composer Joseph Quident, which he performed with Espadero.[5] The high point of the evening was a new tarantella by Gottschalk. This work, which eventually emerged as the *Grande Tarentelle* (op. 67) for piano and orchestra, began life as an improvisation with White and Espadero. It then passed through a two violin version, now lost, and finally emerged in a scoring for orchestra that was performed in Brazil.[6]

Many years later this and many other Gottschalk pieces were issued in unauthorized and often altered editions. The person charged with man-gling them was Arthur Napoleão dos Santos (1843–1925), who arrived in Havana early in 1860. Born in Portugal of parents who decided the name "Napoleon" would do more for a musical career than their Italian origi-nal,[7] Napoleão was a seventeen-year-old former *Wunderkind* at the time he turned up in Havana. Gottschalk crowned Napoleão publicly with a wreath of gold and silver and had only praise for him in private.[8] Flu-ent in several languages and a good chess player, Napoleão had even impressed Dwight, whose journal credited him also with writing novels purely to amuse himself.[9] Napoleão at once assumed the role of Gottschalk's disciple, even though their relationship involved neither les-sons nor joint concerts.

Far more justified in calling himself Gottschalk's protégé was young Ignacio Cervantes (1847–1905), who studied with both Gottschalk and Espadero in 1860 before they sent him off to Paris to complete his train-ing under Gottschalk's old friend Professor Marmontel.[10] Eventually one of Cuba's most renowned composers, Cervantes was formed as an artist in part through these early lessons with Gottschalk.

Amidst this pleasant round of reunions, concerts, and lessons, Gottschalk was invited by the newly appointed captain-general to play at the Palacio on December 19.[11] Moreau recognized in Francisco Serrano y Domínguez a potential patron. Unlike his predecessors, Serrano was linked by marriage to wealthy Creole planter families and was therefore acceptable to Havana society. At the same time, he realized that slavery was doomed on the island and began the long transition to free labor.

Scarcely a week after performing for Serrano, Gottschalk announced to the press that he intended to mount a grand musical festival in honor of the captain-general's forthcoming inauguration.[12] Soon all Havana was talking "often and everywhere" about the event, to be held at the Gran Teatro Tacón.[13] The public welcomed this act of civil boosterism. As the *Gaceta de la Habana* observed:

> Anyone familiar with the international press knows that festivals like this make history in cities where they are held. All Europe will learn of our festival, and no one will be able to disregard Cuba's capital. Thanks to Gottschalk, Havana will take her place among the principal artistic centers of Europe.[14]

The task would be immense, but the newspaper knew that "Gottschalk was the one to do it." Indeed, it concluded, "his name alone offers the best guarantee of the project's most complete success."[15]

Like a modern city hosting the Olympics, Havana mobilized for Gottschalk's festival. The military governor, General Ignacio Planas, made available to Moreau every army band in the local garrison.[16] Maretzek offered the soloists and chorus from his Italian Opera Company. All that was lacking was the music.

Gottschalk's program may have been an exercise in self-advancement, but it also reflects his optimistic belief that high art, provided it was compatible with popular sensibilities, could reach a mass audience. Accordingly, he programmed only three works, all composed by himself and all premiers: *La Nuit des tropiques*; a new mini-opera entitled *Esceñas campestres cubanas* and dedicated to the captain-general's wife; and a solemn *Sinfonía triunfal* in three movements for military band and orchestra. Each had something to stun and delight the Havana public.

Over the preceding months Moreau had prepared a full orchestration of *La Nuit des tropiques*. In spite of the fact that he already commanded a veritable army of musicians, he now had the inspired idea of supplementing his ensemble with the entire band of Afro-Cuban drummers, La Tumba Francesa, whom he had heard six years earlier at the Carnival in Santiago de Cuba. The fact that the Tumba Francesa players were six hundred miles away on Cuba's eastern tip did not faze Gottschalk. He simply let the captain-general know that their presence was required, and soon they were in Havana. Why, though, did Gottschalk not turn to a Havana group for this assignment? The answer is that such elemental drum ensembles were not to be found in the sophisticated capital, even among the many Afro-Cuban musicians there.[17]

Nothing quite like this had ever occurred before. Gottschalk, with his intention to stun the public, teamed a symphonic orchestra with an entire band of folk musicians. To heighten the exotic effect, he placed the leader of La Tumba Francesa directly in front of the orchestra, behind his enormous drum.

The second new work on the festival program was a deliciously charming one-act opera with libretto by the Havana poet and political activist Manuel Ramírez. The whole piece is short—under fifteen minutes—and both Ramirez's scant plot and the music itself sustain a mood of lightness and gaiety. *Esceñas campestres cubanas* vaguely resembles a one-act *opéra comique* by Offenbach, but its true antecedents are less French than Spanish, specifically the form of comic opera in miniature called a *tonadillo escénica*.[18] Ramírez's scene depicts two men, baritone and tenor, who court a peasant lass with their three-string Cuban guitar *(tiple)*. She rejects their advances, however, and as a consolation invites both to dance, flirtatiously telling them "to live is to enjoy; to love is to live" *(Vivir es gozar, amar es vivir)*. From this scant narrative Gottschalk conjured up a wonderful village festival, yet another in the long line of *fêtes champêtre* that runs through the history of romantic music; he had probably first encountered the convention as a boy, on the New Orleans stage.[19]

Gottschalk borrowed the first theme from his own *Danza* (op. 33), one of the Puerto Rico compositions. By the second section, the rhythms begin to shift mercurially. As the various singers enter, each in a different key, the rhythmic subtleties compound further. Finally, as the peasant maiden rejects her suitors, a fresh dance theme breaks out, this time the *zapateado*, a sharply punctuated clog dance common in the Cuban countryside but originally from Spain. The rhythm, "de-*dum*-de-*dum*-dum," is carried not so much by the percussion instruments as by the clarinets and other woodwinds, with counter-rhythms sounding in other parts of the orchestra and in the very Italianate voice parts. Timpani, Caribbean güiros, and the three-string *tiple* add local spice to the rhythms sounded by the woodwinds. A grand finale strongly resembling Schubert's song *The Shepherd on the Rock (Der Hirt auf den Felsen)* brings the scene to a stirring if abrupt close.

The third work on the program, grandiosely labeled a *sinfonía triunfal*, is really three separate pieces for military bands and orchestra that were brought together for this occasion only. The first section constituted a salute by the massed military bands, which added up to some eighty cornets and fifty drums. This composition dropped from sight after the festival and still remains lost. The second movement took the form of a "hymn of triumph based on Gottschalk's finale of the opera *Charles IX*." The third movement was described as a "grand march dedicated to the Prince of Asturias, the two-year-old son of Queen Isabel II."[20]

What was this opera *Charles IX?* As late as Matouba, there is no evidence that Gottschalk was working on any opera besides *Amaiia Warden* and *Isaura di Salerno*. Now he suddenly emerged with a third title, and a very enigmatic one at that. It refers to the French king who ordered the grisly massacre of Protestants on St. Bartholomew's Day, 1572. The story of Charles IX had long since fascinated French romantic writers. The novelist Prosper Mérimée had written a volume on Charles entitled *La Chronique du regne de Charles IX*. Mérimée's book, published in 1829, reads more like an opera libretto than history, and it directly inspired Gottschalk's project. Strange to say, however, the one surviving fragment of the libretto mentions not Charles IX but Romeo and Juliet.[21] Cuban musicologist Jorge Antonia Gonzalez claims to have traced the source of this fragment in Italian to a Spanish-language book on the Montagues and Capulets that was known to several of Gottschalk's friends.[22] However, Gonzales offers no hypothesis on how the story of Romeo and Juliet could have been transported into the world of Charles IX's France.

Whatever the source of Gottschalk's libretto, it is clear that he had undertaken still a third opera and had composed the finale in time for it to be performed by his musical army at the Tacón. This operatic fragment involved a quartet of soloists, a six-part chorus, full orchestra, and military bands. Its two first thematic sections have a strongly Germanic quality, while the brighter third theme is purely Italian. The craftsmanship is good, and the composition as a whole leaves the impression of a young Richard Wagner and Rossini meeting at a Parisian café and setting off together arm-in-arm singing. Especially revealing is the way in which Gottschalk built up the composition from smaller units, like choruses in a song, rather than conceived it as a grander and more integrated whole. Here, once more, he reveals himself as a gifted miniaturist rather than a composer of great sweep and compass. His operas, had he completed any of them, would probably have been in this spirit, so typical of music of the early nineteenth century but not of its second half.

Immense toil was required to prepare parts for the 650 performers. Gottschalk himself labored over twenty-two-hour days writing out the scores and then turned over the job of preparing the hundreds of individual parts to twelve copyists, whom he had hired at his own expense.[23] Next, musicians had to be recruited, and this job also fell to the composer. He was helped by General Planas's offer to dragoon military bands into service and by Max Maretzek's donation of the chorus and soloists from his opera company. Yet even these arrangements required Moreau's personal oversight. The wind band *(charanga)* from the naval warship *Petronila* was also at his disposal, but it fell to Gottschalk to advertise in the press for someone capable of directing it.[24] He also had to send invitations to hundreds of amateur instrumentalists around town, appealing to their loyalty to him personally in order to get them to participate in a non-paying event. Finally, the hundreds of replies sent to his Calle de Aguiar address had to be processed and the number of performers on each instrument sent to the copyists who were preparing parts.[25]

Simultaneously, an army of workmen assaulted the huge Teatro Tacón stage with hammers, nails, and lumber. They reconfigured the hall in order to place the orchestra at the front, with the soloists ranged on the first riser and the 198-voice chorus spread out on two tiers behind them. The highest risers were reserved for all the military bands and for the *charangas*. Down front was constructed a tall black podium, from which the diminutive Gottschalk was expected to impose order on his multitude.

Shortly after the captain-general boasted that the Festival would be the best thing that ever happened on Cuba,[26] newspapers announced a series of rehearsals. These came off without a hitch, although Gottschalk was foolish enough to have scheduled an entirely separate concert in their very midst.[27] Last-minute details included shifting ticket sales to the Calle de Aguiar apartment in order to foil scalpers,[28] arranging mustering points around the Tacón at which the various musical forces would assemble,[29] and, on the day of the concert, issuing a public letter of thanks to all participants.[30]

As the Tacón opera orchestra completed the warm-up section of the program, the musicians assembled: 68 clarinets, 48 violinists, 29 French horn players, 33 tubists, 38 trombonists, 45 drummers, 198 choristers, and 2 triangle players milled about at their designated points on the alleys outside the various classical portals. A huge audience of four thousand already packed the hall, while an even greater crowd filled the streets nearby, hung out of every adjacent window, and perched precariously on adjacent rooftops.

When the Tacón opera orchestra was completing its warm-up pieces in front of the curtain, Gottschalk's musicians took their places on the stage. *La Prensa de la Habana* had already warned the public about the enormous sound it could expect, recommending "that young ladies who are easily frightened or nervous should bring smelling salts, as we predict faintings."[31] Now the moment had come. As the curtain rose, the audience let out a collective gasp. As one viewer put it, "How can anyone possible describe so striking a sight?"[32]

Journalists evaluated the affair the way a general might review a battle, commenting particularly on the coordination and precision of the performance.[33] They noted that the orchestra could not get through *La Nuit des tropiques* without being interrupted by frequent applause, and they judged the finale of *Charles IX* "sublime." Local enthusiasm for the *Esceñas* in particular reached fantastic heights, with one reviewer reporting:

> *Esceñas campestres* has . . . touched both our ears and hearts. Gottschalk has managed to keep the primitive simplicity of the melody, yet he has ornamented it in an indescribable manner. . . Any Cuban hearing this melody while abroad will be reduced to tears.[34]

And so, with further effusions about the "gigantic chords," "heaps of sound," and "oceans of grandiose harmonies," the Havana reviewers judged the Festival a huge success, unprecedented in the annals of Cuban music.

Immediately there were calls for a repeat, especially since a stagehand's failure to lower the curtain after the concluding march had robbed the audience of the opportunity to celebrate with a final thunderclap of applause. The economics favored a repeat as well, for a second performance would have enabled Gottschalk to recover more of the large investment that he, Maretzek, and others had made in the production. But when it was suggested that the repeat performance benefit Spanish veterans of the Moroccan wars rather than the American director and his partners, the subject quietly died.[35]

The Festival turned Gottschalk into a true hero of Cuba. Hymns of praise were dedicated to him.[36] Local grandees like the Marquis Ignacio Larrinaga, with his fine home at 116 Calle de Cuba, begged him to appear in their salons.[37] Popular gathering places like Juan Escauriza's Gran Café de Louvre gained in prestige if Gottschalk simply took coffee there. And if he stayed to improvise on a popular *contradanza*, news would spread rapidly through Havana's intimate central quarter and a large crowd would gather.

Celebrated as a true son of Cuba, Gottschalk no longer felt a need to impress anyone with his Parisian-style virtuosity. Instead, he turned out a group of light and graceful *contradanzas* that celebrate Havana in its own musical voice. Beginning with *El Festival* (nearly identical to *Danza*, op. 33) and *Báilemos (Let's Dance)*, he went on to *Ay! Lunarcitos!* and *Ay Pimpollo no me mates!*, all printed as penny broadsides by Edelmann. He turned out *danzas*, too, including *Inés* and *Las Patitas de mi Sobrina*.[38] Gottschalk dedicated each of these pieces to a different young lady of Havana. The very title of *Vamos a la azotea* (op. 45) was flirtatious, with its invitation "Let's go up on the roof garden."[39] Languid and insouciant, each of these graceful compositions is built on a pair of original melodies in the Havana style, yet each anticipates elements of later American ragtime.

Some of Gottschalk's compositions from this period are most startling, notably the jaunty *Pasquinade (The Clown)*. While the first record of its performance dates only to 1863, this sparkling gavotte almost certainly relates to this same happy post-festival phase of the composer's life in Havana. *Pasquinade* (op. 59) has often been credited with being a forward-looking anticipation of ragtime and jazz. Far more, it is a polished salon piece of great elegance and wit that gains depth thanks to unexpected shifts in tonality and mood. Published posthumously, it was immensely popular throughout Europe and the Americas. In the same exuberant vein, Gottschalk composed *La Gallina (The Hen)* (op. 53). Beginning with an attractive Cuban dance, *La Gallina* slides into some bold dissonances, including unresolved sevenths and minor ninth chords. Critic Harold Schonberg observed of this piece, "The effect is highly Ivesian, even though Charles Ives had as yet not been born."[40]

Local composers responded in kind to Gottschalk's musical salute. Manuel Saumell penned a friendly homage to Gottschalk entitled *Luisiana*, and as the American's *Ojos criollos (Creole Eyes)* gained popularity, a composer identified only as "J. de V. V." issued his own *Ojos negros* dedicated to Gottschalk.[41]

It was a giddy time, with Moreau exchanging photographs with many local beauties. Among them, he singled out Irène de los Ríos y Noguerida, the daughter of a ship's captain whom he had known since 1854.[42] For once he even described this latest flame to his sisters in Paris. He pleaded with Clara to write to Irène, whom he called "the most wonderful being in the world, . . . fine, worthy, virtuous, pretty, and very distinguished." It is impossible to date precisely the composition of any of his pieces from 1860–61, but it is more than likely that the lovely *O ma charmant, épargnez-moi!* (op. 44) pertains to his adored captain's daughter. Published without a dedication, this romance sounds like a forlorn aria from a Creole opera.

Irène de los Ríos disappeared from Gottschalk's life as suddenly as she had entered it, and without the slightest explanation. Immediately afterwards the papers were announcing his imminent departure from Cuba. "We care for him deeply," proclaimed one editorial. "He has written his most melancholy compositions here," the editor continued approvingly, pieces which "float airily into our ears, causing us to close our eyes in dreaming, part our lips with a smile of sublime joy, and pulling a tear and a sigh from our hearts."[43] But now Gottschalk suddenly seemed intent on leaving, In New York the *Musical World* had announced his imminent return as early as April 7. In connection with this impending departure he had even composed the piece *Adiós a la Habana* to supplement his earlier *Souvenir de Cuba* (op. 75).

A month after these heartfelt farewells, Gottschalk was still to be found in Havana, sipping coffee at the Café Louvre and making his usual rounds. For once, this was due neither to his chronic indecision nor to his having duped the public with reports of his departure in order to drum up further ticket sales. He stayed because he and his friend Espadero had combined efforts in order to write down and preserve all of Gottschalk's compositions.

For months Moreau and the reclusive pianist from Calle de Cuba had been inseparable. They concertized together at the Liceo and at the home of Onofre Morejón, secretary of the Liceo.[44] They dropped by the Charles Friedrichs's photographic studio on Calle de Habana to have their pictures taken together.[45] They debated pedagogy and worked on a book of exercises for students that reflect their individualistic notions concerning piano technique.[46] Espadero pumped Gottschalk for his reminiscences of Paris, and when the stay-at-home Espadero published a piece, *La Plainte du poète*, based on a verse by Tasso,[47] Gottschalk responded with a three-part essay detailing his own views on "music, the piano, and pianists."[48]

In the course of this rambling memoir Gottschalk unexpectedly announced, "Today there is no longer any doubt that the taste of the masses is depraved." He railed against artists who allow themselves to become "apostles of the public's ignorance" by flattering its poor tastes. The piano, he intoned, had become a calamity, and its literature was dominated by trash.

What accounts for this astonishing turnabout, which occurred at the very moment of Gottschalk's greatest public triumph? Why did someone who since childhood had been a convinced musical democrat now step forth as a highbrow aesthete, contemptuous of the public and its lowbrow tastes?

The cause is probably to be traced to the influence of Espadero. This reclusive Cuban's aversion to the public was already legendary. Over the years he had developed his fear of society into a philosophy which idolized the inward-looking Chopin and criticized the sociable Liszt for pandering to the mob. In spite of this, Espadero regarded Gottschalk with the deepest affection and was his most loyal champion. Gottschalk reciprocated this friendship and, no doubt because of it, took pains to present himself to Espadero as a more private and inward person than he in fact was. The anti-democratic sentiments expressed in the essay were no doubt heartfelt for now, but they were at the same time a tribute to his sociophobic friend Espadero. Gottschalk's pronouncements were promptly reprinted in Paris and St. Petersburg.[49]

In an act of fealty to his and Espadero's idol, Chopin, Moreau composed several ballades (op. 85, 87), all marked by expressive melodic lines and a total absence of Caribbean flavor. He also wrote out his youthful composition, now lost, based on Byron's *Mazeppa.*[50] In the same breath, as it were, Gottschalk took a pensive melody by Espadero and transformed it into an impressionistic nocturne, *La Chute des feuilles (The Falling Leaves)*(op. 42). This graceful Chopinian sketch is based on yet another elegy by Millevoye:

Fatal oracle . . .
You told me that the leaves
Will again change colors before your eyes
For one last time . . .
Your youth will wither
Before the grass of the meadow,
Before the vines of the hillside.
I am dying! The somber wind
Touches me with its cold breath
And I saw, like a shadow
My fair springtime vanish.
Fall, fall, ephemeral leaf![51]

Espadero sensed that Gottschalk in these months was "troubled with a strange presentiment that his career, so brilliant, would ere long come to a close."[52] Realizing, further, that the majority of Gottschalk's compositions had never been committed to paper, he resolved that he would serve as Gottschalk's amanuensis in order to preserve them for posterity. In assigning himself this task, Espadero consciously assumed the dual role of friend and literary executor that Jules Fontana had played with respect to Chopin.

Espadero sealed this intricate relationship to Chopin by getting Moreau to join him in a correspondence with Fontana in Paris.[53] In a touching letter, Gottschalk dedicated to Fontana two new pieces, *La Gitanella* (op. 35) and a caprice, *Fantôme de bonheur* (op. 36), subtitled *Illusions perdues.* Again, he offered the image of himself as a romantic artist struggling against an uncomprehending society:

> Your thoughts on the inferior music and vulgar, prosaic style of most pianists are exactly the same ones I have myself felt for a long time without daring to express them. Chopin's music has often made me cry while at the same time consoling me during the too frequent hours of melancholy experienced by artists who have the boundless misfortune of not having been born cobblers or molasses merchants.[54]

The task that Espadero had set for himself was formidable. On those rare occasions that Moreau had bothered to write out a composition, he employed a nearly impenetrable shorthand system of numbers and other symbols.[55] These had now to be deciphered. For the majority of pieces that Gottschalk had never written down at all, Espadero prevailed upon him to play each in turn, so they could be set down on paper. Young Arthur Napoleão visited Moreau at this time and found the floor of the room covered with papers and all the chairs piled high with copies.[56] One must question the extent to which the resulting editions reflect Espadero's penchant for elaborate scoring, as opposed to Gottschalk's airier style at the time. Yet had it not been for Espadero's efforts, many of Gottschalk's finest pieces would have vanished. Unfortunately, the task was never completed; scores of pieces were never notated by Espadero, or his own shorthand versions were lost.

Gottschalk's career reached a pinnacle with the great festival at Havana's Teatro Tacón. And then, in the summer of 1860, he entered a period of crisis. One disappointment followed another so that by the time he finally departed from Cuba in February 1862 he had all but abandoned his orchestral, operatic, and conducting careers. Penniless once more, he returned to a United States torn apart by Civil War.

The exact causes of this fateful turn of fortune's wheel remain obscure, but it is clear that both personal and social factors were at work.

The abrupt termination of the relationship with Irène de los Ríos was doubtless a factor, but no evidence as to its causes has yet turned up. About this time, too, Espadero noted that his friend was assaulted by "presentiments of death." Meanwhile, a series of concerts held in May and June demonstrated that the Havana public's immense affection for Gottschalk did not alter the fact that, as the *Diario de la Marina* noted, "concerts, with rare exceptions, never have been in great vogue [here]."[57] The combined effect of these various factors now led Moreau to consider leaving Cuba.

Where should he go? Europe was a possibility. Within several months Moreau's old friend Professor Marmontel was to remind him "not to forget that Paris was the cradle of your reputation and the first to take you to its breast."[58] The Conservatoire had adopted three of Moreau's compositions as set pieces for piano students, but even this did not induce him to return to Europe. He knew his prospects there were uncertain, and many months would be required to re-establish himself.[59]

Normally, the United States would have presented an attractive prospect. Max Strakosch had already offered Moreau a concert tour there for the winter of 1860–61. Moreover, he announced that Gottschalk would be returning to New York with Maretzek and had even publicized the date of his first Manhattan concert with Carlotta Patti.[60] But Lincoln had received the Republicans' nomination for President in May 1860, and talk of civil war was heard on every side. Moreau understood full well what this meant for him. As he explained to his sister Augusta, "the political conditions are such, and the excitement so strong, that I would run a great risk if I showed up in the North, being myself a Southerner. I would inevitably be shot or imprisoned there." A half year before Confederate forces fired on Fort Sumter he foresaw "a war with no way out, like all civil wars, a war that would threaten to last indefinitely and would end only when, as in certain plays by Shakespeare, everyone has been killed."[61]

He also thought briefly of going to Mexico City, where he was already well known thanks to articles on him published in the local press. But more than one musician had encountered great difficulties there. Abandoning this idea, Gottschalk again began dreaming of New Granada, or Venezuela. In early June he was making plans to sail there via St. Thomas.[62] No sooner did his friend General Páez learn of this, however, than he wrote Gottschalk to dissuade him from coming due to the continued fighting in the South American country.[63]

Just as Gottschalk was weighing these ill-starred options, the management of the Gran Teatro Tacón asked him to conduct its Italian opera company during the 1860–61 winter season. He should have sensed that the offer was fishy. Marty, the entrepreneur who built the Tacón, had sold the theater to a group of Havana investors for the lordly sum of six hundred thousand dollars. In a separate deal, Marty slipped ten thousand dollars' worth of Tacón stock to Max Maretzek, on the condition that Maretzek and his own opera company stay away from Havana for two years. Marty assumed that without Maretzek's company the Tacón would fail and its investors be only too willing to resell their shares to Marty at a deep discount. Both Marty and Maretzek would profit greatly by this scheme. The losers would be the Tacón's new owners, who, without Maretzek's troupe, were bound to go into the red. It was these new Cuban owners who hired Gottschalk in the hopes that his popularity would save them from the trap Marty and Maretzek had set for them.[64]

In spite of these intrigues, Gottschalk was attracted by the offer. Opera engaged his passions like nothing else did. Not only was he himself writing several operas, but he penned a long essay on opera for his friend Rafael Mendive at this time.[65] Written in the same chatty style as his earlier essay on pianists, this study passes out judgments with an open hand. Verdi's *Nabucco*, he argued, was "one of his best operas," while *La Traviata* was "nothing more than a mosaic of . . . insufferable vulgarities." Along with such *obiter dicta*, the article provided many insights on Moreau's own life in the wings of the opera world.

When the Tacón's new administrators offered to produce Gottschalk's own operas if he would direct them, and promised him a big budget besides, Gottschalk succumbed.[66] An addition to its other advantages, the arrangement obligated him to complete the writing of several operas, none of which had yet progressed beyond the second act.[67]

Just as he was assuming this formidable burden, Gottschalk's health once more gave way. An "inflammation of the intestines complicated by cerebral congestion" was so serious that his doctor called in two colleagues to help him. On one night alone they applied leeches to his lower body, bled him above, and put cupping glasses on both his front and back sides before soaking him for three hours in a emollient bath from which he emerged scalded from the waist down. After ordering that his possessions be delivered to Paris in the event he died, Gottschalk then fell into an unconscious state, from which he emerged several days later as pale as a ghost and looking like "a lost mummy who has wandered from his sarcophagus."[68]

So worried were his friends that they arranged for him to have a period of complete rest at the sugar plantation Valdespino on the Sierra de Anafe, several hours southwest of Havana.[69] Owned by the local magistrate José Valdespino y Macías, this plantation, approached by a long avenue of palms, was still under construction. The wooden building with exterior gallery was remote even from the nearest village, Caimito, and provided a perfect place to recuperate. In Gottschalk's words, it was a "marvelous paradise in which, unfortunately, only elephants and Eve are lacking."[70] There he passed two months, "smoking, sleeping, drinking coffee, and, above all, breathing the air of the savanna." Daytime was whiled away in a hammock, and nights in the high-ceilinged and open salon among whose rafters nested whole colonies of bats. The transition from day to night was presided over by

> a very ugly Negress, who, after having roasted the coffee, crushed her maize in a hollow piece of wood, recited the Ave Maria before an old colored image of the Virgin, came and squatted down at my feet on the verandah, and there, in the darkness, sang to me in a piercing, wild voice full of strange charm, the *canciones* of the country. I would light my cigar, extend myself in a hammock, and, surrounded by this silent, primitive nature, plunge into a contemplative reverie, which those in the midst of the everyday world can never understand.

Despite his contract to finish several operas, there is no evidence that Moreau composed a note at Valdespino. He emerged in good health, however, and in early September traveled to Cárdenas for a series of concerts. By now he was again in such good spirits that he wrote a detailed description of the booming sugar port. En route back to Havana he stopped at Matanzas, where he visited at the home of friends. There he improvised on the piano deep into the night, so that neighbors got out of bed to listen.[71] Even the grueling train ride back to Havana delighted Moreau to the point that he wrote a droll dialogue between himself and his fellow sufferer, the poor engine.[72]

The idyll was brief, however. In quick succession, two further disasters befell him.[73] First, to his utter surprise Gottschalk discovered that the same story of intrigue at the Swedish court that formed the basis for his own opera *Amalia Warden* had been taken by Verdi as the libretto of his *Un Ballo in Maschera*, premiered the previous winter in Rome. "What a crowning misfortune!" he wrote to his sisters and brothers. "Even if my music were superior to Verdi's, it would be impossible for the same artist to sing two different settings of practically the same text."[74] Upon receiving the news, the Tacón company immediately replaced Gottschalk's unfinished opera with a premiere of Verdi's new work.

Second, while Gottschalk was still in Valdespino, the newspaper of Havana's rival cultural center, Matanzas, had carried an announcement that the impresario Servadio would be bringing from New York his own Italian Opera Company, and that it would include artists of far greater renown than those assembled for the new Lyric Opera Company with which the Tacón's management hoped to fill the void left by Maretzek's departure.[75] Having just been defeated as an operatic composer, Gottschalk was now upstaged as a conductor as well.

No sooner did the Servadio company make its successful debut in Matanzas than the Teatro Variadades in Havana telegraphed with an offer for him to bring his company to the capital.[76] Matanzans objected, of course, and pointed to Servadio's contract with their own Teatro Principal. Servadio was not one to pass up a good deal, however, and, with the kind of masterstroke typical of nineteenth-century operatic politics, he simply divided his company, taking the stronger half to the capital and leaving a rump group to fulfill the contract in Matanzas.[77] Knowing that he would eventually face competition in Havana from the Tacón's company headed by Gottschalk, the ingenious Servadio then offered to break his new contract with the Teatro Variadades and sign on with the Tacón instead. Since the Gran Teatro Tacón was financially pressed, he knew its managers could not refuse. The alternative, after all, was to have their house sit empty until their own company arrived. As to Gottschalk, Servadio engaged him to conduct the half of his company that he had left behind in Matanzas. Since Gottschalk, too, could not afford to refuse, Servadio thus neutralized his competition while gaining control of the biggest theater in Havana.[78]

In a move that was both reckless and foolish, Gottschalk made his debut as an opera conductor in Donizetti's *Les Martyrs* at Matanzas on October 23. The Teatro Principal was newly decorated and featured a special gas jet in the lobby where gentlemen could light their cigars. But the orchestra was abysmal, notwithstanding the fact that "the eminent pianist Gottschalk worked prodigiously to keep the ship on course."[79] Two days later Gottschalk was back in the pit conducting *Lucia de Lammermoor.* This time the Matanzas reviewer was less generous, citing again the underrehearsed orchestra but noting also that "no matter how good Gottschalk is, he must be very careful if he does not want to wreck the ship."[80] By the third night, when the company did *Les Martyrs* again, the theater was only half full and the reviewer grew downright testy. The performance was good, he conceded, but Gottschalk had had to cut out a number of arias his musicians could not handle. Even though the reviewer blamed this not on Gottschalk but on the portly baritone Federico Amodio, the mood by now was definitely hostile. "We want Mr. Amodio to understand that this is not the kind of public to trifle with. . . . We hope this opens his eyes, because we really don't want to fill our pages with bile and ugly thoughts about Mr. Servadio's troupe."[81] The general public accused Servadio of robbing them. After all, they reasoned, since they were paying two centavos per note, each one skipped represented a kind of theft.[82]

Meanwhile, Servadio was facing yet harsher criticism in Havana due to the exorbitant prices he was charging for admission. In an ill-advised effort to save his new patron, Gottschalk announced in Servadio's name that he himself would give a solo piano concert in Matanzas. When Servadio learned of this he promptly canceled the affair, lamely telling the Matanzas press that a grand piano could not be found in their city.[83] Instead, he booked Gottschalk to play between the acts of a later performance of Verdi's *Ernani*. For once, the house was packed, not for Servadio's company, of course, but for Gottschalk, who elicited the first standing ovation of the season and completely upstaged his patron's troupe. Two nights later, with Servadio and company now safely out of town, the "genius of harmony"[84] offered a final concert in Matanzas to benefit local orphans. This elicited extravagant outpourings in verse and confirmed that the local public viewed Gottschalk not as an accomplice of the nefarious Servadio but as his victim.[85] A ball in Gottschalk's honor continued until daybreak.[86]

Having barely survived the Servadio debacle, Gottschalk had now to prove that his own company could do better. His Italian and French soloists were not bad, and the fifty-piece orchestra was at least acceptable. The chorus, however, he judged to be terrible and "the women in it deplorable and ugly. . . . This seems to have been a requirement for the position."[87] Happily for Gottschalk, the troupe made its debut with his beloved *Il Trovatore* by Verdi.

In spite of Gottschalk's deprecation of his female choristers, it was the men who got completely lost at several points during the third performance. The orchestra and soloists fared better, however, and the company as a whole even won praise, thanks to the "intelligent conductor" and "clever maestro" Gottschalk.[88]

By now the Christmas season had begun, and all Havana, including Gottschalk's musicians, threw themselves into the traditional round of partying. Gottschalk had programmed *The Barber of Seville* for a gala Christmas Eve performance but rehearsals proved an impossibility. Most of the orchestral players found better things to do, and when the curtain rose at the Gran Teatro Tacón a disastrously under-rehearsed company greeted the audience. The singers and orchestra wandered off on separate tempos. To keep the various parts together Gottschalk was forced to reduce brisk allegros to a snail's pace. All this dragged out the evening, and by the time the finale sounded half the audience had departed for the Café Louvre next door.[89]

Even though the critics praised Gottschalk's conducting, the chaos that hovered over every performance of this operatic troupe must be traced to his own failures to rehearse the company adequately. One critic understood this clearly. "Gottschalk," he argued, "is a genius as a composer and performer but is temperamentally unsuited to conducting. Indeed, a mediocrity with no pretensions can have more force of will, more energy, and exercise greater dominion over the musicians in order to oblige them to be more punctual and attentive at rehearsals, which is more necessary to obtain results than is a superior intelligence."[90]

The sweetener in Gottschalk's contract with the Tacón was that he was entitled to use the entire orchestra for three concerts to benefit himself.[91] Due to Servadio's incursions and the failure of Gottschalk's own troupe, the management cut this number to one. Having observed local tastes over eight years, Moreau knew that the Havana public preferred a mix of "classical" and more accessible works, particularly those with a Cuban flavor. But Gottschalk stubbornly refused to oblige the public. Instead, he forced the audience to endure his new orchestration of Méhul's *Le Jeune Henri*, the overture to Weber's *Der Freischütz*, and other such "classical" works. All Havana yawned.[92]

Why did Gottschalk commit this latest blunder? Maybe it owed something to the influence of his highbrow friend Espadero. Or perhaps the failed opera season had embittered him on the public's standards. In the essay on opera that he wrote for Mendive, he had gone so far as to propose a hierarchy of taste. In words that could have been penned by Dwight, Gottschalk argued that a Western frontiersman would prefer *Yankee Doodle* to an operatic aria; a Cherokee would favor a tribal war song to *Yankee Doodle*; and a Hottentot would reject the war song in favor of his own primitive drum.[93] Now, for his own benefit concert, Gottschalk deliberately chose works higher on what he had called the "scale of perfection." The benefit was a complete failure.

Among the public who witnessed this disaster was Ada Clare, who had suddenly appeared in Havana at the beginning of February 1861. With characteristic aplomb, she stationed herself prominently in the balcony at the Gran Teatro Tacón for several of the last performances of Gottschalk's operatic troupe, and she was there for his benefit concert as well. The presence of this "great poet and outstanding novelist" was duly noted by the local press, which had obviously been briefed by the artiste herself.[94] Her presence only added to Moreau's trauma.

Even though it coincided with Carnival, this was no mere tourist visit for Ada Clare. Much had transpired in her life since she and Gottschalk parted in 1857. After several extended stays in Paris she had eventually returned to New York, where she again took up acting and also began writing a column for Henry Clapp's *Saturday Press*, founded in 1858 as the voice of radical bohemia. Amidst Clapp's own attacks on temperance, slavery, and Christianity, and his defenses of Walt Whitman's newly published *Leaves of Grass*, Ada dished out acerbic reviews and caustic attacks on the pretensions of males.[95] Fathers came in for particular lambasting as "the ludicrous and therefore the mournful figure in the comedy of life."[96] Yet if she more than ever championed the independence of females, Ada Clare continued to idolize Gottschalk. While still in Paris she had written an essay listing Moreau among the unappreciated geniuses of the age.[97] In an essay from New York she declared, "Who so would teach me how to cease to admire [him] would ensure my enmity for life."[98]

Beset by these conflicting emotions, Ada purchased tickets for herself and her friend Annie Ballard and sailed for Havana.[99] Whatever her hopes for a reconciliation with Gottschalk, however, the mission failed. Nor did she even get him to acknowledge his responsibilities toward Aubrey, if indeed she tried. Ada departed Havana in early March. Gottschalk left no record of her visit, but a friend of his, Tomás Ruiz, composed a *contradanza* entitled *La Seductora* and dedicated it to him.[100]

The Havana public's rejection of his high-toned benefit program threw Gottschalk into confusion. He had followed Espadero down a path that led nowhere. Now, in a cynical move dictated more by his pocketbook than his judgment, he decided to reach out once more to a mass public whose tastes he had just condemned as boorish. As if on cue, a magician named Hermann showed up in Havana with sleight-of-hand tricks, lifelike bird calls, and a wife who sang and performed on the piano. Gottschalk appeared several times with this pair of hucksters, wedged between human and pseudo-aviary warbling.[101] In a further lapse of judgment, he even entertained at a banquet which the conjurer gave at the American Hotel.[102]

Grasping at straws, Gottschalk next decided to recoup his fortunes by pandering to the spectacle-hungry public with a farewell *festival gigantesca* more vast than anything ever witnessed in Havana. He booked the Tacón and rushed to tell the press of his plans. It was not clear whether there would be 450, 500, or 650 musicians—the figure fluctuated daily—but it was obvious that, as one paper concluded, this monster concert would make the earlier festival look "like mere child's play."[103] Beyond doubt there would be forty pianists; that figure, quoted from paper to paper, had doubled to eighty by the time it reached readers in far-off Russia.[104] But that was not all. Having learned from bitter experience that the Havanese love for serious music was limited, he engaged the Robreño *zarzuela* company to punctuate the evening with selections from Spanish light musicals. Moreau's choice of Robreño's troupe was no accident, for it was the company that had lured audiences away from Gottschalk's own performances during his 1854 tour of Cuba.

La Nuit des tropiques provided a warm-up to the orchestral section of this last Havana monster concert. To impart yet more color to this extravaganza, Gottschalk added to the first movement the Spanish folk instrument "harmoniflauta" in order "to portray the calmness and serenity of a tropical region."[105] Then came the *Marche triunfal* and *Finale* from *Charles IX*, souped up with eighty drums and trumpets playing the Spanish *Marcha real* off stage to create an echo effect. Following this, the forty pianists joined the 450-piece orchestra for a new "descriptive symphony" based on Gottschalk's old war-horse, Mehul's *La Chasse du jeune Henri*. Rounding out the evening was a brand new "military fantasy" entitled *Caprichos del arte* and featuring massed regimental bands and a number of *charangas* from naval ships in the harbor.[106] No trace of this *Caprichos* survives.

Virtually every leader of Cuban music was among the forty pianists, including Saumell, Espadero, the young Ignacio Cervantes, the opera composer Aristi, and Carlos Edelmann, whose music store provided the instruments. Even such talents as these required rehearsals, however, and here the good-natured Gottschalk failed again. No more than two dozen of the pianists ever practiced together, and the rehearsals themselves turned into social events.[107] As a result, the pianists were uncoordinated, the orchestra strident, and the off-stage trumpeters so out of tempo as to create "disagreeable noise." Worse, the affair dragged out for five and one-half hours. By eleven p.m. eyes throughout the hall "began to blink as if they were full of little stones." Barely half the audience endured to the last hour.[108]

Gottschalk had no choice but to cancel the repeat of this extravaganza that had been scheduled for a week later.[109] He issued letters of thanks to all participants and sent jewelry to featured performers. But there was no hiding the total humiliation that he had inflicted upon himself. His friend Damian Martinez, one of the forty pianists, dedicated to him a new *contradanza* entitled *La Crisis*, which Edelmann promptly published.[110] Three days after the failed extravaganza the press reported that Moreau was about to sail for New York on the steamer *Catawba*.[111] But five days before the Festival, the first Confederate cannonballs had arched through the sky above Charleston harbor toward Fort Sumter. After receiving five thousand rounds of artillery, the fortress fell, triggering the start of the Civil War. Since the war zone lay astride the *Catawba*'s route, travel to New York became an impossibility. Gottschalk was stuck in Cuba and now completely broke.

With no alternative, he took whatever jobs he could find. This included performances with the acrobats and vaudevillians of the Keller Company, as well as appearances between the acts of Señor Robreño's *zarzuelas*.[112] Wrapped in gloom, he fled Havana for the provincial town of Pinar del Rio. Fine cigars that he would ordinarily have enjoyed now smelled like cabbage, and the local soup tasted to him like "capillary glue."[113] It counted for nothing that the local public serenaded him, for Gottschalk knew that within days the news of his humiliation would reach even this backwater.[114]

For the next four and a half months Gottschalk simply disappeared, surfacing again only in early October 1861.[115] Avoiding his old haunts, he performed twice at a school in the suburban district of Guanabacao.[116] To his amazement he discovered that in spite of the Festival fiasco, members of the Havana public had not wavered in its affection for him and now turned out to welcome his "comeback." They flooded out from town to hear him and to attend the dances that followed each performance.[117] He obliged his public with a new *contradanza* entitled *Di que sí*, to which his loyal friend Saumell responded with his own *Di que no*, dedicated to Gottschalk.[118] He also produced settings for voice and piano of several poems by Rafael Mendive. One, entitled *Serenata à Paulina M*, was later published in English as *Idol of Beauty*. Two others, *A una flor* and *La Músicas de las Palmas*, are lost.[119] Instrumental works from this period include a transcription for piano and two violins of his *Tarentelle* and a *Berceuse* (op. 47), also for two violins and piano but later issued for solo piano. Based on the French cradle song *Fais dodo mon bébé*, this beautifully realized melody later gained immense popularity, giving rise to maternal outpourings from as far afield as Indianapolis and São Paulo.

In further appearances in Matanzas and nearby towns Gottschalk briefly returned to his former self. Audiences showed their enthusiasm by throwing their hats in the air and pounding with canes on the floor.[120] He reciprocated by offering his services to local philanthropists who were working to raise money to build a new opera house.[121] None of this helped cover his costs, however, and by November Gottschalk was so destitute that he could not even afford a steerage class ticket to New York. It was a year since he had written his brothers and sisters that he had "no prospects, no hopes, and no future."[122] Now he could not even delude himself into thinking that a "farewell concert" would refill his coffers and gain him time. The hall was scarcely half full on November 22 for his last Havana appearance, which the press judged only "tolerable."[123]

Some weeks earlier, Gottschalk had written to Pasquale Brignoli in New York, pleading for him to send enough money to cover passage back to the United States. Brignoli, now at the zenith of his American career, reported Gottschalk's plight to Max Strakosch, whose contract offers Moreau had been refusing over four years.[124] When Strakosch responded with yet another offer, Gottschalk seized upon it with pathetic gratitude.

There was one problem, however. Gottschalk was a Southerner. As such, he could not enter New York without first swearing allegiance to the government of the United States and declaring that he was "not in rebellion." This meant renouncing not only his native state of Louisiana but the world that had formed his emotional identity and inspired his art. A year earlier he had first heard the snappy new tune *In Dixie's Land*, fresh from New Orleans, where it had been premiered by Adelina Patti's older brother Carlo. He had even produced variations on *Dixie*, just as he had earlier done with *Yankee Doodle*.[125] Now he had to choose between Dixie and Yankeedom.

On the one hand, there was no conceivable way that Gottschalk could otherwise earn the fifteen hundred dollars a month that Strakosch was offering for the tour. On the other hand, there is clear evidence that Gottschalk resisted taking the inevitable step, procrastinating to the last minute. Well-informed Havana journalists reported this at the time, as did his biographer Fors many years later in Argentina.[126]

Fors, true to form, attributed Moreau's delay in taking the oath to nothing more serious than the lure of a Creole mistress.[127] But were there deeper reasons for this reluctance to take an oath to the Constitution of the United States? If it was due simply to his regional loyalty, it is certainly understandable. Was it, in addition, caused by some blindness regarding the institution of slavery, or worse? After all, he had only recently passed a happy summer on the great "modern" plantation of Plazuela in Puerto Rico and had recuperated at the Valdespino plantation in Cuba without recording any disgust at the practice.

Balancing this, it should be noted that Gottschalk was by no means blind to the evils of human bondage. Later he spoke out against American tourists in Cuba, who

> out of imbecility or bad faith . . . deny the assertions of the enemies of slavery by assuring us that the slaves on the plantations visited by them have a happy air, and that during their stay they had not heard a single blow of the whip. Happy tourists! Suppose that, instead of looking upon those joyous faces that smile in the presence of their master, you had the curiosity to take off the clothes of these unfortunates and to examine their shoulders. You would have learned more in a few seconds by the sight of certain scars badly healed, and perhaps of wounds still bleeding, scarcely healed, than all your observations, founded upon your own suppositions, had taught you.[128]

Since these words were written for publication in the North during the Civil War, one might suppose they were intended to assuage any lingering doubts about his loyalty that may have existed. Yet a private letter to his sisters reflected the same sentiments:

> When you find out what slavery is, when you have observed its horrors as I have, when you have seen thousands of victims die through unmanageable tortures, when your heart has bled like mine has at the sight of myriads of poor human beings, including children and old people, treated like we would not treat an unruly horse or fierce dog . . . then you would condemn without forgiveness the greatest of those inequities which the ages of barbarity bequeathed to us.[129]

Whether prompted solely by Strakosch's offer or by such feelings regarding slavery, Gottschalk finally overcame what the Havana journalist calls his "disgust" at having to choose sides in the Civil War and betook himself to the American consulate to take the oath. Then he finally prepared to depart. The wary Strakosch knew better than simply to send Gottschalk the cash he needed for his trip back to New York. Instead, he asked his cousin Maretzek to book passage for Gottschalk on the same ship on which he and members of his operatic troupe were returning and to make sure that the composer actually boarded.

The plan worked, and on January 17 the *Columbia* steamed past the guns of Morro Castle, with Gottschalk and his valet Firmin Moras among the passengers. Two days later the Havana papers published Moreau's final farewell to his Havana friends, with apologies to all whom he had been unable to take leave of personally. As the *Gaceta de la Habana* explained to its readers, "[Gottschalk] hates farewells, especially if they are forever."[130]

Chapter Twenty

✣ *The Union, 1862*

ONCE again penniless, dreading the winter's cold, and compelled by necessity to board a ship bound for a country at war with itself, Gottschalk had ample cause for dark forebodings. Friends in Havana had warned him about bloody terrorists who were said to prowl Manhattan's streets, of incendiaries who were bombing homes of the rich, and of famine elsewhere in the country.[1]

He was certainly not prepared for what he actually found. New York in February 1862 was a vibrant metropolis, teeming with commerce by day and brilliantly lit by night, offering every sort of entertainment to a public bent on diversion. Union troops had been dying in the siege of Fort Donelsen in Tennessee, but in Manhattan an opera season of 150 nights was about to commence. True, "serious" drama was struggling, but the comedy *Our American Cousin* was drawing gales of laughter at Laura Keene's Theatre, while Charlie Gardiner's *Ethiopian Eccentricities* was packing them in at the American Music Hall. A democratic approach to audiences reigned on Broadway. As the proprietor of one theater boasted in an advertisement, "The Voice of the People is Our Guide."[2] For once Gottschalk's timing was perfect, if accidental.

He stayed briefly at the 14th Street home of lawyer and broker George Henriques. Unlike his previous stay in New York, however, Moreau this time did not settle in at Henriques's or elsewhere and in fact was not even listed in the city directory. In Civil War Manhattan, he was merely a bird of passage.

Another musical transient, Stephen Foster, was living not far away on Hester Street. The two never met. Foster, suffering from alcoholism, was reduced to day-to-day survival and would have shied away from Gottschalk's more fashionable world. And Gottschalk already had his eyes fixed on his opening concert, which the canny Strakosch had set for February 11, the ninth anniversary of his 1853 New York debut.

Five years' absence from New York was a long time, and the public's memory short. To break the ice, Gottschalk's friend Louis Descombes organized an informal musicale at his home on February 8 and invited thirty writers, critics, and musicians. Richard Willis of the *Home Journal* attended, as did Charles Bailey Seymour from the *Times.* Gottschalk's crony Brignoli was there, drinking champagne and applauding, as was Maretzek. These experts concluded that during his years in the West Indies Gottschalk had deepened as a composer and performer and that his earlier "taint of softness and a tendency toward effeminacy" had given way to a new intensity and strength.[3] Willis, anticipating three years of Civil War–era reviews, took up his pen to praise Gottschalk specifically as an American and as one who "discards the old classic forms" the way a river overflows its banks. Gottschalk had demonstrated that "the music of [every] nationality, if distinctive and really *sui generis*, is [worthy] of the attention of a man of sense—or a man of genius."

A series of concerts followed in rapid succession, beginning at Niblo's Saloon and then expanding to Niblo's large hall and finally to the Brooklyn Athenaeum and the new Brooklyn Academy of Music. Maretzek conducted the Academy of Music's orchestra, Richard Hoffman assisted his old friend in several piano duets, and Brignoli not only sang but pitched in as assisting pianist as well. Adding to the general excitement was Carlotta Patti, Adelina's older sister, who had a fine coloratura voice.[4] Again, critics agreed that Gottschalk had entered a new phase: "It is no longer the attractive yet effeminate morbidity of the first period, nor the exuberant virility and tendency to an excess of vigor that followed. Gottschalk seems now to have found the secret of bringing them together."[5]

Every performance in this series was sprinkled with new pieces from the Caribbean. This was a calculated risk, given the presence in the hall of such classicists as George Templeton Strong, who confessed in his diary that he even preferred Hermann the Prestidigitator to Gottschalk.[6] But these sensuous and evocative works perfectly suited the escapist mood of wartime New York and were resoundingly encored.[7]

Amidst the series came news of the first Federal victories at Fort Donelson and at Roanoke, Virginia. On Washington's birthday Gottschalk responded with a thunderous new composition, *The Union* (op. 48), which he premiered at the Academy of Music on a stage draped with American flags. The piece combined elements from the *Siege of Saragossa* and the lost *Bunker Hill* of 1853. To these he added a contemplative quotation from *The Star-Spangled Banner*, which had not yet been declared the national anthem. The popular national air *Hail, Columbia* then entered very quietly, trailing off as a march, only to reappear soon afterward in contrapuntal form interwoven with *Yankee Doodle*. The results were enough to make any piano tremble. Gottschalk was neither the first nor the last composer to exploit *Yankee Doodle*,[8] but he surely achieved the greatest success at it, not least because he was a Southerner who used the work to demonstrate his loyalty to the Union cause. To underscore this, he dedicated the whole confection to General George B. McClellan, head of the Union forces and a great favorite of Francophiles like Gottschalk, who knew he had among his aides a bevy of French aristocrats.

At the second and third concerts at Niblo's Saloon, Gottschalk surprised listeners with a fragment from a work entitled Concerto in F Minor.[9] This may well have been the same "American Concerto" that was begun in Paris and had surfaced again in 1853. Clearly, it was no improvisation, for he programmed it several times in 1862, perhaps after rediscovering it in the bottom of some trunk.

Gottschalk continued his blitz of New York with several more pathbreaking concerts. First, he, Brignoli, and other members of Maretzek's company offered *Don Pasquale* in street clothes.[10] A month later he presented a *matinée d'instruction*, a teaching program for students patterned after a Thalberg program of five years earlier. For this session the piano was installed in the middle of the hall so that the audience of students could be seated around it. This facilitated informal conversation with the artist not only on piano technique but on the music itself.[11]

Capitalizing on his momentum, Gottschalk made appearances in Newark, Philadelphia, Wilmington, Baltimore, and Washington. At the capital Gottschalk found soldiers everywhere, giving the city the appearance of "just having been taken by assault." On the porch of his hotel he observed uniforms from every nation, among them a regiment from the West with hats adorned with squirrel tails.[12]

General McClellan himself had been too busy even to acknowledge the salute of an army band a day earlier but he showed up for Moreau's Washington concert. After introducing Gottschalk to his wife, the commander of the Union forces asked the composer for his photograph. Secretary of State William Seward attended also and delivered to Gottschalk a document signed by President Lincoln giving him free passage to the camp of Brigadier General James Wadsworth, commandant of the Washington Military District at Falls Church, Virginia. Wadsworth received the composer with military honors, and later the Washington banker George Washington Riggs held a banquet for him, attended by half the diplomatic corps.[13] Gottschalk also met an old friend from the Guianas, Francis Jay Herron, now a rising Union officer, who joined in the wartime welcome. In the Federal capital no honor was too great for a Southerner who championed the Union cause.

The series of Gottschalk concerts was an event that even people remote from the world of culture felt obliged to attend. A doughty congressman who missed the first soirée appeared for the second, having
invested in white gloves for the occasion. "Mr. Gottschalk played mighty
pretty," he allowed. "He played slow and then fast, and never seemed to
get his hands tangled up once. He played mighty pretty, but didn't play
nary a *thune!*"[14]

Moreau returned to New York a hero. But would he stay there? In
Paris his loyal friend Professor Marmontel had just published a long arti-
cle proclaiming Gottschalk as the successor of Chopin, now dead, and of
Liszt, who had "retired to his golden tent at Weimar." Marmontel intoned:
"Let L. M. Gottschalk return to us as soon as possible. . . . We want to
shout out 'Honor to the great master!' "[15]

Now all such thoughts of returning to Europe were out the window
as New Yorkers fought to collect the wallet-sized celebrity photographs
of Moreau that were all the rage. To satisfy this burgeoning demand,
Gottschalk rushed to the studios of photographers J. G. Birney and Son
on Broadway and also to Mathew B. Brady's famed salon a few blocks
away at Broadway and 10th.[16] Those who were unable to obtain these
prized collectors' items had to content themselves with gazing at the new
portrait of Moreau just painted by artist Job Vernert and now on exhibit
at the Goupil Gallery.[17] They could also buy the reissued *Life of Louis
Moreau Gottschalk* that was being hawked in pamphlet form or, if they
succeeded in getting tickets to a performance, the deluxe *Gottschalk's
Illustrated Concert Book* that was hot off the press.

All this attention thrust Moreau once more into New York society.
Ada Clare was still very much on the scene, writing for Henry Clapp's
Saturday Press and for the saucy new bohemian paper *Vanity Fair.* She
had thrown herself into the life of an emancipated woman and, according
to Walt Whitman, was "virtuous after the French fashion, namely, [she]
has but one lover at a time!"[18] She hung out with the other Bohemians at
the notorious Pfaff's, a saloon located at 647 Broadway, a few doors
above Bleecker Street.[19] There, in a large basement room extending beneath the sidewalk, Ada Clare reigned as Queen of Bohemia, eating po-
tato pancakes, drinking beer, and exchanging witticisms with writers and
artists at the long table. Off to one side sat Walt Whitman, silent, observing. Whitman described the scene in a notebook:

> The vault at Pfaff's where the drinkers and laughers
>   meet to eat and drink and arouse,
> While on the walk immediately over head pass the myriad
>   feet of Broadway . . .
> Laugh on Laughers!
> Drink on Drinkers![20]

In spite of all that had passed between him and Ada Clare, Gottschalk occasionally attended these soirées. He would go there "to sit by Pfaff's privy and eat sweet-breads and drink coffee, and listen to the intolerable wit of the crack-brains," as a friend put it.[21] Yet if he and Clare sometimes moved in the same circles, he distanced himself from her personally. Taking this as a sign that he disapproved of her, she once more took to the press, this time with an essay entitled "A Few Words About Friendship," in which she lashed out at him for forgetting that friendship "is the acceptance of an individual through whatever errors he may fall into."[22] This failed to move Moreau, who declined to revive their former relationship.

During these same months, he renewed his friendship with Mary Alice Ives, now Mrs. Seymour, to whom he had given lessons in Paris eleven years earlier. From her father, a Brooklyn commission merchant, Mary Alice had meanwhile inherited a considerable fortune. She had attended Gottschalk's 1855 concerts in New York and on that basis had chosen him as a teacher over Thalberg. Well before he departed for Havana she had developed a high-toned and terribly *spirituelle* crush on him. But then he disappeared, and except for occasional letters she lost touch with him. Eventually she married a Reverend Seymour, had a child, and in quick succession endured the death of both.[23] It was probably in response to these deaths that Gottschalk in 1859 had written his *Adieu funèbre* for cello and piano, now lost.

To make matters worse, Mrs. Seymour lost much of her fortune. By the time of Gottschalk's return, she was living in a modest apartment on Sixth Avenue and sustaining herself by giving piano lessons. Bereft of everything but the music to which Gottschalk had introduced her, Mary Alice Ives Seymour now lived for him alone, cultivating a platonic relationship that took its cues from the highly charged love poetry of Elizabeth Barrett Browning.

Mrs. Seymour tried to lure Gottschalk away from what she was sure were debauched evenings with Ada Clare and the bohemians. To vindicate himself, Gottschalk took Mrs. Seymour to what he characterized as a "bohemian soirée." In a clear deception that was no credit to Gottschalk's honesty, they went not to Pfaff's aromatic hole on Broadway but to the fashionable Maison Dorée on 14th Street,[24] a world away. Mrs. Seymour was duly impressed, and duped. This experience enabled her to put the best face on Moreau's bohemian connections when she wrote her lachrymose biography of the composer, but it did nothing to reduce the enmity she felt for Ada Clare.[25]

A confirmed blue-stocking, Mary Alice Ives Seymour was described by George Templeton Strong as "a stout young woman, a . . . rather nervous, fanciful person" who believed in ghosts and was visited on the twenty-fourth of February each year by a particularly eerie specter whom she had first encountered in Great Barrington, Massachusetts.[26] In spite of such eccentricities, she served as a kind of surrogate mother to Gottschalk, who maintained a correspondence with her down to his death.

As if as an antidote to this lugubrious blue-stocking, Gottschalk also enrolled himself as an ardent fan of the most alluring woman in America, actress Adah Isaacs Menken. Born in New Orleans, orphaned at seven, sent onto the stage of the Théâtre d'Orléans as a dancer, and briefly married to a Jewish musician from Cincinnati, Adah Menken arrived in New York in the late 1850s, burning to leave her mark on Gotham.[27] In quick order she joined the bohemian circle at Pfaff's, married (again, briefly) prizefighter John C. Heenan, and invented a role for herself on the stage that was to titillate and outrage Americans throughout the Civil War years.

The vehicle for her dubious triumph was the melodrama *Mazeppa,* based on the same poem of Byron's on which both Liszt and Gottschalk had based compositions for the piano. The climax of this tale occurred when Mazeppa, the fiery Cossack, was discovered by his Polish enemies consorting with a high-born Polish lady. His captors punished him by tying him to the back of a spirited horse and driving him off to his death. Adah Menken took the role of Mazeppa, which she played in flesh-colored tights that made her appear all but naked. She worked with carpenters to design a sweeping wooden ramp leading off stage and personally trained a fiery charger to ascend it with her strapped to its back. After test runs at a theater in Albany, Adah Menken's *Mazeppa* instantly established itself as one of the naughtiest performances ever seen on the American stage.[28]

Between appearances, Adah Menken became a regular at Pfaff's and an intimate friend of Ada Clare's. Aspiring, like Clare, to be a writer, Menken was turning out long poems in free verse patterned after *Leaves of Grass.* It was at this time that Gottschalk met her. Shortly afterwards he began filling page after page of a leather-bound album with *cartes de visite* photos of his fellow New Orleanian. Did their relationship develop further? There is no evidence that it did. Yet the album alone gives the lie to Mrs. Seymour's self-serving claim that he had cut all ties to New York's *demi-monde.*

Of far greater moment than these occasional dalliances were Moreau's business dealings. For a year he had barely been able to keep up payments to his four sisters and two brothers in Paris. The Strakosch contract improved his financial prospects but did not get him out of the woods. To supplement his concert fees he had to sell sheet music. Only days after Gottschalk arrived on the *Columbia*, General Hall delivered to him a new contract.[29] This would have required him to produce from twelve to twenty piano works a year, perform them at concerts, and publish with no other firm without Hall's permission—all for a mere five percent of gross receipts. Worse, if Gottschalk left the country, he would have to forfeit all commissions after six months. Gottschalk balked at this.

While he was considering Hall's proposal, the Boston firm of Oliver Ditson & Co. offered a flat purchase arrangement at one thousand dollars per composition.[30] Besides its generosity, Ditson's offer had the added attraction of coming from the same firm that published *Dwight's Journal of Music*, the mouthpiece of Moreau's arch-enemy. Yet even though Hall's contract was flawed, Gottschalk remained loyal to his old patron, agreeing to promote only his editions while touring. Within the year Gottschalk was to complain about Hall's slowness and his poor distribution. Frustrated, he proposed that Hall and Ditson enter into a co-publication arrangement.[31] Although this was never formalized, Gottschalk nonetheless began sending his new compositions to both Hall and Ditson. At the same time he worked out a separate arrangement with the Escudiers in Paris, who oversaw the issuance of further editions in France, Germany, Italy, Spain, and Russia.[32]

Since Hall continued to pay him by commission, in planning programs Moreau favored pieces published by Hall. Those who chided him for playing only his own compositions were wasting their breath, since a significant part of his income depended on it. The publishers flourished from this arrangement as well. A year and a half after Moreau's return from Havana, the Board of Music Trade announced that Gottschalk's tours had increased gross sales of piano music by a million dollars, a figure that would have been three times larger had it not been for the Civil War.[33]

A second source of supplemental income derived from Gottschalk's contract with the Chickering firm. There was no disputing that Gottschalk's old Boston patron produced excellent pianos. However, by comparison with Érard's new "double escapement action," Chickering's action was somewhat heavy and its damping mechanism imperfect. Nonetheless, Chickering's sales were booming. Gottschalk was therefore only too pleased to sign an exclusive contract with the Bostonians to advertise their pianos in all his concert programs and, working as a commissioned agent, to promote their sales wherever he went.[34] Within a year Chickering produced a new model, which Gottschalk judged superior even to his beloved Érard. The Chickering firm sent two of these mammoth instruments on all Gottschalk's American tours, along with a tuner.[35]

Yet another source of income was royalties from his published essays and travel pieces. While still in New York, Gottschalk proposed that Léon Escudier publish regular reports on the American scene in *La France musicale*, and that he pay his author in printed music, which Gottschalk could then resell.[36] However, the Escudier brothers had quarreled over the ownership of their publishing house, which had just gained exclusive French rights to the works of Verdi. When Marie-Pierre quit, Léon founded *L'Art musical*. It was this new journal that finally took on Gottschalk as a foreign correspondent. Gottschalk's essays for Escudier were reprinted in Russia, Italy, and Germany.

For an American outlet, he turned to his old friends at the *Courrier des États-Unis* in New York. Baron de Trobriand was now a Union officer, but those running the paper in his absence were glad to receive Moreau's regular "Tablettes d'un pianiste", which they ran on the front page. Henry Clapp Jr. and other friends translated these essays into English and arranged for their further issuance in such publications as the *Leader*, the *Home Journal, Once a Month*, and the *Saturday Press*.[37]

That these *Notes of a Pianist* were a money-making project is beyond doubt. They were also a diversion from long and boring hours on the road. Beyond this, the *Notes* had a more elevated purpose. "Ill or well," he wrote, they arose from his realization that "*Art*, so misconceived by some, so maltreated by others, has nowhere a better right to seek just commentators than among her own disciples, be they howsoever awkward with the pen."[38]

When Max Strakosch engaged Gottschalk to tour, he had no intention of sending him on the road as a solo act. He knew the American public better than that. Strakosch therefore turned to his Austrian-born son-in-law, Jacob Grau, and asked him to form an opera company around Gottschalk.

This troupe had little in common with the vast organizations that stage operas today, with their truckloads of scenery and bevies of supporting singers. In fact, Grau's Italian Opera Company never numbered more than six or seven principals. Besides Gottschalk, there were usually three or four singers, an instrumental soloist, and sometimes an assisting pianist to accompany the singers and perform duets with Gottschalk. Supervising the aggregations was a "director," who often doubled as the assisting pianist.

During the Civil War years Gottschalk was the centerpiece for four or five such "opera companies." Such performance groups built a solid basis of public support for opera and maintained their popularity in the American heartland for decades thereafter. Thanks to these traveling aggregations, millions of Americans heard highlights from all the most popular operas of the day. An audience in Rochester, for example, might hear the first and last acts of *Lucia de Lamermoor* in one evening, with plenty of time left for piano solos in between. At times the process of truncating operatic classics became quite ridiculous. Gottschalk chortled that now "*Lucrezia, I Puritani,* and *Il Trovatore* can all be played the same evening!—the whole in two hours and a half, and for fifty cents!"[39] If an orchestra and competent local singers were at hand, a small road troupe might expand for a few evenings into a full opera company. This is how Chicago and other cities of the West saw their first complete operas.[40] Thus, when blackface minstrel companies staged side-splitting parodies of the great operas, they could assume that their audiences had some acquaintance with the real thing.

Whatever Grau's Italian Opera Company lacked in numbers, it more than made up for in quality. The baritone Augustino Susini had already had a splendid career in Europe before reaching American shores. Carlotta Patti's temperament was less fiery than her sister Adelina's, but she was considered to be at least her equal as an artist. Later versions of the company included Carlotta's brother Carlo Patti, a superior violinist of bohemian temperament who had briefly joined the Confederate army. Other well-known artists who participated in the first road company were Carl Bergmann, conductor of the New York Philharmonic, and the conductor and composer Emannuele Muzio.

The greatest successes were achieved when tenor Pasquale Brignoli was with the troupe. Handsome and indolent, Brignoli had been captivating New York audiences since his arrival from Paris in 1856. Walt Whitman hailed Brignoli's "perfect singing voice,"[41] which the artist protected by eating quantities of raw oysters before each night's performance.[42] A captivating personality, Brignoli had a huge following among ladies in the audience and was judged by Ada Clare to be one of New York's "male beauties," along with Carlo Patti and Gottschalk.[43]

There was no opera house on earth that would not have welcomed the singers who participated in Grau's Italian Opera Company and the various successor groups in which Gottschalk participated. Amazingly, these singers gladly performed in villages like Roxbury, Massachusetts, Rockport, New York, Zanesville, Ohio, and Alton, Illinois. They served as living links between the centers of European culture and the rough American frontier. Gottschalk's role in all these companies was to be a bicultural mediator, interpreting each of these worlds to the other. He composed many pieces for his operatic friends, each of them designed to bring out the best features of a classically trained voice by applying it to melodies that meshed with the American spirit. Typical was *Le Papillon*, which he composed for Carlotta Patti. One of his most ambitious songs, *Le Papillon* featured a butterfly-like coloratura part that embroidered the piano melody much as Gottschalk's high treble ornaments embroider his piano pieces.[44]

For Brignoli Gottschalk recast his Cuban song *Serenata à Paulina M* as *Idol of Beauty* (also known as *Viens o ma belle*). For the English tenor George Simpson he composed a *Serenade*, now lost,[45] and for other members of his traveling company he composed such songs as *O Loving Heart, Trust On!; I Don't See It, Mama!; My Only Love, Good Bye!; Slumber On, Baby Dear;* and a second *Berceuse*. Musicologist Richard Jackson has pointed out that these compositions, although they often mismatch text and melody, stand out among American songs of the era for their frequent use of minor keys and for their "startling dissonances repeatedly occurring from the use of suspensions, appoggiaturas, and passing notes among the otherwise lush 'barbershop' harmonies."[46]

In the last week of March 1862 Grau's Italian Opera Company, with Moreau Gottschalk and Carlotta Patti as its featured stars, set out from New York on its first Western tour. At just this time Union troops were massing for their first major encounters with the Confederate army. As Grau's company moved west, the two armies were moving on lines that within weeks would bring them into bloody combat at the Shiloh battlefield at Pittsburgh Landing, Tennessee.

The papers were full of all this as Patti entertained at the Buffalo Opera House with her show-stopping *French Laughing Song* from Auber's *Manon Lescaut* and as Moreau performed his *Columbia* and *Murmures éoliens*.[47] A member of the audience who came in from the countryside concluded that it was "worth the journey to hear the monster piano rave and roar, and plead and pray, and laugh and cry."[48] The artists then traveled to Cleveland, where Carlotta's *French Laughing Song* again stole the show and where the press judged Gottschalk to be "greater than Thalberg."[49] After a pair of concerts in Pittsburgh, they churned down the Ohio by steamboat to Cincinnati, where a "frigidly decorous" opening concert at the Catholic Institute Building was so over-subscribed that the two succeeding concerts were moved to the more commodious Pike's Opera House.[50]

By now it was clear that the audiences came mainly to hear Gottschalk. Grau's Operatic Company was not even being mentioned in the ads for "the Gottschalk Concerts," and even Carlotta Patti was listed in a subordinate role. Thus, Gottschalk was the star, yet he went out of his way to engage local talent. At Cincinnati, for example, he enlisted a young German-born local pianist and student of Thalberg to assist him at the second concert. By featuring this local hero, Charles Kunkel, in advertising, Gottschalk and Grau appealed directly to the public's democratic interests.[51]

While in Cincinnati, Gottschalk learned that he would soon be subject to the draft, which was held by lottery for all males aged twenty to forty. Any man capable of fighting whose name was not drawn in the first round remained on the list and could not leave the country without posting a security deposit of one thousand dollars. Moreau reported anxiously to Clara, "I feel the need to leave. I am no longer living, but what can I do against an insurmountable obstacle?"[52] The local public in this border city knew nothing of these concerns, of course. Cincinnatians hailed him as the "Monte Cristo of piano players" and, above all, as a "true American."[53]

At a pair of concerts in Louisville, Gottschalk unpacked a number of his less frequently performed works, including the *Tennessee Mazurka*.[54] As Grau's troupe then moved by steamboat toward St. Louis, a Confederate army of forty thousand fell on U. S. Grant's thirty-three thousand troops at Pittsburgh Landing, Tennessee. The Confederates initially controlled the battlefield. Then reinforcements reached Grant, and he routed the Confederates in what turned out to be the war's bloodiest battle in the West. Just as Gottschalk arrived in St. Louis, thousands of the wounded from this Battle of Shiloh reached the city. The whole state of Missouri was in commotion. Only months earlier, the militia had split between secessionists and Union sympathizers.[55] Now pro-Union sentiment was at floodtide, not least among the large German population. Gottschalk, with his resounding tribute *The Union*, was able to help the local public celebrate this new affirmation. Newspapers reported that the local "Secesh" crowd heckled him at the first concert but boycotted the second, "having received at the hands of the loyal Gottschalk such a tremendous dose of Union music."[56]

Lists of killed and wounded from Shiloh filled the Chicago papers during Gottschalk's visit there in April 1862.[57] Again *The Union* "excited the liveliest enthusiasm,"[58] but among the politically charged audiences a note of ribaldry was also in the air. At Gottschalk's third Chicago concert a "laughing genius" in the gallery joined Carlotta in her *French Laughing Song* and reduced the whole audience to tears of mirth.[59]

The company then forged on to Milwaukee;[60] Detroit (where Moreau was judged "transcendentally grand");[61] Hamilton, Ontario; Toledo, Ohio; and once more to Cleveland. After a further stop in Lockport, New York, Grau's Italian Opera Company reached Manhattan by April 30. Not pausing to rest, Gottschalk threw himself into ten New York concerts in seven days.[62] In the course of this hectic round at Niblo's Saloon and Irving

Hall, he premiered a new fantasia based on Verdi's *Un Ballo in Maschera*, brought out for the first time in North America his burlesque *Marlborough, s'en va t'en guerre*, and even presented a caprice by Schumann, doubtless as a nod to his supporting pianist that evening, Bostonian William Mason.[63] During this brief interlude he learned that New Orleans had fallen to Federal forces and heard optimistic rumors that the war's end was near.[64]

Fresh from these triumphs, Gottschalk then joined another hastily assembled company under Grau's management to give concerts in Philadelphia, Baltimore, and Washington. Participating with him for this brief tour in May 1862 was the American soprano Clara Louise Kellogg, who left in her memoirs revealing sketches of Gottschalk and his friends. By the time Grau's troupe left for Philadelphia, the railroads were jammed with men in blue heading for the front. Farm boys from Massachusetts and members of New York's aristocratic Seventh Regiment found themselves side by side in the cars, passing along food handed through the windows by volunteer women who had set up soup kitchens at every station.

Patriotic feeling was at fever pitch when Gottschalk performed *The Union* at Philadelphia's Academy of Music on May 26.[65] Union General Nathaniel Prentiss Banks had temporarily thwarted Stonewall Jackson, and many now expected victory to follow victory. Just before Gottschalk arrived in Baltimore, aggressive Unionists nearly lynched a Southern sympathizer there. For the time being, the public's patriotic ardor buoyed Gottschalk's spirits. With sardonic humor he estimated the vast crowds that would assemble if he would promise to play both *The Union* and his variations on *Dixie's Land* on the same program. He was sure that he would reap a quick four thousand dollars, but he also acknowledged that "in the tumult I would probably be the first one strangled."[66] Instead of this repertoire, Gottschalk introduced the song *Idol of Beauty*.[67]

At every grade crossing en route to Washington Gottschalk observed armed sentries. President Lincoln had issued an urgent call for fresh troops to defend the Federal capital, and these were pouring into Washington by rail just as Gottschalk's train steamed in. From Rhode Island alone there came one hundred thousand volunteers, whom Gottschalk encountered as he rode out to visit an academy in Georgetown run by the Sisters of the Visitation. The sisters had one of their piano students perform for Moreau. In a textbook demonstration of poor judgment, the young artiste chosen for this honor was none other than the daughter of Benjamin Butler, the Union general who had just been assigned the job of pacifying Gottschalk's home town of New Orleans. An anti-Semite and a boor, Butler acquired the nickname "Spoons" when silverware began disappearing from the New Orleans homes where he and his officers were quartered. Gottschalk let the incident pass without comment, however.

Returning from Georgetown, Gottschalk encountered a column of wounded rebels captured after Jackson's recent defeat.[68] In spite of such grim signs of war, the entire diplomatic corps turned out for his performances, no doubt taking a cue from Secretary of State Seward's earlier endorsement of the Union patriot from Louisiana. As a joke, Gottschalk interpolated into *The Union* the national anthems of every foreign envoy in the house. To the amusement of all, each dignitary leapt to his feet as he heard his anthem and stayed at attention until the next anthem began.[69]

Such playfulness subsided soon enough, however, for on the return trip to New York Gottschalk's train stopped to pick up a group of wounded soldiers. One, a young officer whose thigh had been shattered by a Confederate bomb, was nearly a skeleton, his face wasted and disfigured by pain.[70] It dawned on Gottschalk that the war would not end soon and that the grim prediction he had made in Havana—that it would grind down both sides to a state of utter exhaustion—was being realized.

As the nation's crisis unfolded, Moreau was drawn into a battle of his own by his old Boston adversary, John Sullivan Dwight. Nine years earlier Dwight had championed the cause of classicism, morality in art, and the German school of composers against romanticism, aestheticism, and the French and Italian school. Gottschalk embodied everything Dwight opposed, and the intervening years had not made him less objectionable to the editor from Boston. Upon Gottschalk's return from Havana, one of Dwight's competitors, the *Boston Musical Times*, had pleaded with him to perform in the Massachusetts capital.[71] Dwight staunchly opposed this invitation. Renewing his old campaign, he published articles from Germany critical of all virtuosos, faulted Moreau for his interest in Spanish music, and again compared him unfavorably to Thalberg.[72]

Gottschalk's defenders correctly interpreted this as an attack on their own taste and responded in kind. The *New York Mercury* was but one of several Manhattan papers that took up cudgels in Gottschalk's behalf. Its critic lampooned Gottschalk's opponents and characterized them as "three cadaverous individuals, evidently from 'down east.' "[73]

This time Gottschalk, too, was prepared to counter-attack. Conspiring with Henry Clapp Jr. and the raucous gang at Pfaff's, he came up with the typical Bohemian pen name of "Jem Baggs." This name was not original with Gottschalk. The actor G. W. Marsh had used it in the farce *The Wandering Minstrel* in 1855. Subsequently, an unidentified friend of the composer had used it (in the form "Jem Bags") to sign several articles that were published in *Dwight's Journal of Music* while Gottschalk was in Cuba.[74] Now Gottschalk took it over and used it for articles that he himself submitted to Dwight's august journal. On February 22, 1862, the new Jem Baggs made his debut on the pages of *Dwight's* with a review of a concert Moreau had recently given in Brooklyn.

"Gottschalk," wrote Gottschalk, "is decidedly the musical Lion of the present. There is something in Gottschalk which pleases me beyond all the pianists I have yet heard. . . . In his inspired moments he sends an electricity through his hearers. . . . But why attempt what I cannot do, for I am not able to write of him as I could wish or as he deserves."[75] Over the next year, the peripatetic Jem Baggs reported on Gottschalk concerts in several cities, always favorably. With exquisite nerve Gottschalk even managed to announce his identity as Jem Baggs on Dwight's own pages. This occurred in the issue of October 17, 1863, when suddenly "Seven Octave" *(sic)*, after a lapse of six years, reappeared with one of his reports on the New York scene. "We have written many indifferent gossiping musical letters in our day," reported Seven Octave–Gottschalk, "and were last known in your paper as *Jem Baggs.* We like our first name [i.e., Seven Octave] better, and with your permission will hereafter be again *Seven Octave.*"[76] This must have evoked thigh-slapping mirth around the tables at Pfaff's!

Gottschalk's next move was to invade Dwight's home territory. For the foray into New England, he and Brignoli assembled a fresh "Italian Opera Troupe." They took this new team to a pre-planned staging point in the Boston suburb of Roxbury. After his disastrous Boston concert in 1853, Moreau had vowed he would never again perform in the Massachusetts capital. He remained true to his vow but now taunted Dwight by sending Brignoli and the troupe into Boston while he gave a series of solo performances in Roxbury, Worcester, and Lowell. All were sold out, and the performance at Mechanic's Hall in Lowell produced an exceptional outpouring of praise from local critics. One rhapsodized, "He plays like a poet. . . . He is [also] the people's man, and in spite of Teutonic abuse [i.e., from Dwight], the people will rush to hear him."[77]

The Boston classicists did not let this pass. One of their mouthpieces, the *Daily Advertiser*, sent its own reviewer to cover the Roxbury concert. In contrast to the critic from Lowell, the *Advertiser's* dismissed Moreau as a "complacent reader of his own works, not the careful, timid, conscientious representative of the mighty dead whose works live after them for our dull sakes." Gottschalk's compositions, claimed the *Advertiser*, were "quite tropical," and a few, it conceded, were "almost worthy to be called works of genius." In spite of all this, the reviewer confided, "Mr. Gottschalk had it not in his power to satisfy the true lover and student of music, [for] he lacks the one great essential—*soul.*"[78]

This was just the line to send the New Yorkers into gales of mirth. The editor of the *New York Leader* confessed he was "so much occupied . . . with a great discovery recently made in Boston that nearly every other matter has gone clean out of my mind": Gottschalk, it turned out, had no soul. "I, for one," confessed the *Leader*, "am disposed to be glad of it, and to exclaim in language which will be shocking to the *Advertiser*, 'Bully for Him!' "[79] Soon the question of Gottschalk's "soul" became a rallying point for musical populists eager to do battle with the elitists and for American nationalists who wanted to lock swords with the Europeanists.

Moving like a guerrilla army, Gottschalk and Brignoli proceeded to "conquer" all the cities in the region surrounding Boston. At Portsmouth, New Hampshire, they won a "complete ovation,"[80] and at Portland, Maine, Moreau's works were judged "some of the richest compositions known to musical language."[81] The troupe spared no effort to win over Salem, Massachusetts, and Providence, Rhode Island, where they offered no fewer than five concerts. Sending a warning to Boston, the *Providence Daily Post* announced that Gottschalk's concerts there were "a complete ovation from beginning to end."[82]

Having won over Boston's hinterland, Gottschalk drew back from the fray, leaving Bostonians anticipating an imminent "attack" on their cultural stronghold but uncertain as to when it would come. Gottschalk chose not to launch his final assault for another four months. Meanwhile, he embarked on a hastily arranged tour to Canada, followed by performances in virtually every city in upstate New York.

Unlike the previous two tours, this one was solo, with assisting pianists who were hired locally. Such aides had to be competent, of course, but if the assistant happened also to be the local piano dealer, as was J. R. Blodgett of Buffalo, or the brother of an important music publisher, as was Charles G. Pond of Rochester, so much the better.[83] At Utica, New York, Moreau hired two assisting pianists as well as a local soprano, Kitty Foster, a stategy that nearly filled the house with relatives of the performers.[84]

This Northern tour proved to be thoroughly pleasant. Gottschalk was delighted by towns like Batavia, Canandaigua, and Geneva, New York.[85] He joined friends for an excursion by canoe on the St. Lawrence River. Traveling as far as Alvarge Islands, the paddlers sang the quartet from *Rigoletto* at the top of their voices. This side-trip probably gave rise to the *Canadian Boat Song*, a four-voice setting of a poem by Thomas Moore (1779–1852) that Moreau dedicated to his friend Charles Vezin's Wissahickon Glee Club in Philadelphia. The Northern tour included other lyrical moments, among them a lovely twilight at Ogdensburg, New York, where Gottschalk listened with tears in his eyes as hymns from a local church floated over the village.[86] But receipts from the tour barely covered expenses.[87]

His attempts to build audiences in Canada got Gottschalk into trouble. At Québec's Théâtre Royal he improvised successfully on a French Canadian air, but at Montreal he went further, inviting the audience to choose works from his entire repertoire.[88] Members of the audience at Nordheimer's Hall accepted the invitation by calling for Gottschalk to play *Dixie*. He answered with *The Union*.[89]

By the time Gottschalk arrived at Saratoga on August 1, 1862, he was exhausted and depressed over the war. Some weeks before, he had finally admitted that his revered General McClellan had proven hopelessly irresolute in battle.[90] Lincoln had tried to regain the upper hand for the Union by issuing the Second Confiscation Act, which freed all slaves of rebel owners who fell under Federal jurisdiction. This ruined several Gottschalk relatives in New Orleans, but Moreau took no notice of it. The same news led to open conflicts among the wealthy vacationers at Saratoga. Border-state moderates from Kentucky and Maryland were driven out of the spa by abolitionists who argued that "Lincoln ought to be hanged for not forcing slaves to murder all the whites of the South."[91]

In spite of these conflicts, money was abundant at Saratoga that summer. Old-timers swore they had never seen so much wealth, so much scandal, or so much hard drinking by ladies as well as by gentlemen.[92] Numerous photographs place Gottschalk squarely in the center of this social whirl. One caught him decked out in a soft straw hat as he crossed a street, while several others show him lounging with dapper men and women in scenes straight out of a painting by Renoir.[93] Yet his energies at the time were directed less to socializing than to mounting a major concert to benefit wounded Union soldiers. Ex-president Millard Filmore and Senator Rufus King of New York lent their support to the project, which had been organized jointly by ladies from the Union, Congress, and Clarendon hotels.[94] The concert, held on August 20, netted eight hundred dollars. Moreau's fellow committeemen presented him with an exquisite gold box, and within days the press of New York and Boston resounded with praise for his patriotism. Both *Vanity Fair* in Manhattan and Dwight's competitor, the *Boston Musical Times*, rhapsodized that the event had to be "chalked, or rather Gottschalked, to his credit."[95] Dwight grudgingly acknowledged Gottschalk's philanthropy, but used the opportunity to take a further jab at him by reprinting in the same issue of his *Journal of Music* an adulatory review of a recent Thalberg concert in London.[96]

Following this working vacation, Moreau headed to yet another fashionable spa, this one at Schooley's Mountain in Morris County, New Jersey. Perched on a high plateau in the Appalachians and surrounded by mineral springs and waterfalls, this rural retreat had been popular for a generation. Gottschalk settled into rooms at the vast wooden Belmont Hall.[97] Even though he found time there to pen several long poems for Mrs. Seymour, he did not really give himself over to leisure.[98] Every day he dressed in his usual grand style, waxed his new pointed mustache "à la Napoléon III," and received English, French, and Spanish journalists who had made the trek from Manhattan in order to interview him.[99]

This pause continued through September, which Gottschalk spent with Louis Descombes at his home *cum* piano showroom at 766 Broadway. His old school friend Nelvil Soulé came through town, having traveled there from New Orleans in an effort to visit his diplomat father, now languishing in a Federal prison.[100] Moreau also frequented Pfaff's, visited with Mrs. Seymour, and fell easily into his old role of man about town. His main project at the time, however, was to tutor a child pianist from Caracas named Teresa Carreño.

This remarkable girl practiced daily at the piano in the Descombes' parlor. Within weeks she was playing *Le Bananier* from memory and even the tortuous *Jérusalem* fantasy, with its chromatic octaves.[101] Gottschalk was generally suspicious of child prodigies and had only consented to hear "Teresita" after a Spanish friend in New York intervened in her behalf. Now he determined that "she *must* be something great, and *shall* be." [102]

He by no means over-estimated this vivacious child. Carreño made her debut at Irving Hall on November 6, 1862, and then proceeded to offer a series of six concerts, evoking ecstatic reviews.[103] Within a year, news of Carreño's breathtaking performances reached President Lincoln, who invited her to perform at the White House. Her all-Gottschalk program ended abruptly when she refused to play further on the dreadfully out-of-tune piano. The Great Emancipator saved the day by asking, "Teresita, do you know my favorite song, *Listen to the Mockingbird?*" She did, and the familiar air brought tears to Lincoln's eyes.[104]

Teresa Carreño, with her overpowering technique and personality, went on to become one of the century's great pianists, "the Walküre of the Piano." [105] To Rossini, it was enough that she was "trained by the celebrated Gottschalk." [106] She in turn taught Edward MacDowell, one of America's greatest academic composers. Throughout her career she championed Gottschalk's music, and her *Gottschalk March* (op. 1) appeared on her concert programs well into the new century.

By mid-September news from the front was more favorable. The Union forces had held off the rebels at the Battle of Antietam, and the

Emancipation Proclamation was sowing confusion behind rebel lines. By October 1 the *New York Times* was predicting that the South would soon run through its supply of manpower. But the impact of mounting casualties was felt in the North as well, as the first draft lists were issued in New York on October 15. In spite of this, the mood of the moment was sufficiently upbeat that Max Strakosch ventured a series of eight concerts at Irving Hall. Situated on Irving Place at 15th Street, this barn-like auditorium had just been refurbished by the English-born tenor and entrepreneur William Harrison. Decked out with frescoes by an Italian artist, the refurbished Irving Hall helped convince New Yorkers that their city would soon surpass the cultural centers of Europe.[107]

There was no opera that season, and only Edwin Forrest's performances in *Spartacus* and Barnum's new exhibition of tropical fish offered competition to Gottschalk.[108] It was therefore Moreau's moment. Whether through Max Strakosch's design or Gottschalk's, the Irving Hall concerts constituted an unprecedented exhibition of American talent. Appearing with Gottschalk were his old protégé Harry Sanderson, a new tenor named William Castle, soprano Lucy Simons, Annie Stockton, and Mrs. Jenny Kempton—all natives of the United States. Directing this aggregation was an aspiring violinist from Brooklyn, Theodore Thomas (1835–1905).[109]

In spite of the presence of several European artists on the bill, it was these Americans, including Gottschalk himself, who captured the public's attention.[110] Moreau had salted the program with his European and Caribbean works, yet he was everywhere described as "Our Gottschalk." This national possessiveness extended even to his piano by Chickering. "It is rather flattering to our national pride," wrote *Vanity Fair*, "that both Mr. Gottschalk and Mr. Thalberg . . . have invariably preferred Chickering's to all others."[111]

With these triumphs at Irving Hall ringing in his ears, Gottschalk decided the moment had come for the final assault on Boston. The enthusiasm in New York had carried a strong anti-Boston cast, as if Manhattan, rather than Beacon Hill, now epitomized the nation's values. *Frank Leslie's Illustrated Newspaper* gloated that "in New York people judge for themselves, and our critics have larger and more catholic views of art and artists." In Boston, by contrast, "a little clique of snarling critics hoodwinks [the public's] judgment to the repression of every generous and genial impulse." Boston, it concluded, was "a city which artists must delight to—leave."[112] The *World* argued that Boston's problem was that it could not perceive anything beyond the music of dead Germans. When Gottschalk played a Mozart sonata with Thomas at one of the Irving Hall soirées, the *World* expressed the hope that Gottschalk "will never so far forget himself again as to play compositions of this kind except at his Boston concerts."[113]

While Federal troops were battling the Confederacy, New York's cultural patriots, drawn up in ranks behind Gottschalk, were bent on final victory over the Massachusetts capital. Moreau had already crushed resistance in the suburbs the previous spring. Now, as the *Boston Morning Journal* recognized, the time had come to steel himself for the final assault, "determined to conquer or die."[114]

Boston had changed since Gottschalk's disastrous debut there in 1853. The Unitarian movement had spent its force of righteousness, and Lincoln had preempted the Abolitionists with his Emancipation Proclamation.[115] The earnest old *Boston True Flag* now carried jokes and fashion columns, while the new *Boston Musical Times*, founded in 1860, offered weekly reports on the Italian and French opera scene.

In contrast to his first assault on Boston, Gottschalk could now claim a kind of fifth column of sympathizers within the city. The firm of Ditson & Co. still issued *Dwight's Journal of Music*, but its biggest profits now came from publishing Gottschalk's works. The Chickering firm, whose founder had once offered charity to a bereaved Moreau, now built its marketing strategy around Gottschalk's endorsement of its new grand piano.[116] Gottschalk had another promoter in the heart of John Sullivan Dwight's territory in the person of Julius Eichberg, his old friend from Geneva. Settled in Boston since 1857, Eichberg championed his colleague from his position as music director at one of Boston's oldest theaters. Eichberg worked by day to undermine Boston's pomposities by composing comic operas.[117] Naturally, Gottschalk enlisted Eichberg for his debut at the Chickerings' new concert hall.

The build-up was immense. On the night of Moreau's first concert Senator Sumner was scheduled to defend the Emancipation Proclamation at a public meeting at Faneuil Hall. This aroused little public interest. By contrast, Bostonians snapped up every seat at Chickering's Hall. As the *Boston Journal* reported, "our musical people are very much exercised in regard to the coming concert of Mr. Gottschalk."[118] Gottschalk had turned the tables.

No one understood this better than John Sullivan Dwight, whom the public now cast as the villain. A writer from the *Boston Musical Times* heard Gottschalk play in private and remarked on "how it would astonish some of our hypocritical friends to hear Gottschalk play a Bach fugue on a pianoforte! And yet he has done so, and in Boston."[119] When Gottschalk performed a pair of Chopin preludes, the *Boston Journal* understood they were "an illustration to a few of our egotistical '*classicists*.'" The writer exulted, "How much superior [Gottschalk] is to them in his ability to appear in *their* exclusive sphere, as well as in one so much beyond them that they may never aspire to it."[120]

The swelling ranks of Gottschalk's champions placed the blame for his long boycott of Boston squarely on John Sullivan Dwight. Dwight tried to justify himself. "The admirers of Gottschalk have talked and written bitterly of the unkind, unappreciative treatment which his talent has received from Boston. This journal has been the especial object of such accusations. . . . We are repeatedly asked: 'Why are you such an *enemy* of Gottschalk?' We have uniformly disavowed all enmity."[121] To exculpate himself, Dwight even republished his old reviews of the 1853 concerts.

The public's response to the concerts at Chickering's Hall was sensational, "a perfect storm of applause" in the words of the *Boston Daily Courier.*[122] The *Journal* reported that the unanimous verdict of local musicians was in Gottschalk's favor.[123] By the third concert Gottschalk was playing *The Last Hope,* the Mozart violin sonata denounced in New York, and *The Banjo,* Dwight's particular *bête noire.* He then moved his concerts to the more commodious Melodeon and packed this hall for several further performances.

Dwight could not restrain himself even in defeat. Grudgingly admitting that Gottschalk was now the best pianist on earth, he renewed his old attack on his music. The operatic transcriptions were "abominable," he charged, full of "trilling and twiddling in piccolo octaves, with senseless, painful repetition." The West Indies pieces were "only a freak, more loud and bright than beautiful." And *The Banjo* was "a humorously close imitation of the vulgar original, good enough for a joke."[124]

Except for the *Boston Evening Transcript,* no other paper echoed these views. Dwight was now alone. While Gottschalk was busy sitting for souvenir photographs at T. R. Burnam's and at Case & Getchell's shop on Washington Street, his friends in New York were celebrating his victory. As for that "twiddling in piccolo octaves," bubbled Richard Storrs Willis in the *Home Journal,* "what a dreadful thing to do! A man who twiddles in piccolo octaves likely as not smokes on the Common when nobody is looking. . . . O, Gottschalk, how could you?"[125]

Shortly after this, the infamous Jem Baggs added insult to injury by publishing yet another favorable review of himself (extolling "the brilliancies of Gottschalk's pianism") in Dwight's own journal.[126] The *Boston Daily Advertiser* summed up the situation: "Mr. Gottschalk has certainly conquered Boston. If there were a prejudice against him, it has faded away or has hid in the minds of the few who cherish it secretly."[127]

Chapter Twenty-one

 The Automaton in Wartime,
1862–65

Gottschalk travels East and West;
Pedals, fingers, know no rest;
Many hearts he conquers where
Freedom's banner streams in air!

The *Union Concert Paraphrase*
Thrills with spirit stirring lays;
Measured footfalls reached the ears,
Martial clangor draws near.

May thy triumphs never cease—
Well earned fame for age increase—
Nobler lines thy story tell;
Child of Genius, fare thee well!

George W. Fox, *Gottschalk*,
from the *Nashua Gazette*
(New Hampshire), 18 July 1863

B Y the autumn of 1862 Gottschalk was piling triumph upon triumph,
and his audience was growing prodigiously. Just then a British entrepreneur named Beal approached him with a whopping contract for a
tour in England.[1] Due to the draft, however, Moreau had to decline. Meanwhile, the irrepressible Max Strakosch and his son-in-law Jacob Grau,
meeting over lunch at an Italian restaurant in Union Square, came up with
an even better offer to put the artist on the road throughout the North.[2]
Thanks to Strakosch's initiative and to several contracts that followed
Strakosch's, Gottschalk was to perform more widely than any other artist
or entertainer during the Civil War.

The Booth family of actors and minstrel troupes like Buckley's Serenaders also claimed large audiences. But none equaled Gottschalk for the
sheer outpouring of fervor they evoked, East and West. The local paper
in Springfield, Illinois, reported that "so large and appreciative an audience of ladies and gentlemen was never before assembled in our city."[3]

The *Detroit Free Press* noted that the concerts there "were greeted with the most unbounded applause, the audience hardly seeming satisfied with even a repetition of every performance,"[4] and in Reading, Pennsylvania, Gottschalk's concert was judged "the most brilliant musical event we have had for years."[5]

As a result of his Civil War tours, Moreau Gottschalk became one of the most widely acclaimed artist in any field, a home-grown hero appealing alike to elite and popular audiences. However much this acclaim testified to his gifts as composer and performer, it was, in equal measure, a testimony to what must surely have been one of the most demanding concert schedules of the era. For three years Gottschalk and variously constituted "opera companies" ceaselessly crisscrossed the country, performing nightly and, when train schedules permitted, even twice daily. This life of constant motion was the sheerest madness, of course. Gottschalk himself called it "la vie de carpet bag."[6] Scarcely had he begun this ceaseless touring when he pronounced it "endless torture without rest. . . . I seem like an uncontrollable machine, and play machine-like, my hands functioning upon the keys with a sickly ardor."[7] In the end, he became the very "automaton pianist" whom Ada Clare had conjured up in 1856 as a jab against him.

Between October 1862 and January 1865, Gottschalk made five extended tours of New England and Canada, three sustained Western tours, several shorter trips to Washington, D.C., and the Middle Atlantic states, and a brief visit to Norfolk, Virginia, after it was reconquered. It is no simple task to reconstruct the route and timing of these tours. The problem traces to Gottschalk himself, who was notoriously careless in dating letters and notebook entries.

By any measure, however, the number of concerts was prodigious. By July 1862 he had given one hundred nine concerts in 120 days.[8] In the single month of November 1862 he presented thirty-three concerts; considering that what Gottschalk called a "Protestant month" has four Sundays with no music, this meant thirty-three concerts in twenty-six days.[9] By June 1864 he was approaching his thousandth concert since returning from Havana.[10] But Gottschalk's own tabulations left out his frequent appearances in benefit concerts arranged by others.[11] Nor did they include informal soirées, such as one that took place in the home of a local notable in Reading, Pennsylvania, following a concert there. At this occasion he performed for the first time an elaboration, now lost, on *The Last Rose of Summer.*[12]

Meeting such a schedule demanded withering amounts of travel. For five months in 1863 Gottschalk performed six days a week without break, shifting cities after every second concert.[13] The miles added up quickly.

As early as the summer of 1862 he had logged fifteen thousand miles since his return from Cuba.[14] With morbid interest he began totaling the miles. When the *Home Journal* reported that he had reached eight thousand, he immediately mailed in a correction, demanding that the editor credit him instead with *eighty* thousand miles.[15] Others soon began taking an interest in this dubious achievement. In September 1863 the Board of Trade of American Music Publishers honored Gottschalk for having racked up ninety-five thousand miles in behalf of the Muse.[16]

It was not unduly difficult to deliver two concerts in different cities on the same day. This whetted Gottschalk's appetite to accomplish the yet greater feat of performing in three different cities on the same day. Fully conscious of the absurdity of it all, he finally attempted to establish this record by appearing at a morning concert in Newark, New Jersey, a matinee in Albany, and an evening performance in Troy, New York. However, when he briefly stepped off the train at Fishkill to help a mother and daughter, the train departed for Albany without him, so he failed to set this record.[17]

The pace of concertizing did not slacken even during vacations. The summer season at Saratoga in 1864, for example, was filled with a steady round of concerts. Moreau's pupil Harry Sanderson was there, and so was his friend George Warren, so it was inevitable that the three pianists would arrange various joint appearances.[18]

The only true rest came when he fled to the home of friends in Baltimore. There, amidst the family of merchant Louis G. Curlett on East Baltimore Street, he found affectionate hospitality and a true oasis. Gossips claimed that one of the Curlett daughters was infatuated with Gottschalk, but Moreau himself denied this. Besides the Curletts, many other friends and activities claimed his attention in Baltimore. The local piano "professor," a Dane named Courlander, named his son for Gottschalk. Moreau also played organ in the Catholic cathedral when he was in town, even composing in his mother's memory an *Ave Maria.*[19]

Except for such brief periods of respite, Gottschalk's life for three years was one of ceaseless travel. In some respects this existence represented a renewal of the vagabond life he had known as a touring artist in America between 1853 and 1857. The smoky trains, grubby hotels, manipulative European impresarios, and money-grubbing managers of concert halls were all still features of his existence. In actuality, however, each element in the system for distributing culture had been transformed by the whirlwind of change that had swept America during Moreau's absence in the Caribbean. An integrated network of concert halls, managers, and critics now existed and needed superstar artists the way a steel mill needs ore. The rail network had been extended as far west as the Wisconsin frontier, enabling a top artist like Gottschalk to be transported swiftly from one cultural mill to the next, each night, as it were, to be poured afresh into a new local mold that was much like all other local molds.

In a moment of enthusiasm, Moreau once exclaimed, "Decidedly these Yankees are the only true travelers in the world."[20] He enthused over the dining cars and the sleeping cars in which "for one dollar more, a magnificent bed is prepared for you, with elastic mattress and pillows." Unfortunately, Gottschalk knew such comforts only rarely. True, he lived on the railroad, and acknowledged that "my home is somewhere between the baggage car and the last car of the train."[21] But his "home" was generally a noisy and soot-filled environment, packed with passengers of every description. On one train near Toledo, Ohio, in 1864 eight hundred passengers were crammed into the narrow cars. On a train in Pennsylvania two thousand passengers were packed "like herrings in a barrel."[22] Since there were no first-class compartments on American trains, the wartime conditions meant that Gottschalk spent countless days in the company of drunken and brawling soldiers.[23] More than once he found himself in the middle of a fracas among recruits. At one point in upper New York state the crowding and noise created such chaos that Gottschalk fled to the baggage car, where he sat between the case of his Chickering grand and two coffins. Alone at last, he resignedly smoked a cigar.[24]

The new and more powerful locomotives of the 1860s made for impressive printed timetables. The war imposed its own schedules, however, with the result that the simplest trips often stretched out endlessly. To his friend Espadero, Moreau complained about a four hour expedition from New York to Philadelphia.[25] The ride from Philadelphia to Baltimore once took six hours, and Boston to Providence seven.[26] Toronto to New York once required forty hours.[27] Delays of all sorts were common. Racing along the main line from Lockport, New York, to Erie, Pennsylvania, in 1865, Gottschalk's train jumped the track. Traveling between Cincinnati and St. Louis, the engine hit a cow, turning that trip into a twenty-two-hour ordeal.[28]

At times he scarcely left the train. In the spring of 1865 Gottschalk spent eleven consecutive nights in a passenger car, leaving only to perform each night in a different town.[29] In these periods, he said, he became like the Chinese in Canton who pass their lives in junks in the harbor, never stepping on land.[30] Sometimes when he did touch land he regretted it. When his train broke down near Joliet, Illinois, in the winter of 1864 he ended up spending the night stretched out in a field adjacent to the tracks, wrapped only in his coat.[31]

His frantic schedule imposed a truly harrowing pace. In a letter to his sisters he recounted several days of a New England tour in April 1864:

Left [Hartford] on the twenty-sixth in the morning for Boston, where I arrived
at five o'clock in the evening. Concert at eight o'clock. Left Boston the next
day at eleven o'clock for Providence, where I played on my arrival at eight
o'clock the same evening. Left Providence at midnight for Boston. Spent the
night in the wagon cars. Arrived at seven o'clock in Boston on the twenty-
eighth. Went to bed in the morning at eight a.m. Slept three hours.[32]

Delays were inevitable and not well received by the public. When he appeared a half hour late for a concert in Detroit in May 1863, his first notes
were greeted with a loud protest from the audience.[33]

Winter snowstorms often disrupted schedules but never worse than
in December 1863, when the temperature in northern Illinois dropped to
twenty-eight degrees below zero and a huge snowstorm engulfed the entire Chicago region.[34] As the snow reached record-breaking depths and
the wind blew it into mountainous drifts, Moreau's train finally gave up
at Harvard, Illinois.[35] There the opera company camped out at the home
of the postmaster. Gottschalk awoke the next day with his mustache covered with ice. Expected for a concert in Chicago that evening, the hardy
band set out for the city. Many passengers suffered frostbite, and several
on the train died from the cold.[36] Meanwhile, at the hall in Chicago local
volunteers tried bravely to hold the audience until Gottschalk's arrival,
which was by no means certain. The minuscule audience was already in
an uproar when suddenly Gottschalk and soprano Angiolina Cordier
strode onto the stage in their overcoats, their faces still red from the
wind. They began performing at once, and within the hour Brignoli and
Behrens, their conductor, wandered in as well. It apparently never occurred to anyone that the concert might have been canceled.

Thanks to the rapid expansion of the rail network, the late 1850s and
early 1860s witnessed the construction of hundreds of new hotels in
cities large and small. These, too, were essential if artists were to tour
nationwide, and hence for the creation of a national market for music
and theater. True, there were some old hostels, like the eighteenth-
century Sun Inn in Bethlehem, Pennsylvania, where Gottschalk not only
stayed but attended a dance in his honor in the second-floor parlor.[37]
However, most were so new that Gottschalk described them in detail in
his newspaper articles, knowing that his readers would be interested. The
great Tremont House in Chicago earned warm praise from him, as did
the imposing Cosmopolitan in St. Louis.[38] Surprisingly, many small towns
also boasted hotels that a grateful Gottschalk could laud in his writings.
Kalamazoo, Michigan, Oswego, New York, and Sandusky, Ohio, all received top billings for their hotels, and Toledo's Oliver House he called
"one of the best in the United States."[39]

Complicating artists' lives was the fact that many of the new hotels were dreadful. Heating posed a grusome problem. The Lindell House in St. Louis was the nation's largest, but cold as an igloo in winter.[40] Gottschalk called the hotel in Harrisburg, Pennsylvania, "Siberian" and complained that at Barnum's Hotel in Springfield, Illinois, he could not warm up after two hours.[41] Crowding posed a worse problem. The vast Burnet House in Cincinnati lodged male guests three to a room, while the arctic Barnum's in Springfield, Illinois, housed guests six per room.[42]

"No one can form an idea of the importance a good hotel has for us," wrote Gottschalk.[43] "Good" meant not waking guests with a gong, as happened in many cities. He was sure this practice was "the last vestige of barbarism."[44] But there were worse vestiges, especially in the area of food. Even though trains arrived at every hour of the day, hotels persisted in offering food only at set mealtimes. As a result, Gottschalk and his musicians frequently went hungry, surviving on apples, stale bread, or frozen eggs. At one pre-concert dinner in Williamsport, Pennsylvania, consisting only of a single herring and some bread for the entire troupe, the conductor, Behrens, brought tears to everyone's eyes by describing in excruciating detail what he would be ordering at Delmonico's were they in New York.[45]

Hunger was their constant companion, causing Gottschalk to view himself as an Alsatian pâté goose in reverse, not stuffed to bursting but starved, so that he could then "exhale harmonious thoughts which the *bons vivants* of mind [in his audience] could taste tranquilly at the banquet of life."[46]

The gastronomic nadir of Gottschalk's life was reached in Cleveland, Ohio, at the Hotel Augier, which he branded "the most frightful, filthy eating house in the world."[47] The Lafitte wine tasted like vinegar, the fish was stale, the soup greasy, the butter rancid, and the tea tasted like chamomile and hay. "Cleveland," he concluded, "is devoted to bad hotels." Then, reflecting further, he realized that "if Cleveland, like me, detested rancid butter, stringy meat, and greasy soup, doubtless the hotel would go bankrupt. If, on the contrary, it prospers, it is because my tastes are not like those of the majority. The hotel is right; it is I who am wrong."[48]

Trains, hotels, and dining rooms defined the daily life of Gottschalk and his operatic troupe, but it was the hundreds of halls in which they performed that constituted their true workplace. The urban revolution fostered by increased population and rail transport extended to performance places as well. Over the decade since Gottschalk's return to America a tide of construction of concert halls, meeting rooms, opera houses, and theaters had swept the land. A few of the old halls he knew before 1856 were still functioning. Most of the halls now were new, vital

links in the chain of institutions that made possible an intense new citi-
fied culture on a national scale.

To be sure, some benighted towns failed to take this last step toward
urbanity. In Dover, New Hampshire, the troupe performed at the city hall,
while in Harrisburg, Pennsylvania, they held forth at the courthouse. The
public in such architecturally laggard cities and towns nonetheless received Gottschalk with great enthusiasm, suggesting that the artistic
tastes of the local citizenry had grown faster than their financial resources.[49]

The evolution of theaters was evident in Indianapolis, Indiana. There
a handsome Masonic Hall had been erected on Washington Street in 1850.
With classical columns across the facade and a gas-lit interior, it was the
scene of concerts and temperance crusades for only eight years before
the fifteen-hundred-seat Metropolitan Hall was built a few doors away.
Meanwhile, Indianapolis's streets were still mud holes. The citizenry
clearly believed that the needs these new concerts halls fulfilled were
more important than paved streets.[50]

It is worth noting that nearly all the new halls were commercial under-
takings. Only a few had the self-conscious purpose of elevating public
taste. The Mercantile Library in St. Louis was one, having been organized
in the 1840s as a membership library. Its building on Locust Street contained a hall that was used for lectures, concerts, and minstrel shows.[51]
Philadelphia and Boston led the country in non-profit halls for concerts.
Gottschalk judged the Academy of Music in Philadelphia as "surely one
of the most beautiful in the world" and considered Boston's new Tremont
Hall and Music Hall as "two of the best."[52]

Whatever Gottschalk's affection for these highbrow establishments,
they were not his true milieu. As a national entertainer, he was linked
with a new nation-wide network of for-profit concert rooms. In nearly
every case these were named for the entrepreneurs who had built them
by selling stock to fellow business people and civic boosters. Brainard's
Hall in Cleveland was typical. The Brainard family moved from New
Hampshire to Cleveland in 1834 and promptly opened a music store there.
By the 1840s they were printing music, and by the following decade they
were well enough established to raise capital to build Brainard's Hall,
where Gottschalk performed more than a dozen times.[53]

The evolution of performing spaces in Chicago reflected that city's
rise as a cultural center. Chicago's first concert occurred when a choir
performed at the City Saloon in 1846.[54] Not until 1850 did a retired actor
and future mayor, John Blake Rice, build a true theater in Chicago. A
year later it burned to the ground and was replaced by the sturdy brick

Metropolitan Hall. Then came a series of auditoriums, all competing for the same acts and audiences. Gottschalk performed frequently at Bryan Hall, built in 1860, and also at Smith and Nixon's. Scarcely did these open their doors than entrepreneurs organized still more joint stock companies to build yet grander halls.[55]

More surprising than the many halls in rich Chicago was the proliferation of such edifices throughout small-town America. Gottschalk found "one of the handsomest little halls I've yet seen in the United States" in Norwalk, Connecticut.[56] He had only praise for Rouse's Hall in Peoria, Illinois, and never passed up an opportunity to play at the Metropolitan Theatre in Utica, New York, where broad seats and good ventilation assured the audience's comfort. Typical of these small-town cultural palaces was Norman Hall in Sandusky, Ohio. Built in 1855, this three-story stone structure took its name from the Norman arches and crenelations that distinguished the building. The room in which Gottschalk frequently performed had been elaborately decorated with frescoes by one Signor Pedretti. The entrepreneurs were hailed by the local press for heightening the glory of this Lake Erie town of eleven thousand. Indeed, the *Sandusky Register* expressed the hope that their investment "would prove a profitable one in every respect."[57]

This was not mere politeness. As competition mounted in the performing arts field, proprietors of concert halls operated on ever slimmer profit margins. No wonder that Gottschalk encountered a sign in the dressing room of the Toledo concert hall warning that the proprietor would turn off the gas if performers had not paid the rent in full before appearing.[58] Pressed for funds, proprietors cut corners by under-heating their halls. After attempting to perform in the icy Mozart Hall in Cincinnati, Gottschalk declared that the only two colder places on earth were Mont Blanc and the Young Men's Association in Detroit, which he suspected of being an ice depot.[59]

This, then, was the world in which Gottschalk was expected to work his magic. Train schedules more rational on paper than in reality, hotels that imposed various forms of torture on their guests, abominable food, and auditoriums run by entrepreneurs whose avarice reflected their anxiety—these were the backstage realities of America's emerging national market for culture. The key role of mediating between these circumstances and the artists fell to impresarios and managers like Max Strakosch.

To be a manager in the arts was risky business, and people in the smaller cities knew it. The *Albany Times and Courier* said its own home town was "so pervertedly penurious that it is hard work to coax any manager of a first-class entertainment to trust his cash box up this way. . . . That Strakosch ventures here tonight [with Gottschalk] is the eighth wonder of the world."[60]

The impresario's task had grown much more complicated since the early days of the flamboyant pioneers like Maretzek, Ullmann, and Maurice Strakosch. The only way managers could now expect to book major talent was to offer contracts that guaranteed scores of performances. Max Strakosch's initial deal with Gottschalk called for one hundred concerts, a huge commitment.[61]

The challenge for a manager of sophisticated talent like Gottschalk was all the greater, for serious music had to go nose-to-nose with a daunting array of popular acts. Even at lordly Irving Hall in New York Gottschalk had to compete with a stereopticon.[62] In Cleveland a ventriloquist provided competition; at Utica's Corinthian Hall he was preceded by one "Professor de Ham"; and during a visit to Cincinnati Barnum's popular midget, Tom Thumb, was on the boards at a theater just across the street. Some of Gottschalk's competitors were old friends like Hermann the Magician of Havana fame, who preceded Gottschalk at a Mercantile Library concert in St. Louis in 1862.[63] The same theater managers who booked Gottschalk were booking such acts as these and carefully calculating their relative profitability.

Balancing these crowd-pleasers were a host of theatrical companies that offered Shakespearean plays. John Wilkes Booth was performing *Hamlet, Othello,* and *Richard III* in Indianapolis on the same nights Gottschalk was giving his 1863 concerts there.[64] Dramatic adaptations of popular novels also offered competition, as, for example, when a version of Alexandre Dumas's *Les Frères Corses* ran opposite Moreau in Cleveland.[65] There were also touring lecturers like Ralph Waldo Emerson, who came into frontal competition with Gottschalk in Indianapolis in January 1863. In this instance Gottschalk prevailed, since Strakosch had stolen the march on Emerson's agent by booking Masonic Hall for the very nights Emerson wanted it. The high-minded Bostonian had to cool his heels "imprisoned in dingy hotel & muddy town" with no choice but to go out and hear the artists who had humiliated him.[66]

Max Strakosch courted risk. Committed to paying Gottschalk's hefty fee for a hundred concerts and to covering the expenses of railroad tickets, hall rentals, and staff, he had to keep the troupe constantly in motion simply to break even. Visits to small-town America figured large on his balance sheet, for so extended a tour could not be sustained in big cities alone.

The intricate schedules that resulted would not have been possible without the telegraph. Practically non-existent back in the 1850s, the telegraph was now an essential tool for Strakosch and other impresarios. His wife in New York constantly wired changes in schedule to the company on the road. The telegraph also enabled the troupe to make concerts that might otherwise have been canceled. In April 1864 Gottschalk found himself stranded alone at Great Bend in Pennsylvania, while the rest of the company awaited him in Binghamton, New York. No sooner did Gottschalk inform Strakosch by telegram of his predicament than the impresario managed to commandeer a special train to pick up the pianist. After Gottschalk confirmed the plan by return cable, Strakosch held the audience until Gottschalk's arrival at Binghamton's station at 9:30 p.m. By 9:40 he was playing his first piece.[67]

Such gymnastics sometimes failed. When the company got stuck in Perth Amboy, New Jersey, Strakosch's advance man read a telegram to the Philadelphia audience confirming that Gottschalk and the others would arrive soon. When they failed to appear, a noisy demonstration broke out and Strakosch was forced to redeem the tickets at a loss of twelve hundred dollars.[68]

Without advertising, Strakosch could never have turned a profit. Marketing was his forte, however. At each station he would wire ahead laudatory reviews of Gottschalk and reports on the company's triumphant progress across the land. Local editors would work these into their stories or even publish them verbatim.

Rare was the concert that did not receive a lengthy review in the local press. Yet inexperienced local critics often floundered for words. The *Utica Advertiser* summed up a performance there in November 1862 by announcing, "Gottschalk played as he alone can play."[69] The *Sandusky Daily Commercial Register* "[did] not propose to waste words in attempting an analytic description of the performance." And the *Missouri Republican* confessed, "Words fail utterly to depict the least merit of his performance."[70]

Some critics went to the opposite rhetorical extreme. The *Buffalo Courier*'s editor came away from a concert saying, "The music talks to you like an inspired prophet, a raving madman, a true friend, a tender lover."[71] No wonder a writer for the *Indianapolis Daily Journal*, in refusing to tout a performance, observed that "critics go into raptures, and pour out streams of melodious and mystical words, but with an effect as slight as that which they fail to describe is astonishing."[72]

Whatever the editor's attitude, it was Strakosch's task to make sure that the first review in each town was favorable. When an editor in upstate New York threw away Strakosch's publicity material on Gottschalk and published instead a malicious attack against music in general, Strakosch appeared at his office, sweet as honey. It turned out that the editor had not received the complimentary tickets he had expected. The vindictive and miserly Strakosch refused to give them to him now, however, with the result that Gottschalk never again dared visit that town.[73]

Strakosch's Neapolitan advance man, Diego de Vivo, outshone his master in marketing. Sent to Philadelphia to drum up an audience amidst a slow theater season, de Vivo had the inspired idea of writing every clergyman in the city and informing them that a ticket would be waiting for them at the box office. Naturally, most ended up buying two or three additional seats, selling out the hall.[74]

Strakosch souped up his marketing of Gottschalk with every promotional trick in the book. Some were familiar, such as the endless "farewell concerts" and the extravaganzas for four pianos or even a dozen.[75] A new setting by Gottschalk of the march from Wagner's *Tannhäuser* became an instant war-horse in this genre. Then there were the invitations for members of the audience to submit requests. Occasionally no requests were forthcoming. At such times Gottschalk went so far as to invite people simply to whistle a tune on which he would improvise. In Indianapolis in 1862 this produced a rousing rendition of the popular tune *We Won't Go Home 'til Morning.*[76] The next day the Indianapolis correspondent for New York's *Home Journal* filed a report in which he asked proudly, "Is it now worthwhile to play 'In the provinces'?"

During a May 1863 visit to Boston, Strakosch went so far as to supplement the troupe with the Brito Brothers, an eleven-year-old violinist and a seven-year-old cornetist. This was too much for John Sullivan Dwight, who judged as "most unnatural" the sight of a seven-year-old playing a cornet nearly as big as himself. "Why should such an infant blow himself bodily through such an instrument?" Dwight asked. But the crowd loved it.[77]

To succeed, Strakosch fought over every cent and engaged in whatever hucksterism he deemed necessary. In the process, the role of impresario-manager was diminished. Max (Strakosch) the Nervous Wreck replaced Max (Maretzek) the Magnificent. Gottschalk still considered Strakosch a "fine fellow" but bridled under his fanatical devotion to making money. A reporter described this strange man as "always in a state of vibration: as a tongue forever in motion and a body never at rest. . . . He has a pronounced foreign accent. When speaking, his voice runs over the entire gamut, only stopping at C-sharp above the lines."[78]

Increasingly, critics attacked Strakosch for presenting Gottschalk in the company of inferior talent.[79] Even the *New York Times* joined the assault, assailing Strakosch for "having made a fortune off the genius of Gottschalk," then using the money to buy a ruined castle in his native Moravia and outfitting himself with the phony title of Baron Max von Strakosch.[80]

Ada Clare. Bancroft Library,
Berkeley, California.

Pages from the travel notebooks.
Gottschalk Collection, New York Public
Library.

Commercial Hotel in St. Thomas, where Gottschalk performed in 1857.
Donald Thompson, "Gottschalk in the Virgin Islands," *Anuario interamericano de Investigacion Musical,* 1970, p. 109.

Firmin Moras, sketch by Gottschalk.
Gottschalk Collection, New York Public
Library.

Ada Clare on the stage. Harvard Theatre Collection.

Baron Philippe Régis Denis de Trobriand, edit
and friend, as Union Army Colonel. *The Guns
1862, The Image of War, 1861-1865*, William
Davis, ed., New York, 1982, 2:164.

Violinist José White of Matanzas,
Cuba. Museo de la Música, Havana.

Manuscript for Marcha Triumfal from Gottschalk's opener *Charles*
Museo de la Música, Havana.

Gottschalk in 1862, by Matthew B. Brady, New York. Collection of the author.

Max Strakosch, Gottschalk's manager.
New York Public Library.

Gaston, Edward, and Moreau Gottschalk,
Saratoga, July, 1863. Glover Collection.

Gottschalk in 1863. Collection of the author.

The Illustrated News, vision of debauched Bohemians at Pfaff's. Museum
of the City of New York.

Gottschalk in 1863. Glover Collection.

A Chickering piano, 1865.
Smithsonian Institution.

Carlotta Patti. New York Public Library.

Gottschalk's crony, tenor Pasquale Brignoli.
Glover Collection.

LOUIS M. GOTTSCHALK,
PRINCE OF PIANO-FORTE.

"Prince of Piano-Forte," *Vanity Fair*, 11 October 1862.
New-York Historical Society.

Gottschalk and friends at Saratoga Springs. Glover Collection.

Poster for a concert in Utica, New York, 1863. Offergeld Collection.

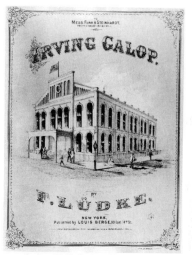

Irving Hall, Irving Place, New York. Museum of the City of New York.

Gottschalk at the time of the Irving Hall concerts. Free Library of Philadelphia.

Triumphant in Boston, 1864. Glover Collection.

Gottschalk with daughters of Louis G. Curlett, Baltimore, 1864. Gottschalk Collection, New York Public Library.

Gaston Gottschalk as a student, 1863. Glover Collection.

Norman Hall, Sandusky, Ohio, built in 1855. Follett House Museum, Sandusky, Ohio.

Cover page to *The Union*, 1863. Collection of the author.

Emanuele Muzio, Verdi's friend and Gottschalk's impresario. New York Public Library.

Medal awarded to Gottschalk in San Francisco, 1865. Glover Collection.

Oakland Female College. *Business Directory of the Pacific Coast, San Francisco, 1871, p. 53.*

The tenor Giovanni Sbriglia, who drew Gottschalk into the Oakland fiasco. Harvard University Theatre Collection.

Ricardo Luis Fors, 1867. Glover Collection.

Gottschalk in Lima. Glover Collection.

...omas Chickering, as a Colonel in the
...ion Army. Glover Collection.

Steamship *Colorado*, on which Gottschalk fled San Francisco.
Bancroft Library, University of California, Berkeley.

Gottschalk performing his Tremolo. Henrique Fleuss, *A Semana Illustrada*, 4 July 1869.

Ricardo Ferreira de Carvalho, student of Marmontel in Paris, colleague of Gottschalk. Glover Collection.

Emperor and patron, Dom Pedro II of Brazil. Bertita Harding, *Amazon Throne, The Story of the Braganzas of Brazil*, New York, 1941, p. 280.

"Did Gottschalk's concert make a profit of $25,800?" "What a guess. It was probably more, since there were boxes that held 85 people!" Henrique Fleuss, *A Semana Illustrada*, 5 December 1869.

Dr. Severiano Rodriguez Martins as the Roman god of healing, Esculapius. Lange, *Vida y Muerta*, no. 5/6.

Gottschalk in Rio de Janeiro. Angelo Agostini, *A Vida Fluminense*, 12 July 1869, New York
Public Library.

Gottschalk in Rio de Janeiro. *Ba-ta-clan*, 19 June 1869.

Gottschalk conducts 56 pianists playing the March from *Tannhäuser*, 5 October 1869. Angelo Agostini, *A Vida Fluminense*, 2 October 1869, New York Public Library.

Bennett Hotel, Tijuca, Brazil. Glover Collection.

Last portrait, December, 1869. Collection of the author.

The Civil War rendered Gottschalk's breakneck tours infinitely more arduous than they would otherwise have been. The war was a ubiquitous presence in every city in which Gottschalk performed, and even along the rail lines connecting them. Beginning with his encounter with the wounded veterans of the Battle of Shiloh at St. Louis in 1862, the national suffering was constantly before his eyes. In Lockport, New York, he encountered an old man in tears as he waited for the return of the body of his son killed at Shiloh. Reviews of Gottschalk's 1863 concerts in Indianapolis were intermingled with lists of Union dead and a poem entitled *A Wife's Wail.*[81] Over the entire period of this visit, fighting between Unionists and "Copperhead" Southern sympathizers was common on the streets of Indianapolis, as were patriotic meetings.[82]

The New York race riots of April 1863 blew up in the same section of lower Manhattan in which Gottschalk was living. Then in July of that year the violent draft riots sent Gottschalk racing back to New York from Portsmouth, New Hampshire.[83] His concerns were justified, for a colored orphanage only a few blocks from George Henriques's house at 149 West 14th Street had burned to the ground, and black New Yorkers were being beaten in the same neighborhood until finally the Governor imposed martial law.

In the course of his travels Moreau visited the Springfield arsenal in Massachusetts and several military facilities elsewhere. At the time he was performing in Chicago in December 1863, the first units of African-American soldiers were being mustered only a few doors from the concert hall. When he later fled to Baltimore in order to rest, he found himself in a city torn asunder by the war. "[Here one encounters] arrests, denunciations, [and] fathers who have remained faithful to the government burning to see their rebel sons whom they know are at the gates of the city, and fearing to compromise themselves by sending them even one word of affection." As Gottschalk tried to rest, Confederate troops burned the Governor's country house nearby.[84] Soon after this, on the platform at Bethlehem, Pennsylvania, he observed conscripts parting from their wives and children and described the sorrowful scene in detail.[85] And when he visited Hampton Roads, Virginia, late in the war he found a conquered and brutalized country.[86]

Gottschalk was soon drawn into the conflict more directly. Received everywhere as a Republican on account of his *The Union,* he was universally praised by Republican newspapers, including German-language sheets like the *Westliche Press* in St. Louis. Conversely, Democratic papers treated him with extreme coolness.[87]

Carlo Patti embroiled the company in some of its most serious political conflicts. Shortly after he premiered *Dixie* in New Orleans, Carlo volunteered for service in the Confederate army. After only a few weeks spent as a signal corpsman in Mobile, he tired of this and boarded a blockade runner for Havana, only to be captured by a Federal gunboat and taken prisoner. Strakosch engineered his release, but the story soon spread that the dashing violinist remained a Confederate sympathizer. At Buffalo, New York, a newspaper picked up this rumor at the time of Gottschalk's concerts in November 1863. Two hours after the newspaper hit the stands, the local marshal appeared at Gottschalk's hotel to arrest Patti. Fortunately, he produced his citizenship papers, the marshal left, and a planned demonstration at that evening's concert failed to materialize. But the matter did not end there, for a fresh crop of stories appeared, these claiming that Carlo had been an officer on General Beauregard's staff. This made him a hero in places like St. Louis and Cincinnati, where pro-Southern sentiment was strong, but it added an element of tension to concerts elsewhere.[88]

It was probably fortunate that Carlo Patti was not with the company on March 24, 1864, when Gottschalk performed for President and Mrs. Lincoln at Willard's Hall. The papers were full of reports that free people of color in Louisiana were petitioning Lincoln to confirm their civil rights.[89] And at Ford's Theater, tragedian Edwin Forrest was performing in *The Octoroon, or Life in Louisiana,* a tear-jerker that dealt with the same theme.[90] It was therefore fitting at that moment for the President to pay his respects to a Louisiana artist who had sided with the Union.

Lincoln impressed Gottschalk as "remarkably ugly, but with an intelligent air, and his eyes have a remarkable expression of goodness and mildness." Gottschalk claimed to have played very badly and was furious with himself, but the critic for the *Daily Morning Chronicle* declared that he had never played better. Two nights later General U. S. Grant and his entire staff attended a Gottschalk gala at Grover's Theatre, near Willard's Hotel on Pennsylvania Avenue.[91]

The closest Gottschalk came to the fighting front was in June 1863, when Strakosch and his troupe found themselves in Williamsport, Pennsylvania, at the very moment Lee's three columns surged into the state on their way to what was to be the Battle of Gettysburg. Tension was high on the streets of Williamsport as a pitiful five-man band rallied the citizenry. Nonetheless, Gottschalk's concert took place without hitch on June 15. The next morning he set out by train for Harrisburg.

By now everyone was convinced that Lee planned to march directly on the Pennsylvania capital. Everyone but Strakosch. When Gottschalk asked Strakosch whether a conflict between two of the greatest armies in history might not provide grounds for canceling the concert, his stubborn manager objected. They therefore boarded the overloaded passenger train, which forged on toward Harrisburg. Troops finally halted the train as it passed over the long wooden bridge spanning the Susquehanna. Confederate snipers were hiding on the riverbanks, so the passengers huddled in the aisles to avoid their bullets. Gottschalk and Strakosch eventually made their way by foot back to the depot. There, as thousands of Union infantry massed in the nearby streets, Strakosch finally admitted, "Decidedly, our concert is done for."[92]

Under such circumstances, it is a wonder that Gottschalk's concerts took place at all, let alone that they succeeded so brilliantly. Yet nearly everywhere the response was the same. A concert in Utica was "the grandest musical treat to which a Utica audience has listened,"[93] and a Dayton, Ohio, audience was judged to be "by far the most appreciative ever assembled."[94]

Over time, Gottschalk identified towns and cities that were particularly sympathetic to him. Baltimore ranked first, along with Philadelphia and—after he had subdued Mr. Dwight—Boston. Providence, Rhode Island, supported him so strongly that he reciprocated with a composition, now lost, entitled *Souvenir of Providence*.[95] Portland, Maine, and Syracuse, New York, also received him warmly, even though he had no personal friends in either city.[96] Gottschalk also jotted down notes on unusually successful performances in some very small towns, including Rutland, Vermont, and Oswego, New York, where he seems always to have played with pleasure.[97]

There were more than a few failures. At Rome, New York, he faced an empty hall and vowed never to go there again.[98] Manchester, New Hampshire, turned out only fourteen auditors, even though laudatory poems had been addressed to Gottschalk the night before in nearby Nashua. The audience in London, Ontario, numbered only thirty-one, counting Firmin Moras and the tuner.[99] In Wilmington, Delaware, a mere eight tickets were sold.[100]

To his credit, Gottschalk did his best even for small audiences. Yet he chided himself for "a very poor concert" in Troy, New York, and for a "detestable" performance in Schenectady.[101] In Plattsburg, New York, a critic lambasted Gottschalk for playing "very little pleasant and agreeable music—about three cents' worth as near as we could estimate. The remainder of the capital we invested in concert tickets is a Dead Loss."[102]

Such failures are scarcely surprising, considering the formidable obstacles he sometimes faced. At Erie, Pennsylvania, and in Adrian, Michigan, audiences were angered by the ticket price of one dollar. Members of the audience in the latter town indicated their preference for "a good Negro show."[103] In Sandusky, Ohio, the audience disconcerted him by whistling, and at Lockport, New York, by hissing.[104] Gottschalk judged the audience at Toledo, Ohio, to be "stupid," but this was mild in comparison with New Jersey, where in city after city the audience was all but non-existent. "New Jersey," he concluded, "is the poorest place to give concerts in the whole world except Central Africa. . . . New Jersey is incurable."[105]

The ordeal of touring left Gottschalk frequently out of sorts, and occasionally downright rude. After what he thought had been a successful concert in Burlington, Vermont, the local press regretted that he had been in so bad a humor that he did not even complete the announced program.[106] He himself admitted to having been brusque toward the audience in Elmira, New York. At Stratford, Connecticut, he went out of his way to anger the audience. There, with the small public sitting in stony silence, he gave a "deplorable" concert, dispatching eight pieces in a mere twenty-five minutes. "Short and sweet," remarked one young woman as she left the hall. "A great deal shorter than sweet," grumbled her beau.[107] Only rarely did local critics acknowledge that their fellow townspeople may have been partly to blame for such fiascoes. One to do so was a Clevelander, who confessed that the public's indifference extended to all performers and not just Gottschalk.[108] This must have been scant consolation for a grim evening.

On top of all these trials, Gottschalk had to attend constantly to family matters while touring. During the autumn of 1862 his sisters were causing him particular concern. At one point we find him trying (successfully) to talk Blanche out of entering a convent.[109] Clara meanwhile had developed an ovarian tumor, and the whole family, fearing for her life, was urging Moreau to return at once to Paris.[110] He could not, of course, and had to learn by letter of her slow recovery after surgery to remove the thirty-pound tumor.[111]

Scarcely was this crisis behind him than it was discovered that his brother Edward, now aged twenty-six, was suffering from tuberculosis. This time there was no question that Moreau had to take charge, and so in January 1863, accompanied by his younger brother Gaston, Edward arrived in New York, too weak even to leave his shipboard berth.[112] Moreau's first reaction was to charge that Edward's affliction was caused by his "incurable laziness."[113] But Edward was dying, and Moreau put aside all past differences in order to serve his brother. Moreau took him and Gaston to Saratoga, where the three Gottschalk brothers for the first and last time sat together for a photograph. In moving letters to each of his sisters Moreau prepared them for the end. He spent the final weeks in constant vigil at Edward's bedside. After Edward died on September 28, 1863, Moreau dressed him in his own concert outfit and arranged for a funeral at St. Stephen Church on 28th Street.[114]

Yet a third burden on the thirty-four-year-old Gottschalk was his high-spirited younger brother, Gaston. At the time of his arrival from Paris, Gaston barely spoke English and, in Moreau's judgment, suffered from "pathetic ignorance" overall.[115] Gottschalk naively believed that he could establish his brother in a clerkship, but this proved impossible.[116] He therefore sent him up the Hudson to the Poughkeepsie Military Institute, a secondary school noted for its strict regimen. This turned out to be beneficial, and by July 1864 Gaston had graduated and was burning to enlist with the Union army. Moreau was appalled and told his sisters that it was easier to imagine that he himself would be named Pope than that this "baby" could become a soldier.[117] At length, Moreau persuaded his publisher William Hall & Son to hire the young man as a clerk. In due course this arrangement, too, came unraveled for the simple reason that Gaston, like his sisters, wanted to follow Moreau in a musical career. But for the time being Gaston was employed and out of harm's way.[118]

Piled on top of these burdens were Moreau's ever mounting concerns over finances. Not only was he the sole provider for all his grown siblings, but members of the Bruslé family in occupied New Orleans were pleading for help, claiming that they would soon be begging if he did not come to their aid.[119] In the early war years this presented no problem, for as Moreau told his sisters in December 1863, money had never been more plentiful.[120] With his profits, he even purchased a house at 209 East 31st Street in New York and began investing in stocks with the advice of his cousin Congressman Leonard Myers.[121] His expenses were enormous, however, often reaching twelve hundred dollars a week. If receipts were down, as sometimes happened, Strakosch could not pay him.[122] A far more aggravating problem was the rising inflation, which drove up prices for all consumer products and services except, apparently, concert tickets. This, along with heavy taxes levied to support the war, meant that for most of the year 1863 Gottschalk saved nothing.[123]

Yet more crippling was the skyrocketing price of gold, which he had to purchase in order to buy the French francs he sent to his sisters. By spring 1864 Gottschalk was paying twice as many dollars as a year earlier for the French francs he remitted to Paris.[124] By September 1864 he had determined to leave the United States by winter, since "the question of money keeps my nose to the grindstone."[125]

Since his return from Havana, Moreau had lived extravagantly, responding to every appeal for contributions and even sending a set of elaborately tooled rifles from the Broadway firm of Ball, Black & Company to his old friends at the Havana Gun Club.[126] Within two years, however, he was again living from hand to mouth and complaining bitterly. "Without this war I'd be rich and in Europe," he wrote to his sisters. "Gold has cursed me."[127]

Whose health would not have broken under the tribulations created by incessant touring, the hardships of war, and relentless family and financial worries? Nearly every letter written by Gottschalk during the Civil War opens with an update on his health. For the first years they were generally positive, with only occasional bulletins announcing "health below zero."[128] The second Western tour and the impending arrival of Edward and Gaston in early 1863 produced severe attacks of neuralgia in one eye, which forced Moreau to cancel several concerts.[129] Following Edward's death in September of that year Gottschalk was again ill for a month, and also depressed, with no will to do anything beyond looking in occasionally at rehearsals of the Philharmonic Society.[130] By December 1863 he was complaining of nervous strain and chronic fatigue,[131] and shortly afterwards of a buzzing in the ears.[132] His old intestinal disorders also flared up again. Constantly on the move and with no doctors at hand, he treated himself with rhubarb and endless doses of Doctor Seidlitz's Powders.[133]

By 1863 Gottschalk was living on the brink of a nervous breakdown. He complained about "swirling in space" and "distressing monotony."[134] The very sight of a piano gave him nausea, and he ruefully recalled the Alexandre Dumas *fils* story of the man who was forced to eat quail for a month and nearly died.[135] This was the period in which he showed rudeness to audiences and despaired over his fate generally. "So many dead illusions!" he wrote.[136]

Battered by worries and poor health, even Gottschalk's physical appearance began to change. Traveling in New York State, he confessed that he was feeling "old and ugly." Gray hairs began to appear during his thirty-third year, and his former vanity revived only to the degree necessary to record in his notes the progress of baldness. All this was noticeable to his public. A critic for the *Chicago Evening Journal* informed the public, "Gottschalk looks worn and weary," while a Cleveland critic noted that he had grown "crotchety."[137]

Arriving in Philadelphia at two o'clock one morning in June 1863, Gottschalk set down his mental state in words applicable to his entire three years of touring: "We are in Philadelphia. Fifteen and a half hours of railroad in one day, not to mention our emotions! The devil take the poets who dare to sing the pleasures of an artist's life."[138]

By sheer fortitude and endurance Gottschalk not only survived this ordeal but provided solace and joy to hundreds of thousands of Northerners whose sons, husbands, and neighbors were dying at the front. Never before had Gottschalk succeeded in reaching so broad a slice of the

American population. At a concert in Utica, New York, the local critic noticed that the house was filled with "gentlemen and ladies from Waterville, Paris, Boonville, Middleville, as well as the villages nearby."[139] He not only drew such ordinary people into the hall, but he left them whistling the melodies they had heard, as was noted in Brooklyn, Québec, and elsewhere.[140]

The Union continued to be Gottschalk's patriotic staple, but he supplemented it with a resounding caprice based on George F. Root's *Battle Cry of Freedom*. A lesser polka entitled *Drums and Cannon* exuded the same patriotic fervor.

A series of new operatic fantasies gave average Americans glimpses of a cosmopolitan culture beyond their national borders. Adaptations of both the march and waltz from Gounod's *Faust* appeared on programs at this time, as did a fantasia based on Weber's *Oberon* (op. 82), the grand march from Wagner's *Tannhäuser*, and a colorful transcription of the duet from Verdi's *Un Ballo in Maschera*. All who heard these works acknowledged them to be the equal of Gottschalk's *William Tell* transcription.[141]

More purely classical works in Gottschalk's wartime repertoire included piano settings of two movements from Mendelssohn's *Scottish Symphony* and of Scandinavian composer Niels Gade's *Im Hochland*, both composed for the relatively sophisticated public of Philadelphia.

Nothing is more surprising than to see some of Gottschalk's most exuberant Caribbean pieces on programs offered in small-town America, including the concert in Utica to which all those people from neighboring villages thronged. The rag-like *Pasquinade* made its North American debut during these years, as did the many new *contradanza-* and habanera-based compositions. *Ojos criollos* was among his most frequently programmed compositions, and it invariably drew an enthusiastic response from audience and critics. In light of subsequent developments in American music, this bears special emphasis.

Syncopated music and ragtime are often seen as having exploded full-blown in the United States before an astonished public in the late 1890s. However, two generations before this, Moreau Gottschalk had prepared the soil as he performed his own Caribbean-inspired syncopated works before a thousand audiences across Civil War America.

When the public at Norton's Hall in Burlington, Vermont, heard him play *Ojos criollos* on April 26, 1864, it learned of a type of music far different from anything it had known before. Neither *Ojos criollos* nor any other Gottschalk composition can be considered ragtime, which is no surprise considering that Scott Joplin was not yet born. Yet the distance between Gottschalk and Joplin is far less than the gulf separating

Gottschalk from his own musical predecessors in the "American" genre. Thanks to the thousands of concerts presented by Gottschalk during the Civil War, Americans got a strong foretaste of what was to come. By injecting a new syncopated element into American popular music, he changed fundamentally the aural world in which the next generation of urban Americans, both audiences and musicians, existed.

A number of new polkas, waltzes, and schottisches written in the familiar salon genre were also addressed to the public's appetite for vital and exuberant music. The sparkling *Radieuse* (op. 72) and *La Brise* waltzes, and presumably the lost *Unidalla Waltz*, all fit this niche, as did the polkas *La Colombe* (op. 49), *Orfa* (op. 71) and *Polka rédowa* (op. 68). *The Maiden's Blush* (op. 106) was a particularly attractive example of this genre, with a suspenseful introduction followed by a lilting Chopinesque waltz.

Interestingly, few popular songs other than patriotic ones figured prominently in Gottschalk's wartime repertoire. The two exceptions were both unabashedly sentimental, *The Last Rose of Summer* and the evergreen *Home, Sweet Home*. Both were in frequent demand by the public. With their lyrics of love and loss known to every member of the audience, these narrative songs embodied the more tender sentiments that united battlefront and home front, North and South, throughout the Civil War.

Also prominent in Gottschalk's wartime repertoire were his own newly written compositions for voice and piano. Cast in the form of narrative ballads with words by his friend Henry C. Watson, such songs as *My Only Love, Goodbye!* and *Oh Loving Heart, Trust On!* spoke directly to experiences common to thousands in his audience. Yet none was written for amateurs to sing casually around the piano, as could so easily be done with *Home, Sweet Home* or *The Last Rose of Summer*. All were art songs, composed for performance by operatic professionals. The most elaborate of these works, *The Shepherdess and the Knight*, based on Gottschalk's earlier piano piece *Pastorella e cavalliere*, never failed to evoke favorable comment from critics but was too demanding for the amateur public, which bought only a few hundred copies of the sheet music.[142]

Another song adapted from an earlier piano piece from Cuba was the berceuse *Slumber On, Baby Dear*. Now outfitted with words by the indefatigable Henry C. Watson, *Slumber On, Baby Dear* retained the basic melody deriving from the French lullaby *Fais dodo*. As sung by Carlotta Patti at dozens of concerts, it invariably faded away amidst muffled sobs from the audience.[143]

The success of Gottschalk's sentimental compositions from the Civil War years owed much to the fact that he himself shared the emotional world they described. Each of these pieces embodied a moment in his own emotional biography, whether it was a romantic episode, as in *My Only Love, Goodbye!* and *Pensez à moi,* or the experience of loss and commemoration, as in his *Ave Maria,* composed to honor his late mother.

Of all Gottschalk's compositions from the Civil War years, none had such deeply personal origins as his *The Dying Poet,* and none came close to gaining the huge and enduring popularity of this one. If *The Union* expressed Gottschalk's stance vis-à-vis the nation's crisis, *The Dying Poet* expressed Gottschalk's sense of the impact of that crisis on his own life.

In form, *The Dying Poet* could not be simpler. A sixteen-measure melody in six-eight time is played twice. Then follows a Chopinesque bridge, also of sixteen measures, after which the original melody sounds again. A development section then unfolds, modulating upward until the melody re-emerges, this time played in the treble in eighth notes; this was the infamous passage that later became a staple of the much lampooned "nickelodeon" style. The piece ends with the melody played in the left hand as the eighth-note accompaniment slowly fades in the right.

This brief composition promptly went through dozens of editions in virtually every country where music was published in the nineteenth century. Like *The Last Hope,* it was also transformed into a Protestant hymn.[144]

Was *The Dying Poet* a clichéd potboiler written to capture a market niche? It eventually sank to the status of a trite old warhouse after being immensely popular for forty years. Its rich-hued sentimentality, like that of Victorian architecture, became cloying to the sensibilities of the aspiring modernists of 1910. Yet at the time Gottschalk composed it, *The Dying Poet* conveyed genuine emotions through highly expressive techniques. Moreover, *The Dying Poet* was not written merely to seize an opportunity presented by the marketplace. On the contrary, Gottschalk treated it with high seriousness and deep sincerity.

In its musical conception, *The Dying Poet* hearkens directly to Chopin, and especially to his Nocturne in E-flat. Its "text" also derives from French romanticism of an earlier age, specifically from the works of Charles-Hubert Millevoye and Alfonse de Lamartine. Millevoye's *Le Poète mourant* had been published in the same collection of elegies from which Gottschalk had drawn *Le Mancenillier* and *La Chute des feuilles:*[145]

> O my friends! You who were so dear to me.
> Give shelter to the legacy of my flawed songs.
> Rescue from oblivion a few of my verses.

Lamartine's *Le Poète mourant* contained the same sentiments, but evoked the arch-romantic image of the wanderer, so appropriate to Gottschalk's own life during the Civil War:

> The poet passes like the birds of passage o'er,
> Who never stay, nor build their nests upon the shore;
> Nor ever on the boughs within the forest dwell;
> But heedless, cradled on the waves' inconstant flow,
> Pass, singing, far from shore;
> Of whom the world doth know
> Not than their voice alone may tell.[146]

Was Gottschalk aware that these lines had been translated by a back-woods American lawyer in the town of Charleston, Illinois, in 1862, immediately before he composed his piece? Did that rustic litterateur, Henry P. H. Bromwell, perhaps bring his translation to Gottschalk's attention after attending a concert in Springfield or Indianapolis? The record is silent. Yet there can be no doubt that both Millevoye's and Lamartine's verses, with their implication that life's most creative moments had passed, fit Gottschalk's perception of his own circumstances with unsettling precision. Cut off from the Southern sources of his inspiration yet committed to his new environment in the North, Gottschalk seems to have sensed that the decay of his creative powers had begun.

Chapter Twenty-two

America Through Gottschalk's Eyes

SOPRANO Carlotta Patti surely knew Gottschalk as well as anyone did. She toured with him for several years and, after his death, had his coffin opened in order to pay her last respects. So it is of more than passing interest that she once quipped that he was interested only in music, money, and sex.[1] Music? Of course. And the preoccupation with money was undeniable, for he was the sole provider for six siblings. But sex?

The American-born soprano Clara Louise Kellogg echoed Patti's judgment, calling Gottschalk a "gay deceiver whom women were crazy about." She recalled Gottschalk and Brignoli comparing their latest love letters following a matinee concert. One young woman asked Gottschalk for a meeting at any spot he would designate. Brignoli bet Gottschalk that she would not show up if he would specify for their rendezvous so unromantic a place as a ferry landing. Gottschalk gleefully took the bet, and won.[2]

There is no doubt that Gottschalk flirted his way across Civil War America. He never failed to spot an attractive female face in the crowd, and his travel diaries have their share of penciled notes testifying to his activity in the romantic realm. On one page he reminds himself to send a photograph to Camilla Rhodes in Providence; elsewhere he notes the address of a Miss Reed in Geneva, New York, and of Mme. Hull in Elmira.[3] One such entry, written on July 22, 1863, on the train headed for Oswego, New York, records an exchange between Moreau and a certain Mary Raymond of Buffalo, with the conversants penciling in their words so as not to tip off fellow passengers:

    (M.R.)   I love M. G. He does not love me.

    (L.M.G.)   I would be the happiest man in the world if I could believe you.

(M.R.)	Put to a test . . .
(L.M.G.)	Your aunt . . .
(M.R.)	Do not tell her of anything and you will see with a little patience that I'm not fooling you.
(L.M.G.)	You are my little angel. I dreamt of you every night. I will be thinking constantly of the happy time I will have if I can find you somewhere this summer.
(M.R.)	You must come to Buffalo . . .
(L.M.G.)	I would prefer Saratoga on account of the nights.[4]

Does this prove Carlotta Patti's claim? All these scraps of evidence together do little more than establish that Gottschalk amused himself by flirting. In this regard he was still a Parisian dandy. When his friend Offenbach came to the United States, he noted with genuine surprise the "strange fact that no one in New York or in any other city in the United States would venture to take up his line and march behind a youthful Yankee maiden, and still less to speak to her."[5] Gottschalk did both. But little more. Even his arch-critic Dwight noted that in public he assumed an air of being "either indifferent or absorbed . . . and this does not suit our haughty belles, who require homage in return for their devotion."[6] While there is ample testimony to Gottschalk's flirtatiousness, there is scant evidence that he was a libertine.

Various rumors regarding Gottschalk's impending marriage circulated from time to time. One, possibly linked with his fellow train passenger Mary Raymond, referred to a rich heiress whom Gottschalk had met in Saratoga in the summer of 1863.[7] Moreau spoke of this rumor in a letter to Espadero: "I am not married yet. I don't even intend to, although if I wished I could marry tomorrow (confidential) with two million pesos!!— and she is pretty!—and well educated! But I am dissuaded from giving pretexts to slanderous envy."[8] A year later another such rumor arose and then died away. About this time Moreau dedicated his song *O, Loving Heart, Trust On!* to "the fair Turkish maiden Oseilu Lylcek," an anagram for Louise Kelly, possibly the lady in question.[9] As the *New York Times* explained, "Gottschalk is too shy; he has been frightened by the premature announcement, and fears that the world would accuse him of marrying for money."[10]

Once again, his world was proscribed by the sense of duty his father had inculcated in him. His task in life was to work endlessly to earn money for the family, not to fulfill himself. In this context even sex posed a threat, as the affair with Ada Clare had shown. Casual flirtations with young innocents were the sole relations with women that did not jeopardize his almost neurotic devotion to his duty as he understood it. That such encounters did not threaten him sexually may also have been important.

The strongest argument against the fairness of Carlotta Patti's characterization of Gottschalk is the massive evidence on the extent to which his attention was absorbed by events and people in the world around him. A staff member of the touring group recorded that Moreau was constantly reading or writing on the train.[11] Confirming this, bohemian Henry Clapp Jr. wrote of Gottschalk's passionate interest in social and political issues of the day.[12] Corroborating this, too, are the dozens of articles on his travels that he filed with newspapers in New York and Paris and that formed the core of his *Notes of a Pianist*. Indeed, these observations are rich with insights on Gottschalk's perspective on America during the Civil War and provide one of the fullest and most detailed assessments of the life and culture of the United States by any American musician or artist of that era.

Inevitably, the Civil War was Gottschalk's daily companion and constant concern. He encountered it through the parents and wives of soldiers in his audiences and through the troops he met on the trains. Within months of his return from Havana he was already denouncing the conflagration as "our monstrous war."[13] He wrote to Espadero: "Half the Union is bloody, and the other half is aflame." By 1864 he was describing the war as a descent into barbarism:

> We have invented a 'wild-fire' which propels flames for more than six miles. . . . Our hospitals are filled with the sick and wounded. Our cities are overflowing with the maimed, blind, lame, horrible, and glorious remnants of our heroic Army. Our national debt already surpasses that of England. A people who promised to be the greatest on earth has fallen to the same level as the Spanish republics![14]

To his sisters he wrote of the war's horrors and predicted a gloomy future for the country.[15] And as he found himself caught up in the mobilization for Gettysburg, with his cousins from the North and South about to face each other in gory battle, he commented simply, "I do not like war."[16]

As a Southerner who supported the North, Gottschalk became a powerful symbol of the conflict, pulled in two directions at once. He maintained close contact with his pro-Confederate cousin Edward G. Gottschalk in New Orleans, yet he also corresponded with a Union officer assigned the task of pacifying the conquered city.[17] He respected Southern heroism yet despised those of his section who were so rabid in their views that "one can no more discuss the issues with them than with madmen."[18]

Gottschalk's pro-Union sympathies were grounded in far more than mere self-interest. The South, he believed, was fighting a rearguard action against one of the great movements of the nineteenth century, namely, the tendency of all nationalities toward unification. In an age when such countries as Italy and Germany were uniting, disunion made no sense at all. Beyond this, the South proposed to destroy "one of the most beautiful political monuments of modern times—the American Union," and this in the name of slavery. "It is unbecoming indeed for my fellow-citizens of the South to ask for the liberty of reclaiming their independence," he wrote, "when this independence is to be made use of only for the conservation of the most odious of abuses and the most flagrant outrage upon liberty." This, in turn, related to what Gottschalk took to be another first principle of politics, namely, that "no one fraction of a people has the right to reclaim its autonomy if it does not carry with it greater guarantees of progress in civilization than those of the majority enslaving it." Measuring the South by this standard, Gottschalk concluded that the Confederate cause was wrong.[19]

In March 1863 Gottschalk's cousin Leonard Myers was elected to Congress as a Republican from Philadelphia. "He deserves it," Moreau wrote to his sisters. "No one in the House of Representatives is more worthy than our good and talented cousin."[20] In the wake of this family success, Moreau came more directly to support the Republican cause and President Lincoln. He had admired Lincoln from the moment he learned that the Railsplitter had pardoned a young soldier of the Army of the Potomac who had been court-martialed and condemned to death for sleeping on duty.[21] He had also admired General George B. McClellan, however, and long expected him to succeed Lincoln in the presidency. This expectation on Gottschalk's part persisted even after Lincoln removed McClellan from his command of the Union army and after half the country accused this commander of indecision and poor leadership.[22]

Whether or not he knew of General U. S. Grant's anti-Semitic views, Gottschalk came eventually to respect this stern warrior as well, even dedicating a composition, the *Hurrah Galop*, to him.[23] He also came out sharply against anti-war Democrats in New York and against the Knights of the Golden Circle in eastern Pennsylvania, both of whom wanted Lincoln to offer peace to the South.[24] That they based their case on constitutional grounds particularly incensed Gottschalk:

> "The Constitution as it was"—such is their cry. Fools that you are! The Constitution today has become impossible. It would be as unreasonable to require that a man should always wear the clothes of his boyhood and have his limbs shortened in order to accommodate them to his clothes.[25]

As his Republicanism deepened, Gottschalk become more vehement in his defense of the war. With evident pride he described to Espadero the ironclads being constructed to thwart the Confederate navy.[26] He also grew increasingly bitter toward Great Britain and other countries that supported the South. He unloaded his resentment to a Canadian friend, Sheldon Stephens, in a letter of August 1863. England, he charged, had two consciences, according to its interests: it supported freedom for black slaves when it judged that this would bring ruin to the French and Spanish colonies in the Caribbean, and it supported the enslavement of blacks in the American South when it judged that this would diminish its other rival, the government in Washington.[27]

The vehemence of Gottschalk's political convictions stunned more than one gathering during the Civil War years. At a dinner in New York, for example, he took on a Northerner who defended slavery and the South's right to secede. Said a friend who witnessed the encounter, "Gottschalk seemed to have had a spirit of fire descend upon him. He spoke rapidly, brilliantly, with such power, such sweeping eloquence . . . that tears filled my eyes—not mine alone, but all felt his power to uphold the right."[28]

An even more tumultuous outburst occurred in March 1863 at the Fifth Avenue home of William T. Blodgett, a wealthy businessman and art collector. The occasion was the installation in Blodgett's home of the monumental painting *Heart of the Andes* by Gottschalk's old friend Frederic Edwin Church. Painted in 1859, this canvas depicted a towering Andean peak with a dense tropical jungle brooding in the foreground. Here was an evocative celebration of the wild and elemental Americas, as opposed to "civilized" Europe. Here, finally, was a visual paean to the United States' Manifest Destiny. After a grand (and profitable) tour of Europe, the *Heart of the Andes* was exhibited at Goupil's Gallery on Broadway.[29] Both Gottschalk and his pianist friend George Warren studied it there and were so excited that Warren, apparently with Gottschalk's involvement, composed a window-rattling homage entitled *The Andes*.

Church's visual polemic in behalf of the United States' destiny in the Americas was then installed in Blodgett's salon, and a grand feast was organized to celebrate the event. Church was there, as were Warren and Gottschalk. Also present was the Marquis of Hartington, later the Duke of Devonshire, who had been burning up the Manhattan social scene for a month. Vehemently pro-Southern, Hartington had had the effrontery to show up at a masked ball sporting a Confederate flag in his buttonhole.[30] Days later he pulled the same trick at the White House. Lincoln reacted by addressing the good Marquis as "Mr. Partington."[31] Everyone present knew that Mrs. Partington was the fabled lady who had tried to hold back a rising ocean tide with her broom.

Inevitably, Blodgett asked Gottschalk to perform for his guests, and

Moreau obliged. During a pause between pieces Hartington renewed his campaign of insults, this time making a slur against American music.[32] Gottschalk was infuriated. "White as a sheet," as George Warren recalled, he rose to his feet to respond to the arrogant Britisher. But instead of arguing, Gottschalk began speaking calmly of a newly popular song written by his old Paris friend George Frederick Root. Root had written this piece to commemorate Lincoln's first call for volunteers. Entitled *Let's Rally 'Round the Flag, Boys!*, it gained immediate popularity. A contemporary declared that Root's song "put as much spirit and cheer into the army as a victory."[33] By year's end, sheet music of Root's hit was pouring from the presses.[34]

Gottschalk thought his friend's composition should be adopted as the national anthem.[35] Standing at his place at Blodgett's dinner table, he told the guests that this new melody was at that moment being sung by regiments marching down Broadway to embark for Washington. He told them that this melody would soon resound on the battlefield and would sustain the soldiers amidst the toughest fight. Then he sprang to the piano and performed an astounding rendition of *Let's Rally 'Round the Flag, Boys!* George Warren later recalled:

> I never heard anything like it, and never will again. . . . The effect was earth-quakian almost. These men of art were enthusiastic; and they were frantic. The uproar could have been heard a mile. Gottschalk was nearly killed with embraces—and the gentleman from England had departed.[36]

The Battle Cry of Freedom, based on Root's melody, became Gottschalk's second musical war-horse during the Civil War. With its simple *maestoso* statement of the theme, variations in double octaves, contrapuntal passages, and slow and lyrical interludes, it was, along with *The Union*, a musical declaration of Gottschalk's patriotism.

Given the fervor of Gottschalk's national feeling, the torrent of criticism he directed toward elements in the American public is all the more perplexing. Yet throughout his Civil War tours he was bombarded with impressions that led him to judge his compatriots with severity. This negative view began in the concert hall, as he responded to squeaky boots in Chicago and stage whispers from audiences in many other cities.[37] He was aghast at a member of the public who asked how many seconds it took for him to play Weber's *Perpetual Motion*.[38] Gottschalk ascribed all this to pure ignorance. How else to explain the mother and daughter in Zanesville, Ohio, who had no idea what piano pedals were, or the listener in Indianapolis who mistook his piano for a "big accordion"?[39] And what about those who were just plain hostile to music and musicians, people like the coachman in Norwalk, Connecticut, who refused to drive him and Carlo Patti when he saw the latter's violin case?[40] "Let us never listen to the public," he concluded, "[or] we should hang ourselves in despair."[41]

At the very least, Gottschalk wrote, the public was engulfed in "an envelope of indifference to foreign art which is peculiar to Americans."[42] Over and over he tried to explain to himself this lacuna in the American character. At one point he blamed it on the "stiff, starched gait" of Anglo-Saxons and their "lack of the pensive elements so indispensable in the arts."[43] Elsewhere, he blamed it on Americans' practicality, which allowed no room for the exercise of aesthetic impulses. Most frequently, however, he laid it to a rude and brutish quality which he found widespread in America.

When a snowball thrown by rowdies in Erie, Pennsylvania, scored a direct hit on his cheek, Gottschalk exclaimed, "How cruel and brutal the lower class Americans are!"[44] After observing a fellow passenger on the train picking his teeth with his penknife, Gottschalk bemoaned the "abuse that unruly and gross majorities exercise toward intelligent and polished minorities, whether it be in the railroad cars or in politics."[45] But unlike those who sought to rescue Americans through a dose of refinement, Gottschalk's concern was not with mere manners. Manners, he believed, reflected deeper values, and it was these that were amiss. He was not surprised that few people turned out for his concert in Newburgh, New York, for example, since the same public had just tolerated the lynching of an African-American man accused of raping a local Irish girl.[46] For Gottschalk, a developed aesthetic sense was incompatible with such barbarism.

Gottschalk traced the most brutal aspects of American character to alcohol. Soldiers swilled whiskey on the trains, and a reeking "professor" of music found solace in it for his failures as a pianist. Nor was alcoholism confined to the Western frontier. "I have never seen so many tipplers and drinking places, and consequently so many drunkards, as in Washington," he wrote.[47] Whiskey had coarsened Americans and brutalized them. The abstemious Moravian Brethren of Bethlehem, Pennsylvania, stood out as an exception. "This gives [Bethlehem] a place in my memory—a privileged place, the horror which I have for drunkenness not being equaled except by that which Mr. D[wight] has for my music."[48]

Besides the degradation of alcoholism, Gottschalk believed that American men had been brutalized by their "manly" notions of manners. Wild laughter "recalling the neighing of a horse" and the quick resort to violence were the natural consequences of the false notions of manliness widespread among American males.[49] This manly ideal would have reduced the country to primitive boorishness had it not been for the civilizing influence exercised by women. While critical of "emancipated" women and quick to ridicule followers of the notorious Mrs. Bloomer, with their "bloomer" pants, Gottschalk had high praise for the role females played in uplifting the men. "American women," he wrote, "with their delicate sentiments and the intelligence that our system of education develops, . . . will do more than all the legislators in the world to polish men. Without them, whiskey and the revolver would completely overrun us."[50] The very liberty that women enjoyed in the United States, he believed, freed them to exercise the civilizing influence that the society so desperately needed.[51]

This said, Gottschalk was sure that the beneficent influence of American women was due to nurture and not nature. For all his talk of how educated women meliorated the brutishness of their men, he stood in horror before the damage that women's unfettered and uncultivated passions could wreak on society. They were, he believed, good haters, and countless events during the Civil War confirmed him in this view. Friends in New Orleans told him how ladies in his native city were holding handkerchiefs to their noses as they passed occupying Union officers on the sidewalks. He also heard of young women in Baton Rouge who burst into laughter when the funeral procession of a fallen Federal officer passed them. And he recoiled at reports of "strong-minded women" in New England who demanded that those who sympathized with General McClellan's peace party should be hanged. "But for the women," he concluded,

> our Civil War would long ago have been ended. Through their imprudent zeal and the intemperance of their opinions which, in politics as in other things, carry them beyond their mark, they have on both sides contributed to foment the discord and to envenom the strife.[52]

If American men were too loutish and the women too fanatical in their passions to counteract the coarseness of life in the New World, could one expect salvation from any other quarter? Gottschalk was certain that it would not come from any of the various ethnic and immigrant groups. Of Native Americans he knew little beyond the Catlin paintings he had viewed in Paris and the portrait he saw of a Sioux chieftain who had "massacred two men, six women, and eighteen children" in Wisconsin.[53] African-Americans earned his sympathy, but he could not imagine them in conditions of equality. "I do not have any illusions regarding the Negro," he declared. "I believe them very inferior morally to the White, [for] no race so maltreated as this [could be otherwise]."[54]

Nor did Gottschalk hold out much hope for the new immigrants, especially the Irish. In his universe, Irishmen occupied the very bottom rank of humanity. From the lynching in Newburgh and other such incidents he concluded that "the most inveterate enemy of the blacks in the United States are the Irish." After a particularly offensive encounter with some drunken Hibernians on the railroad near Watertown, New York, Gottschalk stated flatly, "Decidedly, I do not like the Irish. They are a rude, ignorant, superstitious race."[55]

Gottschalk's views on the many German immigrants he encountered were more ambiguous. He poured ridicule on the omnipresent Teutonic "professor" of music, with his uncombed hair and inevitable gold spectacles, which Moreau assumed were perched on their noses from birth.[56] He fulminated against the fact that the Germans he met were slovenly, not to mention one in Toledo who threw up on him.[57] Yet he was equally quick to acknowledge the industriousness of German immigrants, and he credited them with the rapid development of Milwaukee, St. Louis, and other cities. He also admitted their role in establishing philharmonic societies in many places.

To deal with this ambiguity, Moreau conveniently referred to the countrymen of Goethe and Mendelssohn as "Germans" and to those "whose only characteristic traits of their mother country are love of beer, cordial hatred of every person who combs his hair regularly and sometimes washes his hands" as "Dutch."[58] Much as he respected Eichberg, the musical Mollenhauer brothers, and the pianist Kunkel from Cincinnati, he was sure that it was the "Dutch" rather than the "Germans" who set the tone in America.

How could so disparate a group of peoples ever come together, let alone be raised to some higher level of culture? What principle or institution could possibly link them and provide the needed uplift? Gottschalk found no evidence of a strong and civilizing folk culture that could play this role. Indeed, Gottschalk detected no generalized American folk culture at all. This is the more surprising since he was attuned since childhood to ferreting out such traditions. Thus, on a train near Toledo he listened with rapt interest to a Scotsman playing a flute in the Lydian mode.[59] Yet even if such fragments of folk culture were to be found here and there, they did not add up to a national culture of the common citizen, let alone one that could uplift American mores generally. As to the ubiquitous and popular blackface minstrelsy, Gottschalk did not consider it to be a folk idiom, even though many travelers from abroad did. To the extent he acknowledged minstrelsy at all he tended to view it as rude and barbarous.[60]

Beyond the absence of folk culture, Gottschalk saw America as lacking the many other conditions that might meliorate the harsh conditions of life. "We have no traditions in America," he explained to French read-

ers. "The worship of the past could not exist in a society born but yester-
day. . . . To look back at the past . . . is a luxury that only old societies
satiated with civilization and discounting the future can indulge in."[61]

Gottschalk gave the appearance of one who supported the Union
cause in principle but turned his back on its flesh-and-blood citizens,
whom he suspected of being boorish louts. Increasingly, he found himself
affirming an America that was far nobler in theory than practice and that
lacked the cultural resources necessary to close the gap between reality
and the ideal.

Could religion provide the unifying and elevating force that was so
badly needed? If by religion one meant Protestantism, Gottschalk vigorously denied it. He equated Protestantism with "concentrated boredom"
and in his *Notes* summarized a Sunday in Boston with the words "ennui,
ennui, ennui."[62] On another Sabbath in the Midwest he moaned, "Sunday
is always a splenetic day in all Protestant countries, but in Cleveland it is
enough to make you commit suicide."[63]

Gottschalk's particular *bête noire* was American prudishness, which
he traced to the influence of Protestantism. He railed against "puritanical
anatomy," which recognized only the feet and the head, but not the
body.[64] And he cheered whenever an upholder of such nonsense fell into
wayward paths. With particular relish he recounted the story of a Protestant minister in Joliet, Illinois, who had been horsewhipped by several
irate husbands.[65]

Seeking the source of the wrong-headed views of American Protestants,
Gottschalk placed the blame squarely on their "free interpretation of the Bible." Protestants manipulated Holy Writ to prove both that slavery was a
divine institution and that it was an abomination, that cigars are evil, and
that "all joy in life must be suppressed."[66] It was not enough that Protestants themselves believed such foolishness, but they felt obliged to impose
it on others. Armed with their Bibles, the militants sallied forth against their
fellow citizens in a "rage for conversion, a fever for proselytism, which con-
stitutes one of the characteristic traits of Americans."[67] He cursed such fa-
natics and wished them a cold-water cure.[68]

It was with sheer delight that Gottschalk recorded every scrap of evidence that puritan zeal was waning.[69] He carefully calculated the ratio of
churches to private dwellings in New London, Connecticut (one to ten), and
compared the situation there to what he experienced in New Haven, where
a large audience of Yale students and Episcopalians turned out for a concert during Lent.[70] But this in no way led Gottschalk to conclude that Protestantism could ever become an uplifting force for the country at large.

Catholicism held no greater promise. To be sure, Gottschalk himself
was a Catholic, and "full of religious sentiment," as one old friend charac-

terized him.[71] He often attended mass, and as his sister Clara faced her life-threatening operation he sought to reassure her with the consolations of faith.[72] But Gottschalk's Catholicism, formed in New Orleans and nurtured in Paris, assumed sermons of greater intellectuality and liturgical music of greater emotional depth than could be found in the immigrant Church of the northern United States.

Time after time Gottschalk voiced his complaints. He objected to the "screaming" of the priest in Auburn, New York, and to the "execrable music" at the same church.[73] A preacher in St. Louis struck him as "evidently intent on emitting the greatest number of words with the smallest possible number of ideas."[74] Such examples convinced Moreau that the Catholic Church could never enlighten the rough-hewn American people.

Was there, then, no hope for the United States? Gottschalk saw it as a raw new country with a diverse population drawn from the lower ranks of societies on Europe's cultural fringes. Dedicated to practical concerns of the moment, could such a population ever take more than a passing interest in what Gottschalk called "the domain of the aesthetics of art"? Acknowledging Americans' "clear and practical judgment and more than ordinary power to understand principles," Gottschalk nevertheless believed, they were easily led astray in artistic matters and quick to fall for the sensation of the moment.[75]

These were Moreau's heartfelt views. Yet he encountered so many exceptions to this gloomy picture that he had eventually to reformulate his conclusions on American culture as a whole. How, for example, could the pessimistic view stand up to the reality of Utica, New York? With a mere thirty thousand people, this town boasted a Mendelssohn Society and Academy of Music, beautifully designed churches with splendid organs built by a local craftsman, three newspapers, and a model insane asylum.[76] Then there were the many towns far smaller than Utica, places founded only seven or eight years earlier, where three or four hundred people would turn out for performances by Gottschalk and his operatic troupe.[77] And, finally, there were the great cities like Philadelphia, with its sophisticated audience, and even doughty Boston. Surely, all this provided support for a more optimistic view of American life?

When Gottschalk returned to the Massachusetts capital following his victory over Dwight, he viewed the city through fresh eyes. He visited the quaint bookstore of Ticknor & Fields and discovered there a reverence for tradition that he had not experienced earlier. He dined with Oliver Wendell Holmes, the genre painter Frank Hunt, and other notables. Even Longfellow paid him court. Departing on December 4, 1862, Gottschalk waxed enthusiastic, declaring his love for the cultured old city and its high-minded people.[78]

It does not require a cynic to associate these laudatory remarks with the fact that Gottschalk had been lionized by Boston's cultural elite and that he was prospering from royalties paid him by a Boston publisher and from a retainer he received from a Boston piano manufacturer. His praise for small-town America can likewise be seen as reciprocity for his having been so warmly received there. When Moreau played in York, Pennsylvania, for example, he "caused the public pulse to flutter."[79] It is understandable that he found reasons to flatter those who flattered him.

Yet Gottschalk's deepening regard for the emerging civilization of the United States went far beyond his response to adulation. The New York Philharmonic never really embraced him, yet he pronounced it "one of the best orchestras in the world."[80] Cleveland, Ohio, was a new and raw industrial city that embodied much of what Gottschalk disliked. But Gottschalk had to admit that the public there was making great strides in its ability to appreciate the finer points of culture. This change in Cleveland led him to generalize about the situation nationally:

> I am daily astonished at the rapidity with which the taste for music is developed and is developing in the United States. At the time of my first return from Europe . . . the public listened with indifference. . . . Now piano concerts are chronic, they have even become epidemic. . . . From whatever cause, the American taste is becoming purer, and with that remarkable rapidity we cite through our whole progress.[81]

To what extent did Gottschalk see such cultural advancement as a by-product of American prosperity? There is no doubt that he stood in awe of America's burgeoning wealth. With wide-eyed wonder he reported on a German tailor who used his meager savings to buy land in Pennsylvania, successfully prospected the area for oil, and quickly sold his holdings for $360,000.[82] In Chicago he learned of fifteen hundred houses under construction there at one time. "Nothing in the world," he wrote Espadero, "not even the greatest imagination, can give any idea of the movement, exuberance of life, and activity of these United States."[83]

Implicit in all these observations is the conclusion that the North would inevitably win the Civil War on account of its economic and technological superiority. He reported to Espadero on the construction of an ironclad ship of seven thousand tons, "capable of achieving great speed and of sinking all the ships of England and France with its steel bow."[84] How could the South win, when a single arms works in Massachusetts could produce twelve hundred rifles a day, or when the movements of enemy troops were being reported by telegraph from balloons hovering over the field of battle?[85]

If the North's economic might could win the war, would it not also elevate the nation's culture? Gottschalk thought not. For all his respect for economic achievement, he could not separate it from tawdry commercialism. When a horse died on Broadway, Gottschalk observed that within minutes its sides were plastered with advertising signs. He was shocked that a Dr. H. would promote his tonic in giant letters painted on rocks overlooking the falls of the Genesee River.[86] Like his father before him, Gottschalk persisted in associating the world of commerce with a hokum and humbuggery incompatible with culture.[87]

Having expressed doubts that either religion or commerce could serve as forces for cultural advancement, Gottschalk then proceeded to embrace something that suffused both the religious and commercial life of America, namely, the spirit of enterprise. However much he criticized some manifestations of this spirit, he observed that individual initiative was the great engine for change in America and as such was the defining feature of the American character. He had observed this quality at close range in his publisher General Hall and in his patron Jonas Chickering. Moreau detected it also in the New Orleans dentist who offered him free dental care in exchange for concert tickets. Such a spirit, he concluded, caused Americans "to reject all speculative theories and [to] arrive at solutions of social problems which in Europe would frighten the greatest economists."[88] No wonder that Gottschalk was, as his friend Henry Clapp Jr. observed, "an out and out free-trader."[89]

Throughout his travels Gottschalk documented evidence of the positive impact on culture of American enterprise and initiative. He detailed the history of College Hill in Poughkeepsie, once a dying boarding school, which was purchased by an enterprising Yankee who transformed it into a booming "college."[90] He detected it in Milwaukee's astonishing cultural progress and also in the work of Dr. Abner Kellogg, the entrepreneurial director of the New York State Insane Asylum at Utica.

In Gottschalk's conception, the spirit of enterprise flowed equally through commerce and culture, enabling at least some Americans to do good as they did well. Aside from his occasional outbursts against the venality of New York impresarios, he admired the countless local entrepreneurs who were building theaters and concert halls or otherwise working to improve their local communities. Indeed, he did not hesitate to include himself in their number:

> We should all, however narrow may be our sphere of action, bear our part in the progressive movement of civilization, and I cannot help feeling a pride in having contributed within the modest limits of my powers in extending through our country the knowledge of music.[91]

For all the humbuggery that Gottschalk perceived in America, he also recognized that an intensely civic mentality suffused the populace. "All

Americans know their country's history in detail," he observed, "all are good speakers, and all are constantly occupied with popular elections, political or religious discussions, and public discourses on every possible subject."[92] The widespread public lectures and lyceum gatherings represented the quintessence of this civic outlook. Acknowledging the link between enterprise, cultural uplift, and financial gain, Gottschalk mused: "The profession of lecturer is one of the most lucrative that I know of."[93]

The reason private gain could foster civic and cultural betterment, Gottschalk believed, was that everyone was free to engage in it on equal terms. A Jacksonian democrat by upbringing, Gottschalk became an outspoken champion of democracy in all spheres of life. To be sure, he ranted incessantly against the tendency of boorish rednecks to sneer at anyone wearing gloves or otherwise putting on airs. Yet he waxed rhapsodic every time he encountered a simple yeoman who manifested Jeffersonian virtues. French readers, he cautioned, "cannot understand or comprehend the character of the American farmers. The orderly and respectable habits that characterize them are too incompatible with the gross turbulence and brutalizing ignorance of European peasants to enable you to find an equivalent of the laboring class of American farmers."[94]

Gottschalk's democratic epiphany took place at a pot-bellied stove at the hotel in Clyde, Ohio:

> I have been talking to an old man who has the appearance of a poor farmer. We are talking—poetry! The United States presents to strangers this remarkable condition of things, that it is impossible for them to conjecture from appearances the rank or position of those they meet on their travels. If they meet some who sparkle with diamonds and blow their noses with their fingers, they will meet, just as likely, superior and cultivated minds concealed under the fur-skin greatcoat of the pioneer of the Far West. My companion is well-versed in the literature of the Bible. He loves poetry and evidently understands it. He speaks to me with enthusiasm of the poetry of David. Lamartine . . . would have been delighted in listening to my old companion.[95]

It is worth noting that Gottschalk accepted this cultivated frontiersman on his own terms, without seeking to gentrify him. This gives the lie to those who would see Gottschalk merely as an apostle of genteel parlor culture. It is undeniable that Gottschalk, as a bearer of French cultural values, came to symbolize cosmopolitan refinement to millions in his audience. However, his own values were far more democratic. He was quick to recognize a cultivated spirit under a raccoon hat, and even his notions of refinement had to do less with wealth than with true gentility of manners.[96]

America's glaring social ills were evident to Gottschalk. At the time of the New York race riots he wondered whether it was appropriate to give concerts in a city in which poverty was so widespread.[97] Yet he believed that the combination of enterprise and democracy opened the way for ordinary citizens to foster social and cultural betterment. The nursing stations and food kitchens provided by volunteer women during the Civil War manifested this spirit, which also accounted for the success of such thriving and cultivated towns as Portsmouth, New Hampshire. A friend to the many movements for social and cultural uplift, Gottschalk faulted his fellow countrymen only for their failure to reduce drunkenness through the application of such voluntaristic methods.[98]

As he burrowed deeper into American life, Gottschalk lost the last traces of his old Parisian dandyism. Critics commented favorably on this. The *Detroit Free Press* compared him to a revised edition of a first-rate author; Cleveland's *Plain Dealer* praised him for having "lost his hauteur"; the *Indianapolis Daily Journal* lauded his " quiet undemonstrative bearing."[99] This won him popular favor throughout the West, where, as the Indianapolis critic observed, "Of all things, 'Hoosiers' hate to see a man 'put on airs.' "

For his part, Gottschalk evolved into an optimist in an optimistic age. America had problems galore, but for every problem there was a means to solve it. And the grandest instrument of all for effecting human betterment and cultural uplift was education. During the Civil War, Moreau Gottschalk became an ardent proponent of democratic education as a kind of social and cultural cure-all. His new interest in education took him to many schools. He became closely familiar with the military academy in Poughkeepsie where Gaston studied; he played benefit concerts for the public schools of Brooklyn; he inspected a new academy in Rockford, Illinois; he dropped by the Archbishop's School in Burlington, Vermont; and he discoursed on pedagogy with his friend Reverend Reed, headmaster of the Walnut Hill School outside Geneva, New York.[100] He also visited Harvard, Yale, the University of Michigan, and Moravian College in Bethlehem, Pennsylvania, strongly favoring the last because of its firm emphasis on moral education and ethics. In the course of his travels Gottschalk also developed a strong distaste for "so-called liberal education," which he criticized for inculcating a belief in the "fictitious superiority of name and money."[101]

Thanks to democratic education in the United States, he believed, Americans of all ranks were coming to respect learning. He noted the countless train passengers reading Victor Hugo's *Les Misérables* in translation. He extolled the public library in Salem, Massachusetts, and the Mercantile Libraries in St. Louis and Cincinnati, with their rich selection of foreign newspapers available to anyone who would pay a modest subscription fee.[102] Education, he concluded, was the essence of American democracy.

This, then, was the answer to all those who dwelt only on Americans' coarseness, practicality, and indifference to culture. Education, not "parlor culture" or "refinement," would lift up the American people and enable them to fulfill their grand destiny. As for the crudities of the present, they were merely like those children of whom Montaigne wrote "who bite the nurse's breast, and whom the exuberance of health sometimes renders turbulent."[103]

This, Gottschalk argued, was what Europeans failed to understand. With mounting indignation he assailed the "clique of imbecile, jealous, and sterile pedants" in Europe who attacked Americans for their alleged failure to appreciate their own great artists like Poe. He denounced the "stupid remarks" of Mrs. Trollope in the widely read account of her travels in America. And he complained about the gross distortions of American life that he had encountered in the foreign press everywhere.[104] The fact was, he concluded, "there were few governments that were not interested in hastening the fall of the American Republic. The least enlightened feared the United States, the more liberal were jealous of it."

Would America's detractors succeed in their campaign of vilification? "Unfortunately for the adversaries of democratic principles," gloated Gottschalk, "the thing [i.e., democracy] so far seems possible, whatever they may do. The truth, carefully sifted by the organs of [the European] press, sometimes reaches the people by fugitive gleams that set them to thinking."[105] Shame on Americanophobes abroad who professed to be "amazed that a nation of merchants could produce a poet [Poe]." And shame, too (and here Gottschalk dredged up a hurt from his own past), on Professor Zimmermann of the Paris Conservatoire, who two decades earlier had dismissed a young pianist from New Orleans without even listening to him play because he came from "un pays de machines à vapeur" (a land of steam engines).[106]

Borne along by these affirmations, Gottschalk emerged as a committed American patriot. He poured out some of his best performances before unschooled frontiersmen in small-town halls and lauded his country's achievements in spheres as varied as city building and mental health care. Like his friend Frederic Edwin Church, he even rhapsodized over American nature, boosting Vermont as equal in beauty to anything in Switzerland and announcing flatly that the Finger Lakes region near Geneva, New York, was "the most beautiful country in the world."[107]

So well known was Gottschalk's patriotism that no one was surprised when, in 1864, he began adding *The Star-Spangled Banner* to his programs and even asked the audience in places like Rochester, New York, to stand and sing the last chorus.[108] Showmanship? Of course. But he expressed the same view privately, as when he wrote his sisters from Cincinnati that "the Americans are definitely a great people."[109] Gottschalk of Louisiana, Gottschalk the Parisian dandy, and Gottschalk the rootless sojourner had become Gottschalk the American.

 California: Anatomy
of a Scandal

I N the spring of 1865 Gottschalk completed his three-year concert tour
of the Northern states and departed for California, where he spent
just under five months. By mid-September he had quit California amidst
a nasty scandal and was on a ship bound for South America, where he
was to spend the last four years of his life.

Gottschalk's stay in California, and especially his hasty departure,
marked a turning point in his career. That he was driven from San Francisco engulfed in scandal has given rise to the notion that, but for the
California experience, Gottschalk might have returned to the East Coast
or Europe and opened a fresh page in his creative life. Such speculation
calls for a closer examination of the entire California episode.

As early as 1864 the demand for concerts on the home front began to
taper off. Max Maretzek and his opera company still held forth at the
Academy of Music in New York, and Niblo's Garden continued to offer a
diet of plays and concerts. But now it was Howe's Great Circus and the
Van Amburgh & Co. Menagerie that drew the biggest crowds. As the Civil
War ground into its last phase, the exhausted public wanted only to be
amused. Audiences at Gottschalk's concerts dwindled.[1] Attendance was
poor at an 1864 performance at Smith & Nixon's Hall in Chicago, the
audience having been composed "mostly of music lovers."[2] As attendance
declined, press coverage fell off as well.[3] Only Dwight persisted, assailing
Gottschalk for "disputing the absolute divinity of Bach," as one of the
composer's friends put it. But now everyone was tired, and that same
friend asked if it would not be more "amiable, more chivalrous, and
dignified for this petty warfare [between Dwight and Gottschalk] to
cease."[4]

Amidst this general slackening, Moreau changed managers. Max Strakosch abandoned Gottschalk to work with the newly imported German pianist Charles Wehle and cellist Helene de Katow, who together upstaged Gottschalk with a series of concerts at Niblo's Saloon.[5] Gottschalk, meanwhile, had gone over to the director, composer, pianist, and now manager Emannuele Muzio (1821–90).

Clara Louise Kellogg described Muzio as "a queer, nervous, brusque, red-headed man . . . from the North of Italy, where the type always seems so curiously German."[6] As Verdi's only pupil, Muzio had served his great master as secretary, confidante, and billiards partner. He had conducted various opera companies in Europe and had written several operas, none of which met with success. As a pianist and accompanist he was judged by Dwight to be "the very worst of that class of musicians that I have ever heard."[7] Yet Verdi revered Muzio's talent as a conductor and later chose him to premiere several of his works, including *Aida*.

This was all in the future. For now, Muzio was trying to enter the field of concert management. In the autumn of 1864 he offered Gottschalk a contract to tour the Midwest, and in late spring 1865 he proposed a trip to "El Dorado."[8] The California deal was attractive. Extending over two months, it assured Gottschalk three hundred dollars weekly, committed Muzio to pay his passage to California and back, and forbade Muzio to transfer the management of Gottschalk to anyone else. And so Gottschalk accepted.[9]

Two years before this, Gottschalk had contemplated an overland trip to the West Coast.[10] By early 1864 he thought better of this and let the New York press know that he would soon depart instead for Europe.[11] However, the drop-off in concert receipts, along with the start of Prussia's wars of unification, killed this plan.[12] Even though the French press had already begun the build-up for Gottschalk's return, the European tour was canceled.[13]

By July 1864 the new possibility with Muzio loomed into view. Napoleon III of France had recently installed the Austrian Archduke Maximilian (1837–67) on the throne of Mexico, thus ending a three-year civil war. Maximilian moved quickly to open commercial banks, confirm property rights, and invite European immigration. When friends in Mexico City reported this to Gottschalk, he resolved to head for Mexico.[14] Soon the papers were announcing that Muzio and Gottschalk would depart for Havana and Mexico City.[15]

Such reports continued into March 1865. Then, with no warning, the Gottschalk-Muzio tour suddenly changed its destination to California. And not only California. An advertisement in the *New York Times* announced that they would proceed from California to Hawaii, and then around the world.[16] *Dwight's* went further, adding among their destinations India, Polynesia, China, Japan, "and who knows where?"[17]

Nothing had yet occurred in Mexico to warrant this sudden change of plan. The only plausible explanation is that Ada Clare had once more appeared in Gottschalk's life. A year earlier she, her son Aubrey, and actor Ossian Dodge, who specialized in both male and female parts, had sailed for the Golden Gate. In San Francisco a fledgling circle of bohemian writers was publishing the *Golden Era*, and its editor offered Ada a job as staff writer.[18] She also lobbied the manager of Maguire's Opera House to permit her to make her stage debut in the play *Camille*, adapted from Dumas *fils*.[19] When the moment of her debut came, however, Ada froze with stage fright and was barely able to croak out her lines. The supporting players, most of whom had been on the receiving end of her critical barbs in the *Golden Era*, reveled in her discomfiture, which only grew as a din of catcalls arose from the rowdy gallery.[20] Within days Ada Clare and Aubrey were en route to New York, where they arrived on February 12, 1865.

Ada Clare's old passion for Gottschalk still burned. In her column for the *Golden Era* she had published a poem, *To Whom*, bemoaning the way he had rejected her seven years earlier.[21] She also began writing a novel, *Only a Woman's Heart*, that was transparently based on her relationship with the composer. It is all but certain that she saw Gottschalk during February and March 1865 and that it was her tales of the West that convinced him to abandon the Mexican project and to go instead to San Francisco.

While Muzio was writing friends in Italy to report on his departure for El Dorado,[22] Gottschalk issued a lugubrious farewell card, which read as if he was heading not for the Golden Gate but the Pearly Gates.[23] With similar presentiments he also bundled up a collection of papers to be opened by his sisters in the event of his death.[24] Finally, he offered a series of testimonial concerts at Niblo's Saloon and at the Academy of Music in Brooklyn. So hectic were his final days in New York that Moreau failed to sign a new contract with his publisher Hall; he stuffed it instead into his baggage, where it was found after his death.[25]

At length, Gottschalk and Muzio departed on April 2 aboard the mail steamer *Ariel*. With them was the American soprano Lucy Simons, the student of Carlotta Patti who had toured with Muzio and Gottschalk during the previous season and who was now engaged to Muzio. Simons and Muzio eventually married, but their union ended in divorce. Also with them were the tenor Giovanni Sbriglia and the baritone Carlo Orlandini.

In those days before the Panama Canal, travelers disembarked at Aspinwall on the Atlantic coast and proceeded by train across the Isthmus of Panama to the Pacific, where they were transferred to a second ship.

The larger *Constitution* seemed palatial at first, and Gottschalk settled into reading his geographical dictionary. He very soon realized that the *Constitution* presented the very picture of Hell: no escape from the oppressive heat; no ice water; a bar that closed at ten p.m.; and bedbugs at night. Well before reaching Acapulco, the Italian singers were quarreling and Moreau was in deep depression. He found the heat in Acapulco stifling and the filth ubiquitous.

Gottschalk briefly brightened when he came across the Louisiana Hotel. He promptly introduced himself to the proprietor, saying "I am from New Orleans."[26] The proprietor soon fanned old memories. He recalled the young Paul Morphy of New Orleans, the chess genius who had demolished Europe's best. And then there was that "other prodigy, Gottschalk, from New Orleans who had promised marvelous things, and whose father sent him to Europe in hopes of making a great musician of him," he continued. "And what became of him?," Moreau asked the hotel keeper. "Nobody has heard anything more about him," came the response. Gottschalk felt as if he were attending his own funeral.[27]

A week after the *Ariel* departed from New York, General Lee surrendered to U. S. Grant at Appomattox Court House. Only days later, on Good Friday, April 14, actor John Wilkes Booth assassinated Lincoln. It took nine more days for news to reach the *Constitution* via another steamer. Gottschalk had seen Booth act in Cleveland, and friends had told him of the actor's "violent and fantastic" character. Now, as word of his deed reached the *Constitution* on a resplendent day, the large deck quickly filled with grieving Americans. Gottschalk reported that all the men seemed "overwhelmed under the weight of an incommensurable grief." Judge Field of the U.S. Supreme Court sat in a corner, weeping with his head in his hands. Many of the women, however, seemed to Gottschalk to recover with unseemly speed.[28]

Passengers and crew of the *Constitution* assembled on deck for a prayer service in memory of the fallen president. The Italian singers performed the *Battle Hymn of the Republic,* and Gottschalk played his *The Union.* Reflecting on the moment, he asked himself:

> Where are now those frivolous judgments of the man whom we are weeping for today? His ugliness, his awkwardness, his jokes, with which we reproached him: all have disappeared in the presence of the majesty of death. His greatness, his honesty, the purity of that great heart which beats no longer, rise up today, and in their resplendent radiancy transfigure him whom we called the "common rail splitter." Yesterday his detractors were ridiculing his large hands without gloves, his large feet, his bluntness; today this type we found grotesque appears to us on the threshold of immortality, and we understand by the universality of our grief what future generations will see in him.[29]

The first person to greet Gottschalk when he disembarked in San Francisco was Mr. Badger, Chickering's representative for California. For once the Chickering firm had not sent an instrument with Gottschalk but had called instead on the firm of Badger & Lindenberger to provide him with one. Badger was a born salesman and turned every Gottschalk performance into a promotional event for his firm. A minor point, to be sure, but within months it turned out to be among the factors contributing to Gottschalk's troubles.

The carriage ride to the Cosmopolitan Hotel revealed few signs of a city into which seventy million dollars in silver and gold had flowed from Nevada over the previous year. Dust was everywhere. City fathers talked of introducing the latest innovation in paving, but efforts to "macadamize" the streets had barely begun.

This schism between a rough-and-ready reality and the more refined dreams of a genteel few ran deep in San Francisco and was to have important consequences for Gottschalk. San Francisco was a crude and raucous town where men far outnumbered women. Those over fifty years of age were few, and four out of five of the white males were bachelors.[30] Such gents wanted entertainment, not culture. They loved minstrel shows and supported several "Ethiopian" troupes. They flocked to the theater in such numbers that news read from the stage reached as many people as did newspapers.[31] They liked sensationalism, too, and preferred plays like *Lady Audley's Secret* to concerts, which, as Gottschalk soon recognized, they dismissed as "dearer and less entertaining than other exhibitions."[32]

During the previous season Adah Menken had revealed through her productions of *Mazeppa* the lascivious heart of San Francisco audiences. By the time of Gottschalk's arrival, no fewer than six *Mazeppas* were playing at once.[33] But why bother with staging the entire show when the only part that counted was the great horseback scene? On this basis, many "exhibitions" were staged "for gentlemen only." On a still lower level such acts as "The Hermaphrodite and the Talking Frog" and "The Learned Pig" competed with Gottschalk for the public's attention.[34]

The whole city of San Francisco had the mood of a downtown saloon on Friday night, and this was reflected in the hoax-loving press. Mark Twain was but one of the many punsters writing for the *Golden Era*. Pranksters also abounded at the *Morning Call*, which once devoted several columns to a detailed account of the funeral of a street dog. There was also the irreverent and savage *Daily Dramatic Chronicle*, where every vendetta in the theatrical world was played out for the public's amusement. Debunking and satire were the heart and soul of young San Francisco. Adah Menken herself had come in for her share when a Miss Fanny Brown organized a burlesque of Menken's hit, this one entitled

Masseppa, or The Wild Mule of Oakland.[35] Considering that so grave an event as the earthquake of October 9, 1865, provided grounds for Mark Twain's mirthful ridicule, it was too much to suppose that a touring virtuoso would get off free.

Dead set against this frivolity was a growing band of San Franciscans committed to making their city respectable and refined. New Englanders by origin and Congregationalist or Unitarian in religion, these earnest folk sought to replicate in the Bay Area the cultivated tedium of their Yankee upbringing. It was they who imposed a Sunday Blue Law on San Francisco and who successfully defended it before the California Supreme Court only six months before Gottschalk's arrival. Their quixotic aim was to transform San Francisco into a bastion of morality. Their leader was the dynamic Unitarian minister Thomas Starr King, revered equally for his patriotism and for his four-square probity. These solid citizens read the stately *Daily Alta California*, founded schools where correct values were taught, and fostered a proper New England respect for music and culture by enrolling their daughters in piano lessons with Charles Ferdinand Von Hartmann, recently arrived from Leipzig.[36]

As outsiders, Gottschalk and Muzio had somehow to negotiate their way along the perilous cultural fissure cleaving San Francisco's cultural life. Even had they wanted to, they could not have done this alone, for the city's leading theaters were under the control of Thomas Maguire, known to all as the "Napoleon of Impresarios."[37] Ruddy and handsome, faultlessly attired, and with a huge diamond on his finger, this former New Yorker appeared superficially to be an Irish version of Max Maretzek.[38] In reality he was a very different type.

Prior to his arrival at the Golden Gate in 1849, Maguire had been a Manhattan cab driver, saloonkeeper, and friend of Tammany Hall politicos. A shrewd businessman, he promptly established "opera houses" in San Francisco and Virginia City, Nevada, where he presented exactly what flush miners wanted to see. Combining the roles of theater owner and impresario, he managed popular acts like Maguire's Eureka Minstrels as well as Adah Menken's *Mazeppa*. Then, having vanquished all rivals in this line, he moved into the realm of high culture. By the time Muzio arrived, Maguire had monopolized Italian opera through his chain of Maguire's Opera Houses, to which he conveniently attached gambling rooms. In 1864 Maguire also built the San Francisco Academy of Music on Pine Street below Montgomery. His operatic troupe was serious by any measure. In the 1865 summer season alone it mounted sixty-eight performances of twenty different operas.[39]

Maguire's domineering presence affected Gottschalk in two important ways. First, he robbed Muzio of his role of independent manager. Muzio

either had to bring Gottschalk under Maguire's wing or forget about concertizing in California. This was even more the case with Muzio's fiancée,
Lucy Simons, and his Italian singers. Maguire thus reduced Muzio to a
cipher.

Second, as Gottschalk's de facto impresario, Maguire promoted the
composer mainly to San Francisco's aspiring highbrows, whom he hoped
would fill his deficit-ridden Academy of Music. It took no time for the
frisky local press to figure out this stratagem. When Muzio invited all
the editors to a dinner at the Cosmopolitan Hotel, only two showed up.[40]
The first of six concerts Gottschalk offered in May 1865 was poorly attended.[41] The two-dollar admission fee did not help matters, nor did the
program, which included Beethoven's "Kreutzer Sonata" performed with
a local violinist and a duet featuring Gottschalk and Muzio. As the *Daily
Dramatic Chronicle* put it, "the piano is not an attractive instrument to
those unskilled in music."[42] This did not prevent the august *Daily Alta
California* from lavishly praising Gottschalk, or the *Mercury* from declaring that "it is beyond doubt that art can go no further."[43]

All this set the pundits twittering. The *Daily Dramatic Chronicle* pil-
loried a critic who had compared Gottschalk's music to "a ripe, downy
peach," declaring that it would take a Philadelphia lawyer to find out
what that meant. Days later it ridiculed critics who were "at their wits'
end to find adjectives enough to do justice to their feelings about the
pianist."[44] As for Mark Twain, he chose to compare Gottschalk with the
banjo players from the Olympic Minstrels, and with his landlady's daughter. "I like Gottschalk well enough," he declared:

> He probably gets as much out of the piano as there is in it. But the frozen fact
> is, that all that he *does* get it out of it is "tum, tum." He gets "tum, tum" out of
> the instrument thicker and faster than my landlady's daughter, Mary Ann; but
> after all, it simply amounts to "tum, tum." As between Gottschalk and Mary
> Ann, it is only a question of quantity; and so far as quantity is concerned, he
> beats her three to one. The piano may do for love-sick girls . . . but give me
> the banjo. Gottschalk compared to Sam Pride or Charlie Rhoades is as a Dash-
> away cocktail to a hot whiskey punch. When you want *genuine music . . .*
> just smash your piano, and invoke the glory-beaming banjo![45]

To reach the lowbrows without offending the highbrows, Gottschalk
gradually added more pianos to his programs. More important, he brought
forth a new waltz, *La Californienne*, which was warmly received. Scored
for piano, violin, and soprano, this was soon followed by another new
composition for the local public, *La Bourbonaise*. Both pieces are now
lost.[46]

Gottschalk was invited across the Bay to perform at the Oakland Female College on May 18, along with Lucy Simons.[47] Oakland at that time

was a bucolic village reached by steam ferry from San Francisco. There, in 1858, Mary K. Blake had opened a seminary for young ladies. Backed by a board of trustees heavy with Congregational clergymen, she banned balls and parties and forbade the young ladies even to leave the school grounds unless accompanied by a parent or guardian.[48] Indeed, the regimen at the Oakland Female College was so strict that it all but invited malicious pranks. When two young men tried to call at the Washington Street institution one Sunday in 1860 and were turned away, they sent out dozens of forged invitations to a party at the school. Mrs. Blake was not amused.[49]

In short, the Oakland Female College epitomized the pious, proper, and moralistic side of San Francisco. The only ambiguous element was to be found in the main-floor parlor, which contained no fewer than four pianos. There the young ladies, after completing their studies in literature, math, logic, and moral philosophy, could drum out *The Last Hope* and *The Maiden's Prayer* to their heart's content.[50]

Once the prudent voice of the *Daily Alta California* had declared Gottschalk the world's best pianist and composer, it was natural that the Oakland Female College should ask him to perform there. How could Mrs. Blake have known that only weeks before she invited him, copies of the *Atlantic Monthly* for February and March 1865 had reached San Francisco, and that people were already passing around Gottschalk's account of what he himself admitted had been his "frightfully immoral" life in the West Indies?[51] Fortunately, the concert at Oakland Female College passed without incident.

Gottschalk's final performance at the Academy of Music culminated with a work in which twelve pianists labored on six grand pianos. Immediately afterwards, Gottschalk, Muzio, and Lucy Simons departed by steamboat for Sacramento.[52] After recovering from the shock of Muzio's two-dollar admission fee, the rough-and-ready Sacramento public was more than appreciative. Besides his new *La Bourbonaise*, Moreau stuck mainly to sentimental pieces, and these hit the mark. "His fame is deserved . . . whether he played to cultivated ears or mining roughs who have 'music in their souls,'" wrote the *Sacramento Daily Union*. "The key to his popularity as a pianist," concluded the same paper, "is . . . the expression of sentiment, exquisitely tender, solemnly reverent, sweetly suggestive, or grandly martial."[53]

Within days the musicians had a chance to test their art on more miners a hundred miles farther east at the bonanza Nevada town of Virginia City. Windswept, dusty, and clinging to the side of bald Mount Davidson, this jerry-built city was devoted solely and unapologetically to making money. A largely male populace took its culture straight up. The local crowd had booed the boy violinist Paul Julien, but Adah Menken had taken the boisterous town by storm and left with a fortune in silver. Mark Twain covered Menken's performance for the local *Territorial Enterprise* in an article under the apt heading "The Menken—Written Especially for Gentlemen."

Menken returned in 1864 with Ada Clare, as well as her nineteen pet dogs and her hapless (third) husband, journalist Robert H. Newell. Adah and Ada invited Twain and his sidekick from the *Territorial Enterprise,* "Dan de Quille," to a private dinner to discuss Menken's proposed novel. Mr. Newell was excluded from the festivities and sulked in the lobby. During the revelry one of the dogs that had not been sedated by Menken's sugar cubes soaked in champagne bit Twain's leg. When Twain struck back with his boot, he connected with a sensitive corn on Adah Menken's foot, sending her shrieking to the couch.[54]

Now it was Gottschalk's turn. The price of silver had just plunged by three-quarters, and the resulting panic heightened the already surly mood.[55] At the time of his arrival, the local newspaper carried a whole column on murders, minute details on a recent dog fight, coverage of a poisoning that led to "convulsions, twisting, and jerking of the nerves," and a review of the previous evening's performance at Maguire's, which featured the shooting of an orange off the head of actor E. W. Clarkson at thirty feet.[56] Amazingly, Gottschalk's concert was judged "meritorious and artistical in the highest degree."[57] Sensing the mood, he improvised a "battle piece," complete with trumpets and musketry. As Gottschalk fired his last salvo he looked around, expecting a committee of miners to advance on the stage for the purpose of lynching him. He was mistaken. Not only did he have to repeat the improvisation several times, but the next day a delegation of miners asked him to replay the entire concert. He did.[58]

In spite of all the adulation he received there, Gottschalk loathed Virginia City. Ill for three days,[59] he bemoaned his fate until a family from New Orleans took him in. "Virginia City," he concluded, "is the saddest, the most wearisome, the most inhospitable place on the globe."[60]

As he moved on to Carson City, Dayton, Gold Hill, Dutch Flat, and Marysville, Moreau's mood grew positively foul. "California is a humbug," he concluded.[61] Once he reached San Francisco he was only too pleased to announce his imminent departure for South America. This was no mere publicity stunt. His contract with Muzio had run out. Muzio himself had long since let it be known that he would be glad to stay in San Francisco to teach and conduct Maguire's opera company.[62] Lucy Simons had by now landed a contract with Maguire and was appearing in *I Puritani.* Gottschalk therefore sent his usual press kit ahead to Lima, Peru, where the papers announced his forthcoming arrival.[63] It remained only for him to give his farewell concerts at Maguire's Academy of Music.

Gottschalk must have been amazed at the reception accorded these concerts. Members of Maguire's Italian opera troupe assisted, and the Academy of Music was so packed that he had to add an additional matinee and then a *matinée d'instruction* as well.[64] Suddenly Gottschalk was again a celebrity. He sat for photographs at Brasley and Rulofson's on Montgomery Street, and a local merchant presented him with a large and opulent carpet with his initials embroidered at the center.[65] The new mood continued during a brief trip to Petaluma, where members of a rural audience, behaving "as if they were in London or Paris," proclaimed Gottschalk "THE FIRST AND GREATEST COMPOSER OF THE AGE."[66]

Even though Gottschalk had booked passage on the steamer *America* for August 17, he still had a few weeks to capitalize on this unexpected upturn in his fortunes. He and a local pianist named Gustave Schott made a quick run to play in Stockton and to visit the local insane asylum there.[67] More important, Gottschalk booked Platt's Hall in San Francisco for a pair of concerts on August 8 and 12. Platt's was an old barn more suited to political rallies than concerts. Gottschalk, acting as his own agent, proposed to fill it with two monster concerts. Since Muzio and his Italian singers had signed with Maguire and were thus out of the picture, Moreau turned to an aspiring local mezzo soprano, Jenny Landesman, to brighten up the affairs. The main feature was a pair of works involving ten pianos. As usual, it was easier to find workable instruments than competent pianists. One of the "artists" who had enlisted on the team proved to be so desperately incompetent that at the performance Gottschalk disconnected the hammers of his instrument, meanwhile forbidding the entire battalion from playing warm-up notes lest the young amateur discover the ruse. During the performance the lad pounded away with gusto, and by the time he realized what had been done to him it was too late.[68]

Critics agreed that Miss Landesman's voice required much cultivation, but otherwise had only praise for the two monster concerts.[69] In fact, the staid *Daily Alta California* went overboard, rhapsodizing over "the poetry of improvisation at [Gottschalk's] command" and declaring him "our American musical genius."[70] The *Daily Dramatic Chronicle* was by no means so pleased, however, but this emerged only later.

Gottschalk seemed to be rolling from triumph to triumph. The *America*'s sailing date came and went as he added yet a third monster concert at Platt's Hall and committed himself to organizing a grand concert to benefit the local Société Française de Secours.[71] Never mind that the third monster concert was poorly attended or that Gottschalk was criticized for improvising his way through Mendelssohn's *Song Without*

Words.[72] He was definitely the man of the hour, and all San Francisco seemed eager to salute him.

This actually happened on August 25, when forty of the city's most prominent citizens offered a splendid banquet in his honor. French consul M. Cazotte was there, as was the mayor. Also present was Mr. Badger, who had missed no chance to promote his firm on every Gottschalk concert bill and program. The banquet was judged "a marvel of gastronomical research and culinary chemistry." The high point of the evening was the presentation of an enormous circular medal of solid gold inlaid with diamonds and rubies. For days before the banquet this dish-sized masterpiece had been exhibited in a jeweler's window on Montgomery Street. Now it was offered to Gottschalk "as a token from his California friends," as the inscription reads.[73]

By now the papers were full of announcements of benefit concerts of all sorts, each featuring "our American musical genius." These were so numerous that the same gentlemen who had organized the banquet placed a letter in the press inviting Gottschalk to offer a final concert for his own benefit.[74] Gottschalk, who had just written his sisters that his concerts "continue to have good results," graciously consented to this invitation for him to enrich himself.[75] Mr. Badger placed a fresh round of self-serving ads. Gottschalk's own announcements made much of the fact that Signori Sbriglia, Orlandini, and Fossati, all former Muzio charges now with Maguire, would participate. Announcements in the *Daily Alta California* made clear that the event, slated for September 8, would break all records for refinement and respectability.

Nor did the concert disappoint. The *Alta California* cooed over the "purity and delicacy of the affair" and, reaching for the sky, pronounced it *"spirituel."*[76] Undeniably noteworthy was the lively new *polka de concert* that Gottschalk premiered that evening, *Ses yeux* (op. 66). Combining a wonderfully variegated melodic line with utter naiveté of form, *Ses Yeux* long remained a Gottschalk standard.

Gottschalk had only one further benefit to perform, on the fifteenth, when he had agreed to assist in a concert to benefit the tenor Giovanni Sbriglia. It was on the night before this event that the Gottschalk scandal unfolded.

By Gottschalk's account, it all began when he dropped by a fashionable San Francisco clothier to buy a hat. Charles Legay, the younger brother of the proprietor and a personal acquaintance of Moreau's, used the opportunity to show him the most recent in a series of anonymous letters he had been receiving from a twenty-year-old young lady in Oakland.[77] She invited Legay for a rendezvous that very evening and suggested he bring a friend with him, either Sbriglia or Gottschalk. Moreau declined to join him. Later, when Legay appealed again, he changed his mind. Legay proceeded at once by the last ferry to Oakland, and Gottschalk, who missed the ferry, hired a small boat to take him across the bay. After the two met up again, they took a carriage to the designated spot and waited there for some time. Finally the girl and a friend appeared. The four left for a nocturnal ride, which continued for several hours until the two men dropped the girls at their residence—on Washington Street.

Unfortunately, this was none other than Mrs. Blake's Oakland Female College, and the girls were both students there. Their absence having been noted, Reverend Walsworth himself confronted them on their return. Both Gottschalk, in a long letter of explanation to the Chickerings, and Walsworth, in a statement to the press, agreed that it was 2:30 a.m.[78]

That Moreau thought little of the matter is attested by the fact that he played for Sbriglia's benefit the next day as planned and even announced that he would offer a "final farewell concert" featuring thirty pianos with orchestral accompaniment.[79] But at two p.m. on the day following the Sbriglia benefit, the scandal exploded. A telegram came into the *Sacramento Daily Bee* reporting on "a bit of scandalous conduct on the part of Gottschalk and his business agent." In this version the girls did not return until after daybreak and had been promptly expelled from the school.[80] Two days later the *San Francisco Examiner* took up the story, but without mentioning either Gottschalk or Legay by name. It made clear that it considered them guilty of seduction, however. "We spare our readers a detailed account of the infamous affair," purred the *Examiner:*

> It is sufficient to say that two young and blooming girls have been forever ruined by two heartless libertines, and that one of the girls has been sent to a convent. The simple-minded girls were dazzled by a flashing exterior, and a somewhat celebrated manner, and fell victim to the hellish lust of the Seducer. We hear of pistols being called into requisition to right the hideous wrong.[81]

Then the *Morning Call* swung into action:

> It's the same old story: a strolling adventurer . . . captivates the fancy of thoughtless young school misses, who, closing their eyes to the terrible future into which they by their one criminal act plunge themselves, . . . give themselves to the embraces of the seducer.[82]

On the next day, September 17, the Oakland Female College reported that "matters are not as bad as they might be." While the girls were guilty of "a very great impropriety and a gross violation of school regulations," this did not amount to anything worse than "very indiscreet conduct." The *Morning Call* began by reporting this calmly but then concluded that Gottschalk and Legay "should be kicked out of the society of every family

of man."[83] The *Daily Dramatic Chronicle* went even further in its call
for retribution; on the morning of the eighteenth it blazed the headline
"L. M. Gottschalk Tar and Feather? Eh?"

These were the themes of articles printed as far afield as Carson City
and Gold Hill, Nevada.[84] Never mind that some newspapers made light of
it all, joking about the many young men in San Francisco who were suddenly taking piano lessons.[85] The situation was dangerous, and
Gottschalk knew it. At two o'clock on September eighteenth, the old U.S.
Pacific Mail steamship *Colorado* was sailing for Panama. Gottschalk
boarded at the last minute disguised as "Mr. John Smith." The *Sacramento Daily Bee* concluded that San Francisco had become "too hot for
him," while the *Daily Dramatic Chronicle*, under the headline "Skedad-
dled," reported: "We are informed that 'Farewell Concert Gottschalk' rid
the State of his pestilential presence by leaving on the steamer yes-
terday."[86]

Gradually San Francisco settled down again. The *Daily Morning
Chronicle* criticized other papers, especially the *Dramatic Chronicle*, for
accusing Gottschalk of "heinous offenses against law and good morals,
when there does not exist a shadow of reliable evidence to sustain its
assertions."[87] The *Golden Era* issued a round-up of the incident that defended the Oakland Female College and charged Gottschalk only with
very poor judgment, a conclusion with which several other newspapers
soon concurred.[88]

After all the exertions to which someone went in order to spread the
story of the scandal throughout the West, one would have thought that a
similar effort would have been directed toward New York and the East
Coast. But this did not occur. Most New York newspapers ignored the
story. In fact, the only papers to cover it were the *New York Weekly Review* and a few penny rags.[89] Nor did Manhattan become the dissemination point for further stories about the scandal. Indeed, the defense of
Gottschalk published by his friend Henry Watson and reprinted by Henry
Clapp Jr., in his *Saturday Press* probably reached as many people as the
few stories in the New York press that reported on the incident.[90]

Back in San Francisco the most flamboyant renditions of the episode
had been discounted in favor of more sober versions, which accused
Gottschalk of indiscretion but not of crime. The accuracy of the more
moderate account is attested by several pieces of evidence. Statements
by the Oakland Female College, letters from San Francisco friends to
Gottschalk, and Gottschalk's own account, as set forth in his long letter
of explanation to Charles Francis Chickering, were in agreement on all
essential points.[91] In addition, Gottschalk's behavior following the incident, when he announced yet a further concert, suggests that he felt he

had nothing to fear. Finally, it is revealing that Charles Legay continued to move easily in proper San Francisco society.[92] Had his adventure with Gottschalk been more damaging, Legay would surely not have continued to be received socially.

What, then, caused what came to be known as the "Gottschalk scandal"? On Gottschalk's side, it was all too typical of his behavior toward women. The two most important women in his life were his mother and Ada Clare, both of them extravagant and strong-willed personalities and both of them self-destructive in ways that affected everyone around them. Frightened, even terrified, by the feminine psyche as he had known it, Gottschalk fled to the company of young girls, sweet and adoring innocents with whom he could enjoy what he believed were nothing more than inconsequential flirtations.

A few prominent San Franciscans whispered that the scandal was a part of some "plot" against Gottschalk,[93] but the confident tone of officials of the Oakland Female Seminary as they worked to exculpate themselves and their students, as well as the later behavior of Legay, suggests that there had been no plot to trap Gottschalk. But the question remains: Once the incident took place, who first spread the story to the press and was responsible for the most damaging version that went out over the telegraph?

It was certainly not Thomas Maguire, even though several writers have pointed fingers in his direction.[94] Though no longer under Maguire's direct management, Gottschalk cooperated with him to the end, gladly participating in programs involving musicians under Maguire's management. Besides, Maguire was himself engaged in a "war of managers" at the time and had no time to trifle with Gottschalk.[95]

A second possibility is that the deed was perpetrated by someone connected with the San Francisco piano merchants Ripley & Kimball. Arriving in San Francisco without his usual Chickering, Gottschalk had been dependent upon the firm of Badger & Lindenburger to provide him with a Chickering grand. With a total lack of subtlety, Mr. Badger had overplayed his hand. On the day of Gottschalk's final concert a local paper snidely announced the "Chickering and Gottschalk Benefit."[96] For days, the same paper had been touting the rival instruments for sale at the firm of Ripley & Kimball, noting that they did not need "the magic touch of a Gottschalk to evoke [their] music."[97] And on the day the scandal broke, the papers were at it again, attacking Chickering as much as Gottschalk and suggesting that San Francisco could do without both.[98] No wonder that Henry Watson in New York placed blame for the scandal squarely on Chickering's rivals in California.[99]

Circumstantial evidence also links Emannuele Muzio, Gottschalk's former manager, to the scandal. Notoriously vindictive, Muzio moved from one terrible fight to the next, often unleashing campaigns of slander against his opponents. This time he had ample cause for frustration. Often the butt of negative reviews in his appearances with Gottschalk, Muzio had done no better as manager. By mid-summer he had parted ways with Gottschalk, and the split was nasty. Moreau himself later accused Muzio of having been "a thieving impresario."[100]

Gottschalk's decision to rent Platt's Hall and mount concerts of his own was an act of defiance against Muzio, who reciprocated by refusing to allow Sbriglia and his other singers to perform in Gottschalk's monster concerts. Watson in New York tried to minimize the conflict by publishing that "Gottschalk parted from Signor Muzio for reasons which concerned the great contracting parties alone."[101] This did not paper over the conflict, however. Circumstantial evidence that Muzio was directly involved in the scandal emerged later in Lima, and then again in Montevideo. In both cities Italian singers previously linked with Muzio refused to perform with Gottschalk and otherwise made trouble for him. It is hard to escape the conclusion that Muzio wrote ahead in an effort further to damage his former "property."

The press took up the issue with glee. However, one San Francisco paper in particular, the *Daily Dramatic Chronicle*, led the charge. It was this gossipy sheet that called for telegrams on Gottschalk to be sent east and that printed the nastiest reports on Gottschalk's flight. Anti-French and anti-Catholic to the core, the *Daily Dramatic Chronicle* began hounding Gottschalk on the day of his arrival. By July it was harping on his "musical failure" when everyone else was heaping praise on him, and by August it was denouncing Gottschalk's "pretensions," claiming that "he is a bilk; a penny-whistle."[102] The same paper refused to cover the monster concerts at Platt's and issued various anti-Chickering pieces instead. The one time it fell silent regarding Gottschalk was on September 16–17, the very days on which telegrams concerning the scandal were flying across California and Nevada.

Why, though, did other papers take up the cry? For one thing, many journalists were eager to ridicule anyone who seemed to be peddling refinement in rough-house San Francisco. As to the more conservative press, it, too, had reason to jump on the anti-Gottschalk bandwagon. At the time of the incident San Francisco papers were full of accounts of court cases involving seduction and rape. Two days before the Gottschalk scandal burst they had reported in detail on the trial of a streetcar conductor accused of raping a young girl. A week later a jury awarded ten thousand dollars to one John Riley, whose daughter Bridget had been seduced by an older man.[103]

Besides all these factors, Moreau Gottschalk fell victim to the public's tendency, widespread in the nineteenth century, to ascribe to virtuoso musicians like Paginini and Liszt diabolic sexual powers.[104] When San Francisco's *Daily Dramatic Chronicle* charged Charles Legay with playing Leporello to Gottschalk's Don Giovanni, it linked Moreau directly with this tradition.[105]

To some extent, Gottschalk understood and appreciated these various considerations. Indeed, his prior experience with the press should have prepared him well. A year before departing for California he had mused to his sisters about the fickle nature of public opinion. "The more improbable an infamy is, the more attractions it can offer when it can tarnish for a moment the luster that surrounds a man who is in the public eye. It is a sensation. Under this heading the newspapers eat it up."[106]

However well he may have understood the perils of public life, Gottschalk proved incapable of reckoning with the situation that erupted so suddenly in San Francisco. Least of all did he acknowledge his own culpability in what was, after all, an unforgivably foolish misadventure. Frightened and beaten down by the storm of abuse directed against him, Gottschalk boarded the *Colorado* a defeated man, crushed by forces he could comprehend but not control.

Chapter Twenty-four

❧ Turmoil and Testimonials: Peru and Chile, 1865–66

E VER since Gold Rush days, the exodus of disappointed adventurers from California had been nearly as impressive as the influx. When the *Colorado* steamed out of San Francisco harbor it was packed with nine hundred passengers,[1] many of them returnees. Among them was the incognito voyager "Mr. Smith," who avoided all contact with his fellow travelers by claiming seasickness and staying below in his berth. In this sweltering purgatory he was spared the comments by those on board who had followed the San Francisco press. It is revealing that Gottschalk, usually so careful in recording statistics in his *Notes*, underestimated the number of his fellow passengers by half.[2] Evidently, he hardly saw them.

The *Colorado* was steaming toward Panama City. There Moreau had to decide whether to forge on to South America or return to New York. The answer turned on two issues. First, he had to estimate the damage caused by the Oakland scandal. As he contemplated this, Gottschalk had knowledge only of the most inflammatory and venomous press accounts from the first three days. He was unaware that the Oakland school had itself issued far more moderate statements and that these had been disseminated on the pages of respected newspapers. Nor had he yet received any of the reassuring letters addressed to him by friends in San Francisco. Still less did he appreciate how little impact the whole affair was having in the East.

Cowering in his bunk and passing the hours by reading Alfonse Karr thrillers, Gottschalk believed his career in the United States was finished.[3] In a letter to Mary Alice Seymour he declared, "It is beneath my dignity as a man of honor to notice such slanders."[4] But notice them he did. On the one hand, he turned his back on the United States, boycotting the whole country as he had once boycotted Dwight's Boston. On the other hand, he went into excruciating detail to defend himself in a letter to the one person whose good will was essential to his survival in South America, Charles Francis Chickering. Frank, as he was called, directed Chickering's New York office and oversaw the company's South American sales. Gottschalk's letter to Chickering, belabored through three drafts, was precisely the response to slander that he had vowed he would never make.[5] Besides setting out his own version of the events, it defended the proposition that it was he, rather than the young ladies, who was the chief victim.

Chickering considered the matter closed. The firm not only continued Gottschalk's retainer but empowered him to set up dealerships wherever he traveled and assured him a percentage of sales. As Chickering reported to Moreau in his letter of response, "The matter is not one half or one tenth part so bad as you think it is."[6]

The second factor affecting Moreau's decision not to return to New York was that he had dreamed of traveling to South America for a decade. Had not Thalberg succeeded there? And what about that old invitation from his friend General Echenique, the former president of Peru? The Lima press had already printed laudatory articles announcing Gottschalk's imminent arrival, so the prospect of travel in South America began to look far less forbidding than any alternative.[7]

Gottschalk approached Latin America at the height of one of the most turbulent and contradictory periods in the region's history. Liberal political reforms were everywhere breaking through the stagnation induced by a generation of conservative governments. Slavery had been abolished everywhere except in Brazil and was being curtailed even there. Exports and international trade were now the engine of economic growth. At the same time, these changes occurred amidst bloody wars. On the west coast the War of the Quadruple Alliance pitted Chile, Peru, Ecuador, and Bolivia against Spain, while on the east coast the War of the Triple Alliance teamed Argentina, Brazil, and Uruguay against Paraguay.[8]

It is inconceivable that Gottschalk was unaware of these struggles when he set out from California. The conflicts in Peru had been thoroughly reported in the San Francisco press, and the Paraguayan war, declared on May 1, was covered almost daily. Yet Gottschalk plunged ahead. The *Colorado* soon reached Panama City, which Moreau found to be a study in wretchedness and decay.[9] Rumors that the city would be invaded by a band of rebels did not break the tedium that reigned among the foreign businessmen and consuls there. Grateful for any diversion, they took up a large subscription for Gottschalk to give them a concert.[10] Playing on an instrument that he considered the product "of an illicit union between a Jew's harp and a large kettle," he serenaded not only the diplomats but thousands of local ragamuffins, who gathered in a large crowd outside the windows of the town hall in which he performed.[11] Gottschalk had nothing but contempt for the indolent president of Panama, said to be the bishop's son, who later received him in slippers at his "nasty, miserable, and unclean little house."[12]

A month after quitting San Francisco Gottschalk arrived in Callao, Peru, the port for Lima. As if to prepare the soil for the development of his anti-clerical views, chance gave him as traveling companions on the steamer several priests from Peru and Poland and sixteen French nuns. He studied them all with a highly critical eye and reported on them in articles he sent off to Paris.[13]

Over the weeks before reaching Callao he had planned every detail of his Peruvian visit, even to the point of ordering from his sisters fresh ribbons for his various medals.[14] However, he did not adequately factor the local politics into his planning, and now he paid for his neglect. For several months Spain had been putting pressure on its former colony of Peru. Peruvians suspected the Madrid government of wanting to regain a foothold in the New World, or at least to strengthen its hand there financially. With his fleet of eight warships, the Spanish admiral José Manuel Pareja seized several islands off the Peruvian coast and ordered Peru to pay an indemnification of three million pesos.[15] When the Peruvian government of General Juan Antonio Pezet buckled to this demand, another general, Mariano Ignacio Prado, unleashed a civil war against him.

Prado's army reached the outskirts of Lima just as the clerk at the fashionable Maurin Hotel was telling Gottschalk that no rooms were available.[16] Desperate, he found lodging with a French pharmacist named Ernest Dupeyron, who lived but two blocks from the Plaza de Armas at No. 159 Jiron de la Union. As the armies maneuvered on the outskirts of town, Gottschalk strolled about the City of Kings and found it to be anything but regal. He observed the streets filled with garbage and dead carcasses and concluded, on the basis of conversations with Dupeyron and his friends, that these were the consequence of universal corruption and a bloated army led by self-seeking and indolent officers. On the basis of a few days' observation he pronounced, "There is not a point in the Peruvian character in which you do not find the gangrene of venality, of ignorance, of corruption, of sloth, and of boasting."[17]

At four a.m. on November 6 Firmin Moras awoke Gottschalk to report that the battle for Lima had begun and that he should take cover. Within moments drums and trumpets were audible. Then an avalanche of revolutionary troops stormed down the street under Dupeyron's windows.

Shooting broke out on the square as Prado's forces stationed a whole battery of artillery directly in front of Dupeyron's shop. Gottschalk watched it all through the blinds of a second story window, taking in impressions with the detached air of a spectator at a romantic opera. The costuming he judged to be excellent, especially that of the revolutionary horsemen, who were "covered with large red ponchos, with large round white hats on their heads, and [who stood] immovable as statues." Suddenly the artillery discharged and there were "cries, oaths, a furious tempest. In the gloom," Gottschalk wrote, "I see a whole world of phantoms."

Any idea that this was merely an aesthetic diversion ended when a musket ball lodged in the wall directly behind Gottschalk's head. Soon the pavement was covered with wounded soldiers, and hand-to-hand fighting broke out immediately outside the doors of the pharmacy. Fresh troops of the revolution arrived, to the accompaniment of trumpets and cymbals. Cannon emplaced in the street in front of Dupeyron's establishment were leveled at the palace across the plaza. Horrible shrieks and tumult filled the air as scores of the wounded, along with dozens of corpses, were dragged into Dupeyron's courtyard.

At this point Gottschalk abandoned the role of spectator and pitched in to help. He pleaded to an immense crowd of Peruvian gapers for assistance in carting the wounded to a hospital. No one stepped forward. "Do you perhaps take me for a Negro?" one Peruvian asked.[18] Moreau took this exchange as clear evidence of the utter degradation of "the precepts of the Gospels." With great bitterness he observed that "these nice fellows take Communion fifty-two times yearly, have five or six hundred Masses said, and follow in all the processions," yet did not understand the most basic principles of their faith.[19]

His bloody introduction to South America both absorbed and repelled Gottschalk. For the first time in his travels he began clipping and saving stories on the political scene from the local press.[20] Here was a full-blown civil war, yet neither side appeared to defend any noble cause. General Pezet's government had been a despicable farce, but did General Prado promise anything better? The United States minister in Lima, Alvin G. Hovey, thought so and urged Secretary of State Seward to recognize Prado as a champion of democratic principles.[21] Gottschalk disagreed and dismissed Prado's revolution as a fraud. Nor could he sympathize with Peru in the war with Spain.[22] The republics of South America seemed to him a cruel joke that gave rise only to ignorance, corruption, and xenophobia.[23]

It was with thoughts like these that Gottschalk began a series of concerts at Lima's ponderous old Teatro Municipal on November 17, 1865.

His repertoire for this and subsequent concerts in South America was standard, with two exceptions. First, he played none of his Spanish compositions and very few pieces dating from his sojourn in Spanish Cuba— only two in the course of eight concerts in Lima. Second, he programmed both *The Battle Cry of Freedom* and *The Union* repeatedly, as if to proclaim his personal belief in the superiority of the political institutions of the United States. Lest anyone miss the point, he also arranged for the stage at all of his later concerts in Lima to be ornamented with the flags of both Peru and the United States.[24]

To Gottschalk's amazement, the response of the Lima public was "beyond description." As soon as he appeared on stage he was greeted with yells, the stamping of feet, and wild applause lasting for five minutes. The papers were full of sonnets and odes in his honor.[25]

This artistic upheaval was followed by a natural one when an earthquake struck Lima and heavily damaged the Teatro Municipal.[26] Gottschalk was in bed when the disaster struck. Being on the top floor in a back courtyard, he was sure that he would not escape a disaster that destroyed large parts of the city.[27] Rumors that Gottschalk had died in the catastrophe soon appeared in Paris and New York.[28]

With no venue in which to perform, Gottschalk traveled to the port town of Callao, where he gave two concerts for a mixed Peruvian-English audience. There he presented two new compositions, variations on *Auld Lang Syne* and *Variaciones de aires nacionales del Perú*.[29] Both are lost now, but newspaper reports confirm that the latter was built around the fiery *zamacuecas* and other local dances.

Where had Gottschalk encountered this music? After the earthquake damaged the Teatro Municipal, the only suitable theater in Lima was one connected with the Salón Otaiza, an indoor-outdoor entertainment center patterned after the Mabille in Paris. Members had access to game rooms, baths, a rifle range, and a dance pavilion. A Peruvian writer reported that the dances at the Salón Otaiza were attended largely by the "lower classes."[30] The masked balls in particular scandalized members of respectable Lima society, for they featured, in Gottschalk's words, "the stormy *zamacuecas* and other indigenous dances that, although very picturesque, are not such as prudent mothers permit their daughters to indulge in."[31] To attract a highbrow public to such a spot Gottschalk had to raise ticket prices astronomically and get well-placed friends to make a show of buying the first tickets.

The two compositions drawing on the *zamacuecas* were almost the only use Gottschalk made of the indigenous music of South America. Gottschalk's turning away from folk themes paralleled his changing assumptions about society. His early works had been informed by Jacksonian assumptions about democracy, specifically, that popular tastes could suffuse even high culture. His experiences in South America disabused him of this notion. How could one celebrate local cultures when they included such powerful elements of brutality and ignorance that should be changed? Gone from Gottschalk's outlook was the idea of noble savages who played simple but expressive music. In their place were rude brutes who were resistant to progress. Instead of celebrating indigenous culture, Gottschalk wanted now to change it. His great objective in life became to uplift and transform the South American public. This, he was sure, could be achieved best by exposing it to elevated music and education.

Beginning in Lima, Gottschalk became an active crusader for free public education. Contributing 150 pesos to a Lima free school for poor youths, he addressed the director in the following words:

> To spread the light of education through all classes here is a work of patriotism and charity that contributes effectively to the prosperity and happiness of the nation.
>
> As a son of the great republic of the United States of the North, I have, like all my compatriots, a real interest in all that is related to the future of its younger brothers in South America. As modest as my offering may be, consider it as evidence of my good will toward the school you have founded.[32]

During his Lima concerts, Gottschalk carried his educational ideals into the concert hall. At the Teatro Municipal he had needed only one assisting artist, since he was appearing between the acts of a play. Once he moved to the Salón Otaiza, the whole program was in his hands. Prompted in all likelihood by letters from the vindictive Muzio in California, the Italian singers of Lima declared themselves unavailable. Gottschalk therefore enlisted local musicians and composed three operatic works, one based on *Un Ballo in Maschera*, another on *William Tell*, and the third a *Grande Méditation poétique sobre "Faust" de Gounod*. All were scored for available talent, namely two violins, harmonium and piano. On harmonium was the young William (Guillermo) Tate, a bulwark of the musical scene in Lima for decades thereafter and a perpetuator of Gottschalk's memory after his death.[33] Gottschalk also loaned his Chickering grand to the aspiring Chilean artist Josefina Filomeno when she played a concert to benefit war victims.

Gottschalk's abhorrence of both populism and chauvinism grew during the Lima concerts. He railed against the "hundred hoarse and probably drunken patriots" who burst in on one of his performances to sing the Peruvian national anthem.[34] In 1855 Moreau had written the mazurka *Souvenir de Lima* (op. 74) for his friend General José Rufino Echenique, ex-president of Peru. Now that he was actually in Lima Gottschalk avoided his old friend entirely. Doubtless, he had discovered that as president the reactionary Echenique had fostered the very venality and corruption that Moreau now so vigorously denounced.[35]

Gottschalk's cool attitude toward the victorious forces led General Prado eventually to send twenty soldiers to arrest him. Only when Gottschalk threatened to call in the American minister did Prado drop the plan. The alternatives to Prado were no better, however, and when a general who was trying to overthrow him asked Gottschalk to compose a triumphal march for his cause, Moreau refused.[36] "What republics!" Gottschalk wrote. "What scorn and what outrage upon the principles of liberty, equality, and fraternity are cast by these pseudo-presidents of democracies, who trample upon right, justice, and equality in order to wallow in those turpitudes which recall the decadence of Rome and the Saturnalia of the later Empire!"[37]

The impact of Gottschalk's Lima concerts and of his efforts in behalf of public education eclipsed whatever ill will may have arisen from his liberal politics. Critics judged his new works "sublime" and "true slices of life." Members of the Club Nacional de Lima held a Lucullan banquet in his honor and presented him with a large gold medal inscribed to "al eminente artiste L. M. Gottschalk."[38] Laurel wreaths of silver were also bestowed upon him. The newspaper *El Comercio* concluded that Gottschalk's visit to Peru marked "a new era for our society."[39]

After composing a waltz entitled *Marguerite* (op. 76) in honor of his hostess, Madame Dupeyron, Gottschalk sailed on an English steamer toward Arequipa, Peru's second city, 450 miles farther down the coast. With its Spanish patrician families and its large European population, this cultivated center would normally have been an obvious target for Gottschalk. But en route he learned that the local theater had no roof, which spelled trouble as the rainy season approached. He therefore continued with the intention of proceeding to the Chilean port of Valparaíso.

On March 23, 1865, he reached the Peruvian town of Arica, the ancient jumping-off point for trade with the mining centers of Bolivia.[40] On the next day Admiral Pareja issued an ultimatum to the government of Chile as part of his effort to punish that country for siding with Peru against Spain. Pareja's demands were simple: either Chile would signal its acceptance of Spain's conditions by firing a twenty-one gun salute, or his squadron of seven warships would destroy Valparaíso.[41] After receiving no response from the Chileans, Pareja made good on his threat. In three hours of attack on March 31, 1866, the Spanish launched some twenty-six hundred bombs and projectiles over the city. The population, which fled to the nearby hill, watched in horror. In the process of bombarding Valparaíso, Pareja destroyed several million dollars' worth of property be-

longing to United States citizens. After this incident Gottschalk abandoned all thoughts of reaching Valparaíso and instead dallied at Arica—
or, more specifically, at the town of Tacna, forty miles inland and hence
safe from Spanish artillery shells.

Tacna was a one-carriage town, enlivened by little more than the passage of mule teams bearing silver and copper ore from the Bolivian interior to the coast. Moreau quickly made contact with leaders of the "micro-
scopic circle" of educated residents, mainly Germans, Swiss, and a
smattering of Peruvians. Through methods worthy of P. T. Barnum he
managed to drum up an audience for three concerts, and he probably
used the opportunity to try out a new *Marcha*, in E-flat major, which he
later elaborated in Chile. And then Holy Week set in.[42]

"Small towns are boring everywhere," Moreau confessed to his sisters,
"but in Peru they are deadly."[43] But for all his spleen about the locals,
Gottschalk revealed that in one respect his old curiosity regarding indigenous life and art was as alive as ever. With no little wonderment he listened to an old Indian violinist who accompanied Tacna's priest as he
sang the Lamentations on Good Friday. Like Gottschalk himself, this rustic virtuoso frolicked around the melody, playing arpeggios, trills, plunging chromatic scales, and even obbligatos in the high treble.[44] With the
same ethnographic zeal, Moreau took notes on another Indian's reed flute
or *tristos* and documented the colorful manner in which local residents
adorned their church for Easter Sunday. He carefully observed the local
salon dances, too, including the polka, waltz, lancers, and habanera,
which in Tacna was danced entirely differently than in Havana. The local
quadrille or *mecapaqueña* particularly fascinated him, not only with its
minor keys and eccentric rhythms but also with its almost Arabic-
sounding melodies.[45]

Clearly, Gottschalk's susceptibility to local color had not waned since
Martinique, Cuba, or even New Orleans. What had changed was his more
severely moralistic critique of the society that produced these dances.
Due to this, he felt little disposed to celebrate this indigenous music by
adapting it for performance in the concert hall.

By early May 1866 Gottschalk was eager to move on. But where
should he go? An acquaintance had proposed an expedition inland to Bolivia. However, the five-hundred-mile trip by mule to Chuquisaca (Sucre),
the Bolivian capital, seemed out of the question. Besides, he had learned
that the president of Bolivia, General Melgarejo, was a monster who had
cut off the ears of his adjutant with a saber and hacked at an aide-de-
camp with an axe. "He burns, sacks, and gluts himself like a ferocious
beast in the midst of all the excesses to which his savage and sanguinary
appetites drive him," wrote Gottschalk.[46]

The second alternative was to return directly to Panama, and thence to New York.[47] By now he had received Frank Chickering's letter in response to his own detailed account of the incident in Oakland. In addition to reporting that the California scandal was by no means as grave as Gottschalk believed, Chickering stated bluntly, "I am ready to negotiate with you for a professional season for the winter of '66 & '67. And my candid advice to you is to *come to New York.* Your [version] of the S. F. matter is fast being understood."[48]

The third alternative was potentially the most dangerous, namely, to forge ahead to Valparaíso, Chile, and thence to the Chilean capital, Santiago. This had been his original plan, and since Admiral Pareja's naval squadron was now hundreds of miles up the coast near Lima, Gottschalk decided to risk it. When word reached him in Tacna that many in Chile were already expecting him, all doubts vanished and he embarked at once for Valparaíso, eight hundred miles further down the coast.

Local papers complained about the fact that Gottschalk was only passing through Valparaíso on his way to Santiago, seven hours inland by train, and would not stay long enough even to offer one performance.[49] Actually, he did appear at a musical soirée hosted by several Germans. The next day he climbed the steep hills around the arc-shaped harbor and was intrigued by the ubiquity of stairways rather than streets. While Gottschalk was reconnoitering the port city, he received a letter from the United States ambassador in Santiago, former Union army general Judson Kilpatrick, urging him to come at once to the capital and stay at the embassy in a suite of rooms that had just been refurbished for his use.[50] Kilpatrick's motives were not merely social. Thanks to the fact that the Spanish squadron had destroyed American property at Valparaíso and then seized an American ship at Callao, the United States now actively sided with the South Americans against their former colonial rulers. This assertion of the Monroe Doctrine was welcomed by the Chilean government in Santiago, where both continental and hemispheric solidarity were much in vogue. Ambassador Kilpatrick found in the bilingual and bicultural Gottschalk a convenient way to express this new amity. Gottschalk, for his part, reveled in a role for which his whole life had prepared him.[51]

Santiago, where Gottschalk arrived on the fifteenth, presented a welcome contrast to Lima. Gottschalk would have agreed with Herman Melville's characterization of Lima as "the saddest city on earth," but Santiago had reason to be among the happiest. The snow-capped Andes looked down on a burgeoning center grown rich from the seemingly inexhaustible silver and copper mines of northern Chile. Santiago was the hub of South America's first rail network and boasted new public buildings, sumptuous homes, and gas-lit streets. And in sharp contrast to Peru, Chileans boasted a durable constitution that had survived several unsuccessful attempts to disrupt it.[52] Never mind that the government was oligarchic. It was at least stable, and under the current president, José Joaquín Pérez, an elderly, indolent, but benevolent patrician, religious toleration, free trade, and other liberal reforms were all being advanced.[53]

Economic and political progress enlivened Santiago's cultural life. The large British colony sponsored many good works that benefited the city, while German immigrants had established their usual concert groups and singing societies. By 1857 the great new Teatro Municipal opened its doors.[54] The city also boasted a philharmonic society, an opera company, and a conservatory of music.[55] Only education lagged, with a mere 18 percent of the population literate.[56] This provided a perfect outlet for Gottschalk's philanthropic energies.

These conditions were so positive that it was unnecessary for him to offer the usual warm-up concerts in a small hall. Instead, Gottschalk went directly to the Teatro Municipal, making his debut there on May 31, 1866. Eventually the series in Santiago extended to fifteen concerts, with a *crescendo* to ten-piano affairs and finally a grand festival or "monster concert."[57]

Ambassador Kilpatrick's hopes were realized at the second concert on June 3, when Gottschalk presented a new work, *L'Alianza*, dedicated both to the quadruple alliance of South American countries against Spain and to the alliance between these four countries and the United States.[58] Now lost, this composition can be seen as a kind of analogue to *The Union*, in that it used music to affirm solidarity in the face of a military foe. It is no wonder that it was greeted with shouts and cheers since, as one critic rhapsodized, "it combined the Chilean and Peruvian national anthems with a *zamacuecas* and a most beautiful American tune."[59] The innovative use of the *zamacuecas* on a concert program "pleasantly surprised us," a critic wrote, "and filled us with patriotism."[60]

Two other new pieces were introduced at these concerts: solo variations on the aria *Spirito gentil* from Donizetti's opera *La Favorita*, and solo variations on Karl Gottlieb Reissiger's fifth *Danse brilliante*.[61] Since neither of these survives, it is impossible to judge their musical merit. Their existence, however, gives the lie to anyone who would claim that in South America Gottschalk abandoned composition for the life of a touring virtuoso.

By now he had made contact with those in Santiago who were involved with the furtherance of education. Gottschalk dedicated profits from one concert to a Society for Primary Education.[62] He also played benefit concerts for three Catholic secondary schools, one of them French.[63] Soon every philanthropy in town wanted to tap Gottschalk's fund-raising magic. To accommodate them he came up with the novel idea of offering a single great benefit concert and asking the city council to divide the profits among worthy philanthropic agencies, much as a community foundation might do today.[64]

More than ever before, Gottschalk extended his support to young local musicians. The long list of beneficiaries included Guillermo Deichert, Enrique Rudolphy, Carlos Stamm, and Adolfo Yentzen, all of whom figured prominently in the later history of Chilean music.[65] Another Gottschalk protégé from Chile was the flautist Juan Jacobo Thomson, who performed with the North American guest in several concerts and later used his magazine *Las Bellas Artes* to preserve Gottschalk's memory.[66] Particularly notable among his Chilean students was young Federíco Guzmán (1837–85), later one of South America's most notable romantic composers.[67] So impressed was the North American with the fifteen-year-old Guzmán that he not only gave him lessons and urged him to continue his training in Paris but solicited money from the Chilean public to pay for the trip. Later influenced by Schumann and Chopin, Guzmán nonetheless remained a loyal Gottschalk disciple, as is evident in piano pieces like his *Rappelle-toi* and the symphonic poem *América*.[68] To promote his young protégé, Gottschalk with various partners played Guzmán's two-piano march *La Victoriosa* across South America.

Gottschalk's hemispheric patriotism, his contribution to education, and his support for local artistic talent went to the heart of Santiagans. A leading paper announced that Gottschalk was "the best pianist in the universe," and a series of receptions and banquets was mounted, at which he was presented with gold pins, silver plaques, dolls, and gold medals.[69]

Chilean president Pérez invited Moreau several times to his home and also brought him to the opening of the parliament, where he was seated with the ambassadors from France and the United States.[70] At the Sacre Coeur School the French priests feted Gottschalk as he sat under a canopy adorned with his portrait crowned with laurels. All this hullabaloo was accompanied by a steady bombardment of poems and sonnets celebrating Gottschalk's "celestial harmony," "tender hands," and so on. Typical of these florid verses was one by Manuel Cuartín, who concluded his strophes with:

> Your piano becomes an instrument of God.
> And what will the cold atheist say?
> He will say "there must be a God, and in His mercy I believe."[71]

By now the fervor had reached such a pitch that Gottschalk proposed a festival or monster concert for Santiago. Civic boosters leaped at the idea of being the first capital on the South American continent to sponsor such an event. The editor of *El Ferrocarril* was in ecstasy and published a budget proving that the good-hearted composer was bound to lose money on the project. No matter, Gottschalk responded. "Chile," he declared, "offers to the rest of the Americas a rare example of order joined with liberty."[72] The show must go on.

The program for the *gran festival*, held on August 12, 19, and 26, called for 350 musicians. Several of the pieces were straight out of Gottschalk's first monster concert in Havana, but the finale, a *Gran Marcha solemne*, was composed especially for the occasion.[73] Much later the Brazilian pianist Arthur Napoleão claimed to have helped Gottschalk recast this work for use at a festival in Rio. This led musicologist Francisco Curt Lange to characterize the *Gran Marcha solemne* as an "elastic, migratory product," a matrix into which could be dropped the national anthem of whatever country Gottschalk happened to be in at the time.[74] Since the Chilean and Uruguayan variants of this work are lost, and since only a rough piano reduction by Napoleão of the Brazilian version has survived, it is impossible to judge the accuracy of Lange's claim.[75] Gottschalk, in a letter from Santiago, referred to "a tight contrapuntal section leading to the national anthem of Chile with cannon fire and drums," which corresponds to part of Napoleão's version.[76] But in Santiago, at least, the entire extravaganza was fresh, and no one doubted that it was an ode to Chilean liberty.

Among the thirty-five hundred guests who mobbed the concert hall were the President and ministers, the entire diplomatic corps, and even the Archbishop of Santiago, no music lover, whose presence one newspaper judged to be "a miracle."[77] As the battle section of the *Gran Marcha solemne* unfolded, the audience understood it was experiencing again the bombardment of Valparaíso, now elevated to the level of art.[78] All were certain that the original march that preceded and followed the bombardment section would become a national classic and that "our bands will repeat it endlessly." Then, when the Chilean anthem burst out following the final fugue, it was "like an electric ray that communicated an enthusiasm that radiated frenetically [through the theater]."[79] The immense crowd leaped to its feet, and by the finale the President, ministers, and entire public were waving their handkerchiefs. Men threw their hats into the air. Women wept.[80]

Nor did it end there. When, after repeating the entire performance, Gottschalk finally left the concert hall, 250 bandsmen met him at the stage door. With the musicians blaring his *Gran Marcha solemne* and forty drums marking time, Gottschalk marched at the head of a crowd of several thousand people in a torch-lit procession to his rooms at the American embassy. Cries of "Viva Gottschalk" resounded en route. Even after he had disappeared into the building the crowd refused to disperse. Finally, Gottschalk, standing on a chair lifted aloft by friends, appeared in the window one last time to wish the throng goodnight.

What should we make of this extravagant event? Was it merely another manifestation of Latin exuberance, or was it more? The music can be judged best by its effect on the audience, which was stupendous. Whatever its other qualities, the *Gran Marcha solemne* somehow communicated what the public most wanted to hear. What was that message?

For a country at war, the military motif and especially the "bombardment" passage stole the show. When the Chilean anthem finally emerged after all the cacophony, everyone equated it with victory at arms. But what about the "solemn march" itself, Gottschalk's original theme? Assuming it bore some resemblance to the theme later transcribed by Napoleão, this march was indeed stately and serious. As such, it was probably understood as a reflection of the solid and enduring political order that Chile, alone among its neighbors on the west coast of South America, had established. This march, moreover, lacks all Spanish or regional tinges and could, in fact, have been adopted as easily by Sweden of Austria as by Chile. Chile, in other words, was part not just of South America but of the larger civilized world and offered itself to be judged by the cosmopolitan standard of progress. Finally, the fact that the *Gran Marcha solemne* was composed by a citizen of the United States, who conducted it while standing beneath the entwined flags of the two American republics,[81] implied for the first time that Chile and the United States were on equal footing and were linked by the shared values unique to liberal republics.

Chileans were accustomed to public festivals, but mainly of a religious character. The liberal republic, for all its successes, had failed to provide adequate secular channels for the public expression of its ideals. It therefore fell to Gottschalk to mount the country's, and also the continent's, first large-scale public celebration of nationalism and liberalism—the two great ideological forces of the era. These were Gottschalk's own values, and they perfectly fit the moment. Wrote *El Mercurio*, "Gottschalk's triumph exceeds anything ever known in Chile."[82]

Leaving Santiago, Moreau expected to stop only briefly in Valparaíso before visiting the wealthy mining district in the north of Chile.[83] He misjudged Chile's second city, however, and soon was immersed in a fresh round of concerts and benefits.[84] Citizens of Valparaíso demanded their own festival and insisted that it be at least equal in scale to what had just taken place in Santiago. Gottschalk obliged[85] by simply reproducing the Santiago festival *in toto*. However, three subtle shifts in the presentation did not pass unnoticed.

First, the back of the stage of the Teatro de la Victoria was ornamented with two suns surrounded by dazzling stars. This symbolized the hegemony of the United States and Chile on their respective continents. The two flags were surmounted by a giant eagle—a blunt reference to the Monroe Doctrine and a not very subtle hint to Spain. The "liberty and honor" of Valparaíso and Chile would henceforth never go undefended, declared *La Patria*.[86]

Second, amateur orchestras participated this time, and scores of enthusiasts from small towns in the Chilean interior flooded into Valparaíso "with the sole end purpose of participating in the great event."[87]

Third, the Valparaíso festival highlighted more local talent.[88] A local journalist responded appreciatively, saying, "This American artist knows how to do justice to our compatriots and has encouraged all those who have ability and feel a calling to music, so they may in turn free us some day from our foolish dependence upon whomever arrives here from the outside."[89]

Thanks perhaps to these touches, the crowd nearly tore down the doors of the theater to get in and began cheering even before the performance commenced.[90] The Valparaíso audience did not need to be coached. It listened with appropriate rage to "the unjust aggression of the Spanish squadron"[91] against the city and swelled with pride at Chile's eventual victory. "Never has anyone excited warmer or more spontaneous enthusiasm," wrote *El Mercurio*.[92] Nor was this merely the excitement of the moment. More than a century later the Chilean scholar Luis Merino wrote that Gottschalk had "exerted a major causal impact on the culture of Valparaíso and of Chile, especially through his grand promotion of a national music."[93]

Throughout his travels in South America Gottschalk was his own manager. Since his goal was to set aside enough money in investments that he could eventually support himself fully, he had to make unwelcome choices. Such was his decision to head back up the Chilean coast to the so-called Norte Chico district, the rough and dynamic semi-desert region in which the great mining fortunes were being made. "I will go up and down the whole coast and get the most possible out of it," he declared to his sisters.[94] And so he stopped to perform in La Serena, whose only claim to fame was that it was rich enough for the government of Chile to have established a mint there. By mid-January 1867 he was in Copiapó, the Virginia City of Chile.

Booming since its establishment in 1843, Copiapó boasted sidewalks, a theater, and a large foreign-born population.[95] Moreau delivered three concerts there and lingered for fully three months. Gone, however, were the generous impulses that prompted him in Valparaíso and Santiago. Except for boosting the career of the local prodigy Tomás Ródenas, he focused mainly on amassing money.[96] The local paper criticized him for sharing his talents only with the very wealthy.[97] He promptly corrected this, but his overall focus did not change. Soon he was taking a side trip clear across the Atacama desert to the fabulous silver mine La Buena Esperanza.[98] Not realizing that this El Dorado had already peaked, he invested in a mine there and eventually lost his money, just as he had done in California when he invested in an oil company there.[99]

The Copiapó adventure can perhaps be dismissed as a naive attempt by a fundamentally impractical man to be worldly. Gottschalk had just scored triumphs as composer, conductor, and performer beyond anything known to that time on the entire continent. He seemed charged by fresh energy. And, if his latest compositions were not masterpieces, they at least were received as such. In such an exultant mood, it is understandable that he might have thought it possible to remove in one stroke the financial burden that had weighed on him since his father's death in 1853.

Yet at this very moment, a distinct note of anxiety began to enter Gottschalk's letters. Writing to his sisters, he spelled out his financial situation and complained—in Copiapó of all places—at being over-charged for the use of the theater.[100] To his friend Charles Vezin in Philadelphia he wrote anxiously about the possibility of a lawsuit involving his Manhattan house and criticized his New York law firm, Coudert Brothers for its handling of the affair.[101] In practically the same breath, he groused about "all those maneuvers that are indispensable to the artist's success": the obsequious visits to editors, calls on members of the local elite, and the need to "beg for the good will of pretentious and all-powerful fools."[102]

Gottschalk had registered such complaints many times in the past, of course, but in South America his tone darkened. To his sisters he wrote, "Life is full of real sorrows."[103] A photograph of him taken in La Serena reflects this mood. The photographer posed him standing casually by a chair, with one of the gold medals from Santiago pinned to his chest. But where earlier he might have looked out at the camera with a nonchalance approaching smugness, his expression now was heavy, tired, and without light.[104] The sweetly nostalgic *Home, Sweet Home* and his own lugubrious *The Last Hope* figured prominently in all his concert programs now, and he frequently gave voice to a longing for a stability in his life that his wandering life disallowed.[105]

It was while in this mood that Moreau recorded a "sad but picturesque incident." At the home of the local French consul in Copiapó he had met a distinguished Frenchman who had once studied at the prestigious École Polytechnique but was now utterly destitute. Several days after this dinner the old man died. Since the Frenchman had no family to claim his body, members of the local French colony took matters into their own hands. In accordance with local custom, they assembled at midnight to bear the coffin off to the cemetery. Gottschalk joined them.

With great effort they heaved the wooden coffin onto a horse-drawn hearse. As the pitiful little procession wound up the rocky hillside the poor beast that was pulling the hearse stumbled, and then its harness snapped. When the taciturn Indian driver refused to go further, Gottschalk and several of the others detached the harness and themselves dragged the hearse the rest of the way. Deep in the desert night they reached the cemetery. An old dodderer wearing a black skullcap silently opened the door to a vault and received the coffin.

A few hours later Gottschalk was back in his room at the Hotel Marcadet, mulling over the sad fate of those who die far from hearth and home. Amidst these morose ruminations, he experienced ominous presentiments of his own death. "It is a nightmare," he wrote. "I shall not sleep tonight."[106]

Chapter Twenty-five

✕ A Pan-American on the Rio de la Plata, 1867–68

W ITH the approach of Holy Week in April 1867, Gottschalk finally left Copiapó and sailed south to Valparaíso, where he picked up the Pacific Steam Navigation Company's packet to Argentina. In spite of his morbid depression in Copiapó he was sad to leave, knowing he would never respond to the jaunty pleas of friends there for him to come again.[1] He was awaited in Argentina, however, and this finally dispelled his gloom.[2]

On May 18 Gottschalk's ship put in at Punta Arenas at the mouth of the Straits of Magellan in Tierra del Fuego. Two and a half centuries earlier Magellan had found the impaled corpses of two hundred Indians on this site, which now served as a mustering point for ships preparing to navigate the treacherous straits. Gottschalk joined other passengers for a brief shore visit and met remnants of the Tehuelches tribe, renowned for their extraordinary stature.

On May 25, 1866, the steamer sailed into the broad estuary of the Rio de la Plata. For the next two years this broad river separating Argentina and Uruguay was to be Gottschalk's home, as he shuttled back and forth between Buenos Aires and Montevideo. The eight-hour crossing was often rendered tortuous by the furious storms that blew up on a moment's notice. On one crossing Gottschalk's steamer crashed broadside into a three-masted sailing vessel and nearly sank it. The bow of Gottschalk's ship was destroyed and for several hours the pumps churned furiously. In the end, the ship was saved and the passengers survived. Gottschalk wasted no time sending an account of the near-tragedy to Clara, with the request that she write it up for Henry Watson's *Art Journal*.[3] Clearly, he was beginning to think once more of the United States.

In spite of his prior intentions, Moreau first went not to Argentina but to Montevideo, the capital of Uruguay. It mattered little to him that for most of this period Argentina was ruled by a liberal reformer, Bartolomé Mitre, or that this former professor was creating a national judiciary for Argentina and codifying the nation's laws. These positive factors paled in comparison to the fact that Argentina was at war with Paraguay. Domestic opposition to the war had created virtual anarchy in Buenos Aires, wrecking the economy and ruining Gottschalk's chances of succeeding there.[4] He therefore went straight to Montevideo and settled at the Hotel Americano on Calle de Missiones, near the presidential palace.

The local economy was relatively stronger here. In its politics, however, Uruguay was hardly more stable than Argentina. Its government was shaky and epitomized all that Gottschalk despised in South American politics. Heading it was a classic Latin dictator, Venancio Flores. Flores had several sons who were all notable louts, especially the eldest, Fortunato, who, in spite of his benign name (meaning "Fortunate Flowers"), was a drunkard, a murderer, and the scourge of Montevideo.

When a soldier from Fortunato's private guard failed to stand up straight, Fortunato plunged his saber into the poor wretch's stomach. During a rehearsal at the Comic Opera he asked a French actress to sing one of his favorite songs. When she confessed she did not know it, he beat her unconscious.[5] Fortunato also liked piano music, and soon, in Gottschalk's words, it was "my good fortune to be extraordinary pleasing to him." Meeting Gottschalk in the street one day, Fortunato took him by the arm and called him his dear friend. About the same time, Fortunato and his drinking chums showed up at the Hotel Americano and shot up the lobby, destroying hundreds of glasses and all the mirrors, while Gottschalk cowered in his room upstairs. Another night Fortunato brought guests to the hotel for dinner, argued with them, and threw them all in jail.[6]

Various forces combined to save Montevideo from the kind of anarchy prevailing in Argentina, the most decisive being the French, Spanish, and American gunboats riding in the harbor. The mere presence of their cannon cooled even the hottest Uruguayan blood. The resulting sense of security, along with the up-to-date tastes that arose from the fact that a third of the capital's residents were foreign born,[7] gave Montevideo the edge over Buenos Aires as a musical launching point. Gottschalk understood this well and noted, not without cynicism, "The government here does not dare exercise its evil instincts against foreigners, whose cannon force it into a saintly prudence. At the same time the natives have to withstand a multitude of base acts which dishonor the republican cause."[8]

It did not take Gottschalk long to discover in Montevideo a surprisingly sophisticated musical environment centering around the handsome Teatro Solis, then a decade old.[9] Gottschalk soon met its founding director, the Toulouse-born Count Louis Preti (1826–1902). Preti, a liberal, had fled France after the Revolution of 1848 and was now the doyen of local musicians. Preti introduced Gottschalk around, performed with him in public and private, and later, after Gottschalk's death, championed his memory throughout the southern hemisphere.[10]

Through Preti, Moreau met an elderly French woman, Madame Elise d'Aubigny, who had been a close friend of his mother in Paris. Madame d'Aubigny had frequently heard Moreau in the French capital and now welcomed him as a living link with her own golden years.[11] They reminisced by the hour and together attended a mass in memory of his mother. He helped coach her students, and she knit a wool foot cover for him. Long before Moreau left the Rio de la Plata, Madame d'Aubigny was in tears over his impending departure.[12]

While he was waiting for the Chickerings to send him two new grands, Gottschalk gave his first performances in the small concert hall of the local Sociedad Filarmónica. At the conclusion of his next concert, Madame d'Aubigny's students presented him with a gold medal, a crown of oak and roses, and a gold-embossed sheet of vellum with the names of the donors. "I hardly like this kind of exhibition," Moreau confided to his sisters, "in which the hero always looks foolish."[13]

By the end of this series of concerts, old General Flores had invited Gottschalk to visit him in the presidential palace. "He doesn't look so bad," concluded Gottschalk. "On the contrary, you would take him for an Indian field laborer or a *gaucho*. But they say he has been exceedingly cruel and killed many of his prisoners with his own hands." Only days before this meeting, troops loyal to Flores had discovered four hundred pounds of explosives in a tunnel directly beneath the General's seat in the Council Chamber. Gottschalk observed placidly that had this bomb exploded, "I would have shared the General's fate, since I live only a block from the palace." His broader conclusions on the incident were more pointed. "These poor Latin Americans are incorrigible," he wrote, "It is impossible to lead them on the path of order and equality."[14]

The huge Chickering pianos reached Montevideo by September, and Gottschalk, a salesman *par excellence*, soon had the local press treating them as celebrities in their own right. *La Tribuna* featured the instruments in an article appropriately entitled "Gounod, Gottschalk, and Chickering," and the public responded by buying up every ticket to the concerts announced for the Teatro Solis.[15]

While all this was going forward, a minor storm was brewing. Ever since the episode in Lima when the Italian singers had boycotted one of his performances, Gottschalk had shied away from employing assisting artists from the opera. When he did so now in Montevideo, the same problems reappeared. A tenor named Nerini demanded more time on the program; other singers carped that Gottschalk allowed too little time for applause; while still others told the public it was being taken in.[16] Every effort to appease Nerini and his faction failed, and at least one critic, a Frenchman writing under the name of Dorion, sided with those attacking Gottschalk. Dorion added his own complaint that the American endlessly repeated whatever his public called for.[17] Others, more sympathetic to Gottschalk, complained, "A small band opposed to the famed musician has been born and is operating in a reactionary manner. Where or why it exists is unknown."[18] Is it relevant that the vain Nerini had formerly been associated with Emannuele Muzio? It is consistent with Muzio's character that he would have written also to Montevideo in his effort to defame Gottschalk. No wonder that it was in a letter from the Rio de la Plata that Gottschalk referred to Muzio as his "cheating impresario."[19]

A resounding salvo in Gottschalk's defense came from a twenty-four-year-old Spaniard who had arrived in Montevideo only months before Gottschalk. Luís Ricardo Fors never doubted his special link with destiny, but this familiarity was not reciprocated. Trained as a lawyer in Barcelona, he managed to get himself thrown out of Spain in 1866 for participating in a movement to overthrow Queen Isabel and establish a republic. His first two books had already been published in Spain to no acclaim whatsoever. About this time a Madrid publisher issued a biography of the twenty-eight-year old, probably at this own instigation. A third book—an analysis of Uruguay's government and society—appeared within months of Fors's arrival on the Rio de la Plata. Over the following years, Fors spewed out hastily written books on subjects ranging from civil reform, Freemasonry (like Gottschalk, he was a Mason), railroads, and music. With no awareness of the irony involved, he ended his days celebrating the tercentenary of the appearance of *Don Quixote*.[20] Such was the man who designated himself Gottschalk's biographer.

Gottschalk and Fors met at the Hotel Americano, and immediately the musically illiterate young journalist became Gottschalk's confidante and disciple. Gottschalk introduced Fors to his future wife, and Fors, in his florid and grandiose Spanish, described his hero's every move for the press. When the blow-up with Nerini occurred, Fors let fly with two adulatory essays in *La Tribuna*.[21] The Spaniard never doubted that it was he alone who vanquished Gottschalk's opponents.[22]

This was scarcely the case. Gottschalk himself had already plied the press with reviews written by Berlioz, Victor Hugo, and other notables.

More important, he had had the good sense to present at his Teatro Solis concerts his fifteen-year-old Uruguayan student, Antonio María Celestino (1853–96), whom the local public adored. In a warmly appreciated gesture, he even arranged the prodigy's galop *La Perla oriental* for two pianos and actually performed it with him, lending the boy one of his own Chickering grands for the event.[23]

No less effective was the way Gottschalk courted the local German populace. He accomplished this in part by programming transcriptions from Wagner. This was not a new interest of his. Some years earlier he had written to Espadero of the "admirable, new, picturesque, and unheard of majesty" of Wagner's instrumentation.[24] Throughout South America he had performed his own multi-piano transcription of the march from *Tannhäuser*. By 1865–69 Gottschalk had become, in the words of musicologist Robert Stevenson, "Wagner's best advance publicity agent in both the western United States and South America."[25] In Montevideo he presented himself to the public as a true Wagnerian by programming several times his popular march from *Tannhäuser*.

Gottschalk also appealed to the Germanic part of his audience through more direct means. By the 1860s Germans constituted the solid core of the musical public in Uruguay. Gottschalk included members of the *Frohsinn* club in the Teatro Solis concerts and went out of his way to thank them publicly in the press. In the process he even acknowledged the German nation as "the homeland of those great geniuses who have honored music."[26] With their "sincere love of music combined with intelligence," Gottschalk wrote, Germans had enriched the history of civilization. Days later, the *Frohsinn* group invited him to a soirée and bestowed upon him honorary membership.[27]

Had the German musicians of Montevideo known about the abuse Gottschalk had heaped on their countrymen over many years, they might have treated him differently. This would have been a mistake, though, for Gottschalk himself had changed. Far from disparaging the German "professors," with their unkempt beards and spectacles, he now reached out to them as his most thoughtful audience. He composed a number of *Lieder* for them and later arranged several pieces for them to perform in his concerts. Before long, Moreau was pressing his sister Clara to pay more attention to his many compositions being issued by the firm of Schott & Söhne in Mainz and was also scheming to have Schott translate his writings for German audiences.[28] It is clear that he was laying the groundwork for an eventual visit to Germany.

This rapprochement with Germany paralleled Gottschalk's mounting hostility toward everything French. When his brother Gaston turned up in Mexico and then started talking breezily about obtaining a railroad concession, Moreau blamed it all on his French upbringing. "He is French all over, frenchified down to his spine and unfortunately ignorant and silly *[niais]* as only French people can be."[29] Moreau concluded that being silly and Parisian were practically the same thing and faulted the French for having produced nothing more significant in recent years than Offenbach and champagne.[30]

Beyond these factors, the main reason Gottschalk triumphed over his operatic critics in Montevideo was that the public fell in love with his new *Grande Tarentelle* (op. 67) for piano and orchestra. This work, one of the first compositions by an American for piano and orchestra, delighted the Teatro Solis audience and was encored at every performance, quickly becoming what Gottschalk called his *cheval de bataille*.[31] The spirited dance, with its wild leaps on the keyboard, brisk modulations, arresting chromatic interlude, and, at one point, wild dissonances appeared in concert after concert down to the end of Gottschalk's life, invariably bringing the audience to its feet.[32]

Gottschalk was hardly the first European or American composer to have had fun with the tarantella; Rossini, Auber, Chopin, Thalberg, Weber, and Mendelssohn had all preceded him. But Gottschalk was the first to catch the latest wave of interest in this frenetic Italian dance, and his *Grande Tarentelle* marked the start of a veritable fireworks display of fresh tarantellas by European masters. The following year his old Paris friend Saint-Saëns premiered his Second Piano Concerto, which included a break-neck tarantella in the concluding movement. Soon the Russians caught the fever, as César Cui and Dargomyzhky transcribed tarantellas of their own. Judging from what has come down to us of Gottschalk's, it was less sophisticated and nuanced than these later versions, but what it lacks in elaboration it more than makes up in color and intensity.

But just what has come down to us? Back in Havana in 1860 Gottschalk had presented a tarantella for piano and violin.[33] In New York he performed a tarantella, possibly the same one, now scored for piano, violin, and cello. In 1864 he performed a tarantella for piano and orchestra in Philadelphia, at the Academy of Music. None of these scores survives, but Fors, citing no evidence, claimed they were all one and the same work.[34] This may be so, but Gottschalk more than once composed multiple works under the same title. Besides, he was renowned for never playing a piece the same way twice and for never performing a composition in public in the same form he published it.

We cannot begin to judge what listeners heard in Montevideo, Buenos Aires, or Rio. The surviving piano score is probably barely a sketch of what he actually played, and the few orchestral parts that survive in different variants not only bear the marks of hasty composition but all present intriguing differences. Whatever was heard at the Teatro Solis those nights, however, it stunned the Montevideo audience.

Following these performances, a local poet named Francisco X. de Acha wrote a long poem entitled *Gloria à Gottschalk,* one of many verses in the composer's honor published in the press.[35] De Acha spoke about "El Génio Americano" and in one stanza wrote, "Washington's grand homeland, the American nation, need no longer envy the arts elsewhere, for within [America] is the purest star of the piano, the most brilliant heavenly body of the art of music." Several days later Gottschalk responded to de Acha's praise in a letter widely disseminated by the local press. Writing in fluent Spanish, he offered what amounted to his credo as a citizen of the Americas:

> As a son of the great republic to the north, I grew accustomed from earliest youth to considering the entire Western Hemisphere, irrespective of language or latitude, as the common fatherland of all who desire progress and liberty. As a citizen of the United States, I find myself profoundly grateful for your divination of the basic Americanist urge that drives me forward. Were only my limited abilities the equal of my boundless desires and my limitless patriotic impulse, the art of the New World would soar to new heights.[36]

No artist before Gottschalk had viewed himself as a citizen of the entire hemisphere. No artist before Gottschalk had drawn inspiration from the Caribbean for compositions he performed in the United States, or drawn inspiration from the life of the United States for music to be performed in South America. Curiously, this Pan-Americanism coexisted with his multi-cultural instincts, his keen American nationalism, and his acceptance of the emerging nationalisms within South America. On closer inspection, it is clear that Gottschalk's evolving point of view paralleled that of European liberalism, which, after the failed revolutions of 1848, embraced both nationalism and progressive reform. This, at any rate, was the key both to Gottschalk's music and to his civic activity in Buenos Aires, for which he departed on October 18, 1867.[37]

Detailed reports from Montevideo already published in many Buenos Aires newspapers assured him a warm welcome on the other side of the Rio de la Plata. Within days of settling into rooms on the Calle Esmeralda, Gottschalk found himself dining with the ministers of Finances and Interior, as well as the editors of seven newspapers.[38] Then, on October 27, an Alsatian immigrant and graduate of the Paris Conservatoire named Gustave Nessler (1835–1905) invited Gottschalk to join him and other local musicians for an informal session at his home. No sooner did Moreau walk into Nessler's music room than he spied the orchestral score of a waltz his host had just composed to honor a reigning diva at the local Teatro Colón. Gottschalk casually leafed through the pages and then, setting aside the manuscript, sat down at the piano and played the composition from beginning to end without a lapse.[39] Even in a city that had had a philharmonic society for nearly half a century and boasted a large musical community of Germans, such a feat drew notice and ensured that its perpetrator would be welcomed in every salon.[40]

Adhering to his well-practiced ritual, Gottschalk made contact with Chickering's local representative, a German named Sprunck, and made sure that his music was on sale both at Emilio Cornú's Spanish bookstore and at the English Bookstore on Calle San Martín. He also sought out the best local "professor," Munich-born Albert Buschmeyer (1830–83), to assist him in his concerts.

So confident was Gottschalk that he would meet a warm reception that he dispensed with the usual series of warm-up concerts in a small hall and instead alternated between the mid-sized Coliseo and the great Teatro Colón opera house. Such confidence proved justified when critics bombarded their readers with a barrage of Spanish superlatives and with verses comparing Gottschalk's every note with a drop of divine nectar. One enthusiast went so far as to suggest that the halo surrounding the genius's head emitted electric currents.[41] Even such formulaic notices contained revealing insights, as when the English-language *Standard* spoke repeatedly of the lightness and delicacy of Gottschalk's touch and of his frequent dynamic shifts, which now recalled the "chirp of a cricket" and then suddenly the "scream of a locomotive."[42]

Not until the third Teatro Colón concert on December 1 did Gottschalk bring forth a new composition, his *Souvenir de Buenos Aires*. One critic had faulted him for playing too frequently at the chic Coliseo, where working people felt unwelcome. "Do you believe us unworthy of hearing you? Do you think we are incapable of appreciating you?" asked the critic. "No, no, certainly not. As a republican, you don't think that."[43]

Perhaps it was in response to such folksy chiding that Gottschalk drew on the earthy tango and other Argentinean dances for his *Souvenir de Buenos Aires*. He had performed a tango of his own composition at a Montevideo concert four months earlier, so we can be sure that the composer of *Bamboula* was still to some extent attuned to popular dances and the Afro-American idiom.[44] Two weeks later he premiered two more works at the Colón, this time an *Étude*, now lost, and a fantasy on themes from Flotow's opera *Martha*, scored for two pianos.[45] The series culminated with a rousing performance of the *Grande Tarentelle*.

Gottschalk found himself once more the darling of the local intelligentsia. The English and Italian ambassadors both held banquets in his honor, and Minister of Commerce Varela feted him as a champion of education and the embodiment of Pan-Americanism.[46] Meanwhile, local wags made sport of Gottschalk's heralded ability to conjure up crickets and locomotives. "I wish I could be like Gottschalk," one declared. "If I could, I would evoke a good roast duck wing and a bottle of sherry!"[47]

Moreau himself would not have welcomed such sleight-of-hand. He complained, "All I've done since arriving here is dine, to the detriment of my stomach, which is not strong, and of my temperament, which has difficulty handling official banquets, speeches, et cetera."[48] In spite of all the praise that was lavished on him, he was increasingly disenchanted with Buenos Aires. "It is a very large commercial city with lots of omni-buses, wagons, and carts in the streets. It has industrial wealth, but I doubt that I will be as contented here as in Montevideo, where there is a more carefree spirit and something more picturesque in the people, their manners, and the appearance of the city."[49] Besides, a Spanish *zarzuela* company had just come to town, breaking Gottschalk's monopoly of the entertainment scene.[50]

Worse, the continuing war against Paraguay was again dampening the public's mood. The Argentinean army had proven to be a pompous joke, with more generals, drummers, and buglers than warriors. Gottschalk dis-missed Paraguay's dictator Lopez as a savage but considered Argentina's strife-torn society no more worthy of respect.[51]

Within three months of his arrival in Buenos Aires Gottschalk had concluded that it was "the most badly kept city I have ever seen."[52] Filthy streets, a non-existent fire department, and appalling hygiene exposed the city to scourges of every variety.[53] Just as he was completing his con-certs, an epidemic of cholera broke out and was soon raging throughout the city. Within weeks tens of thousands were dead or dying. Civil order broke down, and a city that was accustomed to concerts and banquets sank once more into anarchy.

The epidemic radicalized Gottschalk's already outspoken views on the country. He observed priests—"cassocked bandits," he called them—who doubled their fee for burying the dead and refused extreme unction to those who had not paid in advance the full cost of their interment. Nor was his assessment of the general populace more positive. As he observed ordi-nary Argentineans preying on the sufferings of others, he wrote:

> What a race! What a people! The populace of the Republic of Argentina is the sewer where all the baseness, corruption, and evil human passions end up. In this nation, abandoned by providence, they are all cowardly, bragging, lying, thieving, covetous, ignorant, and crude. . . . The word "republic" (an outrage to the high principles that this word represents) serves as a veil for every sort of despotism and evil . . . and there you have the Argentine Republic.[54]

Gottschalk spent the entire month of January 1868 in the small rural town of Las Conchas on the El Tigre River, thirty kilometers northwest of the capital. Now a seaside resort, Las Conchas was then a wild spot visited by the jaguars that still inhabited the nearby brush.[55] Even here Moreau could not escape the cholera. A leper who lived near him died of the fever at eight a.m., and by evening his wife, daughter, nurse, and an old Negro woman in the household were all dead as well. Parents abandoned their dying children, and when a priest succumbed in a neighboring village he was left to rot until a *gaucho* lassoed the body and dragged it out of town, there to be consumed by vultures. Gottschalk himself suffered from boils under the arms and on his thighs, and a large tumor began to form in one armpit. Fortunately, he recovered from these symptoms without surgery.[56]

It is astonishing that under such circumstances Gottschalk managed to complete several compositions. He succeeded in writing down his *étude de concert* entitled *Bataille* (op. 64), a trivial *galop* that he had performed in Chile and Buenos Aires. He also penned *Dernier amour* (op. 63), a second *étude de concert*. Based on a beguiling melody that is probably of Gottschalk's own invention, *Dernier amour* is notable for the tango-like rhythm that throbs lazily beneath the catchy tune.[57] It was also in Las Conchas that he wrote out his fantasy on Flotow's *The Last Rose of Summer*, now unfortunately lost, a Mazurka in B Minor, and a new *Pensée poétique*, this time in F-sharp minor.[58] All that remains of another composition for piano, *L'Erube*, is its intriguing title, but a song that he probably penned in Copiapó, Chile, was readied for press at this time. *La Flor que ella me envia* is no masterpiece but, as Richard Jackson has pointed out, contains several features worthy of mention. The setting of the poem by the Chilean romantic poet Guillermo Blest Gana (1829–1905) gains poignance through the use of dissonant ninth chords. Gottschalk's signature use of chromaticism is also notable, as is the stark open fifth chord with which the vocal line begins.[59]

Having recovered from the various maladies that had beset him, Gottschalk returned to Buenos Aires on April 4, 1868. Rumor of his return had circulated since early morning, and by the time his train steamed into the railroad station the waiting hall was packed with fans. This detail, duly reported in *La Nacional* of Buenos Aires, was then reprinted in the Parisian journal *L'Art musical*, from which a London paper translated it, whence it was finally reprinted in *Dwight's Journal of Music* as "a charming specimen of the *highfalutin* rhapsody which follows everywhere in the wake of this sensational pianist."[60]

Given Gottschalk's loathing of Buenos Aires, why did he return there rather than to the friendlier environment of Montevideo? The reason for his choice is that now it was Uruguay's political life that was in complete turmoil. As Gottschalk reported, Fortunato Flores had for some months been relatively sedate, limiting himself to "some broken heads, a few women outraged, and other similar peccadilloes, but no more killings."[61] Suddenly, however, he attacked Uruguay's aging dictator, his own father. Fortunato boxed the old man's ears and would have seized power had not the foreign navies intervened and recaptured the presidential palace for the senior Flores. Finally, on February 19, 1868, General Flores was assassinated, not by his sons but by still other plotters.[62] General uncertainty now prevailed, and it is for this reason that Gottschalk returned to Argentina, cursing it all the while as "the saddest country in the world, a frog that puffs itself up to become an ox."[63]

Buenos Aires was now a city in mourning for the tens of thousands who had perished during the cholera epidemic. Gottschalk's first concert at the Coliseo on March 20 failed to fill the hall, but a subsequent benefit for a school for orphans succeeded. This emboldened him to mount two performances at the Teatro Colón with a hastily assembled regiment of fourteen pianists.[64] His collaborators included two Frenchmen, two Italians, four Spanish Argentineans, four Germans, and even two ladies, discreetly identified only by their initials.[65] A notably cynical feature of these performances, given his views on Argentina, was Gottschalk's solo variations on the national anthem. He probably never wrote down this extended improvisation, identified in the program as *Gran capricho sobre el himno nacional Argentina*. But it produced a "sepulchral silence" throughout the theater, and then a predictable eruption of wild applause.[66]

For no apparent reason other than curiosity, Gottschalk then headed north into the Argentine interior. He traveled by steamboat up the great Parana River, which reminded him of the Mississippi, to the burgeoning port of Rosario. There he was feted by an assembly of drunken Englishmen.[67] From Rosario Gottschalk proceeded to Argentina's second city, Córdoba, and thence to the remote and seductive colonial towns of Salta, Guayaquil, La Concepción, San José, Fray-Bentos, and Paysandu.[68] With his unerring nose for trouble, Gottschalk found himself in the midst of a civil war that was sweeping the Argentine provinces, an "anarchical convulsion" in which gangs led by the gaucho bandit Perez were beheading half the male population of country towns, seizing the women, and generally spreading ruin and death. Everywhere Gottschalk went he encountered mobs proclaiming, "Death to the Liberals, Protestants, Jews, and other agents of the Devil."[69] Returning to his hotel after a concert one evening, he stumbled over a group of policemen sleeping on the ground with their loaded rifles before them. Being a foreigner he was excused for his clumsiness, but when several local youths again awoke the sleepers only minutes later, the police opened fire. One placed his musket on the ear of an offender and blew his head off.[70]

As if he had not already encountered problems enough, Gottschalk returned to Buenos Aires just as the relentless "Pampero" wind was inundating the city with a hurricane of dust. The temperature was not cold, but he shivered under the humid, penetrating gale.[71] With no clear plan of action, he hastily organized a benefit at the Coliseo for the Association for the Protecton of Orphans of Cholera. Orphaned children were everywhere, wandering alone through the streets or huddling together in groups. Members of the local benevolent association had tried in vain to raise money to help them, and only when Gottschalk stepped in did their campaign succeed. "Gottschalk is the Yankee of pianists," declared the Association's president, S. Estrada, as he presented the composer a gold medal.[72]

Immediately after this, Gottschalk put together three further benefit concerts at the Coliseo, one each for the British, French, and German hospitals. The English-language press candidly admitted that the musical tastes of the local British community were undeveloped, a judgment that was more than borne out when the organizers of the benefit for the British Hospital decided to balance Gottschalk's effusions with a blackface minstrel named Champagne Charlie.[73] President Mitre of Argentina showed up for the event, and clearly preferred Champagne Charlie's pranks to the performance by Gottschalk and his young aide-de-camp, Celestino. The concert for the French Hospital was more notable for the gracious vacuities uttered by the chairman of the organizing commission than for the music.[74] This left the prize for best concert to the Germans, who enriched their program with soloists and singing societies drawn from their community. The English-language *Standard* admitted that their own concert had been a "child-like effort" compared to "the glorious program of the Germans" and conceded this was inevitable "because Luther was something of a musician, [while] our Reformers sang psalms through their noses."[75] Gottschalk would have agreed.

The public gratitude for Gottschalk's philanthropy was huge, and it grew when he offered a final concert at the Colón for the Spanish group La Asociación Protectora de los Inválidos.[76] These acts of benevolence also confirmed Moreau's status as a matinee idol, to the extent that when he had a haircut the ladies of Buenos Aires purchased his shorn locks from the barber and sported them in little gold *relicarios* that became the fashion rage of this bizarre season.[77] Nor were local males less enthusiastic, although they preferred to treat him as *el inteligente pianista*, a kind of thinking man's artist.[78]

His high standing among the male elite of Buenos Aires was confirmed on June 10 when Gottschalk hosted a men-only banquet at the Hotel de Louvre. After performing his new *Dernier amour* and other works, he then invited the assembled gentlemen of many nations to a feast, the menu for which filled a full column in the press the next day.[79] The eloquence of Gottschalk's toast moved many of the forty men to tears. With goblet raised, he recalled the aged Italian count whom he had met en route to Cuba in 1854 and related how, when the two parted, the old man told him not to write, since he probably had little time left to live, but instead to think of him whenever Moreau spotted a certain star, which the Count pointed out to him. Now Gottschalk asked the same of his friends, except that he pleaded for those present to recall him in the future whenever they heard one of his compositions played. At five a.m. the entire assembly walked Moreau back to his rooms in the Calle Esmeralda. The usually sharp-tongued critic of *El Mosquito* declared flatly, "Tonight was the finest day of my life!"[80]

In contrast to this bonhomie, the streets of Buenos Aires were by now extremely dangerous. Robberies and muggings were common, and Gottschalk never went out without his pocket pistol and a sword disguised in a walking stick. More than once he had to draw his pistol, and on one occasion he had to use his sword-stick on a drunken Frenchman who attacked him.[81] Amidst this grim anarchy and on the very eve of his departure for Montevideo, Gottschalk attended a final soirée in the rooms of a visiting singer at the Hotel San Martín. Surrounded by several musicians and the Chilean poet Blest Gana, now a government minister, Gottschalk for the first time unveiled a new composition, a dirge-like lamentation entitled *Morte!!*.[82] Over the next year this simple yet effective sixteen-bar melody, played over drum-like chords in the deep bass and intermingled with brief modulations to the major, evoked a torrent of high romantic pathos among all who heard it. Eventually published as op. 60, *Morte!!* achieved a popularity in South America that surpassed all his other compositions. Moreau himself characterized *Morte!!* as "that rather disconsolate of my last effusions." Irony aside, he considered it "my favorite now, . . . neither better nor worse than my old *The Last Hope*."[83]

Thanks to the fertile imagination of his friend Luís Ricardo Fors, Gottschalk's *Morte!!* has been linked with the California scandal.[84] The idea is beguiling: a maiden from California, confined to a nunnery for having fallen in love with Gottschalk, dies behind the monastic walls. News of her death supposedly threw Moreau into inconsolable grief. Unfortunately, there is not a shred of evidence to support this connection other than Fors's claim. Gottschalk himself hinted that the piece memorialized the death of some old flame, but he left no hint as to her identity.[85]

Whatever news may have triggered the writing of *Morte!!*, the inspiration for this piece traces almost certainly as much to literary as to autobiographical sources. Among the group at the Hotel San Martín were two poets, the Chilean Gana and one J. Sienra y Carranza, both of whom published verses based on Gottschalk's piece.[86] While it cannot be confirmed, Gottschalk himself almost certainly had been inspired by several stanzas of poetry contained in Victor Hugo's *Les Orientales*. This is the same source upon which he had previously drawn for themes that he developed musically.[87] The passage by Hugo, beginning "Elle est morte," mourns the death of an adored fifteen-year-old, one of those fair innocents to whom Moreau had always been drawn in his inability and failure to form more enduring relationships with women. Never again did he turn to this theme, as he grew resigned at age thirty-nine to bachelorhood and old age.[88]

When Gottschalk returned to Montevideo in early August 1868, it was rumored that the Paraguayan war was ending and that Uruguay itself was calming down.[89] This was scarcely the case. After the excitement surrounding the assassination of Flores, Montevideo was outwardly calm, yet an ominous instability hung in the air. Gottschalk, well aware that a number of revolutionary movements were brewing in the provinces, stayed on guard.[90] When he chanced upon Fortunato Flores on the street on August 14 they exchanged cordial greetings, but Gottschalk kept his distance. He was well aware that this madman and his brother Eduardo had already broken the necks of several innocent Spaniards accused of complicity in their father's assassination and that Fortunato himself had recently tried to rape an actress in Rio at gunpoint.[91]

A further coup seemed imminent. The host of a particularly opulent ball felt compelled to publish a notice in the press on the day of his extravaganza that a rumored insurrection would not take place during the festivities.[92] The press, meanwhile, engaged in the most sordid scandalmongering, leading Gottschalk to conclude that "everything in this country has gone astray. One cannot say the moral code is corrupted, for it no longer exists, or perhaps never existed."[93]

Moreau himself accidentally fell victim to this mood of civic decay one night in early September. He had dined with an elderly American named Horne and was walking back to his rooms. It was past midnight. Just as Gottschalk was about to pass through the darkened market he sensed that he was being followed. The spot was perfect, he thought, "for a murder or at least a total robbery." Having sized up his adversary, Moreau grabbed him by the collar and threw a choke hold around his neck. The poor wretch pleaded for mercy. He explained that he was a servant of the good Mr. Horne, who had sent him to follow Gottschalk home in case he might be attacked by genuine thieves.[94]

In this violent and surreal environment Moreau offered several concerts at the Teatro San Felipe. Then, in mid-October, he mounted a fifteen-piano extravaganza at the Teatro Solis, during which he performed several unidentified new pieces.[95] All this was preparatory to a pair of monster concerts planned for the Teatro Solis on November 10 and 16.[96] Once more he assembled an army of musicians, this time including three regimental bands, two theater orchestras, an ensemble of amateurs, a choir, twenty-six drummers, twelve pianists, and, to fill any acoustic gaps, "about thirty musicians hired for the occasion."[97] The full list of performers covered a whole column in the press.

The entire square surrounding the Teatro Solis was illuminated several nights before the performance. The new president of Uruguay, whom Gottschalk characterized as "an old beast," attended but was upstaged by the commanders of the naval squadrons from Brazil and the United States. It is appropriate that among the officers from the United States was Alfred Thayer Mahan, later the apostle of naval power and an ardent champion of gunboat diplomacy.[98]

Several of the featured works had already been performed in Chile. The chief difference was that Moreau now reworked the *Marcha solemne* to include an extended exposition of the Brazilian national anthem. This addition was less peculiar than it may seem. In addition to the fact that Brazil led the four-power coalition that was at war against Paraguay, Moreau was already looking ahead to a visit to that country.[99] The local press treated the revised *Marcha* in purely military terms, referring to Gottschalk's "musical army" of performers and praising each "soldier" for knowing precisely when to "shoot."[100] The actual war was grinding on without resolution, but Gottschalk "as a genius and a Yankee was triumphant in his musical paraphrase of the events." He knew how "to conquer the thousand problems" that had stymied the alliance's commanders in the field and therefore emerged a hero.

Both the pre-performance promotions and post-concert reviews agreed that the festival's high point was the premiere of Gottschalk's new work, the "*2me symphonie romantique*," entitled *Á Montevideo*. Here, finally, was the tribute to Uruguay to balance the unexpected salute to Brazil in the *Marcha solemne* on the same program. Its modest length— under thirteen minutes—and the absence of developmental passages disqualifies *Á Montevideo* as a true symphony. Gottschalk's second symphony is in fact a delightful overture in three parts. It begins with a languid *andante*, followed by a sparkling *presto*, which evolves, after a series of fanfares, into a grand *maestoso* section built around the Uruguayan national anthem but prominently featuring both *Yankee Doodle* and *Hail, Columbia!*.[101] Ever the lyricist, Gottschalk introduced his symphony with a seductive melody reminiscent of the nature painting in the opening movement of his first symphony, *La Nuit des tropiques*. The *presto* is an effervescent dance melody with an unexpected snap in its last measures. Both movements would make superb ballet music, and they manifest Gottschalk's great but undeveloped potential in that genre. The third movement, introduced after a series of chromatic modulations, moves swiftly from anthem to anthem and drew on the full battalion of brass players assembled in the Teatro Solis.

Does the symphony *Á Montevideo* have a narrative program? While Gottschalk himself never spelled it out, it is likely that he again intended to "tell a story" or paint a series of genre pictures in the work. If so, one can surmise that the first movement was intended to describe the gentle and bucolic landscape in which the Uruguayan capital is situated; the Offenbach-like second section celebrated the city's dance-crazy society; while the third part saluted both the country of Uruguay and, with *Hail, Columbia!*, the beneficent relationship Gottschalk hoped to establish between that country and the institutions of the United States.

At the time Gottschalk was writing his symphony, he was also involved in a major project for educational reform in Uruguay. Two local friends, Dr. Carlos Ramirez and José Pedro Varela, had recently returned from the United States and, like Gottschalk, were convinced that popular education was the key to the transformation of Uruguay and Argentina. Gottschalk had already supported the local Society for the Education of Orphans and he now threw himself into Ramirez's and Varela's project to expand popular education. In connection with the work of this society he delivered many public speeches and became the Society's first donor by mounting a large benefit concert in its behalf.

Gottschalk and his friends anticipated the seminal educational reforms of Argentine president Domingo Faustino Sarmiento, which were also based on careful study of education in the United States. In a letter to Ramirez, Gottschalk spoke about popular education as a subject "of vital interest to the progress of the new American nations":

> Those favored by fortune can always educate themselves in any country. It is for that reason that America's founders did not concern themselves with the aristocratic element of society, but rather with the lowest ranks of the great mass of people, whom they struggled to enlighten, comprehending that education ought not to be a privilege, but something which belongs to all, as much as the air we breathe. . . . However great Prescott, Longfellow, Everett, Bancroft, and many others may be, these noble characters are less noteworthy than the enlightenment of the collective whole—the "people." [102]

Gottschalk's support for public education and a republican form of government did not end with his involvement in Ramirez's and Varela's society. He also lent his backing to Luís Ricardo Fors's Comité Democrático Ibérico, which advanced the cause of republican government and pop-

ular education in Spain.[103] Gottschalk's efforts to transplant the United
States' system of free public education to the lands of the Rio de la Plata
were commended by all, and they explain the programmatic logic of his
insertion of *Hail, Columbia!* and *Yankee Doodle* into the concluding section of his symphony *Á Montevideo.*

Amidst these earnest concerns, Gottschalk seems also to have become
involved with a French singer and actress named Clélie. When pro-
republican revolutionaries in Cádiz arose to overthrow the Spanish monarchy, Fors's society for Iberian democracy celebrated in Montevideo
with a grand banquet. Gottschalk attended, and afterwards, in response
to an invitation from the singer, he and Fors visited this Clélie in the
Calle del Cerrito. Gottschalk apparently became entangled with her.[104]
Fors claims that at least two doctors eventually advised him to break off
this liaison, but Gottschalk refused, and when Clélie followed him to Brazil, his doom was sealed.

Lange poked holes in nearly every fact in Fors's account of the
Gottschalk-Clélie relationship and concluded that it was all a fabrica-
tion.[105] Indeed, not one piece of evidence has yet been found to support
Fors's claim that Clélie followed Gottschalk to Brazil. Yet Lange himself
substantiates that Clélie actually existed and that she was connected with
the Théâtre Lyrique Français in Montevideo.[106] Nor does he discredit the
authenticity of at least one letter by Gottschalk in which he refers to her.
Clélie's existence and Gottschalk's connection with her in late 1868 cannot, therefore, be denied.

In November he crossed over to Buenos Aires to offer several final
concerts at the Teatro Colón. By now local critics were pleading with
him to include as many Argentinean tunes as possible in his programs.
"Because Gottschalk possessed a marvelous talent for improvisation,"
they reasoned, "it would be easy for him to accede to our wishes."[107]

Immediately after completing these performances, Moreau sought refuge from the summer's heat in the village of San Isidro, situated on the
coastal pampas some twenty kilometers by rail up the Rio de la Plata
from Buenos Aires. He arrived at this barren and windswept spot on December 30, 1868.[108] As was his custom since the start of his career, he
had accepted the hospitality of friends, in this case an American named
Ford, who provided a surrogate family environment in which he could
rest and compose.[109] Exhausted from his monster concerts and having
suffered an attack of tonsillitis some weeks before, Moreau was grateful
For the chance to recover his health.[110]

For the first month he lived "the life of a hermit," sitting for hours on
the lawn overlooking the immense and muddy Rio de la Plata, writing
letters, and visiting occasionally with the local priest, whom he described

as "a fine man who is not very enlightened but who at least inspires an evangelical faith." After a few weeks he began practicing four hours a day—an investigative reporter from the capital credited him with twelve hours daily—and by February he was not only restored to good health but was providing lessons to six students who had come out from Buenos Aires with their families to study with him. The same reporter claimed there were twenty, all of them young ladies.[111]

Once his health had recovered, Moreau also devoted himself to composing. His old repugnance for writing down his compositions persisted, as did his perpetual fear that if written scores of his music circulated prior to publication they would be appropriated and published by others.[112] Nonetheless, the three months in San Isidro were unusually productive, and Gottschalk's output from this time reveals a marked shift in his musical interests. Folk elements are wholly absent from his work of this period, and a new classicism is evident. Among the compositions in this vein were several new *études*, only three of which he set down on paper: *Dernier amour* (op. 62–63), the recently rediscovered *Vision*, and *Hercules* (op. 88), the classical name Gottschalk had once applied to Beethoven.[113] Also in this group was *Tremolo* (op. 58).[114] Inspired by a composition of the same title by the Belgian violinist Charles-Auguste de Beriot (1802–70), Gottschalk's *Tremolo* proved so immensely popular that he featured it prominently in nearly all of his final concerts.[115]

Of an entirely different order is the *Impromptu*, dedicated to his old Montevideo friend Madame Elise d'Aubigny. This sparkling and elegant piece of Chopiniana shows Gottschalk at his stylish best. It is lyrical, airy, and devoid of those ponderous and tendentious qualities that spoiled so much American music of the Victorian era. The same can be said of the *Grand Scherzo* (op. 57), a sweeping tribute to Chopin's E-Major *Scherzo* but with a nostalgically lyrical middle section that is pure Gottschalk. It is unfortunate that the San Isidro septet for piano and strings is lost, as it was almost certainly composed for the German musical community of Montevideo and would therefore probably have been brought to a high level of finish.[116] Gottschalk's several San Isidro *Lieder* and his variations on Gottlieb Reissiger's *La Dernière Pensée*, which would surely be of interest for the same reason, are also lost. No more is known of the dozen mazurkas and waltzes he finished at this time, but the one survivor of this group, a mazurka entitled *Caprice élégiaque* (op. 56), does not rise above the level of ordinary salon pieces. As for his *Mouvement perpétuel, Ballade*, and a piece under the previously used title *Solitude (Méditation)*, one can do no more than guess about their character.

During the last two years of his life, Gottschalk was increasingly preoccupied with compositions for full orchestra. In one letter he referred to "two symphonies for orchestra," only one of which, Á *Montevideo*, is extant.[117] In a letter to his sisters, Gottschalk left eloquent testimony to this turn toward the composition of works for orchestra:

> I was born for the orchestra. When I write symphonic music, I find more expansive and manifold sensations than when I write for the piano. To direct and print your own movements, to transcribe your sensations, to [lead the musicians] under your command, constitutes true creativity, like giving birth. All this is a sovereign act of power.[118]

Luís Fors, who was in close contact with the composer throughout this period, insisted that Gottschalk had also returned to his old passion for opera and was working on several while in Argentina and Brazil. Similarly, an English paper, the *Observer*, published a notice shortly after Gottschalk's death in which it reported, on the basis of a report from a correspondent in Rio, that he had again been toiling to complete his old opera *Isaura di Salerno.*[119]

Whatever the extent of Gottschalk's compositional work in this period, there is no doubt that he had paid an artistic price for the time spent in South America. Wagner premiered *Tristan* and *Die Meistersinger* in this period, Bruckner his First Symphony, and Saint-Saëns his Second Piano Concerto. Verdi entered a new phase with *Don Carlos* in 1867, while in far-off Russia, Rimskii-Korsakov, Tchaikovsky, and Borodin were all writing their first symphonies. Isolated in South America, Gottschalk missed all this. He had perused a score of Verdi's *Don Carlos* in Montevideo with great curiosity and pleaded for his sisters to send him information on Gounod's *Romeo and Juliet.*[120] Such works reached South America only slowly, with the result that Gottschalk lost the stimulation that contact with music by the most advanced composers of the day might have provided.

By mid-March 1869 Gottschalk was once more in Montevideo, fully rested and with his thoughts focused on the future. At a farewell concert on April 4 he premiered his piano septet. A few days later he shipped to his sisters a trunk filled with the trophies he had accumulated during his travels in South America. These included medals, cigar cases, gold and silver wreaths, rugs, gold pens, embroidered handkerchiefs, gold pencil holders, artificial crowns, and an ostrich egg.[121]

Since his departure from Havana in 1862, the direction of Gottschalk's entire life had been ordained more by outside forces—notably the Civil War and his family's financial needs—than by the requirements of his art. Even before the California scandal, Moreau had exhibited a listless resignation regarding the future. In Peru and Chile he had labored relentlessly but with no clear long-term direction. Indeed, the only apparent

plan he had throughout his travels in South America was to plod methodi-
cally from one city to the next, accumulating what capital he could and
dreaming of some vague freedom. Only now, as he prepared to leave
Montevideo, did he give any indication that he had in mind for himself a
more substantial future.

What were Gottschalk's plans during that last spring in 1869? Soon
after his death, the legend arose that he had intended to honor a deathbed wish of his mother by making a pilgrimage to the Holy Land.[122] That
he dedicated his *Grande Tarentelle* to the wife of the heir-apparent to the
crown of Italy has been taken as evidence of his intention of undertaking
a Mediterranean journey. Yet this colorful theory does not hold up. First,
there is no direct evidence that his mother had ever enjoined him to journey to the Holy Land. Second, Gottschalk did indeed dedicate his *Grande
Tarentelle* to Princess Margherita of Savoy, but for the sole reason that
he was urged to do so by a piano-playing diplomat in Buenos Aires, Count
Jionnini, minister to the King of Italy. Moreau and Jionnini had been inseparable friends since they first met in December 1867, and when Jionnini left for reassignment in Europe he pleaded with the American to
make the dedication, assuring him that the princess would bestow on him
the order La Stella d'Italia. Margherita obliged, but the award never
reached Gottschalk.[123]

Even if Moreau was not heading for the Holy Land, did he intend to
return to Europe? His numerous appeals to Clara to disseminate news on
his travels suggest as much, as do his efforts to get his German publisher,
Schott & Söhne, to sell his compositions there.[124] Similar attempts to find
a British publisher for his works imply that he may ultimately have intended to visit that country as well.[125]

Even if these were Gottschalk's eventual goals during his final year, a
European trip was not in the immediate offing. In a letter to his sisters
from San Isidro he explained the reasons for his reluctance to return to
the scenes of his earlier triumphs:

> All of you have reproached me for not coming back to Europe. Alas, dear
> sisters, it is too late for me ever to regain the position that I could have had
> and that others have filled in my absence. My only hope now is that in my
> older days I might be able, if I can accumulate an independent fortune, to
> compose some operas.[126]

If he was not going to Europe, where did Gottschalk expect to build
his future life? At the moment, he had urgent reasons to return to the
United States. For more than a year he had been sending his earnings to
Philadelphia so that Charles Vezin could invest them with the help of
Coudert Brothers. Moreau's faith in "dearest old Charlie" was absolute, to

the extent that he called him "the *one good* man in this world I know of."[127] Unfortunately, Vezin himself was disastrously over-extended and had dipped into several trust funds he managed, including Gottschalk's, in a desperate attempt to save himself. All this came out only later. For now, Gottschalk was frustrated by the unexplained silence from Vezin's quarter and anxious about the substantial funds he had placed in his friend's hands.[128]

At the same time, Gottschalk's relations with the Chickering firm were turning sour. He had good reason to believe that his efforts during the Civil War had saved the company from collapse.[129] More recently, he had turned down a lucrative offer from the Steinways and had vigorously promoted Chickering pianos throughout his South American travels. Gottschalk claimed he had spent over twenty-five hundred dollars on shipping costs alone, none of which had been reimbursed by the company. By 1869 Gottschalk believed the firm owed him, in addition, the lordly sum of fifteen thousand dollars in commissions.[130] Addressing an equally serious problem, he complained that the Chickering agent in New York had failed on several occasions to ship the concert grands in time for scheduled concerts, with the result that Gottschalk had to postpone or cancel.[131]

The Chickering firm's neglect of Gottschalk is understandable. The Boston company had received a gold medal at the great Paris Exposition of 1867, and Charles Francis Chickering had been made a Chevalier of the Legion of Honor. In the resulting flurry of promotion and sales, a single American composer wandering across South America might have seemed insignificant indeed. But Gottschalk, as he prepared to leave the Rio de la Plata, pelted the company with letters and grew convinced that his old patrons had abandoned him.

Just as his anxieties over Vezin and the Chickerings were mounting, Gottschalk received several requests to return to his homeland. His old manager Max Strakosch wrote him in April 1868, proposing a concert tour of the United States and England at the princely rate of twenty-five hundred dollars per month.[132] A few months later Charles Levy, a promoter whom Gottschalk considered "poor but honest" but whom Strakosch had once fired for dishonesty, approached the composer through his sister Clara.[133] Then in the spring of 1869 Strakosch appealed again.[134]

It is clear that Gottschalk willingly succumbed to these attractive offers. In fact, he used his sister Clara to pepper the New York press with reports on his activities, even as he entreated old friends to prepare the way for his return to the United States. Typical was a letter to the pianist Francis G. Hill, who acted as his unofficial press agent in Boston. "I hope," wrote Gottschalk, "you will occasionally keep the friendly portion of our public posted up about poor old Gottschalk, who is and has been ill-used very often, and is certainly not half as bad as some would make him out to be." [135]

Clearly, Gottschalk was now determined to return to the United States. Once there, he would take only those concert engagements necessary to sustain himself financially and otherwise concentrate his energies on composing. However, Brazil lay directly across his route from Montevideo to New York, and Moreau was not one to pass up so tempting an opportunity.

He had no friends in Rio so when the British minister to Buenos Aires was reassigned to the Brazilian capital, Gottschalk asked him to intervene in his behalf with the Brazilian emperor, Don Pedro II. He sent Ambassador Matthews the bound manuscript of his *Marcha solemne*, now reconstructed around the Brazilian national anthem. [136] The dedication to the Emperor achieved its purpose, and Gottschalk received back an album bound in sculpted ebony and inlaid with his own initials. This "veritable marvel of art," as the press called it, signaled that during Gottschalk's visit to Brazil he would receive royal patronage. [137] The summer heat and a banking crisis in Rio delayed Moreau's departure for a month, but on April 21 he boarded the steamship *Kepler* for the last journey of his life. [138]

Chapter Twenty-six

Brazil, 1869: "Prestissimo del mio Finale"

G OTTSCHALK arrived in Rio de Janeiro on May 3, 1869,[1] five days
short of his fortieth birthday and just over twenty years after the
Paris premieres of *Bamboula* and *La Savane*. In the meantime he had
composed scores of works of varying description and given thousands of
concerts from Paris to Petaluma. He had written the equivalent of several
volumes of essays and travel notes. He had been lionized by kings, presidents, and dictators and had been applauded by everyone from Hector
Berlioz to Illinois farmers and musical amateurs in Chile. No New World
artists in any field had ever made half this impact on every geographical
and cultural zone of the hemisphere.

During his last months on the Rio de la Plata, Gottschalk had made
clear that he intended to return to the United States in order to open an
entirely new phase of his career. His flighty younger brother, Gaston, was
now twenty-two and on his own. All his four sisters were either married
or launched on careers as pianists and composers.[2] The modest fortune
that he had set aside through sheer hard work amidst three wars and
several revolutions ensured him a greater degree of financial security
than he had ever known. This security had come at a huge price, but at
forty years of age he had finally achieved the freedom from want that
Mendelssohn, Saint-Saëns, Schumann, and Bizet had known from birth. It
remained to be seen whether Gottschalk was capable of utilizing this
boon to create significant operas and symphonic works, as he dreamed
of doing. The test would come once he was back in New York. Gottschalk
was still relatively young, though, and had many years of potential growth
before him. The only hurdle yet to be surmounted before reaching this
new stage in life was the series of concerts he hoped to give in Brazil.

His prospects in Rio de Janeiro seemed good. He arrived in the Brazilian capital with the promised support of Dom Pedro II. Though an emperor rather than an elected president, Dom Pedro admired the United States. He had translated Longfellow and Whittier into Portuguese; he shared Gottschalk's keen interest in education; and he was an enthusiastic amateur musician, as was his wife.[3] When the great Harvard scientist Louis Agassiz had visited the monarch a few years earlier, he had been impressed by his "simplicity and frankness" and was pleased to discover in him "so liberal a spirit."[4] Moreau could only welcome the backing of this musician and linguist whom he had met briefly in Paris twenty years earlier, and whose patronage he had sought even then.

There were also grounds for concern. Dom Pedro's army was still bogged down in the ruinous war against Paraguay. The American minister in Rio reported that all classes of society were "tired if not disgusted" with a war that brought no glory to Brazil and was ruining its economy.[5] Brazilian reformers opposed the war, and in their Masonic lodges and newspaper offices that quietly discussed whether the country could be saved without first establishing a republic. Such conspiratorial stirrings did not pass unnoticed. Only six months before Gottschalk's arrival the Emperor, in a kind of imperial *coup d'état*, purged all liberals from his government.[6] Anti-monarchical feeling was running high, and the public mood was glum. A Rio newspaper reported on how "the most intelligent part of the public, men with good hearts, saw with sad eyes the invasion of evil which, as the plague corrupts the body, has come to corrupt our souls."[7]

Adding to the challenges facing Gottschalk were the strained relations between Brazil and United States. To be sure, Brazilian liberals looked to the northern republic as a model and protector. But at the official level relations between the two great continental powers were soured by the continuation of slavery in Brazil and by the fact that Dom Pedro's country had provided refuge to several thousand émigrés from the American South.[8] Once more Gottschalk found himself in a tricky diplomatic situation. While insisting on presenting himself as a citizen of the United States and a representative of its values, he at the same time courted the good will of a government that was at odds with his own.

Gottschalk brushed aside these considerations and plunged into the unknown world of Brazil, in the end scoring a personal triumph that exceeded even what he had experienced in Chile. And yet there were unsettling signs from the outset. En route to Rio, a beam broke lose from the mast of the English steamer *Kepler* and crashed to the deck. Gottschalk was sitting in the saloon below when this occurred. The shock shattered a window, and a flying fragment of glass hit a finger of his left hand, cutting the vein and penetrating to the bone. Only the presence of a surgeon on board saved the day.[9] Then, when he arrived in Rio, Moreau expected to find two Chickering grands waiting for him. They never arrived, however, and Gottschalk was frantic. "I absolutely *cannot* play Érards," he reported. "I do not like their touch at all. And the modern Pleyels are very inferior to the old ones. Besides, I don't believe I can get any, since pianos are one of the things South Americans are least willing to lend."[10] Forced to delay his concerts, Gottschalk settled in to the Hotel des Frères Provençaux on the bustling Rua do Ouvidor and waited.[11]

Just as Gottschalk was beginning to despair, the Emperor sent his chamberlain to summon Gottschalk to the palace. It took no time to discover that the entire royal family had long played his music and that they wished to attend all his concerts in Rio.[12] The conversation continued for several hours, with Gottschalk speaking English and French with the Emperor and Italian with the Empress. They covered everything from the politics of the United States to spiritualism, Wagner, and the fine arts. By the end, Gottschalk judged Dom Pedro II to be a true *savant*. "We are a bit over-inclined to fancy that a monarch *must* be just short of a monster," he wrote his sisters. "The Emperor of Brazil is an honest man, loving his country and full of liberal ideas which he does not put into practice as readily as he would like on account of the obstacles deriving from the climate, the habits, the people, and the traditions of the Portuguese cradle." Spotting a diplomatic opening, Gottschalk asked his sister Clara to publish these laudatory words in the United States and to send him a copy at once, since "it may be of great service to me *here*."[13]

Still without his Chickerings but with the Emperor's personal support, Gottschalk made the rounds of Rio's most cultivated salons. First among them was that of Dr. Severiano Rodriguez Martins, a learned mulatto medical doctor who was the Emperor's personal physician and also a competent pianist and descendant of the Brazilian composer Padre José Mauricio Nunez Garcia (1767–1830).[14]

Among the other prominent figures in Brazilian cultural life whom Gottschalk met during those first weeks was the actor, pianist, and impresario Luiz Cándido Furtado Coelho, who managed to persuade Gottschalk to include in several concerts his own musical invention, the copophone.[15] He also made contact with the aristocratic Ricardo Ferreira de Carvalho, who had studied with Professor Marmontel in Paris, and the New Orleans-born African-American pianist and composer Lucien Lambert, whom Moreau had known from childhood.[16]

Most important, he encountered his young friend from Cuba, Arthur Napoleão, now a successful Rio businessman.[17] Napoleão represented the

French piano maker Érard in Rio and was therefore Chickering's competitor there until he, too, became a Chickering agent. Further, his firm Narciso, Arthur Napoleão & Cia was an aggressive music publisher. Napoleão became Moreau's constant companion, assisting pianist, and assistant arranger. Gottschalk reciprocated this friendship, inviting Arthur for billiards with letters such as the following:

> Illustrious Arthur,
>
> Do you want to transform this hour of sinister isolation into a radiant and charming one? Come with me to the salon where we have already measured in courtly contest our billiard cues, and where, by propelling the spheric ivory o'er the green mat, we will see time and worries take wing.[18]

Nowhere else in South America had Gottschalk encountered so effervescent a musical world as in Rio.[19] With a population of 230,000, Rio boasted a philharmonic society (the Sociedade Philarmonica Fluminense), the Club Mozart, a Conservatório do Música, and a national opera. There were several thriving German singing societies, including the solid and competent Liedertafel. Six publishing houses churned out sheet music to meet all this demand.[20]

Within a month of his arrival, Gottschalk had been received by all the most serious patrons and amateurs and had been welcomed as an honorary member of Rio's most active musical societies. Even a sophisticated salon like that of Dr. Severiano Martins mixed European and Afro-Brazilian dance music, so there can be no doubt that Gottschalk was exposed to such local dances as the *lundu*. At this stage of his life, however, he gravitated increasingly toward high culture, with the result that the earthier forms left no mark on his Brazilian compositions. By contrast, the active involvement of the polished choir of the Liedertafel society in these concerts and the participation of musicians like Bernhard Wagner (who later dedicated a composition to Gottschalk's memory) and H. G. Tiepke attested to the growing place of German music in Gottschalk's musical consciousness.

By late May Gottschalk had given up on the Chickerings and borrowed an English Broadwood grand that filled his needs. Thus equipped, he offered to perform concerts for the Philharmonic Society. Demand for the tickets was so great that for the first two performances the society booked the vast and unornamented Theatro Lyrico Fluminense, by far the largest hall in the Brazilian capital. Thereafter they had to move to the smaller Theatro Gymnasio Dramatico, since the Lyrico had already been reserved by others.[21] The Emperor and his family attended every performance at both venues, however.[22] Tickets were scalped at saloons along the Rua do Ouvidor, with boxes going for fifty and even seventy-five dollars each.[23] The press printed letters pleading for the series to be extended, but demand for seats only mounted further.[24]

The public of Rio gave evidence of its passion for music even before Gottschalk's first performance, when letters to the editor demanded specific compositions, especially *Murmures éoliens* and, above all, *Morte!!*.[25] This new piece had gone straight to the heart of the public. A typical commentary referred to the "vague terror it spills onto one's soul" and called *Morte!!* "shocking because of the profound inner turmoil it provokes."[26]

There is no clearer evidence of the musical renewal that Gottschalk was undergoing than the fact that he programmed so many new compositions for these Rio concerts. In addition to the macabre effusions of *Morte!!*, he played on his audience's emotions with *Tremolo* to such an extent that a local weekly illustrated paper published a droll caricature of this pot-boiler.[27] *The Last Rose of Summer*, a new fantasy for two pianos on themes from Bellini's *Norma*, *Dernier Amour*, *Bataille*, and his reworking of Donizetti's *Spirito gentil* were also among the more recent works he offered. Eclipsing all these, however, were his *Grande Fantaisie triomphale sur l'hymne national brésilien* (op. 69) for solo piano and his *Variations de concert sur l'hymne portugais du Roi Luis I* (op. 91) for piano and orchestra.

Francisco Manuel da Silva had composed the Brazilian national anthem in 1831.[28] More an operatic aria than a patriotic hymn, da Silva's anthem provided a perfect vehicle for Gottschalk's variations. Only Napoleão's sketched version of the piano part survives, but even this outline conjures up the dramatic effect that Gottschalk must have achieved. As usual with Gottschalk's variations, he treated each one as he might have a separate *pas* in ballet, framing it with the main theme. This by now tired convention of the virtuoso era greatly weakened the work, but the manneristic distortion of the melody would be at home in a work by Mahler, while the dense scoring for brasses took full advantage of the brilliant tone of the new piston-valved instruments.

By contrast, the second set of variations on the Portuguese national anthem is based on a rather weak march theme. The only claim it had to Gottschalk's attention—but a strong one—was that it had been composed by none other than the Emperor's father, Pedro I.[29] The Portuguese motif was appropriate in other ways for it also paid homage to the Emperor's thirty-one-year-old relative, the reigning Portuguese monarch Luis I. Gottschalk enlivened the Italianate march with frequent chord substitutions and contrasts of mood.

Unfortunately, the orchestration, as opposed to the piano part, showed all the marks of haste and amateurishness. The piece was composed to meet a deadline, and Gottschalk probably farmed out the orchestration to local acolytes and enthusiasts. At any rate, there is far too much doubling of parts, and the voicing throughout is simplistic, even when striking chords are introduced. Gottschalk's own piano variations are conventional but thoroughly engaging, and would be more so were they not framed by orchestral passages featuring leaden brasses and anemic strings. Not until the first slow variation does the work really come alive, but then it briefly attains a romantic sweep that brings to mind similar works by early Bohemian national composers. The Brazilian public responded warmly to both of these salutes from their North American guest and demanded that he program them often during his last months in their country.[30]

Following this series of concerts, Gottschalk dropped from sight for several weeks, re-emerging in Rio only on July 18. A local weekly was sure he had gone "to rest in the solitude of the forests," but several writers have placed him in the village of Tijuca in the hills above Rio involved in an amorous adventure either with the elusive Clélie or with a "strange and somewhat faded" French actress named "La Reine."[31] The true cause of Gottschalk's retreat from visibility was the June 18 arrival in Rio of the Italian tragedienne Adelaide Ristori. Hailed as the first actress of the modern world, Ristori offered passionate performances of *Medea, Phaedra*, and other classical plays.[32] Gottschalk himself confirmed that he suspended concerts because Ristori's agents had booked the Theatro Lyrico Fluminense. A friend recalled later that he considered the alternative spaces either too small or inconvenient.[33] Moreau did not leave Rio, however, nor was he wallowing in idleness. In a letter to his sisters he professed that he was so busy composing that he did not have time even to write a column for *L'Art musical.*[34]

It was at this time that he probably wrote out his *Variations de concert sur l'hymne portugais*, op. 91, and his *Grande Fantaisie triomphale sur l'hymne national brézilien*, op. 69. Lesser compositions from Gottschalk's final period of health and repose include the mazurka *Forget Me Not (Ne m'oubliez pas), Regarde moi (Idylle)*, a romance for voice and piano entitled *L'Esule*, and various operatic transcriptions.

So great was the reception accorded Ristori that a cartoon showed members of her audience emerging from the Lyrico with enormous hands, swollen from clapping.[35] This did not slow the burgeoning Gottschalk cult, however, which soon went to excesses even beyond those committed in Buenos Aires. His compositions had long been known in the Brazilian capital, but now stores could not keep his music in stock. Satirical papers issued droll caricatures of the public's new idol, while the more dignified press lured readers with frameable prints of the American composer. "Gottschalk Cakes" appeared at confectioners, while restaurant keepers added "Beefsteak à la Gottschalk" to their menus.[36] The public consulted Gottschalk's wisdom on every conceivable subject and credited his music with everything from calming overwrought nerves to bringing about the reconciliation of at least one feuding couple.[37]

The Freemasons of Rio invited Gottschalk to visit their "Grand Orient" lodge. A deputation accompanied Moreau from his hotel to the meeting rooms, where he was joined by delegations from every other Masonic lodge in the city, all marching behind their banners. The members of several lodges were clothed in long black mantles embroidered with death's heads and surmounted by large black hoods, the effect of which, Gottschalk mused, was "phantasmagoric and conducive to nightmares." Surrounded by all this exotica, the Grand Master honored Gottschalk with a discourse that "breathed a fervent love for American institutions."[38]

The same liberal spirit of reform and Pan-Americanism was evident during Gottschalk's visit on July 19 to the Colegio Episcopal de São Pedro de Alcântara, a venerable secondary school that flourished under imperial patronage. A brass band played as Gottschalk entered the palace that was used by the school, and the six hundred uniformed students formed a double line leading to the banquet hall.[39] In a pearl of baroque oratory, the president depicted Gottschalk as no mere musician but as a representative of "the great Republic." Never mind that Brazil was an empire and Gottschalk the Emperor's guest. What counted to this subversive representative of the Brazilian establishment was that a revered champion of the republican form of government was in their midst. As had so often happened in his life, Gottschalk was hailed as a symbol of political values that could not otherwise be openly expressed. He responded to this panegyric with a speech in Spanish "about education, free schools, the duties and rights of citizens, &c."[40] Summing up the event for readers of the *New York Times*, Gottschalk stated smugly:

> The United States, particularly since the [Paraguayan] war, are the object of the enthusiasm of all South America, which is proud of the Monroe doctrine and of the Americanism to which it has given rise. I believe that these South American Republics understand that, sooner or later, the United States will be the arbiter of taste.[41]

This round of festivities culminated in a soirée given by the Emperor on July 30 at his handsome Italianate palace of San Christorão, set in a hillside grove on the northeast edge of the city. Moreau had been a frequent visitor at San Christorão, but the Emperor had never before asked him to perform, since he considered the palace piano to be unworthy of his guest. Now Gottschalk had his borrowed English Broadwood installed in the main salon, and there he played the night away.[42]

Amid such adulation, Gottschalk fell in love with Brazil. Speaking of Rio, he told a friend that "here everything sings."[43] But the singing soon ended. As he left the San Christorão Palace at dawn on July 31, a hard rain was falling, and he had to wait some time for his carriage. Gottschalk was chilled to the bone, and by the next day was in bed with a fever. Over the next five days his condition worsened. Several doctors hovered over him. Newspapers offered daily bulletins on his condition, and more than two hundred people called at the hotel each day to inquire about his health. On the fifth day of August a rumor raced through Rio that Gottschalk was dying. At eight p.m. the Emperor's carriage rolled up to the door of the Hotel des Frères Provençaux, and Dom Pedro II's chamberlain disembarked in full court regalia. By now Moreau was barely conscious. As he heard the chamberlain recite the words of condolence with which the Emperor had charged him, he was engulfed by his old terror of dying without family or friends in a foreign land. He felt "absurd and dismal."[44]

For four days and four nights Gottschalk's fever raged. In his delirium he sang, delivered speeches, and was convinced that he would soon "emigrate from this planet to parts unknown."[45] Dr. Severiano Martins diagnosed yellow fever, which was rampant at the time in Rio. A second expert pronounced it to be "pernicious fever." Does this refer to malaria? Whatever the disease, the doctors administered massive doses of quinine, which left Gottschalk "a little deaf."[46] By mid-August his health turned for the better, and Dr. Severiano Martins urged him to leave Rio and take complete rest in a more salubrious climate.[47]

Following his doctor's advice only halfway, Gottschalk accepted an invitation from citizens of the mountain town of Valençe in the Serra da Mantiqueira, northwest of Rio de Janeiro. On the way there he rested for a few days at the Vista Alegre ranch owned by the musical amateur Joaquim Gomes Pimentel.[48] Then he proceeded to Valençe itself, where his arrival was signaled by a rocket fired from the church belfry. By the time Moreau alighted from his carriage, an ensemble consisting of cornet, clarinet, and bass drum had assembled, and when he appeared on the balcony of his hotel a few minutes later he sighted a trombonist, flautist, and tuba player panting up the street to join the welcoming committee.[49]

After giving a single subscription concert in Valençe, Moreau returned to Rio and took a steamer down the coast to Santos, where he boarded the new British-built railroad for São Paulo.[50] Still a college town of thirty thousand, São Paulo was home to several thousand Confederate émigrés.

The United States minister, Henry T. Blow, had recently visited these dis-
placed Southerners and reported that most were destitute and plagued
with "disappointments, misfortunes, and regrets."[51] Some former planters
were reduced to doing manual labor. Even though Moreau was received
warmly by a former Thalberg student, Professor Gabriel Giraudon, the
local expatriates boycotted him as a Union sympathizer.[52] There was also
a nasty incident involving some students who resented the fact that they
had to give up their fraternity house for Gottschalk's second concert. One
flung a heavy sandbag at Moreau, catching him squarely in the chest and
injuring him.[53] Within days Gottschalk reported to his sisters that he was
again in good health,[54] but the incident may have figured in his decision
to cancel a second São Paulo concert and return at once to Santos for a
last performance there.[55] After attending a ball held in his honor,
Gottschalk then sailed once more for Rio, arriving there by September
11.[56]

Acting as his own impresario, he applied every trick he had learned
over twenty years in order to bring together at the climactic moment the
largest assemblage of musicians and music lovers South America had
ever seen. The first step to this end was to make good on his earlier
promise to offer a second concert series featuring himself and selected
artists from Rio. Organized with the help of Arthur Napoleão and Ricardo
Ferreira de Carvalho, these concerts on September 21, 26, and 29 featured
well-known Gottschalk works, including his *Impromptu*, op. 54, and his
Caprice élégiaque, op. 56. The one innovation was the rollicking *Pasquinade*, op. 59. Performed earlier as an improvisation in Havana and in
Philadelphia, this good-natured and syncopated work was singled out for
praise by the local press.

Following the template that had worked so successfully in Buenos
Aires, Gottschalk next organized three much larger performances, this
time involving two full orchestras and thirty-one pianists playing on sixteen pianos. With only seven days to prepare before the first of these
events on October 5, Moreau had to work frantically.[57] He had misplaced
his orchestrations from Buenos Aires and therefore had to write out all
the parts anew, working from memory.[58] Fortunately, every pianist in Rio
seemed eager to participate in this production. Thirteen members of the
group, presumably women, modestly declined to have their full names
listed in the program. A third of the rest were German, including the
president of the Liedertafel group. Among them also were Ricardo de
Carvalho and Arthur Napoleão. Lucien Lambert and his son Lucien-Léon
represented New Orleans on one piano, while other performers came
from the Spanish, Italian, and French musical communities.[59]

On the eve of the first concert, a prophesy spread through Rio that a vast storm would inundate the city on the day of the performance. Fortunately, this cataclysmic event did not come to pass, and the concert went off without a hitch. The Emperor turned out to hear the program, which culminated in a performance of Gottschalk's fantasies on the marches from *Faust* and *Tannhäuser*, pounded out on some three thousand quivering piano strings. In an reprise of his entire career, Gottschalk also hauled out his old *Carnival of Venice* variations and even his early *La Jota aragonesa.* The audience responded warmly, and at the conclusion of the third concert the stage of the Theatro Lyrico Fluminense was inundated with a rain of colored scraps of paper, each bearing a printed poem honoring the composer.[60] The Club Mozart also paid homage to Moreau, and a popular cartoonist marked his latest triumph with a cartoon entitled "The City of Pianos."[61]

Continuing to apply his well-tested formula, Gottschalk then moved swiftly to organize six philanthropic concerts. The beneficiaries included several aspiring artists from Rio, a society for Brazilian monarchists and philanthropists, and a patriotic group dedicated to helping invalid veterans of the war in Paraguay.[62] A cartoonist at *A Semana Illustrada* recorded the event with a naive allegorical drawing showing a one-legged veteran on crutches laying a wreath at Gottschalk's piano with the assistance of the muse Clio.[63]

By now the stage was fully set for the inevitable culminating spectacle, a *concerto monstro* assembling all the musical forces of the Brazilian capital. Viewed from a European perspective, such mass festivals were already something of an anachronism. Thanks to Gottschalk's efforts in South America and to the work of close friends of his in the United States, however, they were only now reaching their peak in the New World.

That very summer Gottschalk's old friend from Geneva, Julius Eichberg, had joined with the Boston bandmaster Patrick Sarsfield Gilmore to organize a mammoth Jubilee Concert in the Massachusetts capital.[64] Its purpose was to celebrate the return of the Southern states to a once-more-glorious union. Gottschalk considered it "a great undertaking" and could have taken pride in the fact that nearly every work on the program was drawn directly from the repertoires of his own earlier festivals and concerts.[65] But Gottschalk's *concerto monstro* had a yet grander purpose, namely, to celebrate the drawing together of all the nations of North and South America into a sublime union of free peoples.

To enable his American guest to accomplish this grand design, the Emperor appointed Gottschalk Director General *pro tem* of all bands within the Brazilian army, navy, and national guard. Dom Pedro II also ordered his chiefs of staff to obey all orders issued by Gottschalk.[66]

Armed with this extraordinary commission, Moreau set about his huge task, assuming the roles of organizer, composer, fund raiser, conductor, accountant, promoter, and soloist. He enlisted the services of four national guard bands, one band each from the Brazilian navy and army, two German orchestras, one professional orchestra consisting of seventy "professors," and even the pit orchestra from the infamous Alcazar, the bawdiest theater in Rio.[67] Parts for 650 musicians had to be copied out by hand. The enthusiastic Arthur Napoleão pitched in, and eleven copyists were hired to work around the clock in shifts.

Nor was the work purely musical. Budgets had to be drawn up, contracts with the professionals drafted and signed, and the vast expanses of the Theatro Lyrico Fluminense redecorated so as to be worthy of the epochal event. Eleven mammoth chandeliers were added to the hall, along with hundreds of additional gas jets to light them. The entire stage had to be reconstructed in tiers to hold the 650 musicians. Enormous flags of Brazil and the United States were hung behind the stage, and a profusion of flowers and tropical plants was placed around the hall. Finally, a group of cannons had to be installed backstage in such a way that they could all discharge with a mighty roar as the massed band struck up the Brazilian national anthem. As the sole leader of the gigantic enterprise, Gottschalk had to oversee each of these tasks.

Gottschalk's schedule during the month preceding the festival's debut performance on November 25, 1869, was packed with activities stretching from dawn to dawn. To an interviewer from a local paper Moreau declared:

> I go from one barracks to the next. I am a symphonic voltaic pile, a steam engine in human form. If I do not go insane it will be neither my fault nor that of my troops. My room is a Capharnaum, my heart a volcano, my head chaos![68]

At the very time he was assembling his festival, Moreau was also laying careful plans for the future. At the end of September he sent the manuscript for his *Impromptu* to his sisters with detailed instructions for its publication by Schott & Söhne in Mainz.[69] He also mailed the manuscript of *Morte!!* to his New York publisher Hall[70] and worked to put his finances in order.[71]

Nor did Gottschalk ever express the slightest doubt that he would be returning soon to the United States. The local press had often reported this as a certainty,[72] and Gottschalk himself wrote the *New York Times* to expect him back in early spring, while informing Henry Watson that he would arrive in February.[73] The erstwhile "King of Bohemia," Henry Clapp Jr., had also heard from him and was making plans for his arrival.[74]

Gottschalk seemed utterly confident about the future, and with good reason. Not only were two New York agents vying for his talents, but his friend Edward Mollenhauer had founded a National Conservatory of Music in New York and was eager for Gottschalk to join him as professor of piano.[75] This all left him in a very positive frame of mind.

In letters to his sisters on September 27 and October 8, he reported confidently on his good health. The bout of illness in August had passed without consequences other than a slight lingering deafness.[76] If the sandbag incident in São Paulo had left any trace—an abscess in his pericardial sac, for example—it was in no way evident. In subsequent letters to friends in Boston and New York he reported on his hard work and lack of sleep, but he did so in a tone of exhilaration rather than of despair. An Englishman who visited Gottschalk at this time found him working over parts for the Festival, to all appearances in good spirits. "He seemed languidly to enjoy the climate and tropical grandeur of Rio," reported the visitor.[77]

For all his optimism, however, Gottschalk was under great strain, and his behavior showed it. Once, while rehearsing his army of musicians, he exploded in frustration and blurted out that they were all "imbeciles." Offended, the musicians stalked off the stage, leaving Gottschalk alone at the keyboard. He began to improvise quietly. Gradually his musicians returned to their places. Moreau, trembling and with tears in his eyes, addressed them in French, saying, "Pardon me, my children, for what I said in haste. Can we recommence?"[78]

Even more erratic was his handling of his business affairs with Chickering. After months of delay, the two grand pianos arrived from Boston at the end of September. From this date forward Gottschalk advertised Chickering pianos in every announcement for the festival and gave every indication that all problems with his longtime patrons had been resolved. This impression is strengthened by the fact that Arthur Napoleão had now signed on as a Chickering representative and was doing a brisk trade in the American pianos from his shop at Rua dos Ourives No. 62.[79]

Given this, it is all the more perplexing that at this very moment, on October 23, Gottschalk suddenly drafted a long and bizarre letter to his former patron in Paris, the piano manufacturer Camille Pleyel, proposing to return to the fold.[80] With uncharacteristic arrogance he declared, "Whether it be right or wrong, I make or break the reputation of a piano manufacturer by playing or not playing his instruments." It is unclear whether this extraordinary letter was actually sent, but both its contents and form suggest that Gottschalk was not in a stable frame of mind when he wrote it.

Supporting this impression is a lithograph of the composer issued by the satirical journal *Ba-ta-clan* just after his death.[81] Apparently based on a photograph taken a few months earlier, the image reveals a somewhat fleshy face grown puffy from fatigue. More alarming, his eyes seem unfocused and vacant, indeed, all but dead.

Whatever his physical and mental state, however, Gottschalk had only to survive two, or at most three, performances of his Festival to complete his tour of Brazil. Throughout his travels in South America he had always suspended activity during the torrid months after Christmas and fled to some quiet spot to rest. One week more and he would be free to recuperate.

As Gottschalk was completing his final preparations, the Empress became dangerously ill. Reporting this to Washington, the American minister in Rio added his view that the entire populace was disgusted with the war in Paraguay and in grim spirits.[82] Several members of the public complained that the price of tickets for the festival was exorbitantly high, to which Gottschalk responded in print by publishing an itemized list of his expenses—an uncharacteristically defensive move on his part.[83]

Whether in spite or because of the high price, the concert attracted the entire elite of Rio de Janeiro. One attendee recorded later that "in the Rua do Ouvidor, in the drawing rooms, in conversations among friends, nobody talked of anything except the gala at the Theatro Lyrico."[84] Scalpers were in evidence as the crowd poured through the doors. No seat was vacant, and extra seating lined the back of the vast hall. As the Emperor made his appearance, hundreds of pairs of opera glasses focused upon him and then turned to scan the boxes, where elegant ladies showed off the latest designs from Guignon, Guimarães, and other fashionable Rio designers.

The program opened with a brief theatrical performance. Then, as the curtain parted to reveal the 650 musicians, the public let out a gasp of surprise. Facing them was a veritable sea of multi-colored dress uniforms, interspersed with players attired in formal dress or national costumes. When Gottschalk finally made his appearance, the entire audience of several thousand rose to greet him with a great cheer accompanied by a mad waving of hats and handkerchiefs. It was an orgy of Pan-American pride and affection.

The program seemed like a mosaic of Gottschalk's career. It opened with martial renditions of fantasies based on the marches from *Faust* and *Le Prophète*. Then Moreau offered several piano solos from his earliest repertoire. After these, the full ensemble performed the *andante* from his *La Nuit des tropiques* and then his *Grande Tarentelle*. The evening ended with an electrifying performance of Gottschalk's *Gran Marcha solemne*, now retitled *Humaitá*, the name of a colorful Brazilian parrot.[85]

No sooner did a long, quiet passage draw to a close then the massed brasses blared out the main theme at *fortissimo* and the off-stage cannon unleashed an ear-splitting volley of thunder. At this crowning moment the entire audience sprang once more to its feet, and wild enthusiasm prevailed as Gottschalk was called out again and again to receive the ovation.[86] For the moment, at least, it seemed to all that Brazil had emerged triumphant from the war still grinding on in the field and that the entire Western Hemisphere was suddenly united in the great cause of liberal reform.

The next day, November 25, Gottschalk was exhausted and remained prostrate in his room at the Hotel des Frères Provençaux. However, he had long since volunteered to appear that night in a regular concert of the Philharmonic Society. After staying in bed all day, he ordered a carriage and made his promised appearance at the Theatro Lyrico Fluminense.[87] As he walked slowly onto the stage, the entire public rose to salute him. He then opened his part of the program by playing *Morte!!*, so beloved by Rio audiences. In acute pain, he barely made it through this lamentation. Then, just as he was playing the first measures of his *Tremolo*, Gottschalk collapsed at the keyboard. The stunned audience watched in horror as friends rushed to his side and bore him off the stage and back to his hotel.

The second performance of the festival program had been scheduled for the following night, November 26. The papers had announced that ticket prices would be reduced in order to reach a broader public, and an enormous crowd assembled, swollen no doubt by reports of the previous evening's drama. Gottschalk was by now in agony and had spent the entire day in bed. Yet he was determined to go on with the performance and actually showed up at the theater, dressed in white tie and tails and with his usual collection of medals pinned to his lapel. The evening began with a performance of a Spanish comedy. When the moment came for him to mount the podium, Gottschalk again collapsed. Acting quickly, Firmin Moras dismissed the 650 musicians and informed the frightened audience that the price of tickets would be refunded.[88] Gottschalk meanwhile had been carried nearly lifeless to his hotel, where the Emperor's personal physician awaited him. From that moment until Moreau's death three weeks later, the loyal Dr. Severiano Martins attended him constantly.

What had stricken Gottschalk? According to an announcement issued on the twenty-seventh by Dr. Severiano Martins, he was suffering from *enteralgia*, in other words, gastroenteritis, or simple food poisoning.[89] Gottschalk was convinced that his condition was far more serious, however, and after lying in agony for five more days he finally requested a second opinion, at which point Dr. Costa Ferrer was called in. Meanwhile, dark forebodings beset the composer, and he dictated a letter to his friend Luís Ricardo Fors in Montevideo, pleading for him to come at once. "Perhaps you cannot do so," he wrote. "It would be a true disappointment, for I find myself in *prestissimo del mio finale.*"[90]

Day by day Gottschalk's condition deteriorated. Wracked by fever and agonizing pain in his abdomen, he writhed in the torrid summer heat until December 8. On that day the two doctors and Firmin Moras conveyed him by carriage to the hillside village of Tijuca, eight miles inland from Rio de Janeiro and eighteen hundred feet above the steamy capital. In this picturesque spot an Englishman named Robert Bennett had established a comfortable, cottage-like hotel, where a fortunate few could escape the heat, enjoy the waterfalls and rustic gardens, and share Bennett's interest in botany.[91] Unfortunately, Gottschalk's condition only worsened at Tijuca.

By now it seemed as if everyone in Rio was following the mortal struggle of this foreigner who had appeared so suddenly in their midst only seven months before. Dom Pedro II was far away at his summer palace in Petropolis, tending to the needs of his own recuperating spouse. He had been informed of Gottschalk's condition, though, and sent two of his courtiers to the Hotel Bennett in order to convey the Emperor's deepest concern.[92]

Suddenly, on December 14 Gottschalk's fever subsided and he began to feel better. In the judgment of his two doctors this upturn had been occasioned by the fact that an "abscess" in his abdomen had broken. There were no grounds for rejoicing, however, for the "abscess" was most probably Gottschalk's appendix, which on that day had ruptured.

It is rare for a forty-year-old to develop appendicitis, but not unheard-of. All Gottschalk's symptoms since the night of the Philharmonic concert point toward appendicitis. Curiously, medical experts have yet to identify the precise factors that trigger this condition. On one point they are clear, however: appendicitis is not induced by stress alone. If this is so, then Gottschalk's death cannot be attributed solely to exhaustion caused by his work on the festival, nor can it be laid to the disease that had stricken him during the previous August. His appendicitis was a chance event, like so much in Gottschalk's life. Had it not struck, the composer would in all likelihood have completed his last two concerts in Rio and returned to whatever destiny awaited him in New York.

This was not to be. It is common for those who suffer a ruptured appendix to experience lowered fever and a brief period of lucidity immediately after the event. Shortly thereafter, however, the secondary infection of peritonitis usually sets in, affecting first the lining of the abdomen and finally the entire body. This is what happened to Gottschalk, and his two doctors could do no more than look on helplessly. At midnight on December 17, Gottschalk predicted that within four hours he would be dead.[93] He attempted to dictate a will but was too weak to sign it. By four a.m. on the eighteenth his life was ebbing fast.

Barely able to speak, he addressed his last words to Dr. Severiano Martins: "I have traveled much and have often been dangerously ill, but never have I found a friend as devoted as you. A father or brother could not have done more. Your efforts are truly superhuman."[94] This said, he made the sign of the cross over the doctor's forehead and kissed his hand. At sunrise on December 18, 1869, Louis Moreau Gottschalk died in Tijuca, Brazil.

The record of Gottschalk's death that the music-loving Dr. Severiano Martins filed in the archives of the Misericordia Hospital was brief and laconic: "I attest that Sr. Moureaud *[sic]* Gottschalk, American, single, forty years old, being treated at the Hotel Bennett in Tijuca, died today of an incurable galloping pleuropneumonia. His illness lasted twenty-one days and his body may be buried."[95]

Chapter Twenty-seven

✕ Post-Mortem: Gottschalk through the 125 Years

E VEN before his death, Gottschalk had been the subject of much image-making and theorizing. After his death this activity gained momentum. The first posthumous images of the composer were the several portrait busts of him made in Rio de Janeiro. One of these was intended for installation in a Rio park, and another found its way to the United States, where it was patented and widely sold in plaster miniature.[1] Meanwhile, a bronze statue of the composer was planned for Central Park in New York but never installed.[2] And in far-off Seville the Belgian ambassador installed a sculptural monument to Gottschalk in his private garden.[3]

While sculptors attempted to capture Gottschalk's physiognomy in stone, composers throughout the Western Hemisphere dedicated musical monuments to his memory. A German tunesmith in Rio recalled Gottschalk's spontaneity at the keyboard in a piece entitled *Improviso.*[4] In Havana, Manuel Saumell penned a wistful *Recuerdos de Gottschalk,*[5] Nicolás Ruiz Espadero imagined a visit to the Brooklyn grave in his *Élégie sur la tombe de Gottschalk,* and Adolfo Quesada conjured up a grander mood in his *Marcha apoteosis.* Meanwhile Richard Hoffman in New York composed *In Memoriam L.M.G.*

As these memorials and tributes faded, the more important task of issuing Gottschalk's unpublished compositions loomed up. The first "posthumous work" by Gottschalk was a *Marche funèbre* issued by Charles Kunkel of St. Louis. The fact that Gottschalk, still quite alive, had himself mailed the piece to the publisher did not inhibit Kunkel from treating it as a requiem.[6] Other publishers commissioned "original" two-piano transcriptions of solo works. Lucien Lambert, Gottschalk's mulatto friend and disciple from New Orleans, produced several of these.[7]

Sheer caprice played a major role in establishing "standard" editions of Gottschalk's works. Nothing exemplifies this better than the fate of his *Célèbre Tarentelle de bravura* or *Grande Tarentelle*. Since the composer left behind no finished manuscript, a friend in Rio tried to reconstruct the work from memory.[8] Meanwhile, Arthur Napoleão issued his own version, which resembled an edition issued in Paris by Escudier. As if this was not complicated enough, the composer had deposited yet another sketch of the *Tarentelle* in Havana with Espadero, who published his own "definitive" edition in 1874.[9] Eventually, no fewer than twenty-five editions of various forms of this work appeared.

Arthur Napoleão saw a gold mine in Gottschalk. Over the years following the composer's death, his firm issued sixty-five Gottschalk compositions for piano. Some were new. Napoleão based his legal claim to them on the fact that he had made available to Gottschalk a private room in Rio where the composer had spent long hours writing. Napoleão drew others from the trove he purchased at the estate sale.[10] Many of the remaining Gottschalk pieces on Napoleão's list were simply pirated from authorized Schott editions in Germany. It took the Schott firm nearly a half century to figure out why its sales were so poor in Brazil, by which time Arthur Napoleão had died a rich man.

Even as the Napoleão brothers were churning out their "Complete Works of Gottschalk," Espadero was fulfilling a promise to Gottschalk to issue the posthumous works. Along with what he claimed was the "definitive" edition of the *Tarentelle*, Espadero had in his possession sixteen pieces for piano, which he now polished up for publication. Beyond this, he claimed to have "fixed in [my] memory with the most scrupulous fidelity ten or twelve meritorious pieces which were never written down but which, having heard him play many times. [I] have been able to transcribe [these] from the first bar to the last without omitting a single detail, nuance, or note."[11] It is fair to ask just where Gottschalk's music leaves off and Espadero's begins. These Havana editions of 1874 were promptly issued by the Escudier firm in Paris, but not without editing Espadero's introduction in such a way as to play down the Cuban's editorial role in their manufacture.[12]

Are these minutiae at all important? W. F. Apthorpe of the *Atlantic Monthly* argued: "A 'posthumous work' by Gottschalk is in itself a sort of ghastly joke, rather like a posthumous performance on the tightrope; for Gottschalk's music has died with him without hope of resuscitation in this world."[13]

In spite of this, hundreds of editions of Gottschalk works, both authentic and mutilated, poured forth from presses on three continents over the decades following the composer's death. The "complete works" issued in Argentina;[14] the editions published by Vidal y Roger in Spain, Edelmann in Havana, Mackar & Noël in Paris, or J. Rivière in London; and the five posthumous works edited and brought out by his sister Clara Gottschalk Peterson—all add new layers of complexity to the task of establishing Gottschalk's musical persona.[15]

The United States that had lionized Gottschalk before his precipitate departure in 1865 was still a raw-boned land. Now it was striving for respectability. Men who had amassed fortunes during the Civil War were now building Renaissance palazzos on Main Street, while their women squirmed into boned corsets and bustles, all for the sake of "good manners" and "culture."

The very memory of Gottschalk posed a challenge to this proper world. Besides his "reputation of being a dangerous lothario,"[16] his music dealt more with ecstasy than with uplift. To survive in the new Victorian climate, Gottschalk's reputation had to be sanitized. It was not enough for the press to claim, as one paper did, that "there was a great deal of exaggeration in the reports of his amorous exploits."[17] His entire life story had to be refurbished.

Who better to accomplish this than the respectable widow of an Episcopal clergyman? Writing under the name of Octavia Hensel, Mary Alice Ives Seymour rushed into print a *Life and Letters of Louis Moreau Gottschalk*, based on her friendship with him.[18] She devoted long pages to the composer's generosity and sense of duty. Her main task, however, was to give the lie to all those who saw him merely as a debauched bohemian. The tactic backfired. The real voluptuary turned out to be Mrs. Seymour herself, for she described her hero as impulsive, "tropical," and driven by a strange tension between "luxuriance and deep reasoning power, passionate longing and calm self-control."[19]

Other friends of the composer mercilessly savaged the book. One of them tore into Hensel's "boudoir rhapsodies" and her effort to "change the dead genius into an anemone."[20] The same friend also charged her with "overlooking those deeper and more enduring traits of character which constituted his real individuality."

A few years later Luís Ricardo Fors set out to present his version of the composer's life. Fors had in his possession many Gottschalk letters that gave value to the biography independent of the many factual errors it contained. Fors had two axes to grind, and both stemmed from his outlook as a Spanish-born liberal. First, he wanted to present his friend as a free spirit untrammeled by the morality espoused by the Catholic Church. Second, he wanted to rescue Gottschalk's musical romanticism from the clutches of belittling classicists. Spewing fountains of extravagant Spanish prose, he labored not to win over his opponents but to pul-

verize them. One of the milder epithets he hurled at Gottschalk's detractors was to call them "moral pygmies and slaves to musical
routine."[21]

To present his paragon of moral freedom, Fors packed his hero's life
with encounters with lusty women. Among these was Dina, a raven-haired
lovely from a harem on the Black Sea who Fors claimed had been en-
slaved by a wicked Boston businessman and liberated by the manly
Gottschalk.[22] One wonders if the composer himself fed this juicy tale to
the gullible Fors as part of his own ceaseless effort to discredit Boston
Puritanism, or if Fors fabricated it on his own.

Clara Gottschalk Peterson issued an English-language edition of her
brother's travel notes. Most of the text had already appeared in print,
whether in French- or English-language newspapers. Now Clara gathered
these together, along with selected letters and a biography. The resulting
Notes of a Pianist revived old controversies and gave rise to new ones.
Some readers considered Clara's "Biographical Sketch" a loving homage,
but most of Gottschalk's friends derided its "hysterical and nauseating
exaggeration."[23] More serious were its myriad errors of facts, which were
to be repeated in Gottschalk studies for a century.

Clara more than compensated for her sloppiness in the "Biographical
Sketch" by the care she took in editing the travel notes.[24] She resisted
the temptation to censor or improve her brother's words. A comparison
of the original published articles and Clara's edition of them reveals that
she faithfully transcribed the originals, reorganizing them or providing
bridges only when essential.[25] To be sure, she relied mainly on
Gottschalk's published texts rather than on his handwritten notebooks,
but the main differences between these texts were the work of Moreau
himself, and not Clara. The one major flaw in her edition of the *Notes* is
that the English translation by her husband, Robert E. Peterson, is an
appallingly anemic rendering of Gottschalk's pungent French prose.

Even in Peterson's neutered translation, Gottschalk's book shocked
many Americans and led some to conclude that he was more French than
American. The *Philadelphia Press*, for example, considered the *Notes*
"more worthy of a French novel than of a book to be put into the hands
of a school girl" and rued that the text had not been "condensed and
expurgated."[26] Others noted Gottschalk's "foreign eyes" with approval,
realizing that his cosmopolitan perspective had enabled him to perceive
aspects of American society that were invisible to locals.[27]

For all its flaws, Clara's edition of the *Notes* enabled the public to
peer behind the mask of aloofness that Gottschalk invariably wore before
the public. Suddenly, he emerged as an ironic commentator on everything
from politics to religion. The arch-romantic was revealed as a keen-eyed

realist, while the "tropical" dreamer was transformed into a quick-witted intellectual.[28] Champions of the European classics may not have been silenced, as a Chicago reviewer claimed,[29] but Gottschalk's own words generated a new interest in the composer as a person. A review for the *New York Times* found the *Notes* "exquisitely amusing" and discovered a delicacy and "subdued pathos" in the author's music that he had heretofore not appreciated.[30] Another reviewer, less generous, confessed that the earlier Gottschalk-mania had left a residue "not unlike that which follows a debauch of candy."[31] After discovering new levels of subtlety in the man, however, the reviewer professed renewed interest in his compositions.

This presented problems of its own. Unless a music is played, and played well, it dies. One of the few points on which friends and foes agreed was that Gottschalk's performance of his own music was inimitable. As the more muscular German-Russian school of piano playing conquered America, the lighter Gottschalkian style dropped away. True, his sisters Clara, Celestine, and Blanche all tried to carry on the tradition, as did his brother Gaston, who ran a music school in Chicago for more than three decades.[32] But since Moreau had not actually taught any of his siblings, they could scarcely be expected to play like him. Nor did they.

Several North American pianists who knew Gottschalk's style best died young. The one exception was Philadelphia-born John Francis Gilder. Over several decades this cultivated musician with the Gottschalk mustache crisscrossed the country playing his master's works.[33] Also on the concert circuit were W. Henry Palmer, who made a practice of passing off Gottschalk compositions as his own,[34] and the self-taught African-American pianist Thomas Green Bethune known as "Blind Tom" (1849–1908), who featured a number of Gottschalk works in his repertoire.[35]

A few pianists of the first rank perpetuated Gottschalk's memory. Among them were European-born Annette Leschetisky Friedheim and the great Josef Hofmann, who kept *Le Bananier* in his repertoire for several years after his American debut as a child prodigy in 1887. So did the American pianist Amy Beach, who programmed Gottschalk's *Berceuse* and other works throughout her career.[36] Far more significant in the long run was Teresa Carreño (1853–1917), the Venezuelan-born virtuoso and Gottschalk pupil who preserved something of his style of performance down to her death in 1917. Similarly, both the brilliant Cuban composer and Gottschalk student Ignacio Cervantes (1849–1905) and the Brazilian composer Brasilio Itiberé de Cunha (1846–1913) continued to champion Gottschalk's music into the twentieth century.

Did Gottschalk exert any influence on major composers who came after him? Bizet performed Gottschalk's works as a young man, and his library contained many Gottschalk compositions.[37] Gottschalk's Latin tinge may even have carried over to the *Habanera* in *Carmen,* although the Cuban link is just as likely to have come through Gottschalk's New Orleans contemporary Ernest Guiraud.[38] The search for Gottschalk's influence on other composers leaves one grasping at straws. Is it significant that the dean of Italian critics, Filippo Filippi, after hearing the La Scala premiere of Verdi's *Aida,* declared that the brilliant finale to the second act recalled "the American Gottschalk"?[39] Probably not. Far more intriguing is evidence presented by the Russian critic Sergei Dianin that Gottschalk's *Le Bananier* "played an exceptionally important part in the formation of the themes for the Polovtsian [Dances]" in Borodin's opera *Prince Igor.*[40] Dianin went on to show how Borodin copied out *Le Bananier* by hand and returned repeatedly to this source in his quest for exotic materials for his opera.

Beyond this, there are few leads. One might note the direct appropriation of Gottschalkian themes by the American composer John Knowles Paine in his 1875 sonata for violin and piano or Charles Ives's quotation of Gottschalk's *The Last Hope* in his setting of Psalm 90. But the very paucity of such influences proves the larger point, namely, that European and American classicists of the late nineteenth and early twentieth centuries had little use for Gottschalk's music. When Carreño programmed several Gottschalk works in a London concert in the 1890s, George Bernard Shaw faulted her for showing bad taste. "Certainly [Carreño] is a superb executant . . . , but Gottschalk!—good gracious!"[41] Luís Ricardo Fors had to admit that even in France "there existed a certain indifference and coldness concerning Gottschalk and his works."[42] Nor was the situation better in Germany. When a respected German pianist of the last century was asked to list his heroes, he immediately cited Anton Rubinstein and Sigismund Thalberg. "How about Gottschalk?" asked an American guest. "Ah! yes, I had forgotten him." replied this master. "He certainly belongs with the other two."[43]

Oblivion would have been a better fate than what Gottschalk received at the hands of late-nineteenth-century American highbrows. Edward MacDowell had studied with two Gottschalk disciples.[44] But as a tenured professor of composition at Columbia University (the first American to be so honored, or handicapped) he was more inclined to follow in the tracks of solid European classicists than of an itinerant American who had appealed to the tastes of the domestic public. Others gave Gottschalk the back of their hand. The nineteenth-century critic W. S. B. Mathews averred, "It seems puerile now that in his concerts Gottschalk could have made an effect with his famous piece, *The Banjo.*" Conceding that Gottschalk possessed "an original and characteristic genius," Mathews went on to class him with John Philip Sousa, whose music, regrettably, also possessed an "inherently popular character."[45]

The *Nation* had set down the party line on Gottschalk as early as 1882, when it announced that the composer had "accommodated himself, to a certain extent, to the demands of the public, and in so doing he partly sacrificed his artistic principles."[46] Frédéric Ritter, an Alsatian-born critic from Boston, codified this stereotype by declaring that Gottschalk had "spent his best forces while endeavoring to entertain musically-inexperienced and uninspired audiences."[47]

It must have galled such critics that the public continued to love Gottschalk's music. Editions of his hits rested on the music racks of parlor pianos from coast to coast and in South America as well. "Even today," wrote a turn-of-the-century Philadelphian, ". . . it is Gottschalk's music, with his portrait on the cover, that still remains supreme among 'fashionable pieces.' "[48] John Philip Sousa's transcription of *Marche de nuit* was popularized by the U.S. Marine Band,[49] and *The Last Hope* echoed through Protestant choir lofts as the hymn *Mercy* or *Gottschalk*. Those who wanted to play works like *The Dying Poet* but could not handle the intricacies of Gottschalk's style could buy simplified versions, which were issued in great numbers.[50]

The sales records of Gottschalk's publisher Oliver Ditson & Co. of Boston document the public's continued affection for his music. The list of works in print shrank in the first generation after his death. It grew again thereafter, reaching fifty-five by 1915. Among perennial favorites were *Tremolo, Scintilla, Marche de nuit, Ojos criollos, Pasquinade, O Loving Heart, Trust On, Radieuse, Berceuse,* the transcription of the *Miserere* from *Il Trovatore, The Banjo,* and, of course, *The Dying Poet* and *The Last Hope.*[51] Other publishers also churned out Gottschalk editions. Among the several dozen American houses to capitalize on his name was that of Scharfenberg & Luis, whose founder, William Scharfenberg, had once tried to ban Gottschalk from membership in New York's Philharmonic Society.

Nor was Gottschalk merely for pianists. Just before the turn of the century, the Regina Company of Rahway, New Jersey, issued a large metal disk of *The Last Hope* for use in its music boxes. And when player pianos were invented, piano rolls of Gottschalk's compositions were issued with great frequency, often with half a dozen versions of a given work on the market at one time.[52] Firms in Cuba, South America, and Europe also issued piano rolls of his music.[53]

Whether thumped out on parlor pianos, cranked out on music boxes, or pumped out on player pianos, Gottschalk's melodies became the stereotyped mode in which Americans expressed many common emotions.

Rare was the silent film which did not specify for the pianist to play *Tremolo* at moments of rising emotion, *The Dying Poet* as the hero and heroine parted, and *Morte!!* as the heroine expired. In South America Gottschalk compositions were performed before the movie as well, in order to set the tone.[54] In the end, these Gottschalk compositions became so utterly clichéd that his music had to be rescued from its own success.

A host of Gottschalk's friends and admirers rose to the challenge. Between 1890 and 1915 a dozen aging Gottschalkians published memoirs containing affectionate accounts of the man and his music. These by no means neutralized the deprecations cast by highbrows nor dispelled the aura of banality generated by the endless repetition of Gottschalk's potboilers. But they helped reclaim Gottschalk's place in American culture at a time when a sacralized high art seemed everywhere in control. It did not hurt that the respected William Mason recalled with pride his friendship with Gottschalk, or that George F. Root, the revered author of *Battle Cry of Freedom*, praised Gottschalk's mastery of Bach and defended his compositions as having contributed to the musical education of the nation.[55]

Not all these reminiscences cast Gottschalk in the best light. One, for example, reported that the composer had confessed that he played certain of his own pieces "because people liked them [and] because he needed the money they brought him."[56] Diego de Vivo, who had served as an assistant tour manager in the 1860s, pined for the lost days of his youth in another memoir entitled "De Vivo's Jolly Season." "It is hard to believe," he wrote, "how soon after the performance the women would rush to the stage door."[57] But even these memoirs helped kindle among a new generation some of the excitement formerly evoked by Gottschalk's name.

Parallel to this *fin de siècle* memoir boom came several more systematic defenses of Gottschalk against his critics. As early as 1892 the journal *Music* issued a lengthy study entitled "Gottschalk—a Successful American Composer."[58] The author, W. S. B. Mathews, had long been one of Gottschalk's most severe detractors but was now prepared to reclaim him as an American original. Here and elsewhere Mathews acknowledged that with Gottschalk "a new accent entered the musical world, an accent distinctly American and personal to Gottschalk."[59] Another expert discoursed on Gottschalk as one of "The World's Greatest Pianists,"[60] while still another simply passed over him because, as he said, "Gottschalk's niche is forever secured in the Temple of Fame."[61] By 1908 the *Musician* devoted an entire number to Gottschalk, and a widely reprinted newspaper piece explained how "Gottschalk Comes to His Own Again."[62] At almost the same time that Teddy Roosevelt's Rough Riders were ascending San Juan Hill in

Cuba, Gottschalk had become the standard-bearer for musical nationalists who were seeking to affirm an authentic American music.[63]

While the North was reclaiming Gottschalk as America's first national voice in music, people in his home town were emphasizing his pioneering status as a regionalist and local colorist. Long before Antonin Dvořák urged American composers to mine their indigenous traditions for inspiration, the gimlet-eyed writer and wanderer Lafcadio Hearn had shown how Gottschalk had done just this.[64] It was Hearn who interested the New Orleans novelist George Washington Cable in Gottschalk, and Cable in turn further enhanced Gottschalk's standing as a leading local colorist. Most of Cable's essays and stories on Creole New Orleans were published by *Scribner's*, whose editor was a brother of Gottschalk's disciple Francis Gilder. Sensing an opening, Gottschalk's tireless sister Clara made contact with *Scribner's* and for the rest of her life campaigned to confirm her brother's standing as the bard of Creole New Orleans. It was she who encouraged a drab New Orleans insurance man, William H. Hawes, to collect every scrap of Gottschalk memorabilia and present them to the City of New Orleans. The bewildered mayor had to endure endless visits from Hawes, who doggedly checked to make sure that Gottschalk's bust was prominently displayed in City Hall.[65]

In the end, the regionalists' campaign succeeded. The new notion of Gottschalk as Creole bard supplanted the more cosmopolitan image that had prevailed during his lifetime and the nationalist image that held sway for a generation thereafter. When in 1906 a Philadelphia publication touted the music of New Orleans, it assured readers that Gottschalk's compositions represented the very essence of that city's culture.[66] New Orleans novelist Grace King went even further, stating that "no music imported by money from abroad can ever speak to the native heart as [Gottschalk's] does. It is the atavism of the soil in sound."[67]

The transformation of Gottschalk into the authentic voice of Southern regionalism coincided with the popularity of ragtime music in the years 1899–1914. A number of observers detected that Moreau Gottschalk had anticipated this rambunctious syncopated music by half a century. Thus a certain W. O. Eschwege penned an article entitled " 'Rag Time' as Old as the Hills," in which he identified Gottschalk as the direct progenitor of this new fad:[68]

> "Rag time" sympathized singularly with [Gottschalk's] idiosyncrasies as a composer, as is indicated clearly in every bar of his *Pasquinade*, a composition deemed by leading pianists of the present day worthy to be included in programs of a high order. The measures [are] fairly dense with wild, constant changes of rhythm which constitute the foundation of what we are pleased to call "rag time," probably a contraction of "ragged time."

In September 1899, the month in which Scott Joplin's *Maple Leaf Rag* was published in Sedalia, Missouri, the indefatigable Hawes demonstrated to Clara Gottschalk Peterson how her brother had invented ragtime. Mrs. Peterson responded, "I approve of your verdict about rag time songs," and asked, "Why do they call by such a name simple syncopation or Spanish rhythm, I wonder?"[69]

Only much later did scholars inquire into the precise channels through which Gottschalk's music might have been transmitted to early ragtime composers. One biographer of Scott Joplin speculated that Joplin heard "the currently popular tunes played in syncopated style, most notably those of Louis Moreau Gottschalk."[70] Another Joplin biographer focused on his early study with a German "professor" in Texarkana, Texas. He argued that this anonymous piano teacher "no doubt" introduced Joplin to Gottschalk's works, and went so far as to suggest that *Ojos criollos* and other Caribbean pieces by Gottschalk had exerted a particularly strong influence on the composer of the *Maple Leaf Rag*.[71] Other writers developed these points further, but none produced more than circumstantial evidence in support of their claims.[72]

Nor is there more conclusive evidence today. However, it is worth noting that all of the Gottschalk works that contain the most conspicuous proto-ragtime elements—*Ojos criollos, Pasquinade, Souvenir de Porto Rico*, etc.—were not only in print throughout the period in which ragtime composers were growing up, but also selling well.[73] Moreover, the major ragtime composers—Scott Joplin, Eubie Blake, Artie Matthews and others—had all benefited from classical training in music. Far from being primitive folk artists, Joplin aspired to write opera, Blake revered Liszt's rhapsodies, and Matthews was devoted to Chopin.[74] All had ample opportunity to play Gottschalk's compositions and probably did so.

No ragtime composer exploited Caribbean and Creole syncopated rhythms more thoroughly than Jelly Roll Morton, born Ferdinand le Menthe. Did Morton know Gottschalk's pioneering works in this genre? It is all but certain, since Morton's teacher, J. Nickerson, moved in the same circle of classically trained black Creole musicians as several Gottschalk contemporaries. Moreover, novelist Grace King confirmed that Gottschalk's works were widely played among the French-speaking population of New Orleans.[75] There is strong evidence also that the operatic repertoire for piano made famous by Gottschalk was passed down to Morton. "Jelly Roll" prided himself on his ability to "rag" the *Miserere* from *Il Trovatore*, which he almost certainly learned from Gottschalk's transcription. Elsewhere he spoke of playing the *Sextet* from *Lucia*, another piece from Gottschalk's repertoire.[76] Morton also recalled a cutting contest among several of the best ragtime composers in which each participant tackled the *Miserere*, Gottschalk's most popular operatic transcription.[77] Clearly, the participants all sprang from the pianistic world that Gottschalk first defined and knew both the operatic pieces he featured and almost certainly his more accessible ballads and syncopated works as well.

A similar process took place in Rio de Janeiro. There the Afro-Brazilian musician Ernesto Júlio Nazaré (1863–1934) studied piano with New Orleans–born Lucien Lambert, a Gottschalk disciple. Nazaré went on to include many Gottschalk works in his repertoire.[78] At the same time Joplin, Morton, and other North American composers were creating ragtime, Nazaré produced a series of rag-like dances with startling parallels to their better-known cousins from the United States. Nazaré probably knew the works of ragtime pioneers from North America, and he undoubtedly was influenced by purely Brazilian traditions of Afro-American music as well. But is it an accident that the one South American composer to write music in an authentic ragtime vein came from the one city on the continent in which Gottschalk's syncopated music was best known and was himself actually a disciple of one of Gottschalk's musical heirs?

All consideration of Gottschalk's relation to ragtime was swept aside by the explosion of popular interest in jazz after 1917. More than ever before, this new music polarized American taste between popular and classical, lowbrow and highbrow. Gottschalk's music had always mediated between these opposing realms, but now musicians like Irving Berlin and Paul Whiteman assumed this role, eclipsing the New Orleanian. By 1925 the *Christian Science Monitor* called Gottschalk "a forgotten pioneer," and a few years later he was simply "a forgotten American musician."[79] The centennial of his birth was noted in Cuba but not in his native country, and when a Caribbean-oriented writer rediscovered him in 1934, he gave his article the mortuary title "An Early Pan-American Exhumed."[80]

Up to 1935 only three people tried to rescue the composer from oblivion. The most ambitious was Gertrude Tucker, a schoolteacher from Clinton, New Jersey, who set out to write his biography. She had access to a few letters in the possession of collateral descendants of Gottschalk but was soon daunted by the task and gave up.[81] The second was a young pianist, John Kirkpatrick, whom critics considered "practically alone in attempting to stir Gottschalk's deeply-imbedded coffin."[82] In spite of valiant efforts, it took Kirkpatrick another twenty years to find an audience for Gottschalk's forgotten works.

The third was the conductor of the New York Sinfonietta, Quinto Maganini, who produced a free transcription of *The Banjo*, which critics judged "an amusing number, certain to delight a popular program."[83] Maganini had caught the bug, however, and yearned to find original Gottschalk scores. He advertised a prize for whoever could turn up the manuscript for the symphony *Night in the Tropics*.[84] The quest proved fruitless, so Maganini orchestrated the work from a surviving piano reduction.

In 1948 the New York Public Library purchased a number of manuscripts that had once belonged to Nicolás Ruiz Espadero. Among them was Espadero's own two-piano reduction of *Night in the Tropics*. The redoubtable Kirkpatrick, along with historian Arthur Loesser, gave this work its North American premiere at the New York Times Hall in December 1948. A review in *Musical America* reported that when the two players hit the lively and syncopated second movement "the audience burst forth into uncontrollable laughter . . . for the formal devices of the classical symphony were never more woefully out of place."[85] Olin Downes of the *New York Times* found it to be "frippery, yet romantic in color, exotic in mood."[86]

Also in the New York Public Library's purchase was a manuscript of the complete score for *Night in the Tropics*. The original had included four-part choirs for each instrument. This had presented no problem in Havana, where Gottschalk had at his disposal an opera orchestra and numerous military bands. It was an impossibility for twentieth century New York, however, so Howard Shanet of Columbia University transcribed the piece for a more reasonably sized orchestra. Shanet also reconstructed the missing final measures. On May 6, 1955, Columbia's orchestra presented the North American premiere of the full symphony. Thereafter, the New York Philharmonic programmed the work from time to time.

Reviews were mixed. The *Times*, for example, considered the symphony "an amazingly modern-sounding piece," but the *Herald Tribune* judged it "less interesting."[87] The party line was that Gottschalk's musings were appropriate for Young People's Concerts and Promenade Concerts, but not for the regular season.

The condescension went deep. The Philharmonic would not have dared emasculate Berlioz's *Symphonie fantastique* by performing it without the complement of instruments specified by the composer. Yet it was all right to do this with music by Berlioz's one American disciple. The same rationalization underlay conductor Andre Kostelanetz's practice of skipping the *andante* movement in order to get right to the boisterous *finale*, which he treated as a Cuban street scene in some Caribbean *Oklahoma!*. In this way, Gottschalk became a musical version of a travel magazine, rich with surface sheen but devoid of darker tones and pathos. Americans had rediscovered Gottschalk, but at the price of trivializing him.

This process was particularly evident in dance. Beginning with the Denishawn Dancers' *Pasquinade* in 1920, the world of ballet turned increasingly to Gottschalk's music.[88] Lincoln Kirstein, George Balanchine, Lynne Taylor, Merce Cunningham, Paul Taylor, and the Royal Danish Ballet all choreographed Gottschalk works with great success. This reached a high point when Balanchine's *pas de deux* to the *Tarentelle* was featured in a performance broadcast live by television from the White House.[89]

It was no small achievement to get Gottschalk into the dance repertoire. When Lincoln Kirstein first suggested that his music be used for New York City Ballet's *Cakewalk*, no one in the company had even heard of the composer. The one exception was George Balanchine, who remembered that Gottschalk's music had been popular in his native Russia.[90] Kirstein engaged Hershy Kay to produce a score. Kay, an expert on Chinese cuisine, succeeded in purging every Gottschalkian element from the music and replacing it with Hollywood schlock. Dance critic Clive Barnes dismissed Kay's product in a review entitled "Bouncy Creole Tunes Get New Setting."[91] Orchestrator Victoria Bond took condescension to new heights with her score for the ballet *Great Galloping Gottschalk*, which the American Ballet Theater performed successfully.[92]

A more complex appreciation of Gottschalk and his music first emerged in South America. In 1950 the German-born Uruguayan scholar Francisco Curt Lange published his book-length monograph on the composer's last year in Rio de Janeiro.[93] Lange's subsequent studies on Gottschalk in Uruguay and Argentina demonstrated his significant contributions to the culture of South America.[94] Other authors in Chile and Brazil picked up the same theme.[95]

The first North American to plunge as deeply into the world of Gottschalk was John Godfrey Doyle, who completed a dissertation on the piano music in 1960.[96] Hard on Doyle's heels came the Philadelphia pianist Jeanne Behrend, who prepared a new edition of *Notes of a Pianist* in 1964. She also issued what remains one of the best recordings of Gottschalk's piano music. Here for the first time was Gottschalk without burlesque or kitch, and without the ham-handed overplaying that has ruined nearly every other recorded performance.[97]

With the approach of the centennial of Gottschalk's death in 1869, a burst of research turned up lost works and forgotten details of his life. Even before Lange published his research on Gottschalk in Rio, an isolated devotee in the Mohawk Valley of New York had issued a microscopically detailed study of "Gottschalk in Utica."[98] Now an epidemic of "Gottschalk in X" articles appeared. A veritable industry was born, extending eventually to Puerto Rico, Buenos Aires, the Virgin Islands, Cuba, Spain, Norfolk (Virginia), Québec, Burlington (Vermont), and Brooklyn.[99] Together, these investigations showed that Gottschalk established artistic and intellectual ties nearly everywhere he went and was anything but the gypsy lothario of myth.

As his persona gained new facets, so did his music. Robert Offergeld was a contributor to *Stereo Review* whose life revolved around the exchange of witticisms with Virgil Thomson and other American composers who had once called Paris home. His *Centennial Catalogue of the Published and Unpublished Compositions of Louis Moreau Gottschalk* broke new ground by showing that only a small percentage of Gottschalk's compositions were ever published and that even manuscripts for most of the rest were missing.[100] However, the list of published works was so much longer than anyone imagined that musicologists began suspecting that a whole chapter in American music had been missed.

In an effort to fill this blank, music historian Vera Brodsky Lawrence issued a facsimile edition of 112 Gottschalk compositions for piano.[101] For the first time, an American composer was honored with something approaching a "collected works" in the Germanic tradition. These facsimiles of old sheet music drew would-be performers like a land rush. Unfortunately, what critic Alfred Frankenstein said of Alan Mandel's recording of forty Gottschalk works[102] could be said of nearly all the post-centennial recordings: "Lord knows the cannonading octaves of the big show pieces are banged out grandly enough, but it lacks elegance and atmosphere. [Mandel] gives us plastics instead of red plush."[103]

The most exciting development of the centennial year was the United States premiere of a whole series of newly rediscovered Gottschalk works. Twenty years earlier, Francisco Curt Lange had located a trove of Gottschalk manuscripts in Rio de Janeiro. John Godfrey Doyle made contact with the owner and discovered that he was willing to sell.[104] Eventually pianist Eugene List, another ardent Gottschalkian (by now *all* Gottschalkians were ardent), raised the money to enable the New York Public Library to make the purchase. On February 25, 1969, List premiered works from this collection at a landmark concert with the New Orleans Symphony Orchestra.[105] In one heady evening List performed *Concert Variations on the Portuguese National Anthem*, the *Montevideo* symphony, *March triunfal*, and the brief operatic delight *Esceñas campestres*.

Later in the centennial year List brought together twenty performers on ten pianos to do a reconstructed version of Gottschalk's *Siege of Sara-*

gossa,[106] and by the time the sesquicentennial of Gottschalk's birth was celebrated in 1979 he had doubled his army for a true monster concert. *Time* reported that the effect "was like a giant hurdy-gurdy."[107]

The centennial vastly broadened the parameters of Gottschalk's life and works, but it also produced its share of nonsense. This was the era of Stokeley Carmichael and black radicalism, and it was perhaps inevitable that someone would claim that Moreau Gottschalk was himself black. One to do so was Florence Robinson of Clark College in Atlanta, who argued that, even though Gottschalk never identified ethnically with blacks, he was of mixed blood.[108] Dr. Robert Pritchard, a pianist and founder of the Pan-American Association, shared this conviction and in 1969 held a conference with representatives of a group called the Black Liberation Front to discuss such issues.[109] A deft organizer, Pritchard persuaded the Organization of American States to sponsor the First Louis Moreau Gottschalk International Piano Competition at Dillard University in New Orleans. Even though the advisory committee included Leopold Stokowski, Pablo Casals, and George Balanchine, the competition passed with scarcely a trace and was not renewed.

That so basic an issue as Gottschalk's genealogy could have been in doubt attested to the continuing need for a full biography. Since it required the use of several languages and materials in ten countries, this presented a real challenge. By 1950 a scholar from Brown University, David James, had plunged into this task. Unknown to James, Vernon Loggins of Columbia University had also taken up the challenge. The two met by accident in Paris when they sat opposite each other at the Bibliothèque Nationale. Both had ordered the same book, and when the librarian brought it to their table and told them to share it, James was so thunderstruck that he abandoned the project.[110] Loggins meanwhile got ever more excited. Convinced that he had the makings of a Hollywood spectacular, he milked his subject for drama and filled inconvenient gaps in evidence by fabricating conversations and events. The book was severely criticized when it appeared in 1958.

When Robert Offergeld announced plans for a Gottschalk biography, he became the third modern writer to attempt the project, and the sixth overall. Diligent research led him to Otto Rhome, an eccentric recluse who lived in a Philadelphia brownstone. Offergeld suspected this man had in his possession a trunk of Moreau Gottschalk's papers. Rhome was a grandson of Gottschalk's sister Blanche and indeed had the papers in his basement. But he refused to receive Offergeld, and when Rhome died it fell to a young fourth-generation Gottschalk descendant, Lawrence B. Glover, to go through the family's papers. Happily, Glover took an interest in these documents, and when he found an unopened letter from Offergeld in the trunk, he contacted him. Most of this trove of Gottschalki-ana eventually took its place in the New York Public Library.[111]

Offergeld was so overwhelmed by the vastness of his goldmine that he simply avoided it and died before writing the first line of his book. Richard Jackson of the New York Public Library's staff published a de-scriptive guide to the Rhome collection, but it long remained an unassimi-lable mass. By then the task had become yet more complex, thanks to John Godfrey Doyle, who had assembled a formidable bibliography of source material, much of it previously unknown; to Francisco Curt Lange, who located unknown Gottschalk correspondence in Buenos Aires; to Clyde W. Brockett of Christopher Newport College, who discovered yet more manuscripts in Spain; and to Rita Maria Castro y Maya of the Museo de la Música, Havana, who came across new Gottschalk materials in Cuba.

Twelve decades after Moreau Gottschalk's death, he had once again become a celebrity of sorts in his native country, in several countries of South America, and, to a lesser extent, in France.[112] Massive documenta-tion on his life was at hand, and more of his works were available than during his own lifetime. Yet the picture of this enigmatic composer re-mained strangely out of focus. Whole segments of his busy career were still obscure, and prevailing views of the known parts were often contra-dictory. For example, two thoughtful writers reached diametrically op-posed conclusions about his personality. Garry E. Clarke considered Gottschalk an "intuitive composer who lacked intellectual commitment and who was plagued by a sense of his own inferiority,"[113] while Daniel Kingman depicted him as "extroverted and self-confident, but suffering from an identity crisis" in his last years.[114]

If Gottschalk's personality has proven elusive, his place in American culture is even more problematic. Gilbert Chase, the prominent American musicologist, assigned him a position on the "exotic periphery" of Ameri-can life, while H. Wiley Hitchcock placed Gottschalk solidly in a "culti-vated tradition" within the mainstream of American music.[115] Still another specialist, Wilfrid Mellers, agreed with Chase's notion of the "exotic pe-riphery" but detected a "Yankee swagger" lurking in Gottschalk's Creole and Latin-tinged pieces.[116]

These writers seemed to think that the choice was to place Gottschalk either in an effete mainstream or on the colorful margins. Barbara Zuck and John Tasker Howard accepted the regional textures of Gottschalk's music but argued that these very qualities established him at the begin-ning of what is today the mainstream of American culture.[117] As Zuck put it, he "looms as one of our most significant figures because he was able to absorb and weave into his music the colorful and exotic melodies and

rhythms of Creole and Latin-American songs." Irving Lowens, in a percep-
tive article in the *New Grove Dictionary of Music and Musicians*, acknowledged that Gottschalk was "by no means an 'advanced' musician,
even in terms of his own day, [yet] his sensitivity to esoterica enabled
him to forecast, with uncanny prescience, American musical developments which did not actually take place until the end of the nineteenth
century."[118]

Harold Schonberg of the *New York Times* split the difference, conceding that Gottschalk was indeed a ground-floor romantic during his Paris
years, but frowning on him for descending to the writing of sentimental
potboilers after his return to America. By this judgment, Gottschalk's
tragedy was to have failed to lay the foundations for a secure "classical"
tradition in the New World. Less clear is whether he succeeded at some
other unspecified task. Did he, for example, pioneer a new music that
drew on European classicism but was at the same time the authentic
voice of American culture? Was he the first great multi-culturist and democrat in American music, who accepted America's diversity and built
from it a corpus of music that embodied some deeper unity? Or was he—
again, that creeping suspicion—merely a colorful hack?

Serious people reached different conclusions on these questions, not
least because the quality of "seriousness" itself was at issue. To an uncanny degree, Gottschalk's life forced those writing about it to reveal
themselves, to put their cards on the table. For a century, Gottschalk had
been a truthful mirror reflecting the changing face of American culture.

The controversy over Gottschalk is part of the warp and woof of the
larger debate over high culture and popular culture in America. Even the
very contradictory quality of Gottschalk's legacy has proven enduring. His
music today evokes the same expressions of regret over an opportunity
lost that were heard a century ago, the same frustration, condescension,
and even indignation. But in other quarters its lyricism and distinctive
textures call forth the full range of emotions to which a diverse and
many-sided culture gives rise and crystallize those deeper feelings of vitality and pathos that flow directly from the American experience. In both
his achievements and in his shortcomings, Gottschalk was an American
original.

Notes

1. A Death in Rio

1. On all aspects of Gottschalk's death and funeral see Francisco Curt Lange, "Vida y muerte de Louis Moreau Gottschalk en Rio de Janeiro (1869)," pt. 1 and 2, *Revista de Estudios Musicales*, 1950, no. 4, 5–6, especially pt. 2, pp. 100–256. See also Octavia Hensel, *Life and Letters of Louis Moreau Gottschalk*, Boston, 1870, pp. 181–85, 207; Louis Moreau Gottschalk, *Notes of a Pianist*, Clara Gottschalk Peterson, ed., Philadelphia, 1881, pp. 75–79.

2. On the death mask see *Jornal do Commercio* (Rio de Janeiro), 19 December 1869; also Lange, "Vida y muerte," no. 5–6, pp. 108ff.; also John G. Doyle, *Louis Moreau Gottschalk, 1829–1869: A Bibliographic Study and Catalog of Works*, Detroit, 1982, pp. 190, 201.

3. Dr. França Junior, *Diario do Rio de Janeiro*, 21 December 1869; Lange, "Vida y muerte," no. 4, p. 141 and no. 5–6, p. 101.

4. Henri Préalle to Clara Gottschalk, 23 December 1869, Glover Collection.

5. *Ba-ta-clan*, 25 December 1869; Lange, "Vida y muerte," no. 5–6, pp. 118–19.

6. See D. Moreira de Azevedo, *Rio de Janeiro*, 2 vols., Rio de Janeiro, 1877, 1:229ff.

7. Draft of letter from Gottschalk to Léon Escudier, n.d. (1857), Miscellaneous Letters, Gottschalk Collection, NYPL.

8. Allegorical drawing by Angelo Agostini, *A Vida Fluminense*, 25 December 1869.

9. Henri Préalle, letter to unknown "Gentleman and Friends," 23 December 1869, Miscellaneous Letters, Gottschalk Collection, NYPL.

10. Gilberto Freyre, *Order and Progress: Brazil from Monarchy to Republic*, New York, 1970, p. 78.

11. *Jornal da Tardé*, 18 December 1869.

12. "A Gottschalk," *Jornal da Tardé*, 21 December 1869.

13. *Diario do Rio de Janeiro*, 23 December 1869; Lange, "Vita y muerte," no. 5–6, pp. 115–16.

14. *Ba-ta-clan*, 25 December 1869.

15. The latter was implied by the *Anglo-Brazilian Times*, which started this rumor, 23 December 1869. The American Minister, Henry T. Blow, was not in Rio at the time.

16. Lange, "Vida y muerte," no. 5–6, p. 176.

17. Henry T. Blow to Hamilton Fish, 9, 19 November 1869, Despatch no. 46, vol. 37, Domestic Despatches, Brazil, General Records of the Department of State, Record Group 59, U.S. National Archives.

18. *Certiduo ole obito,* no. 651, Santa Casa da Misericordia, copy in Glover Collection.

19. Arthur Napoleão, *Autobiographia,* cited by Lange, "Vida y muerte," no. 5–6, p. 102. Henri Préalle to Clara Gottschalk, 23 December 1869, Glover Collection.

20. Lange, "Vida y muerte," no. 5–6, pp. 171–75.

21. Luís Ricardo Fors, *Gottschalk,* Havana, 1880, pp. 177–95.

22. Lange, "Vida y muerte," no. 5–6, pp. 127–49.

23. Brasilio Machado in *Correio Paulistano* (São Paulo), 24 December 1869; quoted by Carlos Penteado de Rezende, "O Poeta do piano," *Investigações: Revista do Departamento de Investigações* (São Paulo), December 1951, p. 41; Lange, "Vida y muerte," no. 4, p. 116.

24. Santiago Estrada, "Luis M. Gottschalk *[sic],*" *Revista Argentina,* January 1870, 6:57–64.

25. N. R. Espadero, "À propos de Gottschalk," *L'Art musical,* 31 March 1870, pp. 141–42.

26. Léon Escudier, "Mort de Gottschalk," *L'Art musical,* 27 January 1870, pp. 25–27; also Gustave Chouquet, "Les Dernières Oeuvres de Gottschalk," *L'Art musical,* 19 May 1870, pp. 197–98.

27. *Morning Post* (London), 23 February 1870.

28. *Illustrated London News,* 29 January 1870.

29. *Orchestra,* 28 January 1870.

30. Amy Fay, *Music Study in Germany,* New York, 1965, p. 42.

31. "Nekrolog," *Literaturnoe pribavlenie k Nuvellistu,* April 1870, pp. 28–29.

32. *Dwight's Journal of Music,* 29 January 1870, p. 184.

33. Henri Préalle to Charles Vezin, *Daily Evening Bulletin* (Philadelphia), 25 January 1870, reprinted in *New York Observer,* 6 February 1870.

34. *L'Abeille,* 23 January 1870; "Morte de Gottschalk," *L'Epoque,* n.d., unfiled clipping, Gottschalk Collection, NYPL.

35. See Vincente Gesualdo, *Historia de la música en la Argentina,* 2 vols., Buenos Aires, 1961, 1:259, fn. 17.

36. *New York World,* 22 January 1870.

37. See *Watson's Art Journal,* 29 January 1870, 25 June 1870.

38. *Orpheonist and Philharmonic Journal,* n.d. 1870, Offergeld Collection.

39. "Figaro on Gottschalk," *Leader,* n.d. 1870, unmounted clipping, Gottschalk Collection, NYPL.

40. *Leader,* n.d. 1870, unmounted clipping, Gottschalk Collection, NYPL.

41. Henry T. Blow to Charles Vezin, 24 August 1870, Diplomatic Despatches, Brazil, vol. 37, General Records of the Department of State, Record Group 59, U.S. National Archives.

42. Henry T. Blow to Department of State, 30 September 1870, Diplomatic Despatches, Brazil, vol. 37, General Records of the Department of State, Record Group 59, U.S. National Archives.

43. Henri Préalle to Clara Gottschalk, 23 December 1869, Miscellaneous Letters, Gottschalk Collection, NYPL.

44. Henri Préalle to Clara and Celestine Gottschalk, 22 March 1870, Miscellaneous Letters, Gottschalk Collection, NYPL.

45. Registry of Wills, City and County of Philadelphia, 4 June 1855, Gottschalk Collection, NYPL.

46. Clara G. Peterson to W. H. Hawes, 30 June 1901, Historic New Orleans Collection, New Orleans.

47. Firmin Moras to Charles Vezin, 26 July 1870, Gottschalk Collection, NYPL.

48. No sooner did a Rio piano dealer purchase the Chickering grands than the Boston firm of Chickering & Sons wrote to report that the instruments had not belonged to Gottschalk in the first place and to demand their immediate return. Henry T. Blow to Viscount de São Vicente, 28 October 1870, copy in letter of Blow to Hamilton Fish, Diplomatic Despatches, Brazil, vol. 37, General Records of the Department of State, Record Group 59, U.S. National Archives.

49. Lange, "Vida y muerte," no. 5–6, p. 222.

50. Francisco Curt Lange, "Louis Moreau Gottschalk (1829–69)," *Die Musikkultur Lateinamerika im 19. Jahrhundert,* Robert Günther, ed., Regensburg, 1982, p. 449.

51. Henry T. Blow to F. M. Cordiero, 21 May 1870, Diplomatic Despatches, vol. 37, no. 81, Record Group 59, Department of State, U.S. National Archives.

52. Hamilton Fish to Henry T. Blow, 18 July 1870, no. 29; also Robert Clinton Wright to Hamilton Fish, 24 May 1871, no. 176; Diplomatic Instructions of the Department of State, 1801–1906, vol. 77, U.S. National Archives.

53. Firmin Moras to Charles Vezin, 26 July 1870, Gottschalk Collection, NYPL.

54. Gottschalk to Charles Vezin, 15 December 1868, Gottschalk Collection, NYPL.

55. "The Vezin Case," "Startling," "Charles Vezin: Further Details in Relation to the Recent Commercial Scandal," *Evening Telegraph* (Philadelphia), *New York Herald,* etc., undated clippings, 1870–71, Scrapbook no. 12, Gottschalk Collection, NYPL.

56. On 24 August 1870, Henry T. Blow had returned Vezin's power of attorney on the grounds that U.S. consuls had no right to act in that capacity.

57. James R. Partridge to Leonard Myers, 25 November 1871, 25 January 1872, Domestic Letters, vol. 89, General Records of the Department of State, Record Group 59, U.S. National Archives.

58. Unsigned and undated fragment, Gottschalk Collection, NYPL.

59. Gottschalk Memorial Fund Concert, Union League Club, 21 May 1870, handbill, Picture Collection, NYPL; *Watson's Art Journal,* 12 March 1870, p. 138.

60. See accounts in the *Herald, Tribune, Sun, World,* and *New York Times,* 4 October 1870; *Courrier des États-Unis,* 10 October 1870; *Orpheonist and Philharmonic Journal,* 5 November 1870.

61. Diary of George Templeton Strong, 3 October 1870, courtesy of Vera Brodsky Lawrence.

62. *Watson's Art Journal,* 8 October 1870.

63. Marguerite F. Aymar, "Gottschalk's Grave," *Musical Bulletin,* February 1871, pp. 25–26.

2. Origins

1. Arnold Myers to Fleurette Gottschalk Myers, n.d. (27 December 1829), Glover Collection.

2. *Acte de baptême,* 22 December 1830, Folio 210, no. 13, Records of St. Louis Cathedral, New Orleans.

3. Aimée Gottschalk to Fleurette Gottschalk Myers, Glover Collection.

4. W. Thomas Marrocco, "Gottschalkiana: New Light on the Gottschalks and the Bruslés," *Louisiana History,* 1971, no. 1, pp. 60–63.

5. James Pitot, *Observations on the Colony of Louisiana from 1796 to 1802,* Baton Rouge, 1979.

6. Bertram Wallace Korn, *The Early Jews of New Orleans*, Waltham, Massachusetts, 1969, pp. 110–27.

7. Carlile Pollock, 24 May 1828, New Orleans Notarial Archives (hereafter NONA).

8. Hugues J. de la Verge, 1 January 1823, NONA.

9. *Courrier de la Louisiane* , 5 June 1830, p. 2.

10. Carlile Pollock, 5 July 1830, NONA.

11. Carlile Pollock, 13 March 1830, NONA.; Felix de Armas, 27 April 1830, 7 May 1830, NONA.

12. Felix de Armas, 7 February 1830, NONA.

13. Carlile Pollock, 15 July 1830, NONA.

14. Louis Moreau Gottschalk, *Notes of a Pianist*, Jeanne Behrend, ed., New York, 1964, p. 47.

15. Gottschalk, "Souvenirs de Gottschalk," *Home Journal,* n.d. 1863, uncataloged clipping, Gottschalk Collection, NYPL.

16. Léon Escudier, *Les Virtuoses*, Paris, 1868, pp. 175–76.

17. *Orchestra* (London), July 1877, p. 372.

18. Susan Dabney Smedes, *Memorials of a Southern Planter*, New York, 1888, pp. 97–98.

19. Alexis de Tocqueville, *Democracy in America*, 2 vols., New York, 1945, 1:350, fn. 21.

20. Theodore Clapp, *Autobiographical Sketch and Recollections During Thirty-five Years Residence in New Orleans*, Boston, 1857, pp. 122–35.

21. Hensel, *Life and Letters*, pp. 38–39.

22. Gottschalk, *Notes of a Pianist*, p. 292.

23. Alfred Einstein, *Music in the Romantic Era*, New York, 1947, pp. 28–30.

24. Gottschalk, *Notes of a Pianist*, p. 46.

25. Clara Gottschalk Peterson, "Biographical Sketch," pp. 26, 28–29.

26. Cf. Ills. 14, 15, and 16. Publication date unknown, Offergeld Papers, property of the author.

27. Bertram W. Korn, "A Note on the Jewish Ancestry of Louis Moreau Gottschalk, American Pianist and Composer," *American Jewish Archives*, November 1963, pp. 117–19.

28. Korn, *The Early Jews of New Orleans*, p. 174.

29. Arthur Barnett, "Eliakim ben Abraham (Jacob Hart): An Anglo-Jewish Scholar of the Eighteenth Century," *Transactions of the Jewish Historical Society of England*, London, 1935–39, 14:207–20.

30. Arthur Barnett, *The Western Synogogue Through Two Centuries*, London, 1961, pp. 46–48 quoted in Korn, "A Note on the Jewish Ancestry," p. 118.

31. Barnett, "Eliakim ben Abraham," p. 216.

32. Korn, *The Early Jews of New Orleans*, p. 174.

33. "Paris News," *Morning Post* (London), 23 February 1870.

34. Escudier, *Les Virtuoses*, p. 175. It has also been claimed that Edward Gottschalk studied at Cambridge University, but there is no evidence to support this.

35. It may also be relevant that Edward's older brother, Joseph Victor Gottschalk, went at an early age to Prussia's Baltic province of Pomerania, where he married. Succession of Joseph Victor Gottschalk, Louisiana Court of Probate, Successions and Probate Records, 1805–46, Part 99 (1836–37), Louisiana Division, New Orleans Public Library.

36. See Todd M. Endelman, *The Jews of Georgian England, 1774–1830*, Philadelphia, 1879, p. 149.

37. William Boswell, 23 May 1828, NONA.

38. Korn, "A Note on the Jewish Ancestry," pp. 118–19.

39. Edward Gottschalk's account book, 23 September 1854, Album no. 8, Gottschalk Collection, NYPL.

40. Louis Moreau to Clara Gottschalk, 24 May 1863(?), Family Letters, Gottschalk Collection, NYPL.

41. Hensel, *Life and Letters*, pp. 45–46.

42. Alan Kendall, *Paganini, a Biography*, London, 1982, p. 95.

43. Clara Gottschalk Peterson, "Biographical Sketch," p. 29.

44. The first evidence of Edward Gottschalk in New Orleans is an advertisement in the *Louisiana Gazette*, 12 June 1823.

45. Cecil Roth, *A History of the Jews in England*, Oxford, 1928, pp. 241ff.

46. Morris U. Schappes, ed., *A Documentary History of Jews in the United States, 1654–1875*, New York, 1950, pp. 141–47.

47. *Passenger Lists of Vessels Arriving at New Orleans (1820–1902)*, Louisiana Department, New Orleans Public Library.

48. Carlile Pollock, 25 April 1829, NONA.

49. Korn, *The Early Jews of New Orleans*, p. 176; Succession of Dr. Joseph Victor Gottschalk, Court of Probate, Orleans Parish, Part 99, 1836–37, Louisiana Department, New Orleans Public Library.

50. Achille Chiapella, 17 July 1852, NONA.

51. Henry Cohen, "Settlement of the Jews in Texas," *Publications of the American Jewish Historical Society*, New York, 1894, p. 150.

52. Among "Israelite Donors" to the first Jewish congregation in New Orleans in 1828 were Hyam Harris, A. H. Harris, and Moses Harris. Morris U. Schappes, *A Documentary History of the Jews in the United States 1654–1875*, p. 609, n. 4. *The Constitution and Bylaws of the Israelite Congregation Shangarai-chasset*, New Orleans, 1828.

53. Carlile Pollock, 15 July 1823, also 28 September 1825 and 26 June 1826, etc., NONA; Marc Lafitte, 10 October 1823, NONA.

54. Korn, *The Early Jews of New Orleans*, pp. 162–65.

55. Cf. James E. Winston, "The Free Negro in New Orleans, 1803–1860," *Louisiana Historical Quarterly*, October 1938, pp. 1075–85.

56. Last Will and Testament of Judith Françoise Roubio, Hilary B. Cenas, 19 July 1834, NONA.

57. John A. Paxton, *New Orleans Directory and Reporter*, New Orleans, 1830, lists Vilson Robio, coach and harness maker, while S. E. Perry, *The New Orleans Directory*, New Orleans, 1832, lists Chantal Rubio, a music teacher.

58. Carlile Polock, 28 September 1825, 26 June 1826, NONA, ; Felix de Armas, 19 May 1827, NONA; William Boswell, 7 August 1827, 7 February 1830, 7 May 1830, NONA; etc.

59. Last Will and Testament of Judith Françoise Roubio, Hillary B. Cenas, 19 July 1834, NONA.

60. Carlile Pollock, 28 September 1825, NONA.

61. Achille Chiapella, 11 October 1852, NONA; Last Will and Testament of Florette *(sic)* Gottschalk, Jean Agaisse, 25 June 1855, NONA. The identity of this boarding school is not yet known.

62. *New Orleans Bee (L'Abeille)*, 21 October 1834.

63. Célestine Louise Gottschalk, quoted in Hensel, *Life and Letters*, p. 38; also Marrocco, "Gottschalkiana," p. 60–62.

64. Louis Moreau Gottschalk to Aimée Gottschalk, 15 February 1855, Family Letters, Gottschalk Collection, NYPL.

65. Korn, *The Early Jews of New Orleans*, p. 132; Pierce Butler, *Judah P. Benjamin*, Philadelphia, 1906, p. 34.

66. Clara Gottschalk Peterson to William L. Hawes, 30 June 1901, Historic New Orleans Collection.

67. Clara Gottschalk Peterson, "Biographical Sketch," p. 32; H. Remsen Whitehouse, *The Life of Lamartine*, 2 vols., London, 1918, 2:132.

68. Gottschalk, *Notes of a Pianist*, p. 12.

69. Eric Williams, *From Colony to Castro: The History of the Caribbean, 1492–1969*, New York, 1984, p. 239.

70. Ph. Wright and G. Debren, "Les Colons de Saint-Domingue passés à la Jamaïque (1792–1835)," *Bulletin de la Société d'Histoire de la Guadeloupe*, 1975, no. 4, p. 33; also Roulhac Toledano and Mary Louise Christovich, "Faubourg Tremé and the Bayou Road," *New Orleans Architecture* (Gretna, Louisiana), vol. 6, 1980, p. 5.

71. Médéric-Louis-Elie Moreau de Saint-Méry, *Description topographique, physique, civile, politique et historique de la partie française de l'Isle Saint-Dominque*, 2 vols., Philadelphia, 1797–98, 1:234.

72. Pierre de Vaissière, *Saint-Domingue, La société et la vie créoles sous l'ancien régime (1629–1789)*, Paris, 1909.

73. Moreau de Saint-Méry, *Description topographique*, 1:17–22; see also Helene d'Aquin Allain, *Souvenirs d'Amérique et de France, par une Créole*, Paris, 1883, p. 137.

74. Williams, *From Colony to Castro*, p. 240; Vaissière, *Saint-Domingue*, pp. 93ff.

75. François Alexandre Stanislaus de Wimpffen, *A Voyage to Saint-Domingo in the Years 1788, 1789, and 1790*, London, 1797, pp. 315–16.

76. Gottschalk, *Notes of a Pianist*, Clara Gottschalk Peterson, ed., p. 68.

77. Louis Moreau Gottschalk to his sisters, 7 February 1869, Family Letters, Gottschalk Collection, NYPL.

78. Gottschalk, *Notes of a Pianist*, p. 10.

79. C. L. R. James, *The Black Jacobins*, New York, 1963, p. 93.

80. Gottschalk, *Notes of a Pianist*, p. 12.

81. Wright and Debren, "Les Colons de Saint-Domingue," pp. 33, 56.

82. Gottschalk, *Notes of a Pianist*, p. 10.

83. Gabriel Debren and René le Gardeur Jr., "Les Colons de Saint-Dominque refugies à la Louisiane," *Bulletin de la Sociète de l'Histoire de la Guadeloupe*, 1975, no. 1, p. 99.

84. Gottschalk, *Notes of a Pianist*, pp. 12–13.

85. On the Deynaults see Allain, *Souvenir d'Amerique et de France*, p. 14.

86. Wright and Debren, "Les Colons de Saint-Domingue," pp. 89–91.

87. Frances Sargeant Childs, *French Refugee Life in the United States, 1790–1800*, Baltimore, 1940, pp. 171–72.

88. They were officers in the so-called Second d'Aquin Battalion, named for the husband of one of Aimée Bruslé's Deynault aunts and consisting of mulatto soldiers. See Marion John Bennett, *Louisiana Soldiers in the War of 1812*, Baton Rouge, 1963, pp. 9–12.

89. Thomas Fiehrer, "Saint Domingue–Haiti: Louisiana's Caribbean Connection," *Louisiana History*, 1989, no. 4, pp. 431–34.

90. L'Étoile Polaire #5 to S.C.F. S.C. Bruslé, 5823, 19 November 1823, Glover Collection.

91. *New Orleans in 1805: A Directory and Census* (New Orleans, 1805, reprint

1936) lists Camil Brusli *(sic)* at 65 St. Anne Street; he was established as a customs inspector by 1806 (Narcisse Broutin, 25 February 1806, NONA); also *Whitney's New Orleans Directory*, 1811 (New Orleans, 1810), lists Bruslé as "inspecteur" living on St. Louis Street.

92. John Lynd, 5 September 1806, NONA; Estevan de Quinones, 13 November 1812, 21 October 1813, 28 November 1814, NONA; Marc Lafitte, 28 April 1814, NONA.

93. Marc Lafitte, 21 September 1818, NONA; Philippe Pedesclaux, 6 August 1818, NONA.

94. Hugues J. de la Vergne, 6 January 1823, NONA.

95. John Smith Kendall, *History of New Orleans*, 3 vols., Chicago and New York, 1922, 1:123, 137.

96. Marrocco, "Gottschalkiana," pp. 61–62.

97. Carlile Pollock, 25 April 1831, NONA. The property was between Bienville and Conti, now the 400 block.

98. "Purchases and Sales of Real Estate by Mrs. Aimée Bruslé, wife of Edward Gottshalk, From the Year 1837 to her Death, and also the Purchases and Sales Made by Edward Gottschalk from 1827 to His death"(MS), Glover Collection.

99. See the records of Carlile Pollock, for the years 1831 and 1832, NONA.

100. *New Orleans Bee*, 20 March 1833, p. 2.

101. Reference to court order of 19 August 1834 in Carlile Pollock, 22 September 1834, NONA.

102. *New Orleans Bee*, 5 November 1834, p. 2.

103. Allain, *Souvenirs d'Amerique et de France*, p. 21.

104. Clara Gottschalk Peterson's French draft for her brother's *Notes of a Pianist* (MS), Gottschalk Collection, NYPL.

105. *New Orleans Bee*, 1 January 1835, p. 2.

106. Carlile Pollock, 15 April 1835, NONA.

107. Gottschalk, *Notes of a Pianist*, pp. 10–11.

108. *Ibid.*, pp. 11–12.

109. The city directories for 1837 list Joseph Victor Gottschalk at 25 Conti Street. By 1838 Edward appears at 18 Conti Street, where he and the family remained until 1842. There is no evidence that Edward owned the house at 18 Conti or that he bought or inherited the house at 25 Conti, as claimed by Vernon Loggins, *Where the Word Ends*, Baton Rouge, 1958, p. 33.

3. Young Gottschalk and Musical Democracy in New Orleans

1. Death Record of Charles Deynaud *(sic)* Bruslé, 20 October 1837, Recorder of Births, Marriages, and Deaths, Orleans Parish, Louisiana, vol. 7, folio 346; succession of Dr. Joseph Victor Gottschalk, 24 February 1838, Orleans Parish, Court of Probate, Succession and Probate Records, 1805–46, pt. 99, 1836–37, New Orleans Public Library.

2. Gottschalk, *Notes of a Pianist*, pp. 11–12.

3. On this oft-told story and on Bras Coupé, see Harriet Martineau, *Retrospect of Western Travel*, New York, 1838, pp. 136–43; Henry C. Castellanos, *New Orleans as It Was: Episodes of Louisiana Life*, New Orleans, 1895, pp. 53–62; Lyle Saxton, *Fabulous New Orleans*, New York and London, 1928, pp. 212–13; and George W. Cable's novelistic account in *The Grandissimes*, New York, 1957, pp. 219–52. See also George W. Cable, *Strange, True Stories of Louisiana*, New York, 1889, pp. 192–232.

4. Carlile Pollock, 22 September 1834, NONA.

5. The statement is translated and published in Saxton, *Fabulous New Orleans*, pp. 212–13.

6. See Henry Bradsher Fearon, *A Sketch of America*, London, 1819, reprinted in *The World From Jackson Square*, Etolia S. Brasso, ed., New York, 1948, pp. 92–93.

7. Clapp, *Autobiographical Sketches and Recollections*, pp. 231, 235, 241.

8. *Michels' New Orleans Annual and Commercial Register*, New Orleans, 1834; obituary for George Harby, *Bee*, 25 June 1862.

9. *New Orleans City Directory*, New Orleans, 1838.

10. Hensel, *Life and Letters*, p. 39.

11. Clara Gottschalk Peterson, "Biographical Sketch," p. 29.

12. *Michels' New Orleans Annual and Commercial Register*, New Orleans, 1834.

13. Clara Gottschalk Peterson claims Moreau played unassisted (p. 29), but her sister Celestine (Hensel, *Life and Letters*, p. 39) denies this.

14. F. J. Narcisse Letellier, *Dois-je parler? Dois-je me taire?*, New Orleans, n.d., and *La Créole*, New Orleans, 1838. Alfred Lemmon of New Orleans has established that Letellier was not a regular or paid organist at the cathedral, so this must have been an exceptional appearance there or an organist other than Letellier was involved (personal communication to the author).

15. On Elie (sometimes wrongly identified as Eli) see Aimée Gottschalk to Louis Moreau Gottschalk, 21 May 1842, Gottschalk Collection, NYPL. An N. Elie, "artist, Orleans Theatre," was living at 93 St. Ann Street in 1841 (*New Orleans Directory for 1841*, New Orleans, 1840). Clara Gottschalk Peterson incorrectly identifies yet another Frenchman, Felix Miolan, as Moreau's violin teacher (Gottschalk, *Notes of a Pianist*, Clara Gottschalk Peterson, ed., p. 29).

16. Lubov Keefer, *Baltimore's Music: The Haven of the American Composer*, Baltimore, 1962, pp. 132–33.

17. *Bee*, 18 November 1837.

18. Far the best treatment of this subject is Henry A. Kmen, *Music in New Orleans: The Formative Years, 1791–1841*, Baton Rouge, 1966.

19. Kmen, *Music in New Orleans*, p. 163.

20. *Ibid.*, p. 142.

21. *Picayune*, 5 April 1837, quoted by Kmen, *Music in New Orleans*, p. 151.

22. Kmen, *Music in New Orleans*, pp. 72ff.

23. Albert J. Pickett, *Eight Days in New Orleans in Feburary 1847*, Montgomery, Alabama, 1847, p. 27.

24. On Dédé and Lucien Lambert see Paul Glass, "A Hiatus in American Music History," *Afro-American Studies*, 1970, pp. 118–19; also Lester Sullivan, "Composers of Color of Nineteenth-Century New Orleans," *Black Music Research Journal*, 1988, no. 1, pp. 51–82.

25. Al Rose, *Born in New Orleans*, Tuscaloosa, Alabama, 1983, p. 23.

26. Desdunes, *Nos hommes et notre histoire*, p. 114; on Lambert's identification of himself as a protégé of Gottschalk see *St. Thomas Tidende*, 26 November 1859.

27. Hensel, *Life and Letters*, p. 182.

28. Kmen, *Music in New Orleans*, p. 15.

29. Oliver Daniel, "The Man Who Wrote (the recitatives to) Bizet's *Carmen*," *Stereo Review*, September 1975, pp. 80–81.

30. Among Gottschalk's operatic works are *Isaura di Salerno* (RO-125), *Carlos IX* (RO-52, D-3), *Amalia Warden* (RO-4, D-3), *Esceñas campestres (Cubanas)* (RO-77, D-

47). See also *Marcha triunfal y final de opera* (RO-157, -97, D-87). The designation "RO" refers to listings in Robert Offergeld, *The Centennial Catalogue of the Published and Unpublished Compositions of Louis Moreau Gottschalk*, New York, 1970; The designation "D" refers to listings in John G. Doyle, *Louis Moreau Gottschalk 1829–1869: A Bibliographical Study and Catalog of Works*, Detroit, 1983.

31. Kmen, *Music in New Orleans*, pp. 36–41.

32. Mina Curtiss, *Bizet and His World*, New York, 1958, p. 19.

33. Kmen, *Music in New Orleans*, pp. 133–39.

34. Gottschalk, *Notes of a Pianist*, Clara Gottschalk Peterson, ed., p. 26.

35. Hensel, *Life and Letters*, p. 195; L. M. Gottschalk, "Gottschalk Correspondence," *Home Journal*, 4 June 1864.

36. Charles R. Suttoni, "Piano and Opera: A Study of the Piano Fantasies Written on Creative Themes in the Romantic Era" (Ph.D. diss., New York University, 1973), p. 309.

37. Quoted by Gottschalk, *Notes of a Pianist*, p. 345.

38. Leann F. Logsdon, "Gottschalk and Meyerbeer" (MS), courtesy of the author, p. 11.

39. Kmen, *Music in New Orleans*, pp. 134–36.

40. *Ibid.*, p. 239.

41. Kaye de Metz, "Minstrel Dancing," *In Old New Orleans*, W. Kenneth Holditch, ed., Jackson, Mississippi, 1983, pp. 34–35.

42. John G. Doyle, "The Piano Music of Louis Moreau Gottschalk (1829–1869)" (Ph.D. diss., New York University, 1960), p. 132.

43. Jason Berry cites the influence of *Bamboula* on later composers without mentioning Gottschalk. Cf. "African Cultural Memory in New Orleans Music," *Black Music Research Journal*, 1988, no. 1, pp. 3–4, 19–20.

44. Loggins, *Where the Word Ends*, pp. 13–15.

45. Gilbert Chase, *America's Music from the Pilgrims to the Present*, New York, 1956, p. 310.

46. James Creecy, n.d., quoted by Dena J. Epstein, *Sinful Tunes and Spirituals: Black Folk Music to the Civil War*, Urbana and Chicago, 1977, p. 135.

47. On the history of Congo Square see Jerah Johnson's excellent "New Orleans' Congo Square: An Urban Setting for Early Afro-American Culture Formation," *Louisiana History*, 19:136–39.

48. Johnson, "New Orleans' Congo Square," pp. 145–48.

49. H. Didimus, *New Orleans as I Knew It*, New York, 1849.

50. H.D., *Biography of Louis Moreau Gottschalk, American Pianist and Composer*, Philadelphia, 1853, pp. 6–7.

51. See Eric Hobsbawm, "Mass-Producing Traditions: Europe, 1870–1914," *The Invention of Tradition*, Eric Hobsbawm and Terence Rangwer, eds., Cambridge, England, 1983, p. 263.

52. Arlin Turner, *George W. Cable, a Biography*, Durham, North Carolina, 1956, pp. 228ff.

53. George W. Cable, "The Dance in Place Congo," *Century Magazine*, February 1886, p. 529.

54. Clara Gottschalk Peterson to William L. Hawes, 11 June 1899, 19 April 1908, Manuscript Division, Historic New Orleans Collection .

55. Lafcadio Hearn, *The Life and Letters of Lafcadio Hearn*, Elizabeth Bisland, ed., Boston, 1906, 1:325, 356.

56. "Those Congo Melodies," *New York Sun*, 9 September 1909.

57. Clara Gottschalk Peterson to William L. Hawes, 11 June 1899, Manuscript Division, Historic New Orleans Collection.

58. George W. Cable, "Creole Slave Songs," *Century Magazine*, April 1886, p. 809.

59. Gottschalk, *Notes of a Pianist*, pp. 202–3; P. J. Reale, "The Belle of the de Joinville Ball," *Yankee*, November 1965, pp. 182–23.

60. Escudier, *Les Virtuoses*, pp. 177–78; Powell A. Casey, *Louisiana in the War of 1812*, Baton Rouge, 1963, pp. i, xv.

61. Gottschalk to his sisters, 27 September 1868, Family Letters, Gottschalk Collection, NYPL.

62. Kmen, *Music in New Orleans*, p. 195.

63. *New Orleans Bee*, 20 May 1840, p. 2.

64. *Ibid.*, 23 May 1840.

65. Hensel, *Life and Letters*, pp. 40–41. *New Orleans Directory for 1841*, New Orleans, 1840; see also obituary for Gabriel Boyer, *New Orleans Bee*, 16 September 1867.

66. Paul Arpin, *Biographie de L. M. Gottschalk, pianiste américain*, New York, 1853, p. 6, claims Moreau met the Irish virtuoso and composer William Wallace at this time. Clyde Brockett refutes this in "Autobiographer versus Biographer: How Factual is Gottschalk?," *Sonneck Society Bulletin*, Summer 1993, pp. 4–7.

67. Hensel, *Life and Letters*, p. 41.

68. *Courrier de la Louisiane*, 17 April 1841; *New Orleans Bee*, 21 April 1841; Gottschalk, *Notes of a Pianist*, Clara Gottschalk Peterson, ed., pp. 30–31.

69. *Courrier de la Louisiane*, 22 April 1841.

70. *Daily Picayune*, 25 April 1841; Gottschalk, *Notes of a Pianist*, Clara Gottschalk Peterson, ed., p. 31.

71. For a review of evidence on the May 1 date see Brockett, "Autobiographer versus Biographer," pp. 4–7.

4. A Creole in Paris

1. Hensel, *Life and Letters*, p. 42.

2. Jacques Hillairet, *Dictionnaire historique de rues de Paris*, 2 vols., Paris, 1967, 1:359–60.

3. See S. Kracauer, *Orpheus in Paris*, New York, 1938, p. 5; T. E. B. Howarth, *Citizen King: The Life of Louis Philippe, King of France*, London, 1969.

4. Edward Gottschalk to Moreau Gottschalk, 13 January 1842, Family Letters, Gottschalk Collection, NYPL.

5. Edward and Aimée Gottschalk to Moreau Gottschalk, 25 September 1841, Glover Collection. Edward and Aimée Gottschalk to Moreau Gottschalk, 13 January 1842, 21 May 1842, Family Letters, Gottschalk Collection, NYPL. Aimée Gottschalk to Moreau Gottschalk, 4 Feburary 1843, 9 Feburary 1843; Moreau Gottschalk to "Mes chers parents," 8 June 1842, Manuscript Division, Historic New Orleans Collection.

6. Moreau Gottschalk to his parents, 8 June 1842, Historic New Orleans Collection.

7. Ordres des Quatre Empereurs d'Allemagne et du Lion de Holstein-Limbourg, 1842, Glover Collection.

8. Gottschalk, *Notes of a Pianist*, p. 373.

9. Hensel, *Life and Letters*, p. 43; Clara Gottschalk Peterson, "Biographical Sketch," p. 8.

10. Moreau Gottschalk to his parents, 8 June 1842, Historic New Orleans Collection.

11. *Ibid.*

12. Edward Gottschalk to Moreau Gottschalk, 13 January 1842, Family Letters, Gottschalk Collection, NYPL.

13. Aimée Gottschalk to Moreau Gottschalk, 25 September 1841, Glover Collection.

14. Aimée Gottschalk to Moreau Gottschalk, 9 Feburary 1843, Family Letters, Gottschalk Collection, NYPL.

15. Aimée Gottschalk to Moreau Gottschalk, 25 September 1841, Glover Collection.

16. Aimée Gottschalk to Moreau Gottschalk, 4 February 1843, Family Letters, Gottschalk Collection, NYPL.

17. Edward Gottschalk to Moreau Gottschalk, 13 January 1842, Family Letters, Gottschalk Collection, NYPL.

18. This portrait, now owned by Carmen D. Valentino of Philadelphia, had arrived in New Orleans by February, 1843, as confirmed by Aimée Gottschalk's letter to her son, 9 February 1843. It remained in the possession of Edward Gottschalk Sr. to his death in 1853, after which it passed first to an Italian family named Ciolina with whom he boarded, and then to the actor Richard Mansfield, who purchased it at a New Orleans antique store. After Mansfield's estate was disbursed in 1905 it passed through various hands until reaching Mr. Valentino. See William L. Hawes to Mrs. Clara G. Peterson, 13 December 1906, and William L. Hawes to Mrs. Richard H. Mansfield, 3 April 1908, Manuscript Division, Historic New Orleans Collection.

19. Kracauer, *Orpheus in Paris*, p. 14.

20. Lester Sullivan, "Composers of Color of 19th Century New Orleans," p. 62.

21. Gottschalk, *Notes of a Pianist*, pp. 52, 221.

22. Moreau Gottschalk to his parents, 8 June 1842, Historic New Orleans Collection.

23. Aimée Gottschalk to Moreau Gottschalk, 13 January 1842, Family Letters, Gottschalk Collection, NYPL; Sir Charles Hallé, *Life and Letters of Sir Charles Hallé*, London, 1868, p. 91.

24. *Gazette musicale*, 10 November 1845, quoted in Arthur Loesser, *Men, Women, and Pianos: A Social History*, New York, 1954, p. 386.

25. Loesser, *Men, Women, and Pianos*, p. 367.

26. Jacques Barzun, *Berlioz and the Romantic Century*, Boston, 1950, p. 142.

27. L. M. Gottschalk, "La Música, el piano, los pianistas, Espadero y 'La Plainte du Poète,'" *Liceo de la Habana*, 27 April 1860, 28 April 1860, 3 May 1860; all future references are to reprinted complete version in Fors, *Gottschalk*, pp. 323–52.

28. Alan Walker, *Franz Liszt*, 2 vols., New York, 1983, 1:187.

29. Carl Dahlhaus, *Nineteenth-Century Music*, Berkeley and Los Angeles, 1989, pp. 134ff.

30. Quoted by Loesser, *Men, Women, and Pianos*, p. 376.

31. Ernst Burger, *Franz Liszt*, Princeton, 1989, p. 152.

32. When Gottschalk's student Teresa Carreño visited Liszt, he told her that he knew of Gottschalk only by hearsay (Marta Milinowski, *Teresa Carreño*, New Haven, 1940, p. 69); but when Moreau's brother Gaston visited Liszt, he was told that Liszt knew Moreau "intimately" (Offergeld, *Centennial Catalogue*, p. 24, RO-162).

33. Gottschalk, "La Música, el piano, los pianistas," Fors, *Gottschalk*, p. 342.

34. Quoted in Fors, *Gottschalk*, p. 344.

35. Hallé, *Autobiography*, p. 59.

36. Walker, *Franz Liszt*, 1:232.

37. Suttoni, *Piano and Opera*, pp. 151–208.

38. Gottschalk, "La Música, el piano, los pianistas," Fors, *Gottschalk*, pp. 340–45.

39. Walker, *Franz Liszt*, 1:235ff.; Burger, *Franz Liszt*, p. 88; Franz Liszt, *An Artist's Journey*, reprinted Chicago, 1989, pp. 22–27.

40. Gottschalk, "La Música, el piano, los pianistas," Fors, *Gottschalk*, p. 350.

41. A. Marmontel, *Pianistes célèbres*, Paris, 1878, pp. 98–107; Reginald R. Gerig, *Famous Pianists and Their Techniques*, Washington and New York, 1974, pp. 131–36; Schonberg, *The Great Pianists*, New York, 1963, pp. 110–14; Loesser, *Men, Women, and Pianos*, pp. 296–98.

42. Hallé, *Autobiography*, p. 52.

43. Schonberg, *The Great Pianists*, p. 112.

44. Moreau Gottschalk to his sisters, n.d. 1869, Family Letters, Gottschalk Collection, NYPL.

45. Gottschalk, "La Música, el piano, los pianistas," Fors, *Gottschalk*, pp. 338–39.

46. Clara Gottschalk Peterson, "Biographical Sketch," p. 32.

47. Marmontel, *Pianistes célèbres*, pp. 214–23; Amédée Mereaux, *Variétés littéraires et musicales*, Paris, 1878, pp. 138–41.

48. Camille Saint-Saëns, *Musical Memories*, Edwin Gile Rich, trans., Boston, 1919, pp. 8–13.

49. *Ibid.*, pp. 11–12.

50. Gottschalk to Aimée Gottschalk, undated fragment no. 29 (1850?), Gottschalk Collection, NYPL.

51. Gottschalk, *Notes of a Pianist*, p. 355.

52. *La España* (Madrid), 5 October 1851.

53. Clara Gottschalk Peterson, "Biographical Sketch," p. 32.

54. Gottschalk, *Notes of a Pianist*, p. 325.

55. Prosper Mérimée, *La Chronique du regne de Charles IX*, Paris, 1829.

56. Gottschalk, *Notes of a Pianist*, p. 86.

57. *Ibid.*, p. 54.

58. *Ibid.*, p. 35.

59. Escudier, *Les Virtuoses*, p. 178.

60. Lange, "Vida y muerte," no. 5–6, p. 41.

61. Gottschalk, *Notes of a Pianist*, pp. 140, 221, 292.

62. Hector Berlioz, *Memoirs of Hector Berlioz from 1803 to 1865*, Ernest Newman, ed., New York, 1947, p. 349 fn.

63. *Ibid.*, pp. 352ff.; Barzun, *Berlioz and the Romantic Century*, pp. 224–25.

64. Allen Lott, "A Berlioz Premiere in America: Leopold de Meyer and the *Marche d'Isly*," *Nineteenth-century Music*, Spring 1985, p. 227.

65. Neil Harris, *Humbug: The Art of P. T. Barnum*, Chicago, 1973, p. 100.

66. Lois Marie Fink, *American Art at the Nineteenth-century Paris Salons*, Washington, D.C., 1990, pp. 52–53.

67. Behrend Gift, Music Division, Free Library of Philadelphia.

68. Carlile Pollock, 8 October 1844, NONA.

69. Carlile Pollock, 30 November 1844, NONA.

70. Clara Gottschalk Peterson, "Biographical Sketch," p. 68.

71. H.D., *Biography*, p. 6.

72. *Revue et gazette musicale*, 30 March 1845, p. 104.

73. "A Louisianian," *Courrier de la Louisiane*, 17 May 1845, reprinted in *Musical Courier*, 11 September 1901, p. 17.

74. H.D., *Biography*, p. 6.

75. *Ibid.*

76. Escudier, *Les Virtuoses*, p. 179.

77. Clara Gottschalk Peterson, "Biographical Sketch," p. 33.

78. Gottschalk, *Notes of a Pianist*, pp. 220–21; also "La Música, el piano, los pianistas," Fors, *Gottschalk*, p. 339.

79. *Revue et gazette musicale*, 8 April 1845, p. 108.

80. Quoted in "A Louisianian," *Courrier de la Louisiane*, 17 May 1845.

5. *Bamboula* and the Louisiana Quartet

1. Henri Herz, *My Travels in America*, Henry Bertram Hill, trans., Madison, Wisconsin, 1963, p. v.

2. Berlioz, *Memoirs*, pp. 420–21.

3. Clara Gottschalk Peterson, "Biographical Sketch," pp. 33–34; William L. Hawes, "Reminiscences of Louis Moreau Gottschalk," *Musical Courier*, 21 March 1900, p. 15.

4. Clara Gottschalk Peterson to William L. Hawes, 15 July 1909, Gottschalk Collection, Historic New Orleans Collection.

5. Gottschalk's participation in these performances is asserted by Hensel (*Life and Letters*, p. 45) and Behrend (*Gottschalk, Notes of a Pianist*, p. xxv, n. 9); cf. also L. M. Gottschalk, untitled note, *Gaceta de la Habana*, 7 January 1860.

6. See Guides-Cicerone, *Paris Illustré*, Paris, 1856, pp. 13ff.

7. Alfred Cortot, *In Search of Chopin*, London and New York, 1951, pp. 12–13.

8. Reproduced by Behrend in *Gottschalk, Notes of a Pianist*, p. 56.

9. Glover Collection.

10. Property of Lily Glover, New Jersey, great-granddaughter of Aimée.

11. Moreau Gottschalk to his brothers and sisters, 2 November 1860, Family Letters, Gottschalk Collection, NYPL.

12. Edward Gottschalk to Moreau Gottschalk, 8 January 1848; Edward Gottschalk to Arnold Myers, 14 April 1850; both, Glover Collection.

13. As with virtually every other Gottschalk composition, the work is variously dated. See RO-243, D-143, and *Gottschalk's Illustrated Concert Book*, New York, 1862, in which Gottschalk himself assigned this piece to 1843; yet another variant collection of dates are those in Gottschalk's hand in a ("Liste des compositions . . .)," unfiled MS, Gottschalk Collection, NYPL.

14. See also RO-163–165, D-93.

15. RO-107.

16. Clara Gottschalk Peterson, "Biographical Sketch," pp. 38–39.

17. Albert Guérard, *Napoleon III*, Cambridge, Massachusetts, 1943, p. 77.

18. Arsène Houssaye, *Man About Paris: The Confessions of Arsène Houssaye*, Henry Knepler, trans., New York, 1970, p. 122.

19. *Revue et gazette musicale*, 2 April 1848, p. 102; 9 April 1848, p. 113.

20. Clara Gottschalk Peterson, "Biographical Sketch," pp. 34–35; also Arpin, *Biographie*, p. 41.

21. Gottschalk, "La Música, el piano, los pianistas," Fors, *Gottschalk*, pp. 330–31. Gottschalk himself erroneously dated these appearances as 1849, but his identification of Lamartine as head of the Provisional Government at the time refutes this.

22. Hensel, *Life and Letters*, p. 87.

23. Firmin Didot Fréres, *Nouvelle biographie générale*, Paris, 1862, pp. 779–83.

24. Gottschalk, "La Música, el piano, los pianistas," Fors, *Gottschalk*, pp. 329–

30; Gottschalk, *Notes of a Pianist*, pp. 222–23; also Kracauer, *Orpheus in Paris*, p. 4.

25. Claude Teillet, "Le Centre Hospitalier Specialisé de Clermont de l'Oise," *Comtes rendus et memories de la Société archéologique et historique de Clermont-en-Beauvaisis*, 1978–82, pp. 90–96.

26. Dr. Eugéne S. Woillez, *Archéologie des monuments religieux de l'ancien Beauvaisis pendant la métamorphose romaine*, 2 vols., Paris, 1839–49.

27. Hensel, *Life and Letters*, p. 87.

28. Sylvie Martin, "Les sociétés musicales Clermontoises," *Comtes rendus et memories de la Société archéologique et historique de Clermont-en-Beauvaisis*, 1988–90, p. 60.

29. Gottschalk, *Notes of a Pianist*, pp. 110–11.

30. *Ibid.*, pp. 207, 264, 317.

31. Théophile Gautier, *La Presse* (Paris), 31 March 1851.

32. Gottschalk, "La Música, el piano, los pianistas," Fors, *Gottschalk*, pp. 342–46.

33. R. G. Kiesewetter, "La Musique des Arabes," *Revue et gazette musicale*, 11 May 1845, pp. 145ff.

34. Offergeld (RO-132) notes the possibility that this work, now lost, may have been one of the Ossianic ballades. It could also be the piece known as *La Lai du dernier ménestrel;* cf. Clara Gottschalk Peterson, "Biographical Sketch," p. 33.

35. Gottschalk, *Notes of a Pianist*, p. 105.

36. RO-32, D-52. Gottschalk dedicated *La Chute des feuilles* to Thomas.

37. Lois Marie Fink, *American Art at the Nineteenth-century Paris Salons*, Washington, D.C., 1990, p. 34.

38. *Revue et gazette musicale*, 17 December 1848, p. 398.

39. Opus 10, pub. by M. Schlesinger, Paris, 1845 (Bibliothèque Nationale Fonds du Conservatoire, Folio 0.406); see Cecilio Tieles, "Julián Fontana: El introductor de Chopin en Cuba," *Revista de Musicologia* (Madrid), January-June 1988, pp. 1–28; also Natalio Galan, *Cuba y sus sones*, Valencia, 1982, pp. 245–56. The Belgian violinist Henri Vieuxtemps had arranged a Creole tune for violin and piano during an 1844 visit to New Orleans, but his *Danse Negro Créole* remained unpublished during his lifetime; see John H. Baron, "Vieuxtemps (and Ole Bull) in New Orleans," *American Music*, Summer 1990, pp. 216–24.

40. Clara Gottschalk Peterson, "Biographical Sketch," p. 36. Clara dates this event to "after his mother's arrival," i.e. the mid-1840s; Arpin *(Biographie)* dates *Bamboula* to 1847, as does "H.D." (E. H. Durell), *Biography*. Escudier (*Les Virtuoses*, p. 180) assigns it to 1845. Gottschalk himself *(Gottschalk's Concert Book)* claims 1844! However, *La France musicale* announced publication on 25 March 1849, and there is no evidence that Gottschalk played this piece in public before 1848. Since we know typhoid raged in Clermont-sur-l'Oise during Moreau's residence there, and that he prolonged his stay there unexpectedly, this is the most likely date of composition for *Bamboula* (Teillet, "Le Centre Hospitalier," p. 94).

41. See the excellent discussion in Doyle, "The Piano Music of Louis Moreau Gottschalk," pp. 122–27.

42. Allain, *Souvenirs d'Amerique et de France*, p. 142.

43. Walker, *Franz Liszt*, 1:298ff.

44. See Doyle, "The Piano Music of Louis Moreau Gottschalk", pp. 129–32; Chase, *America's Music*, pp. 314–15.

45. *La France musicale*, 22 April 1849.

46. Carl Dahlhaus, *Nineteenth-century Music*, Berkeley and Los Angeles, 1989, pp. 14, 149–50.

47. *La France musicale*, 20 January 1850.

48. *Ibid.*, 6 April 1851.

49. Millevoye, *Oeuvres complètes*, 1:91–93.

50. Doyle, "The Piano Music of Louis Moreau Gottschalk," pp. 132–35.

51. Clara Gottschalk Peterson to William H. Hawes, 11 June 1899, Gottschalk Collection, Historic New Orleans Collection.

52. *La France musicale*, 11 March 1849.

53. William Mason, *Memories of a Musical Life*, New York, 1902, p. 206.

54. Niecks, *Chopin, Man and Musician*, 2:102; Hallé, *Autobiography*, p. 54.

55. Doyle, *Louis Moreau Gottschalk*, D-28, p. 195.

56. Lauro Ayestarán, *La Música en el Uruguay*, 2 vols., Montevideo, 1953, 1:425–33.

57. Serge Dianin, *Borodin*, London and New York, 1963, p. 310.

58. Schonberg, *The Great Pianists*, p. 206.

6. Celebrity

1. *La France musicale*, 21 January 1849.

2. Gottschalk, *Notes of a Pianist*, pp. 288–89.

3. Fors, *Gottschalk*, p. 77 fn.; this work, entitled in Spanish *La Caceria*, is almost certainly an expanded version of Gottschalk's adaptation of *La Chasse du jeune Henri*.

4. Walker, *Franz Liszt*, 1:192–94.

5. Gottschalk, *Notes of a Pianist*, p. 48.

6. Serafin Ramirez, *La Habana artística: Apuntes historicos*, Havana, 1891, pp. 35–55; Eduardo Sanchez de Fuentes, *El Folk-lore en la música cubana*, Havana, 1923, pp. 136–39.

7. Gerardin, *Celebrated Salons*, p. 172.

8. Gottschalk, "La Música, el piano, los pianistas," Fors, *Gottschalk*, p. 329.

9. Gerardin, *Celebrated Salons*, p. 185.

10. Gottschalk, "La Música, el piano, los pianistas," Fors, *Gottschalk*, p. 329.

11. Gottschalk, *Notes of a Pianist*, p. 204.

12. *La France musicale*, 11 March 1849, translation in Clara Gottschalk Peterson, "Biographical Sketch," pp. 37–38.

13. *La France musicale*, 22 April 1849. See also *Revue et gazette musicale*, 20 April 1849, p. 134.

14. Aimée Gottschalk to Moreau Gottschalk, 30 October 1849, Miscellaneous Family Letters, Gottschalk Collection, NYPL.

15. *La France musicale*, 1 April 1849.

16. *Ibid.*, 27 May 1849; Gottschalk, *Notes of a Pianist*, p. 52.

17. Arpin, *Biographie*, p. 37.

18. Clyde W. Brockett, "An Influential American in Paris," *Sonneck Society Bulletin*, 1989, no. 1, pp. 3–4.

19. *La France musicale* reported on 17 June 1849 that *La Savane* was in print by that date.

20. *Ibid.*, 20 May 1849, 24 June 1849.

21. *Ibid.*, 3 June 1849, 2 September 1849.

22. *Ibid.*, 4 November 1849, 11 November 1849.

23. Aimée Gottschalk to Moreau Gottschalk, 30 October 1849, Family Letters, Gottschalk Collection, NYPL.

24. *La France musicale*, 13 January 1850.

25. Even though the two-piano version appeared first, it is likely that this began as a piano solo. See Doyle, *Louis Moreau Gottschalk*, D-32, D-32a, D-32b, p. 274.

26. See the discussion by Doyle, *Louis Moreau Gottschalk*, pp. 141, 322.

27. Théophile Gautier, *Voyage en Espagne*, Paris, 1845.

28. Robert Stevenson, "Liszt at Madrid and Lisbon: 1844–45," *Musical Quarterly*, October 1979, pp. 493–512.

29. Kracauer, *Orpheus in Paris*, p. 58.

30. Hensel, *Life and Letters*, p. 44.

31. *La France musicale*, 23 December 1849.

32. *Ibid.*, 13 January 1850.

33. *Ibid.*, 24 February 1850, 31 February 1850.

34. *Ibid.*, 17 March 1850.

35. *Ibid.*, 24 March 1850.

36. T. C. Evans, *Of Many Men*, New York, 1888, p. 174.

37. D-14; RO-169.

38. *La France musicale*, 10 February 1850, 10 March 1850, 5 May 1850.

39. *Ibid.*, 5 May 1850.

40. *Ibid.*, 26 May 1850.

41. *Ibid.*, 31 March 1850, 7 April 1850.

42. *Ibid.*, 9 June 1850.

43. H.D., *Biography*, pp. 12–13.

44. *Confederation suisse*, 28 July 1850.

45. *La France musicale*, 18 August 1850.

46. Clara Gottschalk Peterson, "Biographical Sketch," pp. 44–45; H.D., *Biography*, p. 13.

47. *De la Paroisse de Grandson*, 1857, no. 204, p. 162, Archives Cantonales Vaudoises, Chavannes près Renens; *Le Petit paysan* (Vaud), January 1986, pp. 1–5.

48. *La France musicale*, 18 August 1850; or H.D., *Biography*, pp. 13–14.

49. Rufus Learsi, *Jews in America: A History*, New York, 1972, p. 83.

50. *Journal de Genève*, 22 July 1850.

51. *Gazette de Genève*, 25 July 1850; *Journal de Genève*, 30 July 1850; *La France musicale*, 4 August 1850.

52. Gottschalk, *Notes of a Pianist*, p. 158.

53. *La France musicale*, 18 August 1850.

54. *Ibid.*, 18 August 1850. Cf. Doyle, *Louis Moreau Gottschalk*, D-76, p. 293.

55. *La France musicale*, 1 September 1850.

56. *Journal de Genève*, 23 August 1850; unfortunately, Gottschalk's violin duet is lost. See Doyle, *Louis Moreau Gottschalk*, D-160, p. 331; also RO-297.

57. *Revue de Genève*, 9 August 1850.

58. *Journal de Genève*, 9 August 1850.

59. *Revue de Genève*, 17 August 1850.

60. *Journal de Genève*, 12 August 1850, 22 August 1850.

61. *Revue de Genève*, 23 August 1850.

62. *Journal de Genève*, 17 September 1850.

63. *Ibid.*, 9 September 1850.

64. *Ibid.*, 17 September 1850.

65. *El Orden* (Madrid), 15 June 1852.

66. Gottschalk to his sisters, 1 January 1869, Family Letters, Gottschalk Collection, NYPL; also Fors, *Gottschalk*, pp. 316–20.

67. *Saratoga Daily News*, 14 July 1862; *Journal de Genève*, 24 September 1850.

68. *Revue de Genève*, 30 October 1850.

69. *La France musicale*, 6 October 1850. The violinist Vieuxtemps was to pen his own flashy *Yankee Doodle* variations a year later; *Revue et gazette musicale*, 2 February 1851, p. 109.

70. Arpin, *Biographie*, p.43.

71. Paul Nettl, *National Anthems*, New York, 1952, pp. 79–104; Percy A. Scholes, *"God Save the King!"*, Oxford, 1942, p. 61.

72. *La France musicale*, 18 August 1850.

73. Edmond Barde, *Anciennes Maisons de campagne genevoises*, Geneva, 1937, pp. 87ff.; "Alville," *La Vie en Suisse de S.A.I. la Grande Duchesse Anna Feodorovna*, Lausanne, 1942, pp. 169–78.

74. Apville, *La Vie en Suisse*, pp. 169–78.

75. Gottschalk, *Notes of a Pianist*, p. 51.

76. *La France musicale*, 1 September 1850.

77. Gottschalk, "La Música, el piano, los pianistas," Fors, *Gottschalk*, pp. 337–38.

78. Doyle, *Louis Moreau Gottschalk*, MS-34.8; also RO-124, 183, 199, 293.

79. *La France musicale*, 13 May 1850.

80. *Saroni's Musical Times*, 24 August 1850.

81. *Le Nouvelliste vaudois*, 28 October 1850.

82. *La France musicale*, 10 November 1850; *Le Nouvelliste vaudois*, 9 November 1850.

83. *Le Nouvelliste vaudois*, 31 October 1850.

84. C. H. Schriwaneck, *Gazette de Lausanne*, 28 November 1850.

85. *La France musicale*, 12 January 1851.

86. *Le Nouvelliste vaudois*, 12 November 1850; *La France musicale*, 12 January 1851.

87. *Courrier suisse*, 30 October 1850.

88. Hensel, *Life and Letters*, p. 195. Gertrude Tucker to Lily Glover, 13 October 1938, Glover Collection.

89. *Journal de Genève*, 15 November 1850, 23 November 1850.

90. *Courrier Suisse*, 20 November 1850.

91. *Gazette de Lausanne*, 28 November 1850.

92. *Siècle*, 1 November 1850.

93. *Revue et gazette musicale*, 2 February 1851, p. 36. Also *La France musicale*, 16 February 1851.

94. D-153; RO-162; I am indebted for this information to John G. Doyle (cf. D-153) and to Clyde W. Brockett, "Gottschalk in Madrid: A Tale of Ten Pianos," *Musical Quarterly*, 1991, no. 3, p. 38.

95. 26 February, 12 and 20 March, and 10 April. In modified form this hall exists today as Theatre Gymnase Marie Bell, on Boulevard Bonne Nouvelle.

96. *La France musicale*, 16, 18 March 1851.

97. A series of misdatings by Clara Gottschalk ("Biographical Sketch," pp. 40–41; also Hensel, *Life and Letters*, p. 50, and by Pleyel workers themselves (Letter to Moreau Gottschalk, 22 April 1850 *(sic)*, Album no. 7, Gottschalk Collection, NYPL) wrongly assigned this incident to 1850.

98. *La France musicale*, 27 April 1851; also Pleyel workers to Gottschalk, 22 April 1851, Album no. 7, Gottschalk Collection, NYPL.

99. *L'Assemblé nationale*, 29 April 1851.

100. *La France musicale*, 23 March 1851.

101. *Revue et gazette musicale*, 3 May 1851.

102. *Corsaire*, 16 March 1851.

103. *Constitutionnel*, 30 March 1851.

104. *Le Charivari*, 22 March 1851.

105. *Siècle*, 7 April 1851.

106. *La Presse*, 31 March 1851.

107. *Journal des débats*, 13 April 1851.

108. Quoted by Fors, *Gottschalk*, p. 272.

109. Clara Gottschalk Peterson, "Biographical Sketch," p. 43.

110. Jules Lory, *Journal du plaisir*, 19 April 1851.

111. *La France musicale*, 6 April 1851; Gottschalk, *Notes of a Pianist*, p. 300.

112. Clara Gottschalk Peterson, "Biographical Sketch," p. 43.

113. Julie du Marguerittes, *The Ins and Outs of Paris*, Philadelphia, 1855, p. 334.

114. Maunsell B. Field, *Memories of Many Men and of Some Women*, New York, 1874, p. 65.

115. George F. Root, *The Story of a Musical Life*, Cincinnati, 1891, pp. 49, 65.

116. *Courrier des États-Unis*, 6 March 1862.

117. Houssaye, *Man About Paris*, p. 76.

118. *Ibid.*, p. 80.

119. Patrick Favardin and Laurent Bouëxière, *Le Dandysme*, Paris, 1988, pp. 37ff.

120. Kracauer, *Orpheus in Paris*, p. 23.

121. Gottschalk to his sisters, 7 February 1869, Family Letters, Gottschalk Collection, NYPL.

122. Gottschalk to his sisters, undated letter no. 31 (ca. 11 December 1864), Family Letters, Gottschalk Collection, NYPL; also *Notes of a Pianist*, p. 53.

123. Clara Gottschalk Peterson, "Biographical Sketch," p. 40; C. Barbey-Boissier, *La Comtesse Agénor de Gasparin et sa famille*, 2 vols., Paris, 1902, 1:402 n.

124. Hensel, *Life and Letters*, p. 193.

125. July 1850, 24 August, etc.

126. Doyle, *Louis Moreau Gottschalk*, C-20; D-5; RO-197.

127. Nicholas Till, *Rossini, His Life and Times*, New York, 1983, p. 108.

128. Adolphe Adam, *Souvenirs d'un musicien*, Paris, 1857.

129. Berlioz, *Memoirs*, p. 477.

130. Hector Berlioz, *New Letters of Berlioz, 1830–1868*, Jacques Barzun, ed., New York, 1954, p. 85.

131. H.D., *Biography*, pp. 9–10; Gottschalk to Benacci, 3 August 1850, Gratz Collection, Historical Society of Pennsylvania; also in Carl Honerlin Collection, New York; Doyle, *Louis Moreau Gottschalk*, C-17, D-14.

132. H.D., *Biography*, p. 10.

133. Gottschalk to Benacci, n.d. (October 1850), Collection of Dr. B. Franklin Diamond, Rydal, Pennsylvania.

134. Gottschalk to "M. Hartman," 12 August 1852, Historical Society of Pennsylvania.

135. Berlioz, *Memoirs*, p. 352.

136. Loesser, *Men, Women, and Pianos*, p. 377.

137. See Saint-Saëns, *Musical Memories*, p. 29.

138. Gottschalk Collection, Folder no. 18, NYPL.

139. Margery Morgan Lowens, "The New York Years of Edward MacDowell," (Ph.D. diss., University of Michigan, 1971) p. 110.

7. The Siege of Spain

1. *Le Mémorial bordelais*, 16 May 1851. Originals of all newspaper citations in this chapter, unless otherwise noted, are preserved in Scrapbook no. 7, Gottschalk Collection, NYPL.

2. *L'Ami des arts* (Bordeaux), 25 May 1851.

3. *Courrier de la Gironde* (Bordeaux), 16 May 1851.

4. *L'Indicateur* (Bordeaux), 14 May 1851.

5. *Le Mémorial bordelais*, 16 May 1851.

6. *L'Ami des arts* (Bordeaux), 25 May 1851.

7. *Courrier de la Gironde*, 31 May 1851.

8. *Ibid.*, 19 June 1851.

9. *Ibid.*, 20 June 1851.

10. *L'Ami des arts*, 15 June 1851.

11. Unidentified review, ca. 9 June 1851, Scrapbook no. 7, Gottschalk Collection, NYPL.

12. *L'Agent dramatique* (Bordeaux), 8 June 1851.

13. *Mémorial bordelaise*, 19 June 1851; *La Guienne* (Bordeaux), 19 June 1851; *L'Incidental* (Bordeaux), 19 June 1851.

14. Edward Gottschalk to Arnold Myers, 14 April 1850, Glover Collection.

15. Edward Gottschalk to Arnold, Leonard, and Annie Myers, 7 August 1851, Glover Collection.

16. *Courrier de la Gironde*, 12 July 1851.

17. *L'Ami des arts*, 17 July 1851, 30 July 1851.

18. *La France musicale*, 27 July 1851; D-77; Arpin, *Biographie*, p. 46; Archbishop Donnet, "Sir Louis Moreau Gottschalk de Lislet," n.d., Gottschalk Collection, NYPL.

19. "Feuilleton," unidentified clipping, Scrapbook no. 7, Gottschalk Collection, NYPL.

20. *Mémoriale des Pyrenees* (Pau), 31 July 1851.

21. *L'Éclaireur des Pyrénées* (Bayonne), 7 September 1851.

22. For Liszt in Spain and Portugal see Robert Stevenson's excellent articles "Liszt at Madrid and Lisbon: 1844–45," *Musical Quarterly*, October 1979, pp. 493–512; "Liszt in the Iberian Peninsula, 1844–1845," *Inter-American Music Review*, 1986, no. 2, pp. 3–22.

23. Gottschalk, *Notes of a Pianist*, p. 38.

24. *Cronica de Guipuzcoa* (Saint Sebastian), 23 September 1851. Clyde W. Brockett, "Gottschalk in Biscay, Castile and Andalusia" (MS), courtesy of the author. For all aspects of Gottschalk in Spain the reader should refer to this study and to Brockett's companion piece, "Gottschalk in Madrid," pp. 279–315.

25. Brockett, "Gottschalk in Biscay," pp. 2–3.

26. *Ibid.*, p. 3.

27. Gottschalk, *Notes of a Pianist*, p. 17.

28. Charles Gautier, *Wanderings in Spain*, London, 1853, pp. 46–49.

29. *La Nacion* (Madrid), 26 October 1851.

30. *La France musicale*, 9 November 1851.

31. Gottschalk to Baron de Bock, 23 October 1851, Gottschalk Collection, NYPL.

32. *El Constitucional*, 31 October 1851; *La España*, 30 October 1851.

33. Basil Rauch, *American Interest in Cuba: 1848–1855*, New York, 1948, p. 126.

34. U.S. Minister Daniel M. Barringer to Secretary of State Daniel Webster, 1851

September 18, Despatch no. 58, Despatches of American Ministers and Counsular Officers in Spain, 1851–52, Diplomatic Records, U.S. National Archives.

35. *El Clamor Publica*, 18 September 1851, translated by Barringer, Despatch no. 58, p. 1.

36. Barringer to Webster, no. 62 (14 October 1851) and no. 67 (17 November 1851).

37. See Charles E. Chapman, *A History of Spain*, New York, 1918, pp. 497–502.

38. Gottschalk to Edward Gottschalk, 17 November 1851, Clara Gottschalk Peterson, "Biographical Sketch," p. 59; also Brockett, "Gottschalk in Madrid," pp. 279–80. Riansares and Cristina were secretly married.

39. Gautier, *Wanderings in Spain*, p. 81.

40. Alexandra Orlova, *Glinka's Life in Music: A Chronicle*, Ann Arbor, 1988, p. 459.

41. José Ortega Zapata, untitled article, *El Orden*, 1852 May 30.

42. Including the lost *Canto de huérfanos*, Fors, *Gottschalk*, pp. 230–32.

43. Fors, *Gottschalk*, pp. 235–39.

44. *Daily Enquirer*, 7 June 1855.

45. Rauch, *American Interest in Cuba*, p. 170.

46. Clara Gottschalk Peterson, "Biographical Sketch," p. 59.

47. Theodore Aronson, *Royal Vendetta: The Crown of Spain, 1829–1965*, New York, 1966, p. 73.

48. Clara Gottschalk Peterson, "Biographical Sketch," pp. 59–61.

49. *El Heraldo*, 22 November 1851; *El Clamor Publico*, 23 November 1851; *El Observador*, 20 November 1851; *Los Novidades*, 22 November 1851.

50. Scrapbook no. 7, Gottschalk Collection, NYPL; also Clara Gottschalk Peterson, "Biographical Sketch," pp. 61–62; also Arpin, *Biographie*, p. 47.

51. Barringer to Webster, 12 December 1851, Diplomatic Despatches, no. 70.

52. *El Heraldo*, 14 December 1851; *La Nacion*, 18 December 1851; Brockett, "Gottschalk in Madrid," p. 283.

53. Anon., *The Attaché in Madrid; or, Sketches of the Court of Isabela II*, New York, 1856, p. 87.

54. See Doyle, *Louis Moreau Gottschalk*, D-153; also Brockett, "Gottschalk in Madrid," p. 294.

55. Brockett, "Gottschalk in Madrid," pp. 293–94.

56. *La Nacion*, 18 December 1851.

57. Brockett, "Gottschalk in Madrid," pp. 294–302; Doyle, "The Piano Music of Louis Moreau Gottschalk," pp. 141–43; and Fors, *Gottschalk*, pp. 240–44.

58. Gautier, *Wanderings in Spain*, pp. 50–54.

59. "Gottschalk à Valladolid," *La France musicale*, 1 February 1852, p. 46; Arpin, *Biographie*, p. 47.

60. Clyde W. Brockett, "Footnotes of a Pianist: A Waltz for a Living Princess,"*Sonneck Society Bulletin*, Spring 1991, p. 24; for this and the related waltz *Vallisolitana* see Brockett, "Gottschalk in Biscay," pp. 11–13, 25–26, 61–66.

61. Edward Gottschalk to Annie Myers, 31 March 1852, Glover Collection.

62. *La España*, 28 January 1852.

63. *La France musicale*, 15 February 1852, p. 63.

64. *El Orden*, 29 January 1852.

65. *Gacetade*, 28 January 1852. To be sure, *Desgracia* has the less pointed secondary meaning of "misfortune" or "mishap."

66. Escudier, *Les Virtuoses*, p. 184.

67. Clara Gottschalk Peterson, "Biographical Sketch," pp. 63–64.

68. Escudier, *Les Virtuoses*, p. 184.

69. Fors, *Gottschalk*, pp. 235–39.

70. Gottschalk, *Notes of a Pianist*, p. 137; Clara Gottschalk Peterson to William H. Hawes, 30 June 1901, Gottschalk Collection, Historic New Orleans Collection.

71. Escudier, *Les Virtuoses*, p. 183; Clara Gottschalk Peterson, "Biographical Sketch," p. 63.

72. H. Wiley Hitchcock, *Music in the United States: A Historical Introduction*, Englewood Cliffs, 1988, pp. 39–41.

73. *El Orden*, 27 June 1852. For a detailed analysis of this work and its sources see Brockett, "Gottschalk in Madrid," pp. 302–10.

74. Gottschalk Collection, NYPL.

75. *La Jota aragonesa*, op. 14. See Doyle, "The Piano Music of Louis Moreau Gottschalk," pp. 142–43.

76. *La France musicale*, 11 April 1852.

77. Letter of conferral to Gottschalk, 20 July 1852, Glover Collection. Brockett, "Gottschalk in Biscay," pp. 13–16, 52–53.

78. Barringer to Marquis de Miraflores, February 1852, Despatches of American Ministers and Consular Officers in Spain, 1851–52, Diplomatic Records, U.S. National Archives.

79. Letter of appointment, J. Espin to Gottschalk, 30 May 1852, Scrapbook no. 7, Gottschalk Collection, NYPL; also *El Orden*, 8 June 1852; *El Heraldo*, 8 June 1852; *El Diario Español*, 9 June 1852, etc.

80. *La France musicale*, 27 June 1852, p. 214; *La Opinion de Madrid*, 14 June 1852.

81. Brockett, "Gottschalk in Madrid," p. 284.

82. H.D., *Biography*, p. 20.

83. *Ibid.*, p. 29; *La France musicale*, 27 June 1852; *El Orden*, 15 June 1852; *El Heraldo*, 15 June 1852.

84. *El Heraldo*, 25 June 1852, 1 July 1852; *La Epoca*, 29 June 1852.

85. "Sir L. M. Gottschalk Lislet" (MS), Gottschalk Collection, NYPL.

86. *El Heraldo*, 30 June 1852.

87. José Redondo to Gottschalk, 26 June 1852, Glover Collection; Clara Gottschalk Peterson, "Biographical Sketch," p. 65.

88. *La Esperanza*, 30 July 1852.

89. *El España*, 23 May 1852; *La France musicale*, 4 July 1852; *La Epoca*, 28 July 1852.

90. Arpin, *Biographie*, pp. 53–54.

91. Stevenson, "Liszt in the Iberian Peninsula," p. 8.

92. *Revue et gazette musicale*, 5 September 1852, p. 295.

93. *La France musicale*, 29 August 1852.

94. *The Little Book of Louis Moreau Gottschalk*, Richard Jackson and Neil Ratliff, eds., New York, 1975, pp. 18–19; also Leann F. Logsdon, "Gottschalk's *Workbook*: Notations of a Pianist" (MS), courtesy of the author. Doyle, *Louis Moreau Gottschalk*, MS-9.5; MS-33.26; D-28.

95. Gautier, *Wanderings in Spain*, p. 193.

96. The hypothesis on the rhythmic shift was proposed by Doyle (D-86) and elaborated in detail by Cecilio Teiles, Havana, personal communication to the author.

97. Gautier, *Wanderings in Spain*, p. 260.

98. Fors, *Gottschalk*, p. 241.

99. Brockett, "Gottschalk in Biscay," pp. 28–29.

100. Brockett, "Gottschalk in Madrid," pp. 295–96.

101. *La France musicale,* 17 October 1852.

102. Hensel, *Life and Letters,* p. 47; for interesting speculation on the fate of this work see Brockett, "Gottschalk in Biscay," pp. 44–45, fn. 68.

103. Dates for these events were established through the research of Clyde W. Brockett, "Gottschalk in Biscay," p. 24.

104. Fors, *Gottschalk,* p. 61.

105. "Lola Montez and Gottschalk," *Trinidad Sentinel,* 26 August 1858, Scrapbook no. 4, Gottschalk Collection, NYPL. Escudier, *Les Virtuoses,* pp. 184–86.

106. "Gottschalk," *Orchestra,* July 1877, p. 372.

107. Barringer to Daniel Webster, 6 November 1852, Despatches of American Ministers and Consular Officers in Spain, 1851–52, no. 110, Diplomatic Records, U.S. National Archives.

108. 14 October 1852, Rauch, *American Interest in Cuba,* p. 232.

109. Anon., *Attaché in Madrid,* p. 73.

110. Gottschalk, *Notes of a Pianist,* pp. 138–39.

111. *Ibid.,* p. 140.

112. *La France musicale,* 5, 19 December 1852.

113. D-132.

8. "Financial Music" and Democracy

1. *Boston True Flag,* October 1853.

2. Berlioz, *Memoirs,* p. 397.

3. Max Maretzek, *Crotchets and Quavers,* reprinted in *Revelations of an Opera Manager in Nineteenth-Century America,* New York, 1968, p. 180.

4. *Ibid.,* p. 181.

5. Hensel, *Life and Letters,* p. 99.

6. Gottschalk, *Notes of a Pianist,* p. 45.

7. Maurice Strakosch, *Souvenirs d'un impresario,* Paris, 1887, p. 262.

8. Andrew C. Minor, "Piano Concerts in New York City, 1849–1865" (M.A. thesis, University of Michigan, 1947), pp. 10, 43; *Albion* (New York), 18 January 1851, p. 32.

9. Maretzek, *Revelations of an Opera Manager,* p. 37.

10. Clara Louise Kellogg, *Memoirs of an American Prima Donna,* New York, 1913, p. 40.

11. Maretzek, *Revelations of an Opera Manager,* p. 221.

12. W. G. Armstrong, *Record of the Opera in Philadelphia,* Philadelphia, 1884, p. 78.

13. Russell Sanjek, *American Popular Music and Its Business, the First Four Hundred Years,* New York and Oxford, 1988, 2:67.

14. *Ibid.,* pp. 66–67.

15. Herz, *My Travels in America,* pp. 38–39.

16. *Ibid.,* pp. 42–43.

17. Maretzek, *Revelations of an Opera Manager,* pp. 311–13.

18. *Ibid.,* p. 44.

19. Herz, *My Travels in America,* pp. 90–91.

20. Maretzek, *Revelations of an Opera Manager,* p. 148.

21. Harris, *Humbug,* p. 54.

22. N. Parker Willis, *Famous Persons and Places,* New York, 1854, pp. 392–97; N.

Parker Willis, *Hurry-graphs: or Sketches of Scenery, Celebrities and Society, Taken from Life*, New York, 1851, p. 353.

23. Lind in 1849 characterized the French as a nation "shut out from the common portion of God's blessing upon men, and deservedly so." Of an Italian she encountered she declared, "I am trying to conquer myself—to bear with him—but—he is a *Roman Catholic!*" Quoted by Henry Pleasants, *The Great Singers from the Dawn of Opera to Our Own Time*, New York, 1966, pp. 199, 204.

24. W. S. B. Mathews, *A Hundred Years of Music in America*, Chicago, 1889, pp. 284ff.

25. Loesser, *Men, Women, and Pianos*, p. 492.

26. "About Gottschalk," *Mercury* (New York), 23 March 1862.

27. On de Meyer see Vera Brodsky Lawrence,*Strong on Music: The New York Music Scene in the Days of George Templeton Strong*, vol. 1, *Resonances*, New York, 1988, pp. 309–12.

28. Herz, *My Travels in America*, p. 53.

29. *Ibid.*, p. 30.

30. Robert D. Faner, *Walt Whitman and Opera*, London and Amsterdam, 1951, p. 97.

31. Minor, "Piano Concerts in New York City," p. 461.

32. *Dwight's Journal of Music*, 22 January 1853.

33. Schonberg, *The Great Pianists*, pp. 187–88; also Vera Brodsky Lawrence, "Reverberations: 1850–1856" (MS), vol. 2 of *Strong on Music*, courtesy of the author, p. 353.

34. *New York Times*, 16 November 1851.

35. Lawrence, "Reverberations", pp. 317–19.

36. Delmer Dalzell Rogers, "Nineteenth-century Music in New York City as Reflected in the Career of George Frederick Bristow" (Ph.D. diss., University of Michigan, 1967), pp. 71ff.; also Lawrence, "Reverberations," pp. 205–7.

9. New York Debut

1. "District of New York—Port of New York, Manifest of Passengers, Davis Lines' *Humboldt*," 10 January 1853, copy in Offergeld Papers. Ramon's presence was noted in the *Daily Tribune*, 11 January 1853.

2. Richard Hoffman, *Some Musical Recollections of Fifty Years*, New York, 1910, p. 131.

3. Gottschalk, *Notes of a Pianist*, p. 137.

4. Charles Lockwood, *Bricks and Brownstone: The New York Row House, 1783–1929*, New York, 1972, pp. 161ff.

5. Milton Goldin, *The Music Merchants*, London, 1969, p. 45.

6. Thomas Ryan, *Recollections of an Old Musician*, New York, 1899, p. 61.

7. Junius Henri Browne, *The Great Metropolis; A Mirror of New York*, Hartford, 1869, pp. 92–95.

8. Browne, *The Great Metropolis*, pp. 23–29; George W. Walling, *Recollections of a New York Chief of Police*, New York, 1887, pp. 280, 284.

9. Browne, *The Great Metropolis*, p. 28.

10. *Mirror*, 20 November 1852. Cited by Lawrence, "Reverberations," pp. 460–61.

11. Harris, *Humbug*, p. 51.

12. *New York Herald*, 24 January 1853.

13. "Editor's Easy Chair," *Harper's New Monthly Magazine*, September 1862, p. 419.

14. *Evening Mirror*, 18 January 1853.

15. Harris, *Humbug*, p. 51.

16. L. M. Gottschalk to Aimée Gottschalk, 15 February 1853, Family Letters, Gottschalk Collection, NYPL.

17. Arpin, *Biographie*.

18. Paul Arpin, *Life of Louis Moreau Gottschalk*, Henry C. Watson, trans., n.d., issued initially in *Graham's Magazine*.

19. H.D., "Biography of Louis Moreau Gottschalk," *Graham's Magazine*, January 1853, pp. 61–69. On Durell-Didimus, see *National Cyclopaedia of American Biography*, New York, 1906, 13:121.

20. Richard Henry Stoddard, *Recollections, Personal and Literary*, New York, 1903, p. 80.

21. Bayard Taylor, *The Echo Club, and Other Literary Diversions*, Boston, 1876, p. 53.

22. Walling, *Recollections of a New York Chief of Police*, p. 48.

23. Elihu Vedder, *The Digressions of V.*, Boston, 1910, p. 201.

24. Anne C. L. Botta, *Memoirs of Anne C. L. Botta*, New York, 1894, p. 240.

25. James D. McCabe, *Lights and Shadows of New York Life*, Philadelphia, 1877, p. 595.

26. Abram C. Dayton, *Last Days of Knickerbocker Life in New York*, New York, 1882, pp. 227–29.

27. Arthur Pougin-William Vincent Wallace, *Étude biographique et critiques* Paris, 1866; W. H. Grattan Flood, *Memoir of W. V. Wallace*, London, 1912.

28. Hector Berlioz, *Evenings in the Orchestra*, New York, 1929, p. 356.

29. L. M. Gottschalk to his sisters, undated letter no. 34, (ca. 11 December 1864), Family Letters, Gottschalk Collection, NYPL.

30. Gottschalk, *Notes of a Pianist*, p. 44; Hoffman, *Some Musical Recollections*, pp. 130–36.

31. Oscar Comettant, "Musical America 1850 as Seen Through a French Squint," Ivor D. Spencer, trans., *Music Educators' Journal*, February 1969, 55:43.

32. *New York Herald*, 24 January 1853.

33. *Daily Mirror*, 18 January 1853.

34. Lawrence, "Reverberations," pp. 603–27; William Treat Upton, *William Henry Fry: An American Journalist and Composer-Critic*, New York, 1954; Barbara A. Zuck, *A History of Musical Americanism*, Ann Arbor, 1980, pp. 18–35.

35. *Dwight's Journal of Music*, 24 April 1852, p. 22.

36. *New York Daily Times*, 17 November 1852.

37. William Treat Upton, *William Henry Fry*, p. 45.

38. *Tribune*, 7 January 1853.

39. *Ibid.*

40. Richard Storrs Willis, "Mr. Fry's Lectures," *Musical World and Times*, 19 February 1853, pp. 114–15.

41. *Dwight's Journal of Music*, 12 March 1853, pp. 180–82.

42. *Mirror*, 18 January 1853; *Courrier des États-Unis*, 8 February 1853.

43. Frederic Louis Ritter, *Music in America*, New York, 1890, p. 292.

44. Unidentified clipping, Scrapbook no. 4, Gottschalk Collection, NYPL.

45. *Albion*, 19 February 1853.

46. *New York Herald*, 12 February 1853.

47. *Ibid.*

48. *Ibid.*

49. *Ibid.*

50. *Home Journal,* 19 February 1853.

51. *New York Herald,* 12 February 1853.

52. *New York Times,* 12 February 1853.

53. *Courier and Enquirer,* 12 February 1853.

54. *Ibid.*

55. *Home Journal,* 19 February 1853, p. 158.

56. *Musical World and Times,* 19 February 1853, p. 116.

57. *New York Tribune,* 12 February 1853.

58. *Ibid.*

59. *Ibid.*

60. *Home Journal,* 12 February 1853.

61. *New York Herald,* 19 February 1853.

62. *New York Times,* 20 February 1853.

63. Hoffman, *Some Musical Recollections,* p. 133.

64. *New York Times,* 20 February 1853.

65. *Courier and Enquirer,* 19 February 1853.

66. *Albion,* 19 February 1853.

67. *Musical World and Times,* 26 February 1853, p. 131.

68. *New York Herald,* 19 February 1853.

69. Gottschalk, *Notes of a Pianist,* p. 46.

70. *Musical World and Times,* 5 March 1853.

71. Edward Gottschalk to Aimée Gottschalk, 1 October 1853, Family Letters, Gottschalk Collection, NYPL. "The United States," he confided to her, "is ruined for artists."

72. Gottschalk, *Notes of a Pianist,* p. 46.

73. *Ibid.*, p. 66.

74. *Daily Mirror,* 25 February 1853; *Courrier des États-Unis,* 22 February 1853.

75. Robert A. Gerson, *Music in Philadelphia,* Philadelphia, 1940, pp. 67–68.

76. Sigmund Spaeth, *A History of Popular Music in America,* New York, 1948, p. 91.

77. Unidentified clipping, Philadelphia, 1870, Scrapbook no. 12, Gottschalk Collection, NYPL.

78. *Pennsylvania Inquirer,* 1 March 1853.

79. *Sunday Dispatch,* 27 February 1853.

80. RO-31.

81. Robert Stevenson, "The Latin Tinge: The Impact of Latin Music in the United States," *Inter-American Music Review,* Spring-Summer 1980, pp. 139–40.

82. Lawrence, "Reverberations," pp. 312–14.

83. *Enquirer* (Cincinnati), 29 May 1853.

84. *Ibid.*, 2 June 1853.

85. John Tasker Howard, *Stephen Foster, America's Troubadore,* New York, 1934, p. 205. Fors (*Gottschalk,* p. 77) asserts that these three works were included in a version of *Recuerdos de mi patra* performed at Havana, February 1854.

86. Howard, *Stephen Foster,* pp. 142–44.

87. Evelyn Foster Morneweck, *Chronicles of Stephen Foster's Family,* 2 vols., Pittsburgh, 1944, 2:381.

88. *Louisville Courier,* 21,22 March 1853.

89. Gottschalk to José de Olavarria, 15 June 1853, Gottschalk Collection, NYPL. On this visit in early 1853 see William L. Hawes, "Gottschalk in New Orleans, 1853," *Times-Democrat* (New Orleans), 8 May 1899; also Willy Prophit, "The Crescent City's Charismatic Celebrity: Louis Moreau Gottschalk's New Orleans Concerts, Spring 1853," *Louisiana History*, 1971, no. 3, pp. 243–54.

90. See Robert C. Reinders, *End of an Era: New Orleans, 1850–1860*, New Orleans, 1964, pp. 51–58.

91. *Daily Picayune*, 3 April 1853.

92. Herz, *My Travels in America*, pp. 87–88.

93. *L'Abeille (New Orleans Bee)*, 4 April 1853; also *Courrier de la Louisiane*, 5 April 1853.

94. George P. Upton, *Musical Memories: My Recollections of Celebrities of the Half Century 1850–1900*, Chicago, 1908 p. 78.

95. *Courrier de la Louisiane*, 10 April 1853; Hawes, "Gottschalk in New Orleans."

96. *Courrier de la Louisiane*, 2 April 1853; *Daily Picayune*, 2 April 1853.

97. *Courrier de la Louisiane*, 6 April 1853.

98. Hawes, "Gottschalk in New Orleans." See also Berthe Harwood, "Reminiscences of Louis Moreau Gottschalk," *Musical Courier*, 13 May 1908, p. 39; and review by Placide Canonge, *Courrier de la Louisiane*, 7 April 1853.

99. Josephine Mandeville to Rebecca Mandeville, 9 April 1853, 16 April 1853. Henry D. Mandeville Papers, Louisiana State University Archives, Baton Rouge.

100. *Daily Picayune*, 14 April 1853.

101. *Buffalo Commercial* (Buffalo, New York), 24 March 1862.

102. *Courrier de la Louisiane*, 29 April 1853, 3 May 1853.

103. *Ibid.*

104. *Ibid.*, 10 May 1853. On *Le Rêve (The Dream)*, see D-40, D-141.

105. D-129. John G. Doyle has noted to the author that this was listed as a *Nocturne* in the *Picayune*, 11 May 1853. The 1857 publication is dedicated by anagram to an unknown Bertha Gans.

106. *Courrier de la Louisiane*, 13 May 1853; *Musical World and Times*, 9 July 1853, pp. 149–50. An engraved facsimile appeared in a program for a concert in Lancaster, Pennsylvania, in November 1855 (Glover Collection); the medal is now lost.

107. *Courrier de la Louisiane*, 18 May 1853.

10. Defeat in New England

1. Gottschalk to his sisters, 1 January 1869, Family Letters, Gottschalk Collection, NYPL.

2. *Courrier de la Louisiane*, 19 May 1853.

3. Edward Gottschalk's notebook, Album no. 8, Gottschalk Collection, NYPL.

4. L. M. Gottschalk to José de Olavarria, 15 June 1853, Gottschalk Collection, NYPL.

5. *Enquirer* (Cincinnati), 7 June 1853.

6. *Ibid.*, 7 June 1853.

7. Gottschalk, *Notes of a Pianist*, pp. 202–3.

8. *Courrier de la Louisiane*, 7 July 1853.

9. Gottschalk, *Notes of a Pianist*, p. 123; D-58.

10. George W. Walling, *Recollections of a New York Chief of Police*, New York, 1887, p. 375.

11. N. Parker Willis, *Hurry-graphs*, p. 319.

12. R. F. Dearborn, *Saratoga Illustrated*, Troy, New York, 1872, p. 12.

13. *Evening Express* (New York), 25 August 1853.

14. *Dwight's Journal of Music*, 10 September 1853, p. 193.

15. Handwritten list of works by L. M. Gottschalk, n.d., Gottschalk Collection, NYPL.

16. See the excellent edition, with introduction, of this work by Richard Jackson and Neil Ratliff, *The Little Book of Louis Moreau Gottschalk: Seven Previously Unpublished Piano Pieces*, New York, 1975, p. 17.

17. Dena J. Epstein, *Sinful Tunes and Spirituals: Black Folk Music to the Civil War*, Urbana, 1977, p. 45.

18. David Ewen, *All the Years of American Popular Music*, Englewood Cliffs, 1977, p. 24.

19. Ralph Keeler, "Three Years as a Negro Minstrel," *Atlantic Monthly*, July 1869, p. 85.

20. *Courrier de la Louisiane*, 23 February 1853.

21. *Albion*, 27 May 1853; *New York Times*, 27 May 1853.

22. Paul Ely Smith, "Gottschalk's 'The Banjo,' op. 15, and the Banjo in the Nineteenth Century," *Current Musicology*, 1992, no. 50, pp. 47–61.

23. "Seven Octaves" (L. M. Gottschalk), *Morning Times*, undated clipping, Gottschalk Collection, NYPL. I am indebted to Réginald Hamel of the Université de Montrèal for pointing out this neglected source.

24. *Albion*, 15 December 1855, p. 595.

25. See Hans Nathan, "Early Banjo Tunes and American Syncopation," *Musical Quarterly*, 1956, no. 41, pp. 455–71.

26. Sigmund Spaeth, *History of Popular Music in America*, New York, 1948, p. 107; Guy D. Johnson, *Folk Culture on St. Helena Island*, Chapel Hill, 1930, p. 119.

27. W. K. Batchelder, *Immitation of The Banjo*, 1854; T. Franklin Bassford, *Banjo Dance* (dedicated to L. M. Gottschalk), 1853; D-16.

28. *Sacramento Daily Union*, 1 June 1865.

29. Hensel, *Life and Letters*, pp. 157–58.

30. Frank Converse, *Frank Converse's Banjo Without Master*, New York, 1865, preface.

31. Kendall, *History of New Orleans*, 1:176.

32. *Pennsylvania Inquirer*, 23 August 1853.

33. *Daily Picayune*, 4 September 1853.

34. Scrapbook no. 4, Gottschalk Collection, NYPL.

35. Miss Flash and Miss Terrill to Mr. Moreau Gottschalk, 1853 September 22, Miscellaneous Papers, Gottschalk Collection, NYPL.

36. Theodore Thomas, *Theodore Thomas: A Musical Autobiography*, George P. Upton, ed., Chicago, 1905, p. 26; Ryan, *Recollections of an Old Musician*, p. 66.

37. Quoted in Maretzek, *Revelations of an Opera Manager*, p. xx.

38. Adam Carse, *The Life of Jullien*, Cambridge, England, 1951, pp. 18–33.

39. *Dwight's Journal of Music*, 5 November 1853, p. 37.

40. *New York Tribune*, 15 December 1853.

41. *Dwight's Journal of Music*, 24 June 1854, p. 91; 5 November 1853.

42. *Daily Delta* (New Orleans), reprinted in *Dwight's Journal of Music*, 20 May 1854, p. 55.

43. *Musical World and Times*, 22 October 1853, p. 60; *New York Herald*, 13 October 1853.

44. Edward Gottschalk's account book, Album no. 8, Gottschalk Collection, NYPL.

45. John G. Doyle first identified the Gottschalk-Helmsmuller link, letter to the author, 10 April 1991; see also *New York Times*, 6 September 1853; *New York Mirror*, 12 September 1853.

46. *Gleason's Pictorial Drawing-Room Companion*, 9 October 1853.

47. *Ibid.*, 29 October 1853, p. 285.

48. Mark Twain, *Letters*, 1:168.

49. Ryan, *Recollections of an Old Musician*, p. 186.

50. *Ibid.*, p. 135.

51. Simon Schama, *Dead Certainties: Unwarranted Speculations*, New York, 1991, p. 79.

52. Herz, *My Travels in America*, p. 16.

53. See Paul DiMaggio, "Cultural Entrepreneurship in Nineteenth-century Boston: The Creation of an Organizational Base for High Culture in America" and "Cultural Entrepreneurship in Nineteenth-century Boston: Part II: The Classification and Framing of American Art" *Media, Culture and Society*, 1982, no. 4, pp. 33–50, 303–22; Michael Broyles, "Music and Class Structure in Antebellum Boston," *Journal of the American Musicological Society*, 1991, no. 3, pp. 451–93.

54. Broyles, "Music and Class Structure," p. 475.

55. *Ibid.*, p. 482.

56. Quoted by Kmen, *Music in New Orleans*, pp. 115–16.

57. *Boston Daily Courier*, 19 October 1853.

58. *Bacon's Dictionary of Boston*, Boston, 1886, pp. 256–57.

59. *Commonwealth*, 19 October 1853; also *Boston Post*, 25 October 1853; *Dwight's Journal of Music*, 22 October 1853, p. 22.

60. *Boston Post*, 19 October 1853.

61. *Daily Evening Transcript*, 20 October 1853.

62. *Boston Daily Courier*, 21 October 1853.

63. *Boston Post*, 19 October 1853; see also *Boston Daily Advertiser*, 19 October 1853.

64. *Boston Post*, 25 October 1853.

65. *Boston Traveler* quoted by Hensel, *Life and Letters*, p. 69.

66. *Boston Transcript*, 19 October 1853.

67. *Commonwealth*, 19 October 1853.

68. *Dwight's Journal of Music*, 22 October 1853, p. 22.

69. Unidentified review, Scrapbook no. 4, Gottschalk Collection, NYPL. See also *Boston Transcript*, 22 October 1853.

70. Gottschalk, *Notes of a Pianist*, p. 47.

71. Gottschalk to Aimée Gottschalk, n.d. (August 1853), Family Letters, Gottschalk Collection, NYPL.

72. Unidentified review, Scrapbook no. 4, Gottschalk Collection, NYPL. See also *Boston Transcript*, 22 October 1853.

73. Certificate of Burial, Edouard (*sic*) Gottschalk, Archives of the Archdiocese of New Orleans; *Daily Picayune*, 25 October 1853.

74. Gottschalk, *Notes of a Pianist*, p. 47; see Hensel's erroneous account, *Life and Letters*, pp. 66–68.

75. Gottschalk, *Notes of a Pianist*, p. 47.

76. Gottschalk to his sisters, 1 January 1869, Family Letters, Gottschalk Collection, NYPL.

77. *Ibid.;* also undated fragment no. 85, Gottschalk Collection, NYPL; "Figaro on

Gottschalk," *Leader*, n.d. February 1870, unmounted clipping, Gottschalk Collection, NYPL.

78. Ryan, *Recollections of an Old Musician*, pp. 108–10; Richard G. Parker, *A Tribute to the Life and Character of Jonas Chickering*, Boston, 1854; Gary J. Kornblith, "The Craftsman as Industrialist: Jonas Chickering and the Transformation of American Piano-Making," *Business History Review*, Autumn 1985, p. 365.

79. *Watson's Weekly Art Journal*, 22 April 1865, p. 1.

80. Christine Merrick Ayars, *Contributions to the Art of Music in America by the Music Industries of Boston, 1640–1936*, New York, 1937, pp. 117–22.

81. Kornblith, "The Craftsman as Industrialist," pp. 360–64.

82. Herz, *My Travels in America*, p. 55.

83. Cf. Edward Gottschalk's account book, Album no. 8, Gottschalk Collection, NYPL.

84. *Providence Daily Post*, 22 October 1853, November 7.

85. Edward Gottschalk's account book, 8 November 1853, Album no. 8, Gottschalk Collection, NYPL.

86. *Providence Daily Post*, 2 November 1853.

87. *Ibid.*, 7 November 1853.

88. Edward Gottschalk's account book, 8 November 1853, Album no. 8, Gottschalk Collection, NYPL..

89. Gottschalk, *Notes of a Pianist*, p. 48.

90. Fragment no. 85, Gottschalk Collection, NYPL. In the process of translating the French original, the decimal point also migrated, reducing Gottschalk's losses to $1600 (Gottschalk, *Notes of a Pianist*, p. 48).

91. Concerts were offered in Baltimore, Brooklyn, Hoboken, Jersey City, Chester (Pennsylvania), Albany, and Troy in the weeks after November 12. Edward Gottschalk's account book, Album no. 8, Gottschalk Collection, NYPL.

92. "Jenny" in the *Brooklyn Union* (29 March 1864) refers to the "den of sharpers into which he had fallen" at this time.

93. *Albion*, 19 November 1853.

94. L. M. Gottschalk, fragment no. 85, Gottschalk Collection, NYPL.

95. Edward Gottschalk to Leonard Myers, 10 November 1853, Gottschalk Collection, NYPL.

96. Gottschalk to Aimée Gottschalk, undated letter no. 12 (November-December 1853), Family Letters, Gottschalk Collection, NYPL.

97. Edward Gottschalk to Leonard Myers, 10 November 1853, Family Letters, Gottschalk Collection, NYPL.

98. *Brooklyn Union*, 29 March 1864.

99. *Courrier de la Louisiane*, 21 December 1853.

100. *Ibid.*, 30 December 1853.

101. *Ibid.*, 20 January 1854.

102. For a careful exposition of these two variant editions see Doyle, *Louis Moreau Gottschalk*, D-90, D-90a, D-90b, D-90c.

103. *Courrier de la Louisiane*, 27–28 January 1854.

104. *Ibid.*, 31 January 1854.

105. *Ibid.*, 2 February 1854.

106. Henzel, *Life and Letters*, p. 197.

107. Gottschalk, *Notes of a Pianist*, pp. 55–56.

108. Theodore Guyol, 10 February 1852, NONA. Other slave sales pertaining to the Gottschalk and Bruslé families in this period are recorded in Theodore Guyol, 12

February 1852; Achille Chiapella, 17 July 1852; A. A. Baudouin, 15 July 1852 and 11 October 1852; Octave de Armas, 15 October 1852; all in New Orleans Notarial Archives. See also sheriff sale, 20 January 1854, COB 63–499, Orleans Parish Conveyance Office.

109. Maretzek, *Revelations of an Opera Manager*, p. 149.

11. Mr. Dwight's Crusade

1. Gottschalk, *Notes of a Pianist*, p. 168.

2. On the Dwight-Gottschalk controversy see Kenneth Abraham, "Mr. Dwight's Blind Spot: Louis Moreau Gottschalk," *Musart*, Winter 1973, pp. 47–50; Marcia Wilson Lebow, "A Systematic Examination of the *Journal of Music and Art* Edited by John Sullivan Dwight: 1852–1881, Boston, Massachusetts" (Ph.D. diss., University of California, Los Angeles, 1969), pp. 241–58; and Irving Lowens, *Music and Musicians in Early America*, New York, 1964, p. 228.

3. *Dwight's Journal of Music*, 9 April 1853, p. 7.

4. *Ibid.*, 22 October 1853, p. 22.

5. *Ibid.;* see also the follow-up review on Gottschalk's Worcester concert, *Dwight's Journal of Music*, 12 November 1853, p. 44, which *Dwight's* describes as a "clever hit at modern virtuosity."

6. *Ibid.*, 29 October 1853, p. 30.

7. Hallé, *Autobiography*, p. 58. Liszt's hoaxes were even reported in *Dwight's Journal of Music*, 4 August 1855, p. 140.

8. Louis Moreau Gottschalk, "Notes by a Pianist, III," *Standard* (Buenos Aires), n.d. 1868 (?), Scrapbook no. 5, Gottschalk Collection, NYPL.

9. W. S. B. Mathews, "John S. Dwight: Editor, Critic, and Man," *Music*, 1899, 15:525–40; also W. S. B. Mathews, "Louis Moreau Gottschalk, the Most Popular American Composer," *Musician*, October 1908, 13:440. Loggins (*Where the Word Ends*, pp. 136–39) bases his account of this incident on Mathews, while Irving Lowens (*Music and Musicians in Early America*, New York, 1964, p. 228) places the hoax in the 1860s, by which time Gottschalk's general relations with Boston were considerably improved. See also William Smythe Babcock, "Louis Moreau Gottschalk: The Most Popular of American Composers," *Musician*, 13/10, October 1908, pp. 439–40. Schonberg (*The Great Pianists*, p. 210) parallels Lowens. For a contemporary reference to Gottschalk's hoax see *New York Dispatch*, 9 March 1861, which states that the substituted piece was by Chopin.

10. George Willis Cooke, *John Sullivan Dwight*, Boston,.1898, p. 35.

11. See Arthur M. Schlesinger Jr., *The Age of Jackson*, Boston, 1945, pp. 342–85.

12. *Dwight's Journal of Music*, August 1852, p. 142; Mathews, *A Hundred Years of Music*, p. 374.

13. John Sullivan Dwight, "Chamber Concerts of the Harvard Musical Association," *Harbinger*, 28 November 1846, 3:394–95.

14. John Sullivan Dwight, "Address Delivered Before the Harvard Musical Association, 25 August 1841," *Hatch's Musical Magazine*, 1841, 3:265.

15. *Dwight's Journal of Music*, 20 August 1853, p. 156.

16. Berlioz, *Memoirs*, p. 411.

17. John Sullivan Dwight, "Music a Means of Culture," *Atlantic Monthly*, September 1870, 26:322.

18. Lawrence, "Reverberations," p. 732. Dwight contracted his mania for Beethoven from Brook Farmer Margaret Fuller, who preceeded him in this cult; cf. Ora Frishberg Saloman, "American Writers on Beethoven, 1838–1849," *American Music*, 1990, no. 1, pp. 15–23.

19. Gottschalk, *Notes of a Pianist*, pp. 75, 159.

20. Hensel, *Life and Letters*, p. 60.

21. *Dwight's Journal of Music*, 1 November 1856, p. 38.

22. Gottschalk, *Notes of a Pianist*, p. 174.

23. George P. Upton, *Musical Memories*, p. 77.

24. William Mason to Clara Gottschalk Peterson, 14 October 1900, Glover Collection; also Gottschalk, *Notes of a Pianist*, p. 183.

25. *Dwight's Journal of Music*, 10 January 1857, p. 118.

26. Gottschalk, *Notes of a Pianist*, p. 75.

27. *Dwight's Journal of Music*, 10 January 1857, p. 118.

28. The strength of anti-Catholicism at the nominally tolerant Brook Farm is evident from the hostile reception there of Orestes Brownson, a recent convert.

29. *Dwight's Journal of Music*, 19 September 1857, p. 198.

30. Gottschalk, *Notes of a Pianist*, pp. 260–61.

31. On this theme see the excellent volume edited by Michael R. Marrus, *The Emergence of Leisure*, New York, 1974. On sacralization see Lawrence W. Levine, *Highbrow/Lowbrow: The Emergence of Cultural Hierarchy in America*, Cambridge, Massachusetts, 1988, pp. 118ff.

32. Allen Lesser, *Enchanting Rebel: The Secret of Adah Isaacs Menken*, Fort Washington, New York, 1947, p. 38.

33. *Daily Globe* (Toronto), 17 July 1862.

34. Fragment of an article by L. M. Gottschalk, Scrapbook no. 6, Gottschalk Collection, NYPL. This is a much stronger version of the passage preserved in *Notes of a Pianist*, pp. 75–76.

35. Harris, *Humbug*, pp. 134–35.

36. For Dwight on Berlioz see *Dwight's Journal of Music*, 6 April 1861, p. 3.

37. Mathews, *A Hundred Years of Music in America*, p. 62.

38. George C. D. Odell, *Annals of the New York Stage*, 7:453; Maretzek, *Revelations of an Opera Manager*, p. vii; *Dwight's Journal of Music*, 13 December 1856, p. 84.

39. Kellogg, *Memoirs of an American Prima Donna*, p. 36.

40. Walt Whitman, quoted in John Burroughs, *Whitman: A Study*, Boston and New York, 1896, p. 26.

41. Fragment of an article by L.M. Gottschalk, Scrapbook no. 6, Gottschalk Collection, NYPL.

42. *Dwight's Journal of Music*, 15 November 1856, p. 51.

43. *Ibid.*

44. *Ibid.*

45. Quoted in Lebow, *A Systematic Examination*, p. 139; *Neue Zeitschrift für Musik*, 17 June 1853.

46. *Dwight's Journal of Music*, 5 April 1856, p. 7.

47. Cortot, *In Search of Chopin*, p. 116.

48. *Dwight's Journal of Music*, 11 March 1854, p. 182.

49. Gottschalk, *Notes of a Pianist*, p. 119.

50. *Ibid.*, p. 149.

51. *Dwight's Journal of Music*, 29 November 1856, p. 70.

52. *Ibid.*, 25 February 1854, p. 165.

53. William Foster Apthorp, *Musicians and Music-Lovers and Other Essays*, New York, 1897, p. 277.

54. Dwight, "Address Delivered Before the Harvard Musical Association," pp. 257–72.

55. See Peter Dobkin Hall, *The Organization of American Culture, 1700–1900*, New York, 1982, pp. 194–97; also Levine, *Highbrow/Lowbrow*, pp. 120–23.

56. L. M. Gottschalk, "La Música, el piano, los pianistas," Fors, *Gottschalk*, pp. 326–28.

57. L. M. Gottschalk, "Notes by a Pianist, III," *Standard* (Buenos Aires), n.d. 1868 (?), Scrapbook no. 5, Gottschalk Collection, NYPL.

58. L. M. Gottschalk, letter to the editor, *Standard* (Buenos Aires), n.d. 1869, Scrapbook no. 2, Gottschalk Collection, NYPL.

59. Hensel, *Life and Letters*, p. 176.

60. Gottschalk, *Notes of a Pianist*, pp. 232–34.

12. An Untimely Visit to Cuba, 1854

1. Undated letter (1854), Notebook no. 8, Gottschalk Collection, NYPL.

2. Escudier, *Les Virtuoses*, p. 187.

3. José Garcia de Arboleza, *Manual de la isla de Cuba*, 2nd edition (Havana, 1859), p. 279.

4. Rauch, *American Interest in Cuba*, pp. 262–66. For a comprehensive, detailed, and judicious account of both of Gottschalk's Cuban sojourns see Libby Antarsh Rubin, "Gottschalk in Cuba" (Ph.D. diss., Columbia University, 1974).

5. *Ibid.*, pp. 269–73.

6. *Ibid.*, p. 274. See Samuel R. Walker, "Cuba and the South," *De Bow's Review*, November 1854, pp. 519–25.

7. On Pezuela see D. M. Estorch, *Apuntes para la Historia sobre la administración del Marqués de la Pezuela en la isla de Cuba*, Madrid, 1853, pp. 14–54.

8. *Ibid.*, pp 45ff.; Rauch, *American Interest in Cuba*,. pp. 279–81.

9. Gottschalk, *Notes of a Pianist*, pp. 6–7.

10. *Diario de la Marina*, 15 February 1854; Fors, *Gottschalk*, p. 74.

11. This, according to local tradition reported to the author by Raúl Martínez Rodríguez of Havana.

12. Notebook no. 8, Gottschalk Collection, NYPL.

13. Rauch, *American Interest in Cuba*, p. 241.

14. Richard Henry Dana Jr., *To Cuba and Back*, Boston, 1859, pp. 233–34.

15. Anselmo Suárez Romero (1818–78), *Francisco*, begun in 1832 but published only in 1880; Cirilo Villa Verde (1812–94), *Cecilia Valdés o la Loma del Angel*, begun in 1839 and published in 1882.

16. Raúl Martínez Rodríguez, "Edelmann y la impresión musical en Cuba," *Revolución y Cultura*, June 1989, pp. 47–49; also Serafin Ramírez, *La Habana artística*, Havana, 1891, pp. 64–67.

17. *Diario de la Marina*, 15 February 1854; Fors, *Gottschalk*, p. 76.

18. Ramirez, *La Habana artística*, pp. 57ff.

19. Alejo Carpentier, *La Música en Cuba*, Havana, 1988, pp. 196ff.; Gaspar Agüero y Barreras, "El Compositor, Nicholás Ruiz Espadero," *Revista Cubana*, April-June 1938, pp. 160–78; Gottschalk, "La Música, el piano, los pianistas," Fors, *Gottschalk*, pp.

323–25; see also the essay "Gottschalk et Espadero" extracted from the journal *España musical* by *L'Art musical*, 1874, pp. 401–2; for the definitive biography of Espadero see Cecilio Tieles Ferrer, "Lo Nacional en la vida y la obra de Nicolás Ruiz Espadero" (MS), Havana, 1992.

20. Fors, *Gottschalk*, pp. 74–75.

21. Carpentier, *La Música en Cuba*, p. 196.

22. Tieles, "Julián Fontana," pp. 148–49.

23. Quoted in Carpentier, *La Música en Cuba*, p. 203–4; also Tieles, "Lo Nacional en la vida y la obra de Nicolás Ruiz Espadero," pp. 79–87.

24. Ramirez, *La Habana artística*, pp. 79–86.

25. *Ibid.*, pp. 75–79.

26. Rafael Mendive, "Al Pianista habanero, P. Desvernine," *Revista de la Habana*, 1854, 2:159.

27. *Gaceta de la Habana*, 16 February 1854.

28. *Diario de la Marina*, 27 February 1854.

29. See Zoila Lapique Becali, *Música colonial cubana en las publicaciones periódicas (1812–1902)* 2 vols., Havana, 1979, 1:37.

30. *Diario de la Marina*, 2, 10, 11 March 1854; *Gaceta de la Habana*, 3, 4, 5, 7, 12 March 1854.

31. Lapique, *Música colonial cubana*, 1:145.

32. *Diario de la Marina*, 13 March 1854; translated in Rubin, "Gottschalk in Cuba," pp. 181–82.

33. *Ibid.*, 14 March 1854.

34. *Revista de la Habana*, 15 March 1854. This issue also includes a poem *A Gottschalk* by R. Zambrana and a sonnet *A Gottschalk* by "N.N."

35. Doyle, "The Piano Music of Louis Moreau Gottschalk," pp. 149–51; Rubin, "Gottschalk in Cuba," pp. 169–80; Bacardí y Moreau, *Crónicas de Santiago de Cuba*, p. 426; and, above all, Carlos Borbolla, "El Cocoyé, un canto omtarsero qua origino un potpourri con zaloe historico" (MS, Havana, 1954), Museo de la Música, Havana.

36. See P. Desvernine, "Baile Haytiano," *El Cucuyé*, Havana; Borbolla, *El Cocoyé*, p. 33. S. Trias also published a version of *El Cocoyé*, issued by Edelmann from his shop at Obrapia 12 before 1852–53.

37. Fors, *Gottschalk*, p. 76, claims that it was Espadero who taught Gottschalk this melody. Whether or not this was the case, it was Espadero who transcribed Gottschalk's unissued shorthand version of the piece and published it in his posthumous collection of the composer's works.

38. Rauch, *American Interest in Cuba*, p. 279.

39. *Diario de la Marina*, 25 March 1854.

40. *Ibid.*, 28, 29 March 1854. The other pianists were Barandice, Norrona, Torres, and Alfred Schmidt, who later settled in Lake Charles, Louisiana (William L. Hawes to Mrs. Clara G. Peterson, 13 September 1899, Historic New Orleans Collection).

41. Maretzek, *Revelations of an Opera Manager*, pp. 151–54.

42. Dana, *To Cuba and Back*, p. 47.

43. William L. Hawes to Mrs. Clara G. Peterson, 13 September 1899, Gottschalk Collection, Historic New Orleans Collection.

44. *Diario de la Marina*, 2 April 1854, reprinted in Rubin, "Gottschalk in Cuba," pp. 183–84; RO-2; the relationship of this work to Gottschalk's *Recuerdos cubanos* is not known.

45. *Gaceta de la Habana*, 4 April 1854; *Courrier de la Louisiane*, 13 April 1854; *Diario de la Marina*, 3 April 1854.

46. *Diario de la Marina*, 1 April 1854.

47. RO-158; Rubin, "Gottschalk in Cuba," pp. 205–6; the woman celebrated in this tune was the same mulatto from Santiago de Cuba who originally popularized *El Cocoyé* in that city back in the 1830s.

48. *Gaceta de la Habana*, 6 April 1854. In addition to playing his *El Cocoyé* and *Adios á Cuba*, Gottschalk performed his *Old Folks at Home* variations.

49. P. T. Barnum, *Struggles and Triumphs*, p. 321.

50. Rauch, *American Interest in Cuba*, pp. 285–86.

51. "A Gottschalk" (MS), by J. Heriberto Garcia de [name illegible], 12 May 1854, Gottschalk Collection, NYPL.

52. *Diario de la Marina*, 11, 12, 22, 25 April 1854; *Gaceta de la Habana*, 27 April 1854, 3, 5 May 1854. Gottschalk to Blanchette, undated letter no. 15, Family Letters, Gottschalk Collection, NYPL.

53. *Diario de la Marina*, 15 April 1854.

54. Rubin, "Gottschalk in Cuba," p. 209. This work, identified as RO-221, was performed in New York on 31 January 1856 but is now lost.

55. The *Gaceta de la Habana* (4 May) and *Diario de la Marina* (5 and 20 May) had reported that Gottschalk was returning to the United States and would then leave for Europe.

56. *Gaceta de la Habana*, 20 May 1854; *Diario de la Marina*, 15 April 1854, reported that the sculptor was Sr. Garbeille.

57. Samuel Hazard, *Cuba with Pen and Pencil*, Hartford, 1871, p. 284.

58. *Diario de la Marina*, 4, 5, 13, 20 May 1854; *Prensa de la Habana*, 5 May 1854.

59. *Gaceta de la Habana*, 21 May 1854.

60. Ramirez, *La Habana artística*, pp. 175–91; Paul Glass, "A Hiatus in American Music History," *Afro-American Studies*, 1970, 1:112–13.

61. Ramirez, *La Habana artística*, p. 179.

62. *La Aurora del Yumurí* (Matanzas), 20, 24 May 1854; *Diario de la Marina*, 20 May 1854.

63. Martha Reyes Carballido, "Las Sociededas Philarmonicas en Matanzas" (MS, Havana, 1989), p. 1.

64. *Ibid.*, p. 4.

65. *La Aurora del Yumurí* (Matanzas), 20 May 1854.

66. León Argeliers, *Del Canto y el tiempo*, Havana, 1974, p. 256.

67. James E. Alexander, quoted in Galan, *Cuba y sus sones*, p. 123.

68. See Raúl Martínez Rodrígues, "La Habanera," *Cuba en el ballet*, October-December 1982, 1:19–22; Gerard Béhague, *Music in Latin America: An Introduction*, Englewood Cliffs, 1979, pp. 99ff.; Carpentier, *La Música en Cuba*, pp. 109–22; on Spanish elements see Gilbert Chase, *The Music of Spain*, New York, 1959, pp. 268–69.

69. Lapique, *Música colonial cubana*, 1:179ff.

70. Rubin, "Gottschalk in Cuba," p. 150.

71. Maria Castro y Maya of the Museo de la Música in Havana to the author, 20 December 1991.

72. See Hilario González, "Manuel Saumell y la contradanza," in *Manuel Saumell: Contradanzas*, Havana, 1980, pp. 5–36; Carpentier, *La Música en Cuba*, pp. 165–78; Francisco Calcagno, "Manuel Saumell Robredo," *Diccionario biográfico cubano*, New York, 1878, p. 120.

73. Galan, *Cuba y sus sones*, p. 271.

74. *Recuerdos de Gottschalk*. See Lapique, *Música colonial cubana*, 1:292.

75. Hazard, *Cuba with Pen and Pencil*, p. 318.

76. Gottschalk to "Mon cher localista," n.d. 1860, Unidentified Letters, Gottschalk Collection, NYPL.

77. See *Gaceta de la Habana*, 21 May 1854.

78. *Ibid.*, 7 June 1854; Gottschalk, *Notes of a Pianist*, p. 51.

79. *Diario de la Marina*, 7, 15 June 1854.

80. *Gaceta de la Habana*, 6 July 1854.

81. *Ibid.*, 13 July 1854; *Diario de la Marina*, 18 July 1854.

82. *Gaceta de la Habana*, 8 June 1854.

83. *Diario de la Marina*, 9 July 1854.

84. Aimée Gottschalk to Leonard Myers, 10 October 1854, Family Letters, Gottschalk Collection, NYPL.

85. *Diario de la Marina*, 10, 12 July 1854.

86. *Gaceta de la Habana*, 19 July 1854.

87. Junta Municipal de Caridad de la Villa de Cienfuegos to Gottschalk, 5 August 1854, MS, Glover Collection.

88. Edward Gottschalk's account book, Scrapbook no. 8, Gottschalk Collection, NYPL.

89. *Recuerdos cubanos. Hoja Economica*, 17 July 1854; see Rubin, "Gottschalk in Cuba," p. 55.

90. *Diario de la Marina*, 20 July 1854.

91. Hazard, *Cuba with Pen and Pencil*, p. 440.

92. Gabriel Debren, "Les Colons des Saint-Domingue refugies á Cuba, 1793–1815," *Revista de Indías*, 1953, 12:559–605; 1954, 14:11–36; see also Laureano Fuentes, *Las Artes en Santiago de Cuba: Apuntes históricos*, Santiago de Cuba, 1893.

93. On Tumba Francesa see María Teresa Linares, *La Música y el pueblo*, Havana, 1974, pp. 85ff. Tumba Francesa and other such groups in Santiago were permitted to hold dances in the public assembly rooms or *cabildos*, from which they took their name (Hazard, *Cuba with Pen and Pencil*, p. 196).

94. *El Redactor de Cuba* (Santiago), 19, 25 August 1854.

95. Hazard, *Cuba with Pen and Pencil*, p. 438.

96. Gottschalk to José Angelet, 29 August 1854, Fors, *Gottschalk*, pp. 82–83.

97. Fuentes, *Las Artes en Santiago de Cuba*, p. 75.

98. *El Redactor de Cuba*, 31 September 1854.

99. *Ibid.*, 15 September 1854. This work seems not to have been recorded in earlier catalogues.

100. Scrapbook no. 9, Gottschalk Collection, NYPL.

101. Emilio Bacardi y Moreau, *Crónicas de Santiago de Cuba*, 2nd edition, Santiago de Cuba, 1973, 3:120.

102. Gottschalk to José Angelet, 29 August 1854, p. 83.

103. *El Redactor de Cuba*, 6 October 1854.

104. For example, RO-37, -105, -109, etc.

105. Gottschalk to Aimée Gottschalk, 10 October 1854, Glover Collection.

106. Fuentes, *Las Artes en Santiago de Cuba*, p. 127.

107. Rauch, *American Interest in Cuba*, pp. 291–99; Eric Williams, *From Columbus to Castro: The History of the Caribbean, 1492–1969*, New York, 1970, pp. 413–14.

108. Hazard, *Cuba with Pen and Pencil*, pp. 511–17.

109. Gottschalk to José Angelet, 15 November 1854, Fors, *Gottschalk*, pp. 83–84.

110. Gottschalk to José Angelet, 23 November 1854, Fors, *Gottschalk*, pp. 84–85.

111. Fors, *Gottschalk*, pp. 87–89.

112. Misdated articles from Puerto Príncipe, Scrapbook no. 9, Gottschalk Collection, NYPL.

113. *Recuerdos de Puerto Príncipe* involved six pianos. See *Fanal* (Puerto Príncipe), 6 December 1854. Rubin, "Gottschalk in Cuba," p. 210. His *Caprichos on danses de Puerto Príncipe* included *La Caringa* and *María Lancero.* See RO-43.

114. Fors, *Gottschalk*, pp. 90–92.

115. *El Redactor de Cuba*, 10 February 1855; *Diario de la Marina*, 15 February 1855.

116. *Diario de la Marina*, 13 February 1855.

117. *La Prensa de la Habana*, 22 February 1855.

118. *Diario de la Marina*, 26 January 1855; also *Gaceta de la Habana*, 25 Feburary 1855.

119. Gottschalk to Aimée Gottschalk, 25 January 1855, Family Letters, Gottschalk Collection, NYPL.

120. *El Redactor de Cuba*, 10 February 1855.

121. *Gaceta de la Habana*, 25 February 1855.

13. Last Hopes, Dying Poets

1. William Mason, *Memories of a Musical Life*, p. 208. H. P. Main to William Hawes, 16 February 1899, Gottschalk Papers, Historic New Orleans Collection.

2. Mason, *Memories of a Musical Life*, p. 208.

3. William L. Hawes, a late-nineteenth-century insurance man in New Orleans, devoted dozens of letters and months of his life to finding a copy of the original *The Last Hope*. At length he succeeded. His report on "The Original *The Last Hope*" is in *Musical Record*, 1 July 1899, p. 13.

4. "Gottschalk's Western Experiences," unidentified newspaper, n.d., Scrapbook no. 2, Gottschalk Collection, NYPL.

5. Gottschalk, *Notes of a Pianist*, p. 96; a fuller version of this incident is in "Gottschalk's Western Experiences," unidentified newspaper, n.d., Scrapbook no. 2, Gottschalk Collection, NYPL.

6. *La France musicale*, 17 February 1856.

7. "La Última esperanza: fragment de la vida de un Artista," by Luís Ricardo Fors, unsigned, *La Tribuna* (Buenos Aires), 20 November 1868; also Fors, *Gottschalk*, pp. 205–14.

8. For all aspects of this and the following passage see Robert Offergeld, "More on the Gottschalk-Ives Connection," *Newsletter of the Institute for Studies in American Music*, May 1986, 6:1–2, 13.

9. A thorough review of the publishing history is to be found in Doyle, *Louis Moreau Gottschalk*, D-80, pp. 295–96.

10. Sanjek, *American Popular Music*, 2:69.

11. George P. Upton, *Musical Memories*, p. 77.

12. Gottschalk to William Hall, 24 October 1869, Hensel, *Life and Letters*, p. 175.

13. Lionel D. Wyld, *Low Bridge! Folklore and the Erie Canal*, Syracuse, 1962, pp. 77ff.

14. *Christy's Minstrels' 145 New Songs and Choruses in Vocal Score*, J. Wade, ed., London, n.d.

15. Howard, *Stephen Foster*, pp. 376–78.

16. Russell, *Cheer! Boys Cheer!*, p. 198.

17. Robert Offergeld, notes to "The Music of Democratic Sociability" (MS), Offergeld Papers, property of the author.

18. Sanjek, *American Popular Music*, 2:52–55.

19. RO-117.

20. Dieter Hildebrandt, *Piano Forte: A Social History of the Piano*, Harriet Goodman, trans., New York, 1988, pp. 121–27.

21. No musicologist has expounded this view more cogently than Chase, *America's Music*, ch. 9, "The Genteel Tradition"; a similar analysis is to be found in H. Wiley Hitchcock's chapter, "Cultivated and Vernacular Traditions and the Impact of Romanticism," *Music in the United States: A Historical Introduction*, Englewood Cliffs, 1988, pp. 43–82.

22. George T. Ferris, *Great Violinists and Pianists*, New York, 1895, p. 285.

23. Wilfred Mellers, *Music in a New Found Land*, New York, 1965, p. 253.

24. *Ibid.*, p. 250.

25. Schonberg, *The Great Pianists*, p. 219.

26. Mellers, *Music in a New Found Land*, p. 253.

27. Chase, *America's Music*, p. 166.

28. Fors, *Gottschalk*, p. 117.

29. Hensel, *Life and Letters*, p. 76.

30. *Ibid.*, pp. 157–58.

31. Gottschalk, *Notes of a Pianist*, p. 181.

32. Gottschalk, "Un Pianiste en Amérique," *L'Art musical*, 14 July 1864; also printed in *Standard*, 14 May 1864.

33. Gottschalk, "La Música el piano, los pianistas," Fors, *Gottschalk*, p. 334.

34. Clara M. Brinkerhoff, quoted in Hensel, *Life and Letters*, p. 191.

35. *Gottschalk's Concert Book*, New York, 1862, list of compositions.

36. Hensel, *Life and Letters*, p. 28; see also pp. 132–33.

37. Whitney R. Cross, *The Burned-over District*, Ithaca, 1950, ch. 1–3.

38. Gottschalk, *Notes of a Pianist*, pp. 238–39.

39. N. R. Espadero, "Prefatory Remarks by an Artist Friend of the Great Composer," *Posthumous Works of Louis Moreau Gottschalk*, Boston, 1872.

40. *Daily Courier* (Buffalo), 22 July 1862, NYPL. Peter J. Rabinowitz has argued that the experience of listening to Gottschalk was visual, rather than verbal: " 'With Our Own Dominant Passions'; Gottschalk, Gender and the Power of Listening," *Nineteenth-century Music*, Spring 1993, 16:247–49.

41. See "Pen, Pallet, and Piano," unsigned essay, *New York World*, 23 January 1865, pp. 117–21; copy preserved in Gottschalk clipping file, Music Library, NYPL. Also "Gottschalk," *Orchestra* (London), July 1877, pp. 371–73.

42. Op. 32, RO-190; D-114; D-114–A.

43. *Daily Globe* (Toronto), 17 July 1862.

44. Doyle, "The Piano Music of Louis Moreau Gottschalk," pp. 139–40.

45. Ferris, *Great Violinists and Pianists*, p. 285.

46. *Ibid.*, pp. 105–6.

47. *Godey's Lady's Book*, 1855, p. 89.

48. See Ruth E. Finley, *The Lady of Godey's: Sarah Josepha Hale*, Philadelphia and London, 1931, ch. 11, 12.

49. See Kathryn Kish Sklar, *Catherine Beecher: A Study in American Domesticity*, New Haven, 1973.

50. Maretzek, *Revelations of an Opera Manager*, p. 71.

51. *Ibid.*, p. 71.

52. See Kenneth A. Bernard, *Lincoln and the Music of the Civil War*, Caldwell, Idaho, 1966, pp. 196–97, fn. 14.

53. *Daily Alta California* (San Francisco), 13 May 1865.

54. *Ibid.*, 11 May 1865.

55. *Ibid.*, 2 August 1865.

56. *Ibid.*, 1 June 1865; see also *Daily Union* (Sacramento), 31 May 1865.

57. See the excellent discussion of this theme by Edward Shorter, "Towards a History of *La Vie Intime:* The Evidence of Cultural Criticism in Nineteenth-century Bavaria," *The Emergence of Leisure*, Michael R. Marrus, ed., New York, 1974, pp. 64–67.

58. Robert Offergeld, "Gottschalk and Company: The Music of Democratic Sociability" (MS), Offergeld Papers, possession of the author, courtesy of Dr. Marc L. Spero.

59. Loesser, *Men, Women, and Pianos*, p. 501.

14. Taking Root in New York, 1855

1. *Courrier de la Louisiane*, 10 March 1855.

2. *Daily Picayune*, 11 March 1855.

3. *Courrier de la Louisiane*, 13 March 1855.

4. *Daily Picayune*, 22 March 1855.

5. Fors, *Gottschalk*, p. 97.

6. *Courrier de la Louisiane*, 25, 27 March 1855.

7. *Ibid.*, 14 March 1855; *L'Abeille*, 13 March 1853.

8. This undocumented report is in Loggins, *Where the Word Ends*, p. 147.

9. *Daily Picayune*, 11 March 1855.

10. *Ibid.*, 28 March 1855.

11. *Courrier de la Louisiane*, 27 March 1855.

12. *Ibid.*, 2 April 1855; *Bee*, 2 April 1855; *Bee*, 24 April 1855, reports on a third trip that ended on Burthe Street in Carrollton.

13. Op. 61/62 (no. 2); D-117; Fors, *Gottschalk*, pp. 95–98, also pp. 219–21.

14. *Courrier de la Louisiane*, 2, 4, 5 May 1855; *Daily Picayune*, 2, 6 May 1855.

15. *Courrier de la Louisiane*, 10 June 1855.

16. N. Parker Willis, *Trenton Falls, Picturesque and Descriptive*, New York, 1851, p. 3.

17. Op. 40; D-125; RO-214.

18. *Trow's New York City Directory*, New York, 1856, p. 325.

19. Gottschalk to Aimée Gottschalk, undated letter, Family letters, Gottschalk Collection, NYPL.

20. Gottschalk photograph album, Glover Collection.

21. "America's First White House" (MS), no author, New-York Historical Society.

22. Copy of agreement between Firth Pond & Co. and an unnamed person, probably George Henriquez, 12 May 1854. Gottschalk Collection, NYPL.

23. On Hall see Sanjek, *American Popular Music*, 2:59–67.

24. Tawa, *Sweet Songs for Gentle Americans*, Bowling Green, Ohio, 1980, p. 112.

25. *New York Music Review*, 12 January 1856, p. 10.

26. Gottschalk, *Notes of a Pianist*, p. 69.

27. See references to this in William Hall's draft contract of 20 February 1862, Gottschalk Collection, NYPL.

28. Gottschalk's own chronological listing of his works, preserved in *Gottschalk's Concert Book*, following p. 10, includes for 1855 *The Banjo* (dating actually from 1853); *Marche de nuit; Rayons d'azur; Fantasie sur la Lucie; Fantasie sur "La Fille du Régiment"*; and *Isolement (Solitude)* (RO-239; D-139).

29. Escudier (*Les Virtuoses*, p. 188) lists eight works for 1855.

30. Gottschalk to Leonard Myers, n.d. 1855, Family Letters, Gottschalk Collection, NYPL.

31. *New York Times*, 20 March 1855.

32. Ritter, *Music in America*, pp. 296–98; for a splendid account of this farcical episode see Lawrence, "Reverberations," pp. 920–34.

33. Gottschalk to Espadero, n.d., Fors, *Gottschalk*, p. 398.

34. Lawrence, "Reverberations," p. 1054.

35. Hensel, *Life and Letters*, pp. 186–94.

36. *Dwight's Journal of Music*, 20 May 1854, p. 54; 23 September, p. 198; 30 September, pp. 203–4.

37. William Mason, *Memories of a Musical Life*, pp. 124ff.; also Kenneth G. Graber, *The Life and Works of William Mason (1829–1908)* (Ph.D. diss., University of Iowa, 1976), pp. 9ff.

38. Diploma dated 3 April 1855, Gottschalk Collection, NYPL.

39. Oscar Comettant, "Musical America 1850 as Seen Through a French Squint," Ivor D. Spencer, transl., *Music Educators Journal*, February 1969, 55:45.

40. Theodore Hagen, *Review & Gazette*, 3 November 1855, p. 366, quoted by Lawrence, "Reverberations," p. 344, fn. 166.

41. M. G. Maurique, "A Gottschalk"; Raphael Tombo, "A Gottschalk" (MS); both in Glover Collection.

42. Doña Hermegilda Benavente de Echenique, *El General Echenique, presidente, despojado del Perú en su vindicació en New York 1855;* also *El General Echenique, memorias para la historia del Peru (1808–1878)*, 2 vols., Lima, 1952.

43. R. E. Cunninghame Graham, *José Antonio Páez*, London, 1929, p. 291.

44. On Páez's musical interests see Francisco Curt Lange, "La musicalidad del general José Antonio Páez," *Revista Nacional de Cultura* (Caracas), January-March 1991, pp. 13–30. Lange suggests (p. 27) that Gottschalk first met Páez in Paris in 1851–52.

45. Gottschalk to Clara Gottschalk, 20 July 1863, Family Letters, Gottschalk Collection, NYPL.

46. Gottschalk to Aimée Gottschalk, 14 January 1856, Family Letters, Gottschalk Collection, NYPL.

47. Hensel, *Life and Letters*, p. 187.

48. Gottschalk to George Warren, 10 November 1855, Hensel, *Life and Letters*, pp. 71–72.

49. William H. Gerdts, *American Neo-Classical Sculpture: The Marble Resurrection*, New York, 1973, pp. 44–46.

50. Hensel, *Life and Letters*, p. 203.

51. *The Andes, Marche di Bravura, Homage to Church's Picture "The Heart of the Andes,"* W. A. Pond & Co., New York, 1863.

52. On Church see David C. Huntington, *The Landscapes of Frederic Edwin Church*, New York, 1966; Gerald L. Carr, *Frederic Edwin Church: The Icebergs*, Dallas, 1980.

53. D-160; F. E. Church to George Warren, 24 April 1856, Emmet Collection, Manuscript Division, NYPL.

54. Franklin Kelly, *Frederic Edwin Church*, Washington and London, 1988, p. 98.

55. See the essay from *New York World*, 23 January 1865(?), in Hensel, *Life and Letters*, pp. 202–3.

56. Gottschalk to Leonard Myers, n.d. (Spring 1857), Family Letters, Gottschalk Collection, NYPL; see also Frederic E. Church to Sen. [Leonard] Myers, 21 February 1857, Archives of American Art, copy at Olana State Historic Site, Hudson, New York.

57. F. E. Church to George Warren, 12 February 1857, Archives of American Art, copy at Olana State Historic Site, Hudson, New York.

58. Undated fragment no. 61, Gottschalk Collection, NYPL.

59. James L. Ford, *Forty-Odd Years in the Literary Shop*, New York, 1921, pp. 197ff.

60. William Winter, *Old Friends: Being Literary Recollections of Other Days*, New York, 1909, p. 62.

61. Don C. Seitz, *Artemus Ward (Charles Farrar Browne)*, New York and London, 1919, p. 125.

62. W. D. Howells, *Literary Friends and Acquaintances*, New York and London, 1900, p. 69.

63. L. M. Gottschalk, notebook entry, 13 July 1863, Notebook for 28 June–31 July 1863, Gottschalk Collection, NYPL.

64. Winter, *Old Friends*, p. 59.

65. Van Wyck Brooks, *The Times of Melville and Whitman*, Boston, 1947, p. 135.

66. See Charles Haywood, introduction to Maretzek, *Revelations of an Opera Manager*, pp. xxx–xxxi.

67. *Ibid.*

68. Winter, *Old Friends*, p. 96.

69. Gottschalk to Aimée Gottschalk, 16 November 1855, Family Letters, Gottschalk Collection, NYPL; on the conversion see Léon Beauvallet, *Rachel and the New World*, New York, 1856, p. 178.

70. Gottschalk to Aimée Gottschalk, 16 October 1855, Family Letters, Gottschalk Collection, NYPL.

71. *New York Times*, 29 November 1855.

72. *Ibid.;* also Lawrence, "Reverberations," pp. 1043–48.

73. *Ibid.*

74. Thomas, *A Musical Autobiography*, pp. 38–39.

75. Beauvallet, *Rachel and the New World*, pp. 118, 142.

76. Gottschalk to Aimée Gottschalk, 16 November 1855, Family Letters, Gottschalk Collection, NYPL.

77. Program, Glover Collection.

78. "Another Concert," unidentified Lancaster newspaper, ca. 15 November 1855, Scrapbook no. 4, Gottschalk Collection, NYPL.

79. Gottschalk to George William Warren, 10 November 1855, Clara Gottschalk Peterson, "Biographical Sketch," p. 71.

80. Clara Gottschalk Peterson, "Biographical Sketch," p. 71.

81. Barzun, *Berlioz and the Romantic Century*, p. 332.

82. Gottschalk to Aimée Gottschalk, 16 November 1855, Family Letters, Gottschalk Collection, NYPL.

83. Gottschalk to Aimée Gottschalk, 5 August 1856, Family Letters, Gottschalk Collection, NYPL.

84. *Sunday Dispatch* (Philadelphia), 11, 15 November 1855; *Pennsylvania Inquirer*, 12, 15 November 1855.

85. *Pennsylvania Inquirer*, 15 November 1855.

86. Gottschalk to "My Dear General [Hall]," n.d., Theater and Music Collection, Museum of the City of New York.

87. Gottschalk, *Notes of a Pianist*, p. 268. This offer was made originally in May 1855. See Gottschalk to D. José Angelet, 18 May 1855, Fors, *Gottschalk*, p. 98.

15. American Triumph: The Dodworth's Hall Concerts and the Great Non-Battle with Thalberg

1. Gottschalk, *Notes of a Pianist*, p. 49. Gottschalk conflated the dates of his first meeting with Hall and Hall's decision to sponsor the Dodworth's Hall Concerts. But Hall would have had no reason to mount the concerts unless he could be sure they would promote the sale of Gottschalk editions actually available through him.

2. *Albion* (New York), 17 November 1855.

3. *Courrier des États-Unis*, 12 December 1855.

4. *New York Times*, 15 December 1855.

5. Gottschalk to Leonard Myers, 29 December 1855, Family Letters, Gottschalk Collection, NYPL.

6. *Courrier des États-Unis*, 20 December 1855.

7. Quoted by Lawrence, "Reverberations," p. 1052. I am indebted to Vera Brodsky Lawrence for her comprehensive review of the critical response to the Dodworth's Hall series.

8. *Frank Leslie's Illustrated Newspaper*, 29 December 1855, p. 42.

9. Gottschalk to Leonard Myers, 29 December 1855, Family Letters, Gottschalk Collection, NYPL.

10. *New York Times*, 22 December 1855.

11. *Review & Gazette*, 29 December 1855, p. 432.

12. Gottschalk to Leonard Myers, 29 December 1855, Family Letters, Gottschalk Collection, NYPL.

13. *Evening Post*, 29 December 1855. Naturally, Dwight's anonymous New York correspondent faulted Gottschalk for his rendition of Weber's *Concertstück* (*Dwight's Journal of Music*, 5 January 1856, p. 108).

14. *Spirit of the Times*, 5 January 1856, p. 564.

15. Gottschalk, *Notes of a Pianist*, pp. 67–68. Also Gottschalk to Aimée Gottschalk, 14 January 1856, Family Letters, Gottschalk Collection, NYPL.

16. Hensel, *Life and Letters*, p. 190.

17. Hagen in *Review & Gazette*, 23 February 1856, p. 50.

18. *New York Times*, 9 January 1856.

19. *Review & Gazette*, 9 February 1856, p. 34.

20. *Frank Leslie's Illustrated Newspaper*, 19 January 1856, p. 30.

21. *Musical World*, 26 January 1856, p. 37.

22. *Atlas* (New York), 27 January 1856.

23. Op. 65, RO-239; D-139; also known as *Isolement*.

24. *Gottschalk's Concert Book*, n.d., following p. 10.

25. *Courrier des États-Unis*, 22 January 1856; *Atlas*, 27 January 1856, reports that the program took place on the 29th and included the harpist Aptomas.

26. *Courrier des États-Unis*, 4 February 1856.

27. *Frank Leslie's Illustrated Newspaper*, 16 February 1856, p. 151.

28. *New York Times*, 7 February 1856.

29. *Ibid.*, 14 February 1856.

30. Op. 77, RO-220; D-128.

31. *Albion*, 1 March 1856, p. 103.

32. *Frank Leslie's Illustrated Newspaper*, 8 March 1856, p. 199.

33. *New York Times*, 26 February 1856.

34. Lawrence, "Reverberations," p. 1062.

35. *Courrier des États-Unis*, 25 February 1856; *Atlas*, 24 February 1856.

36. Lawrence, "Reverberations," p. 1066.

37. *Ibid.*, p. 1067.

38. *Atlas*, 30 March 1856.

39. *Priére au soir*, D-80; the *Galop di bravura* is based on an original by Alfred Quidant (1815–93). A one-piano version of this work entitled *Tournament Gallop* was published in 1854.

40. Described in the program of 7 June as *Rayons et ombres, sérenade*, the name Gottschalk assigned to a series of twelve works, of which only four were published.

41. *Atlas*, 13 April 1856.

42. *Courrier des États-Unis*, 28 February 1856.

43. *Ibid.*, 2 June 1856; *New York Times*, 23 May 1856.

44. *Atlas*, 2 March 1856.

45. *Ibid.*, 6, 23 March 1856.

46. Jacques Offenbach, *Offenbach in America*, Paris, 1877, p. 147.

47. *Courrier des États-Unis*, 4 February 1856.

48. Diego de Vivo, "Gottschalk, the Adored," *New York Sun*, 14 March 1897, p. 71.

49. Fitz-James O'Brien, *The Poems and Stories of Fitz-James O'Brien*, William Winter, ed., Boston, 1881, p. 123.

50. *New York World*, n.d., quoted by Fors, *Gottschalk*, p. 142; also "Gottschalk à New York," *L'Art musical*, 15 May 1862, pp. 189–90.

51. Hensel, *Life and Letters*, p. 109.

52. *Frank Leslie's Illustrated Newspaper*, 3 May 1856, p. 327.

53. See Harris, *Humbug*, ch. 2.

54. *Chicago Journal*, December 1862, Scrapbook no. 4, Gottschalk Collection, NYPL.

55. Hoffman, *Some Musical Recollections of Fifty Years*, pp. 133–34. Also undated review, Scrapbook no. 4, Gottschalk Collection, NYPL.

56. The Russian critic Stassov, quoted in Sacheverell Sitwell, *Liszt*, New York, 1967, p. 105.

57. Clara Brinkerhoff, quoted in Hensel, *Life and Letters*, p. 190.

58. George P. Upton, *Musical Memories*, p. 78.

59. Schlesinger Jr., *The Age of Jackson*, p. 277.

60. N. Parker Willis, *Hurry-graphs*, p. 341.

61. Root, *The Story of a Musical Life*, p. 94; Carse, *The Life of Jullien*, p. 32.

62. Dayton, *Last Days of Knickerbocker Life*, p. 120.

63. N. Parker Willis, *Famous Persons and Places*, p. 434.

64. Richard Storrs Willis, *Musical World*, 5 January 1856, p. 1.

65. *New York Times*, 22 December 1855.

66. "Gottschalk's Posthumous Works," *Music*, March 1875, quoted by Doyle, *Louis Moreau Gottschalk*, p. 69.

67. *Daily Commercial* (Cincinnati), 2 April 1862.

68. *Daily Courier* (Cincinnati), 31 March 1862.

69. Hoffman, *Some Musical Recollections of Fifty Years*, p. 135.

70. *Chicago Tribune,* 18 April 1862.

71. *Daily Alta California,* 11 May 1865.

72. *New York Times,* 22 December 1855.

73. *Ibid.*

74. *Daily Journal* (Detroit), 7(?) January 1863, Scrapbook no. 4, Gottschalk Collection, NYPL.

75. Hensel, *Life and Letters,* p. 210.

76. *Daily Courier* (Cincinnati), 31 March 1862.

77. Unidentified Chicago newspaper, 13(?) December 1864, Scrapbook no. 4, Gottschalk Collection, NYPL.

78. *New York Times,* 3 May 1862.

79. *Trow's New York City Directory,* New York, 1856, p. 325.

80. L. M. Gottschalk, Last Will and Testament, 14 June 1856, Gottschalk Collection, NYPL.

81. Gottschalk to Aimée Gottschalk, 6 August 1856, Family Letters, Gottschalk Collection, NYPL.

82. Original place unknown, but partially quoted in letter to George Warren, n.d., Hensel, *Life and Letters,* p. 71.

83. This was the title of a Broadway entertainment offered in 1853 and 1855. Max Maretzek appropriated the title for his own memoirs.

84. The only known articles by "Seven Octaves" to appear under the heading "Crotchets and Quavers" are from undated numbers of *Morning Times,* and are preserved in Scrapbook no. 2, Gottschalk Collection, NYPL.

85. Richard Jackson, "An American Muse Learns to Walk: The First Organization Devoted to the Performance of Concert Music Composed in This Country" (MS), 1992, courtesy of the author. See also Zuck, *A History of Musical Americanism,* pp. 36–37.

86. Jackson, "An American Muse" p. 7.

87. *Ibid.,* p. 4. Also Cooke, *John Sullivan Dwight,* p. 182

88. *Dwight's Journal of Music,* 20 December 1856, p. 93

89. Lawrence, "Reverberations," p. 1177.

90. *Musical World,* 23 February 1856, p. 85.

91. *Ibid.,* 12 April 1856, p. 173.

92. *Ibid., Alone* is based on a text by General William Hopkins Morris (1827–1900). See Richard Jackson, ed., *The Complete Published Songs of Louis Moreau Gottschalk,* Newton Centre, Massachusetts, 1993, p. 13.

93. *Courrier des États-Unis,* 10 June 1856.

94. *Musical World,* 12 May 1855, p. 13.

95. George P. Upton, *Musical Memories,* p. 101.

96. These bizarre episodes are superbly described by Lawrence, "Reverberations," pp. 967, 1013.

97. *Daily Pennsylvanian* (Philadelphia), 29 April 1856; *Courrier des États-Unis,* 5 May 1856; Gottschalk to Leonard Myers, n.d., Family Letters, Gottschalk Collection, NYPL.

98. *New York Herald,* 7 June 1856; *Courrier des États-Unis,* 16 June 1856.

99. *Courrier des États-Unis,* 4 August 1856.

100. Johannes Magendanz, "Gottschalk in Utica," *Town Topics of the Mohawk Valley,* November 1932, p. 20.

101. Unidentified newspaper, Montreal, 14 July 1856, Scrapbook no. 5, Gottschalk Papers, NYPL.

102. Gottschalk to Aimée Gottschalk, 5 August 1856, Family Letters, Gottschalk

Collection, NYPL. For the definitive treatment of Gottschalk's Canadian ventures see Réginald Hamel, *Louis Moreau Gottschalk, son temps (1829–1869)*, Montreal, 1994, ch. 7.

103. *Courrier des États-Unis*, 4 August 1856.

104. Gottschalk to Aimée Gottschalk, 5 August 1856, Family Letters, Gottschalk Collection, NYPL.

105. *Courrier des États-Unis*, 11, 18 August 1856.

106. *Atlas*, 12 October 1856.

107. *Dwight's Journal of Music*, 18 October 1856, p. 23.

108. *Ibid.*, 13 September 1856, p. 191.

109. *Courrier des États-Unis*, 8 September 1856.

110. *Ibid.*, 19 September 1856; *Frank Leslie's Illustrated Newspaper*, 20 September 1856, p. 227.

111. *New York Times*, 22 September 1856.

112. Charles G. Leland, *Memoirs*, New York, 1893, p. 227.

113. *Chopin's Letters*, E. L. Voynich, ed., New York, 1931, p. 133.

114. *New York Herald*, 6 October 1856.

115. *Dwight's Journal of Music*, 11 October 1856, p. 14.

116. Schonberg, *The Great Pianists*, pp. 172–77.

117. Hoffman, *Some Musical Recollections*, p. 129.

118. Gottschalk to Aimée Gottschalk, 10 October 1856, Glover Collection.

119. *New York Times*, 14 November 1856.

120. Quoted by Lawrence, "Reverberations," p. 1110.

121. Gottschalk to (Léon?) Escudier, undated letter no. 41, Gottschalk Collection, NYPL.

122. Posters for their appearance in Baltimore (23 November) and Philadelphia (13 December) are preserved in the collection of Harold Linebach, St. Louis.

123. *Sunday Times*, 18 January 1857.

124. *New York Herald*, 11 November 1856.

125. *New York Times*, 11 November 1856.

126. *Atlas*, 16 November 1856.

127. *Ibid.*, 14 December 1856.

128. Lawrence, "Reverberations," p. 1110.

129. *Review & Gazette*, 29 November 1856, p. 371.

130. *Dwight's Journal of Music*, 15 November 1856, p. 55.

131. *Atlas*, 16 November 1856.

132. *Sunday Times*, 18 January 1857.

133. Kellogg, *Memoirs of an American Prima Donna*, p. 106.

134. *Atlas*, 23 November 1856.

135. *New York World*, 22 January 1870; *Courrier des États-Unis*, 24 November 1856.

136. *New York Times*, 26 December 1856.

137. *Atlas*, 1 March 1857; *New York Times*, 19 March 1857.

138. *Ibid.*, 1 March 1857.

139. *Ibid.*, 7, 12 December 1856; also *Dwight's Journal of Music*, 20 December 1856, p. 92.

140. Gottschalk to Aimée Gottschalk, 10 October 1856, Glover Collection.

141. Doyle, *Louis Moreau Gottschalk*, p. 262.

142. Herman Klein, *The Reign of Patti*, New York, 1920, ch. 1; Louis Engel, *From*

Mozart to Mario, 2 vols., London, 1886, 1:248ff.; Maurice Strakosch, *Souvenirs d'un impressario,* Paris, 1887, pp. 11ff.

143. *La Prensa* (Havana), 19 December 1856.

144. *New York Times,* 10 December 1856.

145. *Courrier des États-Unis,* 18, 22 December 1856.

146. *New York Times,* 27 December 1856.

147. Hoffman, *Some Musical Recollections,* pp. 130–31.

148. Even this was not the last Gottschalk-Thalberg performance, as the two teamed up again in Albany on 27 January.

149. *Courrier des États-Unis,* 10 January 1857; *Atlas,* 11 January 1857.

150. *New York Times,* 13 January 1857; *Dwight's Journal of Music,* 17 January 1857, p. 125.

151. *New York Musical Review and Gazette,* 24 January 1857, pp. 18–19.

152. Photograph no. 62, Iconography Folder 1, Gottschalk Collection, NYPL.

153. *La France musicale,* 2 August 1857.

154. Gottschalk to Arnold Myers, n.d., Family Letters, Gottschalk Collection, NYPL. These materials have not been found.

155. Frederick Edwin Church to George Warren, Emmet Collection, Manuscript Division, NYPL, copy at Olana State Historic Site, Hudson, New York.

16. Ada Clare

1. See Return of a Birth, no. 317638, 1881 August 7, Bureau of Vital Statistics, Health Department, City of New York; also Loggins, *Where the Word Ends,* pp. 150–71. The evidence for the 1859 date is reviewed by Gloria R. Goldblatt in her excellent but regrettably unpublished biography, "Ada Clare, Queen of Bohemia" (MS), 1990, pp. 116–18. Aubrey's contrary claim was asserted in 1881, when his son was born. The only published study on Clare is Albert Parry, *Garrets and Pretenders: A History of Bohemianism in America,* New York, 1933, pp. 14–27. Cf. also *Notable American Women,* 1:339–40.

2. Thomas Butler Gunn, "Diaries" (MS), Missouri Historical Society, St. Louis, vol. 13, December 1859, 13 April 1860. Courtesy of Gloria R. Goldblatt, St. Louis.

3. A. L. Rowson, "A Bygone Bohemia," *Frank Leslie's Popular Monthly Illustrated,* January 1896, p. 102.

4. Goldblatt, "Ada Clare," p. 119.

5. Marie Howland to Edmund Clarence Stedman, Fair Hope, Alabama, 21 April 1907, Special Collections, Butler Library, Columbia University.

6. The Clapp-Whitman view is implicit in their claim that Aubrey was born before Ada departed for Paris in January 1857. Clara Barrus, *Whitman and Burroughs: Comrades,* Boston and New York, 1931, p. 2.

7. Charles Warren Stoddard, quoted by Emily Hahn, *Romantic Rebels: An Informal History of Bohemianism in America,* Boston, 1967, p. 4.

8. Parry, *Garrets and Pretenders,* p. 360.

9. New York City directories, 1883–87; Marie Howland to Edmund C. Stedman, 21 June 1894, Special Collections, Butler Library, Columbia University. Aubrey's stage name was A. C. Noyes.

10. Ada Clare to William Stuart, n.d. (8 January 1867, 25 March 1867), Harvard Theatre Collection, Harvard College Library.

11. Charles Warren Stoddard, "Ada Clare, Queen of Bohemia," *National Magazine*, September 1905, p. 641.

12. Obituary, *New York Clipper*, 14 March 1874; also *Leslie's Weekly*, 14 March 1874; Marie Howland, "Biographical Sketch of Edward Howland," *Credit Fonçier* (Mexico), 15 June 1891, pp. 117–19.

13. Howells, *Literary Friends and Acquaintances*, p. 72; see also William Winter, "Ada," *Wanderers*, New York, 1892, pp. 157–59.

14. Horace Traubel, *With Walt Whitman in Camden*, New York, 1914, 3:117; Walt Whitman, *The Correspondence*, Edwin Haviland Miller, ed., New York, 1961, 2:285.

15. George Howe, *History of the Presbyterian Church in South Carolina*, Columbia, 1870, pp. 302, 611–13.

16. Goldblatt, "Ada Clare," pp. 2–7.

17. Daniel Moley McKeithan, "Paul Hamilton Hayne and the *Southern Bivouac*," *University of Texas Studies in English*, no. 17 (1912), pp. 112–31.

18. *The Correspondence of Bayard Taylor and Paul Hamilton Hayne*, Charles Duffy, ed., Baton Rouge, 1945.

19. *The Era*, 19 June 1864; Goldblatt, "Ada Clare," pp. 13ff.

20. *Ibid.*

21. A.A.M. (Ada McElhenney), "The Rationale of Watering Places," *Charleston College Magazine*, November 1854, pp. 168–73.

22. Diary of Edward McCrady Sr., May-June 1854, McCrady Papers, Manuscript Collection, South Carolina Historical Society, Charleston, South Carolina; Goldblatt, "Ada Clare," p. 27.

23. William Hayne to Marie Howland, 16 February 1897.

24. Ada Clare, "To Thee Alone," *Charleston College Magazine*, 1954, p. 267; reprinted in *Atlas*, 7 December 1856.

25. Ada Clare, "Whips and Scorns of Time," *Atlas*, 7 December 1856.

26. A.A.M. (Ada McElhenney), "Tennyson's *Princess*," *Charleston College Magazine*, May 1854, pp. 45–49.

27. *National Era*, 1854, no. 399.

28. Ada McElhenney to Julian Mitchell, 1 September 1854, South Carolina Historical Society.

29. Ray Reynolds, *Cat's Paw Utopia*, El Cajon, California, 1972, pp. 37ff.; also Goldblatt, "Ada Clare," pp. 50–55.

30. Madeleine B. Stern, *The Pantarch: A Biography of Steven Pearl Andrews*, Boston, 1968, pp. 86–89.

31. Stern, *The Pantarch*, p. 90.

32. Charles Dickens, *Bleak House*, reprint, New York, 1977, p. 29.

33. Ada McElhenney to Julian E. Mitchell, 25 September 1854, Julian Mitchell Papers, Mitchell-Pringle Collection, South Carolina Historical Society.

34. Goldblatt, "Ada Clare," pp. 43–44.

35. Barrus, *Whitman and Burroughs: Comrades*, p. 2.

36. Paul Hayne to Richard H. Stoddard, 28 August 1855, quoted by Goldblatt, "Ada Clare," p. 46. For Ada Clare's version see Ada Clare to Julian Mitchell, 1 September 1855, Julian Mitchell Papers, Manuscript Collection, South Carolina Library, University of South Carolina, Columbia, South Carolina.

37. *Atlas*, 2 December 1855.

38. Goldblatt, "Ada Clare," p. 56.

39. *Ibid.*, p. 70.

40. Zavarr Wilmshurst (William Bennett), "To Ada Clare," *Atlas*, 2 November 1856.

41. *The Complete Poetical Works of Percy Bysshe Shelley*, Boston, 1901, p. 53.
42. Alastor, "Model Concerts," *Atlas*, 16 November 1856.
43. Alastor, "Brewers of Small Beer," *Atlas*, 23 November 1856.
44. Alastor, "The Automaton Pianist," *Atlas*, 30 November 1856.
45. Alastor, "Whips and Scorns of Time," *Atlas*, 7 December 1856.
46. *Atlas*, 28 December 1856.
47. Alastor, "Ada Clare on Suicide," *Atlas*, 4 January 1857.
48. Ada McElhenney to Julian Mitchell, 12 November 1854, Julian Mitchell Papers.
49. *Ibid.*, 29 November 1854, Julian Mitchell Papers.
50. *Atlas*, 4 January 1857.
51. Goldblatt, "Ada Clare," p. 86.

17. Souvenir de Porto Rico

1. *Prensa de la Habana*, quoted in *Courrier de la Louisiane*, 19 December 1856.
2. *Diario de la Marina*, 12 February 1857; *Gaceta de la Habana*, 14 February 1857.
3. Hensel, *Life and Letters*, p. 73.
4. Goldblatt, "Ada Clare," p. 91.
5. *Gaceta de la Habana*, 20 February 1857.
6. *New York Times*, 25 May 1857.
7. Hensel, *Life and Letters*, p. 75.
8. Gottschalk, *Notes of a Pianist*, p. 121; cf. undated fragment from *Standard*, unfiled clippings, Gottschalk Collection, NYPL.
9. *Voyage musical en Allemagne et en Italie*, 2 vols., Paris, 1844.
10. Albert H. Smyth, *Bayard Taylor*, Boston, 1896, p. 95.
11. Gottschalk, *Notes of a Pianist*, p. 39.
12. *New York Times*, 30 December 1856.
13. Ramirez, *La Habana artística*, p. 262.
14. *Gaceta de la Habana*, 20, 22 February 1857.
15. *Ibid.*, 28 February 1857.
16. *Ibid.*, 4 March 1857.
17. Gottschalk to "Clarinett" (Clara) Gottschalk, 12 March 1857, Family Letters, Gottschalk Collection, NYPL.
18. Undated fragment no. 62, Gottschalk Collection, NYPL.
19. *Diario de la Habana*, 26 March 1857.
20. Undated fragment no. 62, Gottschalk Collection, NYPL.
21. *Ibid.*
22. *L'Abeille*, 29 June 1857; *Diario de la Marina*, 5 April 1857.
23. Laureano Fuentes Matons, *Las Artes en Santiago de Cuba*, Havana, 1981, pp. 193–95.
24. *L'Abeille*, 15 June 1857.
25. *Diario de la Habana*, 11, 13 May 1857.
26. Gottschalk, *Notes of a Pianist*, pp. 16–18.
27. *Prensa de la Habana*, 31 May 1857; *Gaceta de la Habana*, 31 May 1857. For all aspects of Gottschalk on St. Thomas see Donald Thompson, "Gottschalk in the Virgin Islands," *Anuario: Yearbook of Inter-American Musical Research*, Austin, 1970, pp. 95–104.
28. *La France musicale*, 24 January 1858.

29. Gottschalk, *Notes of a Pianist*, p. 10.

30. *Ibid.*, p. 18. Thompson, "Gottschalk in the Virgin Islands," pp. 95–97, questions the date of this visit and rightly notes the absence of firm corroborating evidence. Yet no other chronology appears possible.

31. Graham, *José Antonia Páez*, p. 298.

32. 23 June–July 1857; Thompson, "Gottschalk in the Virgin Islands," pp. 98–102. *La France musicale*, 9 August 1857, p. 264.

33. Gottschalk, *Notes of a Pianist*, p. 15.

34. Gottschalk to Arnold Myers, 10 July 1857, Family Letters, Gottschalk Collection, NYPL.

35. Gottschalk, *Notes of a Pianist*, p. 16.

36. Gottschalk to Arnold Myers, 10 July 1857, Family Letters, Gottschalk Collection, NYPL.

37. Thompson, "Gottschalk in the Virgin Islands," p. 102.

38. *Boletin mercantil de Puerto Rico*, 5 August 1862; Donald Thompson, "Nineteenth-century Musical Life in Puerto Rico," *Die Musik Kultur in Lateinamerika im 19. Jahrhundert*, comp. Robert Günther, Regensburg, 1982, p. 329; on Gottschalk in Puerto Rico, see Emilio J. Pasarell, "El Centenario de los conciertos de Adelina Patti y Luis Moreau Gottschalk en Puerto Rico," *Revista del Instituto de Cultura Puertorriqueña*, January-March 1959, pp. 52–55; Emilio J. Pasarell, *Orígenes y desarrollo de la afición teatral en Puerto Rico*, San Juan, 1970, pp. 101–5; and Donald Thompson, "El Joven Tavarez: Nuevos Documentos y nuevas perspectivas," *La Revista de Centro de Estudios Avanzados de Puerto Rico y el Caribe*, July-December 1990, pp. 71–72.

39. *Biografia de las Riquezas de Puerto Rico*, 7 vols., San Juan, 1902, 1:26–27; *Gaceta de Puerto Rico*, 17 October 1878; also Denisse Pulliza, "Azucar en Puerto Rico, Central Plazuela, La Plazuela" (Master's thesis, Centro de Estudios Avanzados de Puerto Rico y el Caribe, San Juan).

40. Gottschalk, *Notes of a Pianist*, pp. 19–20; Gottschalk to "Julio," undated letter no. 72, Gottschalk Collection, NYPL.

41. "Bayamon d. Cornelio Kortright," *Gobernadores Españoles*, Box 102, Record Group 186, Puerto Rico General Archive.

42. Logsdon, "Gottschalk's *Workbook.*"

43. Fors, *Gottschalk*, pp. 370–71. See also Hensel, *Life and Letters*, pp. 75–76; Gottschalk, *Notes of a Pianist*, p. 306.

44. Gottschalk to Leonard Myers, n.d. (1857–?), Family Letters, Gottschalk Collection, NYPL.

45. *Ibid.*

46. *Democrat Gazette*, n.d. 1863, Scrapbook no. 4, Gottschalk Collection, NYPL.

47. *Di qui sí*, Edelmann, no. 23 Obrapia, Havana, Museo de la Música, Havana.

48. Gottschalk to Edward Gottschalk Jr., 8 January 1858, Family Letters, Gottschalk Collection, NYPL.

49. Lapique, *Música colonial cubana*, p. 195.

50. Hector Campos Parsi, "La Música en Puerto Rico," *La gran enciclopedia de Puerto Rico*, San Juan, 1976, 7:82–88.

51. Garcia de Arboleya, *Manual de la isla de Cuba*, Havana, 1859, p. 260; also Argeliers, *Del Canto y el tiempo*, pp. 217–21.

52. Pasarell, "El Centenario de los conciertos de Adelina Patti y Luis Moreau Gottschalk," pp. 52–53.

53. Doyle, "The Piano Music of Louis Moreau Gottschalk", pp. 146–48.

54. Gottschalk to Blanche Gottschalk, 9 December 1857, Family Letters, Gottschalk Collection, NYPL.

55. Luis Veglio Merle, interviewed by Gloria Vega of the Biblioteca General de Puerto Rico, said that his great grandfather, Bernardo Merle, born at Mayagüez, was Patti's principal suitor, that it was he who brought the musicians to Puerto Rico, and that their travels there were defined by the locations of his various homes. This is not confirmed by other evidence. Professor Donald Thompson points to a body of literature establishing that the Ríos' family home was not in Mayagüez but in the town of Humacao. Cf. *New York Evening Journal*, 11, 18, 25 June 1927; *El Tiempo* (San Juan), 19 July 1927.

56. Gottschalk to Arnold Myers, 18 December 1857, Family Letters, Gottschalk Collection, NYPL.

57. *La France musicale*, 25 October 1857, 8 November 1857.

58. Gladys E. Tormes, Archivo Municipal, Ponce.

59. Emilio J. Pasarell, *Esculcando el siglo XIX en Puerto Rico*, Barcelona, 1967, pp. 131–32.

60. Gottschalk to "Julio," undated letter no. 72, Gottschalk Collection, NYPL.

61. Linares, *La Música y el pueblo*, p. 53.

62. Offergeld, *Centennial Catalog*, p. 30, RO-263. See also Doyle, *Louis Moreau Gottschalk*, regarding *El Silvidio*, possibly from Ponce, p. 250.

63. Pasarell, *Orígines y desarrollo*, p. 103.

64. Gottschalk to Edward Gottschalk Jr., 8 January 1858, Family Letters, Gottschalk Collection, NYPL.

65. Pasarell, *Orígenes y desarrollo*, p. 104.

66. Gottschalk to Arnold Myers, 5 August 1858, Family Letters, Gottschalk Collection, NYPL.

67. The sole source of information on the incident is Fors, *Gottschalk*, pp. 223–29.

68. Later performed at Basse-Terre, Guadeloupe, 8 June 1858, but now lost. *Gazette officielle de la Guadaloupe*, 14 June 1858.

69. *El Fénix* (San Juan), 29 May 1858; *La France musicale*, 13 June 1858.

70. *Courrier de la Louisiane*, 8 June 1858.

71. RO-211, -215, -283; Logsdon, "Gottschalk's *Work Book*," Example 11; Pasarell, *Origines y desarrollo*, pp. 105ff.

72. Gottschalk to Arnold Myers, 5 August 1858, Family Letters, Gottschalk Collection, NYPL.

18. Matouba: Nights in the Tropics

1. Gottschalk to Arnold Myers, 5 August 1858, Family Letters, Gottschalk Collection, NYPL.

2. See account sheet from Martinique and Trinidad, Scrapbook no. 9, Gottschalk Collection, NYPL.

3. Fors, *Gottschalk*, pp. 230–32.

4. *Barbados Globe* (Bridgetown), 2 August 1858. This and other clippings are preserved in Scrapbook no. 4, Gottschalk Collection, NYPL.

5. Gottschalk to Arnold Myers, 5 August 1858, Family Letters, Gottschalk Collection, NYPL.

6. Gottschalk to "Charly" (Charles Vezin), n.d., uncatalogued letters, Gottschalk Collection, NYPL.

7. Gottschalk to Charles Vezin, n.d., uncatalogued letters, Gottschalk Collection, NYPL; invitation from Gottschalk to Governor Lyons, n.d., Glover Collection; concert program of 24 August 1858, Gottschalk Collection, NYPL. For information on Gottschalk's Jewish contacts I am grateful to Réginald Hamel of Montreal.

8. Gottschalk to Arnold Myers, 5 August 1858, Family Letters, Gottschalk Collection, NYPL.

9. Loggins, *Where the Word Ends*, p. 175.

10. Gottschalk, *Notes of a Pianist*, p. 40; Gottschalk to "Maria," n.d. (summer 1860, Caimito, Cuba), Undated Letters, Gottschalk Collection, NYPL.

11. Gottschalk, *Notes of a Pianist*, p. 54. Réginald Hamel of the Université of Montréal has examined newspapers in Georgetown and New Amsterdam and found no confirmation of Gottschalk's presence in either city, thus leaving us dependent on one reference in *Notes of a Pianist*.

12. Alan Kimball, *Paganini, a Biography*, London, 1983, p. 21.

13. Gottschalk, *Notes of a Pianist*, p. 25.

14. Lafcadio Hearn, *Two Years in the French West Indies*, New York, 1923, p. 26.

15. Gottschalk to Arnold Myers, June 1859, undated letter no. 36, Family Letters, Gottschalk Collection, NYPL.

16. Gottschalk to Léon Escudier, n.d., uncatalogued letters, Gottschalk Collection, NYPL; Gottschalk, *Notes of a Pianist*, pp. 22–23.

17. Undated fragment no. 71, Gottschalk Collection, NYPL.

18. *La France musicale*, 20 February 1859; cf. *Muzykalnyi svet*, April 1859, pp. 25–27, where this work leads an essayist to call Gottschalk the "colorist of the piano."

19. *La France d'outre-mer*, 25 February 1859.

20. *La France musicale*, 20 February 1859.

21. Gottschalk, *Notes of a Pianist*, p. 21.

22. RO-128.

23. *Gazette officielle de la Guadeloupe*, 14 June 1859.

24. Preface to William Hall & Son edition, New York, 1863.

25. Clara Brinkerhoff, quoted in Hensel, *Life and Letters*, p. 190.

26. *Dwight's Journal of Music*, 31 October 1856, p. 23.

27. See Offergeld's hypothesis on this opera, *Centennial Catalogue*, RO-125.

28. *Reforma* (Rio de Janeiro), 21 December 1869.

29. Gottschalk to his sisters, 2 November 1860, Family Letters, Gottschalk Collection, NYPL.

30. See Doyle, *Louis Moreau Gottschalk*, MS-2, D-3.

31. Julian Budden, *The Operas of Verdi*, 3 vols., New York, 1979, 2:360–66.

32. Gottschalk to his sisters, 2 November 1860, Family Letters, Gottschalk Collection, NYPL.

33. Boudin, *The Operas of Verdi*, 2:365.

34. Gottschalk to Arnold Myers, undated letter no. 36, Family Letters, Gottschalk Collection, NYPL.

35. *La France musicale*, 8 May 1859.

36. Rubin, "Gottschalk in Cuba," p. 77. Réginald Hamel has suggested in a letter to the author that Gottschalk's departure was also hastened by conflicts with the French governor, M. de Maussion de Candé.

37. Gottschalk to Arnold Myers, undated letter no. 36, Family Letters, Gottschalk Collection, NYPL; *La France musicale*, 26 June 1859.

38. *Gazette officielle de la Guadeloupe*, 7 June 1859.

39. *Ibid.*, 14 June 1859.

40. *La France musicale*, 21 August 1859.

41. *Ibid.*

42. Gottschalk, *Notes of a Pianist*, p. 42.

43. Hensel, *Life and Letters*, p. 75.

44. Marguerite F. Aymar, quoted by Hensel, *Life and Letters*, p. 196.

45. *La France musicale*, 4 September 1859; "Notes of a Pianist," *Atlantic Monthly*, February 1865, pp. 177–80 and March 1865, pp. 350–52; Gottschalk, *Notes of a Pianist*, pp. 40–42.

46. Gottschalk, *Notes of a Pianist*, pp. 41–43. (Syntax corrected by author.)

47. *Ibid.*, pp. 40–41.

48. P. Ballivel, *Nos paroisses de 1635 à nos jours*, Basse-Terre, Guadeloupe, n.d., pp. 131–35.

49. See Fabre, *De clochers en clockers: Saint-Claude*, Basse-Terre, 1977. The bottling works for L'eau Matouba now stand on the site of Gottschalk's retreat.

50. Gottschalk, *Notes of a Pianist*, p. 53.

51. Jackson and Ratliff, *The Little Book of Louis Moreau Gottschalk*, pp. 20–21.

52. Quoted by Hensel, *Life and Letters*, p. 103.

53. *Life of Louis Moreau Gottschalk*, New York, 1863, p. 11.

54. Fors, *Gottschalk*, p. 443; Jackson and Ratliff, *The Little Book of Louis Moreau Gottschalk*, pp. 16–17.

55. *Life of Louis Moreau Gottschalk*.

56. *Ibid.*

57. *La France musicale*, 4 September 1859.

58. Doyle, *Louis Moreau Gottschalk*, D-38.

59. *O ma charmante, épargnez-moi!*, op. 44, Hall edition, 1862.

60. Jackson and Ratliff, *The Little Book of Louis Moreau Gottschalk*, pp. 17–20.

61. Hensel, *Life and Letters*, pp. 76–77.

62. RO-47.

63. RO-68, -72, -93, -145.

64. William E. Korf, *The Orchestral Music of Louis Moreau Gottschalk*, Henryville, Pennsylvania, 1983, pp. 62–85; John Cary Lewis, "A Study and Edition of Recently Discovered Works of Louis Moreau Gottschalk" (D.M.A. diss., University of Rochester, 1971), pp. 35ff.; Clyde Brockett Jr., "L. M. Gottschalk: Symphonie romantique 'La Nuit des tropiques' " (MS), courtesy of the author.

65. Carpentier, *La Música en Cuba*, p. 89.

66. *Revue et gazette musicale de Paris*, 14 March 1847, p. 86.

67. Hearn, *Two Years in the French West Indies*, p. 57.

68. Carr, *Frederic Edwin Church*, p. 28.

69. *La France d'outre mer*, 1 November 1859; *La France musicale*, 11 December 1859; undated fragments no. 77–79, Gottschalk Collection, NYPL; Gottschalk, *Notes of a Pianist*, pp. 23–25.

70. *La France musicale*, 23 October 1859, 13 November 1859.

71. *Ibid.*, 8 January 1860.

19. Havana Twilight

1. Gottschalk's photo album, Glover Collection.

2. *Gaceta de la Habana*, 29 November 1859, 4 December 1859.

3. *Ibid.*, 13 December 1859; misdated by Hensel, *Life and Letters*, p. 78.

4. *Gaceta de la Habana*, 20, 24 December 1859; *La Prensa de la Habana*, 20 December 1859.

5. *Gaceta de la Habana*, 29 January 1860.

6. Fors (*Gottschalk*, pp. 233–34) is the sole source for this dating; *Gaceta de la Habana* first mentions it (as a trio) on 17 October 1861.

7. Sanches de Frias, *Arthur Napoleão, resenha comemorativa*, Lisbon, 1913, pp. 130–31; Luiz Heitor Correa de Azevedo, "Arthur Napoléon, 1843–1925," *Arquivas de Centro cultural português*, Paris, 1971, 3:576ff.

8. *Gaceta de la Habana*, 28 February 1860; Hensel, *Life and Letters*, pp. 75–76.

9. *Dwight's Journal of Music*, 19 February 1859, pp. 375–76.

10. Antoine Marmontel to Gottschalk, 31 January 1866, Miscellaneous Letters, Gottschalk Collection, NYPL.

11. *Gaceta de la Habana*, 22 December 1859.

12. *Ibid.*, 25 December 1859.

13. *Ibid.*, 7 January 1860.

14. *Ibid.*

15. *Ibid.;* see Rubin's competent history of this event, *Gottschalk in Cuba*, pp. 81–89.

16. *Gaceta de la Habana*, 25 February 1860.

17. Personal communication from María-Teresa Linares, Director, Museo de la Música, Havana.

18. Chase, *The Music of Spain*, p. 128. On *Esceñas* see Lewis, "Recently Discovered Works of Gottschalk," pp. 1–26; Korf, *Orchestral Music*, pp. 87–104.

19. In 1840 a New Orleans promoter organized a ball on the *fête champêtre* theme; see Kmen, *Music in New Orleans*, p. 24.

20. *La Prensa de la Habana*, 16 February 1860.

21. On this controversy see Doyle, *Louis Moreau Gottschalk*, pp. 226; Korf, *Orchestral Music*, pp. 105–16; Edwin T. Tolon and Jorge A. Gonzalez, *Operas cubanas y sus autores*, pp. 46–51; "Aparece un tesoro musical," *Carteles*, 14 June 1942, p. 40. The author acknowledges the insights that Clyde W. Brockett gained from his examination of the manuscript in Havana. The study soon to be released by Rita Castro y Maya of Havana should resolve many points of uncertainty.

22. Jorge Antonio Gonzales, *La Composicion operastica en Cuba*, Havana, 1986, p. 78.

23. Gottschalk, *Notes of a Pianist*, pp. 26–27.

24. *Diario de la Marina*, 26 January 1860.

25. Fors, *Gottschalk*, p. 104.

26. *Gaceta de la Habana*, 10 February 1860.

27. *Ibid.*, 15 February 1860.

28. *Ibid.*, 8 February 1860.

29. *Diario de la Marina*, 17 February 1860.

30. *Gaceta de la Habana*, 17 February 1860.

31. *La Presna de la Habana*, 16 February 1860.

32. *Diario de la Marina*, 19 February 1860.

33. *Gaceta de la Habana*, 19 February 1860.

34. *Ibid.*, 27 May 1860.

35. *Ibid.*, 21 February 1860.

36. T. Secura, "Himno triumfal," 28 March 1860, unidentified newspaper, Scrapbook no. 4, Gottschalk Collection, NYPL.

37. Edwardo Jones, *Directorio de la ciudad de la Habana y estramuros*, 1840; Gottschalk, *Notes of a Pianist*, p. 26.

38. Jackson and Ratliff, *The Little Book of Louis Moreau Gottschalk*, pp. 21–22.

39. Published also as *Suis moi!*. *Gaceta de la Habana*, 4 August 1861.

40. Harold C. Schonberg, "The Whiff of a Vanished Age," *New York Times*, 18 October 1960.

41. *Gaceta de la Habana*, 16 December 1860.

42. Gottschalk to "Clarinette" (Clara Gottschalk), 3 March 1860, Family Letters, Gottschalk Collection, NYPL.

43. *Eco del Comercio*, 17 April 1860.

44. *Gaceta de la Habana*, 18, 21, 25, 27, 29 April, 7 June, 1860.

45. Photograph no. 65, Gottschalk Collection, NYPL.

46. "Ejercicios, pasages, arpegios, por L. M. Gottschalk y N. R. Espadero" (MS), Gottschalk Collection, NYPL. Cf. also *Étude de force en B major*, RO-82.

47. *Gaceta de la Habana*, 13 March 1860.

48. Gottschalk, "La Música, el piano, los pianistas," Fors, *Gottschalk*, pp. 323–52.

49. *Muzykalnyi svet*, 1861, no. 1, pp. 1–4.

50. Fors, *Gottschalk*, p. 113.

51. *Oeuvres de Millevoye*, 2 vols., Paris, 1880, 1:76–77.

52. N. R. Espadero, "Preferatory Remarks, by an Artist Friend of the Great Composer," *Posthumous Works of Louis Moreau Gottschalk*, Boston, 1872; see also Gottschalk to "Maria," summer 1860, undated letter no. 11, Gottschalk Collection, NYPL.

53. Fors, *Gottschalk*, pp. 215–18.

54. Gottschalk to Fontana, 4 July 1860, Gottschalk Collection, NYPL.

55. Logsdon, "Gottschalk's *Workbook*," pp. 9–11.

56. Napoleão, *Autobiographia*, pp. 85–86; also Doyle, *Louis Moreau Gottschalk*, pp. 236–242.

57. *Diario de la Marina*, 22 June 1860; the concerts that gave rise to this observation were Gottschalk's "farewell" of 25 May and the farewell concerts of singers named Lacosta and Abel Drouillon on 31 May and 20 June (*Gaceta de la Habana*, 27 May 1860, 30 May 1860, 20 June 1860.

58. *Diario de la Habana*, 15 September 1860, cited by Rubin, *Gottschalk in Cuba*, pp. 106–7.

59. Gottschalk to his brothers and sisters, 2 November 1860, Family Letters, Gottschalk Collection, NYPL.

60. *New York Times*, 1 April 1861. For the response in New York to Gottschalk's postponement of the concerts for Strakosch see *New York Times*, 26 May 1861.

61. Gottschalk to Augusta Gottschalk, 23 September 1860, Family Letters, Gottschalk Collection, NYPL.

62. *Gaceta de la Habana*, 20 June 1860, 10 July 1860.

63. Gottschalk to Augusta Gottschalk, 23 September 1860, Family Letters, Gottschalk Collection, NYPL.

64. Max Maretzek, *Crotchets and Quavers*, New York, 1855, pp. 49–50.

65. *El Siglo*, 29 August 1863, reprinted in Fors, *Gottschalk*, pp. 124–34.

66. Gottschalk to his brothers and sisters, 2 November 1860, Family Letters, Gottschalk Collection, NYPL; *Gaceta de la Habana*, 1 June 1860.

67. *Gaceta de la Habana*, 10, 12 June 1860.

68. Gottschalk to "Isadore," 26 July 1860; Gottschalk to "Maria," undated letter no. 11, Gottschalk Collection, NYPL.

69. Ireneo Díaz, *Caimito del Guayabal*, Havana, 1931, pp. 126–29.

70. Gottschalk, "Souvenirs de voyage," *L'Art musical*, 31 July 1862, pp. 279–80; *Gaceta de la Habana*, 20 July 1860; Gottschalk, *Notes of a Pianist*, pp. 34–37.

71. Dolores María de Ximeno y Cruz, *Aquellos tiempos memorias de Lola María*, 2 vols., Havana, 1928, 1:124; *Aurora del Yumurí* (Matanzas), 11 September 1860.

72. Gottschalk, *Notes of a Pianist*, pp. 32–33.

73. Libby Rubin, "Louis Moreau Gottschalk and the 1860–1861 Opera Season in Cuba," *Inter-American Music Bulletin*, July-October 1971, pp. 1–5.

74. Gottschalk to his brothers and sisters, 2 November 1860, Family Letters, Gottschalk Collection, NYPL.

75. *Aurora del Yumurí* (Matanzas), 18 August 1860.

76. *Ibid.*, 19 October 1860.

77. *Gaceta de la Habana*, 21 October 1860.

78. *Aurora del Yumurí*, 21 October 1860.

79. *Ibid.*, 10, 25 October 1860.

80. *Ibid.*, 27 October 1860.

81. *Ibid.*, 30 October 1860.

82. *Ibid.*

83. *Ibid.*, 10 November 1860.

84. *Ibid.*, 22, 24 November 1860.

85. *Ibid.*, 1 December 1860.

86. *L'Art musical*, 10 December 1860.

87. Gottschalk to Augusta Gottschalk, 8 December 1860, Family Letters, Gottschalk Collection, NYPL.

88. *La Prensa de la Habana*, 9, 14, 20 December 1860.

89. *Ibid.*, 26 December 1860.

90. *Ibid.*, 25 February 1861; see also Rubin, "Louis Moreau Gottschalk," p. 5.

91. Gottschalk, "La musique à la Havane," *La France musicale*, 28 October 1860, p. 426.

92. *La Prensa de la Habana*, 25 February 1861; *Gaceta de la Habana*, 26 February 1861.

93. *El Siglo*, 29 August 1863.

94. *Gaceta de la Habana*, 10 February 1861.

95. Ada Clare, "Thoughts and Things," *Saturday Press*, 22 October 1859.

96. *Ibid.*, 28 January 1860.

97. Ada Clare, "Letter from Paris," *Atlas*, 15 April 1857; see also *La France musicale*, 5 April 1857.

98. Ada Clare, "Thoughts and Things," *Saturday Press*, 4 February 1860.

99. Goldblatt, "Ada Clare," pp. 141–47.

100. *Gaceta de la Habana*, 1 September 1861.

101. *Ibid.*, 2, 21 February 1861; *La Prensa de la Habana*, 17 January 1861.

102. *Gaceta de la Habana*, 17 March 1861.

103. *Ibid.*, 21, 31 March 1861, 10 April 1861.

104. *Sankt-Peterburgskie vedemosti*, 1861, no. 143.

105. *Gaceta de la Habana*, 13 April 1861; cf. *Diccinario tecnico de la música*, Felipe Pedrell, ed., Barcelona, 1894, p. 24.

106. *Diario de la Habana*, 15 April 1861.

107. *Gaceta de la Habana*, 11 April 1861.

108. *Ibid.*, 19 April 1861.

109. *Ibid.*, 20, 25 April 1861.

110. *Ibid.*, 28 April 1861.
111. *Ibid.*, 20 April 1861.
112. *Ibid.*, 30 April 1861.
113. Gottschalk to a friend in Havana, Fors, *Gottschalk*, pp. 122–23.
114. *Gaceta de la Habana*, 9, 18 May 1861.
115. For details on this period see Rubin, "Gottschalk in Cuba," pp. 130–38.
116. *Gaceta de la Habana*, 3, 17 October 1861.
117. *Ibid.*, 3, 10 October 1861.
118. *Ibid.*, 25 November 1861.
119. Rubin, "Gottschalk in Cuba," p. 211.
120. *Aurora del Yumurí*, 20 November 1861.
121. *Gaceta de la Habana*, 9 November 1861; *Aurora del Yumurí*, 8 November 1861.
122. Gottschalk to his brothers and sisters, 2 November 1860, Family Letters, Gottschalk Collection, NYPL.
123. *Gaceta de la Habana*, 25, 27 November 1861.
124. Personal communication from William L. Seward, New York; also report from Brignoli's secretary, De Vivo, "Gottschalk, the Adored," p. 71.
125. RO-291; Gottschalk, *Notes of a Pianist*, p. 66.
126. *La Prensa de la Habana*, 19 January 1862.
127. Fors, *Gottschalk*, pp. 123–24.
128. Gottschalk, *Notes of a Pianist*, p. 9.
129. Gottschalk to his sisters, 12 December 1863, Family Letters, Gottschalk Collection, NYPL.
130. Gaceta de la Habana, 19 January 1862.

20. *The Union*, 1862

1. Hensel, *Life and Letters*, p. 95.
2. *New York Herald*, 17 February 1862; Odell, *Annals of the New York Stage*, 7:448.
3. *Courrier des États-Unis*, 10 February 1862; Richard Storrs Willis, "Gottschalk at Home," *Once a Month*, 18 February 1862.
4. *New York Herald*, 12 February 1862; "Gottschalk à New-York," pp. 189–90
5. *Courrier des États-Unis*, 26 October 1863; also *New York Herald*, 12 February 1862; *Daily Tribune*, 14 February 1862; *Albion*, 15 February 1862; *Vanity Fair*, 22 February 1862; *Frank Leslie's Illustrated Newspaper*, 22 February 1862.
6. *The Diary of George Templeton Strong*, Allan Nevins and Milton Halsey Thomas, eds., 4 vols., New York, 1952, 3:208.
7. *New York Herald*, 17 February 1862.
8. William Mason, *Memories of a Musical Life*, p. 236.
9. *New York Times*, 26 February 1862, 1 March 1862.
10. *Courrier des États-Unis*, 19 February 1862.
11. *New York Times*, 18 March 1862; *Frank Leslie's Illustrated Newspaper*, 15 March 1862; *Albion*, 12 March 1862; *Dwight's Journal of Music*, 22 March 1862, p. 408.
12. Gottschalk, *Notes of a Pianist*, pp. 54–55.
13. *Diario de la Marina*, 23 March 1862; Gottschalk, *Notes of a Pianist*, pp. 54–56.
14. Virginia Clay, *A Belle of the Fifties*, New York, 1904, pp. 49–50.
15. "Les Pianisists contemporains," *L'Art musical*, 6 February 1862, p. 78.
16. *Vanity Fair*, 15 March 1862, p. 134.

17. *Courrier des États-Unis,* 6 March 1862. This portrait is now in the posession of Lawrence Glover.

18. Barrus, *Whitman and Burroughs,* p. 3.

19. *Trow's New York City Directory,* New York, 1858. Pfaff's later moved to 653 Broadway. Cf. Martin D. Hyman, " 'Where the Drinkers & Laughers Meet:' Pfaff's Whitman's Literary Lair," *Seaport,* Spring 1992, pp. 57–61, where Pfaff's is mislocated at 647 Broadway.

20. Cited by Henry Seidel Canby, *Walt Whitman, an American,* New York, 1943, pp. 139–40.

21. Traubel, *With Walt Whitman in Camden,* p. 416.

22. *Leader,* 15 February 1862.

23. Hensel, *Life and Letters,* pp. 53–63.

24. *Ibid.,* pp. 133–36.

25. *Ibid.,* p. 118.

26. *The Diary of George Templeton Strong,* pp. 14–15.

27. Charles Warren Stoddard, "La Belle Menken," *National Magazine,* February 1905, pp. 479–80.

28. Lesser, *Enchanting Rebel,* pp. 75–247; Odell, *Annals of the New York Stage,* 7:233–35.

29. William Hall to Gottschalk, 20 February 1862, Glover Collection.

30. Sanjek, *American Popular Music,* 2:71.

31. Gottschalk to Thomas Hall, 3 March 1863, Theatrical and Music Collection, Museum of the City of New York.

32. Gottschalk to Léon Escudier, 20 February 1862, Gottschalk Collection, NYPL.

33. "Music Publishing in America," n.d. (September 1863), Scrapbook no. 4, Gottschalk Collection, NYPL.

34. C. F. Chickering to Gottschalk, 3 April 1863, Glover Collection.

35. *Dwight's Journal of Music,* 10 January 1863, p. 325.

36. Gottschalk to Léon Escudier, 18 March 1863, Free Library of Philadelphia.

37. Gottschalk to Clara Gottschalk, 2 August 1863, Family Letters, Gottschalk Collection, NYPL.

38. Gottschalk from "Barnum's Hotel," St. Louis [actually Springfield, Illinois], *Home Journal,* n.d. (April 1862), Scrapbook no. 4, Gottschalk Collection, NYPL.

39. Gottschalk, *Notes of a Pianist,* p. 230.

40. George P. Upton, *Musical Memories,* pp. 232–34.

41. Walt Whitman, "The Dead Tenor," Faner, *Walt Whitman and Opera,* p. 92.

42. Kellogg, *Memoirs of an American Prima Donna,* pp. 24–25.

43. Ada Clare, "The Male Beauties," *Leader,* n.d. (October 1862), Scrapbook no. 4, Gottschalk Collection, NYPL.

44. Jackson, *The Complete Published Songs,* intro., pp. 87–88.

45. Gottschalk, *Notes of a Pianist,* p. 60.

46. Jackson, *The Complete Published Songs,* intro., p. 3.

47. *Buffalo Commercial Advertiser,* 25 March 1862.

48. *Buffalo Express,* 26 March 1862.

49. *Cleveland Herald,* 28 March 1862.

50. *Cincinnati Enquirer,* 1 April 1862.

51. *Ibid.,* 2 April 1862; Patricia Gray Tipton, "The Contribution of Charles Kunkel to Musical Life in St. Louis" (Ph.D. diss., Washington University, 1977), pp. 15–18.

52. Gottschalk to Clara Gottschalk, undated Letter no. 30, (1 April 1862), Family Letters, Gottschalk Collection, NYPL.

53. *Cincinnati Enquirer*, 2 April 1862.

54. *Louisville Journal*, 5 April 1862.

55. James Neal Primm, *Lion of the Valley: St. Louis, Missouri*, Boulder, 1981, pp. 246–59.

56. *Daily Missouri Democrat*, 8, 11, 12 April 1862; also *Westliche Post*, 9 April 1862.

57. *Chicago Evening Journal*, 14 April 1862.

58. *Chicago Tribune*, 15 April 1862.

59. *Chicago Evening Journal*, 18 April 1862.

60. Gottschalk, *Notes of a Pianist*, p. 57.

61. *Detroit Advertiser*, 21 April 1862.

62. Gottschalk to Clara Gottschalk, 24 May 1862, Family Letters, Gottschalk Collection, NYPL; *New York Times*, 30 April 1862, 2 May 1862.

63. *New York Times*, 5 May 1862; *New York Herald*, 20 May 1862.

64. *New York Herald*, 30 April 1862; *New York Times*, 3 May 1862.

65. Gottschalk, *Notes of a Pianist*, p. 66.

66. *Ibid.*

67. *Baltimore Sun*, 12 May 1862.

68. Gottschalk, *Notes of a Pianist*, pp. 70–71.

69. *Ibid.*, p. 74.

70. *Ibid.*, p. 73.

71. *Boston Musical Times*, 7, 14 February 1862.

72. *Dwight's Journal of Music*, 25 January 1862, 15 February 1862, 2 March 1862.

73. *New York Mercury*, 23 March 1862.

74. *Dwight's Journal of Music*, 1 December 1860, pp. 285–86; 18 January 1861, p. 343; 27 July 1861, 134–35. The author is indebted to Vera Lawrence Brodsky for pointing these out. Cf. Lawrence, "Reverberations," p. 1025.

75. *Ibid.*, 22 February 1862, p. 374.

76. *Ibid.*, 17 October 1863, p. 120.

77. *Lowell Daily Citizen*, 3 June 1863.

78. Reprinted in *Dwight's Journal of Music*, 12 July 1862, p. 120.

79. *New York Leader*, 6 September 1862.

80. *Portsmouth Daily Chronicle*, 5, 6 June 1862.

81. Clipping of June 1862, preserved in Scrapbook no. 4, Gottschalk Collection, NYPL.

82. *Providence Daily Post*, 9 June 1862.

83. *Rochester Daily Democrat*, 23 July 1862. Gottschalk dedicated his *Orfa, grande polka* (op. 71) to J. R. Blodgett .

84. *Utica Herald*, 1 August 1862; Magendanz, "Gottschalk in Utica," *Town Topics of the Mohawk Valley*, October 1932, p. 13.

85. Gottschalk, *Notes of a Pianist*, pp. 87–88.

86. *Ibid.*, pp. 82, 86.

87. Gottschalk to Augusta Gottschalk, 20 July 1862, Family Letters, Gottschalk Collection, NYPL.

88. Paul Letondal, "Gottschalk à Théâtre Royal," *L'Ordre* (Québec), 9 July 1962; Gottschalk, *Notes of a Pianist*, p. 83; *Boston Musical Times*, 6 September 1862.

89. Quoted in *Daily British Whig*, Kingston, Ontario, 16 July 1862.

90. Gottschalk, *Notes of a Pianist*, p. 90.

91. *New York Express*, 27 August 1863.

92. *Boston Daily Journal*, 20 August 1862.

93. Iconography folder no. 1, Gottschalk Collection, NYPL.

94. *Boston Daily Journal,* 20 August 1862; *Daily Saratogian,* 16 August 1862; *New York Herald,* 6 September 1862.

95. *Boston Musical Times* (from *Vanity Fair*), 6 September 1862.

96. *Dwight's Journal of Music,* 16 August 1862, p. 153.

97. *History of Morris County, New Jersey,* New York, 1862, pp. 79–80.

98. Hensel, *Life and Letters,* pp. 104–6.

99. "Gottschalk en el desierto," *El Continental* (New York), 18 September 1862.

100. Gottschalk to Annie Myers, 23 August 1862, Gottschalk Collection, NYPL.

101. L. G. Gottschalk, "Carreño and L. M. Gottschalk," *Music,* February 1897, p. 458; Mathews, *A Hundred Years of Music,* p. 118.

102. Milinowski, *Teresa Carreño,* p. 31; Gottschalk to L. J. Harrison, 12 December 1862, George Sherman Dickinson Music Library, Vassar College.

103. *Frank Leslie's Illustrated Newspaper,* 8 November 1862; Odell, *Annals of the New York Stage,* 7:528.

104. Milinowski, *Teresa Carreño,* pp. 61–62.

105. Schonberg, *The Great Pianists,* p. 328.

106. Herbert Weinstock, *Rossini,* New York, 1968, p. 338.

107. *Frank Leslie's Illustrated Newspaper,* 4 October 1862.

108. *New York Times,* 6 October 1862.

109. Ezra Schabas, *Theodore Thomas,* pp. 19–20.

110. *Weekly Stage,* New York, 21 October 1863.

111. *Vanity Fair,* 11 October 1862, p. 178.

112. *Frank Leslie's Illustrated Newspaper,* 8 November 1862.

113. *World,* 25 October 1862.

114. *Boston Morning Journal,* 6(?) November 1862, Scrapbook no. 4, Gottschalk Collection, NYPL.

115. Van Wyck Brooks, *New England: Indian Summer, 1865–1916,* Garden City, 1944, p. 19.

116. *Boston Daily Courier,* 25 October 1862; *Boston Gazette,* 5 October 1862; *Home Journal,* 6 December 1862; etc.

117. Sanjek, *American Popular Music,* 2:111.

118. *Boston Journal,* 10 October 1862.

119. *Boston Musical Times,* 11 October 1862, p. 134.

120. *Boston Journal,* 13 October 1862.

121. "Gottschalk in Boston—Then and Now," *Dwight's Journal of Music,* 11 October 1862, p. 222.

122. *Boston Daily Courier,* 12 October 1862.

123. *Boston Journal,* 10 October 1862.

124. *Dwight's Journal of Music,* 18 October 1862.

125. *Home Journal,* 12(?) November 1862, Scrapbook no. 4, Gottschalk Collection, NYPL.

126. *Dwight's Journal of Music,* 8 November 1862, p. 255.

127. *Boston Daily Advertiser,* 13 November 1862.

21. The Automaton in Wartime, 1862–65

1. *El Continental* (New York), 11 October 1862.

2. De Vivo, "Gottschalk, the Adored."

3. *Illinois Journal,* 9 January 1863.

4. *Detroit Free Press,* 22 November 1862.

5. *Reading Democrat,* 12 June 1863.

6. Gottschalk, "Souvenirs de voyage," 31 July 1862, pp. 279–80; cf. Gottschalk, *Notes of a Pianist,* p. 120.

7. Gottschalk, "Souvenirs de voyage,", 31 July 1862, pp. 279–80.

8. *Ibid.*

9. Gottschalk to Augustine Gottschalk, 7 December 1862, Family Letters, Gottschalk Collection, NYPL.

10. Gottschalk, "Un Pianiste en Amérique," pp. 260–62.

11. See, for example, benefit for Mrs. Marie Abbot, Brooklyn Athenaeum, 13 April 1863; or for the New York Sanitary Fair at the home of Mrs. Belmost, Gottschalk to his sisters, 13 March 1864, Family Letters, Gottschalk Collection, NYPL.

12. *Reading Democrat,* 12 June 1863.

13. Gottschalk to Blanche Gottschalk, 28 February 1863, Family Letters, Gottschalk Collection, NYPL.

14. Gottschalk, "Souvenirs de voyage,", 31 July 1862, pp. 279–80.

15. Gottschalk, *Notes of a Pianist,* pp. 218–19.

16. "Fast Traveling," undated letter no. 66 (12? June 1864), Gottschalk Collection, NYPL.

17. Gottschalk, *Notes of a Pianist,* pp. 103–4.

18. *New York World,* 13 August 1864; *Watson's Weekly Art Journal,* 23 August 1864.

19. Gottschalk to Clara Gottschalk, 19(?) April 1864, Family Letters, Gottschalk Collection, NYPL. Information on the Curletts provided by Francis O'Neill, Maryland Historical Society. Keefer, *Baltimore's Music,* p. 157.

20. Gottschalk, *Notes of a Pianist,* p. 70.

21. *Ibid.,* p. 99.

22. *Ibid.,* p. 242.

23. *Ibid.,* p. 235.

24. *Ibid.,* p. 261.

25. Gottschalk to Espadero, 19 November 1862, Fors, *Gottschalk,* p. 409.

26. Gottschalk, *Notes of a Pianist,* p. 291; Gottschalk to his sisters, 3 March 1864, Family Letters, Gottschalk Collection, NYPL.

27. Gottschalk, *Notes of a Pianist,* p. 242; Gottschalk to Augusta Gottschalk, 5 January 1865, Family Letters, Gottschalk Collection, NYPL.

28. Gottschalk, *Notes of a Pianist,* pp. 263, 247.

29. Gottschalk to his sisters, 6 January 1865, Family Letters, Gottschalk Collection, NYPL.

30. Gottschalk to Espadero, 20 November 1862, Fors, *Gottschalk,* pp. 410–11.

31. Gottschalk to his sisters, 6 January 1865, Family Letters, Gottschalk Collection, NYPL.

32. Gottschalk to his sisters, 3 March 1864, Family Letters, Gottschalk Collection, NYPL.

33. *Detroit Daily Journal,* 8 May 1863.

34. Gottschalk, *Notes of a Pianist,* pp. 150–55; *Chicago Post,* 5 January 1864.

35. Gottschalk, *Notes of a Pianist,* p. 148.

36. *Chicago Journal,* 5 January 1864.

37. Gottschalk, *Notes of a Pianist,* p. 177. The Sun Inn still stands.

38. *Ibid.,* pp. 112, 242, 292.

39. *Ibid.*, pp. 208, 209, 253, 256.

40. *Ibid.*, p. 247; *Encyclopedia of the History of St. Louis*, William Hyde and Howard L. Conard, eds., St. Louis, 1899, 3:1287.

41. Gottschalk, *Notes of a Pianist*, pp. 114, 256.

42. *Ibid.*, pp. 114–15.

43. *Ibid.*, p. 238.

44. *Ibid.*, p. 214.

45. *Ibid.*, pp. 187–88.

46. *Ibid.*, p. 200.

47. *Ibid.*, p. 93.

48. *Ibid.*, pp. 238–39.

49. *Ibid.*, pp. 78–79.

50. *Indianapolis Daily Journal*, 22 January 1863; Jeannette Covert Knowland, *Hoosier City: The Story of Indianapolis*, New York, 1943, p. 285; Edward A. Leary, *Indianapolis: A Pictorial History*, Virginia Beach, 1980, p. 44.

51. Clarence E. Miller, "Forty Years of Long Ago: Early Annals of the Mercantile Library Association, 1846–1886" (MS), 1935, St. Louis Mercantile Library.

52. Gottschalk, *Notes of a Pianist*, p. 234.

53. Sanjek, *American Popular Music*, 2:131–33.

54. Alfred Theodore Andreas, *History of Chicago*, 3 vols., Chicago, 1884–86, 1:497.

55. *Chicago Times*, 14 December 1864; Andreas, *History of Chicago*, 2:598–99.

56. Gottschalk, *Notes of a Pianist*, p. 165.

57. *Sandusky Register*, 1853, n.d., Theater File, Sandusky Public Library.

58. Gottschalk, *Notes of a Pianist*, p. 92.

59. *Ibid.*, pp. 246–47.

60. *Albany Times and Courier*, 21 November 1862.

61. *Dwight's Journal of Music*, 3 October 1863, p. 112.

62. *Wilkes' Spirit of the Times*, 3 October 1863.

63. Miller, *Forty Years of Long Ago*, p. 56.

64. *Indianapolis Daily Journal*, 26 January 1863.

65. Miller, *Forty Years of Long Ago*, p. 62; *Cleveland Plain Dealer*, 25 November 1862.

66. *Indianapolis Daily Journal*, 22, 26–27 January 1863; *The Letters of Ralph Waldo Emerson*, Ralph L. Rusk, ed., 6 vols., New York, 1939, 5:311.

67. Gottschalk to Clara Gottschalk, 19 April 1864, Family Letters, Gottschalk, NYPL.

68. De Vivo, "Gottschalk, the Adored."

69. *Utica Advertiser*, 22 November 1862.

70. *Sandusky Daily Commercial Register*, 5 December 1862; *Missouri Republican*, 9 April 1862.

71. *Buffalo Daily Courier*, 25 March 1862.

72. *Indianapolis Daily Journal*, 16 December 1862.

73. Gottschalk, *Notes of a Pianist*, p. 216.

74. De Vivo, "Gottschalk, the Adored."

75. Chicago, 25 December 1862; New York, 28 September 1863.

76. *Home Journal*, 22 December 1862. This work is the same as Gottschalk's lost *Marlborough, s'en va t'en guerre* (RO-160).

77. *Dwight's Journal of Music*, 16 May 1863, p. 31; *Boston Daily Journal*, 6 May 1863.

78. Quoted by Magendanz, "Gottschalk in Utica," *Town Topics of the Mohawk Valley*, November 1932, p. 13.

79. *Brooklyn Eagle*, 8 March 1863; "Gottschalk at Aquarial Hall," unidentified clipping, Scrapbook no. 4, Gottschalk Collection, NYPL.

80. "America and Noblemen," *New York Times*, n.d. May 1864, Scrapbook no. 4, Gottschalk Collection, NYPL.

81. *Indianapolis Daily Journal*, 26 January 1863.

82. *Indianapolis Daily Gazette*, 23, 27 January 1863.

83. Gottschalk to Clara Gottschalk, 18 July 1863, Family Letters, Gottschalk Collection, NYPL.

84. Gottschalk to his sisters, 19 July 1864, Family Letters, Gottschalk Collection, NYPL.

85. Gottschalk, *Notes of a Pianist*, pp. 179–80.

86. Clyde W. Brockett, "Gottschalk at Hampton Roads" (address delivered to the Sonneck Society, April 1991), MS courtesy of the author.

87. *Westliche Press* (St. Louis), 9–10 January 1863; *Indianapolis Daily Sentinel*, 18 December 1862.

88. Gottschalk to his sisters, 25 December 1863, Family Letters, Gottschalk Collection, NYPL; Gottschalk, *Notes of a Pianist*, pp. 198–99.

89. *National Morning Chronicle* (Washington), 22 March 1864.

90. *National Intelligencer* (Washington), 25 March 1864.

91. Gottschalk, *Notes of a Pianist*, pp. 170–71; *National Intelligencer*, 26 March 1864; *Daily Morning Chronicle*, 25 March 1864; Bernard, *Lincoln and the Music of the Civil War*, pp. 202–4.

92. Gottschalk, *Notes of a Pianist*, pp. 129–37.

93. *Utica Advertiser*, 16 February 1865.

94. *Dayton Daily Journal*, 14 December 1862.

95. "Musical," 18(?) June 1862, Scrapbook no. 4, Gottschalk Collection, NYPL.

96. Gottschalk, *Notes of a Pianist*, p. 209.

97. *Ibid.*, pp. 198, 207.

98. Magendanz, "Gottschalk in Utica," *Town Topics of the Mohawk Valley*, October 1932, p. 25.

99. Gottschalk, *Notes of a Pianist*, p. 254.

100. *Ibid.*, p. 257.

101. *Ibid.*, pp. 193, 195.

102. *Plattsburg Sentinel*, 29 April 1864.

103. Gottschalk, *Notes of a Pianist*, pp. 262, 155.

104. *Ibid.*, pp. 93, 263.

105. *Ibid.*, pp. 92, 163.

106. *Burlington Free Press*, 7 July 1862. Jane Ambrose, "Louis Moreau Gottschalk's Visit to Vermont in 1862," *Vermont History*, Spring 1971, pp. 125–27.

107. Gottschalk, *Notes of a Pianist*, p. 161.

108. *Cleveland Plain Dealer*, 1 December 1863; *Cleveland Herald*, 27 March 1862.

109. Gottschalk to Blanche Gottschalk, 8 September 1862, 1 December 1862, Family Letters, Gottschalk Collection, NYPL.

110. George Gottschalk to Augusta Gottschalk, 10 September 1862, Glover Collection.

111. Sophie Maurigy to Annie Myers, 7 December 1862, Family Letters, Gottschalk Collection, NYPL.

112. Clara Gottschalk Peterson, "Biographical Sketch," p. 70; Hensel, *Life and Letters*, pp. 151–54.

113. Gottschalk to Clara Gottschalk, 20 January 1863, undated letter no. 6, Family Letters, Gottschalk Collection, NYPL.

114. Gottschalk to Celestine Gottschalk, undated letter no. 5, Family Letters, Gottschalk Collection, NYPL; Gottschalk to Augusta Gottschalk, 7 September 1863, Family Letters, NYPL; Gottschalk to Clara Gottschalk, 17 September 1863, Family Letters, Gottschalk Collection, NYPL.

115. Gottschalk to his sisters, 12 December 1863, Family Letters, Gottschalk Collection, NYPL; Hensel, *Life and Letters*, p. 151.

116. Gottschalk to his sisters, 24 February 1863, Family Letters, Gottschalk Collection, NYPL.

117. Gottschalk to his sisters, 20 July 1864, Family Letters, Gottschalk Collection, NYPL.

118. Gottschalk to his sisters, 7 February 1869, Family Letters, Gottschalk Collection, NYPL.

119. Mrs. Camille Bruslé to Auguste (Augustine) Gottschalk, n.d., Family Letters, Gottschalk Collection, NYPL.

120. Gottschalk to his sisters, 25 December 1863, Family Letters, Gottschalk Collection, NYPL.

121. Gottschalk to Leonard Myers, 4 December 1863, Family Letters, Gottschalk Collection, NYPL.

122. Notebook for June–July 1863, Gottschalk Collection, NYPL.

123. Gottschalk to his sisters, 29 March 1864, 8 May 1864, Family Letters, Gottschalk Collection, NYPL.

124. Gottschalk to his sisters, 29 March 1864, Family Letters, Gottschalk Collection, NYPL.

125. Gottschalk to his sisters, 6 September 1864, Family Letters, Gottschalk Collection, NYPL.

126. Undated printed fragment, Scrapbook no. 4, Gottschalk Collection, NYPL.

127. Gottschalk to his sisters, n.d. (11? October 1864), Family Letters, Gottschalk Collection, NYPL.

128. Gottschalk, *Notes of a Pianist*, p. 68.

129. Gottschalk to "My Dear Friend," January 1863, undated letter no. 89, Gottschalk Collection, NYPL; also *The Home Journal*, 7 February 1863.

130. Hensel, *Life and Letters*, p. 155.

131. Gottschalk to his sisters, 17 December 1863, Family Letters, Gottschalk Collection, NYPL.

132. Gottschalk, *Notes of a Pianist*, p. 206.

133. *Ibid.*

134. *Ibid.*, p. 116.

135. Gottschalk to Espadero, 15 June 1864, Fors, *Gottschalk*, p. 148.

136. Undated fragment no. 68, Gottschalk Collection, NYPL.

137. *Chicago Evening Journal*, 29 December 1863; *Cleveland Times*, 21 February 1863; *Cleveland Courier*, 23 February 1863.

138. Gottschalk, *Notes of a Pianist*, p. 143.

139. *Utica Morning Journal*, 19 February 1863.

140. *Brooklyn Daily Eagle*, 21 April 1864; Gottschalk, *Notes of a Pianist*, p. 83.

141. *Wilkes' Spirit of the Times*, 31 October 1863. All these works except the *Valse de Faust* are lost.

142. Jackson, *The Complete Published Songs*, pp. 109–10.

143. Gottschalk, *Notes of a Pianist*, pp. 112–13.

144. *Why Sinks My Soul Desponding*, Ditson & Co., New York, 1874.

145. Millevoye, *Oeuvres complètes*, 1:78–79.

146. Henry P. H. Bromwell, *The Dying Poet*, Denver, 1918.

22. America Through Gottschalk's Eyes

1. Personal communication from William K. Seward, New York, based on his research in unpublished papers of Carlotta Patti in his personal collection.

2. Kellogg, *Memoirs of an American Prima Donna*, p. 107.

3. Travel Diary, 28 June–1 July 1863, Gottschalk Collection, NYPL.

4. Travel Diary, 28 June–1 July 1863, Gottschalk Collection, NYPL.

5. Offenbach, *Offenbach in America*, p. 97.

6. *Dwight's Journal of Music*, 18 June 1863, p. 48.

7. *Home Journal*, 7 January 1863.

8. Gottschalk to Espadero, 1 March 1863, Fors, *Gottschalk*, pp. 392–93.

9. "Musical Review," unidenitified clipping, Scrapbook no. 4, Gottschalk Collection, NYPL.

10. *Sunday Morning Times*, n.d. March 1864, Scrapbook no. 4, Gottschalk Collection, NYPL.

11. De Vivo, "Gottschalk, the Adored."

12. Henry Clapp, "Figaro on Gottschalk," *Leader*, n.d. 1870, unmounted clipping, Gottschalk Collection, NYPL.

13. Gottschalk, *Notes of a Pianist*, p. 73.

14. Gottschalk to Espadero, 14 June 1864, Fors, *Gottschalk*, p. 152.

15. Gottschalk to his sisters, 17 July 1864, Family Letters, Gottschalk Collection, NYPL.

16. Gottschalk, *Notes of a Pianist*, p. 132.

17. Gottschalk to his sisters, 13 October 1864, Family Letters Letters, Gottschalk Collection, NYPL; Gottschalk, *Notes of a Pianist*, pp. 131, 199.

18. Gottschalk to his sisters, 13 October 1864, Family Letters, Gottschalk Collection, NYPL.

19. Gottschalk, *Notes of a Pianist*, p. 56.

20. Gottschalk to his sisters, 13 October 1864, Family Letters, Gottschalk Collection, NYPL.

21. Gottschalk, *Notes of a Pianist*, p. 61.

22. *Ibid.*, p. 137.

23. *Hurrah Galop*, published by Ditson & Co., 1863.

24. Gottschalk, *Notes of a Pianist*, p. 187.

25. *Ibid.*, p. 199.

26. Gottschalk to Espadero, 20 November 1862, Fors, *Gottschalk*, pp. 410–11.

27. Gottschalk to Sheldon Stephens, 2 August 1863, Brian Mann, "A Gottschalk Letter at Vassar College," *Sonneck Society Bulletin*, 1992, no. 1, p. 6.

28. Hensel, *Life and Letters*, p. 188.

29. *New York Times*, 1 March 1863.

30. *The Hone and Strong Diaries of Old Manhattan*, Louis Auchincloss, ed., New York, 1989, p. 220.

31. James Russell Lowell, "On a Certain Condescension in Foreigners," in *Fireside Travels*, Boston, 1904, p. 318, fn. 1.

32. Hensel, *Life and Letters*, pp. 208–9.

33. Henry Stone, "A Song in Camp," *Century Magazine*, December 1887, p. 320. Dena J. Epstein, "The Battle Cry of Freedom," *Civil War History*, September 1958, pp. 307–13.

34. Sanjek, *American Popular Music*, 2:231–38.

35. Gottschalk, *Notes of a Pianist*, p. 181.

36. Hensel, *Life and Letters*, p. 209.

37. *Chicago Evening Journal*, 5 January 1864; Gottschalk, *Notes of a Pianist*, p. 93.

38. Gottschalk, *Notes of a Pianist*, pp. 55, 219.

39. *Ibid.*, pp. 362, 98.

40. *Ibid.*, p. 165.

41. *Ibid.*, p. 60.

42. *Ibid.*, pp. 94–95, 72.

43. *Ibid.*, p. 76.

44. *Ibid.*, p. 262.

45. *Ibid.*, p. 236.

46. *Ibid.*, p. 191.

47. *Ibid.*, p. 263.

48. *Ibid.*, p. 178.

49. *Ibid.*, pp. 162, 177, 246.

50. *Ibid.*, pp. 211–12.

51. *Ibid.*, p. 147.

52. *Ibid.*, pp. 130–31, 283.

53. *Ibid.*, p. 57; cf. "The Indian Massacres in Minnesota," *New York Tribune*, 24 October 1861.

54. Gottschalk, *Notes of a Pianist*, p. 56.

55. *Ibid.*, pp. 86, 191.

56. *Ibid.*, pp. 119, 149.

57. *Ibid.*, p. 60.

58. *Ibid.*, p. 117.

59. *Ibid.*, p. 27.

60. "When a foreigner asks and inquires about national melodies, he is unanimously directed to hear the so-called Negro melodies." Adam Gurowski, *America and Europe*, New York, 1857, p. 179.

61. Gottschalk, *Notes of a Pianist*, p. 233.

62. Gottschalk to his sisters, 13 March 1864, Glover Collection.

63. Gottschalk, *Notes of a Pianist*, p. 91.

64. *Ibid.*, p. 197.

65. *Ibid.*, p. 251.

66. *Ibid.*, pp. 197, 85, 122.

67. *Ibid.*, p. 59.

68. *Ibid.*, p. 97.

69. *Ibid.*, p. 158.

70. *Ibid.*, pp. 159, 167.

71. Hensel, *Life and Letters*, p. 23.

72. Gottschalk to Clara Gottschalk, 2 October 1862, Family Letters, Gottschalk Collection, NYPL.

73. Gottschalk, *Notes of a Pianist,* pp. 180, 211, 250.

74. *Ibid.,* p. 249.

75. *Ibid.,* p. 94.

76. *Ibid.,* pp. 90, 206, 264.

77. *Ibid.,* p. 98.

78. *Ibid.,* pp. 233–34.

79. Letter to the editor of an unidentified New York journal, written from York, Pennsylvania, 7 February 1865, Scrapbook no. 4, Gottschalk Collection, NYPL.

80. Gottschalk, *Notes of a Pianist,* p. 261.

81. *Ibid.,* pp. 238–39.

82. *Ibid.,* p. 237.

83. *Ibid.,* p. 243; Gottschalk to Espadero, 20 November 1862, Fors, *Gottschalk,* pp. 410–12.

84. Gottschalk to Espadero, 20 November 1862, Fors, *Gottschalk,* pp. 410–12.

85. Gottschalk, *Notes of a Pianist,* pp. 76, 80.

86. *Ibid.,* p. 253.

87. L. M. Gottschalk, "Dramatic Feuilleton," June 1863, unidentified newspaper, Scrapbook no. 4, Gottschalk Collection, NYPL.

88. Gottschalk, *Notes of a Pianist,* p. 227.

89. "Figaro on Gottschalk," *Leader,* n.d. 1870, unmounted clipping, Gottschalk Collection, NYPL.

90. Gottschalk, *Notes of a Pianist,* p. 194.

91. *Ibid.,* p. 239.

92. *Ibid.,* p. 154.

93. *Ibid.,* p. 31.

94. *Ibid.,* pp. 153–54.

95. *Ibid.,* p. 241.

96. Richard L. Bushman, *The Refinement of America,* New York, 1992, pp. 273– 78.

97. Hensel, *Life and Letters,* p. 96.

98. *Ibid.,* p. 88.

99. *Detroit Free Press,* 24 November 1862; *Plain Dealer* (Cleveland), 1 December 1863; *Indianapolis Daily Journal,* 17 December 1862.

100. Gottschalk, *Notes of a Pianist,* p. 88; *Geneva Gazette,* 18, 25 July 1862.

101. Gottschalk, *Notes of a Pianist,* p. 60.

102. *Ibid.,* pp. 65, 79, 88.

103. *Ibid.,* p. 52.

104. *Ibid.,* pp. 260, 63.

105. *Ibid.,* p. 51.

106. *Ibid.,* pp. 259, 52.

107. *Ibid.,* pp. 88, 88, 214.

108. *Rochester Union Advertiser,* 17 February 1865.

109. Gottschalk to his sisters, 12 December 1863, Family Letters, Gottschalk Collection, NYPL.

23. California: Anatomy of a Scandal

1. *Buffalo Daily Courier,* 7 February 1865.

2. *Dwight's Journal of Music,* 7 January 1865, p. 372.

3. *New York Times,* 29 February 1864.

4. "Gottschalk", undated clipping from *Watson's Art Journal* (? March 1865), Scrapbook no. 4, Gottschalk Collection, NYPL.

5. Wehle assumed the stage name James Wehli; Odell, *Annals of the New York Stage*, 7:694–96.

6. Kellogg, *Memoirs of an American Prima Donna*, p. 12.

7. *Dwight's Journal of Music*, 4 February 1865, p. 389.

8. E. Muzio, contract with Gottschalk, 15 November 1864, Miscellaneous Letters, Gottschalk Collection, NYPL; "Contract of Agreement Between Mr. Muzio and Gottschalk," undated letter no. 44, Gottschalk Collection, NYPL; Gottschalk to his sisters, 11 December 1864, Family Letters, Gottschalk Collection, NYPL.

9. Gottschalk, *Notes of a Pianist*, p. 268.

10. Gottschalk to his sisters, 25 December 1863, Family Letters, Gottschalk Collection, NYPL.

11. *New York Times*, 23 February 1864.

12. Gottschalk to his sisters, 8 May 1864, Family Letters, Gottschalk Collection, NYPL; *New York Times*, 29 February 1864.

13. Gaston Gottschalk to Augusta Gottschalk, 21 March 1864, Family Letters, Gottschalk Collection, NYPL; *New York Herald*, 21 February 1864; *New York Times*, 23 February 1864.

14. Gottschalk to his sisters, 21 October 1864, Family Letters, Gottschalk Collection, NYPL; *Dwight's Journal of Music*, 29 October 1864, p. 336.

15. *Cleveland Morning Leader*, 7 December 1864.

16. *New York Times*, 27 March 1865; *Courrier des États-Unis*, 24 March 1865.

17. *Dwight's Journal of Music*, 15 April 1865, p. 14.

18. Goldblatt, "Ada Clara," pp. 172ff.

19. Charles Warren Stoddard, "Ada Clare, Queen of Bohemia," *National Magazine*, September 1905, pp. 638–45; Goldblatt, "Ada Clare," pp. 195–209.

20. Stoddard, "Ada Clare," p. 641.

21. Goldblatt, "Ada Clare," p. 183.

22. *Guiseppe Verdi, nelle lettere di Emanuele Muzio ad Antonio Barezzi*, Luigi Agostino Garibaldi, ed., Milan, 1931, p. 373.

23. Reprinted in Gottschalk, *Notes of a Pianist*, p. 269; cf. *Dwight's Journal of Music*, 4 March 1865, p. 407.

24. Fragment dated 22 March 1865, undated letter no. 20, Gottschalk Collection, NYPL.

25. Thomas Hall to Charles Vezin, 14 June 1870, Gottschalk Collection, NYPL.

26. Gottschalk, *Notes of a Pianist*, pp. 276–80.

27. *Ibid.*, p. 281.

28. *Ibid.*, p. 283.

29. *Ibid.*, p. 284.

30. Franklin Walker, *San Francisco's Literary Frontier*, New York, 1943, p. 9.

31. Lois M. Foster, "Annals of the San Francisco Stage" (MS), 4 vols., San Francisco, 1937 (Bancroft Library, Berkeley), 1:149ff.

32. Gottschalk, *Notes of a Pianist*, p. 299.

33. Foster, "Annals of the San Francisco Stage," 1:173.

34. *Daily Morning Call*, 17 May 1865; Gottschalk, *Notes of a Pianist*, p. 293.

35. *Daily Dramatic Chronicle*, 3 April 1865.

36. Anon., *Early Master Teachers, History of Music in San Francisco Series*, New York, 1940, 4:1–4.

37. On Maguire see Lois M. Foster, "Annals of the San Francisco Stage," 1:160–87, and Goldin, *The Music Merchants*, pp. 58–63.

38. Pauline Jacobson, *City of the Golden Fifties*, Berkeley and Los Angeles, 1941, p. 263.

39. *Golden Era*, 10 September 1865.

40. Gottschalk, *Notes of a Pianist*, p. 298.

41. *Daily Dramatic Chronicle*, 20 May 1865; *Daily Morning Call*, 19 May 1865.

42. *Daily Morning Call*, 19 May 1865.

43. *Daily Alta California*, 10, 12 May 1865; *Sunday Mercury*, 14 May 1865.

44. *Daily Dramatic Chronicle*, 9, 12 May 1865.

45. *The Works of Mark Twain*, Edgar Marquess Branch and Robert H. Hirst, eds., 15 vols., Berkeley and Los Angeles, 1981, 2:235.

46. *Daily Dramatic Chronicle*, 26 May 1865; *Daily Morning Call*, 17 May 1865.

47. *Daily Alta California*, 18 May 1865.

48. Edgar J. Hinkel and William E. McCann, eds., *Oakland, 1852–1938*, 2 vols., Oakland, 1939, 1:494; the exact relation of Mrs. Blake and Rev. E. B. Walmsworth, president of a Pacific Female College that apparently merged with Mrs. Blake's school, is unclear. (B. F. Stilwell, *Directory of the Township and the City of Oakland*, Oakland, 1868.)

49. "Ye Olde Oakland Days" (MS), Oakland Free Library, 1937.

50. G. Calderwood and G. T. Loofbourow, *Facts and Figures of Oakland and Alameda County*, Oakland, 1896, p. 125.

51. Gottschalk, *Notes of a Pianist*, p. 42.

52. *Sacramento Daily Bee*, 1 June 1865.

53. *Sacramento Daily Union*, 31 May 1865, 1 June 1865.

54. Nigey Lennon, *The Sagebrush Bohemian*, New York, 1990, pp. 85–87; Goldblatt, "Ada Clare," pp. 185ff.

55. Brent H. Smith, "The History of the Comstock Lode, 1850–1920," *University of Nevada Bulletin*, 1943, no. 3, p. 59.

56. *Virginia Daily Union*, 6 June 1865.

57. *Ibid.*, 7 June 1865.

58. Jacob Kunkel, unidentified fragment, Scrapbook no. 4, Gottschalk Collection, NYPL.

59. *Daily Alta California*, 13 June 1865.

60. Gottschalk, *Notes of a Pianist*, p. 307.

61. *Ibid.*, p. 314.

62. *Golden Era*, 21 May 1865.

63. *Daily Alta California*, 11 July 1865; *El Mercurio* (Lima), 8 August 1865.

64. *Daily Morning Chronicle*, 15, 21 July 1865; *Era*, 16 July 1865.

65. Folder no. 1, Item 12, Gottschalk Visual File, NYPL; *Daily Alta California*, 24 July 1865

66. *Petaluma Journal and Argus*, 7 July 1865.

67. Gottschalk, *Notes of a Pianist*, pp. 316–17.

68. *Ibid.*, pp. 310–13; cf. Herz, *My Travels in America*, pp. 91–92.

69. *Golden Era*, 13 August 1865; *Daily Evening Bulletin*, 9 August 1865.

70. *Daily Alta California*, 17 July 1865.

71. *Courrier de San Francisco*, 30 August 1865.

72. *Daily Alta California*, 21 August 1865.

73. *Courrier de San Francisco*, 21 August 1865; *Daily Alta California*, 29 August 1865.

74. *Daily Alta California*, 3 September 1865.

75. Gottschalk to his sisters, 30 August 1865, Family Letters, Gottschalk Collection, NYPL.

76. *Daily Alta California*, 9 September 1865.

77. The key archival document, Gottschalk's explanatory letter to Chickering, has been published by Richard Jackson, "A Gottschalk Collection Surveyed," *Notes (Quarterly Journal of the Music Library Association)*, December 1989, pp. 34ff.

78. Published by Richard Jackson, "A Gottschalk Collection Surveyed," p. 35.

79. *Daily Alta California*, 16 September 1865, also 26 August.

80. *Sacramento Daily Bee*, 16 September 1865.

81. *San Francisco Examiner*, 16 September 1865.

82. *Morning Call*, 16 September 1865.

83. *Ibid.*, 17 September 1865.

84. *Carson City Appeal*, 17 September 1865; *Gold Hill Daily*, 23 September 1865.

85. *Daily Dramatic Chronicle*, 18 September 1865.

86. *Sacramento Daily Bee*, 18 September 1865; *Daily Dramatic Chronicle*, 19 September 1865.

87. *Daily Morning Chronicle*, 22 September 1865.

88. *Golden Era*, 1 October 1865; *Gold Hill Daily*, 23 September 1865.

89. *New York Weekly Review*, 14 October 1865.

90. *Watson's Art Journal*, 11, 25 November 1865; *New York Saturday Press*, 4 November 1865.

91. (?) Ransom to Gottschalk, 29 September 1865, Miscellaneous Letters, Gottschalk Collection, NYPL.

92. Douglas S. Watson, "The San Francisco McAllisters," *California Historical Society Quarterly*, 1932, no. 2, p. 127.

93. (?) Ransom to Gottschalk, 29 September 1865, Miscellaneous Letters, Gottschalk Collection, NYPL.

94. Loggins, *Where the Word Ends*, pp. 226–29.

95. *Daily Dramatic Chronicle*, 23 September 1865; *New York Herald*, 20 October 1865.

96. *Daily Dramatic Chronicle*, 8 September 1865.

97. *Ibid.*, 5 September 1865.

98. *Ibid.*, 16 September 1865.

99. *Watson's Art Journal*, 2 September 1865, p. 245.

100. Gottschalk to "my dear friend" (Charles Warren?), 9 February 1869, Family Letters, Gottschalk Collection, NYPL.

101. *Watson's Art Journal*, 2 September 1865, p. 297.

102. *Daily Dramatic Chronicle*, 14 July 1865, 5 August 1865.

103. *Daily Morning Call*, 14, 24 September 1865.

104. Alan Kendall, *Paganini*, London, 1982, p. 108.

105. *Daily Dramatic Chronicle*, 20 September 1865; also *Daily Alta California*, 9 September 1865.

106. Gottschalk to his sisters, 19 July 1864, Family Letters, Gottschalk Collection, NYPL.

24. Turmoil and Testimonials: Peru and Chile, 1865–66

1. *New York Times*, 23 September 1865.

2. Gottschalk, *Notes of a Pianist*, p. 321.

3. Undated fragment, Gottschalk Collection, NYPL.

4. Hensel, *Life and Letters*, p. 162.

5. Published by Jackson, "A Gottschalk Collection Surveyed," pp. 37ff.

6. Charles Francis Chickering to Gottschalk, 6 March 1866, Gottschalk Collection, NYPL.

7. *El Mercurio* (Lima), 9 February 1865, 8 August 1865. Unless otherwise noted, all newspaper references in this chapter and in the two subsequent chapters are based on Gottschalk's own clipping files, Gottschalk Collection, NYPL. By far the best treatment of the South American period of Gottschalk's life is to be found in Robert Stevenson's "Gottschalk in Buenos Aires" and "Gottschalk in Western South America," *Inter-American Music Bulletin*, November 1969, 74:1–7, 7–16; for Brazil, see Lange, "Vida y muerte."

8. See David Bushnell and Neill Macaulay, *The Emergence of Latin America in the Nineteenth Century*, New York, 1988, pp. 180–92.

9. Gottschalk, *Notes of a Pianist*, pp. 326–30; Gottschalk to his sisters, 4 September 1868, Family Letters, Gottschalk Collection, NYPL.

10. *New York Herald*, 12 October 1865.

11. Gottschalk, *Notes of a Pianist*, p. 328.

12. *Ibid.;* Gottschalk to his sisters, 10 October 1865, Family Letters, Gottschalk Collection, NYPL.

13. *El Comercio* (Lima), 18 October 1865.

14. Gottschalk to his sisters, 11 October 1865, Family Letters, Gottschalk Collection, NYPL.

15. Robert N. Burr, *By Reason or Force*, Berkeley and Los Angeles, 1965, pp. 92–99.

16. Gottschalk, *Notes of a Pianist*, p. 339.

17. *Ibid.*, p. 343.

18. *Ibid.*, p. 352; Gottschalk to his sisters, 13 November 1865, Family Letters, Gottschalk Collection, NYPL.

19. Gottschalk, *Notes of a Pianist*, p. 352.

20. Gottschalk Collection, NYPL.

21. Alvin G. Hovey to Secretary of State Seward, 13 January 1866, Consular Despatches, General Records of the Department of State, Record Group 59, U.S. National Archives.

22. Gottschalk to his sisters, n.d. 1866 (ca. May 4), Family Letters, Gottschalk Collection, NYPL.

23. Gottschalk, *Notes of a Pianist*, pp. 343–44.

24. Rodolfo Barbacci, "Actividades de L. M. Gottschalk en el Perú (1865–1866)," *Revista de Estudios Musicales*, December 1950–April 1951, pp. 343–50; Stevenson, "Gottschalk in Western South America," *Inter-American Music Bulletin*, November 1969, 74:9.

25. Gottschalk to his sisters, 20 November 1865, Family Letters, Gottschalk Collection, NYPL; *El Comercio*, 18, 21 November 1865.

26. J. Dobrera, "Le Théâtre de Lima," *L'Art musical*, 4 January 1866, p. 39; Gottschalk to his sisters, 4 September 1868, Family Letters, Gottschalk Collection, NYPL.

27. Gottschalk to his sisters, 4 September 1868, Family Letters, Gottschalk Collection, NYPL.

28. Walsh, "Adieux de Gottschalk à Buenos-Ayres," *L'Art musical*, 22 October 1868, pp. 374–75.

29. *El Comercio*, 25 November 1865.

30. Dobrera, "Le Théâtre de Lima," p. 39.

31. Gottschalk, *Notes of a Pianist,* p. 358; see also, *El Comercio,* 2 January 1866.

32. *El Mercurio* (Santiago), 16 December 1865.

33. Stevenson, "Gottschalk in Western South America," p. 10; Gottschalk to his sisters, 13 December 1865, Family Letters, Gottschalk Collection, NYPL.

34. Gottschalk, "Nouvelles de Pérou," *L'Art musical,* 25 January 1866, pp. 61–62.

35. *The Cambridge History of Latin America,* 3:559; *Souvenir de Lima* was not complete in final form until 1860 (D-146).

36. Gottschalk, "Nouvelles de Pérou," pp. 61–62.

37. Gottschalk, *Notes of a Pianist,* pp. 394–95.

38. Stevenson, "Gottschalk in Western South America," p. 10; the medal is preserved in the Glover Collection.

39. *El Comercio,* 25 November 1865.

40. Gottschalk, *Notes of a Pianist,* p. 363.

41. Burr, *By Reason or Force,* p. 99.

42. D-88.

43. Gottschalk to his sisters, 5 May 1866, Family Letters, Gottschalk Collection, NYPL.

44. Gottschalk, *Notes of a Pianist,* p. 366.

45. *Ibid.,* p. 368.

46. *Ibid.,* p. 374.

47. Gottschalk to his sisters, 5 May 1866, Family Letters, Gottschalk Collection, NYPL.

48. Charles Francis Chickering to Gottschalk, 6 March 1866, Assorted Letters, Gottschalk Collection, NYPL.

49. *El Mercurio,* 16 May 1866.

50. Gottschalk to his sisters, 14 May 1866, Family Letters, Gottschalk Collection, NYPL.

51. Eugenio Pereira-Salas, "La Embajada musical de Gottschalk en Chile," *Andean Quarterly,* January 1944, pp. 5–6, 11.

52. Brian Loveman, *Chile, the Legacy of Hispanic Capitalism,* New York, 1988, pp. 140–49.

53. *The Cambridge History of Latin America,* 3:591.

54. Gottschalk to his sisters, 3 June 1866, Family Letters, Gottschalk Collection, NYPL.

55. Eugenio Pereira-Salas, "La Vida musical en Chile en el siglo XIX," *Die Musikkulturen Lateinamericas im 19. Jahrhundert,* Robert Günther, ed., Regensburg, 1982, pp. 241–46.

56. *The Cambridge History of Latin America* 3:608.

57. Gottschalk to his sisters, 23 June 1866, Family Letters, Gottschalk Collection, NYPL.

58. Stevenson, "Gottschalk in Western South America," p. 12.

59. *El Ferrocarril,* 5 June 1866.

60. "Crónica de Santiago," *La Patria* (Valparaíso), 2 June 1866.

61. Stevenson, "Gottschalk in Western South America," p. 11 Doyle points out that other arias from this period survive in op. 68 (D-54), personal communication.

62. Sociedad de Instrucción Primaria; Gottschalk, *Notes of a Pianist,* p. 377.

63. Pereiras, "La Embajada," p. 8; *El Ferrocarril,* 20 July 1866.

64. *El Ferrocarril,* 7 August 1866.

65. Stevenson, "Gottschalk in Western South America," p. 12.

66. *Ibid.*, p. 13.

67. *La Patria* (Valparaíso), 6 June 1866; Eugenio Pereira Salas, *Apuntes biográficos de Federíco Guzmán*, Santiago, 1979.

68. Gesualdo, *Historia de la música*, 2:592–93.

69. *El Ferrocarril*, 5 August 1866; Gottschalk to his sisters, 16 August 1866, Family Letters, Gottschalk Collection, NYPL; undated letter in French from Colegio Santo Ignaco, Scrapbook no. 5, Gottschalk Collection.

70. Gottschalk to his sisters, 10 July 1866, Family Letters, Gottschalk Collection, NYPL.

71. Manuel Blanco Cuartín, "Al Celebre Pianista L. M. Gottschalk," Santiago, n.d., 1866, Scrapbook no. 5, Gottschalk Collection, NYPL.

72. *El Ferrocarril*, 1866 July 7.

73. *El Mercurio*, 15 August 1866; *La República*, 1866 August 10; *El Ferrocarril*, 16 August 1866.

74. Lange, "Vida y muerte," no. 5–6, p. 244; no. 4, p. 137, n. 150.

75. Lewis, "Recently Discovered Works of Gottschalk," pp. 332–47.

76. Gottschalk to his sisters, 16 August 1866, Family Letters, Gottschalk Collection, NYPL.

77. *El Ferrocarril*, 16 August 1866; *El Mercurio*, 1866 November 6.

78. "El Festival del Domingo," Santiago, n.d. 1866, Scrapbook no. 5, Gottschalk Collection, NYPL.

79. *El Independiente* (Valparaíso), 14 August 1866.

80. Gottschalk to his sisters, 16 August 1866, Family Letters, Gottschalk Collection, NYPL.

81. *El Independiente*, 14 August 1866.

82. *El Mercurio*, 15 August 1866.

83. Gottschalk to his sisters, 2 October 1866, Family Letters, Gottschalk Collection, NYPL.

84. *El Ferrocarril*, 5 December 1866; Luis Merino, "Música y Sociedad en el Valparaíso decimónico," *Die Musikkulturen Lateinamerikas*, pp. 199–230.

85. Gottschalk to his sisters, 3 November 1866, Family Letters, Gottschalk Collection, NYPL.

86. *La Patria*, 22 November 1866.

87. *Ibid.*, 19, 22 November 1866.

88. *El Ferrocarril*, 5 December 1866.

89. *Ibid.*, 13 June 1866.

90. *El Mercurio*, 23 November 1866.

91. *Ibid.*, 23 November 1866.

92. *Ibid.*, 24 November 1866.

93. Merino, "Música y sociedad," p. 216.

94. Gottschalk to his sisters, 2 September 1866, Family Letters, Gottschalk Collection, NYPL.

95. Brian Loveman, *Chile: The Legacy of Hispanic Capitalism*, New York, 1979, pp. 141–47.

96. Stevenson, "Gottschalk in Western South America," pp. 12–13.

97. *El Constituyente* (Copiapó), 21 January 1867.

98. Gottschalk, *Notes of a Pianist*, pp. 379–83.

99. Gottschalk to his sisters, 3 February 1867; Gottschalk to his sisters, 6 April 1869 ("list of objects in the parcel"); Gottschalk to a friend, 9 February 1869; all, Family Letters, Gottschalk Collection, NYPL.

100. Gottschalk to his sisters, 3, 9 February 1867, Family Letters, Gottschalk Collection, NYPL.

101. Gottschalk to Charles Vezin, 20 November 1866, Assorted Letters, Gottschalk Collection, NYPL.

102. Gottschalk, *Notes of a Pianist,* p. 384.

103. Gottschalk to his sisters, 7 June 1866, Family Letters, Gottschalk Collection, NYPL.

104. Glover Collection.

105. *El Constituyente,* 1 February 1867.

106. Gottschalk, *Notes of a Pianist,* pp. 377–79.

25. A Pan-American on the Rio de la Plata, 1867–68

1. Gottschalk to his sisters, 25 April 1867, Family Letters, Gottschalk Collection, NYPL.

2. Gottschalk to his sisters, 3 April 1867, Family Letters, Gottschalk Collection, NYPL.

3. Gottschalk to his sisters, 25 May 1868, Family Letters, Gottschalk Collection, NYPL.

4. Bushnell and Macaulay, *The Emergence of Latin America,* pp. 230ff.

5. Gottschalk to his sisters, 13 December 1867, Family Letters, Gottschalk Collection, NYPL.

6. Gottschalk, *Notes of a Pianist,* p. 392.

7. *The Cambridge History of Latin America,* 3:673.

8. Gottschalk to his sisters, 14 August 1867, Family Letters, Gottschalk Collection, NYPL.

9. Ayestarán, *La Música en el Uruguay,* 1:241–44, 607–17; Francisco Curt Lange, "La Música en el Uruguay durante el siglo XIX," *Die Musikkulturen Lateinamerikas,* pp. 333–43.

10. Francisco Curt Lange, "Louis Moreau Gottschalk (1829–1869): Correspondencia recientemente descubierta sobre su personalidad y obra realizada en el Uruguay y el Brasil," *Die Musikkulturen Lateinamerikas,* pp. 371–87.

11. Gottschalk to his sisters, 29 April 1868, 15 August 1868, Family Letters, Gottschalk Collection, NYPL.

12. List of objects contained in parcel, 6 April 1869, Gottschalk Collection, NYPL. Gottschalk to his sisters, 18 August 1868, Family Letters, Gottschalk Collection, NYPL.

13. Gottschalk to his sisters, 28 June 1867, Family Letters, Gottschalk Collection, NYPL; *El Siglo* (Montevideo), 20 June 1867.

14. Gottschalk to his sisters, 12 July 1867, 14 August 1867, Family Letters, Gottschalk Collection, NYPL.

15. *La Tribuna,* 5 September 1867.

16. *Ibid.,* 14 September 1867; *Las Noticias* (Montevideo) 15 September 1867; *El Siglo,* 21, 24 September 1867.

17. Fors, *Gottschalk,* p. 169.

18. *El Siglo,* 20 September 1867. See also Francisco Curt Lange, "Louis Moreau Gottschalk (1869–1969)," *Boletin Interamericano de Música,* May 1970, pp. 7–8.

19. Gottschalk to "My Dear Friend," Gottschalk Collection, NYPL.

20. Francisco Córdova y López, *Apuntes biográficos de Luís Ricardo Fors, miscelanea americana,* Madrid, 1871; *Enciclopedia universal ilustrada europeó-*

americana, Barcelona, 1924, 24:537–538; Lange, "Vida y muerte," no. 4, pp. 50–52.

21. L. R. Fors, "Gottschalk," *La Tribuna*, 24, 26 September 1867.

22. Fors, *Gottschalk*, p. 34.

23. *La Tribuna*, 6 October 1867; *Las Noticias* (Montevideo), 13 September 1867; Robert Stevenson, "Gottschalk in Buenos Aires," *Inter-American Music Bulletin*, 1969, 74:6, fn.14.

24. Gottschalk to Espadero, Buffalo, 1 December 1862; Fors, *Gottschalk*, pp 403–4.

25. Robert Stevenson, "Gottschalk Programs Wagner," *Inter-American Music Review*, 1983, 5:89.

26. *La Tribuna*, 7, 8 October 1867.

27. J. Zisemann and Charles Grimm to Gottschalk, 20 October 1867, Assorted Letters, Gottschalk Collection, NYPL.

28. Gottschalk to his sisters, 28–29 April 1868, 4 September 1868, Family Letters, Gottschalk Collection, NYPL.

29. Gottschalk to his sisters, 6 April 1869, Family Letters, Gottschalk Collection, NYPL.

30. Gottschalk to his sisters, 7 February 1869, 14 March 1869, Family Letters, Gottschalk Collection, NYPL.

31. *El Siglo*, 3 October 1867; *La Tribuna*, 13 September 1867; Hensel, *Life and Letters*, p. 177.

32. Lewis, "Recently Discovered Works of Gottschalk," pp. 32–40.

33. See the excellent summary in Doyle, *Louis Moreau Gottschalk*, pp. 288–90; also Offergeld, *A Centennial Catalogue*, p. 34.

34. Fors, *Gottschalk*, pp. 233–34.

35. *La Tribuna*, 3 October 1867; also Glover Collection.

36. *El Siglo*, 6 October 1867. Translation based on Stevenson, "Gottschalk in Buenos Aires," p. 2; see also L. R. Fors, "Despedida de Gottschalk," *La Tribuna*, 3 October 1867.

37. *La Nacion Argentina* (Buenos Aires), 1867 October 19.

38. Gottschalk to his sister, 11 June 1868, Family Letters, Gottschalk Collection, NYPL; *Le Courrier de la Plata* (Buenos Aires), 24 October 1867.

39. *La Tribuna*, 28–29 October 1867; Stevenson, "Gottschalk in Buenos Aires," p. 2.

40. Lange, "La Música en la Argentina del siglo XIX," pp. 75–81.

41. *La Tribuna*, 22 October 1867, 7 November 1867; *El Pueblo*, 7 November 1867; *La Nacion Argentina*, 7 November 1867.

42. *Standard*, 7 November 1867; Gesualdo, *Historia de la música*, 2:246ff.

43. *Courrier de la Plata*, 8 November 1867.

44. *El Siglo*, 7 July 1867; Stevenson, "Gottschalk in Buenos Aires," p. 3.

45. Gottschalk to his sisters, 13 December 1867, Family Letters, Gottschalk Collection, NYPL.

46. *Courrier de la Plata*, 15 November 1867; Gottschalk to his sisters, 16 November 1867, Family Letters, Gottschalk Collection, NYPL.

47. *El Nacional*, 31 October 1867.

48. Gottschalk to his sisters, 16 November 1867, Family Letters, Gottschalk Collection, NYPL.

49. *Ibid.*

50. *La Nacion Argentina*, 5 November 1867.

51. Gottschalk to his sisters, 19 December 1867, Family Letters, Gottschalk Collection, NYPL.

52. Unidentified letter by Gottschalk, n.d. (December 1867), Gottschalk Collection, NYPL.

53. S. A. Hazeltine, *A Year of South American Travel*, Philadelphia, 1891, p. 91.

54. Gottschalk to his sisters, 3 February 1868, Family Letters, Gottschalk Collection, NYPL.

55. Gottschalk to his sisters, 14, 18 May 1868, Family Letters, Gottschalk Collection, NYPL.

56. Gottschalk to his sisters, 3 February 1868, Family Letters, Gottschalk Collection, NYPL.

57. *Standard* (Buenos Aires), 21 March 1868.

58. Gottschalk to his sisters, 29 April 1868, Family Letters, Gottschalk Collection, NYPL.

59. Richard Jackson, ed., *The Complete Published Songs of Louis Moreau Gottschalk*, 1993.

60. *Dwight's Journal of Music*, 29 August 1868, p. 304.

61. Gottschalk, *Notes of a Pianist*, pp. 392–93.

62. *The Cambridge History of Latin America*, 3:673.

63. Gottschalk, *Notes of a Pianist*, p. 397.

64. *El Nacional*, 21 March 1868; *La Tribuna*, 29 April 1868; Gesualdo, *Historia de la música*, p. 256ff.

65. *Courrier de la Plata*, 1, 26, 30 April 1868, 2 May 1868; Stevenson, "Gottschalk in Buenos Aires," p. 5.

66. *La Tribuna*, 29 April 1868.

67. Gottschalk to his sisters, 14 May 1868, Family Letters, Gottschalk Collection, NYPL.

68. *Courrier de la Plata*, 3 April 1868.

69. Gottschalk to his sisters, 29 July 1868, Family Letters, Gottschalk Collection, NYPL.

70. Gottschalk to his sisters, 24 May 1868, Family Letters, Gottschalk Collection, NYPL.

71. Gottschalk to his sisters, 24 June 1868, Family Letters, Gottschalk Collection, NYPL.

72. S. Estrada, "Gottschalk!," *La Tribuna*, 11, 16 April 1868.

73. *Standard* (Buenos Aires), 21, 28 May 1868.

74. *Courrier de la Plata*, 3, 4 June 1868.

75. *Standard*, 6 June 1868.

76. *Standard*, 9 June 1868; certificate of thanks to Gottschalk, 22 June 1868, Album no. 5, Gottschalk Collection, NYPL.

77. A. Boyez, "L. M. Gottschalk dans le Rio de la Plata," *L'Art musical*, 13 February 1868, p. 85.

78. *La Nacion Argentina*, 19, 20 March 1868.

79. *El Mosquito*, 14 June 1868.

80. *Ibid; Courrier de la Plata*, 11 June 1868; *Standard*, 11 June 1868.

81. Gottschalk to his sisters, 11 July 1868, Family Letters, Gottschalk Collection, NYPL.

82. J. Sienra y Carranza, *"Muerta!!," El Pueblo*, 23 June 1868; "Walsh," in the *Courrier de la Plata*, n.d., Album no. 3, Gottschalk Collection, NYPL.

83. Gottschalk to Francis G. Hill, 22 June 1869, Hensel, *Life and Letters*, p. 171; Gottschalk to William Hall, 24 October 1869, Hensel, *Life and Letters*, p. 175.

84. For a thorough discussion see Clyde W. Brockett, "Louis Moreau Gottschalk and his *Morte!! (She Is Dead)* Lamentation," *American Music*, 1990, no. 1, pp. 29–53.

85. Gottschalk to his sisters, 14 October 1868, Family Letters, Gottschalk Collection, NYPL.

86. Sienra y Carranza, "*Muerta!!*"

87. Victor Hugo, *Morceaux choisis*, Paris, 1899, pp. 63–65.

88. Gottschalk to his sisters, 31 December 1867, Family Letters, Gottschalk Collection, NYPL. The one hint concerning the identity of the subject of *Morte!!* is an undated letter in Spanish, probably written in Chile, in which a bitter Gottschalk breaks off a relationship with a young woman (undated letter no. 82, Gottschalk Collection, NYPL).

89. Gottschalk to his sisters, 29 July 1868, Family Letters, Gottschalk Collection, NYPL.

90. Gottschalk to his sisters, 18 August 1868, Family Letters, Gottschalk Collection, NYPL.

91. Gottschalk to his sisters, 18 August 1868, October 14, Family Letters, Gottschalk Collection, NYPL.

92. Gottschalk to his sisters, 27 September 1868, Family Letters, Gottschalk Collection, NYPL.

93. *Ibid.*

94. Gottschalk to his sisters, 4 September 1868, Family Letters, Gottschalk Collection, NYPL.

95. Gottschalk to his sisters, 29 October 1868, Family Letters, Gottschalk Collection, NYPL.

96. *Standard*, 14 November 1868 (misdated by Hensel, *Life and Letters*, pp. 168–70); *El Siglo*, 12 November 1868; *La Tribuna*, 12 November 1868; *El Orden*, 12 November 1868; *Courrier de la Plata*, 19 November 1868.

97. Gottschalk to his sisters, undated fragment, Family Letters, Gottschalk Collection, NYPL.

98. Gottschalk to his sisters, 13 November 1868, Family Letters, Gottschalk Collection, NYPL.

99. Korf, *Orchestral Music*, pp. 125–33.

100. *El Siglo*, 8 November 1868.

101. Korf, *Orchestral Music*, pp. 135–43; Lewis, "Recently Discovered Works of Gottschalk," pp. 34–35.

102. *El Siglo*, 9 October 1868; Hensel, *Life and Letters*, pp. 165–67.

103. Fors, *Gottschalk*, pp. 253–57.

104. *Ibid.*, p. 256.

105. Lange, "Vida y muerte," no. 5–6, pp. 124, fn. 198; pp. 127–49.

106. *Ibid.*, p. 147.

107. Moisé, "Crónica musical," *La Tribuna*, 13 November 1868.

108. *La República* (Buenos Aires), 20 November 1868; *La Tribuna*, 21 November 1868; *El Nacional*, 22 November 1868; Gottschalk to his sisters, 1 January 1869, Family Letters, Gottschalk Collection, NYPL.

109. *El Nacional* (Buenos Aires), 4 April 1869.

110. Gottschalk to his sisters, 1 January 1869, Family Letters, Gottschalk Collection, NYPL.

111. Gottschalk to his sisters, 26 January 1869, 7 February 1869, Family Letters, Gottschalk Collection, NYPL; *El Nacional*, 4 April 1869.

112. Gottschalk to his sisters, 1 January 1869, Family Letters, Gottschalk Collection, NYPL.

113. Gottschalk, "La Música, el piano, los pianistas," Fors, *Gottschalk*, p. 335.

114. Gottschalk to Francis G. Hill, 14 April 1869, Hensel, *Life and Letters*, pp. 163–64; Gottschalk to George William Warren, 24 October 1869, Hensel, *Life and Letters*, pp. 176–77; Doyle, "The Piano Music of Louis Moreau Gottschalk," p. 85.

115. First performed in March 1868: *La República* (Buenos Aires), 20 March 1868.

116. Possibly based on themes from Verdi's *Un Ballo in maschera;* cf. Gottschalk to his sisters, 13 April 1869, Family Letters, Gottschalk Collection, NYPL.

117. Gottschalk to George William Warren, 24 October 1869, Hensel, *Life and Letters*, pp. 176–77.

118. Gottschalk to his sisters, 27 September 1868, Family Letters, Gottschalk Collection, NYPL.

119. *Observer*, 7 February 1870.

120. Gottschalk to his sister, 12 July 1867, Family Letters, Gottschalk Collection, NYPL.

121. List of contents in the trunk, 6 April 1869, Family Letters, Gottschalk Collection, NYPL.

122. Hensel, *Life and Letters*, pp. 184–85, 197; Lange, "Vida y muerte," no. 5–6, p. 119.

123. Gottschalk to his sisters, 31 December 1867, 13 November 1868, Family Letters, Gottschalk Collection, NYPL.

124. Gottschalk to his sisters, 1 April 1869, Family Letters, Gottschalk Collection, NYPL.

125. Gottschalk to his sisters, 14 October 1868, Family Letters, Gottschalk Collection, NYPL.

126. Gottschalk to his sisters, 1 January 1869, Family Letters, Gottschalk Collection, NYPL.

127. Gottschalk to Charles Vezin, 15 December 1868, Gottschalk Collection, NYPL.

128. Gottschalk to Charles Vezin, 27 May 1868, Gottschalk Collection; Gottschalk to his sisters, 27 September 1868, Family Letters, Gottschalk Collection, NYPL.

129. Gottschalk to his sisters, 1 January 1868, Family Letters, Gottschalk Collection, NYPL.

130. Henri Préalle to Charles Vezin, 24 December 1869, published by Vezin in an unidentified newspaper, Glover Collection.

131. Fragment of draft letter from Gottschalk to the Chickering firm, n.d., uncataloged letter no. 65, Gottschalk Collection, NYPL; Gottschalk to Charles Vezin, 27 May 1868, Gottschalk Collection, NYPL.

132. *La República*, 1 April 1868.

133. Gottschalk to his sisters, 18 August 1868, Family Letters, Gottschalk Collection, NYPL; Gottschalk, *Notes of a Pianist*, p. 146.

134. Gottschalk to Francis G. Hill, 14 April 1869, Hensel, *Life and Letters*, pp. 163–64.

135. *Ibid.*

136. Gottschalk to his sisters, undated letter no. 3, Family Letters, Gottschalk Collection, NYPL.

137. *La República*, 4 December 1868.

138. Gottschalk to his sisters, 14 March 1869, Family Letters, Gottschalk Collection, NYPL.

26. Brazil, 1869: "Prestissimo del mio Finale"

1. Lange, "Vida y muerte," no. 5–6, p. 124, fn. 197; both Henri Préalle (letter to Charles Vezin, 24 December 1869, Gottschalk Collection, NYPL) and Hensel (*Life and Letters*, p. 170) erroneously date his arrival as 10 May.

2. Gottschalk to his sisters, 8 July 1869, Family Letters, Gottschalk Collection, NYPL.

3. Mary Wilhemine Williams, *Dom Pedro the Magnanimous*, Chapel Hill, 1937, p. 217.

4. Quoted by Professor and Mrs. Louis Agassiz, *A Journal in Brazil*, Boston, 1868, p. 52.

5. Henry T. Blow to Secretary of State Hamilton Fish, 23 November 1869, Miscellaneous Letters, General Records of the Department of State, Record Group 59, Brazil, U.S. National Archives.

6. C. H. Haring, *Empire in Brazil*, Cambridge, Massachusetts, 1968, pp. 96–97.

7. "Gottschalk," *A Semana Illustrada* (Rio de Janeiro), 18 July 1869.

8. Henry T. Blow to Secretary of State Hamilton Fish, 1 September 1869, Miscellaneous Letters, General Records of the Department of State, Record Group 59, U.S. National Archives.

9. Gottschalk to his sisters, 8 May 1869, Family Letters, Gottschalk Collection, NYPL.

10. *Ibid.*

11. *A Reforma* (Rio de Janeiro), 19 May 1869; Lange, "Vida y muerte," no. 4, p. 78.

12. Gottschalk to Mary Alice Ives Seymour, August 1869, Hensel, *Life and Letters*, p. 72; *New York Times*, 24 October 1869.

13. Gottschalk to Clara Gottschalk, 15 August 1869; Gottschalk to his sisters, 29 May 1869, Family Letters, Gottschalk Collection, NYPL.

14. *Jornal para Todos* (Rio de Janeiro), 12 June 1868.

15. Lange, "Vida y muerte," no. 4, p. 80.

16. *Ibid.*, no. 5–6, p. 316–17.

17. Renato Almeida, *História da música brasileira*, Rio de Janeiro, 1942, pp. 415–16.

18. Lange, "Vida y muerte," no. 4, pp. 68, 88, 222.

19. Francisco Curt Lange, "A Música no Brasil durante o século XIX," *Musikkulturen Lateinamerikas*, pp. 121–66; Almeida, *História da música brasileira*, pp. 356–70.

20. Lange, "Vida y muerte," no. 4, p. 72.

21. *Ibid.*, no. 4, pp. 62–63.

22. *Jornal do Commercio* (Rio de Janeiro), 9 June 1869.

23. *Ibid.*, 5 June 1869; *A Vida Fluminense*, 5 June 1869. Gottschalk to Francis G. Hill, 22 June 1869, Hensel, *Life and Letters*, pp. 170–71.

24. *Jornal do Commercio*, 4 June 1869. On this series see Lange, "Vida y muerte," no. 4, pp. 77–87.

25. *Jornal do Commercio*, 29 May 1869.

26. *Jornal para Todos*, 25 May 1869; *Jornal do Commercio*, 24, 29 May 1869, 21 June 1869. On the reception of *Morte!!* see Brockett, "Louis Moreau Gottschalk and his *Morte!! (She Is Dead)* Lamentation."

27. *A Semana Illustrada*, 4 July 1869.

28. David P. Appleby, *The Music of Brazil*, Austin, 1983, p. 36. (Op. 69, op. 91, D-157).

29. "Gottschalk in Rio," *Standard*, 23 July 1869; Korf, *Orchestral Music*, pp. 144–48.

30. *A Vida Fluminense*, 19 June 1869.

31. *A Semana Illustrada*, 18 July 1869; Lange, "Vida y muerte," no. 4, p. 87; the case for Clélie is made by Fors (*Gottschalk*, p. 174) and for a Bohemian actress named "La Reine" by Escragnolle-Doria ("Gottschalk," p. 68–71) and Lange ("Vida y muerte," no. 4, pp. 147–48).

32. *Jornal para Todos*, 29 May 1869.

33. Ernest Cibrão, *A Semana Illustrada*, 2 January 1870.

34. Gottschalk to his sisters, 8 July 1869, Family Letters, Gottschalk Collection, NYPL.

35. *A Vida Fluminense*, 3 July 1869.

36. *Standard* (Buenos Aires), 23 July 1869.

37. *Jornal para Todos*, 19 July 1869.

38. Gottschalk to an unknown friend, August 1869; Clara Gottschalk Peterson, "Biographical Sketch," p. 73; *New York Times*, 24 October 1869.

39. *Jornal do Commercio*, 23 July 1869; *New York Times*, 24 October 1869; on the school, see Dr. Moreirade Azevedo, *O Rio de Janeiro*, 2 vols., Rio de Janeiro, 1877, 2:61–96.

40. Gottschalk to Francis G. Hill, 24 July 1869, Hensel, *Life and Letters*, p. 172.

41. *New York Times*, 24 October 1869.

42. William Hepworth Dixon, *New America*, London, 1867, p. 389.

43. *A Semana Illustrada*, 2 January 1870.

44. *New York Times*, 24 October 1869.

45. Gottschalk to Oliver Ditson, 22 August 1869, Hensel, *Life and Letters*, p. 174; Lange, "Vida y muerte," no. 4, pp. 95–104.

46. Gottschalk to his sisters, 8 October 1869, Family Letters, Gottschalk Collection, NYPL.

47. Gottschalk to his sisters, 15 August 1869, Family Letters, Gottschalk Collection, NYPL.

48. Lange, "Vida y muerte," no. 4, p. 101.

49. *New York Times*, 26 October 1869; Clara Gottschalk Peterson, "Biographical Sketch," p. 74.

50. Rezende, "O Poeta do piano," pp. 21–42.

51. Henry T. Blow to Hamilton Fish, 15, 19 January 1870, 21 July 1870, Diplomatic Despatches, General Records of the Department of State, Records Group 59, U.S. National Archives.

52. Rezende, "O Poeta do piano," p. 26.

53. Lange, "Vida y muerte," no. 5-6, pp. 171–75.

54. Gottschalk to his sisters, 4 September 1869, Family Letters, Gottschalk Collection, NYPL.

55. *Revista Commercial* (Santos), 10 September 1869.

56. Lange, "Vida y muerte," no. 5–6, p. 260; Clara Gottschalk Peterson, "Biographical Sketch," p. 74.

57. Lange, "Vida y muerte," no. 4, pp. 118–24.

58. Gottschalk to his sisters, 8 October 1869, Family Letters, Gottschalk Collection, NYPL.

59. Program for Grande Concerto, 5 October 1869, Theatro Lyrico Fluminense, Glover Collection.

60. Gottschalk to his sisters, 8 October 1869, Family Letters, Gottschalk Collection, NYPL.

61. *A Vida Fluminense*, 2 October 1869; Lange, "Vida y muerte," no. 5–6, p. 260.

62. Lange, "Vida y muerte," no. 4, pp. 125–27.

63. *A Semana Illustrada*, 21 November 1869.

64. Ryan, *Recollections of an Old Musician*, pp. 189–97.

65. Gottschalk to Oliver Ditson, 22 August 1869, Hensel, *Life and Letters*, p. 174.

66. Gottschalk to Messrs. William Hall & Son, 24 October 1869, Hensel, *Life and Letters*, p. 175.

67. Lange, "Vida y muerte," no. 4, p. 128.

68. *A Vida Fluminense*, 25 December 1869, quoted by Lange, "Vida y muerte," no. 5–6, p. 107.

69. Gottschalk to his sisters, 27 September 1869, Family Letters, Gottschalk Collection, NYPL.

70. Gottschalk to Messrs. William Hall & Son, 24 October 1869, Hensel, *Life and Letters*, p. 175.

71. Gottschalk to Henri Préalle, 22 October 1869, Gottschalk Collection, NYPL.

72. *Jornal do Commercio*, 21 November 1869.

73. *New York Times*, 21 January 1870; *Watson's Art Journal*, 29 January 1870, p. 10.

74. Henry Clapp Jr., "Figaro on Gottschalk," *Leader*, n.d. 1870, unmounted clipping, Gottschalk Collection, NYPL.

75. *New York Herald*, 24 October 1865; *Watson's Art Journal*, 22 January 1870, pp. 92–93 and 5 February, p. 117.

76. Gottschalk to his sisters, 8 October 1869, Family Letters, Gottschalk Collection, NYPL.

77. "Creole Music," unidentified and uncataloged clipping headed "Music and Drama," 14 April 1883, Gottschalk Collection, NYPL.

78. L. G. Escragnolle-Doria, "Gottschalk," pp. 72–73; Lange, "Vida y muerte," no. 4, p. 132.

79. Program for Grande Concerto, 5 October 1869, Theatro Lyrico Fluminense, Glover Collection.

80. Gottschalk to Camille Pleyel, 23 October 1869, Assorted Letters, Gottschalk Collection, NYPL.

81. *Ba-ta-clan*, 25 December 1869; see also a second version preserved in Museo de la Música, Havana.

82. Henry T. Blow to Secretary of State Hamilton Fish, 19 November 1869, Miscellaneous Letters, General Records of the Department of State, Record Group 59, U.S. National Archives.

83. *Jornal do Commercio*, 22 November 1869; Lange, "Vida y muerte," no. 4, p. 130.

84. Freyre, *Order and Progress*, p. 77.

85. Lange, "Vida y muerte," no. 4, p. 133.

86. Hensel, *Life and Letters*, pp. 178–179.

87. Lange, "Vida y muerte," no. 4, pp. 140, 179; Hensel, *Life and Letters*, p. 179.

88. Lange, "Vida y muerte," no. 4, pp. 141–44.

89. *Jornal do Commercio*, 28 November 1869.

90. Fors, *Gottschalk*, p. 185.

91. Agassiz, *A Journey in Brazil*, pp. 85–86.

92. Lange, "Vida y muerte," no. 4, p. 146.

93. *Reforma*, 21 December 1869; Hensel, *Life and Letters*, p. 184.

94. *A Semana Illustrada*, 2 January 1870.

95. Escragnolle Doria, "Gottschalk," p. 73.

27. Post-Mortem: Gottschalk through the 125 Years

1. A bust intended for a Rio park was completed by Mr. Filippone (Henri Préalle to Clara and Celestine Gottschalk, 22 March 1870, Glover Collection); a second, by Francisco Manuel Chaves Pinheiro, remains unlocated (Lange, "Vida y muerte," no. 5–6, p. 153, fn. 22); a third, unidentified but possibly by Jean Paul Franceschi, is in the Historic New Orleans Collection. Dated 18 December 1869, it was patented on 16 March 1871. A slightly different plaster miniature is in the author's collection.

2. Escudier, "Mort de Gottschalk," pp. 65–67

3. Ambassador Van Montenaecken to Clara Gottschalk, 9 December 1872, Family Letters, Gottschalk Collection, NYPL.

4. Lange, "Vida y muerte," no. 4, p. 83.

5. Lapique, *Música colonial cubana*, 1:292.

6. No copy of the Kunkel edition has yet been found. Fillipone & Tornaghi, Rio de Janeiro, issued a piece with the same title, dedicated to Gottschalk. Lange, "Vida y muerte," no. 5–6, pp. 152, 223.

7. See his two-piano transcription of *Esquisses créoles* and other works, Doyle, *Louis Moreau Gottschalk*, p. 195.

8. Done by Ricardo Ferreira de Corvalho. Cf. Fors, *Gottschalk*, pp. 233–34.

9. Lange, "Louis Moreau Gottschalk (1820–1869)," pp. 381ff.

10. *Madeleine* (D-83), rediscoverd by Doyle; see also Lange, "Vida y muerte," no. 5–6, p. 164.

11. Espadero's introduction to Gottschalk's posthumous works, Fors, *Gottschalk*, pp. 291–92.

12. N. R. Espadero, "Les Oeuvres posthumes de L. M. Gottschalk," *L'Art musical*, 5 February 1874, pp. 11–12.

13. W. F. Apthorp, "New Music," *Atlantic Monthly*, February 1874, p. 256.

14. Issued by the firm of Monguillot in Buenos Aires; cf. Gesualdo, *Historia de la música*, 2:987.

15. By far the most detailed analysis of Gottschalk imprints is that in Doyle, *Louis Moreau Gottschalk*; see also Offergeld, *Centennial Catalogue*.

16. Unidentified clipping (*Watson's Art Journal?*), 20 May 1871, Scrapbook no. 4, Gottschalk Collection, NYPL.

17. *Ibid.*

18. Boston, 1870.

19. Hensel, *Life and Letters*, pp. 22, 26.

20. Nym Crinkle, pseud. for Andrew Carpenter Wheeler (1835–1903), "In Behalf of Gottschalk," *New York World*, n.d 1870, Scrapbook no. 4, Gottschalk Collection, NYPL.

21. Fors, *Gottschalk*, p. 418.

22. *Ibid.*, pp. 245–52.

23. "Louis Moreau Gottschalk," *Musical Leader and Concert-Goer*, n.d. uncatalogued clipping, Gottschalk Collection, NYPL.

24. *American Register* first announced the publication on 23 March 1872.

25. I am indebted to Robert T. Seaman in Oberlin College for carrying out this examination.

26. *Philadelphia Press*, 29 October 1881.

27. *New York Daily Tribune*, 6 November 1881.

28. H. T. Finck, "Gottschalk's Tour in the United States," *Nation*, 5 January 1882, pp. 16–17.

29. Erham., "Gottschalk," *Song Friend* (Chicago), n.d., unfiled clippings, Gottschalk Collection, NYPL.

30. "A Great Musician," *New York Times*, 23 December 1881.

31. Unknown critic, quoted in "Gottschalk as Composer and Pianist," *American Art Journal*, 29 October 1881.

32. Gottschalk family concert programs, Glover Collection.

33. Brandon Murray, "A Disciple of Gottschalk," *Ev'ry Month*, n.d., uncatalogued clippings, Gottschalk Collection, NYPL.

34. Gottschalk to his sisters, 29 September 1868, Family Letters, Gottschalk Collection, NYPL.

35. Sometimes identified as Thomas Greene Wiggins. See Geneva H. Southall, *Blind Tom: The Post–Civil War Enslavement of a Black Musical Genius*, 2 vols., Minneapolis, 1979, 1983, 1:107, 2:164. See also W. S. B. Mathews, "Blind Tom," *Dwight's Journal of Music*, 2 September 1865, p. 96. Also William L. Hawes to Clara Gottschalk Peterson, 12 October 1908, Historic New Orleans Collection .

36. *Boston Herald*, 18 February 1909.

37. Curtiss, *Bizet and His World*, p. 472.

38. Oliver Daniel, "The Man Who Wrote (the recitatives to) Bizet's *Carmen*," *Stereo Review*, September 1975, pp. 80–81.

39. Quoted by Carlo Gatti, *Verdi, the Man and His Music*, New York, 1955, p. 246.

40. Dianin, *Borodin*, pp. 310–14.

41. George Bernard Shaw, *Music in London 1890–94*, 3 vols., London, 1932, 1:25.

42. Fors, *Gottschalk*, p. 383.

43. Apthorp, *Musicians and Music-Lovers*, p. 212.

44. Margery Morgan Lowens, "The New York Years of Edward MacDowell" (Ph.D. diss., University of Michigan, 1971), p. 5.

45. W. S. B. Mathews, "An Evening with American Composers," *Music*, January 1898, 13:351, 354.

46. Henry T. Finck, "Gottschalk's Tour in the United States," *Nation*, 5 January 1882.

47. Ritter, *Music in America*, pp. 380–81.

48. Louis C. Madeira, Philip H. Goepp, *Annals of Music in Philadelphia and History of the Musical Fund Society*, Philadelphia, 1896, p. 161.

49. Paul E. Bierley, *John Philip Sousa: A Descriptive Catalog of His Works*, Urbana, 1973, p. 134.

50. Eclipse Publishing Company, 1900.

51. Quarterly statements of Oliver Ditson & Company to the estate of L. M. Gottschalk, Glover Collection.

52. Doyle, *Louis Moreau Gottschalk*, pp. 365ff.

53. Rita Maria Castro y Maya, Havana, letter to the author.

54. Gérard Henri Béhaque, *Popular Musical Currents in the Art Music of the Early Nationalistic Period in Brazil, circa 1870–1920* (Ph.D. diss., Tulane University, 1966), pp. 138–39.

55. William Mason, *Memories of a Musical Life*, pp. 205–9; Root, *The Story of a Musical Life*, p. 65.

56. George P. Upton, *Musical Memories*, pp. 76–77.

57. Diego de Vivo, "De Vivo's Jolly Season," New York Sun, 4 April 1897.

58. *Music*, June 1892, pp. 117–32. See also "The Great American Composer, the Where, the Why, and the When," *Etude*, July 1906, pp. 422–23.

59. W. S. B. Mathews, *Music*, June 1895, p. 190.

60. T. James Tracy, "The World's Greatest Pianists," *Etude*, September 1907, p. 560.

61. "Virtuoso," *Etude*, May 1899, pp. 133–34.

62. "Gottschalk Number," *Musician*, October 1908; *America*, 12 December 1908.

63. "Gottschalk's Period," *Etude*, June 1914, p. 423.

64. Hearn, *The Life and Letters*, 1:228–29.

65. See the Hawes–Clara Gottschalk Peterson correspondence in the Historic New Orleans Collection.

66. Alice Graham, "Musical Life in New Orleans, A Study," *Etude*, April 1906, pp. 217–18.

67. Grace King, *New Orleans, The Place and the People*, New York, 1925, p. 356.

68. Undated clipping (1899?), Scrapbook no. 12, Gottschalk Collection, NYPL.

69. Clara Gottschalk Peterson to William H. Hawes, 16 September 1899, Historic New Orleans Collection.

70. James Haskins and W. Kathleen Benson, *Scott Joplin*, Garden City, 1978, p. 59.

71. Peter Gammond, *Scott Joplin and the Ragtime Era*, New York, 1975, pp. 22, 29, 33.

72. Eric Thacker, "Ragtime Roots," *Jazz and Blues*, November 1973, pp. 6–7; "Gottschalk and a Prelude to Jazz," *Jazz and Blues*, 12 March 1973, pp. 10–12, 17; Fred Kern, "Ragtime Wins Respectability," *Clavier*, April 1976, pp. 28–30.

73. Sales records of Oliver Ditson & Co., Glover Collection.

74. Gammond, *Scott Joplin and the Ragtime Era*, p. 7.

75. King, *New Orleans, the Place and the People*, p. 356.

76. Lomax, *Mr. Jelly Lord*, pp. 66, 278–279.

77. *Ibid.*, pp. 6, 34, 148–149.

78. Béhaque, *Popular Musical Currents*, pp. 137–40.

79. G. Jean Aubry, "A Forgotten Pioneer," *Christian Science Monitor*, 26 December 1925; Tod B. Galloway, "Forgotten American Musician," *General Magazine and Historical Chronicle*, 1932, pp. 56–64.

80. Nicolás Ruiz Espadero et al., "El Centenario Luis Moreau Gottschalk," *Revista Bimestre Cubano* (Havana), November-December 1930, pp. 254–63. Robert D. Darrell, "An Early Pan-American Exhumed," *Musical Mercury*, January-Febuary 1934, pp. 18–21.

81. See correspondence between Gertrude Tucker and Lily Glover, Glover Collection.

82. Darrell, "An Early Pan-American Exhumed," p. 18.

83. R. M. Knerr, "Publications," *Musical Courier*, 23 September 1933, p. 22.

84. Quinto Maganini, "Letter to the Editor," *New York Times*, 22 May 1932; *New York Herald Tribune*, 15 May 1932.

85. Robert Sabin, "American Piano Musical Collection," *Musical America*, 1 January 1949, p. 5.

86. Olin Downes, *New York Times*, 23 December 1948. For an account of this

concert, see Jackson and Ratliff, *The Little Book of Louis Moreau Gottschalk*, pp. 11–13.

87. *New York Times*, 22 November 1959; *New York Herald Tribune*, 6 May 1955.

88. For a comprehensive review of choreographic treatment of Gottschalk's works, see Doyle, *Louis Moreau Gottschalk*, "Literature and Modern Performances," pp. 17ff.

89. "Balanchine at the White House," *Wall Street Journal*, 13 April 1979.

90. Nancy Reynolds, *Repertory in Review: Forty Years of the New York City Ballet*, New York, 1977, p. 121.

91. *New York Times*, 9 September 1966.

92. Clive Barnes, "ABT's 'Galloping Gottschalk' Romps Home," *New York Post*, 4 May 1982.

93. Lange, "Vida y muerte."

94. Francisco Curt Lange, "Gottschalk en Montevideo" (MS), Montevideo, 1966; "Gottschalk en la Argentina" (MS), Montevideo, 1962.

95. Pereira-Salas, "La Embajada músical de Gottschalk en Chile," pp. 5–11; "Gottschalk," *Jornal de Música* (Rio de Janeiro), February 1952, pp. 4–10.

96. Doyle, "The Piano Music of Louis Moreau Gottschalk."

97. MGM Records, E 3370. See Irving Lowens, "Review of Records," *Musical Quarterly*, April 1957, pp. 270–73.

98. Johannes Magendanz, "Gottschalk in Utica," *Town Topics of the Mohawk Valley*, October-December 1932, January-May 1933.

99. Stevenson, "Gottschalk in Buenos Aires," pp. 1–7. See bibliographic entries under Jane Ambrose, John W. Barker, Clyde Brockett, Libby Antarsh Rubin, and Donald Thompson.

100. New York, 1970.

101. *The Piano Works of Louis Moreau Gottschalk*, Vera Brodsky Lawrence, ed., 5 vols., New York, 1969.

102. Alan Mandel, "Louis Moreau Gottschalk: Forty Works for Piano," Desto Records (DC 6470–73).

103. Alfred Frankenstein, "Gottschalk: Works for Piano," *High Fidelity Magazine*, 1970, no. 2, p. 86.

104. Doyle, *Louis Moreau Gottschalk*, p. 43.

105. Herald C. Schonberg, "Music: Southern Original," *New York Times*, 27 February 1969.

106. Donald Henahan, "Ten Pianists Tuning Up for 'Saragossa,'" *New York Times*, 24 September 1969.

107. Christopher Porterfield, "Monster Rally," *Time*, 14 May 1979, p. 106.

108. Florence Crim Robinson, "A View of Louis Moreau Gottschalk," *Musical Analysis*, Winter 1972, pp. 1–6; see also David M. Baker, "Indiana University's Black Music Committee," *Black Music in Our Culture*, Dominique-René de Lerma, ed., Kent, Ohio, 1970, p. 21.

109. The First Louis Moreau Gottschalk International Competition for Pianists and Composers, Dillard University, New Orleans, 3–7 June 1970.

110. Personal conversation with Robert Offergeld, 1989.

111. Richard Jackson, "More Notes of a Pianist: A Gottschalk Collection Surveyed and a Scandal Revisited," *Notes*, December 1985, pp. 352–75; also, personal communication from Lawrence B. Glover, 1992.

112. *Les voyages extraordinaires de Louis Moreau Gottschalk, pianiste et aventurier*, Serge Berthier, ed., Lausanne, 1985.

113. Garry E. Clarke, *Essays on American Music*, Westport, Connecticut, 1977, pp. 49–72.

114. Daniel Kingman, *American Music, a Panorama*, New York, 1979, pp. 348–54.

115. Chase, *America's Music*, pp. 55, 66; Hitchcock, *Music in the United States*, pp. 69–74, 88.

116. Mellers, *Music in a New Found Land*, p. 254.

117. Zuck, *A History of Musical Americanism*, pp. 39–41; John Tasker Howard and George Kent Bellows, *A Short History of American Music*, New York, 1957, p. 119.

118. Irving Lowens, "Gottschalk, Louis Moreau," *New Grove Dictionary of Music and Musicians*, London, 1980, 7:572.

Bibliography

I. Manuscript Collections

Archivo General, Biblioteca General de Puerto Rico, San Juan
Gregor Benko, Freeport, New York
Biblioteca de la Escola Nacional de Musica, Rio de Janeiro
Biblioteca Nacional José Martí, Departmentio de Música, Havana
Seccíon Manuscritos de la Biblioteca Nacional de Rio de Janeiro
Columbia University, Butler Library, Special Collections
Dr. D. Franklin Diamond, Rydal, Pennsylvania
George Sherman Dickinson Music Library, Vassar College
Escola Nacional de Musica, Rio de Janeiro
Free Library of Philadelphia
Lawrence A. Glover, East Brunswick, New Jersey
Historic New Orleans Collection, New Orleans
Historic Society of Pennsylvania, Philadelphia
Carl Honerlin Collection, New York
Library of Performing Arts, New York Public Library
Harold Linebach, St. Louis, Missouri
Harvard Theatre Collection, Harvard College Library, Cambridge, Massachusetts
Missouri Historical Society, St. Louis
Museo de la Música, Havana
New Orleans Notarial Archives
New Orleans Public Library
New-York Historical Society
Olana State Historic Site, Hudson, New York
Orleans Parish Conveyance Office, New Orleans
St. Louis Mercantile Library
South Carolina Historical Society, Columbia
United States National Archives, General Records of the Department of State, Washington, D.C.

II. Selected Published Music of Louis Moreau Gottschalk

Gottschalk, L. M. *Complete Published Songs of Louis Moreau Gottschalk.* Edited by Richard Jackson. Newton Centre, Mass., 1993.

Gottschalk, L. M. *The Little Book of Louis Moreau Gottschalk*. Edited by Richard Jackson and Neil Ratliff. New York, 1975.

―――. *Obras posthumas de L. M. Gottschalk*. Edited by Nicolás Ruiz Espadero, Havana, 1873.

―――. *The Piano Works of Louis Moreau Gottschalk*. Edited by Vera Brodsky Lawrence. 5 vols., New York, 1969.

III. Selected Published Writings of Louis Moreau Gottschalk

Gottschalk, L. M. *Illustrated Concert Book*. New York, 1862.

―――. "Dramatic Feuilleton," unidentified newspaper, June 1863, Scrapbook no. 4, Gottschalk Collection, NYPL.

―――. "Iz putevykh zametok amerikanskago pianista Gotshalka." *Literaturnoe pribavlenie k nuvellistu*, Moscow, January 1864, pp. 6–7; February 1864, pp. 12–15.

―――. ["Letter-essay"]. *El Siglo*, Havana, 29 August 1863.

―――. "La Música, el piano, los pianistas, Espadero y 'La Plainte du poète.'" *Liceo de la Habana*, Havana, 27, 28 April 1860, 3 May 1860.

―――. "La Musique à la Havane." *La France musicale*, 24 January 1858, 11 December 1859, 28 October 1860.

―――. "Notes of a Pianist." *Atlantic Monthly* 15 (February 1865):177–81, 15 (March 1865):350–52, 15 (May 1865):573–75.

―――. *Notes of a Pianist*. Edited by Jeanne Behrend. New York, 1964.

―――. *Notes of a Pianist*. Edited by Clara Gottschalk Peterson. Translated from the French by Robert E. Peterson, M.D. Philadelphia, 1881.

―――. "Souvenirs de voyage." *L'Art musical*, 31 July 1862; 13, 20, 27 August 1863; 3, 24 September 1863; 15 October 1863; 19 May 1864; 14 July 1864.

―――. *Les voyages extraordinaires de Louis Moreau Gottschalk, pianiste et aventurier*. Edited by Serge Berthier. Lausanne, 1985.

IV. Contemporary Sources and Memoirs

Adam, Adolphe. *Feuilleton* of *L'Assemblée nationale*, Paris, 29 April 1851.

―――. *Souvenirs d'un musicien*. Paris, 1857.

Allain, Helene d'Aquin. *Souvenirs d'Amérique et de France, par une Créole*. Paris, 1883.

"Alville." *La vie en Suisse de S.A.I. la Grande Duchesse Anna Feodorovna*, Lausanne, 1942.

Apthorp, William Foster. *Musicians and Music Lovers*. New York, 1897.

―――. "Recent Music." *Atlantic Monthly* 35 (March 1875):380–81.

Arboleza, José Garcia de. *Manual de la isla de Cuba*. 2nd ed., Havana, 1859.

Arpin, Paul. *Biographie de Louis Moreau Gottschalk, pianiste américain*. New York, 1853.

―――. *Life of Louis Moreau Gottschalk*. Translated from the French by H. C. Watson, New York, 1853.

Aymar, Marguerite F. "Gottschalk's Grave." *Musical Bulletin*, February 1871.

Barival, Mennechet de. "Gottschalk." *L'Art musical*, Paris, 5 April 1857.

Berlioz, Hector. "Gottschalk." *Journal des débats*, Paris, 3 April 1851.

————. *Memoirs of Hector Berlioz from 1803 to 1865*. Edited by Ernest Newman. New York, 1947.

Beauvallet, Léon. *Rachel and the New World*. New York, 1856.

Bromwell, Henry P. H. *The Dying Poet*. Denver, 1918.

Cable, George W. "The Dance in Place Congo." *Century Magazine* 31 (February 1886):517–32.

————. "Creole Slave Songs." *Century Magazine* 31 (April 1886):809.

Camancho, Simon Bolivar. "Gottschalk en Rio de Janeiro." *Jornal do Commercio*, 24 November 1869.

Cardoso de Menezes, Antonio. "Noticiaro Gottschalk." *Diario do Rio de Janeiro*, 22 December 1869.

Clapp, Henry. "Figaro on Gottschalk." undated fragment from *Leader*, Clipping File, Gottschalk Collection, NYPL, 1870.

Clare, Ada. *Only a Woman's Heart*. New York, 1866.

————. "The Pangs of Despised Love." *Atlas*, 28 December 1856.

————. "Thoughts and Things." *Saturday Press* (weekly, 1859–60).

————. "Whips and Scorns of Time." *Atlas*, 7, 14, 21 December 1856.

Clay, Virginia. *A Belle of the Fifties*. New York, 1904.

"Comments on Gottschalk." *Godey's Lady's Book and Magazine*, January-June 1856, p. 377.

Comettant, Jean Pierre Oscar. *Histoire de cent mille pianos et d'une salle de concert (Pleyel)*. Paris, 1890.

————. *Trois ans aux États-Unis*. Paris, 1857.

Comettant, Oscar. *Feuilleton* of *Le Siècle*. Paris, 1 November 1850.

Córdova y López, Francisco. *Apuntes biográficos de Luís Ricardo Fors, miscelanea americana*. Madrid, 1871.

Costa, H. da. "Gottschalk." *Tribune del Pueblo*, Madrid, reprinted in *L'International*, Bayonne, 15 September 1841.

Curtis, George W. "Gottschalk." *Harper's New Monthly Magazine*, 25 September 1862.

Cybrão, Ernest. "Gottschalk." *A Semana Illustrada*, Rio de Janeiro, 6 June 1869, p. 3543.

Dana, Richard Henry. *To Cuba and Back*. Boston, 1859.

Dayton, Abram C. *Last Days of Knickerbocker Life in New York*. New York, 1882.

Delord, Taxile. *Feuilleton* in *Le Charivari*, Paris, 22 March 1851.

Durell, Edward Henry [H[enry] D[idimus]]. "Biography of Louis Moreau Gottschalk." *Graham's Magazine*, January 1853.

Dwight, John Sullivan. "Address Delivered Before the Harvard Musical Association, 25 August 1841." *Musical Magazine*, 1841.

————. "Music a Means of Culture." *Atlantic Monthly* 26 (September 1870).

Eichberg, Julius. *Feuilleton* in *Nouvelliste vaudois*, Geneva, 26 October 1850.

Escudier, Léon. *Les Virtuoses*. Paris, 1868.

————. "Mort de Gottschalk." *L'Art musical*, 27 January 1870.

Escudier, Marie. "Gottschalk à Valladolid." *La France musicale*, 1 February 1852.

————. "Gottschalk en Suisse." *La France musicale*, 27 October 1850.

Espadero, Nicolás Ruiz. "À propos de Gottschalk." *L'Art musical*, 31 March 1870.

————. "Les Oeuvres posthumes de L. M. Gottschalk." *L'Art musical*, 5 February 1874.

————. "Prefatory Remarks by an Artist Friend of the Great Composer." *Posthumous Works of Louis Moreau Gottschalk*, Boston, 1872.

Estorch, D. M. *Apuntes para la historia sobre la administración del Marqués de la*

Pezuela en la isla de Cuba, desde 3 de Diciembre de 1853 hasta 21 de Septiembre de 1854. Madrid, 1856.

Estrada, Santiago. "Luis Moreau Gottschalk." *Revista Argentina* 6 (January 1870):57–64.

Fay, Amy. *Music Study in Germany from the Home Correspondence of Amy Fay.* Edited by Fay Pierce. New York, 1922.

Finck, H. T. "Gottschalk's Tour in the United States." *Nation,* 5 January 1882.

Ford, James L. *Forty-Odd Years in the Literary Shop.* New York, 1921.

Fors, Luís Ricardo. *Gottschalk.* Havana, 1880.

Frias, Sanches de. *Arthur Napoleão, resenha comemorativa.* Lisbon, 1913.

Gates, W. Francis. "A Pioneer American Pianist: Gottschalk." *Etude,* August 1898.

Gerig, Reginald R. *Famous Pianists and Their Techniques.* Washington and New York, 1974.

Gilder, John Francis. "Recollections of Gottschalk." *Etude,* October 1897.

———. "An Appreciation of Gottschalk by One Who Knew Him." *Musical Record,* November 1896; also *Etude,* June 1914.

Gottschalk, L. Gaston. "Carreño and L. M. Gottschalk." *Music* 11 (February 1897):468.

"Gottschalk." *Orchestra,* July 1877.

"Gottschalk Number." *Musician,* October 1908.

"Gottschalk's Period." *Etude,* June 1914.

Gunn, Thomas Butler. "Diaries." MS, Missouri Historical Society, St. Louis.

Hallé, Sir Charles. *Life and Letters of Sir Charles Hallé.* London, 1868.

Hawes, William L. "Reminiscences of Louis Moreau Gottschalk." *Musical Courier* 40 (21 March 1900):14–15.

Hazard, Samuel. *Cuba with Pen and Pencil.* Hartford, 1871.

Hearn, Lafcadio. *The Life and Letters of Lafcadio Hearn,* 2 vols. Edited by Elizabeth Bisland. Boston, 1906.

Herz, Henri. *My Travels in America.* Translated by Henry Bertram Hill. Madison, 1963.

Hoffman, Richard. *Some Musical Recollections of Fifty Years.* New York, 1910.

Howells, W. D. *Literary Friends and Acquaintances.* New York and London, 1900.

Lanas, Juan. "Gottschalk en el desierto." *El Continental,* New York, 18, 22 September 1862.

Landaluze, Victor P. de. "Célebre Tarantella de Gottschalk y obras postumas de este artista." *Diario de la Marina,* Havana, 1874, reprinted in Fors, *Gottschalk,* pp. 284–90.

Leland, Charles G. *Memoirs.* New York, 1893.

"L. M. Gottschalk, Prince of Piano-Forte." *Vanity Fair,* 11 October 1862.

"L. M. Gottschalk." *Watson's Weekly Art Journal,* 11 November 1865.

Maretzek, Max. *Revelations of an Opera Manager in Nineteenth-century America.* New York, 1968.

Marmontel, Antoine François. *Les Pianistes célèbres.* Paris, 1878.

Mason, Lowell. *Musical Letters from Abroad.* New York, 1854.

Mason, William. *Memories of a Musical Life.* New York, 1902.

Mendive, Rafael. "Al pianista habanero, P. Desvernine." *Revista de la Habana* 2 (1854):159.

Menezes, Ferreira de. "Literature: Gottschalk. A morte de Gottschalk." *Correio Paulistano,* São Paulo, 24 December 1869.

———. "O Poeta do Piano." *O Ypirang,* São Paulo, 29 August 1869.

Merlin, La Comtesse María de las Mercedes. *La Havane.* 3 vols., Paris, 1844.

Mérimée, Prosper. *La Chronique du regne de Charles IX.* Paris, 1829.

Napoleão, Arthur. "Autobiographia." MS, Biblioteca de la Escola Nacional de Musica, Rio de Janeiro.

"Nekrolog." *Literaturnoe pribavlenie k Nuvellistu.* Moscow, April 1870, pp. 28–29.

O'Brien, Fitz-James. *The Poems and Stories of Fitz-James O'Brien.* Edited by William Winter. Boston, 1881.

Offenbach, Jacques. *Offenbach in America.* Paris, 1877.

Parker, Richard G. *A Tribute to the Life and Character of Jonas Chickering.* Boston, 1854.

Peterson, Clara Gottschalk. *Creole Songs from New Orleans.* New Orleans, 1902.

Ramírez, Serafin. *La Habana artística.* Havana, 1891.

Ripley, Eliza. *Social Life in Old New Orleans.* New York, London, 1912.

Rodríguez, Raúl Martínez. "Edelmann y la impresión músical en Cuba." *Revolución y Cultura*, June 1989, pp. 47–49.

Root, George F. *The Story of a Musical Life.* Cincinnati, 1891.

Rowson, A. L. "A Bygone Bohemia." *Frank Leslie's Popular Monthly, Illustrated*, January 1896, pp. 96–107.

Ryan, Thomas. *Recollections of An Old Musician.* New York, 1899.

Saint-Saëns, Camille. *Musical Memories.* Translated by Edwin Gile Rich. Boston, 1919.

Seymour, Mary Alice Ives [Octavia Hensel]. *Life and Letters of Louis Moreau Gottschalk.* Boston, 1870.

Stoddard, Charles Warren. "Ada Clare, Queen of Bohemia." *National Magazine*, September 1905.

Stoddard, Richard Henry. *Recollections Personal and Literary.* New York, 1903.

Strakosch, Maurice. *Souvenirs d'un impresario.* 2nd ed., Paris, 1887.

Thomas, Theodore. *Theodore Thomas: A Musical Autobiography.* Edited by George P. Upton. Chicago, 1905.

Tracy, T. James. "The World's Greatest Pianists." *Etude*, September 1907.

Upton, George P. *Musical Memories: My Recollections of Celebrities of the Half Century 1850–1900.* Chicago, 1908.

de Vivo, Diego. "De Vivo's Jolly Season." *New York Sun*, 4 April 1897.

————. "Gottschalk, the Adored." *New York Sun*, 29 March 1897.

Willis, N. Parker. *Famous Persons and Places.* New York, 1854.

————. *Hurry-graphs: Sketches of Scenery, Celebrities and Society Taken from Life.* New York, 1851.

Winter, William. *Old Friends: Being Literary Recollections of Other Days.* New York, 1909.

————. *Vagrant Memories: Being Further Recollections of Other Days.* New York, 1915.

Witterson. "Gottschalk en Lausanne." *La France musicale*, 10 November 1850.

Ximeno y Cruz, Dolores María de. *Memorias de Lola María.* 2 vols., Havana, 1928.

V. Contemporary Newspapers and Journals Consulted

UNITED STATES
  Albany, New York
    Albany Times and Courier
  Baltimore, Maryland
    Baltimore Sun
  Boston, Massachusetts

Boston Daily Courier
Boston Journal
Boston Musical Times
Boston Post
Boston True Flag
Dwight's Journal of Music
Gleason's Pictorial Drawing-Room Companion
Brooklyn, New York
  Brooklyn Daily Eagle
Buffalo, New York
  Buffalo Commercial Advertiser
  Daily Courier
Burlington, Vermont
  Burlington Free Press
Carson City, Nevada
  Carson City Appeal
Chicago, Illinois
  Chicago Evening Journal
  Chicago Tribune
Cincinnati, Ohio
  Cincinnati Enquirer
  Cincinnati Post
  Daily Commercial
  Daily Courier
Cleveland, Ohio
  Cleveland Courier
  Cleveland Herald
Detroit, Michigan
  Daily Journal
  Detroit Advertiser
Geneva, New York
  Geneva Gazette
Indianapolis, Indiana
  Indianapolis Daily Gazette
  Indianapolis Daily Journal
  Indianapolis Daily Sentinel
Louisville, Kentucky
  Louisville Journal
Lowell, Massachusetts
  Daily Citizen
New Orleans, Louisiana
  L'Abeille (Bee)
  Courrier de la Louisiane
  Daily Picayune
New York, New York
  Albion: or British, Colonial, and Foreign Weekly Gazette
  Atlas
  El Continental
  Courrier des États-Unis

Evening Mirror
Evening Post
Frank Leslie's Illustrated Newspaper
Home Journal
Mercury
Musical World
New York Evening Express
New York Herald
New York Musical Review & Gazette
New York Times
New York World
Orpheonist and Philharmonic Journal
Review & Gazette
Saturday Press
Spirit of the Times
Watson's Weekly Art Journal
Petaluma, California
  Petaluma Journal and Argus
Philadelphia, Pennsylvania
  Daily Pennsylvanian
  Evening Telegraph
  Pennsylvania Inquirer
  Sunday Dispatch
Portsmouth, Maine
  Portsmouth Daily Chronicle
Providence, Rhode Island
  Providence Daily Post
Reading, Pennsylvania
  Reading Democrat
Rochester, New York
  Rochester Daily Democrat
  Rochester Union Advertiser
Sacramento, Caliafornia
  Sacramento Daily Bee
  Sacramento Daily Union
Sandusky, Ohio
  Sandusky Register
St. Louis, Missouri
  Daily Missouri Democrat
  Westliche Press
San Francisco
  Courrier de San Francisco
  Daily Alta California
  Daily Dramatic Chronicle
  Daily Evening Transcript
  Daily Morning Call
  San Francisco Bulletin
Springfield, Massachusetts
  Springfield Daily Republican

Washington, D.C.
  National Morning Chronicle
  National Intelligencer
Utica, New York
  Utica Herald
Virginia City, Neveda
  Virginia Daily Union
ARGENTINA
  Buenos Aires
    Courrier de la Plata
    La Nacion Argentina
    Standard
    La Tribuna
BRAZIL
  Rio de Janeiro
    Anglo-Brazilian Times
    Ba-ta-clan
    Jornal do Commercio
    Jornal para Todos
    A Reforma
    Semana Illustrada
    A Vida Fluminense
    Jornal da Tardé
CANADA
  Québec City
    L'Ordre
  Toronto
    Daily Globe
CHILE
  Copiapó
    El Constituyente
  Santiago
    El Mercurio
  Valparaíso
    El Ferrocarril
    El Independiente
    La Patria
CUBA
  Havana
    Diario de la Marina
    Gaceta de la Habana
    Liceo de la Habana
    La Prensa de la Habana
    Revista de la Habana
    El Siglo
  Matanzas
    Aurora del Yumurí
  Puerto Príncipe
    Fanal
  Santiago de Cuba

El Redactor de Cuba
FRANCE
  Bordeaux
    L'Ami des arts
    Courrier de la Gironde
  Paris
    L'Art musical
    L'Assemblée nationale
    Le Charivari
    La France musicale
    Revue et gazette musicale de Paris
    Le Siècle
GUADELOUPE
  Pointe-à-Pitre
    Gazette Officielle de la Guadeloupe
PERU
  Lima
    El Mercurio
RUSSIA
  Moscow
    Literaturnoe pribavlenie k Nuvellistu
  St. Petersburg
    Muzujak'nyi svet
SPAIN
  Madrid
    El Clamor Publica
    La España
    La Nacion
    El Orden
SWITZERLAND
  Geneva
    Gazette de Genève
    Journal de Genève
    Nouvelliste Vaudois
  Lausanne
    Gazette de Lausanne
TRINIDAD and TOBAGO
  Port-of-Spain
    Port-of-Spain Gazette
    Trinidad Sentinel
URUGUAY
  Montevideo
    Las Noticias
    El Siglo

VI. Secondary Works

Abraham, Kenneth. "Mr. Dwight's Blind Spot: Louis Moreau Gottschalk." *Musart*, Winter 1973, pp. 47–50.

Agüero, Gaspar. "El Compositor Nicolás Ruiz Espadero." *Revista Cubana*, Havana, April-June 1938, pp. 160–78.

Almeida, Renato. *História da música brasileira*. 2nd ed., Rio de Janeiro, 1942.

Ambrose, Jane. "Louis Moreau Gottschalk's Visit to Vermont in 1862." *Vermont History*, Spring 1971, pp. 125–127.

Argeliers, Léon. *Del Canto y el tiempo*. Havana, 1974.

"Around the Town." *Williamsport Sun-Gazette* (Pennsylvania), 25 February 1963.

Aubry, G. Jean. "A Forgotten Pioneer." *Christian Science Monitor*, 26 December 1925.

Austin, William W. *"Susanna," "Jeanie," and "The Old Folks at Home": The Songs of Stephen Collins Foster from His Time to Ours*. New York, London, 1975.

Ayars, Christine Merrick. *Contributions to the Art of Music in America by the Music Industries of Boston, 1640 to 1936*. New York, 1939.

Ayestarán, Lauro. *La Música en el Uruguay*, vol. 1. Montevideo, 1953.

Bacardí y Moreau, Emilio. *Crónicas de Santiago de Cuba*. 3 vols., Santiago de Cuba, 1908–1913.

Barbacci, Rodolfo. "Actividades de L. M. Gottschalk en el Peru (1865–66)." *Revista de Estudios Musicales II*, 5 (December 1950–April 1951):343–50.

Barker, John W. "Gottschalk in Brooklyn: A Morbid Epilogue to a Brilliant Career." Paper read at a Midwest chapter meeting, American Musicological Society, Newberry Library, Chicago, 11–12 November 1967.

———. "Gottschalk's Grave." *Stereo Review* 22 (February 1969):6.

Barreda, E. M. "Un Pianista que hace ochenta años hizo la delicia de las porteñas." *Atlantida*, Buenos Aires, February 1948.

Bartlett, Homer N. "First of American Pianists to Gain Recognition Abroad." *Musical America*, 30 January 1915, p. 35.

Barrus, Clara. *Whitman and Burroughs: Comrades*. Boston and New York, 1931.

Barzun, Jacques. *Berlioz and the Romantic Century*. Boston, 1950.

Béhague, Gerard Henri. *Music in Latin America: An Introduction*. Englewood Cliffs, 1979.

———. "Popular Musical Currents in the Art Music of the Early Nationalistic Period in Brazil, circa 1870–1920." Ph.D. dissertation, Tulane University, 1966.

Behrend, Jeanne. "Louis Moreau Gottschalk. First American Concert-Pianist." *Etude*, January 1957.

———. "The Peripatetic Gottschalk, First American Concert Pianist." *Americas* (Pan-American Union) 11/10, 21–26 October 1959. Spanish and Portuguese translation, "El Pianista errante," *Americas* 11/11, 20–26 November 1959.

Bernard, Kenneth A. *Lincoln and the Music of the Civil War*. Caldwell, Idaho, 1966.

Berry, Jason. "African Cultural Memory in New Orleans Music." *Black Music Research Journal*, 1988, no. 1.

Bolling, Ernest L. "Our First Musical Ambassador Louis Moreau Gottschalk." *Etude*, February 1932.

Borbolla, Carlos. "El Cocoyé, un canto omtarsero qua origino un potpourri con zabe historico." MS, Museo de la Música, Havana, 1954.

Brockett, Clyde W. "Autobiographer versus Biographer: How Factual Is Gottschalk?" *Sonneck Society Bulletin*, Summer 1993, pp. 4–7.

———. "Footnotes of a Pianist: A Waltz for a Living Princess." *Sonneck Society Bulletin*, Spring 1991.

———. "Gottschalk at Hampton Roads." Address delivered to Sonneck Society, April 1991. MS courtesy of the author.

———. "Gottschalk in Biscay, Castile, and Andalusia." MS.

———. "Gottschalk in Madrid: A Tale of Ten Pianos." *The Musical Quarterly*, 1991, no. 3, pp. 279–315.

———. "An Influential American in Paris." *Sonneck Society Bulletin*, 1989, no. 1, pp. 8–9.

———. "Louis Moreau Gottschalk and his *Morte!! (She Is Dead) Lamentation*." *American Music*, 1990.

———. "The Madrilene and Vallisolitana: Compositions of L. M. Gottschalk." MS.

Broder, Nathan. "Gottschalk." In *Die Musik in Geschichte und Gegenwart*, edited by Friedrich Blume, vol. 5, columns 571–72. 14 vols, Kassel, 1949–68.

Brooks, Van Wyck. *The Times of Melville and Whitman*. Boston, 1947.

Broyles, Michael. "Music and Class Structure in Antebellum Boston." *Journal of the American Musicological Society*, 1991, no. 3.

Bushman, Richard L. *The Refinement of America*. New York, 1992.

Calcagno, Francisco. "Manuel Saumell Robredo." *Diccionario biográfico cubano*. New York, 1878.

Canby, Henry Seidel. *Walt Whitman, an American*. New York, 1943.

Carballido, Martha Reyes. *Las Sociedadas Philarmonicas en Matanzas*. MS, Museo de la Música, Havana, 1989.

Carpentier, Alejo. *La Música en Cuba*. Havana, 1988.

Carr, Gerald L. *Frederic Edwin Church: The Icebergs*. Dallas, 1980.

Carse, Adam. *The Life of Jullien*. Cambridge, England, 1951.

Castellanos, Henry C. *New Orleans as It Was: Episodes of Louisiana Life*. New Orleans, 1895.

Chapin, Victor. *Giants of the Keyboard*. Philadelphia, 1967.

Chase, Gilbert. *America's Music from the Pilgrims to the Present*. New York, rev. ed., 1966.

———. *The Music of Spain*. New York, 1959.

———. "Review Article: The Music of Gottschalk." *Anuario: Yearbook for Inter-American Musical Research*, 6:105–10.

Chouquet, Gustave. "Les dernières oeuvres de Gottschalk." *L'Art musical*, 1870.

Clarke, Garry E. *Essays on American Music*. Westport, Connecticut, 1977.

Cole, Fannie L. Gwinner. "Gottschalk." *Dictionary of American Biography* 7 (1931):441–42.

Cole, Ronald Fred. "Music in Portland, Maine, from Colonial Times Through the Nineteenth Century." Ph.D. dissertation, Indiana University, 1975.

Converse, Charles Crozat. "Reminiscences of Some Famous Musicians." *Etude*, October 1912.

Cooke, George Willis. *John Sullivan Dwight*. Boston, 1898.

Cooke, James Francis. *Louis Moreau Gottschalk*. Philadelphia, 1928.

Correa de Azevedo, Luis Heitor. "Arthur Napoleon, 1843–1925, un pianiste portugais au Brézil." *Arquivas do Centro Cultural Portugues* 3 (1971):572–602.

Cortot, Alfred. *In Search of Chopin*. Translated by Cyril and Rena Clarke. London, 1951.

Darrell, Robert D. "An Early Pan-American Exhumed." *Musical Mercury*, January-February 1934, pp. 18–21.

Debren, Gabriel. "Les colons des Saint-Dominique refugies à Cuba, 1793–1815." *Revista de Indías* 12 (1953):559–605.

Debren, Gabriel, and René le Gardeur Jr. "Les Colons de Saint-Dominque refugies à la Louisiane." *Bulletin de la Société de l'Histoire de la Guadeloupe*, 1975, no. 1, p. 99.

Dianin, Serge. *Borodin*. Translated by Robert Lord. London and New York, 1963.

Doyle, John G. "Gottschalk: Nationalist Composer, Native Virtuoso." *Music Educators Journal* 56 (December 1969):25–30, 71–73.

————. *Louis Moreau Gottschalk, 1829–69: A Bibliographical Study and Catalog of Works.* Detroit, 1983.

————. "The Piano Music of Louis Moreau Gottschalk (1829–69)." Ph.D. dissertation, New York University, 1960.

Dufour, Charles. "Gottschalk at Fifteen Won Fame." *New Orleans Times-Picayune,* 18 March 1951.

————. "Gottschalk Memorial Concert Honors N.O. Piano Prodigy." *New Orleans States-Item,* 25 February 1969.

Engel, Louis. *From Mozart to Mario.* London, 1886.

Ericson, Raymond. "105 Years Later, It's Gottschalk Time Again." *New York Times,* 7 July 1968.

Escragnolle-Doria, L. G. "Cousas não ditas (Os Gottschalk)." *Revista da semana,* Rio de Janeiro, 8 April 1944.

————. "Gottschalk." in "Cousas do Passado," supplement to vol. 82, Part 2, *Revista do Instituto Histórico e Geográfico Brazileiro,* Rio de Janeiro, 1909, pp. 61–75.

Espadero, Nicolás Ruiz, et al. "El Centenario Luis Moreau Gottschalk." *Revista Bimestre Cubano,* Havana, November-December 1930, pp. 254–63.

Eyer, Ronald. "Louis Moreau Gottschalk, America's First Musical Celebrity." *Musical America* 69:10–12.

Ferrer, Cecilio Tieles. "Julián Fontana: El Introductor de Chopin en Cuba." *Revista de Musicología,* Madrid, January–June 1988, pp. 1–28.

————. "Lo Nacional en la vida y la obra de Nicolás Ruiz Espadero." MS, Havana, 1992.

————. *Espadero, lo Hispánico Musical en Cuba.* Barcelona, 1994.

Ferris, George, T. *Great Violinists and Pianists.* New York, 1895.

Fiehrer, Thomas. "Saint Domingue–Haiti: Louisiana's Caribbean Connection." *Louisiana History,* 1989, no. 4, pp. 431–34.

Finck, Henry T. "Gottschalk's Tour in the United States." *Nation,* January 1882.

Fisher, William Arms. "Louis Moreau Gottschalk. The First American Pianist and Composer. A Life Sketch." *Musician* 13 (October 1908):437–438, 466.

Foster, Lois M. "Annals of the San Francisco Stage," MS, 4 vols. Bancroft Library, Berkeley, 1937.

Frankenstein, Alfred. "Gottschalk: Works for Piano." *High Fidelity Magazine,* 1970, no. 2.

Freyre, Gilberto. *Order and Progress: Brazil from Monarchy to Republic.* Translated and edited by Rod W. Horton. New York, 1970.

Frias, David C. Sanches de. *Arthur Napoleão.* Lisbon, 1913.

Fuentes, Eduardo Sanchez de. *Cuba y sus músicos.* Havana, 1923.

Fuentes, Laureano. *Las Artes en Santiago de Cuba: Apuntes históricos.* Santiago de Cuba, 1893.

Galan, Natalio. *Cuba y sus sones.* Valencia, 1983.

Galloway, Tod B. "Forgotten American Musician." *General Magazine and Historical Chronicle* 35 (October 1932):56–64.

Gates, W. Francis. "The First American Pianist." *Etude,* July 1940.

Gesualdo, Vincente. *Historia de la Música en la Argentina.* 2 vols., Buenos Aires, 1961.

Glass, Paul. "A Hiatus in American Music History." *Afro-American Studies,* vol. 1, 1970.

Goldin, Milton. *The Music Merchants.* London, 1969.

González, Hilario. "Manuel Saumell y la Contradanza." *Manuel Saumell: Contradanzas.* Havana, 1980.

Gonzales, Jorge Ántonio. *La Composicion operástica en Cuba.* Havana, 1986.

"Gottschalk." *Jornal de Musica,* Rio de Janeiro, February 1952.

"Gottschalk." *Musical Standard* 14 (11 August 1900):95.

"Gottschalk Momentoes." *Musical Courier* 40 (7 March 1900):23.

"Gottschalk Momentoes at New Orleans." *Music* 17 (April 1900):663–64.

"Gottschalk's Farewell Concert, New Orleans, 1841." *Musician* 13 (October 1908):441.

Gottschalk, L. G. "Carreño and L. M. Gottschalk." *Music,* February 1897, p. 458.

Graham, Alice. "Musical Life in New Orleans, a Study." *Etude,* April 1906.

Günther, Robert, ed. *Die Musikkulturen Lateinamericas im 19. Jahrhundert.* Regensburg, 1982.

Hahn, Emily. *Romantic Rebels: An Informal History of Bohemianism in America.* Boston, 1967.

Hamel, Réginald. *La Louisiane créole: Littéraire, politique et sociale, 1762–1900,* 2 vols. Ottawa, 1984.

————. *Louis Moreau Gottschalk son temps (1829–69).* Montreal, 1995, forthcoming.

Harris, Neil. *Humbug: The Art of P. T. Barnum.* Chicago and London, 1973.

Harwood, Bertha. "Reminiscences of Louis Moreau Gottschalk." *Musical Courier* 56 (13 May 1908):39–40.

Hawes, William L. "Gottschalk in New Orleans, 1853." *New Orleans Times-Democrat,* 8 May 1899.

————. "Gottschalk's *Last Hope.*" *Musician* 13 (October 1908):440.

————. "Gottschalk's Views Regarding Beethoven's Sonatas." *Musician* 13 (October 1908):440.

————. "Louis Moreau Gottschalk." *Musical Courier* 43 (11 September 1901):17; 54 (1907):24–25.

————. "The Original *Last Hope.*" *Musical Record,* July 1899, p. 1.

————. "The Origin of Gottschalk's *Last Hope.*" *New Orleans Times-Democrat,* 30 April 1899.

Hildebrandt, Dieter. *Piano Forte: A Social History of the Piano.* Translated by Harriet Goodman. New York, 1988.

Hitchcock, H. Wiley. *Music in the United States: A Historical Introduction.* Englewood Cliffs, 1988.

Howard, John Tasker. "American Music." *Harvard Dictionary of Music.* Edited by Willi Apel. Cambridge, Massachusetts, 1944.

————. "Louis Moreau Gottschalk, as Portrayed by Himself." *Musical Quarterly* 18 (1932):120–133.

————. *Our American Music: Three Hundred Years of It.* New York, 1929.

Jackson, Richard. "An American Muse Learns to Walk: The First Organization Devoted to the Performance of Concert Music Composed in This Country." MS, 1992.

————."A Gottschalk Collection Surveyed." *Notes (Quarterly Journal of the Music Library Association),* December 1989.

————. "A Note on Gottschalk Manuscripts in New York." *Anuario: Yearbook for Inter-American Musical Research* 6 (1970):111–12.

Johnson, Jerah. "New Orleans' Congo Square: An Urban Setting for Early Afro-American Culture Formation." *Louisiana History* 19:136–39.

Jullien, Adolphe. "Gottschalk." *Grove's Dictionary of Music and Musicians,* 2nd ed., 2 (1906):205.

Keefer, Lubov, *Baltimore's Music: The Haven of the American Composer.* Baltimore, 1962.

Kellogg, Clara Louise. *Memoirs of an American Prima Donna.* New York, 1913.

Kelly, Franklin. *Frederic Edwin Church and the National Landscape.* Washington and London, 1988.

Kendall, John Smith. "The Friend of Chopin, and Some Other New Orleans Musical Celebrities." *Louisiana Historical Quarterly* 31 (October 1948):856–76.

King, Grace. *New Orleans, the Place and the People.* New York, 1925.

Kingman, Daniel. *American Music, a Panorama.* New York, 1979.

Kirkpatrick, John. "Observations on Four Volumes and Supplement of the Works of Louis Moreau Gottschalk in the New York Public Library." Typescript, n.d. (ca. 1935), Special Collections, Americana Division, Library of the Performing Arts, NYPL.

Klein, Herman. *The Reign of Patti.* New York, 1920.

Kmen, Henry A. *Music in New Orleans.* Baton Rouge, 1966.

Kobbé, Gustav. "Gottschalk." *Appleton's Cyclopedia of American Biography* 2 (1898):691.

Korf, William E. "Gottschalk's One-Act Opera Scene, *Esceñas campestres.*" *Current Musicology* 26 (1978):62–73.

———. *The Orchestral Music of Louis Moreau Gottschalk.* Henryville, Pennsylvania, 1983.

Korn, Bertram W. *The Early Jews of New Orleans.* Waltham, Massachusetts, 1969.

———. "A Note on the Jewish Ancestry of Louis Moreau Gottschalk, American Pianist and Composer." *American Jewish Archives* 15 (November 1963):117–19.

Kugman, Daniel. *American Music, a Panorama.* New York, 1977.

Lange, Francisco Curt. "Gottschalk en la Argentina." MS, property of the author, Caracas, Venezuela, 1962.

———. "Gottschalk en Montevideo." MS, property of the author, Caracas, Venezuela, 1966.

———. "Louis Moreau Gottschalk (1829–69)." *Boletin Interamericano de Música,* May 1970, pp. 3–14.

———. "Louis Moreau Gottschalk (1829–69)." In Robert Günther, ed., *Die Musikkulturer Lateinamerikas im 19. Jahrhundert.* Regensburg, 1982.

———. "La musicalidad del general José Antonio Páez." *Revista Nacional de Cultura,* Caracas, January-March 1991, pp. 13–30.

———. "Vida y muerte de Louis Moreau Gottschalk en Rio de Janeiro (1869)." *Revista de Estudios Musicales* 4 (August 1950), 5 (December 1950), 6 (April 1951).

Lapique Becali, Zoila. *Música colonial cubana en las publicaciones periodicas (1812–1902),* 2 vols., Havana, 1979.

Law, Fredericks. "Some Forgotten Worthies." *Musician* 13 (June 1908):262–63.

Lawrence, Vera Brodsky. *Strong on Music: The New York Music Scene in the Days of George Templeton Strong.* Vol. 1, *Resonances,* New York, 1988; vol. 2, *Reverberations: 1850–56. Chicago, 1994.*

Lebow, Marcia Wilson. "A Systematic Examination of the Journal of Music and Art edited by John Sullivan Dwight: 1852–81, Boston, Massachusetts." Ph.D. dissertation, University of California, Los Angeles, 1969.

Lennon, Nigey. *The Sagebrush Bohemian.* New York, 1990.

Lesser, Allen. *Enchanting Rebel: The Secret of Adah Isaacs Menken.* Fort Washington, New York, 1947.

Levine, Lawrence W. *Highbrow/Lowbrow: The Emergence of Cultural Hierarchy in America.* Cambridge, Massachusetts, 1988.

Lewis, John Cary. "A Study and Edition of Recently Discovered Works of Louis Moreau Gottschalk." D.M.A. dissertation, University of Rochester, 1971.

Liebling, Emil. "Gottschalk and His Period." *Musician* 13 (October 1908):487.

Linares, María Teresa. *La Música y el pueblo.* Havana, 1974.

Lindstrom, Carl E. "The American Quality in the Music of Louis Moreau Gottschalk." *Musical Quarterly* 13 (July 1945):356–366.

Livingston, William. "Gottschalk." *The Encyclopedia Americana,* international ed., 8 (1972):118.

Loesser, Arthur. *Men, Women, and Pianos: A Social History.* New York, 1954.

Loggins, Vernon. *Where the Word Ends.* Baton Rouge, 1958.

Logsdon, Leann F. "Gottschalk and Meyerbeer." Paper read before a meeting of the American Musicological Society, Southern Chapter, 10 March 1978.

———. "Gottschalk's *Work Book:* Notations of a Pianist." MS, New York University, 1977.

———. "Louis Moreau Gottschalk: His Style and Significance." Honors thesis, Newcomb College, Tulane University, 1974.

"Louis Moreau Gottschalk." *Musical Leader and Concert-Goer* 15 (11 June 1908):6.

Lowens, Irving. "The First Matinee Idol, Louis Moreau Gottschalk." *Musicology* 2 (1948):23–34.

———. "Gottschalk, Louis Moreau." *New Grove Dictionary of Music and Musicians,* 7 (1980):570–74.

———. *Music and Musicians in Early America.* New York, 1964.

Maganini, Quinto. "Letter to the Editor." *New York Times,* 22 May 1932.

Magendanz, Johannes. "Gottschalk in Utica." *Town Topics of the Mohawk Valley,* October-December 1932, January-May 1933.

Mann, Brian. "A Gottschalk Letter at Vassar College." *Sonneck Society Bulletin,* 1992, no. 1, pp. 5–7.

Marrocco, W. Thomas. "Gottschalkiana: New Light on the Gottschalks and the Bruslés." *Louisiana History* 12 (Winter 1971):59–66.

———. "Gottschalkiana II: Miscellanea." Paper read at the American Musicological Society Annual Meeting, 29 December 1969, St. Louis.

Martínez Rodriguez, Raúl. "Edelmann y la impresión músical en Cuba." *Revolucion y Cultura,* June 1989.

Mathews, W. S. B. "An Evening with American Composers." *Music,* 13 (January 1898):351–59.

———. "Gottschalk, a Successful American Composer." *Music* 2 (June 1892):117–32.

———. *A Hundred Years of Music in America.* Chicago, 1889.

———. "John S. Dwight: Editor, Critic, and Man." *Music* 15 (June 1899):525–40.

———. "Louis Moreau Gottschalk, the Most Popular of American Composers." *Musician,* 13 (October 1908):439–40.

Mellers, Wilfred. *Music in a New Found Land.* New York, 1965.

Miller, Clarence E. *Forty Years of Long Ago: Early Annals of the Mercantile Library Association, 1846–86.* MS, 1935, St. Louis Mercantile Library.

Milinowski, Marta. *Teresa Carreño.* New Haven, 1940.

Minor, Andrew C. "Piano Concerts in New York City 1849–65." Master's thesis, University of Michigan, 1947.

Morneweck, Evelyn Foster. *Chronicles of Stephen Foster's Family.* 2 vols., Pittsburgh, 1944.

Odell, George C. D. *Annals of the New York Stage,* New York, 1931 and various years.

Offergeld, Robert. *The Centennial Catalogue of the Published and Unpublished Compositions of Louis Moreau Gottschalk.* New York, 1970.

―――. "Gottschalk and Company: The Music of Democratic Sociability." MS, Offergeld Papers, property of the author.

―――. "The Gottschalk Legend. Grand Fantasy for a Great Many Pianos." 1:xiii-xxxiv in Vera Brodsky Lawrence, ed.,*The Piano Works of Louis Moreau Gottschalk,* 5 vols. New York, 1969.

―――. "Louis Moreau Gottschalk." *HiFi/Stereo Review* 21 (September 1968):53–67.

―――. "More on the Gottschalk-Ives Connection." *Newsletter of the Institute for Studies in American Music* 6 (May 1986):1–2.

Parry, Albert. *Garrets and Pretenders: A History of Bohemianism in America.* New York, 1933.

Parsi, Hector Campos. "La Música en Puerto Rico." *La Gran Enciclopedia de Puerto Rico,* vol. 7. San Juan, 1976.

Pasarell, Emilio J. "El Centenario de los conciertos de Adelina Patti y Luis Moreau Gottschalk en Puerto Rico." *Revista del Instituto de Cultura Puertorriqueña* 2 (January-March 1959.)

―――. *Esculcando el siglo XIX en Puerto Rico,* Barcelona, 1967.

―――. *Orígenes y desarrollo de la afición teatral en Puerto Rico* (Editorial de Departamento de Instrucción Pública). Estado Libre Asociado de Puerto Rico, San Juan, 1970.

Pereira-Salas, Eugenio. "La Embajada musical de Gottschalk en Chile." *Andean Quarterly,* Santiago de Chile, Winter 1944, pp. 5–11.

Pleasants, Henry. *The Great Singers from the Dawn of Opera to Our Own Time.* New York, 1966.

Prophit, Willie Sword. "The Crescent City's Charismatic Celebrity: Louis Moreau Gottschalk's New Orleans Concerts, Spring, 1853." *Louisiana History* 12 (Summer 1971):243–54.

Pulliza, Denisse. "Azucar en Puerto Rico, Central Plazuela, La Plazuela." Master's thesis, Centro de Estudios Avanzados de Puerto Rico y el Caribe, San Juan, n.d.

Rabinowitz, Peter J. " 'With Our Own Dominant Passions': Gottschalk, Gender, and the Power of Listening." *Nineteenth-century Music* 16 (Spring 1993):242–52.

Rauch, Basil. *American Interest in Cuba: 1848–55.* New York, 1948.

Ramírez, Serafin. *La Habana artística: Apuntes historicos.* Havana, 1891.

Rezende, Carlos Penteado de. "O Poeta do piano." *Investigações: Revista do Departamento de Investigações,* São Paulo, 3 December 1951, pp. 21–42.

Rigby, Charles. *Sir Charles Hallé.* Manchester, 1952.

Ritter, Frederic Louis. *Music in America.* New York, 1890.

Robinson, Florence Crim. "A View of Louis Moreau Gottschalk." *Musical Analysis,* Winter 1972.

Rogers, Delmer Dalzell. "Nineteenth-century Music in New York City as Reflected in the Career of George Frederick Bristow." Ph. D. dissertation, University of Michigan, 1967.

Rogert, M. Robert. "Jazz Influence on French Music." *Musical Quarterly* 21 (January 1935):67.

Root, George F. *The Story of a Musical Life.* Cincinnati, 1891.

Rubin, Libby Antarsh. "Gottschalk in Cuba." Ph.D. dissertation, Columbia University, 1974.

———. "Louis Moreau Gottschalk and the 1860–61 Opera Season in Cuba." *Inter-American Music Bulletin* 78 (July-October 1971):1–7.

———. "La Música cubana y sus origenes." *Boletin Latino-Américano de Música* 4. Edited by Francisco Curt Lange. October 1938.

Sanjek, Russell. *American Popular Music and Its Business: The First Four Hundred Years.* 3 vols., New York and Oxford, 1988.

Schonberg, Harold C. "Civil War Pianist." *New York Times,* 23 April 1961.

———. "The Delights of Salon Music." *New York Times,* 25 February 1979.

———. "Gottschalk's Monster Concert." *New York Times,* 22 April 1979.

———. *The Great Pianists.* New York, 1963.

———. "Let's Get to Gottschalk." *New York Times,* 1968 Feb. 25.

———. *The Lives of the Great Composers.* New York, 1970.

Shanet, Howard. "En Garde, Vanguard!" *Saturday Review,* 14 March 1964, p. 118; reprinted in *Music Journal,* February 1965, p. 68.

Shpall, Leo. "Louis Moreau Gottschalk." *Louisiana Historical Quarterly* 30 (January 1947):120–27.

Smith, Paul Ely. "Gottschalk's 'The Banjo,' op. 15, and the Banjo in the Nineteenth Century." *Current Musicology,* 1992, no. 50.

Snook, Gerald O'Brien. "The Gottschalk Legacy." Master's thesis, University of Nebraska, Lincoln, 1966.

Sterling, Manuel Marquez. "Gottschalk, Musical Humboldt." *Americas* 22 (January 1970):10–18.

Stevenson, Robert. "Gottschalk in Buenos Aires" and "Gottschalk in Western South America." *Inter-American Music Bulletin* 74 (November 1969):1–7, 7–16.

———. "Gottschalk Programs Wagner." *Inter-American Music Review* 5 (Spring-Summer 1983):89–94

———. "Havana." *New Grove Dictionary of Music and Musicians* 8 (1980):318.

Stone, Henry. "A Song in Camp." *Century Magazine,* December 1887.

Sullivan, Lester. "Composers of Color of Nineteenth-century New Orleans." *Black Music Research Journal,* 1988, no. 1, pp. 51–82.

Suttoni, Charles R. "Piano and Opera: A Study of the Piano Fantasies Written on Opera Themes in the Romantic Era." Ph. D. dissertation, New York University, 1973.

Swayne, Egbert. "Gottschalk: The First American Pianist." *Music* 18 (October 1900):519–29.

Tawa, Nicholas. *Sweet Songs for Gentle Americans.* Bowling Green, 1980.

Teillet, Claude. "Le Centre Hospitalier Specialisé de Clermont de l'Oise." *Comtes rendus et memories de la Société archéologique et historique de Clermont-en-Beauvaisis,* 1978–82.

Thompson, Donald. "Gottschalk in the Virgin Islands." *Anuario: Yearbook of Inter-American Musical Research* 6 (1970):95–103.

Tolón, Edwin T. and Gonzalez, J. A. *Operas cubanas y sus autores.* Havana, 1943.

Traubel, Horace. *With Walt Whitman in Camden.* 6 vols., New York, 1914.

Upton, William Treat. *William Henry Fry: An American Journalist and Composer-Critic.* New York, 1954.

Vaisaière, Pierre de. *Saint-Domingue, la société et la vie créoles sous le ancien régime (1629–1789).* Paris, 1909.

Walker, Franklin. *San Francisco's Literary Frontier.* New York, 1943.

Williamson, Jerry Max. "The Transitional Period Between Romanticism and Realism in the American Arts." Ph.D. dissertation, Florida State University, 1963.

Wright, Ph. and G. Debren. "Les colons de Saint-Domingue passés à la Jamaïque (1792–1835)." *Bulletin de la Société d'Historie de la Guadeloupe*, no. 4, 1975, p. 33.

Zuck, Barbara A. *A History of Musical Americanism.* Ann Arbor, 1980.

Index

General

Places